Glencoe Social Studies
New York Regents Review Series
United States History and Government

Coon • Grant • Miller • Rubin • Sesso

Mc Graw Hill **Glencoe**

New York, New York   Columbus, Ohio   Chicago, Illinois   Peoria, Illinois   Woodland Hills, California

The McGraw-Hill Companies

Send all inquiries to:
Glencoe/McGraw-Hill
8787 Orion Place
Columbus, OH 43240

ISBN 0-07-869394-2

Printed in the United States of America

5 6 7 8 9 10 026 09

TEACHER REVIEWERS

Charles Coon
Adjunct Professor of American History
State University of New York College at Cortland
Cortland, New York

Alice Grant
Educational Consultant
Social Studies Department Chairperson (Retired)
Pelham Memorial High School
Pelham, New York

Joy Miller
Social Studies Teacher
Fairport High School
Fairport, New York

Stuart Rubin
Social Studies Department Chairperson (Retired)
Mepham High School
Bellmore, New York

Gloria Sesso
Director of Social Studies
Patchogue-Medford Schools
Patchogue, New York

CREDITS

TABLE OF CONTENTS

CORRELATION CHART

New York Core Curriculum for United States History and Government	Unit 1	Unit 2	Unit 3	Unit 4
Unit One: Introduction				
A. The physical/cultural setting in the Americas	1		13, 14	
B. Role/influence of geography on historical/cultural development	1		13, 14	
C. Geographic issues today	1			
D. Demographics	1		13, 14	
Unit Two: Constitutional Foundations for the United States Democratic Republic; I. The Constitution: The Foundation of American Society				
A. Historical foundations		2		
B. Constitutional Convention		4		
C. The Bill of Rights		3, 4		
D. Basic structure and function: three branches and their operation		3		
E. Basic constitutional principles		4		
F. Implementing the new constitutional principles		4		
Unit Two: Constitutional Foundations for the United States Democratic Republic; II. The Constitution Tested: Nationalism and Sectionalism				
A. Factors unifying the United States, 1789–1861		5		
B. Constitutional stress and crisis		5		
C. Territorial expansion through diplomacy, migration, annexation and war; Manifest Destiny		5, 8, 9		
D. The Constitution in jeopardy: The American Civil War		9		
Unit Three: Industrialization of the United States; I. The Reconstructed Nation				
A. Reconstruction plans			11	
B. The North			11	
C. The New South			11	
D. End of Reconstruction			11	
E. The Impact of the Civil War and Reconstruction: Summary		10	11	
Unit Three: Industrialization of the United States; II. The Rise of American Business, Industry, and Labor, 1865–1920				
A. Economic transformation and the "search for order"			12	
B. Major areas of growth in business and industry		6	12	
C. Representative entrepreneurs: Case studies in concentrated wealth and effort			12, 13	
D. New business and government practices: Popular and government responses			12	17
E. Labor's response to economic change: Organize		6	12	
F. Agrarian response to economic change: Organize and protest		6		15
Unit Three: Industrialization of the United States; III. Adjusting Society to Industrialism: American People and Places				
A. Impact of industrialization			12	
B. Immigration, 1850–1924		7	12, 13	
C. Reactions to the "new" immigration		7	12, 13	
D. The frontier (1850–1890)			12, 14	
Unit Four: The Progressive Movement: Responses to the Challenges Brought About by Industrialization and Urbanization; I. Reform in America				
A. Pressures for reform		7	13	15, 17
B. Progress: Social and economic reform and consumer protection		7		15, 17
C. Progressivism and government action		7	13	15, 17
Unit Four: The Progressive Movement: Responses to the Challenges Brought About by Industrialization and Urbanization; II. The Rise of American Power				
A. An emerging global involvement				16, 18
B. Restraint and involvement: 1914–1920				16, 18
C. Wartime constitutional issues				16
D. The search for peace and arms control: 1914–1930				16, 18

INTRODUCING THE BOOK

The *Glencoe Social Studies New York Regents Review Series—United States History and Government* book is designed for you, the student, to help you review your United States History and Government course. Each part of the book concentrates on the content that you will need to know to successfully take the Regents Examination in United States History and Government.

The first part of the book familiarizes you with the kinds of questions that are given in the Regents Exam. It provides you with strategies, instructions, and tips that are based on past Regents Exams to help you take the exam successfully.

The second part is an outline and commentary that is based on the student edition of *The American Vision*. It is organized on a unit and chapter basis, and can be used for both reviewing text material and preparing for the Regents Exam. In the margins next to the narrative, you will find test-taking tips and key social studies concepts. Each unit is followed by Regents questions for practice; an answer key is provided in a separate booklet.

The book concludes with three complete Regents Exams to provide complete test practice. This last section also includes a glossary with significant vocabulary terms.

It is a good idea to keep up with your assignments throughout the year so there will be no need to cram for the Regents Exam. Use this Review Book to review the material one chapter or unit at a time. Use questions from your textbook as well as the questions at the end of each unit of this book to help you study.

New York State allows three hours for you to take the Regents Exam in United States History and Government. With proper review, this is ample time to do well on the exam. Get a good night's sleep and eat a well-balanced meal so you will not be tired or hungry during the exam. When the signal is given to begin the exam, skim through the *entire* exam to get an idea of the basic content and structure of the test.

As you can see by past Regents Examinations located at the back of this Review Book, the exam is composed of three parts. Part I consists of 45–50 multiple-choice questions. Part II consists of one thematic essay question, and Part III consists of one document-based question. Part A of the document-based question contains short answer questions based on up to nine specific documents. Part B of the document-based question consists of an essay that requires you to analyze the documents from Part A.

Both the thematic essay and document-based questions are accompanied by a scoring rubric that explains how each will be graded. In order to score a passing grade on the Regents Exam, you must earn at least 65 points.

PREPARING FOR THE REGENTS

This entire book is set up to help you grasp the facts, main ideas, and concepts needed to do well on your Regents Exam. Notes in the margin for this section of the Review Book provide test-taking tips, vocabulary, pointers, and more. The multiple-choice questions and thematic essays in the Regents Practice sections that follow each chapter are taken from past Regents Exams. If you have trouble with any questions, take notes in the margin so that your teacher or classmates can help you with further review strategies.

PART I   MULTIPLE-CHOICE QUESTIONS

General Strategies

Go through the multiple-choice questions the first time, answering only those questions of which you are sure. Read each question very carefully and consider all the possible answers. Underline key words or phrases in each question. Look out for absolute words like "always" and "never." On a second or third reading, answer the remaining questions. Take your time. Think carefully and don't let other students leaving distract or rush you.

Do not leave any spaces on the answer sheet blank. There is no penalty for guessing. But you will definitely lose points for *not* answering a question. As a final review, check your answer key one last time against the questions to make sure that you have marked your answers in the correct spaces on the answer sheet. (It is a good idea to circle answers directly on the exam to make your cross-checking easier.) Be careful about changing your first answers without a good reason for doing so. Your first choices are more likely to be correct.

Multiple-choice questions on the Regents Exam are arranged chronologically, from historical beginnings through the present. You will also find questions that test your knowledge of the relationship between geography and history near the beginning of Part I.

To perform well on the multiple-choice questions in the first section of the U.S. History and Government Regents Examination, you need to have a solid understanding of the vocabulary associated with this course of study, and be ready to apply this knowledge through analysis of different materials.

Several different types of multiple-choice questions may appear on the exam.

- **Recall Questions** When you encounter recall multiple-choice questions, proper preparation and review pay off. Read through the following examples of recall questions. (Answers can be found on page xxi.)

1 Which region of the United States is correctly paired with an industry that is dominant in that region?
   (1) Southwest—timber
   (2) Pacific Northwest—citrus crops
   (3) Great Plains—grain crops
   (4) Atlantic Coastal Plain—iron mining

2 The United States Supreme Court decisions in *Gideon* v. *Wainwright* and *Miranda* v. *Arizona* extended the rights of the accused to
   (1) a speedy trial   (3) legal counsel
   (2) reasonable bail   (4) an impartial jury

3 Since 1823, which United States policy has limited foreign influence in the Western Hemisphere?
   (1) the Eisenhower Doctrine
   (2) popular sovereignty
   (3) imperialism
   (4) the Monroe Doctrine

4 After the Civil War, the poll tax, literacy test, and grandfather clause were used to ensure that
   (1) all citizens exercised the right to vote
   (2) poor people were given equal voting rights
   (3) the voting rights of most former slaves were denied
   (4) the elderly in the South could vote in Federal elections

REGENTS WARM-UP

To answer question 2, you must be familiar with the 26 landmark Supreme Court cases that you studied in your U.S. History and Government course. *Gideon* v. *Wainwright* and *Miranda* v. *Arizona* are two of these landmark cases.

5   In the 1920s, the growth of the Ku Klux Klan and the
    passage of restrictive immigration laws reflected a
    growing American belief in
    (1) nativism
    (2) socialism
    (3) imperialism
    (4) internationalism

REGENTS WARM-UP

Each of the answers in
question 5 is a key social
studies term. Make sure you
know the meanings of these
terms before taking the
Regents Exam.

Types of Recall Questions

There are several types of multiple-choice questions that
appear on most Regents Exams that involve some kind of
thinking skill.

- **Generalizations** A generalization is a broad statement
  about a topic. To be valid, or true, a generalization must
  be based on facts. Sometimes the facts are provided by
  the question itself. Other times you must recall facts that
  support a generalization. (It sometimes helps to jot
  down these facts next to the question.) The following
  questions ask you to identify or evaluate the accuracy of
  generalizations. (Answers can be found on page xxi.)

6   Which statement best describes the economic
    differences between the North and South just prior
    to the Civil War?
    (1) The Northern economy was primarily agricul-
         tural, while the Southern economy was based on
         manufacturing.
    (2) Jobs on plantations attracted more European
         immigrants to the South than to the North.
    (3) Transportation systems were more developed
         in the North than in the South.
    (4) The Southern economy was more diversified
         than the Northern economy.

7   Which statement identifies a change in American
    society during World War II?
    (1) Economic opportunities for women
         increased.
    (2) Government regulation of the economy
         decreased.
    (3) The Great Depression worsened.
    (4) Racial tensions were eliminated.

REGENTS WARM-UP

Think of a generalization as
a summary. Its main purpose
is to draw together the facts
in a general statement. To
allow for the addition of new
facts, generalizations use
such qualifying words as
most, usually, as a rule, and
so on.

REGENTS WARM-UP

In question 6, note the use of
the qualifying word *primarily*
in answer choice (1).

REGENTS WARM-UP

To choose the correct answer
to question 7, ask yourself
which of the statements about
American society during
World War II is *true.*

REGENTS WARM-UP

In question 9, the word *conclusion* means the same thing as "statement," and the word *valid* means "true."

8 What was the experience of most of the "new immigrants" who arrived in the United States from southern and eastern Europe in the late 1800s and early 1900s?
  (1) They lived in urban areas and most held low-paying jobs.
  (2) They obtained free land in the West and became farmers.
  (3) They became discouraged with America and returned to their homelands.
  (4) They were easily assimilated into mainstream American culture.

9 Which conclusion about the civil rights movement of the 1960s is most valid?
  (1) Groups in the movement had common goals but different methods for attaining them.
  (2) Civil disobedience failed to bring about any legislative changes.
  (3) The movement began with violent protests but ended with peaceful demonstrations.
  (4) The movement failed to inspire other groups to work for change.

10 Which statement most accurately describes conditions of American farmers during the economic boom of the mid-1920s?
  (1) Shortages of fertile land and farm equipment lowered farm income.
  (2) Overproduction helped keep farmers from participating in the prosperity of the times.
  (3) Subsidies and other government programs dramatically increased farmers' incomes.
  (4) Higher prices for farm products resulted in a higher standard of living for farmers.

• **Cause and Effect** History is a study of cause-and-effect relationships. As a result, you will find many questions dealing with cause and effect on the Regents Exam. A *cause* is an event or action that brings about a change. There are *immediate causes,* or events that directly trigger an event, and *underlying causes,* or developments that build up over time. There are also immediate and

long-range effects. An *immediate effect* directly results
from a series of causes. A *long-term effect* is a lasting
change that reveals itself over time. For example, if you
begin to exercise, an immediate effect is muscle soreness.
A long-term effect is being more toned and fit. The
following are examples of cause-and-effect questions.
(Answers can be found on page xxi.)

11 What was one result of World War II?
    (1) The arms race ended.
    (2) The Cold War ended.
    (3) Communism was eliminated.
    (4) Two superpowers emerged.

12 What was a major result of Prohibition in the United
    States during the 1920s?
    (1) restriction of immigration
    (2) growth of communism
    (3) destruction of family values
    (4) increase in organized crime

13 The creation of the first political parties in the United
    States resulted from a controversy over
    (1) declaring independence from Great Britain
    (2) recognizing women's equality
    (3) expanding slavery into the newly acquired
        territories
    (4) interpreting the Constitution

14 Territorial expansion during the first half of the
    19th century contributed to
    (1) balancing the Federal budget
    (2) escalating the debate over slavery
    (3) weakening the traditional policy of isolationism
    (4) improving the living conditions of Native American
        Indians

15 The loss of jobs in manufacturing industries has been
    caused by the introduction of
    (1) radio and television
    (2) automobiles and airplanes
    (3) automation and computers
    (4) improved medicine and space travel

REGENTS WARM-UP

In question 11, the word
result means the same thing
as "effect."

REGENTS WARM-UP

In question 14, the words
contributed to means the
same thing as "helped
cause."

- **Comparison** Comparison involves looking for similarities and/or differences between two or more items. On the Regents Exam, you will be asked to compare people, ideas, events, times, and so on. Comparison is the most common form of question used to form links between historical periods. The following questions ask you to make comparisons. (Answers can be found on page xxi.)

16 The Palmer raids following World War I and the McCarthy hearings during the Korean War were similar in that they were caused by fear of
(1) new military weapons
(2) foreign invasions of the United States
(3) communist influence in the United States
(4) economic depression

17 How does the present-day United States' economy differ from the nation's economy of 1900?
(1) Immigrants are no longer a source of labor.
(2) Today's government plays a less active role in the economy.
(3) The United States is less dependent on oil imports.
(4) The growth of service industries is greater today.

18 One similarity between the Articles of Confederation and the United States Constitution is that both documents provide for
(1) a national legislature to make laws
(2) federal control of commerce between the states
(3) federal power to impose and collect taxes
(4) the abolition of slavery

19 One way in which the Chinese Exclusion Act, the Gentlemen's Agreement, and the National Origins Act were similar is that all were expressions of
(1) imperialism
(2) nativism
(3) militarism
(4) Manifest Destiny

20 How did the power of government change during the Civil War and the Great Depression?
(1) Presidential powers were expanded.
(2) Congress exerted greater leadership.
(3) The Supreme Court expanded civil liberties.
(4) Power shifted from the federal government to the states.

REGENTS WARM-UP

Question 19 asks you to compare three pieces of legislation. But to answer it correctly, you also need to know the definition of the key social studies terms listed in the answers.

Data-Based Questions

A special type of multiple-choice question on the Regents Exam asks you interpret some type of data. The data may be in written form or in visual form. Some questions test your understanding of the data. Others involve evaluation of the data. You may also be asked to form generalizations or draw conclusions based on the data.

- **Written Sources** Sprinkled throughout past Regents Exams are various kinds of written data—quotes, mock dialogues, poems, and more. The following are examples of questions that involve the interpretation of written data. (Answers can be found on page xxi.)

Base your answers to questions 20 and 21 on the speakers' statements below and on your knowledge of social studies.

Speaker A: "Our nation has grown and prospered from the ideas and labor of immigrants. The nation has been enriched by immigrants from different nations who brought new ideas and lifestyles, which have become part of American culture."

Speaker B: "United States industries are competing with established European manufacturers. To prosper, American industries need the vast supply of unskilled labor that is provided by immigrants."

Speaker C: "Immigrants are taking jobs at low wages without regard for long hours and workers' safety. American workers must unite to end this unfair competition."

Speaker D: "Immigrants arrive in American cities poor and frightened. They are helped to find jobs or housing. These newcomers should show their gratitude at voting time."

21 Which speaker is most clearly expressing the melting pot theory?
   (1) A   (3) C
   (2) B   (4) D

22 Speaker *D* is expressing an opinion most like that of a
   (1) labor union member
   (2) religious leader
   (3) factory owner
   (4) political party boss

REGENTS WARM-UP

Question 21 tests your understanding of the melting pot theory.

Base your answer to question 23 on the quotation below and on your knowledge of social studies.

> "We conclude that in the field of public education, the doctrine of 'separate but equal' has no place. Separate educational facilities are inherently unequal. . . ."
> —*Chief Justice Earl Warren*,
> Brown v. Board of Education of Topeka, Kansas

23 This quotation illustrates the Supreme Court's power to
    (1) uphold previous decisions
    (2) overrule state laws
    (3) check the powers of the executive branch
    (4) provide for educational funding

Base your answer to question 24 on the headlines below and on your knowledge of social studies.

"U.S. Sponsors Panamanian Revolution" (1903)

"U.S. Establishes Military Rule in Dominican Republic" (1916)

"CIA Supports Overthrow of Guatemala Regime" (1954)

24 These headlines suggest that
    (1) United States interests in Latin America have often led to intervention.
    (2) The United States is willing to fight to maintain the independence of Latin American nations.
    (3) Latin American nations have declared war on the United States several times.
    (4) Latin American nations are able to run their governments without the United States' help.

- **Maps** Many past Regents Exams have asked students to interpret data presented on maps. A series of steps will help you interpret data on a map. First, try to identify the topic or subject of the map. Check to see if the map has a title. Next, you must collect the map's most important facts. The map key or labels on the map will help you with this task. Once you have collected this information, you are ready to interpret the data. The following map and question provide an opportunity to practice your map-reading skills. (The answer can be found on page xxi.)

Base your answer to question 25 on the map below and on your knowledge of social studies.

25 The situation shown in the map threatened the United States policy of
   (1) intervention   (3) neutrality
   (2) containment   (4) collective security

REGENTS WARM-UP

Don't forget to read the map title and labels to get as much information as you can before trying to answer question 25.

- **Political Cartoons** Political cartoons are one of the most commonly used data-based questions in the Regents Exam. Political cartoons, like a newspaper editorial, express an opinion or point of view on an issue. The following question asks you to interpret a political cartoon. (The answer can be found on page xxi.)

Base your answer to question 26 on the cartoon below and on your knowledge of social studies.

The Vultures' Roost

Source: Graff, Henry, *The Glorious Republic*, Houghton Mifflin (adapted)

26 What is the main idea of this cartoon?
  (1) Big business greatly influenced the actions of the Senate.
  (2) The Senate had to continue to pass legislation to support conservation efforts.
  (3) The Senate needed more financial support from monopolies.
  (4) Relations between industry and the Senate benefited the general public.

- **Graphs and Tables** Graphs and tables summarize and organize information in an easy-to-read format. Like other visual data, you begin interpreting a graph or a table by reading its title to find out what the graph or table shows. Then read all the labels shown. Now you are ready to interpret the facts, or data, on the graph or table. The following questions offer practice in interpreting information presented in a graph and a table. (The answers can be found on page xxi.)

Base your answer to question 27 on the chart below and on your knowledge of social studies.

MEDIAN EARNINGS OF MEN AND WOMEN IN THE UNITED STATES, 1960–1990				
Year	Women	Men	Women's Earnings as a Percent of Men's	Earnings Gap in Constant 1990 Dollars
1960	$ 3,257	$ 5,368	60.7	$ 8,569
1970	5,323	8,966	59.4	11,529
1980	11,197	18,612	60.2	11,776
1990	19,822	27,678	71.6	7,856

Source: Bureau of the Census

27 The data in this chart support the conclusion that between 1960 and 1990
   (1) government failed to pass laws that granted women equal access to jobs
   (2) the earnings gap between men and women was only slightly improved
   (3) women's earnings consistently increased faster than those of men
   (4) most higher-paying jobs were still not legally open to women

REGENTS WARM-UP

In question 27, the word *chart* is used as a synonym for "table."

Base your answer to question 28 on the graphs below and on your knowledge of social studies.

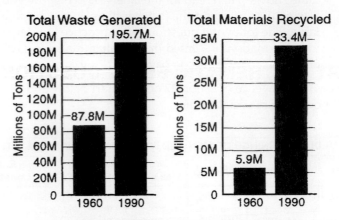

U.S Municipal Solid Waste, 1960 vs.1990

Source: U.S. Environmental Protection Agency

28 Data from the graphs support the conclusion that between 1960 and 1990
   (1) the government failed in its efforts at recycling
   (2) the amount of waste that was recycled increased
   (3) most people favor mandatory recycling efforts
   (4) efforts to recycle waste decreased steadily

Answers to Sample Questions in Part I Multiple Choice

1. (3)   2. (3)   3. (4)   4. (3)   5. (1)   6. (3)   7. (1)   8. (1)
9. (1)   10. (2)   11. (4)   12. (4)   13. (4)   14. (2)   15. (3)   16. (3)
17. (4)   18. (1)   19. (2)   20. (1)   21. (1)   22. (4)   23. (2)   24. (1)
25. (3)   26. (1)   27. (2)   28. (2)

PART II   THEMATIC ESSAY QUESTION

General Strategies

The thematic essay question is an important part of the Regents Exam. A generic scoring rubric is provided with the directions for the thematic essay. The rubric explains how your response to the thematic essay will be graded. The highest possible score is a five; the lowest is a zero.

Each thematic essay question includes a theme and a task. The theme states a broad idea related to an aspect of U.S. History and Government. The task describes what you have to do to complete the essay.

Before you begin to write your thematic essay response, read the theme and the task carefully. Look for clues that will help you identify the information you need to include to thoroughly address both the theme and the task. It's a good idea to underline the parts of the theme and task that you think are most important. Note the number of parts in the task and watch for *italicized* words that call your attention to important points.

It is also important to read the scoring rubric. To receive full credit (5 points) for this section of the Regents Exam, each of the task items must be addressed in your written essay response.

The sample thematic essay question that follows is from the June 2001 U.S. History and Government Regents Examination:

Theme: Territorial Expansion (1800–1900)

> Various events or developments have influenced the territorial expansion of the United States. In 1800, the United States was a new nation of approximately 895,000 square miles of territory. By 1900, the nation had grown to about 3,000,000 square miles of territory.

Task: Identify *two* events or developments that had a significant impact on United States territorial expansion between 1800 and 1900, and for *each* event or development identified:

- Discuss the historical circumstances surrounding the event or development

- Evaluate the importance of the event or development on the growth of the United States

You may use any example from your study of United States history. Some suggestions you might wish to consider include the Louisiana Purchase (1803), completion of the Erie Canal (1825), War with Mexico (1846–1848), Homestead Act (1862), completion of the first transcontinental railroad (1869), and Native American Indian policies (1800–1900).

You are *not* limited to these suggestions.

In the sample thematic essay task, you are asked to *discuss* and *evaluate*. Other tasks might ask you to *describe, show,* or *explain.* Keep these general definitions in mind:

- *Discuss* means "to make observations about something using facts, reasoning, and argument; to present in detail."

- *Describe* means "to illustrate or tell about something in words."

- *Show* means "to point out; to set forth clearly a position or idea by stating it and giving data which support it."

- *Explain* means "to make plain or understandable; to give reasons for or causes of; to show the logical development or relationship of."

- *Evaluate* means "to examine and judge the significance, worth, or condition of; to determine the value of."

Preparing to Write

Before writing, make a chart to organize your thoughts. The rows down the side of the chart should reflect the tasks. The columns across the top should reflect the examples you have chosen to include in your thematic essay.

To get ready to write the thematic essay above, your chart should look like similar to this:

Tasks	Louisiana Purchase	Homestead Act
Task 1: Discuss the historical circumstances surrounding the event or development.		
Task 2: Evaluate the importance of the event or development on the growth of the United States.		

Writing the Essay

When you get ready to write your thematic essay, be brief and to the point. Your thematic essay response should include an introduction, a body of several paragraphs, and a conclusion.

- **Introduction** Your introduction should describe what it is that your essay will show or prove. Do not just copy the theme or task—be sure to state in your own words what your essay will show or prove.

- **Body** The body paragraphs need to include all elements of the task by showing that you understand the theme. The body should incorporate relevant facts, examples, and details in an easy-to-understand way. Use the table that you made before you began to write to organize the body paragraphs of your response.

- **Conclusion** The conclusion to your essay response should be a summation of the theme or problem.

Your thematic essay response should be between one and two pages long. Do not overwrite. When you are finished, proofread your work to make sure that you have addressed all parts of the task.

Sample thematic essay questions are included in the Practicing for the Regents section at the end of each unit and in the Regents Exams at the back of this book.

THEMATIC ESSAY GENERIC SCORING RUBRIC

Score of 5:

- Thoroughly develops all aspects of the task evenly and in depth

- Is more analytical than descriptive (analyzes, evaluates, and/or creates* information)

- Richly supports the theme with many relevant facts, examples, and details

- Demonstrates a logical and clear plan of organization; includes an introduction and a conclusion that are beyond a restatement of the theme

Score of 4:

- Develops all aspects of the task but may do so somewhat unevenly

- Is both descriptive and analytical (applies, analyzes, evaluates, and/or creates* information)

- Supports the theme with relevant facts, examples, and details

- Demonstrates a logical and clear plan of organization; includes an introduction and a conclusion that are beyond a restatement of the theme

Score of 3:

- Develops all aspects of the task with little depth or develops most aspects of the task in some depth

- Is more descriptive than analytical (applies, may analyze, and/or evaluate information)

- Includes some relevant facts, examples, and details; may include some minor inaccuracies

- Demonstrates a satisfactory plan of organization; includes an introduction and a conclusion that may be a restatement of the theme

Score of 2:

- Minimally develops all aspects of the task or develops some aspects of the task in some depth

- Is primarily descriptive; may include faulty, weak, or isolated application, or analysis

- Includes few relevant facts, examples, and details; may include some inaccuracies

- Demonstrates a general plan of organization; may lack focus; may contain digressions; may not clearly identify which aspect of the task is being addressed; may lack an introduction and/or a conclusion

Score of 1:

- Minimally develops some aspects of the task

- Is descriptive; may lack understanding, application, or analysis

- Includes few relevant facts, examples, or details; may include inaccuracies

- May demonstrate a weakness in organization; may lack focus; may contain digressions; may not clearly identify which aspect of the task is being addressed; may lack an introduction and/or a conclusion

Score of 0:

Fails to develop the task or may only refer to the theme in a general way; *OR* includes no relevant facts, examples, or details; *OR* includes only the theme, task, or suggestions copied from the test booklet; *OR* is illegible; *OR* is a blank paper

* The term *create* as used by Anderson/Krathwohl, et al. in their 2001 revision of Bloom's *Taxonomy of Educational Objectives* refers to the highest level of the cognitive domain. This usage of *create* is similar to Bloom's use of the term *synthesis*. Creating implies an insightful reorganization of information into a new pattern or whole. While a level 5 paper will contain analysis and/or evaluation of information, a very strong paper may also include examples of creating information as defined by Anderson and Krathwohl.

PART III   DOCUMENT-BASED QUESTION

General Strategies

Part III of the Regents Exam contains one document-based question, or DBQ. While the DBQ is similar to a conventional essay in many ways, the DBQ also has some additional components. The DBQ has two parts:

Part A presents a series of up to nine documents, some of which you may have seen before, but many of which may be new to you. The documents may be written passages or quotes, political cartoons, paintings, photographs, tables, or graphs. One or more short-answer questions accompany each document, and are directly related to it.

Approach these questions in the same way that you approached the data-based multiple-choice questions in Part I of the Regents Exam. That is, examine each document carefully, being sure to read all titles, labels, captions, or other text before answering the question. Be sure to answer each question with complete sentences.

Part B requires you to write an essay that addresses a specific task and that uses information obtained from the documents as well as your knowledge of social studies. Approach this essay in the same way that you approached the thematic essay in Part II of the Regents Exam. Like the thematic essay, Part B of the DBQ contains a rubric that explains how your response to the essay will be graded. The highest possible score is a five; the lowest is a zero.

The sample document-based question that follows is from the June 2001 U.S. History and Government Regents Examination:

This question is based on the accompanying documents (1–6). This question is designed to test your ability to work with historical documents. Some of these documents have been edited for the purposes of this question. As you analyze the documents, take into account both the source of each document and any point of view that may be presented in the document.

Historical Context: Throughout its history, the United States has followed different foreign policies to promote its interests. These policies have included neutrality, imperialism, containment, and internationalism. Specific actions have been taken and specific programs have been established to carry out these policies.

Task: Using information from the documents and your knowledge of United States history, answer the questions that follow each document in Part A. Your answers to the questions will help you write the Part B essay, in which you will be asked to:

- Describe *two* different United States foreign policies

- Discuss *one* specific action or program the United States has used to carry out *each* foreign policy

- Evaluate the extent to which the action or program used was successful in carrying out *each* foreign policy

Again, keep these general definitions in mind:

- *Discuss* means "to make observations about something using facts, reasoning, and argument; to present in detail."

- *Describe* means "to illustrate or tell about something in words."

- *Show* means "to point out; to set forth clearly a position or idea by stating it and giving data which support it."

- *Explain* means "to make plain or understandable; to give reasons for or causes of; to show the logical development or relationship of."

- *Evaluate* means "to examine and judge the significance, worth, or condition of; to determine the value of."

Preparing to Write

Before writing, make a chart to organize your thoughts. The rows down the side of the chart should reflect the tasks. The columns across the top should reflect the examples you have chosen to include in your DBQ essay.

To get ready to write the thematic essay above, your chart should look like similar to this:

Tasks	Foreign Policy #1	Foreign Policy #2
Task 1: Describe **two** different United States foreign policies.		
Task 2: Discuss **one** specific action or program the United States has used to carry out **each** foreign policy.		
Task 3: Evaluate the extent to which the action or program used was successful in carrying out **each** foreign policy.		

Writing the Essay

Approach the writing of your DBQ essay in the same way that you approached the thematic essay. Be sure to include an introduction, a body of several paragraphs, and a conclusion.

Sample Part A and Part B document-based questions are included in the Practicing for the Regents section at the end of each unit and in the Regents Exams at the back of this book.

DOCUMENT-BASED ESSAY GENERIC SCORING RUBRIC

REGENTS WARM-UP

Remember, the guidelines you are given on the exam are the guidelines for the highest score. Make sure you fully address each of the guidelines given.

Score of 5:

- Thoroughly develops all aspects of the task evenly and in depth

- Is more analytical than descriptive (analyzes, evaluates, and/or creates* information)

- Incorporates relevant information from *at least* the requested number of documents

- Incorporates substantial relevant outside information

- Richly supports the theme with many relevant facts, examples, and details

- Demonstrates a logical and clear plan of organization; includes an introduction and a conclusion that are beyond a restatement of the theme

Score of 4:

- Develops all aspects of the task but may do so somewhat unevenly

- Is both descriptive and analytical (applies, analyzes, evaluates, and/or creates* information)

- Incorporates relevant information from *at least* the requested number of documents

- Incorporates relevant outside information

- Supports the theme with relevant facts, examples, and details

- Demonstrates a logical and clear plan of organization; includes an introduction and a conclusion that are beyond a restatement of the theme

Score of 3:

- Develops all aspects of the task with little depth *or* develops most aspects of the task in some depth

- Is more descriptive than analytical (applies, may analyze, and/or evaluate information)

- Incorporates some relevant information from some of the documents

- Incorporates limited relevant outside information

- Includes some relevant facts, examples, and details; may include some minor inaccuracies

- Demonstrates a satisfactory plan of organization; includes an introduction and a conclusion that may be a restatement of the theme

Score of 2:

- Minimally develops all aspects of the task *or* develops some aspects of the task in some depth

- Is primarily descriptive; may include faulty, weak, or isolated application or analysis

- Incorporates limited relevant information from the documents *or* consists primarily of relevant information copied from the documents

- Presents little or no relevant outside information

- Includes few relevant facts, examples, or details; may include some inaccuracies

- Demonstrates a general plan of organization; may lack focus; may contain digressions; may not clearly identify which aspect of the task is being addressed; may lack an introduction and/or a conclusion

Score of 1:

- Minimally develops some aspects of the task

- Is descriptive; may lack understanding, application, or analysis

- Makes vague, unclear references to the documents or consists primarily of relevant and irrelevant information copied from the documents

- Presents no relevant outside information

- Includes few relevant facts, examples, or details; may include inaccuracies

- May demonstrate a weakness in organization; may lack focus; may contain digressions; may not clearly identify which aspect of the task is being addressed; may lack an introduction and/or conclusion

Score of 0:

Fails to develop the task or may only refer to the theme in a general way; *OR* includes no relevant facts, examples, or details; *OR* includes only the historical context and/or task as copied from the test booklet; *OR* includes only entire documents copied from the test booklet; *OR* is illegible; *OR* is a blank paper.

* The term *create* as used by Anderson/Krathwohl, et al. in their 2001 revision of Bloom's *Taxonomy of Educational Objectives* refers to the highest level of the cognitive domain. This usage of *create* is similar to Bloom's use of the term *synthesis*. Creating implies an insightful reorganization of information into a new pattern or whole. While a level 5 paper will contain analysis and/or evaluation of information, a very strong paper may also include examples of creating information as defined by Anderson and Krathwohl.

UNIT 1 GEOGRAPHY OF THE UNITED STATES

Chapter 1   Human and Physical Geography

Unit 1 Overview

Each nation is shaped by the opportunities offered and limitations imposed by its geography. The United States was formed by its rivers and mountains, by its mosaic of immigrants who came to the nation seeking many different kinds of freedom. Geography has affected patterns of colonization and expansion, as well as wartime efforts. In an increasingly interdependent world, dealing with issues such as aging populations, environmental destruction, and urban challenges is critical. Studying both the human and physical geographic features of the United States will enable you to understand more fully the history of the country.

Unit 1 Objectives

1.   Explain the physical and cultural setting of the Americas.

2.   Describe the factors that shaped the identity of the United States and the physical barriers to expansion that early settlers faced.

3.   Analyze the role and influence of geography on the nation's historical and cultural development.

4.   Discuss current geographic issues.

5.   Summarize demographic issues facing the United States at the beginning of the twenty-first century.

Chapter Overview

The United States spans the continent of North America, stretching from the Pacific Ocean in the west to the Atlantic in the east. Mountains frame its eastern and western edges, cradling a central region of vast grassland plains. These grasslands have been transformed into some of the world's most productive farmlands.

Physical geography affects the distribution and density of the population in the United States. The nation's earliest settlements and largest cities developed along waterways. These waterways, used for transportation and their abundant natural resources, helped the country become industrialized.

Acid rain, smog, and water pollution cause damage to the region's environment and also affect human health. The United States is working to manage its rich natural resources responsibly.

The United States' immigrant roots make the country diverse. The nation has a heritage of religious freedom. People in the United States enjoy a high standard of living. The nation currently faces challenges from an aging population and the effects of the influential baby boom generation.

As you read through this chapter, ask yourself these questions:
(1) Why have rivers played such an important role in the nation's development?
(2) How are population patterns in the United States influenced by the nation's physical geography?
(3) What are some of the environmental challenges facing the United States?
(4) What geographic factors encouraged the **industrialization** and **urbanization** of the United States?

CORE CONCEPTS: PLACES AND REGIONS

Most people in the United States live in urban areas. Major cities are ethnically diverse, reflecting an immigrant heritage. The country's economic strength, however, was built on agriculture. Manufacturing, technology, and service industries have joined agriculture as the nation's primary economic activities.

Main Ideas and Concepts

- **Civic Rights and Responsibilities** In a world of scarce resources, all citizens must help preserve the water, land, and air.

- **Science and Technology** Inventions such as the steel plow and steam tractor made it possible to farm large areas of what had once been **prairie**.

- **Geography and History** During the 1930s poor farming techniques and drought combined to create a Dust Bowl across much of the Great Plains.

- **Culture and Traditions** Early Native Americans practiced a way of life that honored the land and animals.

People, Places, Terms

The following names and terms will help you to prepare for the Regents Exam in United States History and Government. You can find an explanation of each name and term in the Glossary in the back of this book, in your textbook, or in another reference source.

groundwater	megalopolis	steppe
immigration	prairie	urbanization
industrialization	socioeconomic status	

SECTION 1 THE PHYSICAL AND CULTURAL SETTING IN THE UNITED STATES

Size and Location

The United States is located in the Western hemisphere on the North American continent. It shares a northern border with Canada, and a southern border with Mexico and the Gulf of Mexico. On the eastern shore is the Atlantic Ocean; the Pacific Ocean is at the western shore. Its land mass is 3,619,696 square miles (9,375,720 square kilometers).

CORE CONCEPTS: THE WORLD IN SPATIAL TERMS

The United States could fit inside the nation of Canada, which has a landmass of 3,851,809 square miles (9,976,185 square kilometers).

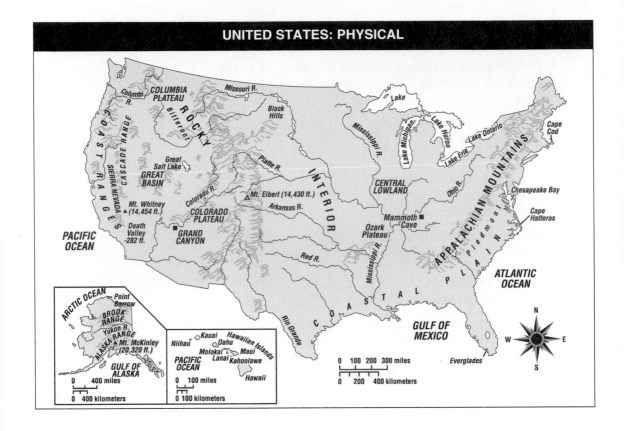

UNITED STATES: PHYSICAL

Major Zones/Areas

The United States can be divided into four major areas. The Western plains and plateaus include the Pacific Ranges, the Rocky Mountains, and the Columbia and Colorado Plateaus. The Great Plains make up the interior landforms. The Eastern mountains and lowlands consist of the Appalachian Mountains, the continent's second-longest mountain range. Islands make up the fourth major zone.

Climate Zones Much of Alaska is part of a subarctic climate. It has long, very cold winters. The climate from southern Alaska to California is marine west coast. Wet ocean air, which the mountains force upward, cools and releases moisture, bringing more than 100 inches (254 cm) of rain yearly in some parts of the region. In southern California, the climate is mild. Between the Pacific Ranges and the Rocky Mountains, the weather is hot and dry, with a desert or **steppe** climate. Moving eastward to the

CORE CONCEPTS: PHYSICAL SYSTEMS

Glaciers and volcanic action shaped the country's landforms. A collision of the North American and Pacific tectonic plates created the mountain chain known as the Pacific Ranges.

Great Plains, the climate is humid, with hot summers and bitterly cold winters. In the east, the climate is humid and subtropical in the south, with a tropical savanna climate in south Florida.

Vegetation Zones Large coniferous forests abound in Alaska. In the west, there are coniferous forests, ferns, and mosses. Little grows in the desert regions. Depending on the latitudes, there may be desert scrub, coniferous forests, or grasslands. The Great Plains is a natural grassland. Tropical rainforests thrive in Hawaii; wetlands and swamps are part of the southeastern United States.

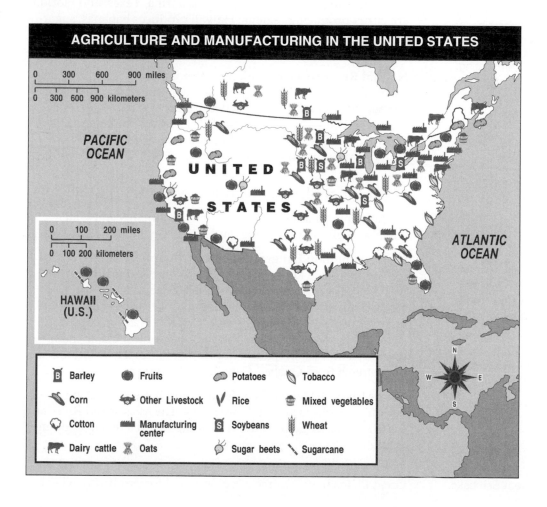

CORE CONCEPTS: ENVIRONMENT AND SOCIETY

One of the ongoing debates in managing timber resources is the matter of controlled burning. Current policy now follows a Native American practice of setting fires in dry areas. This prevents dry brush from becoming too thick and drying out the underbrush or preventing new seeds from germinating.

CORE CONCEPTS: IMMIGRATION AND MIGRATION

One of the mass migrations across the Great Plains took place in the 1830s and 1840s. Followers of Joseph Smith, founder of the Mormon religion, searched for a place to practice their religion freely. After persecution in Ohio, Missouri, and Illinois, they crossed with difficulty into Utah Territory and settled near the Great Salt Lake.

Agricultural Areas About one billion acres (405,000,000 ha) of land in the United States is used for agriculture. Land use is nearly evenly divided between livestock and farmland. Cattle ranches are found throughout the Western, Southern, and Midwestern parts of the nation. In the North-central region, dairy products, hogs, and chickens are leading products. The Great Plains have been converted to the nation's breadbasket, with wheat the major product. The Corn Belt stretches from Nebraska to Ohio. About half of the corn crop is used for animal feed; the remainder is processed into corn oil and sweeteners, or used for human consumption. The Southern states are noted for growing cotton, rice, and tobacco. California, Texas, and Florida are citrus-producing regions; Hawaii produces bananas, sugarcane, and pineapple. Throughout the Midwestern states, farms produce a variety of fruits and vegetables.

Natural Resources The nation's natural resources include fuels such as natural gas, petroleum, and coal. Minerals—including copper, silver, and gold, as well as iron ore—are found in the west. The United States also has forests and woodlands that supply the timber industry. The abundant fish in oceans and inland waters are another resource.

Factors that Shaped the Identity of the United States

The country has been formed by its mountains and waterways, as well as by its fertile land and many natural resources.

Major Mountain Ranges The Rocky Mountains stretch some 3,000 miles (4828 km) from Alaska to New Mexico, linking the United States and Canada. In the past, this relatively young mountain range created major barriers to westward expansion. Some of its peaks are more than 14,000 feet (4,267 m) high. The Appalachian Mountains are the country's oldest major chain, located in the eastern part of the United States. Heavily eroded, they stretch from Quebec, Canada to the state of Alabama.

Major River Systems A wealth of water has supplied the nation's people, farms, and industries. The Mississippi River and the St. Lawrence Seaway are two of the world's major shipping areas.

Great Plains At first dismissed as unlikely to be of any use, the Great Plains have become a region noted for producing wheat.

Atlantic and Pacific Oceans The oceans at both coasts have allowed the United States to ship goods easily to every continent of the world.

Coastlines Settlements along the coasts have become major seaports and centers of the fishing industry.

Climate The majority of the country lies in the temperate zone, with sufficient growing seasons and rainfall. People in some parts of the country regularly face the threat of hurricanes, tornadoes, fires, or floods.

Abundance of Natural Resources The early colonists found timber for making homes, public buildings, and forts. There was land for growing crops and river systems and oceans to ship those crops. The discovery of gold, silver, and copper during the nineteenth century brought wealth to many.

Barriers to Expansion/Development

Physical barriers slowed the westward expansion of the nation. Settlers had to contend with climate, distance, and geographic features to expand into new territory.

Climate The early settlers from England had to deal with harsh winters. As settlers pushed west, they generally tried to time their journeys to escape blizzards and other difficulties of winter weather.

Mountain Ranges Crossing the Appalachians, and then the Rockies, proved a difficult feat for settlers. Daring pioneers and mountain men served as guides over the mountains.

Arid Lands The American Southwest is a desert region that remained sparsely inhabited until modern air conditioning made it a destination for retirees. California's Death Valley holds the record for the highest recorded temperature—134°F (57°C)—of anywhere in the nation.

Great Plains Settlers of the Great Plains often had to deal with drought and frigid winters.

CORE CONCEPTS: ENVIRONMENT AND SOCIETY

The Native Americans who lived in Alaska faced scarce resources and limited farmland. They turned to hunting caribou and other animals for food and clothing.

CORE CONCEPTS: MOVEMENT OF PEOPLE AND GOODS

Archaeologists have long maintained that the first peoples in North America arrived during the Ice Age via a land bridge that linked Asia to Alaska. Recent evidence, however, suggests that nomads from Central and South America may have arrived earlier or at the same time as those coming from Asia.

SECTION 2 THE ROLE AND INFLUENCE OF GEOGRAPHY ON HISTORICAL AND CULTURAL DEVELOPMENT

The history and culture of any people cannot be explained fully without considering the geographical factors that influenced the group.

Influences on Early Native American Indians

Native peoples of the Pacific Northwest enjoyed abundant resources and a mild climate. Their homes and canoes were made of the redwood, cedar, and fir trees of the region. They used nets to harvest salmon from the Pacific.

In the Southwest's high deserts, Native Americans used irrigation to farm. Midwestern tribes followed the buffalo, while Native Americans east of the Mississippi traded extensively, hunted, and grew crops. Groups in the northeastern woodlands hunted and traded.

Influence on Colonization Patterns and Colonial Development

Colonists from major European nations began arriving in North America by the late 1500s. French traders and trappers used the Mississippi River and the St. Lawrence as major trade routes. The Spanish founded military posts and missions at the same time as they started farms and large cattle ranches. English colonies in the northeastern region found farming difficult, although the area offered ample timber for shipbuilding and harbors for trade and fishing. In the middle and southern English colonies, the milder climate was well suited for farming.

Territorial Expansion

The United States continued expanding westward, lured by resources of land and minerals. The former Mexican territory of Texas, which became part of the United States in 1845, was valued for its cattle ranches and cotton production. When gold was discovered in California in 1848, the influx of prospectors soon gave that republic enough citizens to become a state.

Impact During Wartime

The nation has secured important geographic resources to meet economic needs or establish boundaries. For example, the Treaty of Paris (1783), which ended the French and Indian War, secured the Mississippi River as the western border of the new nation of the United States of America.

Effect of Location on United States Foreign Policy

The United States has used its geographical setting within the western hemisphere to define foreign policy. Both the Monroe Doctrine and the Roosevelt Corollary expressed the nation's right to protect its interests and limit foreign intervention throughout the region.

At the beginning of the twentieth century, American know-how completed the Panama Canal, which linked Pacific and Atlantic trade. As a result of the Spanish American War (1898), the United States acquired land for naval bases in Hawaii and Cuba.

SECTION 3 GEOGRAPHIC ISSUES TODAY

Waste Disposal

Industrial and agricultural wastes pose a threat to the nation's waters. Illegal dumping of toxic wastes (byproducts of industrial production) can enter the **groundwater** through small leaks. Thermal pollution results from industries that release heated industrial wastewater into cooler rivers and lakes. Fertilizers and pesticides used in agriculture also make their way into the water supplies.

The signing of the North American Free Trade Agreement (NAFTA) in 1992 has also sparked environmental concerns along the United States–Mexico border. The environment along the Rio Grande is threatened by the rapid industrial growth that resulted from NAFTA.

Water and Air Pollution

In addition to the industrial and agricultural pollution affecting the nation's water supply, acid rain affects a large area of the eastern United States. Acid rain forms when chemical emissions

CORE CONCEPTS: SCIENCE AND TECHNOLOGY

Building the Panama Canal had been a dream of many nations. The French had invested more than a decade attempting the feat, which resulted in the loss of many workers to yellow fever. The canal eventually cost nearly $390 million and took 40,000 workers ten years to complete.

CORE CONCEPTS: ENVIRONMENT AND SOCIETY

In the 1970s, a grassroots movement to protect the environment led to the passage of a number of Congressional Acts and to the first Earth Day celebration.

CORE CONCEPTS: INTERDEPENDENCE

To combat pollution, Canada and the United States signed the Great Lakes Quality Water Agreement in 1972. The Great Lakes span the U.S.–Canadian border. Today, the Commission for Environmental Cooperation monitors NAFTA's environmental effects and makes suggestions for ways to reduce pollution.

from factories, power plants, automobiles, and refineries react with the water vapor in the air. The result of this chemical reaction is that chemicals, such as nitrogen oxide and sulfur dioxide, turn into their acidic forms. Acid rain in the rivers and lakes damages plants and fish. Lakes may become biologically dead, that is, unable to support most organisms.

Shifting Populations

During the 1970s, the American South and Southwest became—and has remained—the fastest-growing section of the nation. Known as the Sunbelt for its mild climate, the region attracts manufacturing, service, and tourism. Lured by the pleasant winters, many retirees choose to relocate to this region. Because the area is close to Caribbean and Latin American nations, many immigrants from those nations arrive there as well.

The historic centers of commerce and industry in the Northeast and along the Great Lakes remain densely populated areas. The Pacific coast is another population cluster; the state of California is the most populous in the nation.

Energy Usage

Throughout the history of the United States, the country has largely relied on fossil fuels, such as oil and coal, to supply energy. However, those resources are not renewable—once they are gone, they cannot be replaced. Over the past few decades, the government and private industry have worked to develop renewable energy sources, such as wind, natural gas, and solar power.

Urban Problems and Challenges

In the late 1800s, the population began to shift from a rural, agricultural base to an urban, industrial one. Cities grew rapidly, facing the challenges of housing, transportation, and sewage. Other problems included violence, crime, pollution, disease, and fire.

SECTION 4 DEMOGRAPHICS

Characteristics

Population in the United States is divided nearly evenly according to gender, with women slightly outnumbering men.

CORE CONCEPTS: URBANIZATION

During the thirty years after the Civil War, the urban population of the United States grew rapidly. The nation in 1840 had a mere 131 cities (defined as settlements with populations of 2,500 or more). By 1900, the number of cities exceeded 1,700. Not only the numbers of cities but their populations have increased. New York City, for example, went from a population of 800,000 in 1860 to 3.5 million in 1900.

There are more than 285 million people living in the nation. About 62 percent of people are between the ages of 18 and 64, according to the 2000 United States Census. People under 18 make up 26 percent of the population and 12 percent are over 65. More than 54 percent of people are married, and 68 percent of households are familes with at least one person over 18 years old. The Caucasian ethnicity makes up 70 percent of the population, with Hispanic and African American ethnicities each around 13 percent.

The Bill of Rights was added to the Constitution in 1791, granting Americans religious freedom. Most of the people in the nation who are part of an organized religion are Christians. Other major religions include Judaism, Buddhism, and Islam.

The United States has a literacy rate of 97%, one of the world's highest. Most people in the country enjoy a high standard of living. Higher **socioeconomic status,** reflected by income and level of education, offers the advantages of opportunities and choice. As is usual in countries with a high standard of living, the birth rate is low, increasing the population about 0.5 percent annually.

Immigration

According to U.S. Census data from 2003, more than 11 percent of the United States population was born in a foreign country. Still considered a land of opportunity, the nation attracts people looking for better employment or education opportunities. Of this group, more than 53 percent came from Latin America, 25 percent came from Asia, and 14 percent from Europe. The remainder (about 8 percent) come from other nations around the world.

Migration

Americans have always been a people who value the right to move around freely. One in six persons relocates in a typical year, often to metropolitan areas.

Population Relationships and Trends Since 1865

The United States has experienced steady growth from **immigration** and birth rate. At times, this growth has been explosive. During the 1840s, for example, about 1.5 million Irish came to the nation to escape the potato famine in their homeland.

CORE CONCEPTS: DIVERSITY

A large Spanish-speaking population has always populated the Southwestern United States. New Mexico is officially bilingual, since all state or local government business may be conducted in either Spanish or English. In many large cities in California, signs are written in Chinese, Korean, or Japanese, as well as in English and Spanish.

CORE CONCEPTS: MOVEMENT OF PEOPLE AND GOODS

African Americans migrated to urban areas from the rural South in two different major movements. The Great Migration during World War I brought between 300,000 and 500,000 African Americans to Northern cities for jobs, altering the ethnic composition of cities such as Detroit, Cleveland, Chicago, and New York. Although the Great Depression slowed the migration, it resumed during World War II.

CORE CONCEPTS: LINKING PAST AND PRESENT

Many Mexicans originally arrived through work programs that encouraged Mexicans to help with farming during World War II. The *Bracero*—"worker" in Spanish—program brought more than 200,000 temporary agriculture workers into the country in 1942. Some workers also helped building railroads. Perhaps as many as 5 million workers took part in the program during the 1950s and early 1960s before it ended in 1964. Today, many Mexicans cross into the United States daily to work. Some remain in the country as illegal aliens, a situation that the governments of the United States and Mexico are seeking to address.

CORE CONCEPTS: REFORM MOVEMENTS

Agricultural workers, many of them Hispanic, organized for better treatment during the 1960s under the leadership of people such as Cesar Chavez and Dolores Huertes. They led a national boycott of grapes, one of the prime farm products of California, in 1965. The boycott lasted for five years, until vineyard owners agreed to improve working conditions and raise wages. The United Farm Workers (UFW), formed in 1966, led to important gains for Latino farm workers.

Population Growth

Distribution Most of the population centers in the United States are along coastal areas where a healthy economy can support many people. More than 80 percent of the people in America live in its 276 metropolitan areas, defined as a city of at least 50,000 inhabitants and its outlying suburbs. Chains of closely linked cities are known as a **megalopolis**, or "great city."

Density The United States has an average population density of 77 persons per square mile (30 people per square km). The population is widely distributed outside urban areas.

Current Issues

In the new millennium, the United States faces several issues related to population. The aging population and the effect of the baby boom generation, as well as the changing composition of the population, are all matters of concern.

Graying of America As a result of both a declining birth rate and improvements in medical technology that enabled people to live longer, the number of senior citizens in the United States began increasing during the 1980s. Older Americans have become a political force, often voting in a block.

Effects of the Baby Boom Generation After World War II, the population of the United States grew rapidly. From 1945 to 1961, more than 65 million children were born. These people are known as the "baby boom generation." A child was born every seven seconds during the height of the baby boom.

The members of the baby boom generation have always been a social and political force. Their large numbers, for example, affected the number of schools that needed to be built during the 1950s through the 1970s. Now that the first members of the group are facing retirement, experts predict a change in retirement patterns and in matters generally related to aging.

Changing Composition of Populations Hispanic Americans are the fastest-growing minority in the United States. The number of Hispanics increased from 3 million to 9 million between 1960 and 1970. Hispanic children, particularly in New York, Texas, and California, have created a need for bilingual education.

The number of Asian immigrants also began to grow following the United States involvement in the Korean War and Vietnam. They often settle in the Pacific coastal states.

PRACTICING FOR THE REGENTS

Part I Multiple-Choice Questions

The following multiple-choice questions come from past Regents High School Examinations. Test your understanding of the geography of the United States by answering each of these items. Circle the number of the word or expression that best completes each statement or question. Test-taking tips can be found in the margins for some questions. For additional help, see Taking the Regents Exam on pages ix–xxxi of this Review Book.

1 The best source of information for identifying the location of the major mountain ranges in the United States is
   (1) an encyclopedia
   (2) an almanac
   (3) an atlas
   (4) a dictionary

2 Which region of the United States is correctly paired with an industry that is dominant in the region?
   (1) Southwest—timber
   (2) Pacific northwest—citrus crop
   (3) Great Plains—grain crops
   (4) Atlantic Coastal Plain—iron ore mining

3 Which geographic factor had the greatest influence on early patterns of industrialization in the United States?
   (1) scarcity of flat land on which to build factories
   (2) shortages of timber and coal
   (3) desires of workers to live in mild climates
   (4) availability of waterpower to operate machines

Base your answer to question 4 on the chart below and on your knowledge of social studies.

**Rural and Urban Populations
in the United States**

Year	Rural	Urban
1860	25,226,803	6,216,518
1870	28,656,010	9,902,361
1880	36,059,474	14,129,735
1890	40,873,501	22,106,265
1900	45,997,336	30,214,832
1910	50,164,495	42,064,001
1920	51,768,255	54,253,282

Source: Bureau of the Census

4 Which generalization about population growth is supported by information in this chart?
   (1) For every census listed, rural population exceeded urban population.
   (2) By 1920, more people lived in cities than in rural areas.
   (3) The Civil War significantly slowed the rate of population growth.
   (4) Most urban population growth was due to people migrating from rural areas.

5 The groups that composed the majority of immigrants to the United States between 1890 and 1920 were called "new immigrants" because they
   (1) were the last immigrants to enter the United States before World War I
   (2) settled in frontier areas of the country
   (3) stayed only for a short time before returning to their homelands
   (4) came from different regions of the world than most of the groups who came before 1890

6   During the first three decades of the twentieth century, what was the main reason many African Americans left the South?
    (1) The Dawes Act made free land available in the West.
    (2) More factory jobs were available in the North.
    (3) Many white landowners refused to accept them as sharecroppers.
    (4) Racial discrimination did not occur outside states in the South.

7   In the 1930s, which geographic factor most influenced the westward migration of thousands of people from the Great Plains?
    (1) extended drought in farming areas
    (2) excessive flooding of the Mississippi River
    (3) serious earthquakes in Pacific coastal areas
    (4) destructive hurricanes in the Gulf of Mexico

8   The Dust Bowl experiences of the Oklahoma farmers during the Great Depression demonstrated the
    (1) effect of geography on people's lives
    (2) success of government farm subsidies
    (3) limitation of civil liberties in times of crisis
    (4) result of the Indian Removal Act

9   A population movement that developed in the United States immediately after World War II was the migration of white, middle-class Americans from
    (1) the west coast to the east coast
    (2) the Northeast to the Sunbelt
    (3) the cities to the suburbs
    (4) the suburbs to renewal areas in inner cities

Base your answer to question 10 on the diagram below and on your knowledge of social studies.

Urban-Suburban Pattern of American Life

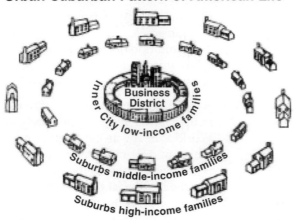

10 Which development following World War II caused the urban-suburban pattern shown in the diagram?
   (1) increase in the number of farms
   (2) expansion of highways and automobile ownership
   (3) movement of most factories to rural areas
   (4) decline in the number of middle-income families

11 Cesar Chavez created the United Farm Workers Organization Committee (UFWOC) in 1966 primarily to
   (1) secure voting rights for Mexican Americans
   (2) improve working conditions for migrant workers
   (3) provide legal assistance to illegal immigrants
   (4) increase farm income

12 Social scientists use the expression "graying of America" to describe the
   (1) aging of the nation's population
   (2) declining political power of older Americans
   (3) possible failure of the Social Security System
   (4) increasing number of babies born to older couples

13 According to the 1990 census, which two areas of the United States include the most densely populated parts of the nation?
   (1) the Great Plains and Texas
   (2) the Northeast and Southern California
   (3) the South and the Rocky Mountain states
   (4) the Appalachian states and the Midwest

14 President Bill Clinton supported the
    North American Free Trade Agreement
    (NAFTA) primarily as a way to
    (1) normalize trade relations with Cuba
    (2) stimulate economic growth in the
        United States
    (3) restrict the flow of drugs into the
        United States
    (4) increase the United States trade
        deficit

REGENTS WARM-UP

Read the directions in Regents essay questions carefully so that you carry out all operations. In the Essay, you are asked to identify *two* events or developments and respond to *two* points for each.

Part II   Thematic Essay Question

The following thematic question comes from past Regents Examinations. Write your answers on a separate sheet of paper. Essay-writing tips appear in the margin. For additional help, see Taking the Regents Exam on pages ix–xxxi of the Review Book.

Directions: Write a well-organized essay that includes an introduction, several paragraphs addressing the task below, and a conclusion.

Theme: Territorial Expansion (1800–1900):

> Various events or developments have influenced the territorial expansion of the United States. In 1800, the United States was a new nation of approximately 895,000 square miles of territory. By 1900, the nation had grown to about 3,000,000 square miles of territory.

Task: Identify *two* events or developments that had a significant impact on United States territorial expansion between 1800 and 1900 and for *each* event or development identified:

> • Discuss the historical circumstances surrounding the event or development
>
> • Evaluate the importance of the event or development on the growth of the United States

You may use any example from your study of United States history. Some suggestions you might wish to consider include the Louisiana Purchase (1803), completion of the Erie Canal (1825), War with Mexico (1846–1848), Homestead Act (1862), completion of the first transcontinental railroad (1869), and Native American Indian policies (1800–1900).

You are *not* limited to these suggestions.

Guidelines: In your essay, be sure to:

- Address all aspects of the *Task*
- Support the theme with relevant facts, examples, and details
- Use a logical and clear plan of organization
- Introduce the theme by establishing a framework that is beyond a simple restatement of the *Task* and conclude with a summation of the theme

Part III   Document-Based Question

This exercise is designed to test your ability to work with historical documents. It is similar to the document-based questions that you will see on the Regents Examination. While you are asked to analyze three historical documents, the exercise on the actual exam will include more documents. Some of the documents have been edited for the purposes of the question. As you analyze the documents, take into account the source of each document and any point of view that may be presented in the document.

Historical Context: On May 5, 1906, an earthquake in San Francisco, California, and a subsequent fire destroyed the city. A second earthquake, on October 17, 1989, lasting 15 seconds, killed an estimated 90 people and caused billions of dollars in damage.

Task: Using information from the documents and your knowledge of United States history and geography, answer the questions that follow each document in Part A. Your answers to the questions will help you write the Part B essay, in which you will be asked to:

> Apply the information given to outline a disaster response policy on a national or international level. The policy should be aimed at people likely to suffer from climate conditions similar to the area discussed in the short answer questions. Include information about likely outcomes and preventive strategies in your plan.

Part A   Short Answer Questions

Directions: Analyze the documents and answer the short-answer questions that follow each document in the space provided.

Document 1

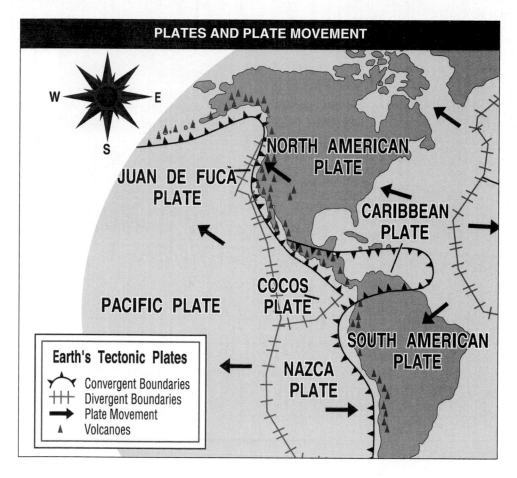

PLATES AND PLATE MOVEMENT

NORTH AMERICAN PLATE

JUAN DE FUCA PLATE

CARIBBEAN PLATE

PACIFIC PLATE

COCOS PLATE

SOUTH AMERICAN PLATE

NAZCA PLATE

Earth's Tectonic Plates
- Convergent Boundaries
- Divergent Boundaries
- Plate Movement
- Volcanoes

1   What two geographic features combine to make this area dangerous?

_____

_____

Document 2

2*a*   What danger to the town of San Francisco appeared after the earthquake?

_____

_____

  b   How would that danger increase the total losses? [Hint: Think about public services available in 1906.]

_____

_____

Document 3

> The old San Francisco is dead. The . . . lightest-hearted, most pleasure-loving city of this continent, and in many ways the most interesting and romantic, is a horde of huddled refugees living among ruins. It may rebuild; it probably will; but those who have known that peculiar city by the Golden Gate and caught its flavor of the Arabian Nights feel it can never be the same. . . . The city lay on a series of hills and lowlands between. These hills are really the end of the Coast Range of mountains which lie between the interior valleys and the ocean to the south.
>
> —Will Irwin, *The New York Sun, April 21, 1906*

3a How does Irwin describe the city after the earthquake?

_____

_____

b What does Irwin predict will happen to the city?

_____

_____

c How does Irwin show his feelings for the city in this article?

_____

_____

Part B   Essay

Write a well-organized essay that includes an introduction, several paragraphs, and a conclusion. Use evidence from at least *two* of the documents in the body of the essay. Support your response with relevant facts, examples, and details. Include additional outside information.

Historical Context: On May 5, 1906, an earthquake in San Francisco, California, and a subsequent fire destroyed most of the city. A second earthquake, on October 17, 1989, lasting 15 seconds, killed an estimated 90 people and caused billions of dollars in damage.

Task: Using information from the documents and your knowledge of United States history and geography, write an essay in which you:

> Apply the information given to outline a disaster response policy on a national or international level. The policy should be aimed at people likely to suffer from climate conditions similar to the area discussed in the short answer questions. Include information about likely outcomes and preventive strategies in your plan.

Guidelines: In your essay, be sure to:

- Address all aspects of the task by accurately analyzing and interpreting at least two documents
- Incorporate information from the documents in the body of the essay
- Incorporate relevant outside information
- Support the theme with relevant facts, examples, and details
- Use a logical and clear plan of organization
- Introduce the theme by establishing a framework that is beyond a simple restatement of the Task or Historical Context and conclude with a summation of the theme

UNIT 2 CREATING A NATION

Unit 2 Overview

In the 1500s, interactions between a variety of cultures shaped America from the colonial era through the American Revolution and beyond. Native Americans struggled to live alongside Europeans and their ever-growing settlements and colonies. Africans tried to adapt to the new continent to which they were brought involuntarily. The United States faced many challenges in these early years. Internal improvements and industrial development began to reshape the nation, but this reshaping also highlighted the growing differences between North and South. Westward expansion generated new conflicts with both Native Americans and Great Britain. The push for social reforms intensified.

The growing sectional crisis in the 1800s led to the Civil War, the most wrenching war in American history. Studying these early cultural interactions and conflicts will help you understand the centuries of history that followed.

Unit 2 Objectives

1. Explain the religious and economic reasons why Europeans became interested in America.

2. Describe colonial culture in the English colonies.

3. Summarize events that fueled colonial discontent.

4. Describe the issues at stake during the Constitutional Convention.

5. Discuss the growing tensions between the nation's developing political parties.

PREPARING FOR THE REGENTS

This entire book is set up to help you grasp the facts, main ideas, and concepts needed to do well on your Regents Exam. Notes in the margin include core concepts, test-taking tips, and more. Use blank spaces in the margins to answer questions raised in the text or to jot down key points. Before each unit of study, skim through the exams at the back of the book to develop a sense of what your state wants you to know about the world.

REGENTS WARM-UP

Early America matured into a rich, diverse society. As you read, consider how the values and traditions of the various European colonists contributed to this diversity.

Chapter Overview

Spanish, French, and English colonists came to North America. The colonies they founded often reflected the values and traditions of their homelands. Over time, an agricultural society developed. In the South, a large number of Africans were enslaved for plantation labor. In the North, commerce took hold, and England's trade policies proved cause for concern. High birthrates and immigration expanded the population as American society began to take shape.

As you read through this chapter, ask yourself these questions:
(1) How was life for European settlers shaped by the values they brought with them and the geography of the regions where they settled?
(2) For what reasons did the English establish colonies along the eastern coast of North America?
(3) How did the economy develop and grow in the New England, Middle, and Southern Colonies?
(4) What was the cause of the increasing tension between the Colonists and Britain?

Main Ideas and Concepts

- **Culture** European colonizers shaped the new cultures of North America.

- **Linking Geography to History** The system of headrights provided settlers with new ways to acquire more land.

- **Culture** Puritan religious beliefs shaped the cultural history of New England.

- **Linking Geography to History** After the English Civil War, England resumed colonizing America, eventually establishing seven new colonies.

- **Culture** The culture of the New England Colonies developed differently from that of the Southern Colonies.

- **Immigration and Migration** Immigrants to the American colonies in the 1700s came from all across Europe or were brought by force from Africa.

People, Places, Terms

The names or terms below will help you to prepare for the Regents Exam in United States History and Government. If you do not know a name or term, look up the identification or definition in the Glossary in the back of this book, in your textbook, or in another reference source.

cash crops	joint-stock	natural rights
English Bill	companies	Pilgrims
of Rights	John Locke	plantations
Enlightenment	Mayflower	presidios
Great Migration	Compact	Puritans
heretics	mercantilism	rationalism
House of Burgesses	Middle Passage	subsistence
indentured servants	Montesquieu	farming

SECTION 1 NATIVE AMERICAN PEOPLES

The culture of most Native Americans developed in response to their environments. By the time the first Europeans arrived, Native Americans were fragmented into many small groups that had adapted to the different regions of North America.

The Southwest The Zuni, Hopi, and other Pueblo peoples lived in small groups and depended on corn to survive. They cultivated several strains that were adapted to the dry climate and also farmed squash and beans.

Sometime around 1500, the Navajo and Apache came to the region from the northwest. Although the Apache remained primarily nomadic, the Navajo learned farming from the Pueblo people and lived in widely dispersed settlements.

The Pacific Coast Many different groups settled on the Pacific Coast. Although they did not practice agriculture, they lived in permanent settlements. The plentiful fish and trees provided food and means for creating shelter. They also hunted deer and small game.

The Great Plains Before 1500, the Great Plains people practiced agriculture. However, when Europeans arrived, they were nomads, possibly driven from their settlements by drought or war. The Sioux people followed migrating buffalo herds on foot and lived in cone-shaped tents called tepees.

The Spanish introduced horses to America in the 1500s. Over the next few centuries, as the animals either escaped or were stolen, they spread northward and some were tamed by the Sioux. In the process, the Sioux became some of the world's greatest mounted hunters and warriors.

The Peoples of the Northeast Most of the people of the Northeast were divided into two major language groups—those who spoke Algonquian languages and those who spoke Iroquoian languages. The Algonquian-speaking people lived mostly in what would become known as New England. These Native Americans were among the first to encounter English settlers.

Stretching west from the Hudson River across what is today New York and southern Ontario and north to Georgian Bay were the Iroquoian-speaking peoples. They included the Huron, Erie, Seneca, Cayuga, Onondaga, Oneida, and Mohawk.

These peoples practiced slash-and burn agriculture, which involved cutting down parts of forests and then burning the cleared land. This left a layer of nitrogen-rich ashes, which they worked into the soil to make it more fertile. Both groups also viewed land as a resource for a group of people to use, and not for one person to buy or sell.

The Iroquois League All Iroquoian peoples had similar cultures. They lived in longhouses in large towns, which they protected by building stockades. The people lived in large extended families called kinship groups, which were headed by the elder women of each clan.

Despite these similarities, war often broke out between different groups. In the late 1500s, five of the nations in western New York formed an alliance that became known as the Iroquois League. The nations agreed to the Great Binding Law, a constitution that defined how the confederacy worked. The women who headed the kinship groups chose the representatives to the council, who were all men.

Peoples of the Southeast Almost all of the people in the Southeast lived in towns that were arranged around a central plaza. Women did most of the farming, while the men hunted.

The Cherokee were the largest group—about 20,000 lived in some 60 towns when the Europeans arrived. Other peoples included the Choctaw, Chickasaw, Natchez, and Creek.

SECTION 2 THE SPANISH AND FRENCH BUILD EMPIRES

The Spanish Settle the Southwest

After conquering Mexico and the Inca Empire of Central and South America, Spanish interest turned to the area that is today the Southwest of the United States. The Spanish gave the name New Mexico to the area north of New Spain (Mexico). They built forts called **presidios** throughout the area to protect the Spanish settlers and to serve as trading posts. Few Spaniards, however, were interested in settling the territory.

The Catholic Church became important in colonizing the area. Spanish priests built missions and spread Christianity to the Native Americans living there. Father Junipero Serra took control of California by establishing missions there. The Spanish priests tried to end traditional Native American practices that were in conflict with Catholic beliefs. As a result, thousands of warriors, led by a Native American religious leader named Popé, destroyed most of the missions in New Mexico in 1680.

Mining and Ranching Although the Spanish did not find gold, they did find silver and set up silver mines all across northern Mexico. They used the Native Americans to work the mines. To feed the miners, the Spanish set up large cattle ranches, called haciendas, in northern Mexico. The men who herded the cattle were called *vaqueros*. Cowhands in the United States later adopted the lifestyles of the vaqueros.

The French Empire in America

New France Is Founded In the 1500s, the French began fishing near North America. Fishermen often traded goods for furs from the Native Americans. Fur had become very fashionable in Europe. As demand for fur grew, French merchants began to expand their fur trade. In 1605 Samuel de Champlain established a colony in what is today Nova Scotia. In addition, he founded Quebec, which became the capital of the French colony of New France.

The colony was made up mostly of fur traders who lived among the Native Americans with whom they traded.

New France Expands

Exploring the Mississippi The French government also began to explore North America. Louis Joliet, Jacques Marquette, and René-Robert Cavelier de La Salle explored the Mississippi River. La Salle claimed the region for France and named it Louisiana in honor of the French king.

Settling Louisiana The French did not permanently settle the region until 1698. The settlers in southern Louisiana realized that the crops that grew there, such as sugarcane and rice, needed hard labor. Few settlers were willing to do that kind of work. As a result, the French brought over enslaved Africans and forced them to work on their plantations.

SECTION 3 ENGLISH COLONIES IN AMERICA

England Takes Interest in America

In the late 1500s, changes in England occurred that led to English colonization in America.

The Reformation Divides Europe One change had to do with religion. In the early 1500s, Western Europe was Catholic. In 1517, a German monk named Martin Luther accused the Church of corruption and founded the Lutheran Church. This started the Protestant Reformation, which spread throughout Europe.

The Reformation Changes England The Reformation in England occurred when the pope refused to annul King Henry VIII's marriage. The king broke with the Church and declared himself the head of England's church, which became known as the Anglican Church. Some people wanted to "purify" the Church of all Catholic elements. These people were known as **Puritans**. They wanted every congregation to appoint its own leaders, rather than having the king appoint them. When the king refused, many Puritans left England for America in order to practice their religion in their own way.

Economic Changes in England England also experienced economic changes.

CORE CONCEPTS: CONFLICT

Before breaking with the Catholic Church, Henry VIII was a strong champion of the Catholic faith. In 1521 Pope Leo X had given Henry the title "Defender of the Faith" for a treatise against Martin Luther, "In Defense of the Seven Sacraments."

When England began producing more wool than Europe would buy, merchants began to look for new markets. They began to organize **joint-stock companies** in which many investors pooled their money to use for large projects. Doing so allowed English merchants to trade with and colonize other parts of the world without financial support from the government.

Jamestown Is Founded

In 1606 King James I granted the Virginia Company, a group of investors, a charter to start colonies in Virginia. The company sent 144 colonists who founded the settlement of Jamestown. Unfortunately, the land they selected was swampy and swarming with disease-carrying mosquitoes. This was just the beginning of many problems the settlement faced.

Early Troubles The colonists knew nothing about farming. Many were not used to manual labor and refused to do it. They also argued with one another and were not able to make decisions. As a result, sickness and food shortages killed many of the settlers.

Captain John Smith, the leader of the settlement, began trading with the Powhatan Confederacy, the local Native Americans. Their chief, Powhatan, helped the colony survive. To increase the population of Jamestown, the Virginia Company offered free land to people who worked for the colony for seven years. About 400 new settlers arrived in 1609. However, there was not enough food for these settlers, and by winter they began to steal food from the Native Americans. In response, the Native Americans attacked the settlers. By 1610 only 60 settlers were still alive.

Tobacco Saves the Colony The Jamestown colonists tried growing tobacco, but the crop grown was too bitter. John Rolfe, one of the colonists, experimented with seeds from Trinidad, a Caribbean island. His tobacco sold for a good price, and the Jamestown settlers began planting large amounts of it. Finally, the settlers had a cash crop that could be sold to England.

The First Assembly In 1618 the head of the Virginia Company gave Jamestown the right to elect its own legislative assembly. The new government included 20 representatives, called burgesses. The assembly was called the **House of Burgesses.** To attract new settlers to Virginia, the company also started the system of headrights. New settlers who bought a share in the

LINKING PAST AND PRESENT

The exact location of Jamestown's fort was not known until 1996. Archaeologists knew, from written descriptions, that the fort lay along the James River, but they did not know its precise location. Researchers believed that the remains of the fort had been destroyed by erosion from the James River. However, in 1996, archaeologists finally discovered evidence of a fortification that matched historical descriptions.

company or who paid for their passage were given 50 acres of land and 50 more acres for additional family members.

Virginia Becomes a Royal Colony The changes introduced by the Virginia Company attracted many new settlers to Virginia. This increase alarmed the Native Americans, and they attacked the settlers. Hundreds of settlers died. The king, upset about the colony's failures, took back the Virginia Company's charter. He made Virginia a royal colony and appointed a governor to run it.

Maryland Is Founded

In England, Catholics did not accept the king as head of the Church. As a result, many were persecuted. In 1632 Lord Baltimore, who was a member of Parliament until converting to Catholicism, was granted an area of land northeast of Virginia, which he named Maryland. Baltimore owned Maryland, making it a proprietary colony. The proprietor, or owner, could govern the colony as he saw fit. Although Lord Baltimore hoped that Maryland would become a refuge for Catholics, most of the settlers were Protestant.

SECTION 4 NEW ENGLAND

The Pilgrims Land at Plymouth

When some Puritans, called Separatists, broke away from the Anglican Church, the English government persecuted them. Some of these Separatists, known today as **Pilgrims**, decided to immigrate to America. They left on the *Mayflower* in 1620. After a storm blew the ship off course, it landed across Massachusetts Bay at a place called Plymouth.

Plymouth Colony Under the leadership of William Bradford, the Pilgrims went to work as soon as they arrived at Plymouth. A Native American named Squanto helped the Pilgrims by teaching them how to farm and fish. He also helped them negotiate a peace treaty with the other Native Americans who lived nearby. The following autumn, the Pilgrims joined the Native Americans in a festival to celebrate the harvest. This festival became the basis for the Thanksgiving holiday.

CORE CONCEPTS: DECISION MAKING

The male settlers aboard the *Mayflower* made plans, prior to landing at Plymouth, for establishing self-government. The document they created and signed declared their intention to create a government and obey its laws. This document, later known as the **Mayflower Compact**, also stated an agreement to discuss matters affecting the community and to make decisions based on majority rule.

The Puritans Found Massachusetts Bay Colony

When King Charles I took the throne in 1625, persecution of the Puritans increased. At the same time, a depression hit England's wool industry. John Winthrop, a Puritan and wealthy attorney, wanted to help the Puritans leave England. He was one of the stockholders in the Massachusetts Bay Company, which had received a charter from the king to create a colony in New England. Winthrop used the charter to find a refuge in America for the Puritans. In 1630 about 900 settlers set sail for America and eventually arrived in Massachusetts.

More settlers followed, and Massachusetts quickly expanded. Several towns were founded, including Boston. As conditions in England worsened, many more people left in what became known as the **Great Migration.**

Church and State The government of Massachusetts was based on the charter of the Massachusetts Bay Company. Those who owned stock in the company were called "freemen," and all of the freemen together made up the General Court. The General Court made the laws and elected the governor. The General Court eventually became a representative assembly. Every year the freemen of each town elected up to three deputies to send to the General Court. Laws required everyone in the colony to attend church services. The government regulated behavior and collected taxes to support the church. The leaders of the Massachusetts Bay Colony did not tolerate differences in religious beliefs. **Heretics**—people whose religious beliefs differed from those of the majority—were considered a threat to the colony.

Rhode Island and Religious Dissent

Roger Williams Founds Providence Roger Williams was a strict Separatist who believed that the Puritans should not have remained a part of the Anglican Church. In 1635 the General Court ordered him to leave Massachusetts because of his criticisms of the Puritan Church. Williams headed south, where he bought land from the Native Americans and founded the town of Providence. There, the government did not involve itself in religious matters and his government allowed all religions to worship freely.

The Colony of Rhode Island Over the years, other Puritans were banished from Massachusetts. They founded the towns of Newport and Warwick. In 1644 these two towns joined with Providence and Portsmouth to become the colony of Rhode Island and Providence Plantations. The colony's charter provided for religious freedom and the separation of church and state.

The River Towns of Connecticut

In 1636 the Reverend Thomas Hooker moved his entire congregation to the Connecticut River valley and founded the town of Hartford. Hooker was frustrated with the government in Massachusetts because he thought that everyone, not just church members, should be allowed to vote. In 1637 Hartford and two other towns joined together and created their own General Court. They adopted a constitution known as the Fundamental Orders of Connecticut. This was the first written constitution of the American colonies. It provided for all adult men, not just church members, to elect the governor and the General Court.

The Pequot were a Native American group who lived in the Connecticut River valley. When two Massachusetts traders were killed in Pequot territory, Massachusetts sent troops to punish the Pequot. A war started, and the Pequot began raiding towns along the river. The Connecticut settlers organized an army. Other Native American groups, enemies of the Pequot, fought alongside Mason's army. Hundreds of Pequot were killed. Those who were captured were sold into slavery or given to other Native American groups as war prizes. The Connecticut government eventually resettled some Pequot in two villages.

New Hampshire and Maine

Some people who disagreed with Puritan authority in Massachusetts moved north of the colony. Massachusetts granted this northern area to two men, who divided the land grant in two. The southern part was named New Hampshire and the northern part was named Maine. Massachusetts claimed both parts, but the two men challenged the claims in court. An English court ruled against Massachusetts in 1677. In 1679 New Hampshire became a royal colony. Massachusetts bought back Maine, which remained a part of Massachusetts until 1820.

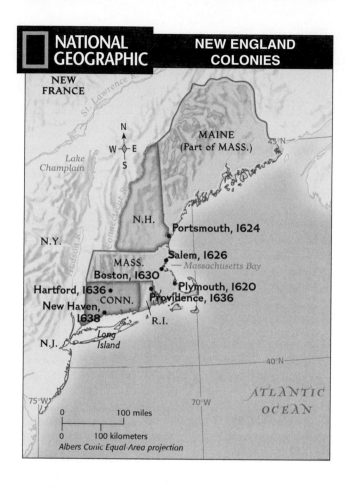

NATIONAL GEOGRAPHIC   **NEW ENGLAND COLONIES**

NEW FRANCE

St. Lawrence R.

N.Y.

Lake Champlain

MAINE (Part of MASS.)

45°N

N.H.

Portsmouth, 1624

Salem, 1626
—Massachusetts Bay

MASS.

Boston, 1630

Hartford, 1636 •
New Haven, 1638 •

CONN.

Plymouth, 1620
Providence, 1636

R.I.

N.J.

Long Island

40°N

75°W   70°W

ATLANTIC OCEAN

0   100 miles

0   100 kilometers

Albers Conic Equal-Area projection

REGENTS WARM-UP

Questions on past Regents Exams have focused on map skills. Study the map on this page. How long after the establishment of Plymouth Colony was Boston founded? Which English settlement was not located directly on the coast?

King Philip's War

After the Pequot War, the Native Americans and New England settlers enjoyed peaceful relations. However, by the 1670s, colonial governments began demanding that the Native Americans follow English law. This demand angered Native Americans, who believed that the English were trying to destroy their way of life.

In 1675 the Plymouth Colony tried and executed three Wampanoag for a murder. The Wampanoag warriors then attacked the settlers. This attack marked the beginning of King Philip's War, named after the Wampanoag leader. The settlers won the war in 1678. After the war, few Native Americans were left in New England. New England now belonged to the English settlers.

New England's Economy

The climate and soil in New England was unsuitable for the development of large plantations. New England farmers practiced **subsistence farming**—farming only enough crops to feed their own families. The main crop grown in New England was corn, which was suitable for the region's short growing season and rocky soil. Farmers also raised livestock.

Fishing and Whaling Because of New England's geography, fishing became a major industry in the region. The Grand Banks lay northeast of New England in the Atlantic Ocean. This is a region where the mixing of the warm Gulf Stream and the cold North Atlantic produced an environment favorable to plankton—an important food for fish and whales. During colonial times, many kinds of fish flourished in the Grand Banks.

Lumbering and Shipbuilding Forests covered much of New England. Waterfalls were used to power sawmills. The lumber was then transported downriver to the coast and then shipped to other colonies and to England. The lumber was used to make goods such as furniture and barrels. It was also used to build ships. Shipbuilding became another important industry in New England.

Life in New England's Towns

Town Meetings The town was the center of New England society. It determined how the land was settled and how the people were governed. The residents of towns met to discuss local problems and issues. These town meetings eventually became the local town government. Anyone could attend a town meeting, but only men who were granted land by the town could vote.

The men who were chosen to run the town's affairs were called selectmen. They appointed other officials the town needed. Town meetings led people to believe that they had a right to govern themselves. Such meetings helped set the stage for democratic government in the colonies.

New England Puritans were expected to attend Sunday worship at the meetinghouse, or church. They were expected to obey strict rules that regulated most activities of daily life. Puritans also felt that they had a duty to watch over the moral behavior of others.

CORE CONCEPTS: CULTURE

Puritans, although often viewed by others as rigid, drank rum, enjoyed music, and liked to wear brightly colored clothing that indicated their wealth and social position. Puritan artisans and architects produced beautiful and elegant works.

Trade and the Rise of Cities

New England produced few products that England wanted. However, England produced many goods that New England colonists wanted. To get these goods, some settlers became merchants.

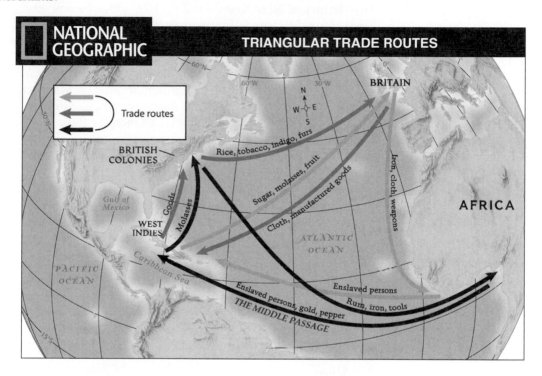

Triangular Trade The only way colonial merchants could acquire the English goods that settlers wanted was to sell New England's goods somewhere else in exchange for goods that England wanted. The sugar plantations in the Caribbean wanted to buy New England's fish and lumber. The planters would pay for the goods by trading sugar or by giving the colonial merchants bills of exchange. These were credit slips that English merchants had given the planters in exchange for sugar. The colonial merchants would take the bills back to New England and trade them to English merchants for their manufactured goods. The three-way trade colonial merchants developed with the Caribbean colonies is an example of triangular trade.

SECTION 5 THE MIDDLE AND SOUTHERN COLONIES

New Netherland Becomes New York

The History of New Netherland In 1609 a Dutch company hired Henry Hudson to find a route through North America to the Pacific. Instead, he found a wide river, known today as the Hudson River. In 1614 the Dutch claimed the region in the Hudson River valley and called it New Netherland. Their major settlement was called New Amsterdam, located on Manhattan Island. Because fur trade was the major activity in New Netherland, the colony grew slowly. To increase the population, the Dutch allowed anyone to buy land in the colony. Settlers came from many countries.

New York and New Jersey King Charles II wanted New Netherland because the territory would link Virginia and Maryland to New England. In 1664 he granted the land to his brother James, who sent warships to seize New Netherland from the Dutch. After taking the land, which he named New York, James gave a large part of it to two of the king's closest advisers and named the new colony New Jersey. To attract people to the new colony, the proprietors offered generous land grants, religious freedom, and the right to elect a legislative body.

Pennsylvania and Delaware

The Quakers Charles II also gave land to William Penn, a wealthy Quaker. Penn used the grant to create a colony in America for Quakers, which he called Pennsylvania. He thought of Pennsylvania as a "holy experiment" where people enjoyed complete political and religious freedom. He signed a treaty with the local Native Americans, who gave the land to the colonists. This action started a time of peace between the European settlers and the Native Americans that lasted more than 70 years. Penn built the capital of Pennsylvania and named it Philadelphia, or "the city of brotherly love."

Pennsylvania had a lawmaking body that was elected directly by voters. All colonists who owned land and believed in Jesus had the right to vote. All Pennsylvanians had the right to practice their religion with no interference. Land was readily available. In addition to English Quakers, many Germans and Scotch-Irish immigrated to Pennsylvania. By 1684 Pennsylvania had more than 7,000 colonists, and Philadelphia became a center for trade. In 1682 Penn bought more land south of Pennsylvania. This land later became the colony of Delaware.

Society in the Middle Colonies

Unlike the New England Colonies, the Middle Colonies had abundant rich soil and a long growing season suitable for farming. Farmers grew a variety of crops, but wheat became the main **cash crop**—crop grown primarily for market.

The Wheat Boom In the early 1700s, Europe experienced a population explosion. Many Europeans immigrated to America, particularly to the Middle Colonies. The increased number of people in Europe created a big demand for wheat to feed these people. As a result, wheat prices in the Middle Colonies soared, making these colonies very profitable.

The boom in wheat prices created distinct social classes in the Middle Colonies, as they did in New England. Wealthy entrepreneurs made up the highest social class. Small farmers who made a small profit from their land made up the middle class. At the bottom of society were people who either rented land or worked for wages.

New Southern Colonies

King Charles granted a territory south of Virginia to several friends. The land was named Carolina. It developed into two separate regions—North Carolina and South Carolina.

North Carolina Most people who came to North Carolina were small tobacco farmers from Virginia. North Carolina did not have a good harbor. As a result, it grew slowly.

South Carolina The proprietors were more interested in South Carolina. They had believed that the land was good for growing sugarcane, but it did not grow well, after all. Eventually, the colony began to capture Native Americans and ship them to the Caribbean as enslaved workers. The first settlers in South Carolina arrived in 1670 and named their settlement Charles Town, which is known today as Charleston.

The Georgia Experiment In the 1720s, James Oglethorpe, a member of Parliament, asked King George II for a colony for people who owed debts to start over. England was eager to give Oglethorpe the land. Not only would it help England's poor, but it would also give England a buffer between South Carolina and

Spanish Florida. The new colony was named Georgia. Settlers from other countries soon objected to the colony's strict laws. The owners of the colony eventually lifted some of the laws and set up an elected lawmaking body. However, in 1751 the owners gave control of the colony back to the king. Georgia became a royal colony.

The Southern Economy

The economy of the Southern Colonies depended on commercial agriculture. Tobacco became the South's first successful cash crop. Rice and indigo were also important cash crops. They needed the right kind of climate and techniques to be grown. This need resulted in the start of **plantations**—large commercial estates where many workers lived on the land and cultivated the crops for the landowner.

Indentured Servants To be profitable, tobacco farmers needed a large workforce to grow a large crop. The Southern Colonies had plenty of land for growing tobacco, but not enough workers. England had many poor tenant farmers without work. Many of these people were willing to sell their labor for a chance to come to America and obtain land. To pay for their journey, they agreed to become **indentured servants**. The American colonists agreed to pay the cost of the passage and provide food, shelter,

REGENTS WARM-UP

To practice your skill at interpreting information in a graph, answer the following question.

Approximately how many pounds of tobacco did England import in 1735?

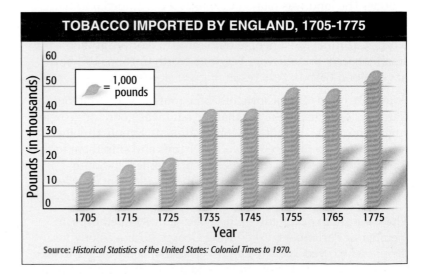

TOBACCO IMPORTED BY ENGLAND, 1705-1775

= 1,000 pounds

Pounds (in thousands)

Year

Source: *Historical Statistics of the United States: Colonial Times to 1970.*

and clothing for the servants until their labor contracts ended. The servants agreed to work for the owners for a certain number of years.

Rice in South Carolina Initially, farmers in South Carolina were unable to grow rice because they did not know how to harvest it properly. Then planters began to grow a new type of rice and decided to import enslaved Africans to raise it. Rice soon became a major cash crop.

Southern Society

Very few planters actually became wealthy. Planters who could afford a large labor force and many acres of land could produce a large crop and extend their estates. This resulted in a wealthy elite who controlled most of the land and needed workers to work the land.

The Southern plantations were self-contained communities which included the planters' houses, the workers' houses, a school, a chapel, and workshops. In the 1600s, plantations were generally small. In the early 1700s, when the planters switched their labor force to slave labor, the size of the plantations increased.

Backcountry Farmers About half of the indentured servants died before receiving their freedom. Even those who became free were rarely able to purchase their own land because of the high cost. As a result, many indentured servants became tenant farmers. They worked lands they rented from the planter elite.

Those indentured servants who were able to purchase land generally bought the land in the "backcountry," farther inland. They practiced subsistence farming on small plots of land and lived in small houses. By the late 1600s, Southern society was divided into a wealthy elite at the top, and poor backcountry farmers, tenant farmers, indentured servants, and enslaved Africans at the bottom.

Bacon's Rebellion

By the 1660s, Sir William Berkeley controlled the House of Burgesses—Virginia's legislative assembly. By assembling a majority of supporters, he arranged for the House to limit the vote to people who owned property. This act cut the number of voters in Virginia by half, which angered the backcountry and tenant farmers.

Crisis Over Land Backcountry farmers wanted to expand their landholding, but the only land left was that claimed by Native Americans. Most wealthy planters did not want to risk war with the Native Americans, so they opposed expanding the colony. This further angered the backcountry farmers.

In 1675 war broke out between backcountry farmers and the Native Americans of the region. Governor Berkeley did not authorize military action.

Nathaniel Bacon Leads a Revolt In April 1676, a group of backcountry farmers led by a wealthy planter named Nathaniel Bacon took action. Bacon organized a militia and attacked the Native Americans. The House of Burgesses then authorized Bacon to raise 1,000 troops to attack the Native Americans. The House also restored the vote to all free men.

Bacon was not satisfied with the changes. In July 1676, he and several hundred armed men returned to Jamestown and took power from Berkeley, charging him with corruption. Berkeley raised his own army, and the two sides fought for control of Jamestown. Bacon's Rebellion ended when Bacon became sick and died.

Slavery Increases in Virginia Bacon's Rebellion showed many wealthy planters that they needed to have land available for backcountry farmers in order to keep Virginia society stable. It also resulted in the planters using enslaved Africans more than indentured servants because they never had to be freed and therefore would never need land. The policies of the English government also encouraged slavery. In 1672 King Charles II granted a charter to the Royal African Company to start a slave trade. The English colonists no longer had to purchase enslaved Africans from the Dutch or the Portuguese.

Slavery in the Colonies

By 1870 between 10 and 12 million Africans were transported by force to the Americas from West Africa. They endured horrible conditions on cramped ships. The passage across the Atlantic Ocean was known as the **Middle Passage**.

When the first Africans arrived in Virginia in 1619, English law did not recognize slavery. As a result, these Africans were treated like indentured servants. As the number of Africans increased in Virginia and Maryland, their status began to change. In 1638 Maryland became the first British colony to recognize slavery. In 1705 Virginia enacted a slave code—a set of laws that formally regulated slavery and defined the relationship between enslaved Africans and free people. Other colonies also enacted slave codes. Under these laws, Africans could not own property and could not meet in large numbers. By the early 1700s, slavery had become an accepted institution, especially in the Southern Colonies, where the work of enslaved Africans was important to the plantation economy.

SECTION 6 THE IMPERIAL SYSTEM

Mercantilism, a set of ideas about the world economy and how it works, was very popular in the 1600s and 1700s. Mercantilists believed that a country could become wealthy by accumulating gold and silver. By selling more goods to other countries than it bought from them, more gold and silver would flow into the country than would flow out. Mercantilists also believed that a country should establish colonies in order to buy raw materials from the colonies and, in turn, sell them manufactured goods. Mercantilism benefited colonies by giving them a ready market for their raw materials. The drawback, however, was that it prevented colonies from selling their goods to other nations. Also, if a colony did not make goods that the home country needed, then it could not accumulate the gold and silver it needed to buy manufactured goods. The New England Colonies had that problem, which made them turn to triangular trade.

The Navigation Acts At first, England did not pay much attention to its American colonies. When King Charles II came to the throne, he decided to regulate trade with the colonies in order to bring wealth to England. In 1660 he asked Parliament to pass a navigation act. The act said that all goods coming in and out of the colonies had to be carried on English ships. The act also listed specific raw materials that could be sold only to England or to other English colonies. The list included the major goods that earned money for the colonies, greatly upsetting the colonists. They believed that it forced them to deal with English merchants who charged them high prices for manufactured goods that caused them to reduce their profits.

Problems with Enforcement Colonial merchants were angry, and many broke the new laws. Parliament set up inspectors in the colonies to report back to England. However, England had a problem enforcing the laws. As a result, King Charles appointed a committee to oversee colonial trade. The members found out

CORE CONCEPTS: IMPERIALISM

Another navigation act said that all merchants bringing European goods to the colonies had to stop in England and pay taxes. The goods then had to be shipped to the colonies on English ships, thus increasing the colonists' costs.

that Massachusetts was ignoring the Navigation Acts. Ships from other countries were docked in Boston harbor and the colonists were smuggling goods to Europe, the Caribbean, and Africa. The Massachusetts governor said that Massachusetts was not required to obey laws unless they benefited the colony. King Charles responded by taking away the colony's charter and making it a royal colony.

The Dominion of New England James II, who succeeded Charles as king in 1685, went even further in punishing the colonies. Under his authority, England merged Massachusetts, Plymouth, and Rhode Island together to create a new royal province called the Dominion of New England. Later, England added Connecticut, New Jersey, and New York to the province.

The Dominion was to be run by a governor-general and councilors appointed by the king. They had the power to make laws and impose taxes. The colonial assemblies were abolished. The king appointed Sir Edmond Andros the first governor-general. His harsh rule made nearly everyone in New England angry.

The Glorious Revolution of 1688

The English people were growing suspicious of King James II. He rejected the advice of Parliament and offended many of them by openly practicing Catholicism. Some people worried that England would experience another civil war.

A Bloodless Revolution Most people expected that James would be succeeded by his Protestant daughter Mary and her Dutch husband, William. However, their hopes were shattered when James's second wife gave birth to a son, who would now be the heir to the throne and would be raised Catholic. News of the birth caused protests. Not willing to risk a Catholic dynasty, Parliament asked William and Mary to take the throne. When William arrived, James fled the country. This bloodless change of power became known as the Glorious Revolution.

In 1689 Parliament enacted the **English Bill of Rights**. It outlined the powers the king did not have and the rights that people did have, such as the right to petition the king and the right to a fair jury. Parliament also passed the Toleration Act, which granted freedom of religion to all Protestants but not to Catholics and Jews.

The Glorious Revolution in America As soon as the Massachusetts colonists learned about James II, an uprising occurred in Boston. The colonists seized Andros and sent him back to England. The new monarchs permitted Rhode Island and Connecticut to resume their previous form of government, but they issued a new charter for Massachusetts. This charter combined Massachusetts Bay Colony, Plymouth Colony, and Maine into the royal colony of Massachusetts. The new charter allowed the people in the colony to elect an assembly, but the governor was to be appointed by the king. Only people who owned property could vote, but they did not have to be members of a Puritan congregation.

The Legacy of John Locke During the Glorious Revolution, a political philosopher named **John Locke** wrote a book entitled *Two Treatises of Government.* In the book, Locke argues that a monarch's right to rule had to come from the people. He said that all people were born with certain **natural rights.** These included the right to life, liberty, and property. He said that people came together to create a government to protect their rights. In return, the people agreed to obey the government's laws. He also said that if a government violated the people's rights, the people were justified in changing their system of government. Locke's ideas influenced American colonists, who would use these ideas to start a revolution against Great Britain.

SECTION 7 A DIVERSE SOCIETY

Family Life in Colonial America

The population of the American colonies increased dramatically by the mid-1700s. People in the colonies were having large families, and many immigrants were arriving in America.

Women in Colonial Society Women in the American colonies had few legal rights, particularly married women. A woman could not own anything, and all the property she brought into the marriage became her husband's. Married women could not make a contract or file a lawsuit. Single women had more rights. They could own property, file lawsuits, and run businesses. By the 1700s, the status of married women in the colonies improved.

Health and Disease American colonists frequently suffered diseases. Colonial cities were hard hit by epidemics. In 1721, a smallpox epidemic swept through Boston. Reverend Cotton Mather, a Puritan leader, used information from his own reading and the knowledge of enslaved Africans to develop an inoculation for smallpox.

CORE CONCEPTS: CONSTITUTIONAL PRINCIPLES

In 1734, John Peter Zenger, a German immigrant, published an article in which he called supporters of New York's royal governor "the dregs and scandal of human nature." He was arrested for printing libel. Although Zenger's acquittal did not change the libel laws, it helped establish the American commitment to freedom of the press.

Immigrants in Colonial America

German Immigrants Arrive in Pennsylvania Many immigrants arrived in the colonies in the 1700s. German immigrants came to Pennsylvania in search of religious freedom. By 1775 Germans, known as the Pennsylvania Dutch, made up about one-third of the population. They became some of Pennsylvania's most prosperous farmers.

The Scotch-Irish Head West The Scotch-Irish were descendants of the Scots who helped England claim control of Northern Ireland. Many left Ireland to escape rising taxes, poor harvests, and religious discrimination. Many Scotch-Irish migrated to the frontier where they occupied vacant land.

Colonial America's Jewish Community Jews first arrived in the Dutch colony of New Netherland in the mid-1600s to practice their religion without persecution. Most Jews lived in colonial cities.

Africans in Colonial America

Africans arrived in the colonies from many parts of West Africa. They tried to keep their own languages and traditions.

Africans Build a New Culture In South Carolina, where rice farming needed a large workforce, Africans worked in larger groups than in other Southern Colonies. Because these Africans were isolated from the white planters, they developed their own language called Gullah. It combined English and African words and allowed Africans from a variety of regions to talk to one another. Using a common language helped Africans develop a new culture in America.

Oppression and Resistance In South Carolina, planters used harsh and cruel means to control the enslaved Africans. Although slaveholders tried to force enslaved Africans to obey, Africans developed many ways to fight back against slavery. Some ran away, others would refuse to work hard, or staged work slowdowns. Sometimes groups of enslaved people banded together to resist slaveholders. In the 1730s, the governor of Spanish Florida promised freedom and land to any enslaved African who fled to Florida. In 1739, 75 Africans gathered near the Stono River, attacked their white overseers, and fled toward Florida. They attacked whites as they traveled. The local militia ended the Stono Rebellion, killing between 30 and 40 of the Africans.

The Enlightenment and the Great Awakening

Two European cultural movements influenced the American colonies. The **Enlightenment** challenged the authority of the church in science and philosophy while elevating the power of human reason and experience. A religious movement, which became known as the Great Awakening, stressed dependence on God.

The Enlightenment The Enlightenment thinkers believed that people could apply natural laws to social, political, and economic relationships, and that people could figure out these laws if they used reason. This emphasis on logic and reasoning was known as **rationalism.**

John Locke was an influential Enlightenment writer. He argued that people were not born sinful, as the Church claimed. Instead he believed that society and education could make people better. Baron **Montesquieu** was an Enlightenment thinker who suggested that the powers of government should be separated into three branches in order to protect people's freedom. The French philosopher Voltaire advocated religious toleration and freedom of thought and expression. Jean-Jacques Rousseau helped spread the idea of political and legal equality for all people—the end of special privileges for aristocrats and elites, the right of all people to participate in the formation of laws and policies. This thinking influenced the writers of the American Constitution.

The Great Awakening Many Americans followed a religious movement called pietism, which stressed an individual's devoutness and union with God. Ministers spread pietism through revivals, which were large public meetings for preaching and prayer. This rebirth of religious feelings became known as the Great Awakening.

A central idea of the Great Awakening was that people had to be "born again," or have an emotional experience that brings a person to God. Churches that accepted the new ideas, such as the Baptists and Methodists, saw an increase in their membership.

The Great Awakening had a great impact on the South. Baptist preachers condemned slavery and welcomed enslaved Africans at their revivals. As a result, thousands of enslaved Africans joined Baptist congregations. This angered the white planters, who feared that they would lose control of their workforce.

CORE CONCEPTS: CIVIC VALUES

The Magna Carta was a charter signed in 1215 by King John of England. This document granted his subjects certain rights, such as the right to a fair trial by a jury of their peers. These rights were extended with the Habeas Corpus Act of 1679. This act requires the government to produce a prisoner in court to justify their imprisonment. English settlers brought their belief in these ideas with them to America, and they were incorporated into the Constitution.

CHAPTER 3   THE AMERICAN REVOLUTION

Chapter Overview

In the early colonial period, the colonies grew accustomed to running their own affairs. When Britain tried to reestablish control, tensions mounted over taxes and basic rights. In 1775 these tensions led to battle, and in 1776 the colonists declared their independence from Britain. With the help of France and Spain, the colonists defeated the British in 1781. The Treaty of Paris formally ended the war.

The Revolutionary War had several important results on American society. The United States of America emerged from the war with new and unique visions of government and culture. Americans continue to value and protect local liberties and the right to representation in government.

CORE CONCEPTS: REFORM MOVEMENTS

American ideals of democracy inspired independence movements in the colonies of Latin America. These colonies overthrew their European rulers one after the other throughout the early 1800s.

As you read through this chapter, ask yourself these questions:
(1) What events fueled colonial discontent?
(2) How did Massachusetts continue to defy Britain after the repeal of the Townshend Acts?
(3) How did European countries aid the Americans in the war for Independence?
(4) What features of the political system of the United States were set up after the Revolutionary War?

Main Ideas and Concepts

- **Civic Values** The colonies used economic protest to fight Parliamentary power.

- **Government** The First Continental Congress acted as a government during the Revolutionary crisis.

- **Linking Geography to History** Hostility between the French and British caused France to support the colonies.

- **Culture** A uniquely American culture arose as the Revolutionary War ended.

People, Places, Terms

The following names and terms will help you to prepare for the Regents Exam in United States History and Government. You can find an explanation of each name and term in the Glossary in the back of this book, in your textbook, or in another reference source.

John Adams	Continental Congress	Intolerable Acts
Samuel Adams	Declaration of	republic
Albany Plan	Independence	Stamp Act
of Union	French and	Townshend Act
boycott	Indian War	George Washington

SECTION 1 CAUSES OF THE REVOLUTION

The French and Indian War

The First Skirmish In the 1740s, both the British and the French became interested in the Ohio River Valley. To block British claims, France ordered forts to be built from Lake Ontario to the Ohio River. **George Washington,** an officer in the Virginia militia, led troops against a French force and a small battle occurred. Washington surrendered, but the fighting that began there would grow into a war involving several European powers.

The Albany Conference The British government had told the colonies to prepare for the coming war and to negotiate an alliance with the Iroquois, who controlled western New York. Seven colonies sent representatives to meet with Iroquois leaders at Albany, New York, in June 1754. This meeting became known as the Albany Conference.

The Iroquois refused an alliance with the British but agreed to remain neutral. The colonies agreed to appoint one commander of all British troops in the colonies. Finally, the conference issued the **Albany Plan of Union.** Formulated by a committee led by Benjamin Franklin, it proposed that the colonies unite to form a federal government. The plan, however, was rejected by many colonies.

The British Triumph In 1755, after Native American and French forces ambushed the British troops and killed the British

CORE CONCEPTS: CHANGE

Although the colonies rejected the Albany Plan of Union, the plan showed that many colonial leaders had begun to think about joining their colonies together.

CORE CONCEPTS: IDENTITY

By the end of the war, the colonies felt less dependent on the British for military support. They became more concerned with their own problems and began to think of themselves as American rather than British.

commander-in-chief, Washington rallied the British troops and organized a retreat. The Native Americans of western Pennsylvania now realized that they could beat the British and began attacking British settlers in their territory.

The **French and Indian War** took place along the frontier. In 1756, the fighting between England and France spread to Europe, where it became known as the Seven Years' War. After the British cut off French supplies to North America, the Iroquois pressured the Native Americans in Pennsylvania to end their attacks on the British. The French were now outnumbered. Spain entered the war on the side of the French, so Britain seized Spain's colonies in Cuba and the Philippines.

The Treaty of Paris finally ended the war in 1763. New France and all of Louisiana east of the Mississippi became part of the British Empire. Spain gave Florida to Britain in exchange for Cuba and the Philippines. The French signed a separate treaty with Spain, giving Spain control of New Orleans and the land west of the Mississippi.

The Colonies Grow Discontented

For many years, England had not really collected taxes and largely ignored the colonies, a policy known as salutary neglect. As a result of the French and Indian War, however, the British government was deeply in debt. The British Parliament believed that the colonists should pay for part of the war. This change in policy angered the colonists and set the two sides on a course of confrontation.

CAUSES OF THE AMERICAN REVOLUTION	
British Action	**What It Meant to the Colonists**
Proclamation Act of 1763	Drew a line from North to South along the Appalachian Mountains and declared no colonists could settle west of the line
Sugar Act	Raised existing taxes and created new ones
Currency Act of 1764	Banned paper money in an effort to slow inflation
Stamp Act	Required stamps on all printed materials; this was the first direct tax on the colonies
Quartering Act	Required colonies to provide shelter for British troops or pay their rent

The Proclamation Act of 1763 Settlers had been moving into western Pennsylvania in defiance of the colony's treaty with the region's Native Americans. In the spring of 1763, several Native American groups united to wage war against the British. British officials did not want to bear the cost of another war. In addition, many owned shares in fur trading companies and did not want to disrupt trade. Until new treaties could be drawn, western settlement was limited. This enraged many colonists.

Customs Reform In 1763, George Grenville, first lord of the Treasury, developed new tax policies to reduce Britain's debt. Grenville convinced Parliament to pass a law that said those accused of smuggling would be tried at a British court in Nova Scotia instead of in colonial courts. Colonial courts were more sympathetic to smugglers.

Protests from angered merchants were ignored. James Otis, a colonist, argued that because colonists had no representatives in Parliament, they could not be taxed for the purpose of raising money. Otis's arguments gave rise to the expression, "No taxation without representation."

Impact of the Stamp Act When the **Stamp Act** took effect in November 1765, the colonists ignored it and **boycotted** British goods. Protest spread throughout the colonies. In New York, 200 merchants signed a nonimportation agreement promising not to buy British goods until Parliament repealed the Stamp Act.

As a result of the boycott, thousands of British workers lost their jobs. The British could not collect money that the colonists owed them. The British repealed the Stamp Act in 1766. Parliament then passed the Declaratory Act. It said that Parliament had the power to make laws for the colonies.

The Townshend Acts

Britain continued to have financial problems. In 1767 Charles Townshend, the new finance officer, set up new laws and taxes, called the **Townshend Acts**. One of the acts was the Revenue Act of 1767. It placed taxes on glass, lead, paper, and tea imported into the colonies. The Revenue Act legalized the use of writs of assistance, general search warrants. They were used to help customs officers arrest smugglers.

Action and Reaction The Townshend Act angered many colonists. The Massachusetts assembly started organizing resistance against Britain. One of the leaders of the resistance

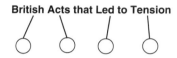

was **Samuel Adams.** He and James Otis wrote a letter that said the taxes in the Townshend Acts would be used to pay the salaries of the government officials. The British government responded by ordering the Massachusetts assembly to dissolve. The merchants of Boston, New York, and Philadelphia signed nonimportation agreements.

The boycott spread through the colonies. Americans stopped drinking British tea and buying British cloth.

The Boston Massacre In the fall of 1768, colonists began harassing British troops who had been sent to keep order. In the commotion that followed, the British troops began firing into the crowd, killing five and wounding six. The shootings became known as the Boston Massacre. News of the violence raced throughout the colonies. A few weeks later, news arrived that the British had repealed almost all of the Townshend Acts. Parliament, however, kept a tax on tea to show it had a right to tax the colonies. The repeal of the Townshend Acts brought a temporary peace to the colonies.

CORE CONCEPTS: JUSTICE

Although John Adams opposed British policies in the American colonies, he defended British soldiers who took part in the Boston Massacre. Adams stated that the soldiers had only obeyed the orders they were given.

SECTION 2 THE REVOLUTION BEGINS

Massachusetts Defies Britain

The Boston Tea Party In May 1773, England's new prime minister decided to help the nearly bankrupt British East India Company. British taxes on tea had caused colonists to smuggle in cheaper Dutch tea. To help the company sell its tea, Parliament passed the Tea Act of 1773, which allowed East India Company tea to be sold at lower prices than smuggled Dutch tea. American merchants were angered. Some tea ships arrived in Boston harbor in December 1773. On the night before the customs officials were planning to take tea ashore, about 150 men, disguised as Native Americans, boarded the ships and dumped 342 chests of tea into the harbor. The raid became known as the Boston Tea Party.

The Intolerable Acts The Boston Tea Party led Parliament to pass new laws that became known as the **Intolerable Acts**. The acts shut down Boston's port and banned most town meetings. They also violated the colonists' right to trial by a jury of one's peers and the right not to have troops quartered in one's home.

The First Continental Congress The colonies responded by calling the First Continental Congress on September 5, 1774.

Fifty-five delegates met in Philadelphia. Although they all opposed the Intolerable Acts, their responses to it varied. Moderates believed a compromise was possible. Radicals believed it was time for the colonies to fight for their rights. After a few days, the delegates approved the Continental Association. This was a plan for every county and town to form committees to enforce a boycott of British goods. The delegates also agreed to hold a second **Continental Congress** if things were not resolved. A petition was sent to the king asking him to restore colonial rights.

The Revolution Begins

While the Continental Congress was meeting, the Massachusetts assembly organized the Massachusetts Provincial Congress. They formed the Committee of Safety, chose John Hancock to lead it, and gave him the power to call up the militia. Militias began to drill and practice shooting.

Loyalists and Patriots Many colonists still felt loyal to the king and believed that the colonists should uphold British laws. Those who backed Britain became known as Loyalists, or Tories. Patriots, or those who believed that the British had become tyrants, were on the other side.

Lexington and Concord The British government ordered British General Gage to arrest the Massachusetts Provincial Congress.

On April 19, 1775, British troops arrived in Lexington, where minutemen were waiting on the village green. The British ordered them to leave. As the minutemen began to back away, a shot was fired. No one is sure who fired it. The British soldiers fired at the minutemen, then headed to Concord. When they tried to cross the bridge on the north side of town, they ran into more minutemen. A fight broke out, and the British were forced to retreat. News of the fighting spread across the colonies. Militia from all over New England came to help fight the British. By May 1775, militia troops had surrounded Boston and had trapped the British inside.

The Second Continental Congress After the battles at Lexington and Concord, the Second Continental Congress met in Philadelphia. The Congress voted to name the militia surrounding Boston the Continental Army. George Washington was appointed general and commander in chief. In the meantime, the British sent in reinforcements and decided to gain control of the area around Boston. However, the Americans turned back two British advances. They showed that the colonists could stand up to the British armies.

The Decision for Independence

The Fighting Spreads As the fighting continued, more and more Patriots began to think that it was time for the colonies to declare independence. By January 1776, public opinion also began to change because of a pamphlet called *Common Sense,* published by Thomas Paine. In the pamphlet, Paine said that the British king was the enemy, not just Parliament. *Common Sense* helped to convince many Patriots and other colonists that it was time to declare independence. On July 4, 1776, a committee approved a document on independence that Thomas Jefferson had drafted. The Continental Congress issued the **Declaration of Independence**, and the American Revolution had begun.

The Declaration of Independence stated that people have certain basic rights and that government should protect those rights. John Locke's ideas strongly influenced the declaration. It also listed colonists' complaints against the British government and declared the colonies "free and independent states" that formed a sovereign nation, "The United States of America." The document was written mainly by Thomas Jefferson, with help from Benjamin Franklin and John Adams. It also expressed ideas that had been voiced throughout the colonies in the preceding months in several dozen other "declarations of independence" that had been drafted by colonial governments and other organizations.

SECTION 3 THE WAR FOR INDEPENDENCE

OPPOSING ARMIES		
	British Army	Continental Army
Size of army	**32,000 men**	**230,000 men (only 20,000 at any time)**
Training	**Disciplined and well-trained**	**Inexperienced**
Supplies	**Well equipped**	**Poorly equipped**
Government	**Strong, central government**	**Weak and divided central government**
Support for war	**Limited support in England for war and its cost**	**Divided loyalties, many deserters**
Military strategy	**Traditional military strategy**	**Guerrilla warfare strategies**
Financial resources	**Wealth of resources from England**	**Support from France and Spain; foreign loans; personal financial support**
Motivation	**Fighting to retain colonies**	**Fighting to gain rights and freedoms**

The Northern Campaign

The British knew that to be successful, they had to win several battles and convince the Americans that the cause was hopeless.

Opening Moves The Continental Congress asked Washington to defend New York City, but the British captured New York and used it as their headquarters. Washington sent Captain Nathan Hale to spy on the British. He was caught by the British and hanged.

The British secured a victory at White Plains, New York. At this time, winter was approaching, which usually ended fighting for a time because of the weather. However, General Washington led his troops across the Delaware River into New Jersey and defeated the British in two small battles. Americans also fought the British to surrender at Saratoga, New York, a victory that improved American morale and convinced France to help the Americans.

France Enters the War In two treaties the French recognized the United States as an independent nation and created an alliance between the two countries. By June 1778, Britain and France were at war.

The Southern Campaign

After being defeated at Saratoga, the British decided to start a campaign in the southern states, where many Loyalists agreed to fight for Britain. However, people living in the Appalachian Mountains had formed a militia. They intercepted British troops at the Battle of Kings Mountain and destroyed the army. The battle was a turning point in the South. General Nathaniel Greene, the new American commander in the region, wanted to wear down the British and destroy their supplies. The plan worked, and by late 1781, the British controlled very little territory in the South.

The War Is Won

The Battle of Yorktown In April 1781, the British marched into Virginia but were soon met with American troops. The British were outnumbered and too far inland, so they retreated to Yorktown. Washington decided to move the American and French troops to Yorktown. With a French fleet nearby, the British could not escape by sea. On September 28, 1781, American and French troops surrounded Yorktown and bombarded the town. On October 19, 1781, the British surrendered.

CORE CONCEPTS: NATIONALISM

Nathan Hale's last words, before he was hanged by the British for spying, were "I only regret that I have but one life to lose for my country."

LINKING PAST AND PRESENT

When the British surrendered after the Battle of Yorktown, a band played "Yankee Doodle." The words were meant to make fun of the inexperienced and poorly trained American troops during the French and Indian War. The American troops, however, liked the song and sang it during the Revolutionary War.

The Treaty of Paris In March 1782, Parliament voted to start negotiations in Paris with the colonists. The Treaty of Paris was signed on September 3, 1783. Under the treaty, Britain recognized the United States of America as a new nation with the Mississippi River as the western border.

SECTION 4 THE WAR CHANGES AMERICAN SOCIETY

New Political Ideas

After the war, American leaders formed a **republic**—a form of government in which power resides with a body of citizens who vote. The citizens elect representatives who are responsible to them.

New State Constitutions American leaders believed that the best form of government was a constitutional republic, in which a system of checks and balances was set up to prevent any one group from getting too strong. American leaders, including **John Adams,** argued that the best government was made up of three separate branches—executive, legislative, and judicial. Adams also argued that the legislature should be bicameral, or made up of two houses. By the 1790s, most states had created consitutions. Some state governments were bicameral; others were unicameral (legislature was made up of only one house).

New York adopted its first constitution on April 20, 1777, and elected its first governor a couple of months later. New York's government is similarly structured to the federal government, as are most of the states. The governor is elected to a four-year term, and the legislature is bicameral, made up of an Assembly and a Senate. All representatives serve two-year terms. There is also a judicial system which includes a Court of Appeals (the highest court in the state) and trial courts known as Supreme Courts. A Bill of Rights was added in 1821 to guarantee New York citizens the freedoms of religion, speech, and the press.

Voting Rights Expand The war showed many farmers and artisans that they were equal to the rich planters and merchants they fought with during the war. It led the lower classes to demand a greater role in choosing their leaders. In most states, the new constitutions made it easier to gain voting rights.

However, people still had to own a certain amount of property to hold elective office.

Freedom of Religion The war led to changes in the relationship between the church and the state. Many American leaders opposed the power of a church to make people worship in a certain way. In 1786 the Virginia legislature passed the Virginia Statute for Religious Freedom. It said that Virginia no longer had an official church and that the state could not collect taxes for churches.

The War and American Society

The ideas of greater freedom applied mainly to white men, and not to most women and African Americans.

Women at War Women played an important role in the Revolutionary War. Some served on the battlefront while other women ran businesses and farms at home when their husbands and sons went to fight.

African Americans Many enslaved African Americans gained their freedom during the Revolution, many more after the war. Emancipation, or freedom from enslavement, became a major issue. Many Northern states took steps to end slavery. As a result, slavery ended in the North over the course of several years. Freed African Americans generally moved to cities to find jobs.

The South still relied heavily on enslaved labor and had no interest in abolishing slavery. In 1782, Virginia, the only southern state to do so, passed a law encouraging manumission, or the voluntary freeing of enslaved persons. Although about 10,000 enslaved people obtained their freedom this way, most did not.

An American Culture Emerges

The Revolutionary War brought Americans from all walks of life together against a common enemy and led to patriotic symbols, stories of heroes, and art.

Changes in Education American leaders knew that an educated public was necessary for a republic to succeed. As a result, several state governments provided for state-funded universities. The University of North Carolina became the first state university in the nation. American elementary schools tossed out British textbooks and began teaching republican ideas.

CORE CONCEPTS: JUSTICE

After the war, women continued to make advances. They could more easily obtain a divorce and get an education. In addition, more schools for girls were started and more women were able to read.

CORE CONCEPTS: BELIEF SYSTEMS

In 1816 African American church leaders formed the first independent African American denomination, the African Methodist Episcopal (AME) Church.

LINKING PAST AND PRESENT

After the Revolutionary War, Noah Webster called for a simplified and Americanized system of spelling. Webster wrote a speller and dictionary that established a national standard of American words and usages.

Chapter Overview

After the American Revolution, the new nation struggled to draw up a plan for government. Americans wanted to make sure the government did not have too much power. Eventually they came up with a way to balance federal and state power and to separate federal power into three branches. Promising to add a bill of rights helped win approval for the Constitution.

REGENTS WARM-UP

The problems faced by developing nations has been a key theme in many essay questions on past Regents Exams. Watch for the problems faced as the new nation struggled to develop a plan for government.

As you read through this chapter, ask yourself these questions:
(1) What were the achievements and weaknesses of the newly formed Confederation Congress?
(2) What issues were at stake during the Constitutional Convention and what compromises were reached?
(3) What were the main points of debate between the Federalists and Anti-Federalists?
(4) How was the Constitution finally ratified?

Main Ideas and Concepts

- **Political Systems** The Articles of Confederation provided a workable but faulty national government.

- **Nation-State** The new Constitution tried to uphold the principle of state authority while providing needed national authority.

- **Government** The state governments approved the Constitution through individual conventions.

People, Places, Terms

The following names and terms will help you to prepare for the Regents Exam in United States History and Government. You can find an explanation of each name and term in the Glossary in the back of this book, in your textbook, or in another reference source.

amendment
Anti-federalists
Articles of
    Confederation and
    Perpetual Union
checks and balances
duty
executive branch

federalism
Federalists
Great Compromise
impeach
judicial branch
legislative branch
New Jersey Plan
Northwest Ordinance

popular
    sovereignty
separation of
    powers
Three-Fifths
    Compromise
veto
Virginia Plan

SECTION 1 THE CONFEDERATION

The Achievements of the Confederation Congress

The Articles of Confederation The Continental Congress
adopted the **Articles of Confederation and Perpetual Union** in
November 1777. This was a plan for a loose union of the states
under the authority of Congress. The states did not want to give
up their independence to a strong central government. As a
result, the Articles set up a very weak central government.

Western Policies The Confederation Congress had some
successes. Because the Confederation Congress could not set
taxes, it raised money by selling the land it controlled west of the
Appalachian Mountains. Congress set up the Land Ordinance of
1785 to establish a system of surveying the lands.

Congress passed the **Northwest Ordinance** in 1787. It provided the basis for governing much of the western territory. It
created a new territory that could later be divided into three to
five states. The ordinance also guaranteed certain rights to those
living in the territory, such as freedom of religion and property
rights, and it prohibited slavery in that area.

The Confederation Congress negotiated several trade treaties
with other countries. By 1790 the trade of the United States was
greater than the trade of the American colonies before the
Revolution.

**LINKING GEOGRAPHY
TO HISTORY**

According to the Land
Ordinance of 1785, western
lands were divided into
townships, which were
subdivided into 36 sections.
Each section was one-mile
square. The Northwest
Ordinance of 1787 was
important because it outlined
the territorial government and
how the territory would
eventually be divided into
new states.

POWERS OF THE FEDERAL GOVERNMENT		
	Articles of Confederation	United States Constitution
Declare war; make peace	✔	✔
Coin money	✔	✔
Manage foreign affairs	✔	✔
Establish a postal system	✔	✔
Impose taxes		✔
Regulate trade		✔
Organize a court system		✔
Call state militias for service		✔
Protect copyrights		✔
Take other necessary actions to run the federal government		✔

Weaknesses of the Articles of Confederation

Problems with Trade Although the Confederation Congress had some successes, it also had some problems. After the war ended, British merchants flooded the United States with British goods, driving many American artisans out of business. Many American states fought back by restricting British imports. However, all the states did not charge the same **duties,** or taxes, on imported goods. As a result, British ships would land at the states with the lowest taxes. States also began taxing each other's goods to raise money, threatening the unity of the new United States. It was clear that a stronger central government was needed.

SECTION 2   A NEW CONSTITUTION

The Constitutional Convention

"Nationalists" were American leaders who believed that the United States needed a strong central government in order to survive. George Washington, Benjamin Franklin, and James Madison were some of these nationalists.

In 1786, Madison convinced Virginia's assembly to call a convention of all the states to discuss the problem they had with trade and taxation. Too few states came to the convention to solve any problems. The next year, Alexander Hamilton called for the Confederation Congress to call a convention in Philadelphia to discuss revising the Articles of Confederation. Every state except Rhode Island showed up to the Constitutional Convention.

The Framers Most of the 55 delegates who attended the convention had experience in colonial, state, or national government. George Washington was chosen as the presiding officer and James Madison (who became known as the Father of the Constitution) kept records of the debates. The meetings were closed to the public to ensure that the delegates were free to discuss issues without political pressure.

The Virginia and New Jersey Plans The Virginia delegation arrived at the Constitutional Convention with a plan for a new national government. The plan, called the **Virginia Plan,** called for scrapping the Articles of Confederation and creating a new national government. It proposed that the government be made up of a legislative, an executive, and a judicial branch, with two houses in the legislative branch. Voters would elect members of the first house. State governments would nominate members of the second house who would then be elected by the first house. In both houses, the number of representatives for each state would depend on the number of people in the state. Because the plan would benefit the larger states, small states opposed it.

The **New Jersey Plan** called for modifying the Articles of Confederation to make the central government stronger. The plan called for a single-house Congress in which each state was equally represented. Congress would also have the power to raise taxes and regulate trade.

REGENTS WARM-UP

Past Regents Exams have asked students to make comparisons. As you read about the decisions made at the Constitutional Convention, think about how the new constitution compares to the Articles of Confederation.

A Union Built on Compromise

As the convention worked on the new constitution, delegates found themselves divided geographically. Smaller states wanted protection against the voting power of the larger states. Northern and Southern states were divided over another issue—how to treat slavery in the new constitution.

The Great Compromise A special committee was chosen to resolve the first issue. Roger Sherman of Connecticut proposed two houses of Congress—the House of Representatives and the Senate. Representation in the House of Representatives would be based on the state's population. In the Senate, each state would have equal representation. This compromise is known as the Connecticut Compromise and the **Great Compromise.**

Compromise Over Slavery To solve the issue of slavery, the committee proposed that each state elect one member to the House of Representatives for every 40,000 people in the state. Southern delegates wanted to count enslaved people as part of the population. Northern delegates opposed this because slaves could not vote and because they felt that if slaves were counted for representation, they should also be counted for taxation. The committee proposed the **Three-Fifths Compromise** which states that every five enslaved people would count as three free persons.

The Southern delegates demanded that the new constitution not interfere with the slave trade. They also wanted a limit on Congress's power to regulate trade. Northern delegates wanted a government that could control foreign imports into the United States. A new compromise stated that Congress could not tax exports and would not ban the slave trade until 1808.

The Confederation Congress approved the new constitution in September 1787. The Constitution now had to be ratified by nine of the 13 states.

A Framework for Limited Government

The new constitution was based on the principle of **popular sovereignty**—authority to govern resides with the people. It set up a representative system of government in which elected officials represented the people. The Constitution created a system of government known as **federalism.** The power of the government is divided between the federal, or national, government and the state governments. The Constitution provided for

CORE CONCEPTS: CIVIC VALUES

While the American Revolution was a battle fought for liberty, acceptance of the Three-Fifths Compromise clashed with this ideal. Slavery deprives individuals and whole classes of people of liberty.

a **separation of powers** among the three branches of federal government. The **legislative branch,** which made the laws, was made up of Congress. The **executive branch,** headed by the president, enforced the laws. The **judicial branch,** made up of the federal courts, interpreted the laws.

Checks and Balances The Constitution also set up a system of **checks and balances** to stop any one branch of government from becoming too powerful.

The president was given the power to **veto,** or reject, acts of Congress. However, Congress had the power to override the veto with a two-thirds vote in both houses. Congress also had the power to **impeach,** or formally accuse the president or other official in the executive or judicial branch of misconduct, and then have him removed.

The legislative and executive branches balanced the judicial branch. The president could nominate members to the judiciary, but Congress had to approve the appointments.

Amending the Constitution The delegates set up a system of making **amendments,** or formal changes, to the Constitution. To prevent the Constitution from being changed too frequently, the system made it difficult for amendments to be adopted.

An amendment could be proposed by two-thirds of the members of both houses of Congress. Additionally, two-thirds of the states could call a constitutional convention to propose an amendment. The proposed amendment then had to be ratified by three-fourths of the state legislatures or by conventions in three-fourths of the states.

SECTION 3 RATIFICATION

A Great Debate

Federalists and Anti-Federalists After the Constitution was written, each state had to elect a convention to vote on it. Those who supported the Constitution called themselves **Federalists,** to indicate that they supported the federal system of government. Those who supported the Federalists included large landowners, merchants, and artisans. They believed that a strong central government would levy taxes on imports, which would help American businesses. Farmers who lived near the coast or along rivers also supported the Federalists.

Those who opposed the Constitution were called **Anti-Federalists**. They supported the need for a national government, but questioned whether the national government or the state governments should be dominant. Anti-Federalists included John Hancock and Patrick Henry. Many Anti-Federalists were farmers who lived far from the coast. They were generally self-sufficient and were suspicious of the wealthy.

The Anti-Federalists conducted a negative campaign. They complained that the Constitution did not protect people's rights, but failed to present their own plan for protecting rights. The Federalists were better organized. Most newspapers supported the Federalists. They presented their program in speeches, pamphlets, and debates. The Federalists explained why the Constitution should be ratified in a collection of essays known as *The Federalist Papers*. James Madison, Alexander Hamilton, and John Jay wrote the essays under the pen name Publius. The papers were originally published in New York newspapers and were later bound and distributed together. The essays, which were very influential, explained how the new Constitution worked.

The Fight for Ratification

The ratifying conventions started in December 1787 but were not completed until 1790. Delaware, Pennsylvania, New Jersey, Georgia, and Connecticut quickly ratified the Constitution.

Massachusetts In Massachusetts, Anti-Federalists held a majority at the convention. One Anti-Federalist, Samuel Adams, objected to the Constitution because he believed it endangered the independence of the states. The Federalists promised to attach a bill of rights once the Constitution was ratified. They also promised to add an amendment that would reserve for the states all powers not specifically given to the federal government by the Constitution. This persuaded Adams, and Massachusetts, to ratify the Constitution.

By June 1788, Maryland, South Carolina, and New Hampshire had also ratified the Constitution. Virginia and New York, however, had not. Federalists believed that without the support of the two large states, the new government would not succeed.

Virginia and New York Federalists, including George Washington and James Madison, presented strong arguments for ratification to the Virginia convention. Finally, the promise to add a bill of rights won Virginia's support. A close vote in New

CORE CONCEPTS: HUMAN RIGHTS

Anti-Federalists would not ratify the Constitution until a promise was made to attach a bill of rights, thus protecting basic liberties and rights including freedom of speech, freedom of the press, freedom of assembly, freedom of religion, and the right to a trial by jury.

York resulted in a Federalist victory. By July 1788, all states except Rhode Island and North Carolina had ratified the Constitution. Because nine states were all that was needed for ratification, the new government could start without those two states. By 1790 both states finally ratified the Constitution.

SECTION 4 BASIC CONSTITUTIONAL PRINCIPLES

The principles outlined in the Constitution were the Framers' solution to the complex problems of a representative government.

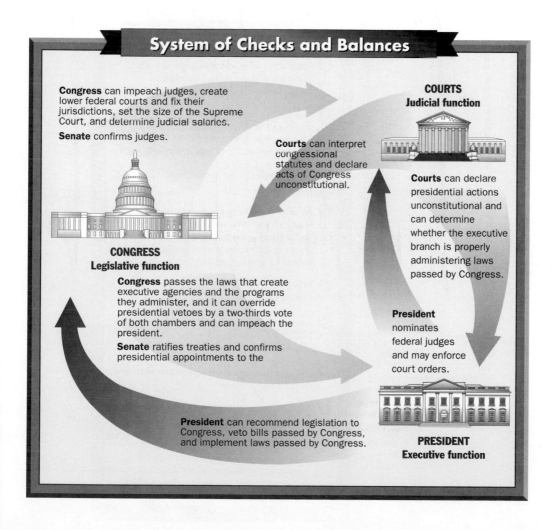

System of Checks and Balances

Congress can impeach judges, create lower federal courts and fix their jurisdictions, set the size of the Supreme Court, and determine judicial salaries.

Senate confirms judges.

COURTS
Judicial function

Courts can interpret congressional statutes and declare acts of Congress unconstitutional.

Courts can declare presidential actions unconstitutional and can determine whether the executive branch is properly administering laws passed by Congress.

CONGRESS
Legislative function

Congress passes the laws that create executive agencies and the programs they administer, and it can override presidential vetoes by a two-thirds vote of both chambers and can impeach the president.

Senate ratifies treaties and confirms presidential appointments to the

President nominates federal judges and may enforce court orders.

President can recommend legislation to Congress, veto bills passed by Congress, and implement laws passed by Congress.

PRESIDENT
Executive function

The Bill of Rights One major objection to the new Constitution was that it did not protect the rights of the people. In 1791 the Framers sent several amendments to the states to be ratified. They became known as the Bill of Rights.

The Bill of Rights limits the power of government. Its purpose is to protect the rights of individual liberty, such as freedom of speech, and the rights of persons accused of crimes, such as the right to a jury trial. Although the Bill of Rights originally applied only to the national government, almost all its provisions have been applied to the states through a series of Supreme Court decisions.

The Bill of Rights

1. Guarantees freedom of religion, speech, assembly, and press, and the right of people to petition the government

2. Protects the right of states to maintain a militia and of citizens to bear arms

3. Restricts quartering of troops in private homes

4. Protects against "unreasonable searches and seizures"

5. Assures the right not to be deprived of "life, liberty, or property, without due process of law," including protections against double jeopardy, self-incrimination, and government seizure of property without just compensation

6. Guarantees the right to a speedy and public trial by an impartial jury

7. Assures the right to a jury trial in cases involving the common law (the law established by previous court decisions)

8. Protects against excessive bail and cruel and unusual punishment

9. Provides that people's rights are not restricted to those specified in Amendments 1–8

10. Restates the Constitution's principle of federalism by providing that powers not granted to the national government nor prohibited to the states are reserved to the states and to the people

Later amendments to the Constitution included amendments to outlaw slavery, ban states from denying any person life, liberty, or property without due process of law, and give women and African Americans the right to vote.

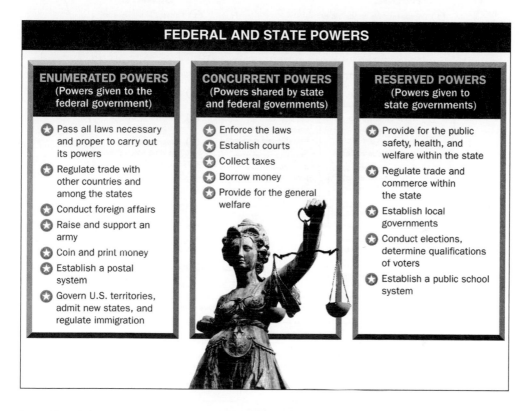

FEDERAL AND STATE POWERS

ENUMERATED POWERS (Powers given to the federal government)	CONCURRENT POWERS (Powers shared by state and federal governments)	RESERVED POWERS (Powers given to state governments)
⭐ Pass all laws necessary and proper to carry out its powers	⭐ Enforce the laws	⭐ Provide for the public safety, health, and welfare within the state
⭐ Regulate trade with other countries and among the states	⭐ Establish courts	⭐ Regulate trade and commerce within the state
⭐ Conduct foreign affairs	⭐ Collect taxes	⭐ Establish local governments
⭐ Raise and support an army	⭐ Borrow money	⭐ Conduct elections, determine qualifications of voters
⭐ Coin and print money	⭐ Provide for the general welfare	⭐ Establish a public school system
⭐ Establish a postal system		
⭐ Govern U.S. territories, admit new states, and regulate immigration		

Presidential Power in Wartime The president shares with Congress the power to make war and is responsible for many key military decisions, including the use of nuclear weapons and the use of troops to control serious disorders within the country.

Foreign Affairs Modern presidents usually conduct foreign affairs by executive agreement, rather than using the treaty process specified in the Constitution. While a treaty is an agreement between nations, an executive agreement is made directly between the president and the head of state of another country. It does not require Senate approval.

HOW A BILL BECOMES A LAW

HOUSE

① Representative hands bill to clerk or drops it in hopper.

② Bill given *HR* number.

SENATE

① Senator announces bill on the floor.

② Bill given *S* number.

Committee Action

① Referred to House standing committee.

② Referred to House subcommittee.

③ Reported by standing committee.

④ Rules Committee sets rules for debate and amendments.

Bill is placed on committee calendar.

Bill sent to subcommittee for hearings and revisions.

Standing committee may recommend passage or kill the bill.

① Referred to Senate standing committee.

② Referred to Senate subcommittee.

③ Reported by standing committee.

Floor Action

① House debates, votes on passage.

② Bill passes; goes to Senate for approval.
OR
A different version passes; goes to conference committee.

① Senate debates, votes on passage.

② Bill passes; goes to House for approval.
OR
A different version passes; goes to conference committee.

Conference Action

★ Conference committee works out differences and sends identical compromise bill to both chambers for final approval.

★ House votes on compromise bill.   ★ Senate votes on compromise bill.

Passage

★ President signs bill or allows bill to become law without signing.*

OR

★ President vetoes bill.

★ Congress can override a veto by a 2/3 majority in both chambers. If either fails to override, the bill dies.

* President can keep bill for 10 days and bill becomes law. If Congress adjourns before the 10 days (Sundays excluded) then it does not become law.

Source: *Congress A to Z*, 2nd ed. (Washington D.C.: CQ Inc., 1993).

CHAPTER 5   FEDERALISTS AND REPUBLICANS

Chapter Overview

In the first government under the Constitution, important new institutions included the cabinet, a system of federal courts, and a national bank. Political parties gradually developed from the different views of citizens in the Northeast, West, and South. The new government faced special challenges in foreign affairs, including the War of 1812 with Great Britain.

As you read through this chapter, ask yourself these questions:
(1) What tensions were growing between the nation's political parties?
(2) What tensions arose between Western settlers and Native Americans?
(3) Why was Washington's Farewell Address important?
(4) What events led to the Louisiana Purchase?
(5) Why did the United States declare war on Britain?

REGENTS WARM-UP

Essay questions on past Regents Exams have asked how the ideas or actions of an individual have shaped history. Underline information in this chapter that shows how George Washington affected the course of American history.

Main Ideas and Concepts

- **Government** George Washington helped define the office of the American presidency.

- **Conflict** Disagreements between political parties threatened citizens' rights.

- **Power** An important Supreme Court decision asserted that the Court had the power to decide whether laws passed by Congress were constitutional.

- **Decision Making** Military leaders helped decide the outcome of the War of 1812.

People, Places, Terms

The following names and terms will help you to prepare for the Regents Exam in United States History and Government. You can find an explanation of each name and term in the Glossary in the back of this book, in your textbook, or in another reference source.

Alien and	embargo	nationalism
Sedition Acts	enumerated powers	sedition
aliens	implied powers	speculators
bonds	judicial review	Tecumseh
cabinet	Meriwether Lewis	Treaty of Ghent
William Clark	Louisiana Purchase	Whiskey Rebellion

SECTION 1 WASHINGTON AND CONGRESS

Creating a New Government

Institutions of Power The first task facing the new government was to organize itself. The Congress set up departments to handle different responsibilities. These departments included the Department of State, the Department of the Treasury, and the Department of War. It also created the Office of the Attorney General. President Washington appointed Thomas Jefferson as secretary of state, Alexander Hamilton as secretary of the treasury, General Henry Knox as secretary of war, and Edmund Randolph as attorney general. This group of advisers to the president became known as the **cabinet.**

Through the Judiciary Act of 1789, Congress established district courts and courts of appeal, as well as six justices for the Supreme Court. Washington chose John Jay as the first chief justice of the United States.

Financing the Government

The Tariff of 1789 After the government was organized, it needed to find ways to raise money in order to operate. Congress passed the Tariff of 1789. It taxed all imports from other countries. It also required shippers to pay tonnage, or tax based on how much their ships carried. Southerners opposed the tariff and the tonnage because they made it costly to ship their products to Europe and to import needed goods.

Hamilton's Financial Program Hamilton supported the Tariff of 1789, but also believed that the government needed the ability to borrow money. To pay for the Revolutionary War, the Confederation Congress issued **bonds,** or paper notes promising to repay money with interest after a certain length of time. By 1789 the United States owed about $40 million to American

CORE CONCEPTS: CIVIC VALUES

The Ninth Amendment states that people have rights other than those listed. The Tenth Amendment states that any powers not specifically listed to the federal government would be reserved for the states.

citizens and about $12 million to several foreign countries. The value of the bonds had fallen, but Hamilton believed that the government should pay these debts in full. Doing so, he believed, would give people confidence in the ability of the government to pay back its loans.

Opposition to Hamilton's Plan Critics argued that Hamilton's plan was unfair to the people who first purchased the bonds. These people feared that they would never be paid, so they sold their bonds to **speculators**—people willing to take a risk in hopes of a future financial gain. Many of these speculators paid very little for the bonds but would now receive full value. Southerners were upset because most of the people who owned the bonds were Northerners, but much of the tax money used to pay off the bonds would come from the South.

The Bank of the United States Hamilton asked Congress to establish a national bank to manage the country's debts and interest payments. The bank would also make loans and issue paper money.

Southerners opposed the bank because they felt that Northern merchants would own most of the bank's stock. Madison argued that establishing a bank was not among the federal government's **enumerated powers**—powers specifically mentioned in the Constitution. Hamilton argued that the Constitution gave the federal government the power to make laws that were necessary for it to execute its responsibilities. He argued that this created **implied powers**—powers not explicitly listed in the Constitution but necessary for the government to do its job. After studying both sides of the debate, President Washington agreed to sign the bill, which created the Bank of the United States.

The Whiskey Rebellion Hamilton also believed that the government had the right to impose direct taxes on the people. In 1791, Congress passed Hamilton's proposal for a tax on the making of American whiskey. This tax angered farmers in the west, where whiskey was used as a medium of exchange because paper money was not available in large quantities. In western Pennsylvania, farmers rebelled against the tax in what came to be known as the **Whiskey Rebellion**. Hamilton wanted to establish the authority of the federal government to collect taxes, so he urged President Washington to send troops to crush the Whiskey Rebellion. The rebels stopped without a fight.

CORE CONCEPTS: DECISION MAKING

In July 1790, Hamilton, Madison, and Jefferson struck a deal. Madison and Jefferson would convince Southerners in Congress to vote for Hamilton's financial plan. In return, the capital of the United States would be moved to the District of Columbia.

CORE CONCEPTS: POLITICAL SYSTEMS

The Constitution grants three types of power to the national government: expressed, implied, and inherent. Collectively, these powers are known as delegated powers, or powers the Constitution grants or delegates to the national government.

CORE CONCEPTS: CHOICE

Political parties are important to democratic governments. There are no strict requirements for membership in political parties in the United States. A person is considered a member of the political party in which they want to belong. When a person registers to vote, he or she may select the party they wish to join.

The Rise of Political Parties

The debate over Hamilton's financial plans split Congress into two sides, which became the nation's first political parties. Those in support of Hamilton were called Federalists. Those who opposed him called themselves Democratic-Republicans, or Republicans.

DIFFERENCES BETWEEN THE FIRST POLITICAL PARTIES	
Federalists	**Democratic-Republicans**
Leader: Alexander Hamilton	**Leader: Thomas Jefferson**
Favored: • Rule by the wealthy class • Strong federal government • Emphasis on manufactured products • Loose interpretation of the Constitution • British alliance • National bank • Protective tariffs	**Favored:** • Rule by the people • Strong state governments • Emphasis on agricultural products • Strict interpretation of the Constitution • French alliance • State banks • Free trade

SECTION 2   PARTISAN POLITICS

Washington's Foreign Policy

The French Revolution began shortly after George Washington was inaugurated in 1789. At first most Americans supported the revolutionaries. French radicals seized control in 1792, however, and executed thousands of people.

The American Response Americans were divided over the French Revolution. The Federalists opposed it, while the Republicans supported it. In 1793 the French declared war on Britain, putting the United States in a difficult position. The Treaty of 1778 with France required the United States to help defend France's colonies in the Caribbean, which meant war with Great Britain. President Washington then declared the United States to be neutral toward both Britain and France.

Jay's Treaty Despite Washington's declaration of neutrality, Britain seized American ships carrying goods to France. To avoid war, Washington sent John Jay to Britain to find a solution. Under Jay's Treaty, the U.S. agreed that Britain had the right to seize merchandise that was bound for France. In return, the British agreed that the U.S. merchants would not be discriminated against when they traded with Britain (called most-favored nation status). Although people were upset with the provisions of the treaty and accused the Federalists of being pro-British, the treaty was ratified.

Pinckney's Treaty Spain joined France in its war against Britain, causing Spain to fear that the British and Americans would seize its landholdings in North America. As a result, the Spanish signed Pinckney's Treaty, which granted the United States the right to navigate the Mississippi River and to deposit goods at the port of New Orleans.

Westward Expansion

By 1790 settlement in the area between the Appalachian Mountains and the Mississippi River had grown rapidly, leading to conflicts with Native Americans in the region. A group of Native American warriors ambushed American troops, killing nearly half of them. President Washington sent General Anthony Wayne to put down Native American resistance. The American troops killed many Native Americans. The Native American nations signed the Treaty of Greenville, giving up part of present-day Ohio and Indiana.

Washington Leaves Office

The Farewell Address President Washington decided to retire at the end of his second term. Before he left office, he wrote a letter to the American people. Washington's Farewell Address warned Americans against sectionalism and political parties. He also warned that the United States should avoid getting involved

CORE CONCEPTS: INTERDEPENDENCE

Western farmers were especially supportive of Pinckney's Treaty because it meant they could continue to use the Mississippi to get crops to market.

CORE CONCEPTS: POWER

In exchange for giving up land and signing the Treaty of Greenville, Native Americans received $10,000 a year from the United States government.

REGENTS WARM-UP

Some data-based questions ask you to make inferences based upon written material. Review Washington's Farewell Address. What two main pieces of advice did Washington give the American people? Which group would be most likely to support his advice—the Federalists or the Republicans?

CORE CONCEPTS: CONFLICT

Prior to suspending trade with France, the United States attempted negotiations. Those negotiations failed when France demanded bribes before they would begin to talk. This act became known as the XYZ Affair.

in Europe and becoming too attached to any foreign nation by military alliance. He was in favor of trade with all nations.

The Election of 1796 In the election of 1796, the Federalists supported John Adams for president. The Republicans nominated Thomas Jefferson. John Adams became the second president of the United States.

The Quasi-War with France

The French were upset with Jay's Treaty and began seizing American ships bound for Britain. In June 1798, Congress stopped trade with France. The U.S. navy was directed to capture armed French ships and soon the two countries were fighting an undeclared war, known as the Quasi-War.

After negotiations, France and the United States signed the Convention of 1800. Under this agreement, the United States gave up all claims against France for damages to U.S. shipping. In return, France released the United States from the Treaty of 1778.

The War Between the Parties

The Alien and Sedition Acts In 1798 the Federalists pushed four laws through Congress that became known as the **Alien and Sedition Acts.** The first three laws were aimed against **aliens,** or people living in the country who were not citizens. Once these immigrants did become citizens, they tended to vote for the Republican Party. One law required that immigrants wait 14 years before they could become citizens. The next two laws gave the president the power to deport any alien believed to be dangerous to the United States. The fourth law was aimed at stopping **sedition,** or encouragement to revolt. This law made it a crime to say or print anything against either Congress or the president.

The Virginia and Kentucky Resolutions In 1798 and 1799, the Republican-controlled legislatures of Kentucky and Virginia passed resolutions criticizing the Alien and Sedition Acts. The Virginia Resolutions introduced the theory of interposition. They said that if the federal government did something unconstitutional, the states could step in between the federal government and the people and stop the illegal action. The Kentucky Resolutions introduced the theory of nullification. This theory states that if the federal government passed an unconstitutional law, the states had the right to declare the law invalid.

The Election of 1800 In the presidential election of 1800, the Republican nominees—Thomas Jefferson for president and Aaron Burr for vice president—campaigned against the Federalists and their laws.

The election was close and had an unexpected outcome. The Constitution called for each state to choose the same number of electors as it had senators and representatives. The group of electors, known as the Electoral College, then votes for the president. Each elector was to vote for two people—the presidential candidate and the vice presidential candidate.

When the vote was counted, Jefferson and Burr had the same number of votes. This meant that the Federalist-controlled House of Representatives had to choose a president. Hamilton urged his fellow Federalists to support Jefferson. This still led to another tie. Then Jefferson convinced one Federalist that if elected, Jefferson would not get rid of Hamilton's policies or fire all Federalists in government. The Federalist cast a blank vote, breaking the tie, and Jefferson became the new president.

CORE CONCEPTS: JUSTICE

The election of 1800 showed that power in the United States could be transferred peacefully despite strong disagreements between the parties.

SECTION 3 JEFFERSON IN OFFICE

Thomas Jefferson Takes Office

Thomas Jefferson tried to create a less formal style of presidency. He tried to bring Republican ideas into the policies that the Federalists had already put in place. Jefferson wanted to limit the power of the federal government. He began to pay off the federal debt and limit federal spending. Instead of a standing army, he relied on the local militia. To end worries that he would get rid of the national bank and do away with Hamilton's financial plan, Jefferson appointed a supporter of Hamilton's plan to head the Department of the Treasury.

The Rise of the Supreme Court

Impeaching Judges Congress passed the Judiciary Act of 1801, which created 16 new federal judges, all of whom were Federalists. After Jefferson took office, Congress repealed the Judiciary Act, thereby removing the 16 judges. The Republicans then tried to remove other Federalists, including Supreme Court

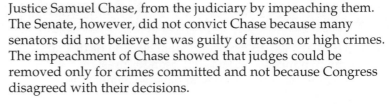

Justice Samuel Chase, from the judiciary by impeaching them. The Senate, however, did not convict Chase because many senators did not believe he was guilty of treason or high crimes. The impeachment of Chase showed that judges could be removed only for crimes committed and not because Congress disagreed with their decisions.

Marbury* v. *Madison President Adams had appointed John Marshall as Chief Justice of the Supreme Court. Before leaving office, President Adams had appointed William Marbury as a judge. Adams signed the appointment, but the documents were not delivered in time. Secretary of State James Madison was to deliver the documents, but Jefferson told him to hold them. Marbury then asked the Supreme Court to order Madison to deliver the documents. He based the request on the Judiciary Act of 1789, which stated that requests for federal court orders go to the Supreme Court.

John Marshall said that the Constitution specified the kinds of cases that the Supreme Court could hear, but a request for a court order was not one of them. He said that that part of the Judiciary Act was unconstitutional and ruled against Marbury. This decision gave the Supreme Court the right of **judicial review,** the power to decide whether laws passed by Congress were constitutional and to strike down those laws that were not.

The United States Expands West

In 1803 Napoleon offered to sell the Louisiana Territory to the United States. By accepting the offer, the United States also gained control of the Mississippi River.

The Lewis and Clark Expedition President Jefferson chose **Meriwether Lewis** and **William Clark** to lead an expedition to explore the Louisiana Territory and to find a route to the Pacific Ocean. Sacagawea, a Shoshone woman, joined the expedition as an interpreter and guide. The group found a path through the Rocky Mountains and eventually traced the Columbia River to the Pacific Ocean.

Federalists opposed the **Louisiana Purchase**. They believed that New England would lose its influence in the nation's affairs, while the South and West would gain influence. Some Federalists known as the Essex Junto drafted a plan to take New England out of the Union.

LINKING PAST AND PRESENT

The *Marbury* v. *Madison* case helped strengthened the Supreme Court because it asserted the Court's right of judicial review—the power to decide whether laws passed by Congress and the actions of the president were constitutional and to strike down laws and actions that were not.

CORE CONCEPTS: SCIENCE AND TECHNOLOGY

Lewis and Clark collected and preserved many previously unknown plant and animal specimens along their journey.

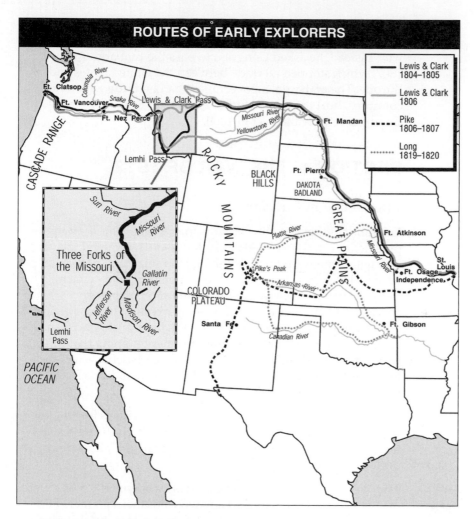

ROUTES OF EARLY EXPLORERS

	Lewis & Clark 1804–1805
	Lewis & Clark 1806
	Pike 1806–1807
	Long 1819–1820

Rising International Tensions

Economic Warfare In 1803 war resumed between Britain and France. At first, the war benefited the United States. It began trading with French colonies in the Caribbean and the British left the American ships alone because the United States had declared neutrality. By 1806, however, both Britain and France blockaded merchant ships going to Europe. Americans were caught in the middle.

In 1807 the British warship *Leopard* stopped the American warship *Chesapeake* to search for British deserters. When the American ship refused to stop, the British ship opened fire, killing three Americans. The British also seized four sailors.

REGENTS WARM-UP

Essays on past Regents Exams have focused on the contributing factors that lead to a major event in history. As you read the following section, take notes on the events that lead to the War of 1812.

Economic Diplomacy Fails Although Americans were enraged, President Jefferson did not want to involve the United States in a war. Instead, he asked Congress to pass the Embargo Act of 1807, which stopped all trade between the United States and Europe. The **embargo,** a government ban on trade with other countries, hurt the United States more than Britain or France. Congress repealed the act in 1809.

SECTION 4 THE WAR OF 1812

The Decision for War

Economic Pressures James Madison, a Republican, won the presidential election of 1808. Like Jefferson, he wanted to avoid war with Britain. To force Britain to stop seizing American ships, he asked Congress to pass the Non-Intercourse Act, which forbade trade with Great Britain and France. Napoleon announced that France would no longer restrict trade, but he did not mention that France would stop the seizure of American ships. Madison accepted the announcement, hoping that this would pressure Britain to stop its trade restrictions. When the British refused, Congress passed a bill to stop imports from Britain.

By 1812 the U.S. refusal to buy British goods was hurting the British economy. In June 1812, Britain's decision to end restrictions on trade came too late, however, because Congress declared war on Great Britain.

The War Hawks Members of Congress who voted for war were nicknamed the War Hawks. They were Southern planters and Western farmers who made much of their money by shipping their products overseas, and they were hurt by British trade restrictions. Eastern merchants made a profit despite British restrictions because they passed the cost of losing ships and goods onto the farmers.

Tecumseh and Tippecanoe Although Western farmers blamed the British for their conflicts with Native Americans, Native Americans were upset about the increased number of settlers on their lands. **Tecumseh,** a Shawnee leader, believed that Native American groups needed to unite to protect their lands. Troops from Indiana Territory clashed with the Native Americans near Tippecanoe River, in the Battle of Tippecanoe. Although there was no clear winner, many Native Americans fled to Canada,

CORE CONCEPTS: ECONOMIC SYSTEMS

In the year prior to the war, the Republicans had closed the Bank of the United States. This made it difficult for the government to borrow money since most private bankers were located in the Northeast, and they were opposed to the war.

which was held by the British. This led many Americans to believe that the British were helping the Native Americans.

Many Americans believed that going to war with Britain would help the United States gain Canada and end Native American attacks. President Madison yielded to the pressure and asked Congress to declare war. The South and the West voted for war, and the Northeast did not.

The Invasion of Canada

Although the United States had declared war, it was not ready to fight. The country did not have enough of the money, troops or equipment necessary to fight a war. Despite these problems, President Madison ordered the military to invade Canada. The plan, however, failed.

The United States had more success on the sea. The U.S. fleet attacked the British fleet on Lake Erie in September 1813. After a four-hour battle, the British surrendered. This victory gave the United States control of Lake Erie. By the end of 1813, however, the United States had still not conquered Canada.

The War Ends

In 1814 the war between Britain and France ended. Britain now turned its attention to the United States.

Raids on Washington, D.C., and Baltimore The British attacked Washington, D.C. They set fire to the White House and the Capitol. They then moved to Baltimore, but the militia there was ready for them, and the British abandoned their plan to attack. The British plan to cut New England off from the rest of the country also failed.

The Battle of New Orleans Then in January 1815, American troops under the command of General Andrew Jackson defeated the British in the Battle of New Orleans. The victory made Jackson a national hero and strengthened **nationalism,** or the feeling of strong patriotism, in the nation. The Federalists lost popularity, and within a few years the party dissolved.

The Treaty of Ghent In 1814 the **Treaty of Ghent** ended the War of 1812. It did not change most existing conditions, but it did increase the nation's prestige overseas and started a wave of patriotism and national unity.

REGENTS WARM-UP

Using a graphic organizer is a good way to gather and remember information about important events in history. Make a cause-and-effect chart similar to those seen earlier in the book to help you remember the causes and effects of the War of 1812. Add to the chart as you finish reading this chapter.

Chapter Overview

After the War of 1812, a new spirit of nationalism took hold in American society. A new national bank was chartered, and Supreme Court decisions strengthened the federal government. New roads and canals helped connect the country. Industry prospered in the North, while an agricultural economy dependent on slavery grew strong in the South. Regional differences began to define political life.

As a result of the developments of this period, many Americans have a strong sense of national loyalty today. In addition, federal authority over interstate commerce between 1812 and 1832 helped create the truly national economy that currently exists.

As you read through this chapter, ask yourself these questions:
(1) How did an increased national pride after the War of 1812 affect the nation's foreign policy?
(2) What were the results of the Industrial Revolution and changes in transportation?
(3) Why did cotton dominate the Southern economy?
(4) What were the major parts of the Missouri Compromise?

Main Ideas and Concepts

- **Continuity and Change** Increased national pride marked the years immediately following the War of 1812.

- **Science and Technology** New manufacturing techniques reshaped the organization of the American workforce and workplace.

- **Change** The invention of the cotton gin made cotton a key part of the South's economy. Cotton farming ensured that slavery continued to shape the South's society and culture.

- **Individuals, Groups, Institutions** The rise of a new political party grew from disagreement between those

who wanted to expand federal power and those who
wanted to limit it.

People, Places, Terms

The following names and terms will help you to prepare for
the Regents Exam in United States History and Government.
You can find an explanation of each name and term in the
Glossary in the back of this book, in your textbook, or in another
reference source.

John C. Calhoun	interchangeable parts	National Road
cotton gin	John Marshall	protective tariff
Democratic-Republicans	Missouri Compromise	revenue tariffs
Era of Good Feelings	Monroe Doctrine	slave codes
Industrial Revolution	Samuel F.B. Morse	Eli Whitney

SECTION 1 AMERICAN NATIONALISM

The Era of Good Feelings

After the War of 1812, Americans had national pride.
Americans had a greater feeling of loyalty toward the United
States than toward their state or region.

The Monroe presidency is described as the **Era of Good
Feelings**. It was a time of political harmony in the country. One
reason for this was because the Republican Party was the only
major political party that had any power. The Federalist Party
had lost political influence and popularity.

Economic Nationalism

American leaders planned a program to bring the nation
together. Their program had three main goals: creating a new
national bank, protecting American manufacturers from foreign
competition, and linking the country together through improvements in transportation.

The Second Bank In 1811 Republicans blocked the rechartering
of the First Bank of the United States. State-chartered banks and
other private banks loaned bank notes that were used as money.
During the War of 1812, prices rose rapidly. The U.S. government had to pay high interest rates on the money it had borrowed to pay for the war. In 1816 **John C. Calhoun** proposed the

bill that was passed by Congress to create the Second Bank of the United States.

Tariffs and Transportation During the War of 1812, an embargo stopped Americans from buying British goods. When the war ended, low-priced British goods flooded American markets. This threatened to put American companies out of business. Congress passed the Tariff of 1816 to protect manufacturers from foreign competition. Earlier **revenue tariffs** provided income for the federal government. The Tariff of 1816 was a **protective tariff.** It helped American manufacturers by taxing imports to drive up their prices.

In 1816 Republican John C. Calhoun sponsored a federal plan to improve the transportation system in the United States. President Madison vetoed it. He said that spending money to improve transportation was not granted by the Constitution. Instead, private businesses and state and local governments paid for road and canal construction.

Judicial Nationalism

Between 1816 and 1824, chief justice of the United States **John Marshall** helped unify the nation. He ruled in two cases that established the power of the federal government over the states.

McCulloch **v.** *Maryland* In 1819 the Court decided in *McCulloch* v. *Maryland* that the Second Bank of the United States was constitutional. The decision said that the "necessary and proper" clause meant that the federal government could use any method to carry out its powers, as long as the method was not expressly forbidden in the Constitution. Marshall also ruled that state governments could not interfere with an agency of the federal government exercising its specific constitutional powers within a state.

Gibbons **v.** *Ogden* In 1824 the Court decided in *Gibbons* v. *Ogden* that the Constitution granted the federal government control over interstate commerce. The Court said that interstate commerce included all trade along the coast or on waterways dividing states. The state could regulate commerce within its own borders. This ruling made it clear that federal law had priority over state law in interstate transportation while states controlled their intrastate commerce.

CORE CONCEPTS: CONSTITUTIONAL PRINCIPLES

The powers that the national government requires to carry out the powers that are expressly defined in the Constitution are called implied powers. The basis for the implied powers is the "necessary and proper" clause (Article I, Section 8). It is also called the "elastic clause" because it allows the powers of Congress to stretch.

REGENTS WARM-UP

Past Regents Exams have asked students to identify the significance of landmark Supreme Court cases. *McCulloch* v. *Maryland* and *Gibbons* v. *Ogden* are two such cases.

Nationalist Diplomacy

Nationalism in Congress and among voters in the United States influenced the nation's foreign affairs. Under President Monroe the United States expanded its borders and became involved in world affairs.

Jackson Invades Florida In the early 1800s, many Southerners were angry with Spanish-held Florida. Runaway slaves fled there, knowing Americans were not allowed to cross the border to look for them. Also, the Seminoles in Florida raided American settlements in Georgia. Spain could not control its border, so many Americans wanted the United States to step in. In a confident show of force against the Seminoles, the United States pressured Spain to sign a treaty in 1819 ceding all of Florida. The treaty also finalized the western border of the Louisiana Purchase lands and the Texas territory.

The Monroe Doctrine Spain's colonies began to rebel in 1809. By 1824, all of Spain's colonies on the American mainland had declared their independence. In the meantime Great Britain, Austria, Prussia, and Russia (and later France) formed the Quadruple Alliance to stop movements against their monarchies in Europe. Members of the alliance, except Great Britain, discussed the possibility of helping Spain regain control of its overseas colonies. In response to this threat, President Monroe issued the **Monroe Doctrine** in 1823. This foreign policy said that the United States would prevent other countries from becoming involved in the political affairs of Latin American countries. The Monroe Doctrine became a long-term foreign policy of the United States.

SECTION 2 EARLY INDUSTRY

A Revolution in Transportation

By the early 1800s, a transportation network of roads, canals, and railroads began to crisscross the country. As a result, great social and economic changes occurred in the United States.

Roads and Turnpikes In 1806 Congress funded the building of the **National Road.** This was a major east-west highway that started in Cumberland, Maryland, and ended in Wheeling, Virginia (now West Virginia). The National Road was the largest federally funded transportation project of its time.

REGENTS WARM-UP

Past Regents Exams have included questions that test your knowledge about shifts in U.S. foreign policy. Until the late 1800s, American foreign policy was based on isolationism—avoiding involvement in world affairs, especially in the affairs of Europe. The Monroe Doctrine extended the meaning of isolationism.

Steamboats and Canals Rivers were a faster, easier, and cheaper way to move goods than were roads but loaded boats and barges could only travel downstream or with the current. In 1807 the steamboat called the *Clermont* traveled upstream on the Hudson River. Use of the steamboat made upstream travel possible and caused an increase in river travel and canal building. The completion of New York's Erie Canal in 1825 spurred a growth of canal building throughout the country. Canals increased trade and stimulated new economic growth.

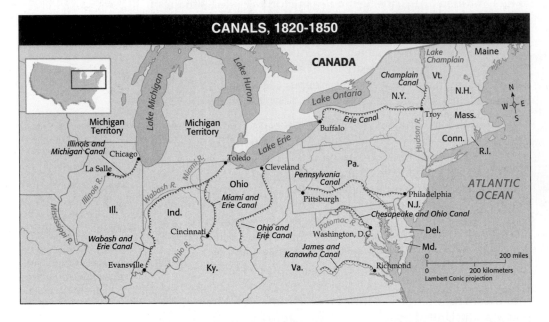

CANALS, 1820-1850

Railroads Railroads were built in America in the early 1800s. Trains were faster than stagecoaches or wagons, and they could go more places than steamboats could. Railroads helped settle the West and expand trade among the nation's regions.

New York By the 1840s, New York had become the leading port in the country. The Erie Canal opened the city of New York to river traffic upstate and linking it to the West. These commercial links made New York a center of manufacturing and trade.

A New System of Production

The **Industrial Revolution** began in Britain in the 1700s. The revolution consisted of several developments in business and industry. Manufacturing moved from hand tools to large, complex machines. Workers went from skilled artisans to workers given specific jobs. Factories replaced home-based workshops. Manufactured goods were sold nationwide and overseas.

Industrialization Industry developed quickly in the United States in the early 1800s. Industrialization began in the Northeast, where swift-flowing streams provided waterpower for textile factories. The Northeast also had entrepreneurs and merchants who had money to invest in industry. Industrialization led to the rise of large cities as thousands of people left farms and villages to seek higher-paying factory jobs in Northeast cities.

Technological Advances Several inventions and technological advances helped industry grow in the United States. **Eli Whitney** made the idea of **interchangeable parts** popular in the gun-making industry. Machines were able to produce large amounts of identical pieces that workers assembled into finished goods. In 1832 **Samuel F.B. Morse** perfected the telegraph and developed the Morse code for sending messages.

Workers Begin to Organize

Working Conditions Working conditions in the factories were better than in England, but they were still difficult. Particularly different were conditions in the factories of Lowell, Massachusetts, where owners employed mostly young women. The women were strictly supervised; they lived in clean boarding houses and dormitories and were well fed. However, the hours were long and the work was difficult and repetitive. In later years (the 1830s and '40s) competition increased and the conditions and wages decreased while hours increased.

By 1860 there were 1.3 million factory workers in the United States. During the late 1820s and early 1830s, many factory workers joined labor unions to improve working conditions. The

CORE CONCEPTS: ECONOMIC SYSTEMS

An important factor in the growth of industry in the United States was free enterprise. In this system, Americans could make money and make their own choices about how to use it. Private ownership of property and competition among businesses are also key factors in the free enterprise system.

unions had little money and, therefore, little power. There were, however, some gains made during this period. President Martin Van Buren lowered the workday for federal employees to 10 hours and the Supreme Court ruled that labor strikes were legal.

Urban Problems With the booming growth in urban population, the number of poor also increased. Some were immigrants who could not find jobs, others were orphans or widows. Many were victims of prejudice, particularly recent Irish immigrants or free blacks.

Middle-Class Life The fastest growing group in American society was the middle class. This was in large part due to the growth of the industrial economy. More people could now open their own businesses, engage in trade, or enter professions. Middle-class women tended to remain in the home and care for children. Although female children were encouraged to attend elementary schools, they were effectively barred from pursuing any higher education.

Households were larger and becoming more elaborate. Many middle-class women could afford to hire domestic help. Many working-class women, however, still had to work outside the home, often hired by middle-class women, who looked down on them.

SECTION 3 THE LAND OF COTTON

The Southern Economy

The economy of the south was based on the farming of several major cash crops, including tobacco, rice, and sugarcane. The major cash crop was cotton. With its focus on agriculture, the South did not industrialize as quickly as the North and had to import most of its manufactured goods.

Cotton Becomes King The invention of the **cotton gin** by Eli Whitney in 1793 greatly increased the production of cotton in the South. Textile mills in Europe were expanding and wanted all the cotton they could get. The demand for cotton also created a huge demand for slave labor. Between 1820 and 1860, the number of enslaved people in the South nearly tripled.

Slavery

Most enslaved African Americans spent their lives in bondage, laboring year after year in rice and cotton fields. While some free African Americans prospered in the cities of the upper South, their rights varied from state to state. Free African Americans in the North, where slavery had been outlawed, still suffered discrimination and had few opportunities. Enslaved African Americans developed their own culture and exercised resistance to cope with the horrors of enslavement.

Slave Codes State **slave codes** forbade enslaved persons from owning property, leaving their owner's land without permission, testifying in court against a white person, and learning how to read and write.

Religious and Cultural Expression African Americans dealt with the horrors of slavery in many ways. Songs were important to many enslaved people. Field workers often used them to lament their bondage, using subtle language and secret meaning. They also played an important part in their religious traditions. By the early 1800s, many were Christians, although they incorporated traditions from Africa into services.

Resistance and Rebellion A former slave, Frederick Douglass became a leader of the antislavery movement. Denmark Vesey was a free African American who was accused of planning a revolt to free the slaves around Charleston, South Carolina. He was tried, convicted, and hanged. White Southern lawmakers enacted even stricter laws regulating slavery.

REGENTS WARM-UP

Past Regents Exams have included questions that test your knowledge of legislation that has limited the rights of various groups. Look at the Regents Exams at the back of the book. Find thematic essay or document-based questions that focus on civil rights.

SECTION 4 GROWING SECTIONALISM

The Missouri Compromise

In 1819 the Union had 11 free states and 11 slave states. Missouri applied for statehood as a slave state. This set off the divisive issue as to whether slavery should expand westward. Admitting any new state would upset the balance in the Senate and start a struggle for political power.

While Congress tried to settle the question of slavery in Missouri, Maine applied for statehood as well. The **Missouri Compromise** (1820) called for admitting Maine as a free state and Missouri as a slave state, thus maintaining the balance of

CORE CONCEPTS: CONSTITUTIONAL PRINCIPLES

The Founders established the Electoral College as a compromise between direct popular vote and Congress choosing the president. The system works well in most elections. However, four times in American history—in the election of John Quincy Adams in 1824, Rutherford B. Hayes in 1876, Benjamin Harrison in 1888, and George W. Bush in 2000—the candidate who lost the popular vote won the election.

free and slave states. The compromise also prohibited slavery in the Louisiana Territory north of Missouri's southern border.

The Election of 1824

The presidential election of 1824 revealed regional differences within the Republican Party. Among the four Republican "favorite sons," Andrew Jackson won the popular vote, but no candidate won a majority of the electoral votes. When the vote went before the House of Representatives, John Quincy Adams was elected president. Jackson's supporters angrily protested the outcome and decided to form a new political party—the **Democratic-Republicans**. The party later shortened their name to Democrats.

CHAPTER 7   THE SPIRIT OF REFORM

Chapter Overview

Reform was a key theme of the 1830s and 1840s. Political reform came with the growth of popular democracy. President Jackson's election symbolized the new power of common citizens. For many Americans, social or religious reform was a goal. Some wanted to end slavery. Others wanted to expand education or women's rights. Throughout this period, sectional rivalries grew more bitter.

As a result of the developments of this period, social and political ideals became important American values.

As you read through this chapter, ask yourself these questions:
(1) How did Jackson's background influence his ideas of democratic government?
(2) How did the nullification crisis spark the debate over states' rights?
(3) What were the goals of different groups active in the Second Great Awakening?
(4) What was the connection between religious and social reform?
(5) How did Northerners and Southerners view abolition?

Main Ideas and Concepts

- **Individuals, Groups, Institutions** The American political system became more democratic during the Jacksonian era.

- **Belief Systems** The Second Great Awakening increased support for many religious groups in the United States.

- **Reform Movements** Reform movements sought to change American society, but in ways that upheld American values and deeds.

- **Human Rights** Abolitionist reformers challenged the morality and legality of slavery in the United States.

People, Places, Terms

The following names and terms will help you to prepare for the Regents Exam in United States History and Government. You can find an explanation of each name and term in the Glossary in the back of this book, in your textbook, or in another reference source.

abolition	Horace Mann	spoils system
caucus system	nativism	Elizabeth Cady
Dorothea Dix	nullification	Stanton
emancipation	secede	Tariff of
Indian Removal Act	Second Great	Abominations
Know-Nothings	Awakening	Trail of Tears

SECTION 1 JACKSONIAN AMERICA

A New Era in Politics

Starting in the early 1800s, the United States saw a growth of democracy. Hundreds of thousands of males gained voting rights. Many of these new voters voted for Andrew Jackson in the 1828 election.

The People's President   Shunning the political elite, Andrew Jackson instituted government reforms that he believed would put political power in the hands of ordinary citizens. He supported the **spoils system,** the practice of appointing people to government jobs on the basis of party loyalty and support. He believed that opening government offices to ordinary citizens increased democracy.

Jackson also wanted to change the way in which presidential candidates were chosen. At the time political parties chose presidential candidates through the **caucus system.** Party members who served in Congress would meet to choose the nominee for president. Jackson believed that this method gave only the well connected the opportunity to hold office. He replaced the caucus with the national nominating convention.

The Nullification Crisis The economy of South Carolina was weakening throughout the early 1800s. Many people blamed the nation's high protective tariffs. South Carolina had to purchase many manufactured goods from Europe. In 1828 Congress placed a new tariff on imports, which people called the **Tariff of**

CORE CONCEPTS: GOVERNMENT

The early caucus became widely criticized as undemocratic because most people had no say in selecting the candidates. The modern caucus system requires openness with the selection process starting at the local level. Nineteen states use caucuses today.

Abominations, which made already expensive European goods even more costly. Many South Carolinians threatened to **secede,** or withdraw, from the Union.

Vice President John C. Calhoun proposed the idea of **nullification.** This idea said that because states created the Union, they had the right to declare a federal law null, or not valid, if they considered it unconstitutional. Jackson considered nullification an act of treason and he was ready to send federal troops to collect the tariff. Compromise ended the crisis, but the debate over states' rights was far from over.

Policies Toward Native Americans

Like many others, President Jackson believed that conflicts with Native Americans would end if they were moved to the Great Plains. In 1830 Jackson pushed through Congress the **Indian Removal Act,** which provided money to relocate Native Americans. Most Native Americans gave in and resettled in the West, but the Cherokee of Georgia refused. They sued the state of Georgia, and their case reached the Supreme Court. The Court sided with the Cherokee, but President Jackson did not support the decision.

Jackson's successor, President Martin Van Buren, sent the army to force the Cherokee from their homes and march them west to what is now Oklahoma. Thousands of Cherokee died on the journey, which became known as the **Trail of Tears.**

Jackson Battles the National Bank

Like most Westerners, Jackson was suspicious of the National Bank, believing it was a monopoly that benefited the wealthy. The bank did serve to keep the currency supply stable, however. In 1832, Jackson's congressional opponents introduced a bill extending the bank's mandate for another 20 years. Jackson vetoed the bill. When he was reelected, he believed that he had a mandate to destroy the bank. His critics would later charge that this move contributed significantly to the financial crises of the future.

A New Party Emerges

Not all Americans thought that Jackson's ideas were best for the nation. By the mid-1830s the Whig Party emerged, advocating a larger federal government and support for industry. In the

1836 election, Democrat Martin Van Buren easily won. Shortly after he became president, an economic depression called the Panic of 1837 hit the United States.

The Whigs had their chance in the White House after the 1840 presidential election, but on key issues President John Tyler acted more like a Democrat.

SECTION 2 A CHANGING CULTURE

The New Wave of Immigrants Between 1815 and 1860, more than 5 million immigrants arrived in the United States. Almost 2 million of them came from Ireland where a potato fungus caused widespread famine. The second largest group of immigrants in this period came from Germany.

Nativism Some immigrants faced discrimination in America. The presence of people with different languages and religions produced a feeling of **nativism,** or hostility toward foreigners. In 1854 several nativist groups formed the American Party. Membership in the party was secret and members were told to answer, "I know nothing" when questioned. The party was nicknamed the **Know-Nothings.**

A Religious Revival The United States experienced a revival of religious commitment in the 1800s that is known as the **Second Great Awakening.** Ministers urged Americans to readmit God into their lives. A number of new religions flourished during this period. The Second Great Awakening preached the message that anything was possible with hard work and prayer. The immigrants' hopes and the revival's message combined to reinforce the belief that people had the ability to redefine their lives.

SECTION 3 REFORMING SOCIETY

Many people in the mid-1800s worked to reform various aspects of American society. Women were among the most visible reformers.

The Imprisoned and Mentally Ill In the 1800s, criminals and the mentally ill were often crowded together in prisons. Reformer **Dorothea Dix** worked to improve conditions for the mentally ill by convincing states to fund state mental hospitals. Others worked for programs to help prisoners rehabilitate themselves.

REGENTS WARM-UP

Past Regents Exams have included questions that test your knowledge about the experiences of different groups of immigrants in the United States during different periods. As you read, pay attention to sections that focus on immigration.

REGENTS WARM-UP

Past Regents Exams have included questions that test your knowledge of legislation that has limited the rights of various groups. Look at the Regents Exams at the back of the book. Find thematic essay or document-based questions that focus on civil rights.

Educational Reform Many reformers began to push for public education, in which government-funded schools were open to all citizens. **Horace Mann** was a Massachusetts legislator who pushed for more education. By the 1850s, tax-supported elementary schools existed in many Northeastern states and soon spread to the rest of the country.

The Early Women's Movement

In the 1800s, people began dividing their lives into two activities—the home and the workplace. Many people believed that home was the proper place for women. Many women believed that women should be treated equally with men.

The Seneca Falls Convention The Seneca Falls Convention (1848) was a gathering of women seeking rights equal to men. This convention declared that all men and women are created equal and women should have equal property and legal rights. Organizer **Elizabeth Cady Stanton** also proposed that women focus on gaining the right to vote.

CORE CONCEPTS: REFORM MOVEMENTS

The Seneca Falls Convention is significant as being the start of an organized women's movement.

SECTION 4 THE ABOLITIONIST MOVEMENT

Throughout American history, many Americans had opposed slavery. The first organizations formed to end slavery started in the early 1800s. Some societies believed that slavery should be ended gradually. Others thought the best solution was to send African Americans back to Africa.

The New Abolitionists In the 1830s, the idea of **abolition**, or the immediate end, of slavery took hold. Abolitionists argued that enslaved African Americans should be freed immediately, with no compensation to former slaveholders. They believed that slavery was an evil for which the country needed to be sorry.

William Lloyd Garrison William Lloyd Garrison was very influential in the development of a national abolitionist movement in the 1830s. He founded Boston's antislavery newspaper, the *Liberator*. He felt the only solution was complete **emancipation**, or the freeing of all enslaved people.

Frederick Douglass and Sojourner Truth Free African Americans also took on significant leadership roles in the

**CORE CONCEPTS:
REFORM MOVEMENTS**

Sojourner Truth may be best-
known for the speech in
which she asked, "And ain't I
a woman?"

abolitionist movement. One of these was Frederick Douglass, who escaped from slavery in Maryland and published his own antislavery newspaper. Another important abolitionist was Sojourner Truth, who helped runaway slaves escape to "free" territories.

The Response to Abolitionism

In the North Many Northerners disapproved of slavery. However, some thought the abolitionist movement was a threat to the existing social system or believed that it would create conflict between the North and the South. Others were afraid that it would lead to the influx of freed African Americans to the North, causing housing and job shortages.

In the South Even though most Southerners did not own slaves, they still viewed slavery as a necessity to the Southern way of life and to its economy. They defended it by claiming that most slaves did not want freedom because they benefited from their relationship with the slaveholders.

In 1831, shortly after Garrison printed his newspaper, Nat Turner, an enslaved preacher, led a revolt that killed more than 50 Virginians. Southerners were furious and demanded that abolitionist material not be circulated in the South. Southern postal workers refused to deliver abolitionist newspapers. The House of Representatives refused to debate all abolitionist petitions.

Chapter Overview

In this period, Americans strove to expand the nation's boundaries. Many believed they had a "manifest destiny" to spread democratic ideals. Others simply wanted to go west to find a new and better life. In Texas, settlers came into conflict with Mexico, while those going west on the Oregon Trail came into conflict with Native Americans.

Developments of the era have left a legacy for Americans—the nation now stretches from the Atlantic to the Pacific Oceans. In addition, some might argue that as a result of this era, Americans remain a restless group of people who are ready to move to pursue economic opportunity; and that many Americans view themselves as destined to succeed and prosper.

As you read through this chapter, ask yourself these questions:
(1) Why were Americans willing to give up their lives in the East to move west?
(2) How did settlers in Texas gain independence from Mexico?
(3) Under what circumstances were Texas and Oregon admitted to the Union?

Main Ideas and Concepts

- **Science and Technology** Several inventions of this period helped make settling the West possible.

- **Individuals, Groups, Institutions** Texans hoped to transplant American institutions to their new homes.

- **Change** The war with Mexico brought new territories under the control of the United States.

People, Places, Terms

The names and terms below will help you to prepare for the Regents Exam in United States History and Government. You can find an explanation of each name and term in the Glossary in the back of this Book, in your textbook, or in another reference source.

Alamo	James K. Polk	John Tyler
annexation	Antonio López	Brigham Young
"Fifty-four Forty	de Santa Anna	
or Fight"	Treaty of Guadalupe	
Manifest Destiny	Hidalgo	

SECTION 1 THE WESTERN PIONEERS

Americans Head West

In 1800 few Americans lived west of the Appalachian Mountains. By 1820 there were about 2.4 million settlers and the population continued to grow quickly. By the time the Civil War started in 1860, more Americans lived west of the Appalachians than lived along the Atlantic coast. Americans moved west for many reasons, including to find religious freedom and to own their own farms.

Manifest Destiny A magazine editor said that the movement west was **Manifest Destiny**—the idea that God had given the continent to Americans and wanted them to settle western lands. Many Americans believed in this concept.

The first settlers to establish farms west of the Appalachians were called "squatters," meaning that they settled on lands they did not own. Squatters wanted to buy the land directly from the government. The Preemption Act of 1830 gave them the right to claim and buy land from the government before it was surveyed and sold by the government to real estate companies.

Plows and Reapers Midwestern farming was made easier by advances in farming technology including a plow with an iron blade and a plow with sharp-edged steel blades that was able to cut through the tough Midwestern sod. These inventions cut in half the labor needed to farm an acre. In 1834 the mechanical reaper made cutting grain much faster and easier.

Settling the Pacific Coast

People who came later to the Midwest pushed on toward California and Oregon. Emigrants thought that the Great Plains had poor land for farming.

Oregon Native Americans and other nations had already claimed parts of Oregon and California. The United States and Great Britain competed to own Oregon. In the late 1830s,

American missionaries came to the Oregon territory to convert local Native Americans to Christianity. These missionaries convinced many Easterners to settle in southern Oregon.

California Beginning in 1821, after gaining independence from Spain, Mexico controlled California. In 1839 the governor of California, wanting to attract more settlers, granted 50,000 acres of land to a German immigrant and trader, John Sutter.

Going West Much of the land that pioneers had to cross was difficult terrain. By the 1840s, mountain men had opened up several east-west passages that acted as "highways" to settlers going west. Among these passages were the Oregon Trail, the Santa Fe Trail, and the California Trail.

Treaty of Fort Laramie Native Americans on the Great Plains feared that the increasing number of settlers moving across their hunting grounds would disrupt the great buffalo herds on which their lives depended. Hoping to ensure peace, the U.S. government and eight Native American groups negotiated the Treaty of Fort Laramie in 1851. The Native Americans agreed to live in certain territories while the government promised that these territories would always belong to the Native Americans.

The Mormon Migration

In 1844 a mob murdered the Mormon founder and leader Joseph Smith. **Brigham Young,** the new leader of the Mormons, decided to take his people west to escape religious persecution. Thousands of Mormons emigrated west on the Mormon Trail, which became an important route to the western United States. In 1847 they stopped at the Great Salt Lake and built a new settlement. The Great Salt Lake is in what is today the state of Utah.

SECTION 2 INDEPENDENCE FOR TEXAS

Opening Texas to Americans

In 1821 Texas came under Mexican control after Mexico won its independence from Spain. Mexico invited Americans and other foreigners to settle in the northern part of the region. They were offered cheap land in return for becoming Mexican citizens and Roman Catholics.

CORE CONCEPTS: IDENTITY

In spite of the fact that early settlers were not inclined to adopt Mexican customs, Texas today draws on a rich history that includes having been a part of Mexico

At first the Americans agreed to Mexican citizenship, but balked at adopting Mexican customs. Very few thought of Mexico as their country. After a rebellion against the Mexican government in 1830, Mexico closed its borders to immigration by Americans. Mexico also banned the import of enslaved labor and placed taxes on goods imported from foreign countries— including the United States. These laws infuriated the settlers.

Texas Goes to War

When Mexico enforced its authority on the colony, outraged Texans prepared for war. Texan forces enjoyed some early victories, but Mexican General **Antonio López de Santa Anna's** superior army soundly defeated the Texans at the **Alamo**—an abandoned mission—and at Goliad.

A surprise attack in the Battle of San Jacinto River led to the capture of Santa Anna and the end of the war. Santa Anna signed a treaty recognizing the independence of the Republic of Texas. In 1836 Texans voted in favor of **annexation**—becoming part of the United States. President Jackson, however, was unwilling to upset Northern leaders, who feared that Texas would be admitted as a slave state.

SECTION 3 THE WAR WITH MEXICO

The Lingering Question of Texas

Disputes over territory between the United States and Mexico dated back to 1803, when the U.S. claimed Texas as part of the Louisiana Purchase. In addition, the ideas of Manifest Destiny and acquiring Mexican territory were popular among Americans. However, Mexico never recognized Texas independence. Mexico considered Texas a Mexican territory.

REGENTS WARM-UP

Previous Regents Exams have included questions on the causes and effects of the war with Mexico. Create a cause-and-effect chart, and fill in the chart as you read this section.

Texas and Oregon Enter the Union

In 1844 Congress voted against annexation of Texas. Many Northerners thought that annexation was a pro-slavery plot.

James K. Polk, a former Congressman and governor of Tennessee, was nominated as the Democratic candidate for the 1844 election. Polk promised to annex Texas and the Oregon territory. He also promised to buy California from Mexico. His platform appealed to both Northerners and Southerners because it expanded the country and kept a balance between free and slave states. Polk won the election.

The Oregon Question President Polk said in public that the United States had a right to Oregon. Those who supported this stand on Oregon used the slogan **"Fifty-four Forty or Fight."** This meant that supporters wanted all of Oregon to the line of 54°40' north latitude. In private, however, Polk agreed to split the territory with Great Britain.

The Annexation of Texas Just before Polk took office, President **John Tyler** pushed a resolution through Congress that annexed Texas. Texas joined the Union in 1845 as a state. This angered Mexico, which broke off diplomatic relations with the United States. Matters between the two countries got worse when Mexico and the U.S. could not agree on the location of Texas's southwestern border.

In November 1845, Polk sent a representative to Mexico City to try to purchase California. Mexico's president refused to meet with him.

The War with Mexico

After Mexico's president refused to discuss the U.S. purchase of California, President Polk ordered U.S. troops to cross the Nueces River. Mexico saw this as an invasion of the country and a force of Mexicans attacked the American troops. Polk declared war with Mexico. Although many Whigs were against the war because they saw it as another plan to extend slavery, Congress voted for the war.

Polk's successful three-part military strategy gained control of California and secured the capture of Mexico's capital city. In signing the **Treaty of Guadalupe Hidalgo,** Mexico gave up much of what became the American Southwest, and the American dream of Manifest Destiny was fulfilled. The United States now stretched from ocean to ocean. The question of whether the new lands would be slave or free would soon lead the country into another civil war.

CORE CONCEPTS: CONSTITUTIONAL PRINCIPLES

States are admitted to the Union by Congress in accordance with Article IV, Section 3 of the Constitution. Texas, however, was admitted as the 28th state under unusual circumstances. Congress passed a joint revolution that provided for immediate statehood, allowing Texas to skip the territorial period.

Chapter Overview

When the nation gained new territory, the slavery controversy intensified. Questions arose concerning whether new states would be slave or free, and who would decide. States that allowed slavery were determined to prevent free states from gaining a majority in the Senate. Political compromise broke down by 1860. When Lincoln was elected president, many Southern states decided to secede.

The political and social debates of this period continue to have influence in the twenty-first century. Older sectional loyalties still define some regions of the country. In addition, the modern Republican Party grew in part from its opposition to slavery.

As you read through this chapter, ask yourself these questions:
(1) How did the government deal with slavery in the territories acquired after the war with Mexico?
(2) How did the Fugitive Slave Act and the transcontinental railroad heighten sectional tensions?
(3) What events led to increased sectional tensions in the 1850s?
(4) What events led to the Civil War and the secession of the Lower South?

Main Ideas and Concepts

- **Geography and History** The acquisition of new lands heightened sectional tensions over slavery.

- **Civic Rights and Responsibilities** As sectional tensions rose, some Americans openly defied laws they thought were unjust. After Lincoln's election, many Southerners placed state loyalty above loyalty to the Republic.

- **Individuals, Groups, Institutions** Due to differing opinions within established parties, Americans forged new political alliances in the 1850s.

People, Places, Terms

The names and terms below will help you to prepare for the Regents Exam in United States History and Government. You can find an explanation of each name and term in the Glossary in the back of this book, your textbook, or another reference source.

abolitionist	Fugitive Slave Act	transcontinental
Compromise	Kansas-Nebraska	railroad
of 1850	Act	Harriet Tubman
Confederacy	popular sovereignty	*Uncle Tom's Cabin*
Jefferson Davis	Republican Party	Underground
Dred Scott decision	secession	Railroad

SECTION 1 SLAVERY AND WESTERN EXPANSION

The Impact of the War With Mexico

Although many slaves managed to escape slavery, they were not safe. Many Southerners believed that they had the right to get a slave back. Northerners believed otherwise and helped enslaved people escape. The war with Mexico opened the new lands of California, Oregon Territory, and Texas to American settlers and again raised the issue of slavery there.

The Wilmot Proviso The Wilmot Proviso proposed that slavery would not be allowed in any of the newly acquired territories. The proposal won the support of Northerners, but outraged Southerners, who believed the decision would threaten slavery everywhere. The Senate refused to vote on the proposal, however, and sent moderates scrambling for a compromise.

Popular Sovereignty One proposal that gained both Northern and Southern support was **popular sovereignty**—the idea that citizens of each new territory should decide the slavery issue for themselves by voting. This idea appealed to many politicians because it removed the issue of expanding slavery from the national government.

Disintegration of the Whig Party In the 1848 election, the Whigs chose General Zachary Taylor as their candidate. The party split over this nomination. Northern Whigs, known as Conscience Whigs, opposed slavery and Taylor because they believed that he wanted to spread slavery westward. Other

REGENTS WARM-UP

Previous Regents Exams have contained questions about how various events dealt with the issue of slavery. Create a chart or other graphic organizer in which you can organize your notes about how events discussed in this section dealt with the issue.

Northern Whigs supported Taylor and voted with the Southern Whigs. The Conscience Whigs quit the party and joined with antislavery Democrats from New York. Finally, Conscience Whigs joined with the Liberty Party to form the Free Soil Party.

The 1848 Election Three candidates ran for president in 1848. Democrat Lewis Cass supported popular sovereignty; Free-Soil Party candidate Martin Van Buren opposed slavery in the territories. Whig candidate Zachary Taylor avoided the slavery issue and won the election.

The Search for Compromise

The 1848 discovery of gold in California brought thousands of prospectors to California. When California applied to join the Union as a free state, Congress again split down sectional lines. Southerners feared losing power in Congress. Though Senator Henry Clay proposed compromises, debates over California led Southerners to threaten **secession.**

Compromise of 1850 Finally, Clay's proposal won the support of the president and Congress. It gave California its statehood as a free state but did not place restrictions on slavery in the rest of the territory from Mexico. Many supporters of Southern rights opposed the compromise. In the end, Congress passed separate bills that became known as the **Compromise of 1850.** Tensions over slavery had temporarily eased.

CORE CONCEPTS: CITIZENSHIP

Henry Clay is known as the "Great Compromiser" because of the significant role he played in the Missouri Compromise, the tariff compromise that ended the nullification crisis in 1833, and the Compromise of 1850.

SECTION 2 MOUNTING VIOLENCE

The Fugitive Slave Act

Resentment over the Compromise of 1850 increased sectional tensions. Southerners applauded the **Fugitive Slave Act,** which required all citizens to help catch and return runaway slaves. If they refused, they could be jailed. Harsh enforcement of the act inspired many Northerners to join the cause against slavery. Harriet Beecher Stowe wrote *Uncle Tom's Cabin* to show the horrors of slavery. Southerners tried, but failed, to have the book banned. The book greatly influenced public opinion about slavery.

The Underground Railroad Antislavery activists—both white and African American—organized the **Underground Railroad.** This was an organized system in which runaways were transported north and given shelter and food along the way. They were moved to freedom in the Northern states or Canada. Many people, particularly **Harriet Tubman,** acted as "conductors." They made dangerous journeys into the South to guide enslaved persons along the Underground Railroad.

The Transcontinental Railroad By the early 1850s, many people were interested in the lands west of Missouri and Iowa. At about the same time, Oregon was opened for settlement and California was admitted to the Union. Many Americans believed that they needed a **transcontinental railroad** to connect the west coast to the rest of the country. Southern leaders pushed for a southern route across the Southwest and through northern Mexico. The Mexicans sold a strip of land—the Gadsden Purchase—to the United States for this purpose.

The Kansas-Nebraska Act Senator Stephen Douglas hurried to organize the Kansas and Nebraska territories for a northern route. Northern leaders were outraged when Douglas's Kansas-Nebraska bill proposed to repeal the Missouri Compromise through popular sovereignty and allow slavery in the new territories. The passage of the **Kansas-Nebraska Act** (1854) set off a bloody territorial civil war between antislavery and pro-slavery settlers in Kansas. When violence over the Kansas issue spread to the floor of the Senate, shocked Northerners strength-ened their resolve to fight the "barbarism of slavery."

SECTION 3 THE CRISIS DEEPENS

Birth of the Republican Party

Reactions to the Kansas-Nebraska Act created sectional divisions within the American Party and the Whigs. Former Whigs and Free-Soil members formed the **Republican Party** to oppose the expansion of slavery. The Republicans wanted to prevent the Southern planters from controlling the federal government. Although Republicans did not agree on whether slavery should be abolished, they did agree that it should be kept out of the territories.

The *Dred Scott* Decision In 1856, voters elected Democrat James Buchanan to the presidency, who believed the best way to save the Union was to make concessions to the South. Buchanan believed that the Supreme Court should decide the issue of slavery in the territories. The case that would decide the issue centered on Dred Scott, an enslaved man whose Missouri slaveholder had taken him to live in free territory before return-

CORE CONCEPTS: CONSTITUTIONAL PRINCIPLES

The Supreme Court's ruling in *Dred Scott* emphasized the rights of the states and the rights of citizens in an increasingly democratic society. The national furor over the *Scott* case damaged the Court and added to the tensions leading to the Civil War.

REGENTS WARM-UP

Past Regents Exams have asked students to identify the significance of landmark Supreme Court cases. The *Dred Scott* Decision, also called *Scott* v. *Sanford*, is one such case.

ing to Missouri. Scott sued to end his slavery, saying that the time spent in free territory meant he was free. In the ***Dred Scott Decision*** (1857), the court ruled against Scott on the grounds that Scott was property, not a citizen and, therefore, could not sue in courts. In addition, the Court ruled that the federal government could not prohibit slavery in the territories, as this was depriving citizens in the territories of their property. The decision made the Missouri Compromise unconstitutional. Northerners opposed the decision. Southerners threatened to leave the Union if Northerners did not obey it.

Continued Conflicts in Kansas When Kansas applied for statehood as a slave state, violent reactions in Congress underscored how deeply the slavery issue had divided the nation. The Senate voted to approve the application but the House of Representatives blocked it. In 1858, settlers in Kansas voted overwhelmingly against allowing slavery in their state. As a result, Kansas did not become a state until 1861.

Lincoln and Douglas

In 1858 Illinois Republicans nominated Abraham Lincoln to run for the Senate against the Democratic incumbent, Stephen A. Douglas. Lincoln asked Douglas to participate in a series of debates. Lincoln believed slavery was wrong and opposed its spread into the territories. Douglas supported popular sovereignty. During the Illinois debates, Lincoln asked Douglas if the people of a territory could ban slavery before becoming a state. If Douglas said yes, then he would be supporting popular sovereignty and opposing the Dred Scott decision. This would cost him Southern support. However, if he said no, that would mean that he no longer supported popular sovereignty, the principle on which he had built his popular following.

The Freeport Doctrine To overcome the dilemma he was in, Douglas gave an answer that became known as the Freeport Doctrine. He said that he supported the *Dred Scott* ruling but believed that people could still keep slavery out by not passing or enforcing laws that were needed to regulate slavery. Douglas won the election.

John Brown's Raid John Brown was an **abolitionist.** In 1859 he developed a plan to free and arm the enslaved people in the area of Harpers Ferry, Virginia. John Brown's insurrection against slaveholders failed. He was tried, convicted of treason, and sentenced to death. While many Northerners viewed Brown's

actions as noble, most Southerners became convinced that
Northerners were plotting the murder of slaveholders.

SECTION 4 THE UNION DISSOLVES

The Election of 1860

Debates over slavery finally split the Democrats, prompting
the fractured party to run two candidates in the 1860 presidential
election. The Southern Democrats wanted the party to uphold
the *Dred Scott* decision and support slaveholders' rights in the
territories. Northern Democrats wanted the party to support
popular sovereignty. The Republicans, who knew they would
not be able to get any electoral votes in the South, turned to
Abraham Lincoln.

Lincoln is Elected With the Democratic vote split, Republican
candidate Lincoln won the presidency. For many Southerners,
having a Republican president meant the end of Southern
society and culture. Beginning with South Carolina, seven
Southern states responded to Lincoln's victory by voting to
secede from the Union.

Compromise Fails As secessionists seized federal property in
their states, Northern members of Congress worked to find a
compromise that would hold the Union together. The Crittenden
Compromise proposed several amendments to the Constitution.
The amendments would guarantee slavery where it existed.
Slavery would be prohibited north of the Missouri Compromise
line and allowed south of it. The compromise did not pass
Congress.

Founding the Confederacy On the same day that Virginia held
a peace conference, delegates from the seceding states declared
the Confederate States of America, or the **Confederacy,** a new
nation. They drafted their own constitution, which guaranteed
slavery in Confederate territory. The Confederacy chose
Jefferson Davis to be president.

The Civil War Begins At his inauguration in March 1861
Lincoln repeated his promise not to interfere with slavery and
urged reconciliation. In April 1861 Confederate troops had
seized Fort Sumter. When Lincoln called up the Union troops to
defend the fort, states in the Upper South decided to side with
the Confederacy. Lincoln prepared for war by quickly taking
steps to keep the slave-holding border states from seceding.

REGENTS WARM-UP

Past Regents Exams have
included questions about
events that led to the start of
the Civil War. Create a chart
or other graphic organizer to
help you list the events that
caused the war to begin as
you read this section.

**CORE CONCEPTS:
CONSTITUTIONAL
PRINCIPLES**

The Founders created a
Constitution that could be
adapted to a future they could
not foresee. One way they
provided for change was to
describe in Article V how
Congress and the states
could amend the Constitution.

Chapter Overview

The Civil War was a milestone in American history. The four-year-long struggle determined the nation's future. With the North's victory, slavery was abolished. During the war, the Northern economy grew stronger, while the Southern economy stagnated. Military innovations, including the expanded use of railroads and the telegraph, coupled with a general conscription, made the Civil War the first "modern" war. The outcome of this bloody war changed the nation: the power of the federal government was strengthened while the Thirteenth Amendment abolished slavery.

As you read through this chapter, ask yourself these questions:
(1) What were the strengths and weaknesses of each region's economy?
(2) How did the progress of war in the East compare to the war in the West?
(3) What were the effects of war on each region's economy?
(4) What was the significance of events at Vicksburg and Gettysburg?

Main Ideas and Concepts

- **Individuals, Groups, Institutions** The Confederacy's weak central government had difficulty coordinating the war effort.

- **Geography and History** The Union hoped to seize the Mississippi Valley and cut the Confederacy in two.

- **Individuals, Groups, Institutions** The Civil War brought great suffering to civilians as well as soldiers on both sides of the conflict.

- **Geography and History** The Union victory at Vicksburg cut the Confederacy into two parts.

People, Places, Terms

The following names and terms will help you to prepare for the Regents Examination in United States History and Government. You can find an explanation of each name and term in the Glossary in the back of this book, in your textbook, or in another reference source.

REGENTS WARM-UP

Begin a chart or other graphic organizer to take notes about the advantages and disadvantages of the North and South. Graphic organizers such as these will help you as you study for your Regents Exam.

54th Massachusetts
Antietam
Clara Barton
John Wilkes Booth
Bull Run
Emancipation
  Proclamation

Gettysburg
  Address
Ulysses S. Grant
greenback
habeas corpus
"Stonewall"
  Jackson

Robert E. Lee
William Tecumseh
  Sherman
Thirteenth
  Amendment

SECTION 1 THE OPPOSING SIDES

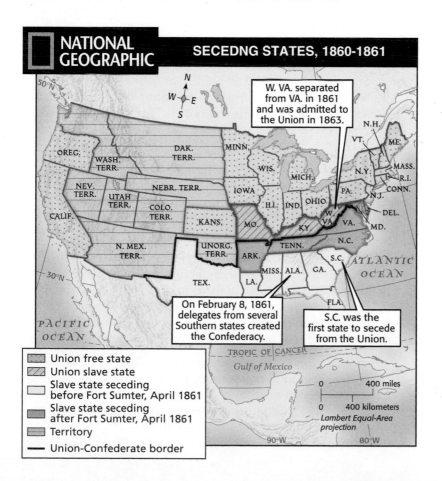

NATIONAL GEOGRAPHIC   **SECEDNG STATES, 1860-1861**

W. VA. separated from VA. in 1861 and was admitted to the Union in 1863.

On February 8, 1861, delegates from several Southern states created the Confederacy.

S.C. was the first state to secede from the Union.

- Union free state
- Union slave state
- Slave state seceding before Fort Sumter, April 1861
- Slave state seceding after Fort Sumter, April 1861
- Territory
- Union-Confederate border

0   400 miles
0   400 kilometers
Lambert Equal-Area projection

Advantages and Disadvantages

The North had several advantages over the South. The North had more people, which made it easier to raise an army and support the war effort. The South had fewer people, and about one-third of them were enslaved. That meant that a greater percentage of its men had to fight, leaving few people to support the war effort.

The Military　About one-third of the total number of officers in the United States joined the Confederacy. Those officers helped the Confederacy to quickly organize a fighting force. In 1860 the South had seven out of the eight military colleges in the United States, which provided the South with a large number of trained officers.

The North had a strong navy. More than three-fourths of the nation's naval officers came from the North along with the crews of merchant ships. They provided the navy with experienced sailors for the Union navy. In addition, the Union controlled most of the navy's warships.

Industry and Agriculture　The North had an economic advantage over the South. It had 80 percent of the nation's factories. Almost all of the nation's firearms and gunpowder were made in the North. To improve the situation, the South began to produce its own weapons and gunpowder.

The South was able to produce a large amount of food, but it had only one railroad line to transport it from the eastern to the western part of the Confederacy. As a result, the Union troops could easily disrupt the South's railroad system and stop the South from moving food and troops by rail.

Finances　The North had financial advantages over the South. The Union controlled the national treasury. It also continued to get money from tariffs. Northern banks had large reserves of cash. They loaned the cash to the government by buying bonds. In February 1862, Congress passed the Legal Tender Act. It created a national currency and allowed the government to print green-colored paper money, known as **greenbacks.**

The finances of the Confederacy, which were never very good, grew worse over time. Southern planters were in debt and could not buy bonds. Southern banks had small cash reserves. The Union's blockade of southern ports reduced trade in the South and, therefore, reduced the amount of money the South could raise through tariffs. To remedy this situation, the South levied

REGENTS WARM-UP

Past Regents Exams have asked students to compare social, political, and economic conditions of the United States in different periods. As you read, think about how the information is similar to what you know about early or later periods in our country's history.

taxes on the people, which many refused to pay. The South was forced to print paper money, which caused a huge rise in inflation.

Party Politics in the North

President Lincoln faced conflict from members of the Republican Party, many of whom where abolitionists. Lincoln's goal in the Civil War was to preserve the Union, not to abolish slavery. The President also had to deal with the Democrats, who challenged his policies. Democrats were divided between those who supported and opposed the war.

Habeas Corpus In 1862 Congress introduced a law that required states to conscript, or draft, people for military service. Many Democrats opposed the law. To enforce the law, Lincoln suspended writs of **habeas corpus.** This refers to a person's right not to be imprisoned unless charged with a crime and given a trial. Lincoln suspended writs for those who supported the Confederacy or who encouraged others to resist the draft.

Weak Southern Government The Confederate constitution stressed states' rights. As a result, the power of the central government was limited. Many Southern leaders opposed Jefferson Davis's policies. They opposed forcing people to join the Confederate army and Davis's suspending of writs of habeas corpus. They also opposed the new taxes placed on Southerners.

SECTION 2 THE EARLY STAGES

Mobilizing the Troops

The Union hoped for a quick victory against the South by striking Confederate forces at **Bull Run.** At first, the attack went well. But when Confederate reinforcements led by **"Stonewall" Jackson** arrived, the Union decided to retreat. This defeat made it clear that the North would need a large, well-trained army to defeat the South.

Excitement about the war drew many Northern and Southern men to enlist at first. When enlistment began to slow down, both sides turned to conscription. In 1863 Congress introduced a national draft to raise the necessary troops. The Confederacy began the draft in early 1862.

CORE CONCEPTS: PRESIDENTIAL DECISIONS AND ACTIONS

During the Civil War, President Lincoln boldly used measures to quiet opposition, even though such measures violated constitutional guarantees of free speech, press, and assembly. For example, he declared martial law and supervised border state elections.

LINKING PAST AND PRESENT

By executive order President Richard Nixon suspended the draft in 1973. Since then membership in the military has been voluntary. Nixon's order, however, did not repeal the law that created the Selective Service System that administered the draft. For that reason, males between the ages of 18 and 25 could be required to serve if conscription is reinstated.

The Naval War

President Lincoln wanted to blockade all Confederate ports. By spring of 1862, the Union had blockaded all ports along the Atlantic, except for Charleston, South Carolina, and Wilmington, North Carolina. Union ships, however, found it difficult to stop all of the blockade-runners—the small, fast ships used by the South to smuggle goods past the blockade.

At the same time that Union ships were blockading Atlantic ports, the Union navy began to prepare to take over New Orleans and gain control of the lower Mississippi River. In April 1862, Union forces bombarded Confederate forts along the lower Mississippi River and captured New Orleans.

The War in the East In the East, major campaigns waged in the Southern states inflicted heavy casualties. Confederate General Robert E. Lee's defeat at **Antietam** led to the bloodiest one-day battle in all of American history.

The Emancipation Proclamation The losses at Antietam, despite the Northern victory, convinced Lincoln to issue the **Emancipation Proclamation**—a decree freeing all enslaved persons in states still in rebellion after January 1, 1863. The Proclamation changed the purpose of the war from preserving the Union to ending slavery.

SECTION 3   LIFE DURING THE WAR

The South's failing economy led to food shortages, riots, and poor morale. In contrast, the North's growing industries supplied Union troops, while innovations in agriculture helped maintain crop production. On both sides, women supported the war effort by working in factories, running farms and businesses, and taking on nursing tasks in army hospitals. When the Emancipation Proclamation officially permitted African Americans to enlist, many rushed to service. The **54th Massachusetts** was the first African American regiment officially organized in the North.

Many Union and Confederate soldiers expected to endure hardships, but most were not prepared for the horrors of war.

The battles produced huge numbers of casualties and wounded. In the camps, infection spread quickly, disease was rampant, and amputations were a common measure to address appalling wounds. **Clara Barton** and many other women nursed soldiers

CORE CONCEPTS: CONFLICT

The Civil War was a total war: a war against an entire society, not just its armies. It is meant to break the will of the people.

on the battlefield. Prisoners of war, especially those held by the South, endured conditions that were especially dreadful.

SECTION 4 THE TURNING POINT

The Union wanted to capture Vicksburg, Mississippi, the last major Confederate stronghold on the river. When General Grant succeeded, the Union victory cut the South in two.

The Road to Gettysburg General Lee's leadership kept Union troops away from the Confederate capital and sent Union troops running in Fredericksburg and Chancellorsville, Virginia. Confident from his victories, Lee decided to launch a northern invasion. When the armies met in Gettysburg, Pennsylvania, however, Union troops overwhelmed the Confederates. More than one-third of the Confederate army died on the fields of Gettysburg. The defeat proved to be the turning point of the war. From that point forward, the Confederacy remained on the defensive. President Lincoln visited the site of the battle and delivered one of the best-known orations in American history—the **Gettysburg Address**.

LINKING GEOGRAPHY TO HISTORY

The Union's capture of New Orleans, near the mouth of the Mississippi River, was a major blow to the Confederacy. It meant that the Confederacy could no longer use the river to carry its goods to sea. Together with Grant's victories to the north, Union forces had split the Confederacy and now had control of almost all the Mississippi River.

SECTION 5 THE WAR ENDS

In May and June of 1864, Union General **Ulysses S. Grant** relentlessly attacked General **Robert E. Lee's** Confederate forces in Virginia.

Sherman's March to the Sea At the same time, Union General **William Tecumseh Sherman** marched from Chattanooga toward Atlanta. Sherman ordered all civilians to leave Atlanta. After Sherman took control of the city, his troops set fires that destroyed more than one-third of the city. From Atlanta, Sherman's army cut a path of destruction that reached to Georgia's coast and north into South Carolina. Sherman exemplified total war. Southerners were demoralized, but Atlanta's capture revitalized Northern support for the war.

The South Surrenders In the 1864 presidential election, voters reelected the president. Lincoln took it as a mandate to end slavery permanently by amending the Constitution. In January 1865, the **Thirteenth Amendment**, which banned slavery in the United States, passed the House of Representatives and was sent to the states for ratification.

CORE CONCEPTS: CONSTITUTIONAL PRINCIPLES

The Thirteenth Amendment is one of three amendments that are known as the Civil War Amendments. The others are the Fourteenth and Fifteenth Amendments.

At the same time, General Lee raced to escape Grant's forces in southwestern Virginia. With his troops surrounded and outnumbered, Lee surrendered to Grant at Appomattox Courthouse.

Lincoln's Assassination Lincoln outlined his plan for restoring the Southern states to the Union, but he would never see his plans through. Although his advisers warned him not to appear unescorted in public, he went to Ford's theater with his wife on April 14, 1865. During the play, **John Wilkes Booth** slipped behind the president and shot him, shocking an already weary nation.

The North's victory saved the Union. It strengthened the power of the federal government over the states. It changed American society by ending the enslavement of millions of African Americans. The war also devastated the society and the economy of the South.

PRACTICING FOR THE REGENTS

Part I Multiple-Choice Questions

The following multiple-choice questions come from or are similar to questions from past Regents High School Examinations. Test your understanding of the geography of the United States by answering each of these items. Circle the number of the word or expression that best completes each statement or question. Test-taking tips can be found in the margins for some questions. For additional help, see Taking the Regents Exam on pages ix–xxxi of this Review Book.

1 The Virginia House of Burgesses was important to the development of democracy in the thirteen colonies because it
   (1) provided an example of a representative form of government
   (2) created the first written constitution in America
   (3) provided for direct election of senators
   (4) began the practice of legislative override of executive vetoes

2 "It is not the cause of one poor printer, nor of New York alone, which you are now trying. No! It may in its consequence affect every free man that lives under a British government on the main [continent] of America. It is the best cause. It is the cause of liberty. . . . Nature and the laws of our country have given us a right to liberty of both exposing and opposing arbitrary power (in these parts of the world at least) by speaking and writing the truth."
   —*Andrew Hamilton, 1735*

   This courtroom summation helped establish which democratic principle in colonial America?

   (1) trial by jury
   (2) equal voting rights
   (3) protection of private property
   (4) freedom of the press

3 The pamphlet *Common Sense*, by Thomas Paine, aided the American cause in the Revolutionary War because it
   (1) convinced France to join in the fight against England
   (2) led to the repeal of the Stamp Act
   (3) created a new system of government for the United States
   (4) persuaded individuals who were undecided to support independence

Base your answers to questions 4 and 5 on the chart below and on your knowledge of social studies.

PREPARATIONS FOR WAR		
	England	**Thirteen Colonies**
Population	Approximately 12,000,000	Approximately 2,800,000
Manufacturing	Highly developed and flourishing	Practically none
Money	Richest country in the world	No money to support the war effort
Army	Large, well-trained army plus mercenary Hessians	All-volunteer forces — willing to fight but poorly equipped
Leaders	Many dedicated and able officers	Few officers capable of leading
Geography	Strange land with long distance to base of supplies	Familiar land with easy access to limited amounts of supplies

4   Which conclusion about the American Revolutionary War is most clearly supported by the information in this chart?
(1) England had few advantages in a war with her American colonies.
(2) The thirteen colonies had more advantages than disadvantages upon entering the war.
(3) England did not believe that the thirteen colonies were worth the expense of a war.
(4) The thirteen colonies had few, but important advantages in the war with England.

5   Which important reason for the American victory in the Revolutionary War is missing from the chart?
(1) naval superiority of the thirteen colonies
(2) aid from foreign nations
(3) control of railroads and canals
(4) greater number of Indian allies

6   Which statement best describes governmental power under the Articles of Confederation?
(1) Power was shared equally by the central government and the states.
(2) A balance of power existed between the three branches of the central government.
(3) A strong chief executive headed a unified central government.
(4) The states had much greater power than the central government.

7   The Northwest Ordinance of 1787 was important because it
(1) ensured universal suffrage for all males
(2) extended slavery north of the Ohio River
(3) provided a process for admission of new states to the Union
(4) established reservations for Native American Indians

8   Which group had the most influence on the ideas stated in the Declaration of Independence and the United States Constitution?
   (1) political leaders of Spain and Portugal
   (2) religious leaders of the medieval period
   (3) writers of the Renaissance
   (4) philosophers of the Enlightenment

9   At the Constitutional Convention of 1787, the Great Compromise resolved the issue of
   (1) representation
   (2) taxation
   (3) slavery
   (4) control of trade

10   Delegates at the Constitutional Convention of 1787 agreed to create a bicameral legislature as a way to
   (1) insure speedy passage of legislation
   (2) assure the right to vote to all adult males
   (3) address the issue of population differences among the states
   (4) satisfy the different interests of the rich and poor citizens

11   Under the United States Constitution, state governments have the power to
   (1) coin money
   (2) license teachers
   (3) regulate interstate commerce
   (4) establish term limits for members of Congress

12   The Constitution assigns the power to ratify treaties exclusively to the
   (1) Supreme Court
   (2) United States Senate
   (3) House of Representatives
   (4) president

13   Which feature of the federal government is specifically described in the United States Constitution?
   (1) president's cabinet
   (2) two-party political system
   (3) congressional committee system
   (4) Senate approval of nominations to the Supreme Court

14   *The Federalist Papers* were published in 1787 and 1788 to help gain support for
   (1) a bill of rights
   (2) the ratification of the Constitution
   (3) a weaker central government
   (4) the abolition of slavery

15   A republican form of government is described as one in which
   (1) there is a two-party system
   (2) representatives are elected by the people
   (3) elected officials have limited terms
   (4) government power is limited by checks and balances

16   The basic purpose of the first ten amendments to the United States Constitution is to
   (1) describe the powers of the three branches of government
   (2) limit the powers of state governments
   (3) guarantee the rights of individuals
   (4) establish a system of checks and balances

17   The due process clause in the Fifth Amendment and the right to an attorney in the Sixth Amendment were designed to
   (1) protect freedom of expression
   (2) assure that laws are properly enacted
   (3) ensure fair treatment for those accused of crimes
   (4) provide for judicial review of laws

18   Which newspaper headline shows the operation of the system of checks and balances?
   (1) **"Senate Rejects President's Choice of Supreme Court Justice"**
   (2) **"Florida to Gain Two Seats in the United States House of Representatives"**
   (3) **"Albany County Receives $4 Million from Congress of Transportation Development"**
   (4) **"New York State Rejects Federal Regulations on Drug Testing"**

19   • Congress proposes an amendment legalizing an income tax.
   • The Supreme Court rules that the income tax is unconstitutional.

   These events illustrate the use of
   (1) delegated powers
   (2) checks and balances
   (3) judicial legislation
   (4) the unwritten constitution

20   One reason the United States Constitution is considered a flexible document is that it
   (1) can be rewritten every ten years
   (2) allows for the creation of a multiparty political system
   (3) gives the states the power to change federal laws
   (4) includes the elastic clause

21   • Alien and Sedition Acts
   • Virginia and Kentucky Resolutions

   These pieces of legislation reflected the conflict between
   (1) Congress and the president
   (2) states' rights and federal supremacy
   (3) the military and the civilian government
   (4) the United States Supreme Court and state courts

22   Most historians consider Alexander Hamilton to have been a successful Secretary of the Treasury because he
   (1) expanded trade with all nations
   (2) established a sound financial plan for the new nation
   (3) eliminated tariffs between the states
   (4) opposed payment of previous federal government debts

23   As a strict constructionist, President Thomas Jefferson questioned the constitutional right to
   (1) receive diplomats from foreign nations
   (2) purchase the Louisiana Territory
   (3) grant pardons to convicted criminals
   (4) veto legislation passed by Congress

24   How did Supreme Court decisions under Chief Justice John Marshall affect government in the United States?
   (1) Federal power increased at the expense of the states.
   (2) Strict limits were placed on congressional use of the elastic clause.
   (3) The impeachment of federal judges was declared unconstitutional.
   (4) State powers under the Tenth Amendment were expanded.

Base your answer to question 25 on the map below and on your knowledge of social studies.

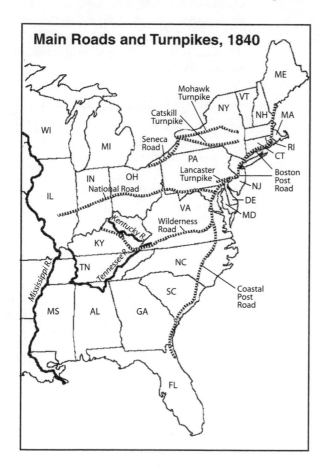

Main Roads and Turnpikes, 1840

25 What was the primary result of road and turnpike development?
  (1) Migration from east to west increased.
  (2) Southern states became more industrialized.
  (3) State government control of transportation was increased.
  (4) Escape from slavery was made easier.

26 President George Washington's Farewell Address influenced future United States foreign policy by advising the nation's leaders to
  (1) practice neutrality toward international conflicts
  (2) place restrictions on the number of immigrants
  (3) stop European colonization of the Western Hemisphere
  (4) limit imports of manufactured goods

27 During the first half of the 19th century, territorial expansion led to
   (1) increased tensions over slavery
   (2) improved relations with bordering nations
   (3) fewer conflicts with Native American Indians
   (4) decreased domestic demand for manufactured goods

28 Which event was most influenced by the principle of Manifest Destiny?
   (1) founding of Jamestown
   (2) defeat of Britain in the Revolutionary War
   (3) purchase of Florida
   (4) acquisition of the Mexican Cession

29 "Resolved. That all laws which prevent woman from occupying such a station in society as her conscience shall dictate, or which place her in a position inferior to that of man, are contrary to the great precept of nature and therefore of no force or authority."
        —Declaration of Sentiments and Resolutions, *Seneca Falls Convention, 1848*

   The writers of this passage were protesting
   (1) British treatment of American colonists
   (2) the absence of a bill of rights in the Constitution
   (3) gender discrimination against women
   (4) lack of legal protection for African Americans

30 "A house divided against itself cannot stand. . . . I do not expect the Union to be dissolved; I do not expect the house to fall; but I do expect it will cease to be divided. It will become all one thing, or all the other. . . ."
        —*Abraham Lincoln, 1858*

   The "divided house" referred to in this speech was caused primarily by
   (1) expansionism
   (2) war with Mexico
   (3) slavery
   (4) the suffrage movement

Part II   Thematic Essay Question

The following thematic essay question comes from past Regents Examinations. Write your answers on a separate sheet of paper. Essay-writing tips appear in the margin. For additional help, see Taking the Regents Exam on pages ix–xxxi of the Review Book.

Directions: Write a well-organized essay that includes an introduction, several paragraphs addressing the task below, and a conclusion.

Theme: The Constitution and Change

The United States Constitution not only provides a basic framework of government, but also allows for the flexibility to adapt to changes over time.

Task:

- Identify *two* basic constitutional principles and discuss how each principle allows the government to adapt to changes in the United States.
- For *each* constitutional principle you discuss, describe a specific historical circumstance when the principle was used to meet the changing needs of American political, social, *or* economic life.

You may use any example from your study of United States history. Some suggestions you might wish to consider include: the amendment process, the elastic clause, judicial review, equality, civil liberties, presidential power in foreign affairs, and presidential power during wartime.

REGENTS WARM-UP

Read the directions in Regents essay questions carefully so that you carry out all operations. In the Essay, you are asked to identify *two* principles and respond to *one* historical circumstance for each.

You are *not* limited to these suggestions.

Guidelines: In your essay, be sure to:

- Address all aspects of the *Task*
- Support the theme with relevant facts, examples, and details
- Use a logical and clear plan of organization
- Introduce the theme by establishing a framework that is beyond a simple restatement of the *Task* and conclude with a summation of the theme

Part III   Document-Based Question

This exercise is designed to test your ability to work with historical documents. It is similar to the document-based questions that you will see on the Regents Examination. While you are asked to analyze five historical documents, the exercise on the actual exam will include more documents. Some of the documents have been edited for the purposes of the question. As you analyze the documents, take into account the source of each document and any point of view that may be presented in the document.

Historical Context: The United States Constitution divides the power to govern among the executive, legislative, and judicial branches of the national government. The Constitution provides for a system of checks and balances to prevent one branch from dominating the other two.

Task: Using information from the documents and your knowledge of United States history, answer the questions that follow each document in Part A. Your answers to the questions will help you write the Part B essay, in which you will be asked to:

- Describe how the system of checks and balances functions
- Show how this system has been applied in specific circumstances in United States history

REGENTS WARM-UP

Describe means "to illustrate something in words or to tell about it." *Show* means "to point out a position or idea by stating it and giving information that supports it."

Part A   Short-Answer Questions

Directions: Analyze the documents and answer the short-answer questions that follow each document in the space provided.

Document 1

> The House of Representatives . . . shall have the sole power of impeachment. . . . The Senate shall have the sole power to try all impeachments.
>
> — United States Constitution, Article 1

1   Which branch of the United States government is responsible for the impeachment process?

_____

_____

Document 2

> He shall have power, by and with the advice and consent of the Senate, to make treaties, provided two thirds of the senators present concur; and he shall nominate, and by and with the advice and consent of the Senate, shall appoint ambassadors, other public ministers and consuls, judges of the Supreme Court, and all other officers of the United States . . . .
>
> — United States Constitution, Article 2, Section 2, Clause 2

2*a*   To whom does "He" refer?

_____

_____

b   Under Article 2, Section 2, Clause 2, what role does the Senate play in the appointment of ambassadors or the appointment of judges to the Supreme Court?

_____

_____

Document 3

Presidential Vetoes, 1901–1990

President	Regular Vetoes	Pocket Vetoes	Total Vetoes	Vetoes Overridden
T. Roosevelt	42	40	82	1
Taft	30	9	39	1
Wilson	33	11	44	6
Harding	5	1	6	—
Coolidge	20	30	50	4
Hoover	21	16	37	3
F. Roosevelt	372	263	635	9
Truman	180	70	250	12
Eisenhower	73	108	181	2
Kennedy	12	9	21	—
L. Johnson	16	14	30	—
Nixon	24	18	42	6
Ford	53	19	72	12
Carter	13	18	31	2
Reagan	39	39	78	9
G. Bush	14	6	20	0

3a   What does this chart indicate about how the president can check the power of Congress?

_____

_____

b   What does this chart indicate about how Congress can check the power of the president?

_____

_____

Document 4

The Ingenious Quarterback

4   In this cartoon, which branch of the government is President Franklin D. Roosevelt trying to change?

_____

_____

Document 5

So if a law be in opposition to the Constitution, if both the law and the Constitution apply to a particular case, so that the Court must either decide that case conformably to the law, disregarding the Constitution or conformably to the Constitution, disregarding the law, the Court must determine which of these conflicting rules governs the case. This is of the very essence of judicial duty . . . .

— Chief Justice John Marshall

5 According to this quotation by Chief Justice John Marshall, what "power" does the Supreme Court have?

_____

_____

Part B   Essay

Directions: Write a well-organized essay that includes an introduction, several paragraphs, and a conclusion.

Use evidence from at least **three** documents in the body of the essay. Support your response with relevant facts, examples, and details. Include additional outside information.

Historical Context: The United States Constitution divides the power to govern among the executive, legislative, and judicial branches of the national government. The Constitution provides for a system of checks and balances to prevent one branch from dominating the other two.

Task: Using information from the documents and your knowledge of United States history, write an essay in which you:

> - Describe how the system of checks and balances functions
> - Show how this system has been applied in specific circumstances in United States history

Guidelines: In your essay, be sure to:

- Address all aspects of the Task by accurately analyzing and interpreting at least three documents
- Incorporate information from the documents in the body of the essay
- Incorporate relevant outside information
- Support the theme with relevant facts, examples, and details
- Use a logical and clear plan of organization
- Introduce the theme by establishing a framework that is beyond a simple restatement of the Task or Historical Context and conclude with a summation of the theme

UNIT 3   THE BIRTH OF MODERN AMERICA

Unit 3 Overview

The period after the Civil War was a time of transformation in the United States. Reconstruction brought great changes to the South and, for a brief decade, hope for African Americans freed from slavery. It also brought a bruising political and constitutional crisis between President Andrew Johnson and Congress. In the decades after the Civil War the West was settled, helped by construction of the transcontinental railroad and the influx of farmers and ranchers to the Great Plains. Changes in technology and favorable economic conditions led to the rapid industrialization of the United States. Industrialization led to the growth of cities and immigration, and new forms of big business.

Studying these great changes in American society will help you understand American history in the first decades of the twentieth century.

Unit 3 Objectives

After studying this unit, you should be able to:

1.   Describe the different plans for Reconstruction;

2.   Explain how the West was settled;

3.   Summarize the main causes and effects of industrialization after the Civil War;

4.   Discuss the growth of American cities and urban culture.

Chapter Overview

The struggle over Reconstruction began before the end of the War. President Lincoln proposed a plan that treated the South leniently. Congressional Republicans (called Radical Republicans) opposed it and proposed a much harsher plan called the Wade-Davis Bill. Lincoln's assassination brought the rivalry between the president and Congress to a head. President Johnson adopted Lincoln's plan but was strongly opposed by Congress. The Election of 1866 strengthened the hand of Congressional Republicans, who set up military districts in the South. When Johnson resisted, Congress impeached him and came within one vote of removing him.

The Freedmen's Bureau helped many former slaves. The Fourteenth Amendment brought the force of federal law to protect the rights of African Americans. Southerners resisted Reconstruction with restrictive laws and violence by such groups as the Ku Klux Klan. Reconstruction was undermined by corruption in the Republican Party, an economic depression, and finally the disputed election of 1876. A deal was made that awarded the presidency to a Republican, Rutherford B. Hayes, in return for a promise to withdraw federal troops from the South. Southern Democratic governments enacted restrictive laws that severely curbed the rights and opportunities available to African Americans.

As you read through this chapter, ask yourself these questions:
(1) What were the different plans for Reconstruction and how did they differ?
(2) How did the Radical Republicans' control of Reconstruction bring them into conflict with President Andrew Johnson?
(3) How did Reconstruction change the South?
(4) How did the decline and end of Reconstruction change Southern life?

Main Ideas and Concepts

- **Change** Reconstruction changed life in the South. For African Americans, it marked a change from slavery to freedom and citizenship. For white Southerners, it meant a change in social life.

- **Constitutional Principles** The Fourteenth Amendment said that no state could deprive anyone of life, liberty, or property without due process of law. The impeachment of President Andrew Johnson marked a sharp conflict between Congress and the Executive Branch.

- **Citizenship** Both the Civil Rights Act of 1866 and the Fourteenth Amendment granted citizenship to African Americans.

People, Places, Terms

The following names and terms will help you to prepare for the Regents Exam in United States History and Government. You can find an explanation of each name and term in the Glossary at the back of this book, in your textbook, or in another reference source.

amnesty	grandfather clause	scalawags
Blanche K. Bruce	Ulysses S. Grant	sharecropping
carpetbaggers	Rutherford B.	Tenure of
Fifteenth	Hayes	Office Act
Amendment	literacy test	Thirteenth
Fourteenth	*Plessy* v. *Ferguson*	Amendment
Amendment	poll tax	
Freedmen's Bureau	Hiram Revels	

SECTION 1 RECONSTRUCTION PLANS

Reconstruction Debate

The North's victory in the Civil War both saved the Union and resulted in widespread destruction in the South, where most of the war was fought. Even before the war ended, there was much debate on how Southern states should be brought back into the

CORE CONCEPTS: PRESIDENTIAL DECISIONS AND ACTIONS

In his Second Inaugural Address, delivered in March 1865, just a month before his death, Lincoln spelled out his conciliatory policy toward the South: *"With malice toward none, with charity for all, with firmness in the right as God gives us to see the right, let us strive on to finish the work we are in, to bind up the nation's wounds . . ."*

CORE CONCEPTS: HUMAN RIGHTS

Howard University in Washington, D.C., was founded by the Freedmen's Bureau to educate newly freed slaves. Today it is the largest predominantly African American university in the United States. The university was named for General Oliver Otis Howard, a Civil War hero and Freedmen's Bureau leader.

Union. Among the questions asked were: "What rights should be granted to freed African Americans?" and "How should Southern states be brought back in to the Union?" Both President Lincoln and the ruling Republican majority in Congress put forth plans. There were many disagreements between the two plans.

Lincoln's Plan As early as December 1863, Lincoln had announced his Ten Percent Plan for Southern states to come back into the Union. Lincoln's plan said that when 10 percent of the voters of a state took a loyalty oath to the Union, the state could form a new government and write a new constitution that banned slavery. Then it would be accepted back into the Union.

Lincoln's philosophy was to encourage Southerners who were loyal to the Union to take over Southern state governments. He did not believe it was useful to punish Southerners. Lincoln offered **amnesty**—a pardon—to all white Southerners who would swear loyalty to the Union. Only Confederate leaders were left out of Lincoln's plan. Lincoln also supported granting the right to vote to African Americans who served in the Union army, but he did not demand that Southern states grant African Americans the same rights as white Americans.

A Rival Plan Congressional Republicans, or Radical Republicans, had strong disagreements with Lincoln's plan. First, they thought Lincoln's plan was too mild and would leave the South largely unchanged. Secondly, they believed that Congress, not the president, should control Reconstruction policy.

The Wade-Davis Bill In July 1864, Republicans managed to pass a plan called the Wade-Davis Bill. It required a majority of Southern white men to take an oath of loyalty to the Union. But it barred any Southern men who had taken up arms against the Union from being delegates to the constitutional convention that each state had to hold to write a new constitution. The Wade-Davis Bill also required the new constitution to ban slavery. Lincoln refused to sign the bill and a standoff ensued.

The Freedmen's Bureau Congress and President Lincoln did agree on a law that created a new government agency to help former slaves, or freedmen. **The Freedmen's Bureau** distributed food and clothing, provided medical services, and set up schools. It also helped freedmen acquire land and work.

Lincoln Assassinated! President Abraham Lincoln was assassinated on April 14, 1865, just five days after the war ended, by John Wilkes Booth, a well-known actor and Confederate sympathizer. Booth shot Lincoln while the president was watching a play at a theater in Washington, D.C. Booth escaped but was soon captured.

A New President Vice President Andrew Johnson from Tennessee became president upon Lincoln's death. Johnson had been the only Southern senator to support the Union during the Civil War.

"Restoration" In May 1865, Johnson announced his own plan that he called "Restoration." Under Johnson's plan, most Southerners would be granted amnesty upon swearing an oath of allegiance to the Union. However, Johnson required that high-ranking Confederate officials and wealthy landowners had to apply personally to the president to be granted amnesty. He appointed governors for the Southern states and required them to hold constitutional conventions. Johnson stated his views when he said, "White men alone must manage the South." Before reentering the Union, each state had to denounce secession and ratify the newly passed **Thirteenth Amendment** to the Constitution, which abolished slavery in all parts of the United States, but Johnson made no other requirements about rights for African Americans. By the end of 1865, all Southern states with the exception of Texas were ready to rejoin the Union.

SECTION 2 RADICALS IN CONTROL

African Americans' Rights

In the fall of 1865, Southern states created new governments, wrote new constitutions, and elected representatives to Congress. More than a dozen of those representatives were former Confederate leaders. When they arrived in Washington, Republican leaders in Congress refused to seat them. They completely rejected Johnson's plan for Reconstruction. Many Northerners thought that Johnson was robbing the North of its victory in the Civil War.

**CORE CONCEPTS:
CITIZENSHIP**

Another effect of the Civil Rights Act of 1866 was to overturn the *Dred Scott* case of 1857. In that case, Dred Scott—a slave—had sued for his freedom because his master had taken him to free territories. The court had denied his suit because it said as a slave, Scott was not a citizen, but instead was the property of his master.

**CORE CONCEPTS:
DECISION MAKING**

Among the leaders of the Radical Republicans were Congressman Thaddeus Stevens of Pennsylvania and Senator Charles Sumner of Massachusetts. Both opposed Lincoln's leniency towards the South. Their ideas about Reconstruction came from their pasts as abolitionists. The Republican Party and Lincoln never favored the outright abolition of slavery before the Civil War, but concerned themselves with limiting its spread in the territories.

Black Codes In late 1865 and early 1866, Southern states passed new laws called black codes whose purpose was to limit the rights of and control African Americans. Laws allowed local officials to arrest unemployed African Americans and make them work for white employers to pay off their fines. Other laws limited the rights of African Americans to own property. To many in the North, the black codes looked as though the Southern states were simply reestablishing slavery.

Challenging the Black Codes Congress responded to the black codes. In early 1866, it extended the life of the Freedmen's Bureau and gave it new powers. The Bureau set up special courts to prosecute anyone who violated the rights of African Americans. Congress also passed the Civil Rights Act of 1866. It granted full citizenship to African Americans and gave the federal government the power to intervene in state affairs to protect their rights. It outlawed the black codes.

President Johnson responded to these actions of Congress with vetoes, but Congress was able to override them, and both acts became law. There was now open rivalry between the president and Congress. Johnson's vetoes persuaded Congressional Republicans that compromise was impossible, and they drafted their own Reconstruction plan.

Citizenship

The Fourteenth Amendment In June 1866, Congress passed the **Fourteenth Amendment**. It granted citizenship to African Americans and said that no state could take away a citizen's life, liberty, or property without "due process of law." It also added that all citizens were entitled to equal protection of the laws. The amendment barred former Confederate leaders from holding office unless they were pardoned by a two-thirds vote of Congress. Congress required Southern states to ratify the amendment to be readmitted to the Union.

Radical Reconstruction

Republicans in Congress were determined to enact a program of Reconstruction that protected African Americans and pun-ished Confederate leaders. Their plan was called Radical Reconstruction.

Reconstruction Acts of 1867

Congress passed the two Reconstruction Acts in 1867.
Among the provisions:

- the 10 Southern states not in the Union were divided into five districts ruled by a military commander
- states had to ratify the Fourteenth Amendment and submit their new constitutions to Congress for approval for readmission to the Union
- military commanders were to begin registering voters and preparing new state constitutional conventions

Many white Southerners refused to participate in the readmission process. Newly registered African Americans helped Republicans win control in Southern states and successfully meet the requirements for readmission to the Union.

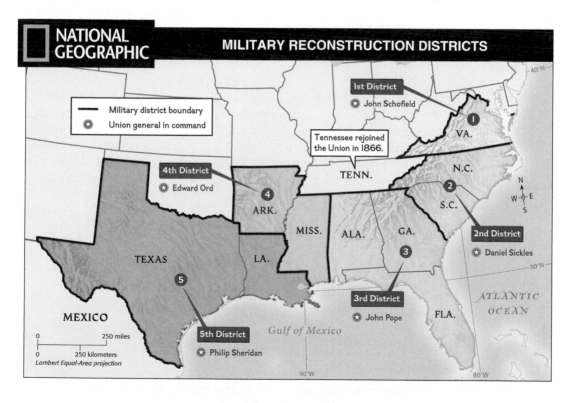

NATIONAL GEOGRAPHIC   **MILITARY RECONSTRUCTION DISTRICTS**

— Military district boundary
⊕ Union general in command

1st District
⊕ John Schofield

Tennessee rejoined the Union in 1866.

4th District
⊕ Edward Ord

2nd District
⊕ Daniel Sickles

3rd District
⊕ John Pope

5th District
⊕ Philip Sheridan

VA.
N.C.
S.C.
TENN.
ARK.
MISS.
ALA.
GA.
TEXAS
LA.
FLA.
MEXICO

ATLANTIC OCEAN
Gulf of Mexico

0   250 miles
0   250 kilometers
Lambert Equal-Area projection

**CORE CONCEPTS:
CONSTITUTIONAL
PRINCIPLES**

The impeachment of Andrew
Johnson was not just about
different ideas about
Reconstruction. It was also
an attempt by Congress to
intrude into and limit the
constitutional powers of the
president and the Executive
Branch.

Congressional Republicans knew that President Johnson was
strongly opposed to their plan. To keep him from interfering,
they passed the **Tenure of Office Act**. It prevented Johnson
from removing government officials—including members of his
own cabinet—without Congressional approval. This new law
passed over Johnson's veto, and violated the tradition that
presidents had the power to remove officials in the Executive
Branch.

Impeaching the President The Tenure of Office Act was an
intrusion into presidential power and it precipitated a crisis. In
1867, Johnson fired Secretary of War Edwin Stanton.
Congressional Republicans did not waste any time in acting.
The House of Representatives voted to impeach President
Johnson for violating the Tenure of Office Act. Johnson's trial in
the Senate began in March 1868 and lasted for three months.
Johnson's supporters argued he was defending presidential
power and that the impeachment was politically motivated.
Republicans accused Johnson of using the veto power as a
weapon against Congress. In May, the Senate voted 35-to-19 to
convict the president. Under the Constitution, the Senate needs
a vote of two-thirds majority to remove the president from
office, so the result was one vote short. Johnson remained in
office.

Election of 1868 Civil War hero General **Ulysses S. Grant** won
the 1868 presidential election in a landslide. Grant won most of
the votes of African American Republicans in the South who
were voting for the first time. After the election, Congress passed
the **Fifteenth Amendment**, which prohibited states and the
federal government from denying the right to vote because of
"race, color, or previous condition of servitude." The amendment was ratified in 1870. Republicans thought that the power of
the ballot gave African Americans the power to protect themselves. Sadly, it was not the case.

SECTION 3 THE SOUTH DURING
RECONSTRUCTION

New Groups Take Charge

The Republican Party dominated Southern politics during
Reconstruction. Its support came mainly from African American
voters and white settlers from the North.

African Americans in Government African Americans, who
just a few years previous to Reconstruction had been slaves, rose
to prominence in politics. As a group, they did not control any
government, but many were elected to office. On the national
level, 16 African Americans were elected to the House of
Representatives. Two African Americans were appointed to the
U.S. Senate—**Hiram Revels**, an ordained minister who was
elected from Mississippi, and **Blanche K. Bruce**, also elected
from Mississippi.

Scalawags and Carpetbaggers Some white Southerners did
support Reconstruction. Many of them were non-slaveholding
farmers or businesspeople who had originally opposed secession. Former Confederates despised them for siding with
Republicans and called them **scalawags**, a term meaning
"scoundrel" or "worthless rascal." Another group hated by
former Confederates were Northern whites who moved to the
South. They were called **carpetbaggers**, a term that referred to
the cheap suitcases made of carpet fabric that many of them
carried traveling to the South. Some carpetbaggers were greedy
people looking to take advantage of business opportunities in
the South. Most were former Union army soldiers or Freedmen's
Bureau employees. Many Southerners accused Republican
governments of corruption—dishonest or illegal actions—and
financial mismanagement. In fact, there was probably less
corruption in Southern state governments than in those in the
North.

Resistance to Reconstruction Most white Southerners opposed
expanded rights for African Americans. Plantation owners tried
to keep control over freed people in many ways. They told them
they were not free to leave the plantations. They refused to rent
freedmen land. Storeowners refused to give African Americans
credit. Employers would not give them work.

The Ku Klux Klan Some white Southerners turned to violence,
forming secret societies whose goal was to terrorize freedmen
from exercising their rights. The most terrifying of these societies
was the Ku Klux Klan, formed in 1866. Klan members wore
white sheets and hoods to disguise themselves. Riding at night,
they burned homes and churches and murdered African
Americans. The Klan used violence before elections to scare
African Americans and keep them from voting. Klan members
were a small minority but a large majority of white Southerners
approved of their actions. Many white Southerners saw the Klan

CORE CONCEPTS: CONSTITUTIONAL PRINCIPLES

Both Revels and Bruce were
appointed to their Senate
posts by the Republican-
controlled Mississippi
legislature. Direct election
of U.S. Senators did not
start until ratification of the
17th Amendment in 1913.

as fighting to resist Republican rule and to restore white supremacy to the South.

Congress passed laws designed to stop the violence but they proved ineffective. Most white Southerners refused to testify against the Klan and others who terrorized African Americans.

Some Improvements

Reconstruction brought important changes to the South, despite the violence. Education was greatly improved for both African Americans and whites. The Freedmen's Bureau and private charities had an enormous impact. By 1870, four thousand schools had been established with two hundred thousand students. Many Northern white women came to the South to teach in these schools. More than half the teachers, however, were African Americans.

Farming the Land Along with education, African Americans needed land to farm to make a living. The Freedmen's Bank, set up in 1865, helped some African Americans buy land, but most were unable to do so. Instead, most turned to **sharecropping**, a system in which landowners rented land in exchange for a share of the crop. Sharecropping kept most African Americans in poverty. After giving the landowner his share of the crop, most farmers had little crop left to sell. For many, sharecropping was little better than slavery.

SECTION 4   CHANGE IN THE SOUTH

Reconstruction Declines

Reconstruction began to decline during the Grant administration for a number of reasons. The leaders of the Radical Republicans began to disappear from the scene. Racial prejudice in the North undermined support. Many Northerners thought that white Southerners should make their own decisions about government. Southerners themselves protested "bayonet rule"—the use of federal troops to support Reconstruction governments. A revolt in the Republican Party emerged in 1872. Horace Greeley, a newspaper editor who favored an end to Reconstruction, ran against Grant, but Grant was reelected.

Democrats Regain Power In the next few years, the Democrats, the party of white Southerners, regained control of state governments throughout the South. Democrats were helped by a series of political scandals in the Grant administration, which further undermined Republican power. An economic depression was blamed on Republican policies. In 1874, the Democrats won control of the House of Representatives, the first time Democrats controlled a part of the federal government since before the Civil War.

The End of Reconstruction

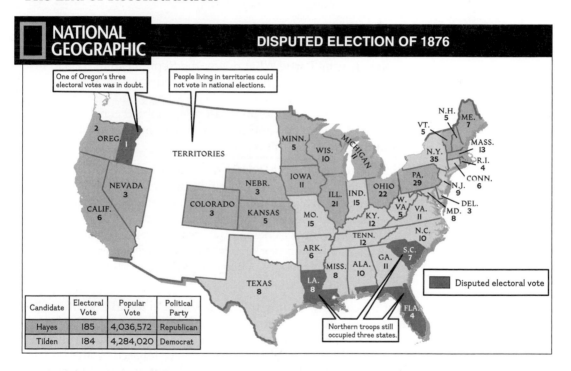

NATIONAL GEOGRAPHIC   **DISPUTED ELECTION OF 1876**

One of Oregon's three electoral votes was in doubt.

People living in territories could not vote in national elections.

TERRITORIES

Northern troops still occupied three states.

Disputed electoral vote

Candidate	Electoral Vote	Popular Vote	Political Party
Hayes	185	4,036,572	Republican
Tilden	184	4,284,020	Democrat

The Election of 1876 The Republicans nominated Governor **Rutherford B. Hayes** of Ohio to run against Democrat Samuel B. Tilden, governor of New York. Tilden appeared to win the election, receiving more than 250,000 more popular votes than Hayes, but returns from Florida, Louisiana, South Carolina, and Oregon (with their 20 electoral votes) were disputed. Congress set up a special commission, or group, to decide which candidate was awarded the disputed votes. The commission was made up of 8 Republicans and 7 Democrats. The commission then voted

8-to-7 along party lines to award all 20 disputed electoral votes, and the election, to Hayes.

Democrats were outraged and threatened a fight. Republican and Democratic leaders held a secret meeting to work out a compromise. The deal, known as the Compromise of 1877, marked the official end of Reconstruction. The main part of the deal was that federal troops would be withdrawn from the South. Republicans also agreed to put a Democrat on the presidential cabinet. Democrats agreed to respect the rights of African Americans and to drop their objections to the commission's vote. Hayes was inaugurated as president.

Change in the South

A New Ruling Party What power the Republican Party had in the South vanished with the pullout of federal troops. Democrats, called "Redeemers" because they had redeemed, or saved, the South from Republican rule, adopted conservative policies of lower taxes and reduced government services, including public education.

Rise of the New South Southerners decided the best way to rebuild the South was to build up industries. In the years after Reconstruction, textile manufacturing, lumbering, and tobacco processing became important industries in the South. Southern industrial growth was helped by a ready supply of reliable workers who would work for low wages. Despite this growth, the South still lagged far behind the North in industry and its economy remained primarily agricultural.

Rural Economy Southern leaders hoped to remake Southern agriculture into small profitable farms raising a variety of crops. However, most large landowners kept control of their plantations, raising a single cash crop—cotton or tobacco. Sharecropping was profitable for landowners, but the tenant farmers, both white and African American, could never earn enough cash from their crop to repay what they needed to borrow to get their next crop in the ground.

A Divided Society

The end of Reconstruction meant the end of African Americans' dreams for justice. Racism became a part of Southern life that severely restricted the freedom and opportunities available to African Americans.

The Supreme Court and Civil Rights Cases In 1883, the United States Supreme Court issued rulings on five different cases that dealt with issues surrounding the Civil Rights Act of 1875 and the Thirteenth and Fourteenth Amendments. Collectively, these decisions came to be known as the *Civil Rights Cases*.

The Court ruled that most of the Civil Rights Act of 1875 was unconstitutional and that the Fourteenth Amendment only prohibited governments from violating civil rights. Individuals not acting on behalf of the state could not be punished for denying others their civil rights.

Voting Restrictions Southern Democrats set up barriers to keep African Americans from voting.

- Many states set up a **poll tax**, meaning people had to pay to vote, effectively barring poor people from voting.
- Potential voters were asked to read and explain complicated parts of the state or federal Constitution. Since many African Americans had little education, this **literacy test** barred them from voting.
- Since the literacy test also barred whites from voting, the **grandfather clause** allowed a person who failed it to vote if their grandfather had voted. This effectively barred African Americans, but not whites, from voting.

Jim Crow Laws These laws effectively established segregation or the separation of the races. The name "Jim Crow" came from a character in a song. In 1896, the U.S. Supreme Court enforced the "separate but equal" segregation doctrine in the case ***Plessy* v. *Ferguson***. The case upheld a Louisiana law requiring passenger trains to have "equal but separated accommodations for the white and colored races." The Court held that the Fourteenth Amendment's equal protection clause required only equal public facilities for the two races, not equal access. In the South, the equal part was rarely enforced, as white facilities were always much better than those provided for African Americans.

Violence Against African Americans Violence against African Americans increased in the years after Reconstruction. One form of violence was lynching, in which an angry mob killed a person, usually by hanging. African Americans were lynched sometimes for just being suspected of a crime or for not behaving in a way that whites approved of.

Reconstruction's Impact Reconstruction was both a success and a failure. It did help rebuild the South and for a few years, gave African Americans hopes for freedom and opportunity. But it failed to make those gains permanent and once it ended, African Americans faced decades of racism, violence, and restrictions on their freedom in the South.

The North

Since most of the battles had taken place in the South, the North did not have to deal with massive rebuilding. Factories producing such goods as guns, ammunition, and clothing flourished during the Civil War, leaving the North with a booming economy. New technology helped to revolutionize agriculture, making it more efficient.

This industrial boom continued for several decades, spurred by advances in technology and transportation.

CHAPTER 12   INDUSTRIALIZATION

Chapter Overview

After the Civil War, the United States—thanks to its abundant natural resources, growing population and business philosophy of free enterprise—expanded into the world's largest industrial power. New inventions such as the telephone and light bulb helped spur the growth of the American economy. The development of railroads across the nation spurred industrial growth. Congressional land grants helped railroads grow, and brought settlers to the Great Plains.

Business leaders like Andrew Carnegie used the modern corporation, economies of scale, and horizontal and vertical integration to create big businesses. Monopolies helped businesses but threatened consumers. Workers in America were threatened by dangerous workplaces, long workdays, low wages, and no right to organize. Employers opposed the growth of unions with every means at their disposal. Railroad workers held big strikes in 1877 and 1894, but the government used federal troops to break the strike each time. Samuel Gompers organized the AFL and preached bread and butter issues. After several years, the AFL grew larger and was able to win some victories for workers.

As you read through this chapter, ask yourself these questions:
(1) What preconditions existed for the growth of industry in the United States after the Civil War?
(2) How did the growth of railroads in the United States after the Civil War change American life?
(3) What changes in how businesses organized themselves led to the growth and power of big business?
(4) What challenges did workers face in their attempts to organize unions?

Main Ideas and Concepts

- **Conflict** Employers clashed with workers who wanted to organize unions.

- **Diversity** Chinese workers were utilized to build the Central Pacific Railroad. Irish were used to build the Union Pacific.

- **Movement of People and Goods** Railroads were important in uniting the nation and its markets.

- **Needs and Wants** The growth of American business supplied goods at lower prices to American consumers.

- **Science and Technology** New inventions like the telephone, the light bulb, and the refrigerated railroad car gave birth to new industries and changed communication.

- **Factors of Production** Big business changed how American business was organized and its productive capabilities.

People, Places, Terms

The following names and terms will help you to prepare for the Regents Exam in United States History and Government. You can find an explanation of each name and term in the Glossary at the back of this book, in your textbook, or in another reference source.

American Federation of Labor	economies of scale	Terence Powderly
	Thomas Alva Edison	John D. Rockefeller
Alexander Graham Bell	entrepreneurs	Leland Stanford
Andrew Carnegie	Samuel Gompers	stock
corporations	Knights of Labor	stockholders
Credit Mobilier	laissez-faire	time zones
department store	monopoly	trusts
	pools	Cornelius Vanderbilt

SECTION 1 THE RISE OF INDUSTRY

The United States Industrializes

Before the Civil War, the United States was largely an agricultural nation. After the Civil War, industry rapidly expanded and millions of Americans left farms to work in factories. By the early 1900s the United States had grown into the world's leading industrial nation.

Natural Resources The reason for the United States' success in industrial growth was its abundance of natural resources, including water, timber, coal, iron, and copper. The discovery of a new resource, petroleum, spurred a new wave of industrial growth.

A Large Workforce The United States was also rich in human resources. The population of the United States tripled between 1860 and 1910. The growing population was due to the prevalence of large families and the millions of immigrants who

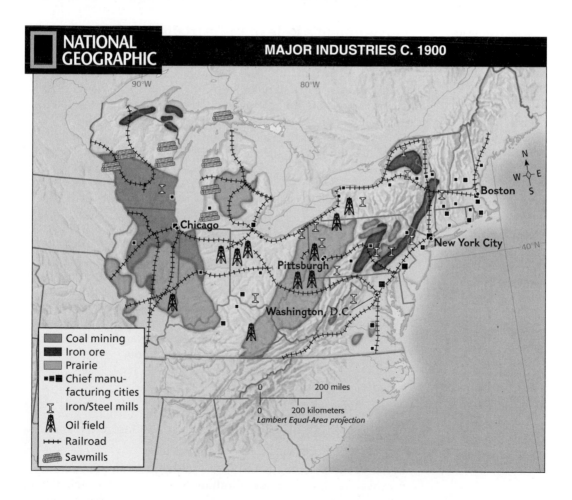

NATIONAL GEOGRAPHIC

MAJOR INDUSTRIES C. 1900

- ▮ Coal mining
- ▮ Iron ore
- ▮ Prairie
- ▪▪▪ Chief manufacturing cities
- ⵣ Iron/Steel mills
- ⚒ Oil field
- ┼┼┼ Railroad
- 🪵 Sawmills

0   200 miles
0   200 kilometers
Lambert Equal-Area projection

CORE CONCEPTS: MOVEMENT OF PEOPLE AND GOODS

From 1870 until 1900, about 12 million immigrants came to the United States. A majority of them came from Germany, England, and Ireland. This was known as the "first wave" of immigration. In the years immediately following (the "second wave"), millions more from Italy, Russia, Poland, and other lands came to America to seek a better life. These new immigrants were able to find jobs in the expanding industries in cities, or cheap land in the Great Plains.

moved to the United States from all over the world. Population growth meant a plentiful supply of workers for a growing economy and increased demand for consumer goods.

Free Enterprise

Economic growth was also spurred by the philosophy of **laissez-faire**, or the idea "to let alone." The United States economy was guided by the market forces of supply and demand, not government regulation of wages and prices. Also, government policy was to keep its spending low so that it did not have to borrow much from banks, leaving money available for business. Businesspeople called **entrepreneurs** took risks to found new businesses.

Government's Role in Industrialism

One exception to the economic policy of laissez-faire was tariffs. Northern manufacturers wanted high tariffs to protect their goods from foreign competition. Southerners wanted low tariffs to promote trade and keep the cost of manufactured goods low. After the Civil War, the Republicans pursued a policy of high tariffs, which helped American business grow but had several negative effects. Foreign goods were priced higher, so American-made goods did not face much competition and thus were able to charge consumers more. High tariffs caused other countries to raise their own tariffs, so that American manufacturers could not sell their goods overseas. Finally, high tariffs caused rural farmers to give up and move to cities to take manufacturing jobs. By 1900, American businesses were so large that business leaders began to see that they were being hurt more than helped by high tariffs.

Other exceptions to the government's laissez-faire policy included giving huge land grants to railroads to help them expand across the country and selling public lands with mineral resources for much less than their market value.

New Inventions

A flood of new inventions in the years after the Civil War helped increase industrial growth, transportation, and communication in the United States.

Bell and the Telephone In 1876, a young Scottish-American inventor named **Alexander Graham Bell** invented the telephone. A year later Bell organized the Bell Telephone Company. Bell

Telephone developed into the American Telephone and Telegraph Company (AT&T), which became one of the largest companies in the nation.

Edison and Electricity Thomas Alva Edison was the most famous inventor of the late 1800s. From his laboratory in Menlo Park, New Jersey, Edison invented the phonograph and perfected the light bulb and the electric generator. Later he invented or perfected the battery, the Dictaphone, and the motion picture. Edison took his inventions into the business world. One of the companies he founded, the Edison General Electric Company, developed into another giant corporation, General Electric (GE).

Technology's Impact Inventions changed American industry. In 1877, the first load of fresh meat was shipped in a refrigerated railroad car. Refrigeration meant that meat and other food items that had only been available locally could now be shipped long distances.

Technology also changed communications. In 1866, a telegraph cable was laid across the Atlantic Ocean, providing instant contact between the United States and Europe. Previously, news could travel only at the speed of the fastest ship. Radio communication developed around the turn of the century. By the 1920s, radios were found in many American homes as a source of news and entertainment.

SECTION 2 THE RAILROADS

Linking the Nation

In 1865, the United States had about 35,000 miles of railroad track, most of it east of the Mississippi. After decades of rapid construction, by 1900 the United States had more than 200,000 miles of track across the entire nation. The boom was set off in 1862 with the Pacific Railway Act. The law called for the building of a transcontinental railroad. Two railroad companies, the Union Pacific and the Central Pacific, were called on to do the job. The government gave both companies huge swaths of land along the right-of-way. As an incentive to each company, the more track they built, the more land they received.

The Union Pacific The Union Pacific pushed westward from Omaha, Nebraska. About ten thousand workers, including Civil War veterans, Irish immigrants, miners, cooks, and ex-convicts, faced harsh weather and, sometimes, angry Native Americans.

CORE CONCEPTS: SCIENCE AND TECHNOLOGY

Edison was a practical man. His genius was applying the discoveries of others through practical experiments. He invented things for the purpose of manufacturing them and making money. He was as much of a businessman as an inventor. His role in founding so many important companies bears out his importance in American business.

CORE CONCEPTS: ECONOMIC SYSTEMS

The invention of the refrigerated railroad car changed the economy of the United States and other industrialized countries. It changed agriculture from a local to a regional and then a national activity. It enabled Southern farmers, with a much longer growing season, to ship produce to the large population centers in the North, where the growing season was months shorter.

The Central Pacific　The Central Pacific, building east from California, faced a shortage of workers, so they hired ten thousand workers from China to help build the railroad. **Leland Stanford**, an investor in the Central Pacific and founder of Stanford University, became governor of California and later served as a United States senator.

Railroads Spur Growth

The transcontinental railroad helped stimulate industrial growth by bringing goods and resources to more markets across the nation. Building the railroads created huge demand for

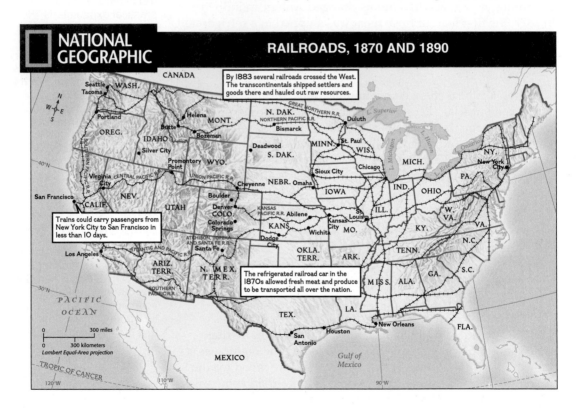

NATIONAL GEOGRAPHIC

RAILROADS, 1870 AND 1890

By 1883 several railroads crossed the West. The transcontinentals shipped settlers and goods there and hauled out raw resources.

Trains could carry passengers from New York City to San Francisco in less than 10 days.

The refrigerated railroad car in the 1870s allowed fresh meat and produce to be transported all over the nation.

goods such as steel and timber to build the tracks, and coal to power locomotives and other machinery. The railroads also physically connected the nation from east to west.

Linking Other Lines The years after the Civil War brought big changes to the railroad business. Large companies built up individual rail lines. Eventually, seven giant systems with terminals in major cities controlled most of the rail traffic. **Cornelius Vanderbilt**, a former boat captain, was the head of the New York Central line. He built Grand Central Terminal in New York City and dominated rail traffic between New York City and Chicago.

The Benefits of a National System Before the 1880s, each community set its clocks by the sun's position in the sky at high noon. As a result, when it was 12:50 p.m. in Washington, D.C., it was 12:09 in Louisville, Kentucky. This way of keeping time interfered with railroad scheduling. In 1883, the American Railway Association divided the country into four **time zones** to standardize time. Large railroad systems were able to operate more efficiently, making travel across the nation easier.

Robber Barons

Some people made a fortune in the railroad business, raising suspicions that some railroad barons had swindled investors or bribed government officials. Bribery was a frequent occurrence, since railroads could make so much money from government land grants.

The Credit Mobilier Scandal **Credit Mobilier** was a construction company set up by investors in the Union Pacific, which overcharged Union Pacific for construction costs. The scam left Union Pacific almost bankrupt. To keep going, the company offered members of Congress additional stock in the Union Pacific at reduced prices in return for more land grants.

SECTION 3 BIG BUSINESS

The Rise of Big Business

Before the Civil War, most businesses were owned by individuals or partners. Businesses were small in scale. By 1900, big business dominated the economy—large companies operated many factories, warehouses, offices and distribution systems.

CORE CONCEPTS: DIVERSITY

Chinese workers were fairly exotic to most Americans in the 1860s and they faced prejudice, discrimination, and violence. The Central Pacific first hired Chinese workers out of desperation. When they saw how productive and disciplined the workers were, they arranged to bring thousands of others from China. The workers for the Central Pacific had to scale the high passes through the Sierra Nevadas and then build across the Nevada and Utah desert. They also worked for low wages. The Chinese workers never faltered.

CORE CONCEPTS: CONSTITUTIONAL PRINCIPLES

The Fourteenth Amendment was adopted to provide citizenship for African Americans and guarantee their rights. However, corporate lawyers saw a way to help corporations in the due process clause of the amendment ("... *nor shall any State deprive any person of life, liberty, or property, without due process of law*"). In the 1886 case *Santa Clara County* v. *Southern Pacific Railroad*, the U.S. Supreme Court said that a corporation had the same rights as a person and therefore could not be summarily denied its rights. The effect of the case was to make it very difficult for states or the federal government to regulate the conduct of corporations.

Economics

The Role of Corporations To succeed, big business needed **corporations**, a form of business that is owned by many people but is treated by law as if it were one person. A corporation is owned by **stockholders** who buy shares of ownership called **stock**. Stock allows corporations to raise large amounts of money and spread out risk. Before 1830, a corporation needed a special charter from a state legislature to exist. But in the 1830s, states began passing incorporation laws, which allowed corporations to form without a state charter.

Economies of Scale Large corporations could operate more efficiently than smaller businesses because they could achieve **economies of scale**.

Corporations have two kinds of costs, fixed and operating. Fixed costs are ones such as mortgage and loan payments as well as the taxes that a company must pay just to exist. Operating costs are the actual costs of running the business, such as wages, raw materials, shipping, and advertising. Big business operations had high fixed costs, but were able to achieve lower operating costs through economies of scale. These advantages resulted in many small businesses either going out of business or being acquired by corporations in the years after the Civil War.

The Consolidation of Industry

Big businesses competed with each other. Each tried to sell at a lower price in order to sell more goods. But low prices, while good for consumers, cut into corporate profits. Business leaders organized **pools**, or agreements with each other not to lower prices. Pools broke apart when one company decided to lower its prices to steal market share from its competitors.

Andrew Carnegie and Steel **Andrew Carnegie** had a spectacular rags-to-riches career. He started as a poor Scottish immigrant working in a textile factory at the age of 12. He later served as the private secretary to the president of the Pennsylvania Railroad. Carnegie invested in companies that served the railroad industry, such as iron mills, locomotive factories, and railroad bridges. By his early 30s, he was earning $50,000 a year and quit his job to concentrate on his own business. Carnegie met the inventor Sir Henry Bessemer, who had invented a process for making steel. Carnegie decided to invest in steel mills.

Vertical and Horizontal Integration To increase manufacturing efficiency, Carnegie took the next step. He started the vertical integration of the steel industry. A vertically integrated business owns the different businesses upon which it depends. Carnegie began buying coalmines, iron ore fields, and limestone quarries.

Carnegie also pushed for the horizontal integration of the steel business. Horizontal integration involves the combining of competing businesses. Carnegie began to buy his competition.

Through horizontal integration, **John D. Rockefeller** of Standard Oil was successful in gaining control of about 90 percent of the oil refining industry in the 1880s. When a company achieves control of an entire industry or market, it is called a **monopoly**. Monopolies are good for business but bad for consumers, because without competition a monopoly can charge whatever it wants for its goods or services.

Trusts Many states passed laws to outlaw monopolies. The laws made it illegal for one company to own stock in another company. Big business got around these laws by forming **trusts**. Instead of directly owning stock, the company sets up trustees, people who own the stock for the company's benefit. In Standard Oil, the first trust, stockholders gave their stock to a group of Standard Oil trustees in exchange for shares in the trust, which entitled them to a share of the trust's profits. Since the trustees were merely managing the shares rather than owning them, no anti-monopoly laws were violated.

Holding Companies In 1889, New Jersey passed a law that allowed New Jersey corporations to own stock in other companies. Many companies used this law to set up a new kind of business called a holding company. A holding company does not produce anything; it just owns the majority of stock in other companies that produce goods, therefore allowing it to control those companies. By 1904, there were 318 holding companies in the United States. These companies controlled over 5,300 factories and were worth more than $7 billion.

Selling the Product Big business led to changes in how products were sold. Large display ads with illustrations replaced simple text messages. Advertising grew to be a big business in its own right.

One new change in selling was the development of the **department store**, which represented a kind of horizontal integration in retailing. John Wanamaker opened the first department store in Philadelphia in 1877. Most shoppers went to small stores that

CORE CONCEPTS: CIVIC VALUES

Carnegie and Rockefeller were denounced in their era as "Robber Barons," people who used their wealth to gain unfair advantage. They each accumulated great wealth. Both men set up foundations, institutions charged with giving their money away to worthy causes. Their foundations are still among the largest in the world and over the years have given billions to worthy causes. Carnegie decided to build libraries. Many cities received the gift of a Carnegie library—many of which are still open today. Carnegie's most famous building is Carnegie Hall, a concert hall in New York City built in 1891.

specialized in individual products—shoemakers, dress shops, coat makers. Wanamaker put it all under one roof: women's, men's, and children's clothing, shoes, and other products. As well as becoming more efficient for consumers and department store owners alike, shopping became a form of entertainment. Chain stores, such as Woolworth's, began building outposts in small towns. Two mail order businesses, Sears Roebuck and Montgomery Ward, brought mail-order shopping to the most remote rural outposts through their catalogs and the mail.

SECTION 4 UNIONS

Working in the United States

Industrial work in the United States after the Civil War was hard and dangerous. Most machinery lacked safety devices, and workers were subject to environmental hazards such as lint, dust, and toxic fumes. However, between 1860 and 1890, average wages for industrial workers rose about 50 percent. Still, the gap between the wealthy owners of big businesses and the workers grew at an alarming rate. In 1900, the average industrial worker made about 22 cents an hour and worked 59 hours a week. Relations between workers and employers were complicated by deflation, which occurs when money increases in value because prices decline. Big business' efficiency caused the price of most goods to decline, so that workers' wages went further. To compensate, employers tried to cut wages, causing tension with workers. Workers decided that the only way to deal with employers was to organize into unions.

Early Unions

There were two basic types of industrial workers in the United States in the late 1800s, craft (skilled) workers and common (unskilled) laborers. Craft workers had special skills and training, and included machinists, iron molders, glassblowers, and printers. Craft workers generally received higher wages and had more control over how they went about their work on the shop floor. Common laborers had fewer skills, received lower wages, and enjoyed less control over their time and how they did their work.

Industry Opposes Unions

Most employers looked upon unions as illegitimate conspiracies that interfered with their property rights. Owners of larger corporations particularly opposed industrial unions, which united all craft workers and common laborers in a particular industry.

Companies used several techniques to keep workers from organizing into unions. They required workers to sign oaths (called yellow-dog contracts) that they would not join a union. They hired detectives to find out who the union organizers were. The organizers were promptly fired and placed on a blacklist, a list of troublemakers circulated to other businesses so no one would hire them. If workers organized a union, employers would use a lockout to break the union. They simply locked workers out of the workplace and didn't pay them. If workers called a strike, employers would hire replacement workers known as strikebreakers or scabs.

Sherman Anti-Trust Act In 1890, Congress passed the Sherman Anti-Trust Act, a law designed to fight large trusts. The key concept of the law was that large trusts act "in restraint of trade." Ironically, the law was used repeatedly against labor unions, which the courts found that by organizing workers they restrained the rights of employers. The first case was in 1894, *U.S. v. Debs* (see p. 153), which ended the Pullman strike of 1894.

United States **v.** *E.C. Knight Co.* In 1892, the American Sugar Refining Company controlled 98 percent of the sugar refining industry. President Grover Cleveland asked the government to sue the company, claiming it was a monopoly. The Supreme Court disagreed, holding that manufacturing was a local activity not subject to the governmental regulation of interstate commerce. The decision limited the power of the government to take action against monopolies.

Political and Social Opposition Union organizers faced formidable challenges. There were no laws that gave workers the right to organize or to protect them from employers' anti-union tactics. Courts frequently sided with employers and declared unions "conspiracies in restraint of trades," subjecting union organizers to fines and jail.

The Struggle to Organize

Workers' attempts to organize industrial unions rarely succeeded in the late 1800s and often led to violence and bloodshed.

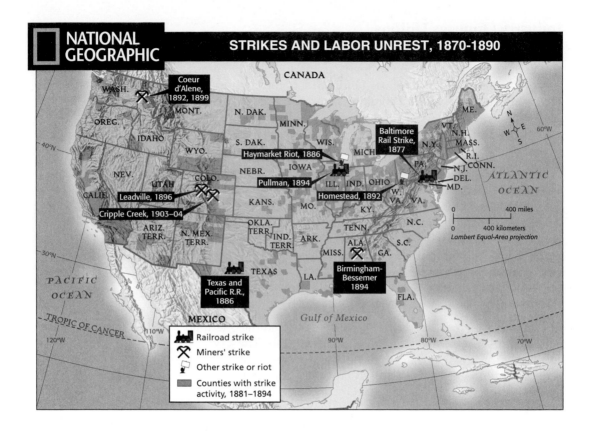

NATIONAL GEOGRAPHIC

STRIKES AND LABOR UNREST, 1870-1890

CANADA

Coeur d'Alene, 1892, 1899
WASH.
OREG.
MONT.
N. DAK.
MINN.
IDAHO
WYO.
S. DAK.
WIS.
Baltimore Rail Strike, 1877
ME.
N.H.
VT.
MASS.
N.Y.
R.I.
CONN.
N.J.
DEL.
MD.
Haymarket Riot, 1886
MICH
NEV.
COLO.
NEBR.
IOWA
Pullman, 1894
ILL. IND. OHIO
PA.
CALIF.
UTAH
Leadville, 1896
KANS.
MO.
Homestead, 1892
W. VA. VA.
KY.
ATLANTIC OCEAN
Cripple Creek, 1903–04
ARIZ. TERR.
N. MEX. TERR.
OKLA. TERR.
IND. TERR.
ARK.
TENN.
N.C.
S.C.
0   400 miles
0   400 kilometers
Lambert Equal-Area projection
MISS.
ALA.
GA.
Texas and Pacific R.R., 1886
TEXAS
LA.
Birmingham-Bessemer 1894
FLA.
PACIFIC OCEAN
TROPIC OF CANCER
110°W
120°W
MEXICO
Gulf of Mexico
90°W
80°W
70°W
60°W
40°N
30°N

Railroad strike
Miners' strike
Other strike or riot
Counties with strike activity, 1881–1894

The Knights of Labor In 1869, **Terence Powderly** formed the **Knights of Labor**, a nationwide industrial labor union that included skilled and unskilled workers, women, and African Americans. The Knights program called for an eight-hour workday, a government bureau of labor statistics, equal pay for women, an end to child labor, and worker-owned factories. The Knights supported the use of arbitration, a process in which a third party helps workers and employers resolve disputes. After a successful strike against a railroad in the early 1880s, membership rose from 100,000 to 700,000 in less than a year. The future of the Knights of Labor looked bright.

The Haymarket Riot The movement for the eight-hour work-day was the primary cause of labor organization in 1886. Following a nationwide strike, a clash between strikers and police resulted in police killing one striker in Chicago. The next night an anarchist group called a protest meeting in Haymarket Square. About 3,000 people were there when someone set off a bomb. Police opened fire and workers shot back. In the gun battle, seven police officers and four strikers were killed. The incident horrified people across the country. The evidence was very weak, but eight men were convicted and four executed, one of whom was a member of the Knights of Labor. The incident hurt the reputation of the Knights of Labor and it began to lose members and power.

The Homestead Strike Trouble erupted at Andrew Carniege's Homestead Mill in Pennsylvania after the plant's manager announced large wage cuts during negotiations with the workers' union. When the union protested, the manager closed the plant and brought in strikebreakers. Union members attacked the strikebreakers, and several men on both sides were killed or wounded. The union eventually capitulated and some workers got their jobs back at drastically reduced wages. Many others were blacklisted and unable to find employment anywhere else.

The Pullman Strike The Haymarket Riot set back the cause of industrial unionism, but in 1893, Eugene V. Debs organized the American Railway Union (ARU). In 1894, the union called a strike against the Pullman Palace Car Company, which made sleeping cars. The company had slashed wages in response to another depression, which had begun in 1893. The union stopped handling Pullman Cars on trains and successfully tied up almost all railroads around the country. The railroad shutdown threatened to paralyze the U.S. economy.

U.S. v. Debs To break the strike, railroad managers attached U.S. Mail cars to every Pullman car. When the union workers refused to handle the Pullman cars, they would be interfering with the U.S. mail, a violation of federal law. President Grover Cleveland responded by calling out federal troops to keep the mail running. A federal court issued an injunction, or a formal court order, directing the union to halt its boycott of Pullman cars. Debs refused and appealed his contempt of court conviction to the Supreme Court. In their decision, the Court unanimously upheld the right of the federal government to halt a strike. The Court reasoned that by disrupting the mail, the strikers were

CORE CONCEPTS: REFORM MOVEMENTS

Eugene Victor Debs (1855–1926) was one of the giants of American labor history. Debs led the Pullman Strike in 1894 and was sent to jail for his activities. In jail he read the writings of Karl Marx and became a socialist. In 1897, he helped found the American Socialist Party. Debs was the party's candidate for president of the United States in four elections. In the election of 1920 he received more than 90,000 votes even though he was in jail for protesting against the government.

interfering with interstate commerce and the "general welfare" of the American people.

The American Federation of Labor

While industrial unions failed in the 1880s, trade unions continued to grow. In 1886, the same year of the Haymarket Riot, delegates from more than 20 trade unions organized the **American Federation of Labor** (AFL), whose first leader was **Samuel Gompers**. Gompers believed that for unions to be successful they had to stay out of politics. The AFL's main goals were to get employers to recognize unions and hire only union members, and agree to collective bargaining. The union also promoted an eight-hour workday.

By 1900, despite its rather slow growth, the AFL was the largest union in the country with more than 500,000 members. Yet the AFL represented less than 15 percent of all non-farm workers. All unions combined represented only about 18 percent of the nation's industrial workers. As the 1900s began, the unions that existed were relatively weak.

Working Women

Women began to join the workforce in increasing numbers after the Civil War. By 1900, women made up 18 percent of the workforce. Society had very definite ideas about what jobs were "women's work." About one-third of women workers were domestic servants. Another third worked as teachers, nurses, sales clerks, and secretaries. The remaining third worked as industrial workers, in such industries as the garment industry and food processing.

Women in all fields of work were paid less than men. For this reason, most unions, including the AFL, excluded women. In 1903, the Women's Trade Union League (WTUL) formed and advocated for an eight-hour workday, a minimum wage, an end to evening work for women, and an end to child labor.

CHAPTER 13   URBAN AMERICA

Chapter Overview

Immigration remade the American nation, leading to population growth and diversity as well as a nativist reaction against foreigners. Immigrants migrated to cities, which grew rapidly. New technology led to changes such as skyscrapers and different methods of urban transportation. Immigration to the cities also led to the growth of political machines that controlled power in return for personal services.

The growth of wealth caused the period from 1870 to 1900 to be called the Gilded Age. Social Darwinism emerged as a philosophy that explained and justified the social conditions of the era. The new conditions of urban life led to the growth of new forms of entertainment. The rapid changes and great disparity in wealth between rich and poor also led to the growth of social critics and reform movements dedicated to helping the poor and changing society.

As you read through this chapter, ask yourself these questions:
(1) What did immigrants to the United States experience in their efforts to make a life in their new country?
(2) What changes took place in American cities after the Civil War?
(3) What was the Gilded Age and how did the growth of big business change American life?
(4) How did Americans react to the growing gap between the rich and the poor?

Main Ideas and Concepts

- **Movement of People and Goods** Immigration reshaped America.

- **Change** The Gilded Age saw rapid economic, cultural, and social change.

- **Science and Technology** New technology in cities resulted in skyscrapers and new transportation systems.

- **Belief Systems** Social Darwinism emerged as a philoso-phy to explain and justify the changes of the era.

- **Culture** New forms of literature, painting, and enter-tainment arose in the cities.

People, Places, Terms

The following names and terms will help you to prepare for the Regents Exam in United States History and Government. You can find an explanation of each name and term in the Glossary at the back of this book, in your textbook, or in another reference source.

Angel Island	individualism	skyscraper
Chinese	nativism	Social Darwinism
Exclusion Act	"new" immigrants	Herbert Spencer
Henry George	"old" immigrants	tenements
Gilded Age	philanthropy	William M.
Gospel of Wealth	political machine	"Boss" Tweed
graft	realism	

CORE CONCEPTS: MOVEMENT OF PEOPLE AND GOODS

From 1870–1900, immigrants helped swell the population of the United States. Foreign-born Americans consistently remained between 15–17 percent of the population in this period. In terms of percentage, the high water-mark was in 1890 when more than 17 percent of Americans were foreign born. In terms of absolute numbers, in 1900 more than 10 million out of a total population of more than 64 million had been born overseas.

SECTION 1 IMMIGRATION

Europeans Flood into the United States

By the 1890s, more than half of the immigrants coming to the United States were from eastern and southern Europe. This wave of immigrants is often known as the "second wave," or **"new" immigrants**. Among them were Italians, Greeks, Poles, Slavs, Slovaks, Russians, and Armenians. They came to get jobs, land, and freedom. Eastern European Jews from several countries made up a good share of the 14 million immigrants. European Jews came to escape religious persecution. It took courage for immigrants to come, but by the 1890s, many legal barriers in Europe had been lowered, and the United States welcomed most immigrants.

The first wave, or **"old" immigrants**, who came mainly from Northern and Western Europe, came with more wealth and education. They assimilated because they had common beliefs, such as Protestantism, and they often spoke some English.

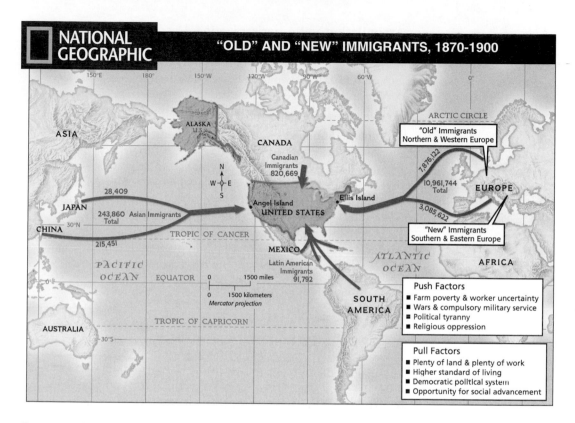

NATIONAL GEOGRAPHIC

"OLD" AND "NEW" IMMIGRANTS, 1870-1900

"Old" Immigrants
Northern & Western Europe

"New" Immigrants
Southern & Eastern Europe

Canadian Immigrants
820,669

Ellis Island

Angel Island

7,876,122

10,961,744 Total

3,085,622

28,409

243,860 Asian Immigrants Total

215,451

Latin American Immigrants
91,792

Push Factors
- Farm poverty & worker uncertainty
- Wars & compulsory military service
- Political tyranny
- Religious oppression

Pull Factors
- Plenty of land & plenty of work
- Higher standard of living
- Democratic political system
- Opportunity for social advancement

ASIA · ALASKA U.S. · CANADA · JAPAN · CHINA · UNITED STATES · MEXICO · EUROPE · AFRICA · SOUTH AMERICA · AUSTRALIA · ARCTIC CIRCLE · TROPIC OF CANCER · EQUATOR · TROPIC OF CAPRICORN · PACIFIC OCEAN · ATLANTIC OCEAN

0　1500 miles
0　1500 kilometers
Mercator projection

Geography

Ethnic Cities Many immigrants settled in cities where jobs and housing were available. Immigrants from the same country tended to settle in the same neighborhoods. In New York City, there was "Little Italy" and the Jewish "Lower East Side." In these ethnic neighborhoods, people spoke their native languages and recreated the neighborhoods, churches, and synagogues of their homelands. Immigrants also worked hard at learning English and adapting to American culture. Immigrants tended to be successful if they arrived with marketable skills or money, or if they settled among members of their own ethnic groups. About one-third of the immigrants who came to the U.S. returned to Europe.

Assimilation and Americanization Despite some substantial differences among immigrant communities, there were some things they all had in common. Most were young and shared the experience of living in cities. They also had to deal with the conflicting influences of their ethnic ties and their desire to assimilate.

Some first and especially second generations of immigrants worked to rid themselves of all vestiges of their old culture, to become thoroughly Americanized. Assimilation was also pushed on immigrants in many ways: schools taught children English and employers insisted that workers speak English on the job. Stores sold American products, forcing immigrants to adapt their diets, wardrobes, and lifestyles to American norms. Church leaders encouraged assimilation and even adapted their theology to make it more compatible with American ways.

Assimilation put pressures on the relations between men and women in immigrant communities. Many came from cultures in which women were even more subordinate to men and some parents still expected to arrange marriages and control their daughters' lives. But either out of choice or economic necessity, many immigrant women (and American-born daughters of immigrants) began working outside the home and developing interests and attachments outside the family.

Asian Immigration to America

Chinese immigration to the United States had multiple causes. China was overcrowded, and food was in short supply. Chinese first came to the U.S. to seek their fortune during the California Gold Rush. When the Taiping Rebellion broke out in China in 1850 and caused widespread suffering, still more Chinese chose to emigrate. In the 1860s, the Central Pacific Railroad recruited Chinese workers to help build its part of the transcontinental railroad.

Chinese immigrants settled mostly in western cities where they worked as laborers, servants, or in skilled trades. Discrimination kept Chinese out of many businesses. Chinese businesspeople opened businesses to serve their own people.

Japanese immigration to America grew in the years between 1900 and 1910. Rapid industrialization and change in Japan disrupted the economy and some Japanese looked to America for a new start. In 1910, California opened an immigration station on **Angel Island** in San Francisco Bay. Immigrants were housed on bunk beds in barracks, sometimes for weeks or months, before they could have an immigration hearing to determine whether they could stay in the United States.

The Resurgence of Nativism

The reaction to the surge in immigration was increased feelings of **nativism**, or extreme dislike of immigrants by native-born people. In the 1840s and 1850s, nativism grew in response to the surge of immigrants from Ireland. In the 1890s, nativism focused on the southern and eastern Europeans and Asian immigrants. Some nativists feared that since so many of the immigrants were Catholic and Jewish, they would be a threat to American Protestants. Native laborers and unions opposed immigration because immigrants would work for lower wages than would American workers. Also, many southern and eastern European immigrants came from nations where socialism was popular, which some Americans thought could put capitalism in danger.

Impact of the Anti-Immigrant Movement Immigration helped the American economy grow, and several presidents vetoed anti-immigrant legislation passed by Congress. In 1882, two anti-immigrant laws were passed. One banned convicts, paupers, and the mentally disabled from entering the United States, and placed a 50-cent tax on each immigrant. That same year, Congress passed the **Chinese Exclusion Act**. This law barred Chinese immigration for ten years and prevented Chinese already in the country from becoming citizens. Chinese immigrants protested this discriminatory legislation, but to no avail. In 1892, the law was extended for another ten years and in 1902 the ban on Chinese immigration was made permanent. In 1890, there were about 105,000 Chinese living in the United States. By 1900, that number had shrunk to 74,000. The Chinese Exclusion Act remained law until it was repealed in 1943.

CORE CONCEPTS: GOVERNMENT

The United States also entered into a "Gentlemen's Agreement" with Japan in 1907. Japan agreed to stop laborers from emigrating to America, and in return, the United States agreed to stop discrimination against Japanese living in America. This agreement was ended in 1924 when Congress passed a law barring Japanese immigration.

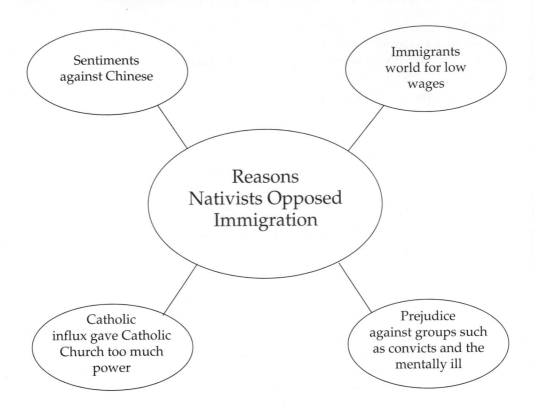

Sentiments against Chinese

Immigrants world for low wages

Reasons Nativists Opposed Immigration

Catholic influx gave Catholic Church too much power

Prejudice against groups such as convicts and the mentally ill

SECTION 2 URBANIZATION

Americans Migrate to the Cities

The urban population of the United States grew tremendously in the three decades after the Civil War. In 1870, there were about 10 million people living in towns of 2,500 or more. In 1900, there were 30 million urban residents. New York City grew from 800,000 in 1860 to almost 3.5 million in 1900. Chicago grew at an even faster rate, from 109,000 to 1.6 million by 1900. In 1840, there were 131 cities in the United States. In 1900, there were 1,700.

Immigrants and people from rural areas accounted for much of the growth. Immigrants settled in cities because there were jobs and housing available, often in ethnic neighborhoods that helped them get started in their new country. Rural Americans also came to cities for jobs, as crop and livestock prices had dropped in the years after the Civil War. They also came for the entertainment, excitement, and conveniences such as indoor plumbing.

African Americans also migrated to cities in large numbers. The vast majority of the country's African American population lived in the rural South in great poverty. Many began moving to escape debt, injustice, or discrimination. They also moved because Northern cities offered more jobs in industry and manufacturing than Southern cities did.

Wages and Working Conditions The average standard of living for workers rose in the years after the Civil War, but for many laborers, the return for their labor remained very small. At the turn of the century, the average income of the American worker was $400 to $500 a year—below the $600 that was considered the minimum for a reasonable level of comfort. Job security was also lacking. Many workers found themselves out of work because of advances in technology or found their wages cut significantly in hard times.

Conditions were difficult as well. Factory laborers worked ten-hour days, six days a week, while steel workers worked twelve hours a day. Many factories were unsafe and unhealthy. If a worker was injured on the job, there was no compensation.

Women at Work With the need for skilled workers decreasing, many business owners hired women and children, whom they could pay less money. Some women were single and were trying to support themselves and their parents or siblings. Many others were married and had to work to supplement their husband's income, which was often not enough to support a family. However, in some communities, the aversion to seeing married women work was so strong—among both men and women— that families struggled on inadequate wages rather than see a wife and mother take a job.

The New Urban Environment

The growth of cities challenged engineers and architects to develop new approaches to housing and transportation.

Skyscrapers Crowded cities drove up the price of land, so landowners started building taller buildings. The first **sky-**

CORE CONCEPTS: SCIENCE AND TECHNOLOGY

Before the mid-1800s, few buildings exceeded four or five stories. The problem with building taller buildings was that the walls would have to be very thick to bear the weight of the structure. Two new developments gave birth to the skyscraper. One was the use of steel girders, which were able to bear the weight of the building so the walls did not have to. The second was the invention of the elevator by Elisha Otis in 1852.

scraper was the ten-story Home Insurance Building built in Chicago in 1885. It was soon dwarfed by taller buildings in New York where limited land on the island of Manhattan encouraged the growth of tall buildings.

Mass Transit In 1890, most transportation in big cities was provided by horsecar, a railroad car pulled by horses. Some cities like San Francisco used cable cars, which were pulled along tracks by underground cables. The largest cities developed additional means of transportation. Chicago built an elevated railroad, while New York built both elevated railroads and underground subways.

Separation by Class

City neighborhoods were divided by definitive boundaries of social and economic class. The wealthiest people built huge, lavish homes—including castles. Middle class people took advantage of new transportation to build homes in "streetcar suburbs." Working class residents crowded into **tenements**, dark and crowded multi-family apartments.

The Growing Middle Class Incomes in the industrial era were rising for almost everyone, although at highly uneven rates. While the most conspicuous result of the new economy was the creation of vast fortunes, more important for society as a whole was the growth and increasing prosperity of the middle class. The salaries of clerks, accountants, middle managers, and other "white collar" workers rose on average by a third between 1890 and 1910.

New marketing techniques and affordable products made consumer goods available to a broad market for the first time. Changes such as canned food, and condensed milk, meant improved diets and better health. Ready-made clothing, available in department stores, resulted in much larger numbers of people becoming concerned with personal style. Middle- and even working-class women could strive to develop a distinctive style of dress. Substantial wardrobes, once a luxury reserved for the wealthy, began to become common at other levels of society as well.

Urban Problems

City living posed threats, including crime, violence, fire, disease, and pollution. These threats were much more prevalent for working class people than others. Native-born Americans blamed immigrants for the rise in crime, but in reality, the crime rate for immigrants was little different from that of native-born Americans. Alcohol contributed to violent crime, as was documented by Jacob Riis, a Danish immigrant who wrote about slum life in his 1890 book, *How the Other Half Lives*. Disease and pollution posed big threats to health. Improper sewage disposal, horse waste, and air pollution from factories and wood fires all contributed to illness and disease.

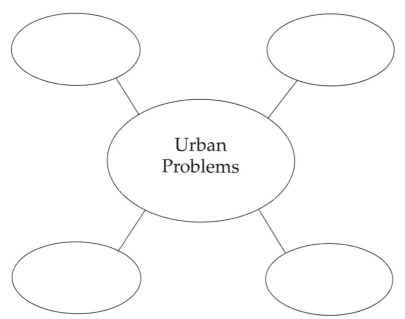

REGENTS WARM-UP

Use a word web like the one shown here to summarize the difficulties that faced new immigrants and others in cities. This skill will be useful as you prepare to answer the two different types of essay questions that appear on Regents Examinations.

CORE CONCEPTS: CIVIC VALUES

Thomas Nast was a cartoonist who brought down the mighty Boss Tweed. For three years from 1868–1871, Nast savagely ridiculed Tweed every week in *Harper's Weekly* with his caricatures that exposed him as the corrupt boss he was. Tweed is reported to have said: "Stop them damn pictures. I don't care what the papers write about me. My constituents can't read. But, damn it, they can see the pictures." In 1871, Tweed and his cohorts were defeated at the polls.

REGENTS WARM-UP

Study the cartoon and answer the following questions:

- What does the caption suggest about Nast's point of view?

- How does Nast feel about Boss Tweed and the men around him?

Urban Politics

A new kind of political system grew in cities, which provided essential city services in return for political power. In cities a **political machine** developed. This was an informal political group designed to keep power by providing services to voters. The machine was run by party bosses. One party boss was George Plunkitt, an Irish immigrant who defended the **graft**, or bribes, as "honest graft" because it was done in return for services. The political machines encouraged corruption, as party bosses not only took bribes but also sold permits to contractors and others doing business with the city. They also paid immigrants to vote a certain way.

Tammany Hall George Plunkitt worked for the New York City Democratic Party machine called Tammany Hall. The leader of Tammany Hall in the 1860s was **William M. "Boss" Tweed**. Tweed's corruption was exposed in the 1870s and he was sent to prison. Opponents of political machines like Thomas Nast, a cartoonist whose work exposed Boss Tweed, raised the issue of the corruption of the political machines. But for many city dwellers, the machines delivered important services and they continued to support them on Election Day.

"WHO STOLE THE PEOPLE'S MONEY?" — DO TELL. N.Y.TIMES. 'TWAS HIM.

Library of Congress

Religion and Politics Religious and ethnic differences shaped party loyalties. The Democratic Party attracted most of the Catholic voters, most of the recent immigrants, and most of the poorer workers—groups that often overlapped. The Republican Party appealed to northern Protestants, citizens of old stock, and much of the middle class—groups that also had considerable overlap. Among the few substantive issues on which the parties took clearly different stands were matters connected with immigrants. Republicans tended to support measures restricting immigration and to favor temperance legislation, which many believed would help discipline immigrant communities. Catholics and immigrants viewed such proposals as assaults on them and their cultures and opposed them; the Democratic Party followed their lead.

Party identification, then, was usually more a reflection of cultural inclinations than a calculation of economic interest. Individuals might affiliate with a party because their parents had done so, or because it was the party of their region, their church, or their ethnic group.

SECTION 3 THE GILDED AGE

A Changing Culture

In 1873, Mark Twain and Charles Warner wrote a novel, *The Gilded Age*. Historians have used its title to refer to the period in American history from 1870–1900. It was a time of rapid industrial growth, and technological and cultural change. By calling the era the **Gilded Age**, Twain and Warner were offering a critical view. Something is *gilded* if it is covered with gold on the outside but made of cheaper material on the inside. Twain, Warner, and other critics were pointing out that underneath the great wealth and progress lay corruption, poverty, crime, and growing disparities in wealth between rich and poor.

The Idea of Individualism One strong idea of the era was that of **individualism**, an idea that remains an important American belief to this day. It declared that no matter how humble one's origins, a person could rise to great heights if he or she simply tried hard enough. The idea was embedded in the belief that there was ample opportunity in American society and that if one did not succeed it was one's own fault.

Horatio Alger The idea of individualism was best expressed by a popular writer named Horatio Alger, a minister who left the clergy and turned to writing. Alger wrote more than 100 novels with the same "rags-to-riches" theme in which a poor person goes to the big city and through hard work, good character, and luck becomes successful. Alger's books were very popular and inspired people to believe that they could have the same results as the heroes of Alger's novels.

Social Darwinism

The idea of individualism was reinforced by the philosophy of Social Darwinism. Its leading proponent was the English philosopher **Herbert Spencer**.

Herbert Spencer Spencer applied Charles Darwin's theory of evolution and natural selection to human society. Darwin had argued that plant and animal life had evolved over the years by a process he called natural selection, in which only the fittest species survived. Those species unable to adapt to changing conditions died out. Darwin's theory was based on millions of years of life. Spencer argued that the same rules applied in the few thousand years of human society. The most successful people were successful not because of social advantages, or power, but because they were inherently better. **Social Darwinism** helped explain the growing disparities in wealth, and helped justify them, too. Spencer's "survival of the fittest" became a catchphrase and helped make Spencer's books best-sellers in the United States.

Business leaders like John D. Rockefeller embraced Social Darwinism. It helped justify their economic theory of laissez-faire capitalism. Social Darwinism helped justify Rockefeller's own success.

Carnegie's Philosophy of Wealth Andrew Carnegie embraced Social Darwinism. Carnegie, however, softened the harsh conclusions of the philosophy with his own ideas about what he called the **Gospel of Wealth**. Carnegie said wealthy Americans bore the responsibility of **philanthropy**—using their great fortunes to further social progress. Carnegie, Rockefeller, and others followed through. Today, their fortunes continue to fund grants to all kinds of social and artistic causes.

Realism

Just as Darwin had looked at the natural world scientifically, a new movement in art and literature known as **realism** attempted to portray people realistically instead of idealizing them as romantic artists had done.

Realism in Art Artists like Thomas Eakins of Philadelphia took everyday events as their subjects and tried to portray them realistically. The style for most of the nineteenth century had been idealistic portrayals of romantic subjects.

Realism in Literature Writers such as Mark Twain tried to capture the world as they saw it. In *The Adventures of Huckleberry Finn*, Mark Twain, whose real name was Samuel Clemens, wrote about the adventures of a boy and his friend Jim, an escaped slave, floating down the Mississippi River on a raft.

Popular Culture

The growth of industry, cities, and technology all changed the way people lived. Many people began to have free time and looked for ways to amuse themselves outside the home.

The Saloon Frank Lloyd Wright, the famous architect, noticed when he moved to Chicago that the city had more saloons than grocery stores. The saloon functioned as a kind of community center for male adults. It was where you went to discuss politics. Saloons offered free toilets, newspapers, water for horses, and even a "free lunch." Salty food was offered to make patrons thirsty so they would order more drinks.

Amusement Parks and Sports The first amusement parks were built in the Gilded Age. Spectator sports also became popular. The first professional baseball team, the Cincinnati Red Stockings, was formed in 1868. The first World Series was played in 1903. Sports such as basketball, golf, and tennis began in this era, as well.

Vaudeville and Ragtime A new popular form of entertainment was called vaudeville, adapted from French theater. It included animal acts, acrobats, singers, and dancers. Its fast-moving acts mirrored the tempo of city life.

A new type of music called ragtime also reflected the fast tempo of city life. It featured syncopated rhythms using the patterns of African American music. Scott Joplin, one of the most important African American ragtime composers, became known as the "King of Ragtime."

CORE CONCEPTS: CULTURE

Professional baseball developed rapidly in the years after the Civil War. The National League was founded in 1876 with teams in eight cities. Other cities founded teams and tried to form a rival league to the National League. The first few attempts to found a rival league did not succeed until the American League was founded in 1901. In 1903 teams from each league met in the first World Series.

SECTION 4 THE REBIRTH OF REFORM

Social Criticism

The tremendous changes of industrialization and urbanization gave rise to a debate about how to best address society's problems. Social Darwinism was challenged by critics who thought that much could be done to help people and improve society.

Henry George was a journalist who wrote a bestseller in 1879 called *Progress and Poverty*. George's idea was to have a single tax on the unearned wealth of land to fund social improvements. George's economic analysis was flawed but he was successful in stimulating debate and challenging the ideas of Social Darwinism and laissez-faire economics.

In 1888, Edward Bellamy's book *Looking Backward* captured the imagination of Americans. Bellamy's book looks backward from the year 2000 and sees an America without crime or poverty, in which the government owns all industry and shares the wealth equally with all Americans. Bellamy's socialist ideas were not shared by all, but like George he helped stimulate debate and challenge the supremacy of Social Darwinism.

Naturalism in Literature

A new style of writing literature known as naturalism also challenged Social Darwinism. Naturalist writers argued that many people failed in life not through any fault of their own, but because they were caught up in circumstances that they could not control. Leaving society and the economy unregulated, as proposed by Social Darwinists, only made things worse, naturalist writers argued. Among the most prominent naturalist novelists were Theodore Dreiser, Stephen Crane, Jack London, and Frank Norris.

Helping the Urban Poor

Naturalist writers and other social critics offered new ideas about society. Others took action and tried to implement ideas they thought would help people and improve society.

The Social Gospel From about 1870 to about 1920, reformers in the Social Gospel movement tried to improve society by using biblical ideas of charity and justice. One leader was Washington

Gladden, who tried to apply what he called "Christian law" to social problems. During a coal strike, Gladden preached about the "right and necessity of labor organizations." Walter Rauschenbusch was a Baptist minister who condemned the influence of competition. Leaders like Gladden and Rauschenbusch inspired other churches to expand their social mission and serve the poor.

The Salvation Army and the YMCA An English minister named William Booth founded a group called Christian Mission. In 1878, the group adopted a military-type organization and it became the Salvation Army. The Young Men's Christian Association (YMCA) also started in England. It set about helping industrial workers and the urban poor by organizing Bible studies, prayer meetings, and citizenship training, and also building dormitories, gymnasiums, and swimming pools.

The Settlement House Movement The settlement house movement was an offshoot of the Social Gospel. Jane Addams among others established settlement houses in poor neighborhoods to help people in need. Addams founded Hull House in Chicago in 1889. Lillian Wald founded the Henry Street settlement in New York's Lower East Side. Settlement houses provided medical care, recreation programs, English classes, hot lunches and other services.

Public Education

Public education spread in this era, not just for altruistic reasons. An expanding industrial economy needed educated workers.

The Spread of Schools The number of children in public schools increased dramatically. In 1870, there were about 6,500,000 children in school. By 1900, that number had risen to 17,300,000. For immigrant children, school was a key to success and to their Americanization. Schools helped assimilate children into American society. They taught immigrant children English, American history, and citizenship. However, school often caused problems for immigrant parents and their children. On the one hand, children often learned English faster than their parents did, and were called upon to help negotiate family business. On the other hand, parents feared children's rapid Americanization could alienate them from their own cultural traditions.

Not everyone had access to school. Rural areas lagged behind and schools were often too far away for some children to attend

CORE CONCEPTS: REFORM MOVEMENTS

Florence Kelley (1859–1932) was a social reformer who helped direct the Settlement House movement into larger national social reform. Kelley first lived at Hull House in Chicago, where she led the fight for laws restricting child labor. She later moved to New York and, from Henry Street Settlement, worked for women's suffrage and civil rights. In 1909 she helped found the National Association for the Advancement of Colored People (NAACP).

regularly. African American children did not have equal educational opportunities. Some African Americans founded their own schools. Booker T. Washington founded the Tuskegee Institute in 1881.

Education for the Workplace City schools helped immigrants assimilate. Schools also helped prepare children for the workplace by drilling them in timely attendance, neatness, obedience, and efficiency—all necessary skills for work. Vocational and technical education in high schools provided students with skills required in specific trades.

Expanding Higher Education Many new colleges and universities were founded in this era. The Morrill Land Grant Act helped found universities in many states. Several women's colleges were founded to provide higher education for women. New women's colleges such as Vassar, Wellesley, and Smith, along with women's colleges on the campuses of Harvard and Columbia Universities, increased the number of women attending college.

Public Libraries Free public libraries expanded in great numbers during the era. Andrew Carnegie played a key role, donating millions of dollars to build libraries in many cities.

CHAPTER 14   SETTLING THE WEST

Section 1   **Miners and Ranchers**
Section 2   **Farming the Plains**
Section 3   **Native Americans**

Chapter Overview

Many of the settlers in the West were miners and ranchers. Miners chased the latest big strike of gold, silver, or copper, hoping to strike it rich. Mining was a boom and bust activity, turning many mining towns into ghost towns. Ranching took hold during the Civil War, when growing demand for beef resulted in rising prices. The expansion of the railroads to Kansas made the long drive—in which cowboys herded cattle hundreds of miles to rail head in Dodge City and Abilene, Kansas—possible.

The Homestead Act helped bring thousands of settlers to farm the Great Plains, a challenging task given the extremes of weather and the lack of rainfall.

Native Americans of the Great Plains saw their way of life threatened by the arrival of settlers and ranchers. Settlers' hunting of buffalo undermined Native Americans main source of food. In wars with the U.S. Army, Native Americans' were defeated and then placed on reservations. In 1887, the government changed its policy to one of assimilation, but it failed to result in a better life for Native Americans.

As you read through this chapter, ask yourself these questions:
(1) How did miners and ranchers help open the West to settlement?
(2) What challenges did farmers on the Great Plains face?
(3) How did the settlement of the Great Plains affect Native Americans?

Main Ideas and Concepts

- **Movement of People and Goods** The Great Plains and Mountain West were settled by miners, farmers, and ranchers who moved from the East.

- **Places and Regions** The Great Plains is a distinct region of the country. Once called the "Great American Desert," it was settled in the years after the Civil War.

- **Human Rights** Native Americans were denied basic human rights, and treaties made with them were broken.

- **Environment** The environment of the Great Plains presented a challenge to settlers. There was little rainfall along with extremes of weather.

People, Places, Terms

The following names and terms will help you to prepare for the Regents Exam in United States History and Government. You can find an explanation of each name and term in the Glossary at the back of this book, in your textbook, or in another reference source.

assimilation	Ghost Dance	reservations
barbed wire	Little Bighorn	Sitting Bull
Dawes Act	long drive	Wounded Knee
dry farming	open range	

SECTION 1 MINERS AND RANCHERS

Growth of the Mining Industry

The West was rich in mineral resources, and miners chased after every big strike. News of the discovery of a deposit of gold, silver, or copper would bring a stampede of prospectors into an area. Individual miners used a process called placer mining, which extracted shallow deposits of minerals through the use of simple tools like picks, shovels and pans. Later, mining corporations would move into the area using quartz mining to dig deep beneath the surface.

Economics

The Big Strike in Nevada In 1859, a miner named Henry
Comstock staked a claim in Six-Mile Canyon, Nevada. The sticky
blue-gray mud turned out to be almost pure silver ore. News of
Comstock's discovery brought more than 30,000 miners to
Virginia City, Nevada, almost overnight. The new town soon
had an opera house, a six-story hotel, shops with the latest
fashions from Europe, and several newspapers. In a few years,
the silver veins were exhausted. Without mining, the town's
economy collapsed and most of the residents moved on—
turning Virginia City into a ghost town. This cycle of boom and
bust was repeated throughout the West.

Ranching and Cattle Drives

Settlers on the Great Plains looked upon the region as a desert.
It certainly wasn't fit for raising cattle, since water was scarce
and the grass too tough for cattle to eat. But in Texas, ranchers
had developed a new breed of cow called the longhorn that
could thrive in the harsh plains environment.

Initially, cattle ranching was not profitable in the Great Plains
because beef prices were low and the cattle too far from Eastern
markets. The Civil War changed all that. Both the Union and
Confederate armies needed meat, and beef prices soared. The
railroad brought a means of getting Western cattle to Eastern
markets. The first **long drive** took place in 1866, when ranchers
drove about 260,000 cattle to the Western end of the railroad at
Sedalia, Missouri. Other trails soon opened.

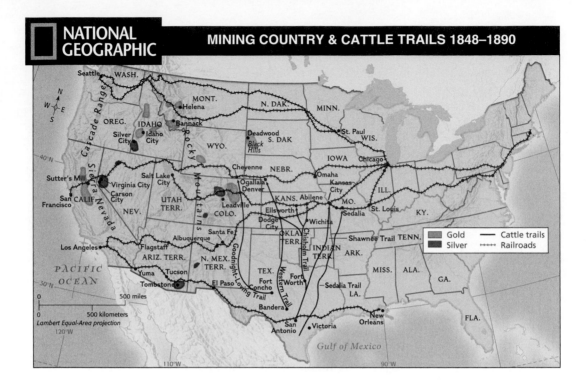

NATIONAL GEOGRAPHIC

MINING COUNTRY & CATTLE TRAILS 1848–1890

The Long Drive The long drive was a big production. In the spring, cowboys rounded up cattle from the **open range**, dividing them into herds according to their brands (a mark indicating ownership). Then cowboys on horseback moved the herds on the long drive to the railheads, a trip that covered hundreds of miles over open country. The combined herds moving on the trail could number anywhere from two hundred to five thousand cattle.

Cowboys were skilled riders who needed hardiness and courage to endure the hardships of long days and nights on the trail in all kinds of weather. Most early cowboys were former Confederate soldiers escaping the harsh life in the South during Reconstruction. Others were Hispanic and African American.

Ranching Becomes Big Business Ranching became a profitable business. It also introduced conflict and changes. Farmers on the Great Plains used a new invention, **barbed wire**, to fence their fields and keep cattle out. Violence often broke out when ranchers cut the wire, wanting to preserve the open range. Later, big ranchers used barbed wire to keep rival herds out of their pastures.

Eventually an oversupply of cattle led to lower prices. The long drive came to an end as railroads came closer to the cattle ranches. In the winter of 1886 and 1887, a blizzard killed thousands of cattle and helped drive still more ranchers out of business. With the end of the long drive, cowboys became ranch hands.

SECTION 2   FARMING THE PLAINS

Geography of the Plains

The Great Plains extends west to the Rocky Mountains. Rainfall on the Plains averages less than 20 inches a year, a very small amount, and trees grow naturally only along rivers and streams. For centuries, the Plains were home to enormous herds of buffalo that were hunted by Native Americans for their hides and meat. Major Stephen Long explored the region in 1819 and called it the "Great American Desert."

The Beginnings of Settlement Railroads opened the Plains to settlement. The railroads had received huge grants of land from Congress and set about selling land to settlers. New settlers were lucky. Rainfall in the 1860s was above average, and farmers got off to a good start. Many settlers came to the Great Plains and received free land under the Homestead Act. By paying a $10 registration fee, settlers qualified to receive 160 acres for free, provided they live on the land for five years. Life on the Great Plains was challenging. With no trees for lumber, settlers built their first homes from sod cut out of the ground. Prairie fires were a constant danger, as were swarms of grasshoppers, extreme summer and winter temperatures, summer thunderstorms and tornadoes, and winter blizzards.

The Wheat Belt

Farmers on the Great Plains used **"dry farming"** methods to farm in the harsh environment. This involved planting seeds deep in the ground where they could take advantage of the moisture held in the earth. New machines such as balers, binders, and threshing machines helped farmers harvest large crops. However, most "sodbusters" (the name given to Great Plains settlers) could not afford the new machines and struggled to make a living. Wealthier large-scale farmers did succeed and soon were growing huge crops of wheat—so large that the Plains became known as the Wheat Belt.

CORE CONCEPTS: POLITICAL SYSTEMS

Education is a core American value and the government has actively promoted education in many ways. A provision of the Homestead Act, also called the 1862 Morrill Act, was to give states large tracts of land on which to set up universities that provided programs in agriculture and education as well as in traditional subjects. Today, every state as well as Puerto Rico has at least one "land grant college." Many well-known state universities originated with the land grants from the Morrill Act.

CORE CONCEPTS: PLACES AND REGIONS

European immigrants played a large role in settling the Great Plains. Railroad companies advertised in Europe about an agricultural paradise in the middle of North America. Thousands of immigrants came. By 1910, more than half the people living on the Great Plains were European-born. The leading ethnic groups settling the Plains were from the Scandinavian countries, Russia, Germany, and Great Britain.

CORE CONCEPTS: SCARCITY

The University of Oklahoma football team is known as the Sooners. The origin of the name comes from the Oklahoma Land Rush. People lined up at the border to rush into the Oklahoma Territory to stake out their claim to free land. The people at the front of the line were surprised to find some people already on the territory who had staked out claims. It turned out these people had snuck into the territory "sooner" than the others, giving rise to the nickname for Oklahomans to this day.

CORE CONCEPTS: ENVIRONMENT AND SOCIETY

The Great Plains were sparsely settled by Native Americans until the 1600s when the Spanish introduced horses to North America. Then the Plains Native American culture evolved into one built around hunting buffalo on horseback. The Native Americans used every part of the buffalo. They ate the meat, made robes from the fur, and used the skin for tipis and the bones for tools.

Economics

Farmers Fall on Hard Times By the 1880s, the United States had become the world's leading exporter of wheat. But in the 1890s, a surplus of wheat on the market caused prices to drop. Some farmers took out mortgages on their farms, getting loans from the bank to make it through hard times. When they could not make their payments, the bank took over the farms, or farmers worked as tenants for a new owner. Farmers also faced the challenge of nature. The good years of sufficient rainfall ended, and by the late 1880s, a drought made farming even more difficult for small farmers.

Closing the Frontier

On April 22, 1889, the government opened one of the last large tracts of unsettled land, which later became the state of Oklahoma. Within hours, more than 10,000 people raced into the region in what became known as the Oklahoma Land Rush.

In 1890, the U.S. Census Bureau reported that the West had been so thoroughly settled "that there can hardly be said to be a frontier line." There were still huge areas of open land. But this "closing of the frontier" was a significant event in American history. The West had always served as a safety valve, where Americans could go to start over. While many Americans continued to do just that in the decades to come, the idea of a wild unsettled frontier was gone.

Life on the Plains remained hard. Successful farmers were able to drill ever-deeper wells to get water. Water was used for crops and to grow gardens and flowers to break the monotony of the ocean of grass that was the Great Plains. Railroads brought lumber and brick to replace sod as a building material for houses. But many settlers found the harsh weather, the drought, and falling prices too much. They gave up their land and moved on.

SECTION 3 NATIVE AMERICANS

Culture of the Plains Indians

Most Native Americans on the Great Plains were nomads who roamed vast distances following herds of buffalo, their main source of food. Despite some differences, the groups of Plains

Indians were similar in many ways. They lived in extended family networks and had a close relationship to nature. Plains Indian nations' populations sometimes numbered several thousand, but were divided into bands of about five hundred. A governing council headed each band, but most members participated in decisions.

Cultures Under Pressure

The arrival of miners, ranchers, and farmers in the West created tension with Native Americans, who saw the arrival of settlers as an invasion of their lands. Groups of Native Americans attacked wagon trains, stagecoaches, and ranches. Settlers attacked and killed Native Americans.

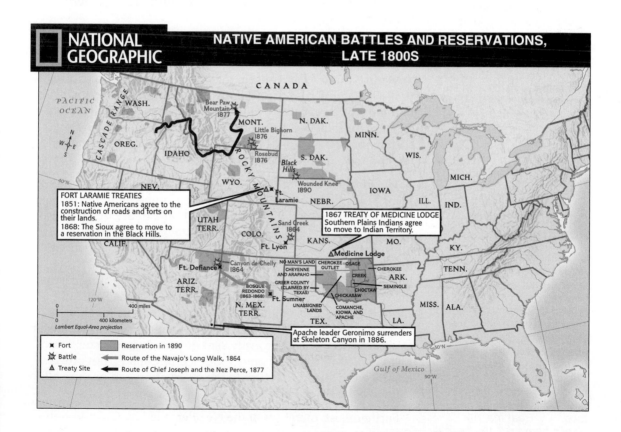

NATIONAL GEOGRAPHIC

NATIVE AMERICAN BATTLES AND RESERVATIONS, LATE 1800S

FORT LARAMIE TREATIES
1851: Native Americans agree to the construction of roads and forts on their lands.
1868: The Sioux agree to move to a reservation in the Black Hills.

1867 TREATY OF MEDICINE LODGE
Southern Plains Indians agree to move to Indian Territory.

Apache leader Geronimo surrenders at Skeleton Canyon in 1886.

- ✕ Fort
- ✳ Battle
- △ Treaty Site
- ▨ Reservation in 1890
- ⟵ Route of the Navajo's Long Walk, 1864
- ⟵ Route of Chief Joseph and the Nez Perce, 1877

CORE CONCEPTS: DECISION MAKING

After the Civil War, the army officer in charge of the Great Plains was Civil War hero General William Tecumseh Sherman. After studying the problem, Sherman realized that, given the vast amount of territory of the Plains and the Native Americans' superior knowledge of the land, it would be difficult to hunt down tribes and engage them in battle. Instead, Sherman chose a strategy that encouraged hunters. His policy was successful—resulting in the near extinction of the buffalo and the defeat of the Plains Indians.

CORE CONCEPTS: HUMAN RIGHTS

Chief Joseph's 1,300 mile retreat revealed his military genius. Vastly outnumbered, he was able to maneuver around U.S. Army attempts to engage him in battle. Upon surrendering, Chief Joseph uttered these eloquent words: *"Our chiefs are killed. . . . The children are freezing to death. . . . My people . . . have no blankets, no food. . . . Hear me, my chiefs; I am tired; my heart is sick and sad. From where the sun now stands I will fight no more forever."*

Lakota Sioux Defend Their Territory The army sent patrols far out into the Northern Great Plains. Instead of keeping the peace, the patrols stirred up trouble with the Lakota Sioux who lived in the area. The Lakota fought hard to control their hunting grounds, which extended from the Black Hills westward to the Bighorn Mountains. Leaders of the Lakota included three great chiefs: Red Cloud, Crazy Horse, and Sitting Bull.

Government

A Doomed Plan for Peace Several violent incidents between Native Americans and settlers convinced Congress that it needed a plan for dealing with Native Americans on the Great Plains. In 1867 Congress formed an Indian Peace Commission that proposed creating two large reservations on the Plains—one in the north for the Sioux and one in the south for Southern Plains Indians.

The Last Native American Wars

Many Native Americans on the Plains refused to go to reservations. They preferred their old life of hunting buffalo. However, that life was threatened by hunters who came to the Great Plains to shoot buffalo. The army encouraged hunters, knowing a scarcity of buffalo would force the Indians to abandon their old life and move to the **reservations.**

Battle of Little Bighorn In 1876, there was a gold rush in the Black Hills of Dakota. Miners and others moved into territory considered sacred by the Lakota, violating a treaty that the government had signed. The Lakota attacked the settlers. The army sent Lt. Colonel George Armstrong Custer, commander of the Seventh Cavalry, to deal with the Lakota. Custer was an impulsive commander who underestimated the fighting capabilities of the Lakota and their Cheyenne allies. In the Battle of **Little Bighorn**, Custer and all 210 of his men were killed by a force of more than 2,500 warriors. Newspapers portrayed Custer as a hero and victim. The army sent more men to pursue the Lakota. **Sitting Bull** and one group fled to Canada, but other Lakota were forced to return to the reservation and give up all claims to the Black Hills.

Farther west, members of the Nez Perce led by Chief Joseph refused an order to relocate to a small reservation in Idaho. In 1877, Chief Joseph and a small band of Nez Perce embarked on a flight of more than 1,300 miles, eluding many army attempts to capture them. Finally, out of food, and with winter closing in, Chief Joseph surrendered.

Wounded Knee Native American resistance to federal authority finally came to an end on the Lakota Sioux Reservation in 1890. The government agent forbade the Lakota from performing a religious ritual called the **Ghost Dance** that celebrated a hoped-for return of the buffalo and the disappearance of settlers. The agent blamed Sitting Bull, who had returned from Canada to the reservation, and sent police to arrest the chief. In a gunfight, Sitting Bull was killed. The Ghost Dance participants fled the reservation and were chased by army troops. On December 29, 1890, army troops killed approximately 200 Lakota men, women, and children; 25 U.S. soldiers were also killed.

Assimilation

Some Americans protested how the government had treated Native Americans. In 1881, author Helen Hunt Jackson published *A Century of Dishonor,* a book criticizing the treatment of Native Americans. Her book triggered discussions in Congress and across the country. Some people believed Native Americans would be better off if they were **assimilated**, or absorbed into American society. In 1887, Congress adopted this policy, passing a law called the **Dawes Act**, which gave land to individual Native American families. The policy failed since many Native Americans had little training or desire to be farmers. Some sold their land and then had no way of supporting their families. The federal Native American policy only made life worse for Native Americans.

PRACTICING FOR THE REGENTS

Part 1 Multiple-Choice Questions

Directions: The following multiple-choice questions come from past Regents Examinations. Test your understanding of global history and geography by answering each of these items. Circle the number of the word or expression that best completes each statement or question. Test-taking tips can be found in the margins for some questions. For additional help, see Taking the Regents Exam on pages ix–xxxi of this Review Book.

1 Following the Civil War, many Southern states enacted Black Codes to
   (1) provide free farmland for African Americans
   (2) guarantee equal civil rights for African Americans
   (3) restrict the rights of formerly enslaved persons
   (4) support the creation of the Freedmen's Bureau

2 What effect did the system of sharecropping have on the South after the Civil War?
   (1) It kept formerly enslaved persons economically dependent.
   (2) It brought investment capital to the South.
   (3) It encouraged Northerners to migrate south.
   (4) It provided for a fairer distribution of farm profits.

3 Following Reconstruction, the term *New South* was most often used to describe
   (1) changes in the Southern economy
   (2) new attitudes in race relations
   (3) the growth of the Republican Party in the South
   (4) the decline of the sharecropping system

4 The underlying reason for the impeachment of President Andrew Johnson was
   (1) the Credit Mobilier scandal
   (2) a power struggle with Congress over Reconstruction
   (3) his refusal to appoint new justices to the Supreme Court
   (4) his polices toward Native American Indians

5 One factor that furthered industrialization in the United States between 1865 and 1900 was the
   (1) development of the airplane
   (2) expansion of the railroads
   (3) mass production of automobiles
   (4) widespread use of steamboats

6   During the late 1800s, industrialization in the United States led to
    (1) the growth of the middle class
    (2) an overall decline in labor union membership
    (3) the creation of affirmative action programs
    (4) a decrease in the use of natural resources

7   In the 19th century, protective tariffs, subsidies for railroads, and open immigration showed that the federal government followed a policy of
    (1) support for economic development
    (2) noninterference in the free-market system
    (3) regulation of unfair business practices
    (4) support for organized labor

8   The term *business monopoly* can best be described as
    (1) the most common form of business in the United States
    (2) government control of the means of production
    (3) an agreement between partners to manage a corporation
    (4) a company that controls or dominates an industry

9   One reason John D. Rockefeller, Andrew Carnegie, and J. Pierpont Morgan were sometimes called robber barons was because they
    (1) robbed from the rich to give to the poor
    (2) made unnecessarily risky investments
    (3) used ruthless business tactics against their competitors
    (4) stole money from the federal government

10 During the late 1800s, leaders of big business gave the greatest support to the passage of
    (1) antitrust laws
    (2) higher tariff rates
    (3) immigration restrictions
    (4) railroad regulation

Base your answers to questions 11 and 12 on the speakers' statements below and on your knowledge of social studies.

Speaker A: "Our nation has grown and prospered from the ideas and labor of immigrants. The nation has been enriched by immigrants from different nations who brought new ideas and lifestyles, which have become part of American culture."

Speaker B: "United States industries are competing with established European manufacturers. To prosper, American industries need the vast supply of unskilled labor that is provided by immigrants."

Speaker C: "Immigrants are taking jobs at low wages without regard for long hours and workers' safety. American workers must unite to end this unfair competition."

Speaker B: "Immigrants arrive in American cities poor and frightened. They are helped to find jobs or housing. These newcomers should show their gratitude at voting time."

11 Which speaker is most clearly expressing the melting pot theory?
   (1) *A*   (2) *B*
   (3) *C*   (4) *D*

12 Speaker *D* is expressing an opinion most like that of a
   (1) labor union member
   (2) religious leader
   (3) factory owner
   (4) political party boss

13 Between 1870 and 1920, the federal government placed few restrictions on immigration primarily because it wanted to
   (1) sell land in the West
   (2) recruit men for the military
   (3) ensure that there would be workers for the factories
   (4) avoid offending foreign governments

Base your answer to question 14 on the chart below and on your knowledge of social studies.

**Rural and Urban Populations
in the United States**

Year	Rural	Urban
1860	25,226,803	6,216,518
1870	28,656,010	9,902,361
1880	36,059,474	14,129,735
1890	40,873,501	22,106,265
1900	45,997,336	30,214,832
1910	50,164,495	42,064,001
1920	51,768,255	54,253,282

Source: Bureau of the Census

14 Which generalization about population growth is supported by information in this chart?
(1) For every census listed, rural population exceeded urban population.
(2) By 1920, more people lived in cities than in rural areas.
(3) The Civil War significantly slowed the rate of population growth.
(4) Most urban population growth was due to people migrating from rural areas.

15 The slogan "Eight hours for work, eight hours for sleep, eight hours for what we will" was used in the late 1800s to promote a major goal of
(1) farmers
(2) politicians
(3) industrialists
(4) organized labor

16 The Indian Wars that occurred between 1860 and 1890 were mainly the result of
(1) disputes over the spread of slavery
(2) conflict with Mexico over Texas and California
(3) the search for gold in California
(4) the movement of settlers onto the Great Plains

17 The aim of the Dawes Act of 1887 was to
(1) restore previously taken land to Native American Indian tribes
(2) maintain traditional Native American Indian cultures
(3) assimilate Native American Indians into American culture
(4) end all governmental contact with Native American Indians

Base your answers to questions 18 and 19 on the cartoon below and on your knowledge of social studies.

Source: Library of Congress (adapted)

18 Which 19th-century business practice does this cartoon illustrate?
(1) forming cooperatives
(2) establishing trade zones
(3) creating monopolies
(4) expanding global markets

19 The cartoonist would most likely support federal government attempts to
(1) pass antitrust legislation
(2) limit regulation of business
(3) establish high tariffs
(4) stop industrial pollution

20 "Transportation being a means of exchange and a public necessity, the government should own and operate the railroads in the interest of the people."

(1892)

Which group showed the greatest support for this idea?
(1) western farmers
(2) union leaders
(3) factory owners
(4) railroad owners

21 **"Labor Leaders Executed for Causing Haymarket Riot"**

"State Militia Called In To End Homestead Strike"

"1,000 Jailed as Silver Miners Protest Wage Cuts"

Which statement about labor unions in the late 1800s is illustrated by these headlines?
(1) Strikes by labor unions usually gained public support.
(2) The government frequently opposed labor union activities.
(3) Labor union demands were usually met.
(4) Arbitration was commonly used to end labor unrest.

22 The 19th-century philosophy of Social Darwinism maintained that
(1) the government should have control over the means of production and the marketplace
(2) all social class distinctions in American society should be eliminated
(3) economic success comes to those who are the hardest working and most competent
(4) wealth and income should be more equally distributed

23 The Jim Crow legal system, which expanded in the South after *Plessy* v. *Ferguson* (1896), was based on the Supreme Court's interpretation of the
(1) due process clause of the 5th Amendment
(2) states' rights provision of the 10th Amendment
(3) equal protection clause in the 14th Amendment
(4) voting rights provision in the 15th Amendment

Part II   Thematic Essay Question

The following thematic essay question comes from past Regents Examinations. Write your answers on a seperate sheet of paper. Essay-writing tips appear in the margin. For additional help, see Taking the Regents Exam on pages ix–xxxi of this Review Book.

Directions: Write a well-organized essay that includes an introduction, several paragraphs addressing the task below, and a conclusion.

Theme: Equality

In United States history, the rights of "life, liberty, and the pursuit of happiness," as stated in the Declaration of Independence, have often been denied to certain groups of Americans.

Task: Identify *one* group from your study of United States history and for that group:

- Use *two* historical examples to show how the group has been denied the rights of "life, liberty, and the pursuit of happiness"
- Identify and discuss *two* efforts that have been made to help the group attain "life, liberty, and the pursuit of happiness"
- Evaluate the extent to which the group has achieved equality today

You may use any group from your study of United States history. Some suggestions you might wish to consider include African Americans, Asian Americans, Native American Indians, women, and persons with disabilities.

You are *not* limited to these suggestions.

Guidelines: In your essay, be sure to:

- Address all aspects of the *Task*.
- Support the theme with relevant facts, examples, and details.
- Use a logical and clear plan of organization.
- Include an introduction and a conclusion that are beyond a simple restatement of the *Theme*.

Part III   Document-Based Question

Directions: This exercise is designed to test your ability to work with historical documents. It is similar to the document-based questions that you will see on the Regents Examination. While you are asked to analyze three historical documents, the exercise on the actual exam will include more documents. Some of the documents have been edited for the purposes of the question. As you analyze the documents, take into account the source of each document and any point of view that may be presented in the document.

Historical Context: The late 1800s was marked by vastly different views of government from different sectors of society.

Task: Using information from the documents and your knowledge of United States history and geography, write an essay in which you:

Discuss two different views of government that are shown in the documents, analyzing how each views what government should and should *not* do.

Part A   Short Answer

The documents below relate to issues of business, labor and politics during the Gilded Age. Examine each document and then answer the questions that follow.

Document 1

> The price which society pays for the law of competition, like the price it pays for cheap comforts and luxuries, is also great; but the advantages of this law are also greater still, for it is to this law that we owe our wonderful material development, which brings improved conditions in its train. . . . and while the law may be sometimes hard for the individual, it is best for the race, because it insures the survival of the fittest in every department. We accept and welcome, therefore, as conditions to which we must accommodate ourselves, great inequality of environment, the concentration of business, industrial and commercial, in the hands of a few, and the law of competition between these, as being not only beneficial, but essential for the future progress of the race.
> —Andrew Carnegie
> *Wealth* 1889

1   How does Carnegie justify the inequality in society between rich and poor?

_____

_____

_____

Document 2

Show me a country in which there are no strikes and I'll show you that country in which there is no liberty.

The periods of unemployment accompanying depression in the business cycle . . . present a challenge to all our claims to progress, humanity, and civilization.

The labor of a human being is not a commodity or article of commerce.

What does labor want? We want more schoolhouses and less jails; more books and less arsenals; more learning and less vice; more leisure and less greed; more justice and less revenge; in fact, more of the opportunities to cultivate our better natures, to make manhood more noble, womanhood more beautiful, and childhood more happy and bright.

—Samuel Gompers

2   What are the responsibilities of government towards labor according to Gompers?

_____

_____

_____

Document 3

> I've been readin' a book by Lincoln Steffens on The Shame of the Cities. Steffens means well but, like all reformers, he don't know how to make distinctions. He can't see no difference between honest graft and dishonest graft and, consequent, he gets things all mixed up. There's the biggest kind of a difference between political looters and politicians who make a fortune out of politics by keepin' their eyes wide open. The looter goes in for himself alone without considerin' his organization or his city. The politician looks after his own interests, the organization's interests, and the city's interests all at the same time. See the distinction? For instance, I ain't no looter. The looter hogs it. I never hogged. I made my pile in politics, but, at the same time, I served the organization and got more big improvements for New York City than any other livin' man. And I never monkeyed with the penal code.
>
> —George Washington Plunkitt in 1905, commenting on journalist Lincoln Steffens' book, *The Shame of the Cities*, which described the corruption in big city political machines.

3   What responsibilities do city politicians have to the people according to Plunkitt?

_____

_____

_____

Part B   Essay

Directions: Write a well-organized essay that includes an introduction, several paragraphs, and a conclusion.

Use evidence from at least *two* documents in the body of the essay. Support your response with relevant facts, examples, and details. Include additional outside information.

Historical Context: The late 1800s was marked by vastly different views of government from different sectors of society.

Task: Using information from the documents and your knowledge of United States history and geography, write an essay in which you:

> Discuss two different views of government that are shown in the documents, analyzing how each views what government should and should *not* do.

Guidelines: In your essay, be sure to:

- Address all aspects of the *Task* by accurately analyzing and interpreting at least *two* documents
- Incorporate information from the documents in the body of the essay
- Incorporate relevant outside information
- Support the theme with relevant facts, examples, and details
- Use a logical and clear plan of organization
- Introduce the theme by establishing a framework that is beyond a simple restatement of the *Task* or *Historical Context* and conclude with a summation of the theme

UNIT 4   RESHAPING THE NATION, *1900–1920*

PREPARING FOR THE REGENTS

This entire book is set up to help you grasp the facts, main ideas, and concepts needed to do well on your Regents Exam. Notes in the margin include core concepts, test-taking tips, and more. Use blank spaces in the margins to answer questions raised in the text or to jot down key points. Before each unit of study, skim through the exams at the back of the book to develop a sense of what your state wants you to know about your nation.

Unit 4 Overview

As the United States ended the nineteenth century, many Americans believed that political corruption prevented government from addressing the nation's pressing needs. As the country entered the twentieth century, it grew to become a world power. While the nation was expanding its territory into other parts of the world, conditions at home gave rise to a widespread Progressive movement. This movement worked for various reforms in government, business, and society. While Americans focused on their own country, Europe slid into a devastating world war that eventually involved the United States as well. These crucial years of domestic change and foreign conflict provided important foundations for the world you live in today.

Unit 4 Objectives

1.   Describe the political response to the economic problems of the late 1800s.

2.   Analyze how a desire for more trade and markets led to political change.

3.   Evaluate the legacy of the Progressive movement.

4.   Analyze how the United States raised an army and won support for World War I.

CHAPTER 15   POLITICS AND REFORM

Chapter Overview

During this period, political parties often focused on party competition rather than on important issues. Rural Americans were suffering economically, and they began to organize to obtain relief. Many states passed laws segregating African Americans and limiting their voting rights.

As you read through this chapter, ask yourself these questions:
(1) How did the even distribution of power between political parties limit the effectiveness of the government?
(2) What problems did Southern farmers face after the Civil War?
(3) How were African Americans in the South disenfranchised?

Main Ideas and Concepts

- **Government** From 1877 to 1896, the Republicans and Democrats were so evenly matched in power that only a few reforms were possible at the national level.

- **Political Systems** In the 1890s an independent political movement called Populism emerged to challenge the two major parties.

- **Economic Systems** Currency and credit problems led to the rise of the Populist movement.

- **Human Rights** In the late 1800s, African Americans stood up to fight against discrimination in the United States.

REGENTS WARM-UP

Several questions on the Regents Exam focus on your understanding of core concepts and themes in United States history. Political systems is an example of a core concept. As you read this chapter, note how political systems affected the ability of the government to govern.

People, Places, Terms

The following names and terms will help you to prepare for the Regents Exam in United States History and Government. You can find an explanation of each name and term in the Glossary at the back of this book, in your textbook, or in another reference source.

William Jennings
  Bryan
greenback
Interstate
  Commerce
  Commission

patronage
Pendleton Act
Populism

Sherman
  Antitrust Act

SECTION 1 STALEMATE IN WASHINGTON

A Campaign to Clean Up Politics

Under the spoils system, or **patronage,** government jobs went to supporters of the winning party in an election. By the late 1870s, many Americans believed that patronage corrupted those who worked for the government. They began a movement to reform the civil service.

The Republican candidates for the election of 1880 were James Garfield for president and Chester Arthur for vice president. They won the election, but President Garfield was assassinated a few months into his presidency. He was killed by a supporter who wanted a civil service job through patronage.

The Pendleton Act In 1883 Congress passed the **Pendleton Act.** This civil service reform act allowed the president to decide which federal jobs would be filled according to rules set up by a bipartisan Civil Service Commission. Candidates competed for federal jobs through examinations. Appointments could be made only from the list of those who took the exams. Once appointed to a job, a civil service official could not be removed for political reasons.

Legislation	Intent
Pendleton Act	filled federal jobs according to Civil Service Commission's rule

REGENTS WARM-UP

Past Regents Exams have focused on important legislation in U.S. history. As you read this chapter, use a graphic organizer such as the one shown here to identify key legislation passed during this period.

Two Parties, Neck and Neck

A major reason that few new policies were introduced in the 1870s and 1880s was because power was divided almost equally between the Democrats and the Republicans. The presidents of this period are often called the Forgettable Presidents.

PRESIDENTS AND THEIR POLITICAL PARTIES

Year	Democrat	Republican
1876		Rutherford B. Hayes
1880		James A. Garfield Chester Arthur
1884	Grover Cleveland	
1888		Benjamin Harrison
1892	Grover Cleveland	
1896		William McKinley

Most presidential elections during that time were very close. The Republicans won four of the six presidential elections between 1876 and 1896. The Democrats controlled the House of Representatives, however, and the Senate was controlled by Republicans who did not necessarily agree with the president on issues. In addition, local political bosses controlled the parties at that time.

A President Besieged by Problems

New York's governor Grover Cleveland was elected in 1884. Many strikes occurred during Cleveland's administration. Small businesses and farmers, who paid high rates for shipping goods, became angry at railroads because they gave large corporations, such as Standard Oil, partial refunds called rebates, as well as lower rates for shipping goods. Democrats and Republicans, however, believed that government should not interfere with corporations' property rights.

Wabash v. *Illinois* The state of Illinois charged more money to passengers or freight that were traveling shorter distances. In 1886, the Supreme Court ruled in the case of *Wabash* v. *Illinois* that Illinois could not restrict the rates that the Wabash Railroad charged for traffic between states. The Court ruled that only the federal government could regulate interstate commerce.

The Interstate Commerce Commission In 1887 President Cleveland signed the Interstate Commerce Act, which created the **Interstate Commerce Commission.** The law was the first to regulate interstate commerce. It limited railroad rates, forbade rebates to high-volume users, and made it illegal to charge higher rates for shorter hauls.

Debating Tariffs Many Americans thought that high tariffs were no longer necessary to protect the nation's manufacturing because large American companies could now compete internationally. They wanted Congress to cut tariffs because these taxes caused an increase in the price of manufactured goods. President Cleveland and Democrats in the House supported tariff reductions, but the Senate supported high tariffs. Congress became deadlocked over the issue.

Republicans Regain Power

The Republican candidate in the 1888 election was Benjamin Harrison. Industrialists who wanted tariff protection contributed greatly to his campaign. President Cleveland and the Democrats were against high tariffs. Harrison won the election by winning the electoral vote, but not the popular vote.

As a result of the election, Republicans gained control of the White House as well as both houses of Congress. The Republicans were able to pass legislation on issues of national concern.

The McKinley Tariff The Republicans addressed the tariff issue by passing the McKinley Tariff. The bill cut tariff rates on some goods but raised rates on others. It lowered federal revenue and left the nation with a budget deficit.

The Sherman Antitrust Act To curb the power of trusts, Congress passed the **Sherman Antitrust Act** of 1890, which made trusts illegal. The courts did little to enforce the act. However, the act was important because it established a precedent in government regulation of big business.

SECTION 2 POPULISM

Unrest in Rural America

Shortly after the Civil War, technology helped farmers produce more crops, which led to lower prices. At the same time, high tariffs increased the price of manufactured goods that farmers needed, making it harder for farmers to sell their products overseas. Farmers also felt they were being treated unfairly by the banks and the railroads.

In the 1890s, a political movement called **Populism** emerged. It aimed to increase the political power of farmers and to work for legislation for farmers' interests.

The Money Supply The nation's money supply concerned farmers. To help finance the Union in the Civil War, the government issued millions of dollars in **greenbacks,** or paper currency that could not be exchanged for gold or silver coins. This rapid increase in the money supply without a rapid increase in goods for sale caused inflation, a decline in value of money. The prices of goods greatly increased.

Deflation Hurts Farmers To get inflation under control, the government stopped printing greenbacks and started paying off bonds. Congress also stopped making silver into coins. As a result, the country did not have a large enough money supply to meet the needs of the growing economy. This led to deflation, or an increase in the value of money and a decrease in the general level of prices.

Deflation forced most farmers to borrow money to plant their crops. The short supply of money caused an increase in interest rates that the farmers owed. Some farmers wanted more greenbacks printed to expand the money supply. Others wanted the government to mint silver coins.

**CORE CONCEPTS:
MOVEMENT OF
PEOPLE AND GOODS**

Another problem with high tariffs was the fact that they forced other nations to raise tariffs as well. When other nations raised tariffs, farmers had a hard time exporting their surpluses.

CORE CONCEPTS: INDIVIDUALS, GROUPS, INSTITUTIONS

The Grange was founded for social and educational purposes. When large numbers of farmers turned to the Grange for help during the recession, the Grange changed its focus to respond to the plight of the farmers.

The Grange Takes Action The first national farm organization was the Grange. When the country experienced a recession and farm income fell dramatically, large numbers of farmers joined the Grange for help. The Grange pressured state legislatures to regulate the railroads in order to reduce rates.

Grangers also put their money together and created cooperatives, marketing organizations that worked to help their members. The cooperatives pooled members' crops and held them off the market to force the prices to rise. Cooperatives also negotiated better shipping rates from railroads.

The Farmers' Alliance The Grange was unable to improve the economic conditions of farmers. By the late 1870s, many farmers left the Grange and joined other organizations that offered to help them solve their problems. One of these was an organization known as the Farmers' Alliance. The Alliance was strong in the South and on the Great Plains. It organized large cooperatives, called exchanges, for the purpose of forcing farm prices up and making loans to farmers at low interest rates.

The exchanges mostly failed. They loaned too much money that was not repaid, and they were too small to dramatically affect world prices for farm products.

The People's Party Some members of the Alliance formed a political party called the People's Party, or Populists, to push for political reforms that would help farmers solve their problems. Most Southern leaders of the Alliance opposed the People's Party because they wanted the Democrats to retain control of the South.

The Rise of Populism

In 1890, the Farmers' Alliance issued the Ocala Demands to help farmers choose candidates in the 1890 elections. The demands included the free coinage of silver, an end to protective tariffs and national banks, tighter regulation of the railroads, and direct election of senators by voters. The demands also included the adoption of a subtreasury plan to set up warehouses where farmers could store their crops, in order to force prices up.

The South Turns to Populism Many pro-Alliance Democrats were elected to office in the South. But when Southern members of the Alliance realized that Democrats were not going to keep their promises to the Alliance, many left the Democratic Party and joined the People's Party.

A Populist Candidate for President The People's Party held its first national convention in July 1892 and nominated James B. Weaver to run for president. Weaver did well in the election, but Democratic candidate Grover Cleveland won.

The Panic of 1893 In 1893 the United States entered a serious economic crisis. The bankruptcy of the Philadelphia and Reading Railroads resulted in a panic. The stock market crashed and banks closed. By 1894, the country was in a deep depression. As the economy worsened, many foreign investors cashed in their U.S. government bonds for gold. This left the government with a very small gold reserve.

The Election of 1896

In the 1896 presidential election, the Democrats nominated **William Jennings Bryan** for the presidential election of 1896. He strongly supported the unlimited coinage of silver. Populists also supported Bryan for president.

Bryan waged an unusually energetic campaign for the presidency, traveling thousands of miles to make speeches. He was a powerful speaker, and he won the nomination with a famous defense of silver, saying he had come to speak "in defense of a cause as holy as the cause of liberty—the cause of humanity." However, Catholic immigrants and other city-dwellers did not care much about the silver issue and disliked Bryan's speaking style. It reminded them of rural Protestant preachers, who were sometimes anti-Catholic.

The Republicans nominated William McKinley for president. He promised workers a "full dinner pail." Most business leaders liked McKinley because they thought the unlimited silver coinage would ruin the country's economy. McKinley won the election.

Populism Declines New gold strikes in Alaska and Canada's Yukon Territory and in other parts of the world increased the money supply. Credit became easier to obtain and the farmers' situation improved. When the silver issue died out, so did the Populist Party.

CORE CONCEPTS: REFORM MOVEMENTS

The Populists' platform in the 1892 election called for:
- unlimited coinage of silver to increase the money supply
- a graduated income tax—one that taxed higher earnings more heavily
- an eight-hour workday
- restriction of immigration
- greater government regulation of big business
- direct election of senators

LINKING PAST AND PRESENT

Although the Populist Party died out, some of its proposals were later adopted and are still in use today. Among them are the federal income tax (Sixteenth Amendment) and direct election of U.S. senators (Seventeenth Amendment).

SECTION 3 THE RISE OF SEGREGATION

Resistance and Repression

After Reconstruction, many African Americans in the South were sharecroppers, or landless farmers who had to give the landlord a large share of their crops to cover the costs for rent and farming supplies.

Exodus to Kansas Because they were always in debt, many African Americans left farming to look for jobs or to claim homesteads in the West. In 1879, Benjamin "Pap" Singleton organized a mass migration of African Americans, called Exodusters, from the rural South to Kansas.

Forming a Separate Alliance Some African Americans who stayed in the South formed the Colored Farmers' National Alliance. This organization helped its members set up cooperatives. Many members joined the Populist Party.

Crushing the Populist Revolt Threatened by the power of the Populist Party, Democratic leaders began using racism to try to win back the poor white vote in the South. By 1890, election officials in the South began using methods to make it difficult for African Americans to vote.

Legalizing Segregation

In the late 1800s, both the North and the South discriminated against African Americans. Segregation, or separation of the races, was legalized in several ways:

- In the South, segregation was enforced by laws known as Jim Crow laws.

- In 1883, a Supreme Court ruling allowed private organizations and businesses to practice segregation.

- After the Court ruling, Southern states passed a series of laws that enforced segregation in all public places.

- The Supreme Court ruling in *Plessy* v. *Ferguson* endorsed "separate but equal" facilities for African Americans. This ruling established the legal basis for discrimination in the South for over 50 years.

CORE CONCEPTS: CONSTITUTIONAL PRINCIPLES

The events that led to *Plessy* v. *Ferguson* involved an African American named Homer Plessy. He was arrested for riding in a whites-only railroad car. Plessy challenged the law as being unconstitutional.

Racial Violence In the late 1800s, mob violence increased in the United States, particularly in the South. Between 1890 and 1899, hundreds of lynchings took place. Most lynchings were in the South, and the victims were mostly African Americans.

The African American Response

In 1892, Ida B. Wells, an African American from Tennessee, began a crusade against lynching. She wrote newspaper articles and a book denouncing lynchings and mob violence against African Americans.

A Call for Compromise Booker T. Washington, an African American educator, believed that African Americans should postpone the fight for civil rights and focus on education and vocations to prepare themselves economically for equality. He explained his views in a speech known as the Atlanta Compromise.

Voice of the Future The Atlanta Compromise was challenged by W.E.B. Du Bois, a leader of African American activists. Du Bois said that white Southerners continued to take away the civil rights of African Americans, even though African Americans were making progress in education and vocational training. He believed that African Americans had to demand their rights, especially voting rights, to gain full equality.

Formation of the Anti-Defamation League In 1913, Sigmund Livingston founded the Anti-Defamation League (ADL) in response to the lynching of a Jewish man in Georgia who had been accused of murder. It was later proved that the man was innocent. The ADL's purpose is to fight anti-Semitism and racism in all its forms. The group spoke out against racist groups such as the Ku Klux Klan, and later, the Nazis in Germany.

CORE CONCEPTS: CULTURE

Booker T. Washington (1856–1915) was born a slave and worked as a child in West Virginia coalmines. At age 16 he walked 500 miles to the Hampton Institute in Virginia because he heard it was one of the few places African Americans could learn a trade. To pay for his education, Washington worked as a janitor. Upon graduation, he worked at Hampton as an instructor. Hampton's founder, Samuel Armstrong, then asked Washington to start a similar school in Tuskegee, Alabama. Washington started the school in 1881 with 40 students in a run-down building. By the time of his death, the school had 2,000 students and over 100 buildings. Washington himself became a national spokesman for the African American community.

REGENTS WARM-UP

Several questions on the Regents Exam focus on your understanding of core concepts and themes in United States history. Presidential decisions and actions is an example of a core concept. As you read this chapter, note how presidential decisions and actions affected the role of the United States in the world community.

Chapter Overview

During the late 1800s and early 1900s, economic and military competition from world powers convinced the United States that it must be a world power. The United States that became an empire when it acquired the Philippines and territory in the Caribbean. American influence in Central and South America grew as the United States took a more active role in Latin American affairs.

As you read through this chapter, ask yourself these questions:
(1) What does it mean to be a world power?
(2) What responsibilities does a world power have to the world community?

Main Ideas and Concepts

- **Power** In the late 1800s, many Americans wanted the United States to expand its military and economic powers overseas. America's growing trade with the world and rivalry with European nations led to a naval buildup and a search for territory overseas.

- **Nationalism** Cubans struggled for independence from Spain, with help from the United States.

- **Imperialism** The United States defeated Spain in a war, acquired new overseas territories, and became an imperial war power.

- **Presidential Decisions and Actions** Under President Theodore Roosevelt, the United States increased its power on the world stage.

- **Economic Systems** The commercial interests of the United States spurred its involvement in distant parts of the world, such as China and Latin America.

People, Places, Terms

The following names or terms will help you to prepare for the Regents Exam in United States History and Government. You can find an explanation of each name and term in the Glossary at the back of this book, in your textbook, or in another reference source.

"big stick" diplomacy	Open Door policy	Roosevelt Corollary
dollar diplomacy	Matthew C. Perry	Theodore Roosevelt
imperialism	Platt Amendment	sphere of influence
jingoism	protectorate	yellow journalism

SECTION 1 THE IMPERIALIST VISION

Building Support for Imperialism

By the 1880s the western frontier was finally filling up. American business leaders began looking overseas to find new markets. Aware that several European countries were expanding their power around the world, many Americans wanted to make the United States a world power.

A Desire for New Markets Several European nations were already expanding overseas. Tariffs had reduced trade between industrial countries, and possibilities for investment in Europe had slowed. As a result, Europeans began investing in industries in other countries, especially in Africa and Asia. To protect their investments in these territories, the European countries began exercising control there. Some areas became colonies, while others became **protectorates.** In a protectorate, the imperial power allowed the local rulers to stay in control and protected them against rebellion or invasion.

This type of expansion is known as **imperialism.** It is the economic and political domination of a strong nation over weaker nations.

A Feeling of Superiority As the United States industrialized, Americans took interest in European imperialism. Many used the ideas of Social Darwinism—that the strongest nations would survive—to defend overseas expansion. Some took the idea even further, stating that English-speaking nations had superior character and systems of government and were therefore destined to control other nations. This idea became known as Anglo-Saxonism.

Expansion in the Pacific

In the 1800s, many Americans began looking to expand across the Pacific Ocean. Business leaders wanted to trade with Japan and China. By the early 1800s, dozens of ships were making the long trip across the Pacific every year.

Matthew Perry in Japan Japan's leaders believed that contact with the West would destroy Japanese culture. As a result, they allowed their nation to trade only with the Chinese and the Dutch.

In 1852 President Franklin Pierce decided to force Japan to trade with the United States. He sent Commodore **Matthew C. Perry** to negotiate a treaty with Japan. Perry entered the Japanese waters with four American warships. Impressed by this show of force, the Japanese realized they could not compete against American technology. As a result, the Japanese opened two ports to American trade.

Annexing Hawaii In addition to China and Japan, Americans became interested in Hawaii. By the mid-1800s, many American business leaders had established sugarcane plantations there.

The queen of Hawaii disliked the influence that Americans were gaining in Hawaii and, in 1891, tried to create a new constitution that reestablished her authority as a ruler of the Hawaiian people. The plantation owners responded by overthrowing the government and forcing the queen to give up her power. They then set up their own government and asked the United States to annex the islands.

Trade and Diplomacy in Latin America

The United States also wanted to increase the sale of its products to Latin America. It wanted Europeans to see the United States as the dominant power in Latin America.

In 1889, the United States invited the Latin American nations to a conference in Washington, D.C., to discuss ways in which the nations could work together to increase trade. The idea of working together became known as Pan-Americanism. The nations in the conference agreed to create an organization that worked to promote cooperation among the nations of the Western Hemisphere. Today, this organization is called the Organization of American States.

Building a Modern Navy

By the late 1800s, the United States was willing to risk war to defend its interests overseas. Many people believed that the United States needed a powerful navy to protect its merchant ships and defend its right to trade. They believed it was necessary for the United States to establish naval bases overseas.

In Congress, two senators, including Henry Cabot Lodge, pushed to build a strong navy. By the late 1890s, the United States was on its way to becoming one of the world's top naval powers.

SECTION 2 THE SPANISH-AMERICAN WAR

The Coming of War

The Cuban Rebellion Begins Cuba, a colony of Spain, provided wealth for Spain with sugarcane plantations. In 1868, Cuban rebels began fighting for Cuban independence. By 1878, the rebellion had failed. The rebels, along with their leader, José Martí, fled to the United States to raise money for weapons and plan a new revolution.

In 1894, after the United States imposed new tariffs on sugar, the economy of Cuba collapsed. Martí and his followers began a new rebellion in February of 1895. They seized control of eastern Cuba, declared its independence, and set up the Republic of Cuba.

Americans Support the Cubans At the start of the Cuban revolution, Americans were neutral. Then two newspapers, the *New York Journal,* published by William Randolph Hearst, and the *New York World,* published by Joseph Pulitzer, tried to outdo each other by reporting outrageous stories of how the Spanish were treating the Cubans. This sensational reporting of exaggerated and sometimes untrue stories, written to attract readers, became known as **yellow journalism.** The gruesome reports caused many Americans to side with the rebels. Meanwhile, Cuban rebels destroyed American property, hoping to encourage the United States to intervene in the war.

Calling Out for War President William McKinley did not want to intervene in the war, fearing it would cost the United States too many lives and hurt the economy. He asked Spain whether the United States could help in negotiating an end to the problem. Spain then offered Cuba self-rule, but not complete independence. Cuba refused. The pressure on McKinley to intervene in the war continued to grow for several reasons:

- The *New York Journal* printed a private letter written by the Spanish ambassador to the United States, Enrique Dupuy de Lôme. The letter described McKinley as weak and seeking the admiration of Americans. Many Americans became angry over the insult.

- In early 1898, McKinley sent the battleship U.S.S. *Maine* to Havana, Cuba, in case Americans had to be evacuated. In February 1898, the *Maine* exploded in Havana's harbor. Although no one knows why the ship exploded, many Americans blamed Spain. Throughout America, people began using the slogan "Remember the *Maine!*" as a rallying cry for war.

- Within the Republican Party, **jingoism,** or an attitude of aggressive nationalism, was very strong. Many members of the Party pressured McKinley to declare war on Spain.

Finally, on April 11, 1898, McKinley asked Congress to authorize the use of force to end the conflict in Cuba. Congress declared Cuba independent and demanded that Spain withdraw. In response, Spain declared war on the United States.

A War on Two Fronts

Spain was not prepared for war. Disease and months of fighting had weakened its soldiers. Spanish warships were old and their crews poorly trained. The United States had more battleships and more naval power. A U.S. Navy squadron

**CORE CONCEPTS:
EMPATHY**

Although the press invented sensational stories to sell newspapers, there is no doubt that the Cuban people did suffer under Spanish rule. Some Americans who supported the Cuban rebellion compared it to the American Revolution.

blockaded Cuba. Another U.S. fleet in Hong Kong was ordered to attack the Spanish fleet in the Philippines, a Spanish colony.

U.S. DEATHS IN THE SPANISH-AMERICAN WAR

385 in battle

2,061 of food poisoning and disease

Source: *The Nystrom Atlas of United States History.*

The United States Takes the Philippines In May 1898, Commodore George Dewey led a squadron that destroyed Spanish warships in the Philippines. President McKinley then sent 20,000 troops to the Philippines and, along the way, seized the island of Guam, a Spanish possession in the Pacific.

American Forces Battle in Cuba The U.S. Army was not as ready for war as the navy was. Poor conditions in training camps resulted in more Americans dying in training than in battle.

In June 1898, American troops landed in Santiago, Cuba. Led by Colonel Leonard Wood with **Theodore Roosevelt** as second in command, the group was known as the "Rough Riders."

The troops and the Rough Riders defeated the Spanish in the battles at Kettle Hill and San Juan Hill. The victories panicked the Spanish commander in Santiago, who ordered the Spanish fleet in the harbor to leave. As the ships left the harbors, the American warships attacked them and sank every ship. The Spanish occupying Santiago surrendered. Soon, American troops occupied the Spanish colony of Puerto Rico. On August 12, 1898, Spain and the United States agreed to a cease-fire.

CORE CONCEPTS: DIVERSITY

Accompanying the Rough Riders in their attack were the 9th and 10th Cavalry Regiments, composed entirely of African Americans. Although their courage was highly praised, they were not considered equals. The U.S. Army did not abolish segregated units until 1948.

An American Empire Is Born

On December 10, 1898, the United States and Spain signed the Treaty of Paris. Cuba was given its freedom as promised. The United States acquired Guam and Puerto Rico, and paid $20 million for the Philippines. This treaty made the United States an imperial power.

The Debate Over Annexation Some Americans supported the annexation of the Philippines. They believed that the Philippines would provide a naval base in Asia, a stopover on the way to China, a large market for American goods, and the ability to teach "less civilized" people how to live properly. Others feared that cheap Filipino labor would drive down wages. Still others believed that imperialism went against American principles of freedom and sovereignty.

Rebellion in the Philippines Controlling its new empire was not easy for the United States. Emilio Aguinaldo, a Filipino revolutionary, ordered his troops to attack American soldiers. The U.S. Army set up reconcentration camps to separate the rebels from the people who supported them, resulting in the deaths of thousands of Filipinos.

Meanwhile, William Howard Taft, the first U.S. civilian governor of the Philippines, introduced reforms in education, transportation, and healthcare to try to win over the Filipino people. Eventually, in 1946, the United States granted independence to the Philippines.

Governing Puerto Rico In 1900, Congress passed the Foraker Act, making Puerto Rico an unincorporated territory. Congress gradually allowed the people a degree of self-government. In 1917, Puerto Ricans were made citizens of the United States. In 1947, the island was allowed to elect its own governor. The debate continues today over whether Puerto Rico should become a state, an independent country, or remain a commonwealth of the United States.

Cuba and the Platt Amendment After the war, the United States set up a military government in Cuba. To ensure that Cuba would remain tied to the United States, McKinley set up conditions for its independence. These conditions became known as the **Platt Amendment**.

CORE CONCEPTS: NEEDS AND WANTS

William Howard Taft's reforms in the Philippines slowly lessened Filipino hostility toward American rule. New railroads, bridges, and telegraph lines strengthened the economy. A public school system was set up, and new healthcare policies virtually eliminated severe diseases such as cholera and small-pox.

Included in the Amendment:

- Cuba could not make a treaty with another nation that would weaken its power or allow another foreign power to gain territory in Cuba.

- Cuba had to allow the United States to buy or lease naval stations in Cuba.

- Cuba's debts had to be kept low to prevent foreign countries from landing troops to enforce payment.

- The United States would have the right to intervene to protect Cuban independence and keep order.

SECTION 3 NEW AMERICAN DIPLOMACY

Theodore Roosevelt's Rise to Power

In the 1900 election, President McKinley asked Theodore Roosevelt to run as his vice president. McKinley won, but was assassinated in September of 1901. Theodore Roosevelt became the youngest person to become president.

Roosevelt was an energetic president. He believed that the United States had a duty to shape the "less civilized" parts of the world. He wanted the United States to become a world power.

American Diplomacy in Asia

By 1899, the United States was a major power in Asia. The United States was very interested in developing trade within the continent. By 1900, American exports to China had quadrupled.

The Open Door Policy In 1894 China and Japan went to war over Korea, which was part of the Chinese empire. Japan won the war. In the peace treaty, China gave Korea independence and gave Japan some territory in Manchuria. The war showed the world that China was weaker than everyone thought.

Japan's increasing power worried Russia, which forced Japan to give back its territory in Manchuria and later made China lease that territory to Russia. This gave Russia control of the territory. Then Germany, France, and Britain each wanted China to lease territory to them. Each part that was leased became the

CORE CONCEPTS: POWER

In 1907 President Roosevelt sent 16 battleships of the new United States Navy, known as the "Great White Fleet," on a voyage around the world to showcase the nation's military might. The tour made a stop in Japan to demonstrate that the United States could and would uphold its interests in Asia. This visit did not help ease the growing tensions between the United States and Japan.

center of a **sphere of influence,** an area where a foreign nation controlled economic development such as railroad building and mining.

These leaseholds worried the United States. The United States proposed an **Open Door policy,** in which all countries would be allowed to trade with China. Secretary of State John Hay called on all countries with leaseholds in China to keep ports open to all nations.

The Boxer Rebellion Meanwhile, secret Chinese societies were working to rid China of foreign control. One of these groups was the Boxers. In 1900 in the Boxer Rebellion, members of the organization seized foreign embassies in Beijing and killed more than 200 foreigners. An international force crushed the rebellion. Some nations wanted to use the rebellion as an excuse to divide China among themselves. This did not happen, however.

A Growing Presence in the Caribbean

LINKING GEOGRAPHY TO HISTORY

Huge quantities of war materials and thousands of troops passed through the Panama Canal during World War II, the Korean War, and the Vietnam War. The strategic location of the canal makes its neutrality critical in times of war.

Roosevelt believed that if the United States displayed its power, it would make other nations think twice about fighting. He believed in the saying "Speak softly and carry a big stick." He applied this "big stick" policy in the Caribbean.

The Panama Canal In 1901, the Hay-Pauncefote Treaty signed by the United States and Great Britain gave the U.S. exclusive rights to build and control a canal across the isthmus in Central America. The United States decided to build a canal through Panama. In 1903 Panama was part of Colombia, which refused Secretary of State John Hay's offer to purchase the land and gain rights to build the canal.

Revolt in Panama Panamanians decided to declare their independence from Colombia and make their own deal with the United States to build the canal. The short uprising against Colombia was supported by the United States, which sent ships to Panama to prevent Colombia from interfering.

The United States recognized Panama's independence, and the two nations signed a treaty to have the canal built. Construction of the 50-mile canal took ten years. It shortened the distance from the Atlantic to the Pacific Ocean by about 8,000 nautical miles. In 1999, control of the canal was transfered to the government of Panama.

The Roosevelt Corollary In 1904, President Roosevelt expanded his **"big stick" diplomacy.** In an address to Congress, he declared the **Roosevelt Corollary** to the Monroe Doctrine. In it, he said the United States would intervene in Latin American affairs when necessary to help keep the Western Hemisphere economically and politically stable. The corollary was first applied to the Dominican Republic when it fell behind in its debt payments to European nations. Latin American nations resented the growing American influence.

President William Howard Taft, Roosevelt's successor, continued Roosevelt's policies. Taft focused more on helping Latin America's industries than on military force. He believed that helping the industries would increase U.S. trade, increase American businesses' profits, and help get Latin American countries out of poverty. Taft's policies became known as **dollar diplomacy.**

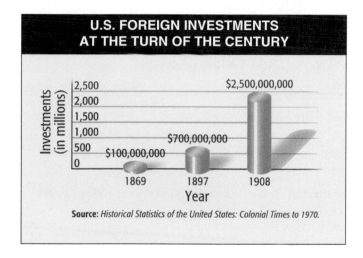

U.S. FOREIGN INVESTMENTS AT THE TURN OF THE CENTURY

Source: *Historical Statistics of the United States: Colonial Times to 1970.*

REGENTS WARM-UP

Past Regents Exams have asked for an interpretation of information on a graph. To practice your graph-reading skills, answer the following questions using the graph:

By how many millions of dollars did U.S. investment in foreign countries increase between 1869 and 1908?

Why do you think such a dramatic increase in foreign investments made the United States feel superior?

REGENTS WARM-UP

Several questions on the Regents Exam focus on your understanding of core concepts and themes in United States history. Reform movements is an example of a core concept. As you read this chapter, note how Progressives worked to reform government so that the government could then work to reform societal problems.

Chapter Overview

Industrialization changed American society. Cities were crowded with new immigrants, working conditions were often bad, and the old political system was breaking down. These conditions gave rise to the Progressive movement. Progressives campaigned for both political and social reforms for more than two decades and enjoyed significant successes at the local, state, and national levels.

As you read through this chapter, ask yourself these questions:
(1) What was the impact of initiative, referendum, and recall, and of the Seventeenth Amendment?
(2) What efforts were made to regulate concentrated corporate power?
(3) Why were Progressives disappointed with President Taft?
(4) What was the legacy of the Progressive movement?

Main Ideas and Concepts

- **Civic Values** Progressive reformers focused on political reforms to try to keep the nation true to its democratic ideals.

- **Presidential Decisions and Actions** Progressive goals were carried to the national level when Theodore Roosevelt became president in 1901.

- **Change** Political differences with Theodore Roosevelt caused President Taft to lose Progressive support.

- **Government** Woodrow Wilson's reforms greatly increased the federal government's role in regulating the nation's economy.

People, Places, Terms

The following names or terms will help you to prepare for the Regents Exam in United States History and Government. You can find an explanation of each name and term in the Glossary at the back of this book, in your textbook, or in another reference source.

arbitration	Nineteenth	referendum
direct primary	Amendment	Square Deal
initiative	prohibition	suffrage
Robert M. La Follette	recall	

SECTION 1 THE ROOTS OF PROGRESSIVISM

The Rise of Progressivism

The era in American history from about 1890 to 1920 is known as the Progressive Era. Progressivism was a collection of ideas and activities focused on fixing the problems within American society. Progressives disagreed among themselves on the solutions, but agreed that the government should take a more active role in solving society's problems caused by urbanization and industrialization.

Progressives believed that the government needed to be fixed and made more responsive to people first, before other problems could be addressed. Progressives also believed that they could fix society's problems by applying scientific principles to society.

Progressives were Democrats and Republicans. Most were urban, educated, middle-class Americans. Many worked as journalists, educators, and politicians.

MUCKRAKERS' FOCUS		
Large Corporations	**Government**	**Social Problems**
Ida Tarbell writes series of articles critical of Standard Oil.	David Graham Philips describes influence of money in the Senate.	Jacob Riis writes How The Other Half Lives, a book that discusses poverty, disease, and crime.
Charles Edward Russell writes about the beef industry.	Lincoln Steffens writes report on vote stealing.	Muckraker articles lead to public debates on social and economic problems.

The Muckrakers Several journalists were the first to express Progressive ideas. These journalists, known as muckrakers, investigated social conditions and political corruption. Their articles led to public debate on social and economic problems and put pressure on politicians to introduce reforms.

Muckraker Jacob Riis focused on social problems in his book *How the Other Half Lives.* The book described poverty, disease, and crime in many immigrant neighborhoods in New York City. Ida Tarbell published articles about unfair practices of the Standard Oil Company, a large corporation.

Making Government Efficient

One group of Progressives believed that problems in society could be solved if government was efficient. They felt that government could become efficient by applying the principles of scientific management. They thought that managing a city required experts, not elected politicians. They wanted to replace the existing system with a commission plan, where a board of commissioners or a city manager with expertise in city services would select and hire specialists to run city departments.

PROGRESSIVES SUPPORT . . .		
Government Reforms	**Business Regulation**	**Social Reforms**
Commission and city-manager forms of government	Consumer protection laws	Child labor laws
The Seventeenth Amendment, which gave voters the right to elect senators directly	The Federal Trade Commission, which was set up to regulate business	Workers' compensation legislation
The Nineteenth Amendment, which gave women the right to vote	The Federal Reserve System, which was set up to control the money supply	The temperance movement, which worked to ban alcohol

Democracy and Progressivism

Some Progressives did not agree with efficiency Progressives. They believed that society needed more democracy, not less. The governor of Wisconsin, **Robert M. La Follette**, criticized how political parties ran their conventions. At the time, party bosses controlled which candidates were chosen to run for office. He pressured the state legislature to require each party to hold a **direct primary**, a party election in which all party members vote for a candidate to run in the general election.

Direct Election of Senators Three new reforms were introduced by Progressives to force state legislators to respond to voters' concerns:

- The **initiative** allowed a group of citizens to introduce legislation and required the legislature to vote on it.

- The **referendum** allowed proposed legislation to be submitted to the voters for approval.

- The **recall** allowed voters to demand a special election to remove an elected official from office.

Another reform affected the federal government. At the time, each state's legislature elected two senators from that state. This system led to corruption. To stop that corruption, Progressives wanted the direct election of senators by all state voters. In 1913, the direct-election amendment, which was suggested by Populists, became the Seventeenth Amendment to the Constitution.

**CORE CONCEPTS:
PRESIDENTIAL
DECISIONS AND
ACTIONS**

The National American
Woman Suffrage Association
supported President Wilson in
the 1916 presidential election.
Although he did not support a
suffrage amendment, he
supported the call for states to
grant women the right to vote.

**CORE CONCEPTS:
CHANGE**

In 1911, a terrible fire swept
through the Triangle
Shirtwaist Company factory
in New York City. Nearly
150 women workers died,
trapped by doors that were
locked from the outside.
Outrage at the deaths caused
New York City to pass strict
building codes dealing with
fire hazards, unsafe machinery, and working conditions.

The Suffrage Movement

The movement for women's voting rights was known as the **suffrage** movement. Suffrage is the right to vote. In 1848, Elizabeth Cady Stanton and Lucretia Mott organized the first women's rights convention. Many Progressives joined the suffrage movement in the late 1800s and early 1900s.

One group of suffragists wanted Congress to pass a constitutional amendment giving women the right to vote. Another group wanted state governments to give women the right to vote. The two groups joined to form the National American Woman Suffrage Association (NAWSA), which used protests to force President Wilson to take action. In 1920 the states ratified the **Nineteenth Amendment**, guaranteeing women the right to vote.

Social Welfare Progressivism

Many Progressives focused on social problems. They created charities to help the poor and disadvantaged, and pushed for laws to help fix social problems. Many adult workers labored in difficult and dangerous conditions. Reformers worked for building codes, workers' compensation laws, zoning laws, and health codes, to make working environments safer. Many also believed alcohol was the cause of many of society's problems. The temperance movement at first worked to reduce alcohol consumption, but later it pushed for **prohibition**—laws banning the manufacture, sale, and consumption of alcohol.

In 1900, over 1.7 million children under the age of 16 worked outside the home. The National Child Labor Committee worked to end child labor.

Lochner **v.** *New York* In 1905, a bakery owner, Joseph Lochner, was fined by the state of New York for permitting an employee to work more than the legal number of hours as permitted by New York law. Lochner appealed, claiming that the limits set by New York infringed on his right to make contracts. In its decision, the Supreme Court held that, although states have the power to regulate health, safety, and public welfare, the New York law was not within the limits of those areas and infringed on Lochner's right to make employment contracts.

Muller **v.** *Oregon* In 1903, Oregon passed a law prohibiting women from working in factories more than ten hours a day. Curt Muller was sued for making a female employee work more than ten hours. He took his case to the Supreme Court, arguing that the Oregon law was unconstitutional. The Supreme Court, however, disagreed, saying that the law took into account the physical differences between men and women. The Court distinguished this case from its Lochner decision based on that reasoning.

Progressives Versus Big Business

A group of Progressives focused on regulating big business, but they disagreed on the solutions. One side believed government should break up big companies to restore competition. The other group wanted the creation of government agencies to regulate big companies and prevent them from abusing their power.

A small minority of Progressives supported socialism, a system in which the government owns and operates industry for the community. Socialism gained some support at the national level. Eugene Debs led the American Socialist Party and was the party's candidate in the 1912 presidential election. However, most Progressives and most Americans believed in the system of free enterprise.

SECTION 2 ROOSEVELT IN OFFICE

Roosevelt Revives the Presidency

During his second term, Theodore Roosevelt's reform program was known as the **Square Deal**. As a Progressive and a Social Darwinist, he felt the government should try to balance the needs of all the groups in American society. He also felt the country needed to be an efficient society that could compete successfully with other nations.

Roosevelt Takes On the Trusts During Roosevelt's first year in office, a fight began over control of the Burlington Railroad. It involved the owners of two other railroad companies. The conflict almost caused a financial crisis. Then the owners agreed to form a new holding company called Northern Securities.

Northern Securities Company v. United States Roosevelt believed that Northern Securities violated the Sherman Antitrust Act, and he ordered a lawsuit filed. The issue before the Court was whether the United States had the authority to regulate the company's effort to eliminate competition. In 1904, the Supreme Court ruled that Northern Securities had violated the Sherman Antitrust Act and unreasonably restricted interstate commerce. It also ruled that the law could apply to any attempts by railroads to eliminate competition.

CORE CONCEPTS: PRESIDENTIAL DECISIONS AND ACTIONS

By intervening in the coal-mining dispute, President Roosevelt used presidential power in a new way. He took the first step toward establishing the federal government as a broker between powerful groups in society.

The Coal Strike of 1902 The United Mine Workers union called a strike of the miners who dug coal. About 150,000 workers from the mines of eastern Pennsylvania demanded a pay increase, reduction in work hours, and recognition for their union. The strike went on for months, threatening a coal shortage as winter approached. Roosevelt urged the union and owners to accept **arbitration**, a settlement imposed by an outside party. The union agreed but the owners did not. Mine owners finally agreed after Roosevelt threatened to have the army run the mines.

Congress Follows Roosevelt Roosevelt believed that most trusts benefited the economy. He did not want to break them up, but he did want to investigate them. In 1903 he convinced Congress to create the Department of Commerce and Labor. Within the department was the Bureau of Corporations, which had the authority to investigate corporations and issue reports on their activities. In 1906 Roosevelt pushed Congress to pass the Hepburn Act. This act was designed to strengthen the Interstate Commerce Commission by giving it the power to set railroad rates and make sure companies did not compete unfairly with each other.

Social Welfare Action

In the early 1900s, consumer protection had become a national issue. Practices in the pharmaceutical and food industries had become serious threats to Americans, forcing new legislation.

In 1906, Upton Sinclair's book *The Jungle* described his observations of unsanitary conditions in meatpacking plants. As a result, the government passed the Meat Inspection Act, which required federal inspection of meat sold and set standards of cleanliness in meatpacking plants. The Pure Food and Drug Act prohibited the manufacture, sale, or shipment of impure or falsely labeled food and drugs.

Conservation

President Roosevelt was especially influential in environmental conservation. In 1902, he supported the passage of the Newlands Reclamation Act, which authorized the use of federal funds from public land sales to pay for irrigation and land development projects. He appointed Gifford Pinchot to head the United States Forest Service to manage the timber resources in the West. The department created regulations controlling lumbering on federal lands. Roosevelt added millions of acres of land as protected national forests. He established new national parks and federal wildlife reservations.

Roosevelt's Legacy

Roosevelt's actions during his presidency caused Americans to look to the federal government to solve the nation's economic and social problems. Roosevelt also increased the power of the executive branch of government.

NATIONAL GEOGRAPHIC

THE PROGRESSIVE MOVEMENT AND STATE GOVERNMENTS 1889–1912

- Reformers control state legislatures
- Reformers influence state government
- Reformers not effective
- 1900 Date reformers came to power

REGENTS WARM-UP

Past Regents Exams have asked for an interpretation of information on a map. To practice your map-reading skills, answer the following question using the map on this page:

What generalization can you make about the Progressive movement in the Great Plains?

**CORE CONCEPTS:
ENVIRONMENT AND
SOCIETY**

President Taft's conservation-
ist contributions actually
equaled or surpassed those
of Roosevelt. Taft set up the
Bureau of Mines to monitor
the activities of mining
companies, expanded the
national forests, and protected waterpower sites from
private development.

SECTION 3 THE TAFT ADMINISTRATION

Taft Becomes President

With the support of President Roosevelt, William Howard Taft
easily won the presidential election of 1908. Taft, a skillful
administrator and judge, had a slow approach to problem
solving that led to conflicts with the Progressives.

Taft, like many Progressives, believed that high tariffs limited
competition, hurt consumers, and protected trusts. He called
Congress into session to lower tariff rates. Speaker of the House
Joseph G. Cannon had the power to push bills through without
discussion. Many Progressives wanted to unseat him because he
blocked their legislation. Taft stopped the campaign against
Cannon, and in return Cannon pushed the tariff bill through the
House. These actions angered many Progressives.

Taft hired Richard Ballinger as secretary of the interior.
Ballinger tried to make nearly a million acres of public forests
and mineral reserves available for private development. Gifford
Pinchot, the head of the Forest Service, charged Ballinger with
trying to turn over valuable public lands to a private syndicate.
Pinchot then leaked the story to the press. Taft fired Pinchot for
insubordination, or disobedience.

The Progressives felt that Taft had "sold the Square Deal
down the river." In the 1910 elections, Democrats took control of
the House and Democrats and progressive Republicans took
control of the Senate.

SECTION 4 THE WILSON YEARS

The Election of 1912

In the presidential election of 1912, conservative Republicans
supported President Taft as the Republican candidate. Theodore
Roosevelt ran as an independent for the Progressive Party and
was supported by many Progressive Republicans. The
Democrats' candidate was Woodrow Wilson. As the governor of
New Jersey, Wilson had made his state a model of progressive
reform.

New Freedom Versus New Nationalism Although Roosevelt
and Wilson were both Progressives, they approached reform
differently. Roosevelt favored legislation to protect women and

children in the workforce and workers' compensation for those injured on the job. He also wanted a federal trade commission to regulate industry. Roosevelt's programs became known as the New Nationalism.

Wilson's plan, called the New Freedom, supported free enterprise and criticized Roosevelt for a program that Wilson felt supported monopolies. He believed that freedom in the economy was more important than efficiency.

Roosevelt and Taft split the Republican vote in the election, giving the presidency to Wilson.

Regulating the Economy

During Wilson's eight years as president, he issued reforms that affected tariffs, the banking system, and trusts. In 1913 the Underwood Tariff reduced the average tariff on imported goods to about half of what it had been in the 1890s. An important part of the Underwood Tariff was the provision for levying an income tax—a direct tax on the earnings of individuals and corporations.

Economic depressions in the 1800s had caused many small banks to close, wiping out customers' savings. To restore people's confidence in banks, Wilson supported the Federal Reserve Act. Under the Federal Reserve system, banks have to keep a portion of their deposits in a reserve to protect customers' money.

In 1914 Wilson asked Congress to create the Federal Trade Commission (FTC) to monitor American business. The FTC investigated companies and issued "cease and desist" orders against companies involved in unfair trade practices. Progressives in Congress went on to pass the Clayton Antitrust Act. This law banned businesses from charging different customers different prices for the same product. Manufacturers could no longer give discounts to those who bought a large volume of goods.

The Legacy of Progressivism

Like Roosevelt, Wilson expanded the roles of the president and the federal government. Before the Progressive Era, most Americans did not expect the government to pass laws to protect workers or to regulate businesses. By the end of the Progressive Era, Americans looked to the government to play an active role

CORE CONCEPTS: CONSTITUTIONAL PRINCIPLES

The Constitution originally prohibited direct taxes unless they were apportioned among the states on the basis of population. In other words, the states would be paying income tax, not individuals, and states with more people would pay more tax. Passage of the Sixteenth Amendment, however, made it legal for the federal government to tax individuals' income directly. This was another Populist idea that became a reality.

CORE CONCEPTS: HUMAN RIGHTS

The 1905 meeting of African American leaders took place at Niagara Falls and led to a movement known as the Niagara Movement. The activists had to meet on the Canadian side of Niagara Falls because no hotel on the American side would accept them.

in regulating the economy and solving social problems. Through the passage of various programs, Progressives did improve the quality of life for millions of people.

The Progressive movement did not, however, address issues facing African Americans. As a result, in 1905, African American leaders met to demand full political rights and responsibilities and an end to racial discrimination against African Americans. African American leaders believed that voting was absolutely necessary to bring about an end to racial discrimination. The meeting led to the founding of the National Association for the Advancement of Colored People in 1909.

CHAPTER 18   WORLD WAR I AND ITS AFTERMATH

Chapter Overview

The United States reluctantly entered World War I after German submarines violated American neutrality. After the war ended, President Wilson supported the Treaty of Versailles, believing its terms would prevent another war. The U.S. Senate, however, rejected the treaty. It did not want the country to be tied to European obligations. Instead, Americans turned their attention to the difficult adjustment to peacetime.

As you read through this chapter, ask yourself these questions:
(1) What caused World War I?
(2) How was the economy controlled to support the war?
(3) What was the American response to the Treaty of Versailles?
(4) What were the effects of the postwar recession on the United States?

REGENTS WARM-UP

Several questions on the Regents Exam focus on your understanding of core concepts and themes in United States history. Uses of geography is an example of a core concept. As you read this chapter, note how knowledge of the geography of Europe is key to under-standing the issues involved in World War I.

Main Ideas and Concepts

- **Interdependence** Ties with the British influenced American leaders to enter World War I on the side of the Allies.

- **Government** To fight the war, the federal government created new agencies to mobilize the economy, draft soldiers, and build public support.

- **Conflict** American troops played a major role in help-ing end the war, while President Wilson played a major role in the peace negotiations.

- **Change** Economic turmoil and fear of communism made the postwar readjustment period a difficult one for the United States.

People, Places, Terms

The following names and terms will help you to prepare for the Regents Exam in United States History and Government.

You can find an explanation of each name and term in the Glossary at the back of this book, in your textbook, or in another reference source.

armistice	League of Nations	self-determination
Franz Ferdinand	propaganda	Treaty of Versailles
Fourteen Points	reparations	Pancho Villa

SECTION 1 THE UNITED STATES ENTERS WORLD WAR I

Woodrow Wilson's Diplomacy

President Woodrow Wilson opposed imperialism. He did, however, believe that the United States should promote democracy. He wanted a world free from revolution and war. His beliefs were put to the test soon after he took office.

The Mexican Revolution In 1911 a revolution in Mexico forced its leader, Porfirio Díaz, to flee the country. General Victoriano Huerta took over. President Wilson refused to recognize the new government and prevented arms from reaching Huerta. In 1914 Wilson sent marines to seize the Mexican port of Veracruz and overthrow Huerta. Anti-American riots broke out in Mexico. **Pancho Villa** led guerrillas, an armed group that carries out surprise attacks, into New Mexico. A number of Americans were killed. Wilson sent General John J. Pershing and his troops into Mexico to capture Villa. Pershing was unsuccessful.

Many nations criticized Wilson's actions in Mexico, which damaged U.S. foreign relations. However, in his first term Wilson sent the marines into Nicaragua, Haiti, and the Dominican Republic to try to set up governments that he hoped would be democratic and stable.

The Outbreak of World War I

By 1914 conflicts among European nations led to an outbreak of war. The roots of World War I can be traced back to the 1860s, when Prussia began a series of wars in order to unite German states. By 1871 Germany was united. The new German nation changed European politics. France and Germany were enemies. Germany formed the Triple Alliance with Austria-Hungary and Italy. Twelve years later, Russia and France formed the Franco-Russian alliance against Germany and Austria-Hungary.

NATIONAL GEOGRAPHIC   **ALLIANCES IN EUROPE**

Lambert Azimuthal Equal-Area projection

Triple Alliance
Triple Entente
Balkans

Britain remained neutral until the early 1900s, when it began an arms race with Germany. This increased tensions between the two countries, causing the British to join with France and Russia into an alliance called the Triple Entente.

The Balkan Crisis Nationalism, intense pride for one's homeland, was a powerful force in Europe in the late 1800s. An important component of nationalism was **self-determination**, the belief that people who share a common culture should have their own national identity and government. This belief led to a crisis in the Balkans, where different national groups within the Ottoman and Austro-Hungarian empires began to seek independence.

A Continent Goes to War In June 1914, the heir to the Austro-Hungarian throne, Archduke **Franz Ferdinand**, was killed by a Bosnian revolutionary who was a member of a Serbian nationalist group. This act set off a chain of events that led to World War I:

- On July 28, Austria declared war on Serbia.

- On August 1, Germany declared war on Russia, an ally of Serbia.

- Two days later, Germany declared war on France, an ally of Russia.

- When Germany crossed neutral Belgium to invade France, Britain declared war on Germany.

The Allies—France, Russia, Britain, and later Italy—fought for the Triple Entente. Germany and Austria-Hungary joined the Ottoman Empire and Bulgaria to form the Central Powers.

REGENTS WARM-UP

Past Regents Exams have focused on the causes of World War I. As you read this chapter, use a graphic organizer such as the one shown here to keep track of the factors that contributed to the war.

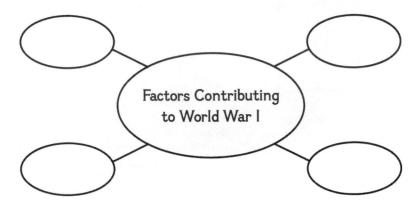

Factors Contributing to World War I

Germany's Plan Fails Germany planned to first conquer France and then focus on Russia. However, Russia quickly mobilized and invaded Germany. When Germany pulled troops out of France to fight the Russians, the Allies took advantage of the situation by stopping the German advance. Both sides became locked in a stalemate that lasted three years. The Central Powers had more success fighting the Russians. They swept across miles of territory and took hundreds of thousands of prisoners.

Americans Take Sides

President Wilson declared the United States to be neutral. However, most of America favored the Allies, for several reasons:

- Wilson's cabinet members believed that an Allied victory would preserve an international balance of power.

- Many Americans valued the heritage, language, and political ideals they shared with Britain, as well as the United States' historic links with France.

- The British skillfully employed **propaganda**, or information used to influence opinion, to gain American support. For example, Germany's harsh treatment of neutral Belgium stirred American sympathy.

- Companies in the United States had strong ties to the Allied countries. Many American banks gave loans to the Allies. The money would be paid back only if the Allies won. As a result, American prosperity was tied to the war.

Moving Toward War

Although most Americans did not want to get involved in the war, several events drew the United States into it.

The British Blockade The British navy blockaded Germany to keep it from getting supplies. The British redefined contraband, or prohibited materials, to stop neutral parties from shipping food to Germany. To get around the blockade, Germany deployed submarines known as U-boats. Germany threatened to sink without warning any ship that entered the waters around Britain. The *Lusitania,* a British passenger liner, was hit by the Germans, killing almost 1,200 passengers, including 128 Americans.

Attacking civilian ships without warning violated an international treaty and outraged the United States. President Wilson demanded that Germany safeguard the lives of civilians and stop U-boat strikes. Not wanting the United States to join the war, Germany promised not to sink any more merchant ships without warning. This promise was called the Sussex Pledge.

The Zimmermann Telegram In January 1917, a German official named Arthur Zimmermann sent a telegram to Mexico. It proposed that Mexico ally itself with Germany in the event of a war between Germany and the United States. In return, Mexico would regain territory it had lost to the United States. British intelligence intercepted the telegram and it was leaked to American newspapers. Furious, Americans concluded that war with Germany was necessary.

The United States Declares War Shortly after the Zimmermann telegram became public, Germany resumed U-boat attacks on merchant ships, including six American merchant ships. President Wilson finally asked Congress to declare war on Germany, which it did on April 6, 1917.

CORE CONCEPTS: IDENTITY, EMPATHY

Although most Americans supported the Allies, many recent immigrants from Germany sided with their homeland. Also, many of the nation's 4.5 million Irish Americans—whose homeland had endured centuries of British rule—sympathized with the Central Powers.

SECTION 2 THE HOME FRONT

Building Up the Military

When the United States entered the war, it was necessary to recruit more soldiers. Many Progressives believed that conscription, or forced military service, was against democratic principles. A new system of conscription, called selective service, required all men between the ages of 21 and 30 to register for the draft. A lottery then randomly decided the order in which they were called to service.

African Americans in the War African American soldiers faced discrimination and prejudice within the army, where they served in racially segregated units under the control of white officers. Many African Americans won praise from their commanders and received war medals.

Women in the Military World War I was the first war in which women officially served. The navy enlisted about 11,000 women, whose jobs included clerics, radio operators, electricians, pharmacists, photographers, chemists, and torpedo assemblers. The army, refusing to enlist women, hired them as temporary employees to fill clerical positions. Army nurses were the only women in the military to go overseas during the war.

Organizing Industry

President Wilson and Congress agreed that the government should not control the economy. Instead, they wanted to establish a cooperative relationship between big business and government to ensure efficient use of resources during the mobilization of the American economy for war.

The War Industries Board In 1917 the War Industries Board (WIB) was created to coordinate the production of war materials. The WIB worked with business leaders, telling industries what they could and could not make.

Food and Fuel The Food Administration, under the direction of Herbert Hoover, was responsible for increasing food production while reducing consumption. Hoover asked people to raise their own vegetables in order to leave more food for the troops. The Fuel Administration encouraged people to conserve coal and oil. Daylight savings time was introduced to conserve energy.

CORE CONCEPTS: DIVERSITY

Although they faced discrimination within their own army, African American soldiers at the battlefront received a warm reception from their French allies. One African American soldier wrote: "I have never before experienced what it meant really to be free, to taste real liberty, in a phrase, 'to be a man.' "

CORE CONCEPTS: SCARCITY

Instead of rationing food during the war, the Food Administration encouraged people to save food on their own. It asked Americans to serve "just enough," and to have Wheatless Mondays, Meatless Tuesdays, and Porkless Thursdays. The Fuel Administration asked people to observe Heatless Mondays.

Paying for the War To raise money to pay for the war, the government raised income taxes and created new taxes. It also borrowed money from the American people through Liberty Bonds and Victory Bonds. By buying bonds, Americans were loaning the government money that would be repaid with interest in a specified number of years.

Mobilizing the Workforce

To prevent workers from striking during the war, the government established the National War Labor Board in 1918. In exchange for wage increases, an eight-hour workday, and the right to organize unions and bargain collectively, labor leaders agreed not to disrupt war production with a strike.

Women Support Industry The war increased the need for women in the workforce. They took factory and manufacturing jobs and positions in the shipping and railroad industries. After the war, women returned to their previous jobs or left the workforce.

African Americans Head North With the flow of European immigrants cut off and large numbers of white workers being drafted, the war opened new doors for African Americans. Between 300,000 and 500,000 African Americans left the South to settle in the North. This "Great Migration" changed the racial makeup of many northern cities.

Ensuring Public Support

Selling the War The government wanted to make sure that the public supported the war. It set up an agency called the Committee on Public Information (CPI) to "sell" the idea of war to the American people. Pamphlets and speeches helped deliver patriotic messages.

Civil Liberties Curtailed Espionage, or spying to acquire secret government information, was addressed in the Espionage Act of 1917. It set up consequences for people who aided the enemy. The Sedition Act of 1918 went a step further by making it illegal to criticize the president or the government.

A Climate of Suspicion Suspicions of disloyalty led to the mistreatment of German Americans. Anti-German feelings sometimes led to violence. Radical labor activists, socialists, pacifists, and anyone appearing disloyal also came under attack.

CORE CONCEPTS: CONSTITUTIONAL PRINCIPLES

The First Amendment specifically states that Congress shall make no law abridging freedom of speech, or of the press. However, the Supreme Court did abridge such freedoms in its ruling on *Schenck* v. *United States*. The Court used as an example of dangerous speech someone untruthfully yelling, "Fire!" in a crowded theater.

The Supreme Court Limits Free Speech In 1917, two people were convicted of violating the Espionage Act. The defendants in the case had distributed leaflets promoting draft resistance. They argued that their First Amendment right to free speech was violated by their conviction. In *Schenck* v. *United States*, the Supreme Court ruled that an individual's freedom of speech could be curtailed if the words spoken created a "clear and present danger." According to the Court, many things that could be said in peacetime might be dangerous during wartime.

SECTION 3 A BLOODY CONFLICT

Combat in World War I

Methods used to wage war changed in World War I. Troops began using rapid-fire machine guns. They also dug trenches as a means of protection from modern weapons. The space between opposing trenches was called "no man's land." Soldiers would charge out of the trenches and race across no man's land to throw grenades into the opposing trenches. This inefficient military move made soldiers easy targets. In major battles, both sides lost hundreds of thousands of men.

New Technology Both sides used new technology in their warfare. Poison gas, first used by the Germans, caused vomiting, blindness, and suffocation. The British introduced the tank, which could roll over barbed wire and trenches. Airplanes were first used in World War I to observe enemy activities, drop bombs, and engage in air battles.

The Americans and Victory

About two million American soldiers, or "doughboys," fought in World War I. Although they were mostly inexperienced, they boosted the morale of the Allied forces.

Winning the War at Sea To avoid having troop ships sunk on their way to Europe, the admiral of the U.S. Navy proposed convoys. Troop ships and merchant ships traveled in large groups, escorted by warships. This system reduced the number of ships lost and ensured that American troops reached Europe safely.

Russia Leaves the War In 1917 riots broke out in Russia over the government's handling of the war. Food and fuel were scarce. When the provisional government set up after the abdication of the czar continued Russia's participation in World

War I, Vladimir Lenin, leader of the Bolshevik Party, overthrew the government and replaced it with a Communist one. Lenin pulled Russia out of the war and agreed with Germany to sign the Treaty of Brest-Litovsk. In exchange for some Russian territory, Germany agreed to remove its army from Russian lands. This helped Germany, which was now free to concentrate its troops on the Western Front of the war.

The German Offensive Falters In March of 1918, Germany launched a massive attack along the Western Front and pushed deeply into Allied lines. But American and French troops blocked the German attack of Paris and held their ground.

The Battle of the Argonne Forest In September of 1918, the American forces launched a massive attack between the Meuse Rive and the Argonne Forest. One German position after another fell to the advancing American troops. By early November, the Americans had shattered the German defenses.

The War Ends On November 11, 1918, Germany finally signed an **armistice**, or cease-fire, that ended the war.

A Flawed Peace

In January 1919, leaders of the victorious Allied nations met to resolve the issues caused by the war. President Wilson's peace plan was called the **Fourteen Points**. The fourteenth point called for an association of nations to be known as the **League of Nations**. The purpose of the League would be to preserve the peace and prevent future wars.

The World Court The establishment of the League of Nations also provided for a World Court that was authorized to make judgments on disputes between nations. However, the nations had to voluntarily submit to the court's authority. The United States never joined the Court because the Senate never ratified the provisions that authorized it. The World Court became the International Court of Justice when the United Nations replaced the League of Nations in 1945.

The Treaty of Versailles The other Allied governments felt Wilson's plan was too lenient toward Germany. The final peace plan, called the **Treaty of Versailles**, weakened or discarded many of Wilson's proposals and treated Germany more harshly than Wilson had proposed. The treaty stripped Germany of its armed forces and made it pay **reparations**, or war damages, in the amount of $33 billion to the Allies. It also required Germany to accept blame for the devastation caused by the war.

CORE CONCEPTS: JUSTICE

President Wilson's Fourteen Points plan was based on "the principle of justice to all peoples and nationalities." Among other things, the plan proposed to eliminate the general causes of war through free trade, disarmament, freedom of the seas, self-determination, and open diplomacy instead of secret agreements.

CORE CONCEPTS: FOREIGN POLICY

Senator Henry Cabot Lodge feared that membership in the League of Nations would hamper the nation's freedom to act independently. He said: "The United States is the world's best hope, but if you fetter her . . . through quarrels of other nations, if you tangle her in the intrigues of Europe, you will destroy her powerful good, and endanger her very existence."

The Senate Rejects the Treaty The Treaty of Versailles was opposed by many United States lawmakers. Instead, the United States negotiated separate peace treaties with each of the Central Powers. A group of senators also rejected membership in the League of Nations, fearing that such an alliance would force the United States to fight in numerous foreign conflicts. The League of Nations, though proposed by President Wilson, took shape without the participation of the United States.

SECTION 4   THE WAR'S IMPACT

An Economy in Turmoil

After World War I ended, the U.S. government removed the controls it had placed on the economy during the war. People quickly bought goods, and businesses increased their prices. Rapid inflation resulted, increasing the cost of living—the cost of food, clothing, shelter, and other essentials people need.

Inflation Leads to Strikes While workers needed higher wages, companies wanted to lower wages due to an increase in operating costs. But membership in labor unions had increased greatly during the war, and unions had become well organized. Business groups associated all labor activity with the work of Communist or radical groups. Business leaders wanted to break the power of unions. The situation resulted in a huge wave of strikes in 1919:

- General strikes—strikes that involve all workers living in a general location, not just workers in a certain industry—worried Americans. Such strikes by Communists and other radicals were common in Europe. A general strike in Seattle involved more than 60,000 people and brought the city to a halt for five days.

- The Seattle strike was followed by a police strike in Boston. About 75 percent of the police walked off the job. The governor of Massachusetts, Calvin Coolidge, called in the National Guard to stop looting. When the police tried to return to work, Coolidge fired them, and a new police force was hired to replace them.

- One of the largest strikes in American history took place when 350,000 steelworkers went on strike for higher pay, shorter hours, and recognition of their union. The strike failed and set back the union cause in the steel industry for almost two decades.

Racial Unrest

In the summer of 1919, race riots occurred in many northern cities. They were caused by the return of hundreds of thousands of American soldiers who needed to find employment. African Americans, who had moved north during the war to work, were now competing with whites for jobs and housing. Racism and frustration led to violence.

The Red Scare

Because the Communists had withdrawn Russia from the war, many Americans associated communism with being unpatriotic and disloyal. Business leaders also feared Communist ideology, which challenged the capitalist system of enjoyment of private property and profit. They used the wave of labor strikes in 1919 to fuel fear that Communists or "Reds" might take control. This led to a nationwide panic called the Red Scare.

The postal service intercepted 30 packages that were addressed to political and business leaders and set to explode. One bomb damaged the home of U.S. Attorney General Mitchell Palmer. In response, Palmer set up the General Intelligence Division (now known as the Federal Bureau of Investigation). He organized raids on various radical organizations, although there was no evidence that any of them was responsible for the packages. Most of the people he rounded up were immigrants, who were then deported, or expelled from the country.

An End to Progressivism

In the 1920 election, the Democratic candidate, James M. Cox, ran on the ideals of Progressivism and Internationalism. Wilson had asked that the election be a referendum on the League of Nations. The major issue in the election was isolationism as opposed to internationalism.

The Republican candidate for president, Warren G. Harding, called for a return to "normalcy." He wanted the United States to return to the simpler days before the Progressive Era and World War I. This idea appealed to most Americans, who were tired of the unrest that had overcome the country. Harding won by a landslide.

CORE CONCEPTS: HUMAN RIGHTS

The Palmer raids were often carried out without concern for people's civil rights. Homes were entered without search warrants. People were jailed indefinitely and not allowed to talk to their attorneys.

PRACTICING FOR THE REGENTS

Part I Multiple-Choice Questions

The following multiple-choice questions come from past Regents Examinations. Test your understanding of United States history and geography by answering each of these items. Circle the number of the word or expression that best completes each statement or question. Test-taking tips can be found in the margins for some questions. For additional help, see Taking the Regents Exam on pages ix–xxxi of this Review Book.

1   Which United States foreign policy was most directly related to the rise of big business in the late 1800s?
    (1) containment
    (2) imperialism
    (3) détente
    (4) neutrality

2   The Interstate Commerce Act and the Sherman Antitrust Act were passed by Congress to
    (1) increase safety in the workplace
    (2) promote fair hiring practices
    (3) improve working conditions
    (4) protect the interests of small businesses

3   A goal of the Granger and Populist movements was to
    (1) expand rights for African Americans
    (2) help western farmers fight unjust economic practices
    (3) provide support for the banking industry
    (4) enable big business to expand without government interference

4   The Populist and Progressive movements were similar in their approaches to reform in that both
    (1) supported the return of powers to the state governments
    (2) promoted the use of violent strikes and protests against big business organizations
    (3) opposed the strict *laissez-faire* attitudes of the federal government
    (4) lobbied for immediate social and economic equality for African Americans

5   In the late 19th century, the major argument used by labor union leaders against immigrants was that immigrants
    (1) took jobs from United States citizens
    (2) contributed little to enrich American life
    (3) placed financial drains on social services
    (4) refused to assimilate into American culture

6   Dorothea Dix, Jane Addams, and Jacob Riis were all known as
    (1) muckrakers
    (2) suffragettes
    (3) political leaders
    (4) social reformers

7   During the 1890s, Joseph Pulitzer and William Randolph Hearst used yellow journalism to generate public support for the
    (1) election of Populist candidates
    (2) presidential candidacy of William McKinley
    (3) goals of workers in the Pullman strike
    (4) Spanish-American War

8   During the late 19th century, Samuel Gompers, Terence Powderly, and Eugene Debs were leaders in the movement to
    (1) stop racial segregation of Native American Indians
    (2) limit illegal immigration
    (3) gain fair treatment of Native American Indians
    (4) improve working conditions

9   Reformers of the Progressive Era sought to reduce corruption in government by adopting a constitutional amendment that provided for
    (1) a maximum of two terms for presidents
    (2) term limits on members of Congress
    (3) voting rights for African Americans
    (4) direct election of United States senators

10   The 1919 Supreme Court decision in *Schenck* v. *United States* established the "clear and present danger" test as a method of
    (1) controlling the activities of organized crime
    (2) determining the limits of freedom of expression
    (3) limiting the powers of the president during wartime
    (4) establishing qualifications for United States participation in the League of Nations

11   Muckrakers contributed to the rise of Progressivism in the early years of the 20th century by
    (1) challenging big government and urging a return to past conditions
    (2) exposing widespread corruption in business and government
    (3) writing favorable biographies about wealthy Americans
    (4) aligning themselves with the women's suffrage movement

12   Passage of the Pure Food and Drug Act and the Meat Inspection act illustrated the federal government's commitment to
    (1) environmental conservation
    (2) workers' rights
    (3) business competition
    (4) consumer protection

13   Which law was passed as a result of muckraking literature?
    (1) Interstate Commerce Act
    (2) Sherman Antitrust Act
    (3) Meat Inspection Act
    (4) Federal Reserve Act

14 In *How the Other Half Lives*, Jacob Riis
    described the living conditions of
    (1) workers in urban slums
    (2) African Americans in the segregated
         South
    (3) the rich in their mansions
    (4) Native American Indians on
         reservations

15 What was a significant impact of the
    Progressive movement on American
    life?
    (1) increased government regulation of
         business
    (2) increased restrictions on presiden-
         tial powers
    (3) decreased influence of the media on
         public policy
    (4) reduced government spending for
         social programs

16 Which action can the Federal Reserve
    System take to fight inflation or
    recession?
    (1) authorize deficit spending
    (2) alter the tariff rates
    (3) adjust the money supply
    (4) require a balanced federal budget

17 The "big stick" policy and dollar
    diplomacy were attempts to
    (1) increase United States power in
         Latin America
    (2) contain the spread of communism
         in eastern Europe
    (3) protect free trade on the Asian
         continent
    (4) strengthen political ties with
         western Europe

18 During the late 19th and early 20th
    centuries, the intervention of the United
    States in Latin American was motivated
    mainly by a desire to
    (1) reduce the influence of communism
    (2) control Latin American indepen-
         dence movements
    (3) promote European colonization of
         the area
    (4) protect growing United States
         investments in Latin America

19 Which statement best summarizes
    President Theodore Roosevelt's views
    about conservation?
    (1) Environmental issues are best
         decided by the private sector.
    (2) Unlimited access to natural
         resources is the key to business
         growth.
    (3) Wilderness areas and their
         resources should be protected for
         the public good.
    (4) Decisions about the use of natural
         resources should be left to the states.

20 Which long-awaited goal of the
    women's rights movement was
    achieved during the Progressive Era?
    (1) right to vote
    (2) right to own property
    (3) equal pay for equal work
    (4) equal access to employment and
         education

21 When Susan B. Anthony refused to pay
    a fine for voting illegally in the election
    of 1872, she stated: "Not a penny shall
    go to this unjust claim." Her action was
    an example of
    (1) anarchy
    (2) judicial review
    (3) civil disobedience
    (4) vigilante justice

Base your answers to questions 22 and 23 on the speakers' statements below and on your knowledge of social studies.

Speaker A: "The [African American] demands equality—political equality, industrial equality, and social equality; and he is never going to be satisfied with anything less."

Speaker B: "Equal but separate accommodations for the white and colored races is for the preservation of the public peace and good order."

Speaker C: "Vocational training will provide the means for African Americans to gain the civil liberties they deserve."

Speaker D: "The best answer for the equality of the [African American] lies in a return to his homeland in Africa."

22 Which speaker most strongly agrees with the beliefs of W.E.B. Du Bois?
    (1) *A*   (3) *C*
    (2) *B*   (4) *D*

23 Which speaker would most likely support the Jim Crow laws that emerged in the 1890s?
    (1) *A*   (3) *C*
    (2) *B*   (4) *D*

Base your answer to question 24 on the cartoon below and on your knowledge of social studies.

24 Which title best describes the message of this cartoon?
    (1) "Neutrality Is the Best Policy"
    (2) "Isolationism: Our Old Ally"
    (3) "Temptations of the Imperialist Menu"
    (4) "The Dangers of Overeating"

25 Which situation was the immediate
cause of the United States entry into
World War I in 1917?
(1) The League of Nations requested
help.
(2) The *Maine* was blown up in Havana
Harbor.
(3) Nazi tyranny threatened Western
democracy.
(4) German submarines sank United
States merchant ships.

26 Which argument did President
Woodrow Wilson use to persuade
Congress to enter World War I?
(1) making the world safe for democracy
(2) retaliating against the Japanese
bombing of Pearl Harbor
(3) assisting the neutral nations with
their defense
(4) removing the Nazi threat from the
Western Hemisphere

27 Why did the Senate reject the Versailles
Treaty (1919)?
(1) to keep the United States free from
foreign entanglements
(2) to express opposition to the harsh
sanctions imposed on Germany
(3) to avoid the dues for membership in
the League of Nations
(4) to reduce United States military
forces in Europe

Part II   Thematic Essay Question

The following thematic essay question comes from past Regents Examinations. Write your answers on a separate sheet of paper. Essay-writing tips appear in the margin. For additional help, see Taking the Regents Exam on pages ix–xxxi of this Review Book.

Directions: Write a well-organized essay that includes an introduction, several paragraphs addressing the task below, and a conclusion.

Theme: Social Change

> Events have influenced social change in American society.

Task: Identify *one* event in United States society that has influenced *social* change, and for the event identified:

> • Discuss the historical circumstances surrounding the event
> • Show how the event was intended to bring about specific social change
> • Evaluate the extent to which the event was successful in bringing about that change

You may use any example from your study of United States history. Some suggestions you might wish to consider include passage of the Civil War amendments; development of the automobile; passage of the Eighteenth Amendment [national Prohibition]; passage of the Nineteenth Amendment [women's suffrage]; passage of the Social Security Act (1935); President Dwight D. Eisenhower's decision to send troops to Little Rock, Arkansas; and the Supreme Court's decision in *Roe* v. *Wade.*

You are *not* limited to these suggestions.

Guidelines: In your essay, be sure to:

- Address all aspects of the *Task*
- Support the theme with relevant facts, examples, and details
- Use a logical and clear plan of organization
- Introduce the theme by establishing a framework that is beyond a simple restatement of the *Task* and conclude with a summation of the theme

Part III   Document-Based Questions

This exercise is designed to test your ability to work with historical documents. It is similar to the document-based questions that you will see on the Regents Examination. While you are asked to analyze five historical documents, the exercise on the actual exam will include more documents. Some of the documents have been edited for the purposes of the question. As you analyze the documents, take into account the source of each document and any point of view that may be presented in the document.

Historical Context: The Progressive movement that began in the late 1800s was an attempt to bring about governmental reforms and to correct injustices in American life.

Task: Using information from the documents and your knowledge of United States history, answer the questions that follow each document in Part A. Your answers to the questions will help you write the Part B essay in which you will be asked to:

- Discuss specific problems or injustices that were present in American life during the late 1800s and early 1900s
- Explain how reforms proposed during the Progressive Era attempted to address these problems

Part A Short-Answer Questions

Directions: Analyze the documents and answer the short-answer questions that follow each document.

Document 1

Our laws should be so drawn as to protect and encourage corporations which do their honest duty by the public and discriminate sharply against [regulate] those organized in the spirit of mere greed, for improper speculative purpose.

— Theodore Roosevelt (1900)

1   What did Theodore Roosevelt say should be done to corporations that operate with little or no consideration for the public good?

_____

_____

Document 2

We propose ... "effective legislation to prevent industrial accidents, occupational
diseases, overwork, and unemployment ... to fix minimum standards of health and
safety in industry ... and to provide a living wage throughout industry. ..."

— Progressive Party platform (1912)

2   State *two* reforms that were proposed in the Progressive Party platform of 1912.

    (1) _____

    _____

    (2) _____

    _____

Document 3

Bosses of the Senate

Source: *A Political Cartoon History of the United States*, Scott Foresman (adapted)

3   According to the cartoon, who were the "Bosses of the Senate"?

_____

_____

Document 4

> The Senate of the United States shall be composed of two senators from each state, chosen by the legislature thereof, for six years; and each senator shall have one vote.
>
>   —United States Constitution (1787)
>
> The Senate of the United States shall be composed of two senators from each state, elected by the people thereof, for six years; and each senator shall have one vote.
>
>   — Seventeenth Amendment to the United States Constitution (1913)

4   How did the Seventeenth Amendment make the selection of United States senators more democratic?

_____

_____

Document 5

> The preamble of the Federal Constitution says: "We, the people of the United States. . . ."
> It was we, the people; not we, the white male citizens; nor yet we, the male citizens; but
> we, the whole people, who formed the Union. And we formed it, not to give the blessings
> of liberty, but to secure them; not to the half of ourselves and the half of our posterity, but
> to the whole people — women as well as men."
>
>   — Susan B. Anthony

5   What argument was used by Susan B. Anthony to support the demand that women be
      given the right to vote?

_____

_____

Part B Essay

Directions: Write a well-organized essay that includes an introduction, several paragraphs, and a conclusion. Use evidence from the five documents in your essay. Support your response with relevant facts, examples, and details. Include additional outside information.

Historical Context: The Progressive movement that began in the late 1800s was an attempt to bring about governmental reforms and to correct injustices in American life.

Task: Using information from the documents and your knowledge of United States history and geography, write an essay in which you:

> • Discuss specific problems or injustices that were present in American life during the late 1800s and early 1900s
> • Explain how reforms proposed during the Progressive Era attempted to address these problems

Guidelines: In your essay, be sure to:

- Address all aspects of the *Task* by accurately analyzing and interpreting the *five* documents
- Incorporate information from the documents in the body of the essay
- Incorporate relevant outside information
- Support the theme with relevant facts, examples, and details
- Use a logical and clear plan of organization
- Introduce the theme by establishing a framework that is beyond a simple restatement of the *Task* or *Historical Context* and conclude with a summation of the theme

UNIT 5   BOOM AND BUST, *1917–1940*

Unit 5 Overview

After World War I, the United States enjoyed a time of prosperity and confidence. The decade of the 1920s saw rising stock prices and increased consumer spending. It also witnessed cultural innovations such as jazz music and motion pictures. At the end of the 1920s, however, several economic problems combined to trigger the Great Depression that began in 1929. Understanding the events of these decades will help you understand American society today.

Unit 5 Objectives

1. Explain the increase in African American political activism.

2. Analyze the growing economic crisis in farming in the 1920s.

3. Identify the causes of the Great Depression.

4. Evaluate President Hoover's attempts to revive the economy.

5. Discuss Franklin Roosevelt's early political career.

6. List three programs of the First New Deal that provided jobs for the unemployed.

7. Analyze how the New Deal affected Americans' sense of security and their attitude toward the role of government.

PREPARING FOR THE REGENTS

This entire book is set up to help you grasp the facts, main ideas, and concepts needed to do well on your Regents Exam. Notes in the margin include core concepts, test-taking tips, and more. Use blank spaces in the margins to answer questions raised in the text or to jot down key points. Before each unit of study, skim through the exams at the back of the book to develop a sense of what your state wants you to know about your nation.

Chapter Overview

The 1920s was an era of rapid change and clashing values. Many Americans believed society was losing its traditional values, and they took action to preserve these values. Other Americans embraced new values associated with a freer lifestyle and the pursuit of individual goals. Writers and artists pursued distinctively American themes, and the Harlem Renaissance gave African Americans new pride. The 1920s left permanent legacies to American culture. During this era, national celebrities emerged in sports and film. Jazz music became part of American culture. F. Scott Fitzgerald and Ernest Hemingway wrote classics of American literature.

As you read through this chapter, ask yourself these questions:
(1) What led to a resurgence in racism and nativism in the 1920s?
(2) What effects did sports, movies, radio, and music have on popular culture in the United States during the 1920s?
(3) What impact did the Harlem Renaissance have on U.S. society?
(4) What factors led to the increase in African American political activism?

CORE CONCEPTS: CHANGE

Women gained new political power in 1920 with passage of the Nineteenth Amendment, giving them the right to vote. Many women who had stepped in to fill the gap in the labor force caused by World War I were reluctant to leave their jobs behind when the fighting men returned. Women increasingly entered the work force, gaining a new freedom.

Main Ideas and Concepts

- **Change** The rapid changes of the early 1900s challenged Americans who wanted to preserve so-called traditional values.

- **Culture** American culture in the 1920s saw a rise in both the arts and popular entertainment.

- **Individuals, Groups, Institutions** African Americans played stronger political and cultural roles in the 1920s than they had in previous decades.

People, Places, Terms

The following names and terms will help you to prepare for the Regents Exam in United States History and Government. You can find an explanation of each name and term in the Glossary at the back of this book, in your textbook, or in another reference source.

Emergency Quota Act	Great Migration	nativism
evolution	Harlem Renaissance	police powers
Fundamentalism	Ku Klux Klan	Sacco-Vanzetti case

SECTION 1 A CLASH OF VALUES

Nativism Resurges

At the start of the 1920s, an economic recession, an influx of immigrants, and racial and cultural tensions combined to create an atmosphere of disillusion and intolerance. Anti-immigrant feelings increased, leading to the growth of racism and **nativism**, the desire to protect the interests of old-stock Americans against those of immigrants. Many Americans viewed immigrants as a threat to the traditional American society. The arrival of millions of immigrants appeared to pose a threat to the four million American servicemen and women who had returned from World War I and who were searching for work in an economy with soaring unemployment and rising prices.

The Sacco-Vanzetti Case In the 1920s, the majority of immigrants came from southern and eastern Europe. They faced ethnic and religious prejudices. The **Sacco-Vanzetti case** is an example of this discrimination. On April 15, 1920, two armed men killed two employees of a factory in Massachusetts and robbed the company of its payroll. Two Italian immigrants—Nicola Sacco and Bartolomeo Vanzetti—were arrested for the crime. Newspapers reported that the two immigrants were anarchists, those who opposed all forms of government, and that Sacco owned a gun similar to the murder weapon. Although no one at the time knew whether the two men were guilty, many people concluded that they were guilty because they were Italian immigrants and anarchists. Other people believed that the case was an example of prejudice against people based on their ethnic origin. In July 1921, Sacco and Vanzetti were found guilty and sentenced to death. They were executed six years later, maintaining their innocence to the end.

Red Scare Fear of Communism grew during this period. The precursor to the FBI, the General Intelligence Division, was established to investigate potential revolutionaries. However, the agents often disregarded the civil liberties of the suspects. Officers entered homes and offices without search warrants. People were mistreated and jailed for indefinite periods of time and were not allowed to talk to their lawyers. When these raids failed to turn up any hard evidence of revolutionary conspiracy, people eventually turned against them.

Return of the Ku Klux Klan At the forefront of the movement to restrict immigration was the **Ku Klux Klan**, or KKK. The old KKK had flourished in the South after the Civil War and used threats of violence to intimidate newly freed African Americans. After World War I, the Klan targeted immigrants, Catholics, Jews, and other groups they believed did not represent traditional American values. Because of a large public campaign, Klan membership skyrocketed in the 1920s, spreading beyond the South and into Northern and Midwestern cities.

The Klan began to decline in the late 1920s, and its membership shrank. Politicians whom the Klan had supported were voted out of office. The Klan never again had a major impact on politics.

CORE CONCEPTS: IMMIGRATION AND MIGRATION

On occasion, immigration quotas led to the separation of families. If one family member had been born in a country whose quota was still open, and another had been born in a country with a closed quota, the former would be admitted and the latter deported.

Controlling Immigration

After World War I, American immigration policies changed in response to the postwar recession and nativist pleas to "Keep America American."

The Emergency Quota Act of 1921 In 1921 Congress responded to nativist demands to limit immigration by passing the **Emergency Quota Act**. The act limited the number of people admitted in a single year to three percent of the total number of people in any ethnic group already living in the United States as determined in the 1910 census. This provision discriminated against people from southern and eastern Europe.

CONTROLLING IMMIGRATION		
Emergency Quota Act	**National Origins Act of 1924**	**Hispanic Immigration**
Signed by President Harding in 1921	Made immigrant restriction a permanent policy	First wave of Mexican immigration followed Newlands Reclamation Act of 1902
Established a temporary quota system	Tightened the quota system to 2 percent of those already in the U.S.	Newlands Act provided funds for irrigation and farm projects in the American Southwest
Only 3 percent of the total number of people in any ethnic group already in the U.S. could be admitted in a single year	Eventually limited immigrants to 150,000 per year	By 1914, more than 70,000 Mexican immigrants had come to the United States due to the Mexican Revolution and job opportunities in U.S.

The National Origins Act of 1924 In 1924 passage of the National Origins Act made immigration restriction a permanent policy. The law also tightened the quota system by setting quotas at two percent of each national group and moving the year back to 1890, essentially allowing immigration only from northwestern Europe.

Hispanic Immigration The reduction in immigration caused a shortage of workers for agriculture, mining, and railroad work. The National Origins Act exempted immigrants from Western Hemisphere nations from the quota system. More than 600,000 Mexicans arrived in the United States between 1914 and the end of the 1920s.

The New Morality

During the 1920s, a "new morality" took over the nation. The new morality challenged traditional ways of thinking. It stressed youth and personal freedom. Ideals of the loving family and personal satisfaction influenced views on relationships. Romance, pleasure, and friendship became linked to successful marriages. Advice books in the 1920s dispensed such hints as "Have lots of pleasure that both husband and wife enjoy . . . and above all, be good friends."

CORE CONCEPTS: MOVEMENT OF PEOPLE AND GOODS

By 1914 more than 70,000 Mexicans had poured into the United States. Many of them were fleeing the terror and aftermath of the Mexican Revolution of 1910.

CORE CONCEPTS: CULTURE

In addition to "The Jazz Age," the 1920s were also called "The Roaring Twenties" because of people's pursuit of pleasure and fun.

Women in the workforce also began to define the new morality. Many women held jobs simply because they needed the wages for themselves or their families. For some young single women in the 1920s, work was a way to break away from parental authority and establish a personal identity.

The automobile also played a part in the new morality. It gave America's young people more independence and made it easier for them to escape parental control and find new forms of entertainment with their friends.

Women in the 1920s A new fashion look started in the 1920s. Women shortened their hair and wore silk stockings. Glamorous stage and screen stars became popular. A flapper was a young, dramatic, stylish, and unconventional woman who smoked cigarettes and drank alcohol. She also dressed in clothes that at that time were regarded as too revealing.

Other women sought financial independence by joining the workforce, many of them as salesclerks or secretaries. Some made contributions in fields such as science, medicine, law, and literature.

The Fundamentalist Movement

Many Americans feared that the new morality threatened traditional values. To these Americans, the consumer culture, relaxed ethics, and growing urbanism symbolized the nation's moral decline. Many—especially those in small, rural towns—joined a religious movement known as **Fundamentalism**.

Fundamentalist Beliefs Fundamentalists rejected Charles Darwin's theory of **evolution**, which said that human beings had developed from lower forms of life over millions of years. Instead, Fundamentalists believed in creationism—the belief that God created the world as described in the Bible.

The Scopes Trial Evolutionists and creationists eventually clashed. In 1925 Tennessee passed a law that prohibited the teaching of evolution. When John T. Scopes, a biology teacher, taught evolution in his high school in Dayton, Tennessee, he was arrested and put on trial. In the Scopes trial, William Jennings Bryan, a Fundamentalist and former Populist presidential candidate, was the prosecutor. Clarence Darrow defended John Scopes. Scopes was found guilty and fined $100. The conviction was later overturned.

CORE CONCEPTS: CHANGE

During the 1920s women increasingly entered the workforce. In 1920 one out of five employed persons was a woman. By 1950 women accounted for 30 percent of the workforce.

CORE CONCEPTS: SCIENCE AND TECHNOLOGY

Florence Sabin's medical research led to a dramatic drop in death rates from tuberculosis. Public health nurse Margaret Sanger, believing that the standard of living could be improved if families limited the number of children they had, founded the American Birth Control League in 1921. This organization became Planned Parenthood in the 1940s.

THE FUNDAMENTALIST MOVEMENT		
Fundamentalism	**Fundamentalist Beliefs**	**The Scopes Trial**
A religious movement	The Bible is literally true without error	Historic 1925 trial where evolutionists and creationists clashed
The name "Fundamentalism" came from the name of a series of pamphlets	Rejected theory of evolution; embraced theory of creationism as written in the Bible	John T. Scopes volunteered to test the Butler Act, which outlawed any teaching of evolution
Grew as a reaction to the "new morality," which caused Americans to lose their traditional values	Billy Sunday and Aimee Semple McPherson preached traditional religious and moral values	William Jennings Bryan represented creationists; Clarence Darrow defended Scopes; Scopes convicted, but conviction later overturned

Prohibition

Throughout the early 1900s, many people began supporting prohibition—laws banning the manufacture, transportation, and sale of alcoholic beverages. Many Progressives believed that prohibition would reduce unemployment, domestic violence, and poverty. The Eighteenth Amendment, which took effect in January 1920, made prohibition the law.

To enforce the amendment, Congress passed the National Prohibition Act, also known as the Volstead Act. Enforcing Prohibition became the responsibility of the U.S. Treasury department, which greatly expanded the federal government's **police powers**. These are a government's power to control people and property in the interest of public safety, health, welfare, and morals. The Treasury Department's new Prohibition Unit made more than 540,000 arrests, but many Americans persisted in ignoring the law. They went to secret bars called speakeasies, where they could buy alcohol. Organized crime supplied and often ran these speakeasies, which were located all over the country.

CORE CONCEPTS: JUSTICE

Al Capone, one of the most successful and violent gangsters of the era, had many police officers, judges, and other officials on his payroll. Capone dominated organized crime in Chicago. Finally, Eliot Ness, the head of a special Treasury Department task force, brought Capone to justice.

The huge profits that could be made from illegally selling liquor led to smuggling. Smugglers brought liquor into the United States from Canada and the Caribbean. Smuggling and the buying of liquor led to an illegal billion-dollar industry. Violence broke out in the streets as gangs fought to control the liquor trade. Crime became big business. Some gangsters made enough money and had enough power to corrupt local politicians. The Eighteenth Amendment was eventually repealed by the Twenty-first Amendment in 1933.

SECTION 2 CULTURAL INNOVATIONS

Art and Literature

Charles Lindbergh's historic solo flight across the Atlantic Ocean in 1927 symbolized American progress in the modern age. The modern age was reflected strongly in American art, literature, and popular culture. During the 1920s, American artists and writers challenged traditional ideas. They explored what it meant to be "modern," and they searched for meaning in the emerging challenges of the modern world.

The Literary Scene Many novelists, affected by the experiences of World War I, wrote about disillusionment and reevaluated the myths of American heroes. Ernest Hemingway was one such writer. His fiction presented a new literary style characterized by direct, simple, and concise language, and novels such as *A Farewell to Arms* reflected the contempt for the war that many in his generation felt. Edith Wharton received the Pulitzer Prize for her novel *The Age of Innocence*, which described the joys and sorrows of upper class Easterners. Willa Cather depicted life on the prairie in *My Antonia* and *Death Comes for the Archbishop*. F. Scott Fitzgerald, perhaps the most famous writer of the era, exposed the emptiness and superficiality of much of modern society in such novels as *The Great Gatsby*.

Popular Culture

Many Americans in the 1920s had more spending money and more leisure time than ever before, which they devoted to making their lives more enjoyable.

The Rise of Hollywood Motion pictures became very popular. Because sound in films was still not possible, theaters had piano players to provide music during the feature, and subtitles revealed the plot and contained some dialogue. Silent film stars Mary Pickford, Charlie Chaplin, Douglas Fairbanks, and Gloria Swanson became famous. The first "talking" picture—*The Jazz Singer*—came out in 1927.

Popular Radio Shows and Music Radio also had a large following during the Jazz Age. Most radio stations in the 1920s played the popular music of the day, but classical music was also offered. Comedy shows had wide audiences.

In addition to providing entertainment, the mass media—radio, movies, newspapers, and magazines aimed at a broad audience—helped to expand people's view of the world. The mass media helped break down narrow focus on local interests. They fostered a sense of shared national experience that helped unify the country and spread the new ideas of the time.

SECTION 3 AFRICAN AMERICAN CULTURE

The Harlem Renaissance

Many African Americans joined in what was called the **Great Migration**, the movement from the rural South to industrial cities in the North. By moving north, African Americans sought to escape the segregated society of the South, to find economic opportunities, and to build better lives. After World War I, the African American population of large northern cities increased greatly. In the New York City neighborhood of Harlem, African Americans created an environment that stimulated artistic development, racial pride, a sense of community, and political organization. This flourishing of African American arts became known as the **Harlem Renaissance**.

The Writers One of the first important writers of the Harlem Renaissance was Claude McKay, whose verse expressed a proud defiance of and bitter contempt for racism, two major character-istics of Harlem Renaissance writing. Another important writer was poet Langston Hughes, who became a leading voice of the African American experience in the United States. His poem *I, Too* describes the disenfranchisement many African Americans felt in the 1920s, and in *The Negro Speaks of Rivers*, Hughes reveals a profound love of his heritage. Zora Neale Hurston wrote the first major stories featuring African American women as central characters, including her work *Their Eyes Were Watching God*.

CORE CONCEPTS: CULTURE

Radio station WWJ in Detroit was the first to initiate regular radio broadcasting, which began in 1920. In that same year, listeners of station KDKA in Pittsburgh learned the news of Warren G. Harding's landslide victory in the presidential election—the first election results ever broadcast. By 1923 more than 500 radio stations were providing millions of listeners with news reports and music.

LINKING GEOGRAPHY TO HISTORY

Although jazz was an American creation, its roots stretched across the Atlantic Ocean to Europe and Africa. The music Louis Armstrong and Duke Ellington helped to make famous originated from the spirituals and work songs of African slaves. These songs were a blend of African rhythms and European melodies and harmonies. This music evolved into ragtime, which, combined with the blues, became jazz.

Jazz, Blues, and the Theater Shortly after Louis Armstrong arrived in Chicago from New Orleans, he introduced an improvisational, early form of jazz, a style of music influenced by Dixieland music and ragtime. Armstrong broke away from the New Orleans tradition of group playing by performing highly imaginative solos. He became the first great cornet and trumpet soloist in jazz music.

Ragtime also influenced the composer, pianist, and bandleader Duke Ellington. He created his own sound, using a blend of improvisation and different combinations of instruments. Like other African American musicians, Ellington got his start at the Cotton Club, one of the most famous Harlem nightspots. Bessie Smith became famous for singing the blues, a soulful style of music that evolved from African American spirituals. Smith performed with many of the top jazz bands of the era.

African American Politics

The racial pride of African Americans that sparked the artistic achievements of the Harlem Renaissance also affected their political and economic goals. The postwar years saw the development of a new sense of dignity and defiance among African Americans, who forged new roles in life and politics.

The Black Vote in the North The Great Migration had a significant effect on the political power of African Americans in the North. As their numbers increased, African Americans became a powerful bloc that could sometimes sway the outcome of elections. Most African Americans voted for Republicans. In 1928 African American voters in Chicago achieved a significant political breakthrough when they helped elect Oscar DePriest, the first African American representative in Congress from a Northern state.

The NAACP Battles Lynching The National Association for the Advancement of Colored People (NAACP) fought against segregation and discrimination. It did so mainly by lobbying politicians and working through the courts. From its beginning in 1909, the NAACP had lobbied and protested against the horrors of lynching. The group's efforts led to the passage of anti-lynching legislation in the House of Representatives in 1922. Unfortunately, the Senate defeated the bill. The NAACP continued lobbying against lynching throughout the 1920s and 1930s. It worked with organized labor and was successful in defeating the nomination of Judge John J. Parker to the U.S. Supreme Court. Parker was known for his racist and anti-labor positions.

Black Nationalism and Marcus Garvey While some people were fighting for integration and improvement in the economic and political position of African Americans, other groups began to emphasize black nationalism and black pride. Marcus Garvey began to call for black separation from white society. He founded the Universal Negro Improvement Association (UNIA), which worked to promote black pride and unity. The movement's message was that African Americans could gain economic and political power through education. Garvey also believed that African Americans should separate themselves from whites. He told his followers that they would never find justice in the United States and urged them to settle in the African country of Liberia. Many African Americans distanced themselves from Garvey and his push for separation. Although Garvey was not successful in gaining support for his movement, he did instill in millions of African Americans a pride in their heritage and a hope for the future. This reemerged strongly during the 1950s and played a vital role in the civil rights movement of the 1960s.

Chapter Overview

Prosperity was the theme of the 1920s, and national policy favored business. Although farmers were going through an economic depression, others remained optimistic about the economy. The middle class bought on credit the many new convenience products available. One of the most popular purchases of the day was the automobile, which had a major impact on how Americans lived.

Important elements of American life that were first seen at this time had a lasting impact. Today the automobile still remains central to transportation in the United States. Credit—a standard means for making purchases in today's world—increasingly began to be used in the 1920s to buy consumer goods.

As you read through this chapter, ask yourself these questions:
(1) What problems did President Harding face during his administration?
(2) How did Calvin Coolidge restore public confidence after assuming the presidency?
(3) How did the growing importance of the automobile and other new industries improve the standard of living in the United States?
(4) How did Andrew Mellon's strategies for maintaining prosperity encourage economic growth in the United States and how did they contribute to causing the Great Depression?

REGENTS WARM-UP

Essays on Regents Exams often test your understanding of cause-and-effect relationships. As you read this chapter, jot down notes that could be used in a response to this essay item:

Identify *three* factors that helped promote the growth of the economy during the 1920s and discuss how each contributed to this growth.

Main Ideas and Concepts

- **Government** The "Ohio Gang" of the Harding administration were involved in scandals that created political upheaval.

- **Science and Technology** New technology, such as the automobile and radio, helped reshape American lifestyles.

- **Economic Systems** After World War I, the United States had to pay down a large amount of war debt while maintaining economic growth.

People, Places, Terms

The following names and terms will help you to prepare for the Regents Exam in United States History and Government. You can find an explanation of each name and term in the Glossary at the back of this book, in your textbook, or in another reference source.

assembly line	mass production	trickle-down
isolationism	normalcy	economics
Kellogg-	Teapot Dome	welfare
Briand Pact	scandal	capitalism

SECTION 1 PRESIDENTIAL POLITICS

THE HARDING ADMINISTRATION		
Warren G. Harding	**The Ohio Gang**	**The Teapot Dome Scandal**
Became president of the United States in 1920	Group of Harding's poker-playing friends with whom he smoked and drank	Secretary of Interior Albert B. Fall allowed private interests to lease lands belonging to the government
Believed he lacked the intellectual capacity for the job of president	Some used their position and influence to sell government jobs, pardons, and protection from prosecution	Fall received bribes from private interests; bribes exceeded $300,000
His charm and genial manner endeared him to the nation	Harding felt Ohio Gang had betrayed him and complained bitterly	Senate investigated; Fall became first cabinet officer to go to prisoner

The Harding Administration

Warren G. Harding was elected president in 1920. After the horrors of World War I, Americans yearned to go back to simpler and steadier times. Harding tailored his presidency to this goal. He ran on the campaign slogan "Return to **Normalcy**"—a return to "normal" life after the war.

CORE CONCEPTS: PRESIDENTIAL DECISIONS AND ACTIONS

Most historians rank President Warren G. Harding as one of the country's weakest presidents. They believe he failed as president because he was weak-willed and a poor judge of character.

The Ohio Gang Harding made several distinguished appointments to the cabinet, but many other appointments were a disaster. Harding gave many cabinet posts and other high-level jobs to friends and political allies from his native Ohio. These people became known as the Ohio Gang. Some of these appointees used their positions to sell government jobs, pardons, and protection from prosecution. Charles R. Forbes, whom Harding chose to run the Veterans Bureau, sold scarce medical supplies from veterans' hospitals and kept the money for himself.

In June 1923, amid the scandal in the Veterans Bureau and rumors of other unethical behavior, Harding and his wife left Washington to tour the West. On the trip, he fell ill and died, shortly before news of the Forbes scandal became public.

The Teapot Dome Scandal Harding's secretary of the interior, Albert B. Fall, secretly allowed private companies to lease lands at Teapot Dome, Wyoming, and Elk Hills, California, containing U.S. Navy oil reserves. In return, Fall received bribes from these companies totaling more than $300,000. Eventually the Senate investigated what the newspapers named the **Teapot Dome scandal**, and Secretary Fall became the first cabinet officer in U.S. history to go to prison.

The Coolidge Administration

Vice President Calvin Coolidge became president after Harding's death. Coolidge was very different from Harding. His simple and frugal nature came as a welcome change from the Harding administration's corruption.

"Silent Cal" Takes Over Coolidge quickly distanced himself from the Harding administration and worked to restore integrity to the presidency. In the year following Harding's death, Coolidge's presidency avoided scandal and continued to encourage the nation's expanding economy.

Coolidge believed that the country would prosper if business prospered. His focus was on prosperity through business leadership with as little government interference as possible. Coolidge easily won the Republican Party's nomination for president in 1924.

The Election of 1924 The Democrats were divided between supporters from the urban East and those from the rural South and West. As a result, they had a difficult time choosing a candidate. They finally agreed on John W. Davis of West Virginia.

CORE CONCEPTS: GOVERNMENT

The increasing number of women candidates for office distinguished the election of 1924. Women were elected to the governorships of Texas and Wyoming, and 123 were elected to state legislatures.

The Republicans campaigned on the slogan "Keep Cool with Coolidge," and they urged Americans to keep the party that favored business in office.

Some people who did not want to choose between the Republican and Democratic candidates left their parties to form a new Progressive Party to address the reform agenda of the pre-World War I period. They nominated Wisconsin senator Robert M. La Follette as their candidate. He and Davis combined could not keep the Republicans from winning the election. Coolidge won easily with more than half the popular vote.

SECTION 2 A GROWING ECONOMY

The Rise of New Industries

By the 1920s, the automobile had become an accepted part of American life. The automobile was just one part of a rising standard of living that many Americans experienced in the 1920s. These Americans were earning more money than ever before and their wages increased as their work hours decreased.

At the same time, the rise of **mass production**, or large-scale product manufacturing usually done by machinery, made more products available and lowered the cost to the consumers. This formula changed the American economy. Innovation thrived, and new industries emerged.

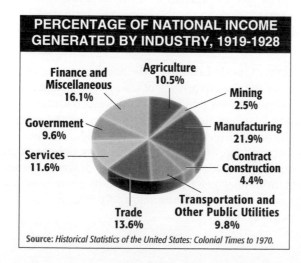

PERCENTAGE OF NATIONAL INCOME GENERATED BY INDUSTRY, 1919-1928

Finance and Miscellaneous 16.1%
Agriculture 10.5%
Mining 2.5%
Government 9.6%
Manufacturing 21.9%
Services 11.6%
Contract Construction 4.4%
Trade 13.6%
Transportation and Other Public Utilities 9.8%

Source: *Historical Statistics of the United States: Colonial Times to 1970.*

CORE CONCEPTS: FACTORS OF PRODUCTION

Henry Ford increased workers' wages and reduced the workday to gain workers' loyalty and to undercut union organizers. Ford's decision to increase his workers' wages also enabled them to buy the cars they were producing and thus contributed further to the prosperity of the Ford Motor Company.

The Assembly Line Another major industrial development enormously increased manufacturing efficiency. First adopted by carmaker Henry Ford in 1913, the **assembly line** divided operations into simple tasks that unskilled workers could do, and cut unnecessary motion to a minimum. After Ford started using this system, the time it took to build a car decreased dramatically. Whereas in 1913 the task had taken 12 hours, in 1924 workers were building an automobile every 93 minutes. By 1925, a Ford car came off the assembly line every 10 seconds.

Ford's assembly-line product was the Model T. In 1908, the Model T's first year, it sold for $850. By 1924, thanks to improved assembly-line methods and the high volume of sales, Model Ts were selling for $295.

The low price of cars created a huge demand. By the mid-1920s other car manufacturers, such as General Motors and Chrysler, were competing with Ford. Auto industry growth spurred growth in other industries, such as rubber, plate glass, nickel, and lead. Automaking took 15 percent of the nation's steel. The number of cars on the roads led to a tremendous expansion of the petroleum industry.

The Social Impact of the Automobile Just as the automobile changed the way manufacturing was done, it also changed American life. The automobile created an increase in small businesses such as garages and gas stations. It eased the isolation of rural life by putting urban areas within reach of people in rural areas, and the countryside within reach of city dwellers. Cars also let people live farther away from work. A new kind of consumer and worker, the auto commuter, appeared. Commuters lived in growing suburban communities and drove to work in the city.

The Consumer Goods Industry Many other new goods came on the market to take advantage of rising disposable income. Americans bought new products such as electric razors and frozen foods. New appliances advertised as labor-savers changed the home. Electric irons, vacuum cleaners, washing machines, and refrigerators changed the way people cleaned their homes and prepared meals. Products designed to appeal to consumers' concerns with fashion and hygiene—such as mouthwash, deodorants, cosmetics, and perfumes—became popular in the 1920s.

The Consumer Society

The higher wages and shorter workdays of Americans in the 1920s gave them increased buying power. Americans now accepted their new role as consumers.

Easy Consumer Credit One notable aspect of the economic boom was the growth of individual borrowing. The apparent prosperity of the 1920s gave many Americans the confidence to go into debt to buy new consumer goods.

Credit had been available before the boom, but most Americans had considered debt to be shameful. Now, however, American attitudes toward debt started changing as people began believing that they would be able to pay back their debts over time. Many racked up debts to buy the family car, radio, furniture, washing machine, and vacuum cleaner. Some started buying on credit at a faster rate than their incomes rose.

Mass Advertising One problem that inventors faced was making people aware of a new product. To create a market, manufacturers turned to advertising, another booming industry in the 1920s. Advertisers created appealing, persuasive messages that linked their clients' products with the ideals of the modern era.

Welfare Capitalism Industrial workers also prospered in the 1920s, partly owing to rising wages and partly because some corporations introduced what came to be called **welfare capitalism**. Companies allowed workers to buy stock, take part in profit sharing, and receive benefits such as medical care and pensions. With benefits covering some of their basic needs, workers were able to spend more of their income on consumer goods.

Benefits programs made unions seem unnecessary to many workers. In the 1920s unions lost both influence and membership. At the time, there was no federal legislation to protect union activity. Employers promoted the open shop—a workplace where employees were not required to join a union.

The Farm Crisis Returns

American farmers did not share in the prosperity of the 1920s. As a group, they earned less than one-third of the average income for workers in the rest of the economy. Technological advances allowed them to produce more but also increased their costs. However, demand for farm products did not increase with the increasing yield, which resulted in lower prices.

REGENTS WARM-UP

To practice your skills at reading a graph, answer the following question:

Approximately how far did farm wages fall between 1920 and 1930?

(1) $35
(2) $15
(3) $20
(4) $10

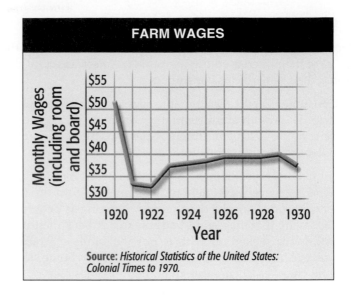

FARM WAGES

Source: *Historical Statistics of the United States: Colonial Times to 1970.*

CORE CONCEPTS: CULTURE

Heavy borrowing on the part of farmers for purchase of land and new technology (such as the gasoline-engine tractor) led to a rise in farm mortgage debt from $7.8 billion in 1920 to $10.8 billion in 1923.

Changing Market Conditions Many factors contributed to this depression in American agriculture. During the war, the government had urged farmers to produce more to meet the great need for food in Europe. Many farmers went deeply into debt to buy new land and new machinery in order to raise more crops. Sales were strong, prices were high, and farmers made money. After the war, however, Europeans began producing more farm products of their own. Debt-ridden European countries had little money to spend on American farm products. Congress unintentionally made matters worse by passing the Fordney-McCumber Act in 1922. This act raised tariffs to protect American industry from foreign competition. Europeans reacted by no longer buying American agricultural products. American farmers could no longer sell as much of their output overseas, and prices fell.

Helping Farmers Some Progressive members of Congress tried to help farmers sell their surplus, calling for the federal government to purchase surplus crops and sell them abroad. The argument was that this would raise the domestic price of crops and help farmers. Congress passed the bill twice, but President Coolidge vetoed it both times. He argued that the bill would encourage farmers to produce even greater surpluses that the government would not be able to sell. As a result, American farmers stayed in recession throughout the 1920s.

SECTION 3 THE POLICIES OF PROSPERITY

Promoting Prosperity

Andrew Mellon became the chief architect of economic policy in the United States in the 1920s. He served as secretary of the treasury in three Republican administrations. His policies encouraged growth and led to a stock market boom, but ultimately contributed to the Great Depression.

The Mellon Program When Mellon took office he had three major goals—to balance the budget, to reduce the government's debt, and to cut taxes. He began by cutting government spending. One major expense was the interest on the national debt. World War I costs had increased the debt from $5.7 billion in 1917 to almost $26 billion by 1920. Mellon refinanced the debt to lower the interest. He also persuaded the Federal Reserve to lower its interest rates as well. These steps helped reduce the debt by $7 billion between 1921 and 1929.

Mellon also worked to reduce tax rates. He believed that lowering taxes would allow businesses and wealthy consumers to spend and invest their extra money. This would cause the economy to grow. As the economy grew, Americans would earn more money. The government would actually collect more taxes at the lower rate than it would if it had kept tax rates high. This idea is known today as **trickle-down** (or supply-side) **economics**. By 1928 Congress had drastically lowered the tax rates.

Mellon's tax policy favored the wealthy investing class and placed the tax burden on the middle and working classes. His trickle-down theory promised that the lower classes would eventually benefit from investment growth. Furthermore, his tax policy had a negative impact on middle and lower class consumption.

Hoover's Cooperative Individualism Other government programs also promoted economic growth. Secretary of Commerce Herbert Hoover tried to balance government regulation with his idea of cooperative individualism. This idea encouraged manufacturers and distributors to form trade associations that would voluntarily share information with the government. These trade associations were devices used to circumvent the Sherman and Clayton Antitrust laws and reflected the Republican alliance with big business—an alliance reminiscent of the 1880s and 1890s.

Trade and Arms Control

Before World War I the United States had owed billions of dollars more to foreign investors than foreigners owed the United States. By the end of the war, the situation had reversed. By the 1920s the United States had become the world's dominant economic power.

Isolationism After the war, most Americans favored **isolationism**. They wanted to be left alone to pursue prosperity. This sentiment had contributed to Harding's victory in 1920 as Americans rejected Wilson's call to make the election a referendum on the League of Nations and internationalism. The United States, however, was too powerful, too economically interconnected with other countries, and too widely involved in international affairs to retreat into isolationism. Although American delegations took part in conferences held by the League of Nations, it was United States policy to promote peace through agreements with individual countries rather than doing so through the League's efforts.

The Dawes Plan The United States' former wartime allies had difficulty repaying their huge war debts. They claimed that the tariffs the American government had placed on European goods closed the United States to European imports, which slowed down Europe's economic recovery. The United States argued that American taxpayers should not have to assume the debts of others. American officials argued further that America's allies had gained new territory as a result of the victory over Germany, while the United States had gained nothing. They also pointed out that European nations were receiving reparations—huge cash payments that Germany was required to make as punishment for starting the war and causing so much destruction.

The payments, however, were crippling the German economy. In 1923, Germany defaulted on their reparations payments. When the French invaded the Rhine to extract payment, German workers refused to work; runaway inflation and economic collapse ensued.

CORE CONCEPTS: JUSTICE

The Treaty of Versailles (1919) provided for an admission by Germany of its guilt in causing the war. Great Britain and France had presented Germany with a bill of $33 billion as reparations for damages caused by the war.

The United States wanted European economies to be stable so that the Europeans could buy American exports and repay their war debts. In 1924 Charles G. Dawes, an American banker, negotiated an agreement with France, Britain, and Germany to resolve the German economic problems. Under the agreement, American banks would loan money to Germany to help it meet its reparation payments. At the same time, Britain and France would accept less in reparations while paying more on their war debts. Although the plan achieved initial success in easing the reparations crisis, in the long run, it actually put Britain, France, and Germany more deeply in debt to American banks and corporations.

The Washington Conference Despite their economic problems after the war, the major powers were involved in a costly naval arms race. To help stop this arms race, the United States invited representatives from eight nations—Great Britain, France, Italy, China, Japan, Belgium, the Netherlands, and Portugal—to Washington to discuss disarmament. Secretary of State Charles Evans Hughes proposed a ten-year moratorium, or pause, on the building of major new warships. He also proposed a list of warships in each country's navy to be scrapped, beginning with some American battleships.

The conference resulted in three agreements. In the Five-Power Naval Limitation Treaty, Britain, France, Italy, Japan, and the United States essentially agreed to Secretary Hughes's proposals for mutual reduction. The Four-Power Treaty among the United States, Japan, France, and Britain recognized each country's island possessions in the Pacific. In the Nine-Power Treaty, all the participating countries guaranteed China's independence and territorial integrity.

The conference, however, did not place a limit on land forces. It also angered the Japanese because it required Japan to keep a smaller navy than either the United States or Great Britain.

THE WASHINGTON CONFERENCE, NOVEMBER 1921–FEBRUARY 1922			
Treaty	**Signers**	**Terms**	**Weaknesses**
Four-Power Treaty	United States, Great Britain, France, Japan	• All agreed to respect the others' territory in the Pacific • Full and open negotiations in the event of disagreements	• Mutual defense of other co-signers not specified
Five-Power Treaty	United States, Great Britain, France, Japan, Italy	• All agreed to freeze naval production at 1921 levels and halt production of large warships for 10 years • U.S. and Great Britain would not build new naval bases in the western Pacific	• No restrictions on the construction of smaller battle craft such as submarines and naval destroyers • Did not place restrictions on the ground forces
Nine-Power Treaty	United States, Great Britain, France, Japan, Italy, Belgium, China, the Netherlands, Portugal	• All agreed to preserve equal commercial rights to China—a reassertion of the "Open Door Policy"	• No enforcement of the terms of the "Open Door Policy" specified

CORE CONCEPTS: INTERDEPENDENCE

Sixty-two nations eventually signed the Kellogg-Briand Pact. The U.S. Senate passed the pact by a vote of 85 to 1. However, many people were skeptical about its possibilities for success because it provided no means of enforcement.

Abolishing War The apparent success of the Washington Conference gave support to the belief that written agreements among nations could end war altogether. U.S. Secretary of State Frank Kellogg and French Foreign Minister Aristide Briand proposed a treaty to outlaw war. The United States and 14 other nations signed the **Kellogg-Briand Pact** on August 27, 1928. The treaty stated that all signing nations agreed to abandon war and to settle all disputes by peaceful means. The pact was hailed as a victory for peace.

CHAPTER 21   THE GREAT DEPRESSION BEGINS

Chapter Overview

Prosperity in the United States seemed limitless before the Great Depression struck. Overproduction and agricultural problems contributed to the economic catastrophe. President Hoover looked to voluntary business action and limited government relief as solutions, but these efforts failed. Meanwhile, millions of Americans lost their jobs and life savings. Artists and writers depicted this suffering, and many people turned to lighthearted films to escape their difficult lives.

The Great Depression left several lasting effects on American society. Hoover's model of business-government cooperation is still influential. John Steinbeck's novel *The Grapes of Wrath* and Grant Wood's painting *American Gothic* are permanent artistic legacies from this era.

As you read through this chapter, ask yourself these questions:
(1) What were the causes of the Great Depression?
(2) How did the Great Depression affect American families?
(3) How did President Hoover attempt to revive the economy?
(4) What were the limitations of Hoover's recovery plans?

REGENTS WARM-UP

Questions on past Regents Exams have explored how events or policies in one part of the world have affected regions elsewhere. As you read this chapter, identify ways in which U.S. government policies and the events of the Great Depression affected European economic development.

Main Ideas and Concepts

- **Economic Systems** The Great Depression was caused by a combination of economic problems and government policies.

- **Culture** Radio and motion pictures provided ways to escape the worries that plagued people during the Depression's early years.

- **Individuals, Groups, Institutions** In a limited way, President Hoover began using new government agencies to improve the nation's slumping economy.

People, Places, Terms

The following names and terms will help you to prepare for the Regents Exam in United States History and Government. You can find an explanation of each name and term in the Glossary at the back of this book, in your textbook, or in another reference source.

Black Tuesday	**margin**	**speculation**
Bonus Army	**public works**	**stock market**
Dust Bowl	**relief**	
foreclose	**shantytown**	

SECTION 1 CAUSES OF THE DEPRESSION

The Election of 1928

In the election of 1928, the presidential candidates tried to paint a rosy picture of the future. Republican Herbert Hoover went so far as to say, "We are nearer to the final triumph over poverty than ever before in the history of any land."

The Candidates Calvin Coolidge decided not to run for president in 1928. This cleared the way for Herbert Hoover to head the Republican ticket. Hoover had spent eight years as secretary of commerce in the Harding and Coolidge administrations. The Democrats chose Alfred E. Smith, four-time governor of New York. Smith was the first Roman Catholic ever nominated to run for president.

Campaign Issues By 1928 Prohibition had become a major issue among voters. Hoover favored the ban and was considered a "dry." Smith was opposed to the ban and was a "wet." Many Protestants believed that if a Catholic were elected president, the Pope would rule the White House. This belief damaged Smith's candidacy. Smith's biggest problem was the apparent prosperity of the 1920s, for which the Republicans took full credit. As a result, Hoover won in a landslide victory.

CORE CONCEPTS: PRESIDENTIAL DECISIONS AND ACTIONS

On March 4, 1929, an audience of 50,000 stood in the rain to hear Herbert Hoover's inaugural speech. Sound movie cameras covered the event for the first time, and radios broadcast the address worldwide. "I have no fears for the future of our country," Hoover said. "It is bright with hope."

ELECTION OF 1928		
Issue	**Herbert Hoover**	**Alfred E. Smith**
Prohibition	Favored ban on liquor sales	Did not favor ban on liquor sales
Religion	Quaker; embarrassed by charges against Smith and tried to quash them	Catholic; many believed Catholic Church would rule the U.S. if Smith was elected
Economy	Promised to continue the trend of prosperity; "two cars in every garage"	Smith's biggest problem was the strength of the economy

The Long Bull Market

After the election, stock prices rose to new highs. The **stock market** was established as a system for buying and selling shares in companies. Sometimes, events lead to a long period of rising stock prices, known as a bull market. In the late 1920s a long-lasting bull market convinced many Americans to invest heavily in stocks.

As the market continued to rise, many investors began buying stocks on **margin**. They made a small cash down payment and took out a loan from a stockbroker to pay for the rest. The stockbroker earned both a commission on the sale and interest on the loan. Buying on margin was safe as long as stock prices kept rising. The problem came if the stock price began to fall. To protect the loan, a broker could issue a margin call. This was a demand for the investor to repay the loan at once. If prices fell, investors had to sell quickly, or they might not be able to repay their loans.

Before the late 1920s, the prices investors paid for stocks had in general reflected the stocks' true value. If a company made a profit, its stock price rose. A drop in earnings could cause the stock price to fall. In the late 1920s, large numbers of new investors bought stocks without regard to the company's earnings. Hoping to make a fortune quickly, buyers engaged in **speculation**. Instead of investing in the future of the companies whose shares they bought, they took risks. They were betting that the market would continue to climb, which would let them sell the stock at a higher price and make money quickly.

The Great Crash

By mid-1929, the stock market was running out of new customers, and stock prices stopped rising. In September, professional investors sensed danger and began to sell off their holdings. Prices slipped. Other investors sold shares to pay the interest on their loans from brokers. Prices fell further.

Crash! Brokers began making margin calls to customers. Frightened customers put their stocks up for sale at a frantic pace. Prices dropped drastically. On October 29, 1929, a day later called **Black Tuesday**, prices took their steepest dive. By mid-November stock prices had dropped by over one-third. The stock market crash was not the major cause of the Great Depression, but it made the economy less able to survive its other weaknesses.

Banks in a Tailspin Banks also were weakened as a result of the stock market crash. Many banks had lent money to stock speculators. Many had also invested depositors' money in the stock market in hopes of getting higher returns. When stock values collapsed, the banks lost money on their investments and speculators could not repay their loans. Many banks cut back severely on the loans they made. Consumers and businesses were not able to borrow as much money as they had before. This helped to put the economy into a recession.

Many banks were forced to close because of their losses. At that time, the government did not insure bank deposits. If a bank closed, customers lost their savings. News of bank failures led many depositors to withdraw their money all at once. This is called a bank run. The run on the banks caused many banks to collapse. During the first two years of the Depression, more than 3,000 banks were forced to close.

CORE CONCEPTS: INTERDEPENDENCE

The economic crash and the resulting Great Depression were global events. American banks had made large loans to affiliated banks overseas. European as well as American banks failed and caused others to fail. Worldwide, many businesses closed. Unemployment rates throughout the world soared. In Germany, for example, 6 million workers were unemployed in 1932—one quarter of the workforce.

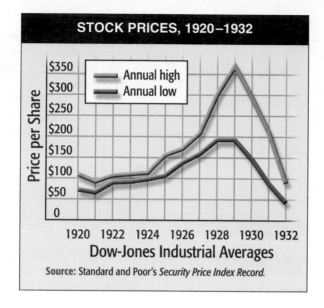

STOCK PRICES, 1920–1932

— Annual high
— Annual low

Price per Share

$350
$300
$250
$200
$150
$100
$50
0

1920 1922 1924 1926 1928 1930 1932

Dow-Jones Industrial Averages

Source: Standard and Poor's *Security Price Index Record.*

REGENTS WARM-UP

To practice your graph-reading skills, answer the following question:

Stock prices peaked in 1929. Before this peak, when did they begin to rise sharply?

(1) 1922
(2) 1924
(3) 1926
(4) 1928

The Roots of the Great Depression

The stock market crash alone did not cause the Great Depression. Other forces were at work. The roots of the Great Depression were deeply entangled in the economy of the 1920s.

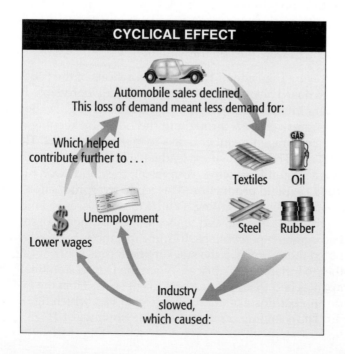

CYCLICAL EFFECT

Automobile sales declined. This loss of demand meant less demand for:

GAS

Textiles   Oil

Steel   Rubber

Industry slowed, which caused:

Unemployment

Lower wages

Which helped contribute further to . . .

REGENTS WARM-UP

The following question from a past Regents Exam tests your ability to recognize cause-effect relationships.

Which economic trend of the 1920s helped cause the Great Depression?

(1) rising cost of mass-produced goods
(2) increasing income tax rates
(3) falling tariff rates
(4) widening income gap between the rich and the poor

CORE CONCEPTS: NEEDS AND WANTS

While manufacturing output per person-hour rose 32 percent, the average worker's wage increased only 8 percent. In 1929 the top 5 percent of American households earned 30 percent of the nation's income. Almost two-thirds of families earned less than $2,500 a year.

The Uneven Distribution of Income Overproduction was a key cause of the Depression. More efficient machinery increased the production of both factories and farms. Most Americans did not earn enough to buy all the goods that were produced. Andrew Mellon's tax policies made it more difficult for wage earners to purchase consumer goods. During the 1920s, many Americans bought high-cost items, such as refrigerators and cars, on the installment plan. People made a small down payment and paid the rest of the price in monthly installments. Some buyers reached a point where they had to reduce their purchases in order to pay their debts. When sales slowed, manufacturers cut production and laid off employees. The slowdown in one industry affected other industries, putting more and more Americans out of work.

The Loss of Export Sales During the 1920s, U.S. banks made high-interest loans to stock speculators instead of lending money to foreign companies. Without these loans, foreign companies purchased fewer products from American manufacturers. Matters grew worse after June 1930, when Congress passed the Hawley-Smoot Tariff. It raised the tax on imports to the highest level in American history. Although the tariff protected American manufacturers from foreign competition, it damaged American sales abroad. Because imports now cost much more, Americans bought fewer of them. Foreign countries then raised their tariffs against American products, which caused fewer American products to be sold overseas. American companies and farmers were hurt by this situation.

Mistakes by the Federal Reserve The actions of the Federal Reserve Board also contributed to the Great Depression. Instead of raising interest rates to stop speculation buying, the Board kept its rates very low throughout the 1920s. By keeping rates low, it encouraged member banks to make risky loans. The low interest rates misled business leaders, who thought that the economy was still growing. As a result, they borrowed more money to expand production. This led to overproduction at a time when sales were falling. Failure of businesses to invest in research, development, and higher wages for their workers, also had economic repercussions. In some instances, businesses also gambled their profits in the stock market, thus contributing further to inflated stock prices. When the Depression finally hit, companies had to lay off workers to cut costs. Then the Fed made another mistake. It raised interest rates, which tightened credit. The economy continued to slide downward.

SECTION 2 LIFE DURING THE DEPRESSION

The Depression Worsens

The Depression grew steadily worse during Hoover's administration. By 1933 more than 9,000 banks had failed. Some 30,000 companies went out of business and more than 12 million workers were unemployed, about 25 percent of the workforce.

Lining Up at Soup Kitchens People without jobs often went hungry. They joined bread lines to receive a free handout of food and lined up outside soup kitchens that private charities had set up to provide meals to poor people.

Living in Makeshift Villages People who could not pay their rent or mortgage lost their homes. Those who could not or would not move were given an eviction notice. Court officials called bailiffs threw nonpaying tenants and their belongings onto the streets. Many newly homeless people put up shacks on unused or public lands, forming communities called **shanty-towns**. Blaming the president for their situation, people called such places Hoovervilles.

Many homeless and unemployed Americans began to wander around the country in search of work or a better life. They walked, hitchhiked, or "rode the rails"—sneaking rides in empty railroad cars. These wanderers, mostly boys and young men, were called hobos, and the camps they made near rail yards were called hobo jungles.

The Dust Bowl Farmers soon faced a new disaster. In order to plant vast wheat fields, Midwestern farmers had plowed up the wild grasses that had held the soil's moisture. When crop prices dropped in the 1920s due to overproduction, lessening demand and high tarrifs, however, farmers left many of their fields unplanted. In 1932 a severe drought struck the Great Plains. With neither grass nor wheat to hold the scant rainfall, the soil turned into dust. From the Dakotas to Texas, America became a **Dust Bowl**. Winds whipped up the dry soil, blowing it aloft and blackening the sky for hundreds of miles. Dust buried crops and livestock and piled up against farmhouses. As the drought continued, the number of dust storms grew each year.

REGENTS WARM-UP

As you read through this chapter, make a chart listing changes in society resulting from the Great Depression.

CORE CONCEPTS: ENVIRONMENT AND SOCIETY

Kansas was hit hardest by the loss of soil in the Dust Bowl years. Other states affected by the drought and soil loss were North and South Dakota, Nebraska, Colorado, Oklahoma, Texas, and a small part of New Mexico. Oklahoma, Kansas, Nebraska, and South Dakota suffered population losses as a result.

Some farmers managed to hold on to their land, but many had no chance. Unable to pay their mortgages, they had to turn their farms over to the banks. Many families packed their belongings into old cars or trucks and headed west to California, hoping for a better life. In California, they lived in makeshift roadside camps and remained homeless and in poverty. Since many migrants were from Oklahoma, they became known as "Okies."

African Americans and the Depression For the most part, African Americans had not shared in the prosperity of the previous decade, but the Depression was devastating for them nevertheless. They experienced more unemployment, homelessness, malnutrition and disease than they had in the past, and considerably more than most whites.

As the Depression deepened, whites in many southern cities began to demand that all African Americans be dismissed from their jobs. In other areas, whites used intimidation and violence to drive African Americans from jobs. By 1932, over half the African Americans in the South were without employment.

Mexican Americans in Depression America Similar patterns of discrimination confronted Mexicans and Mexican Americans. In the 1930s, there were approximately 2 million Latinos (or Hispanics) in the United States. Many filled the same menial jobs in the West and elsewhere that African Americans filled in other regions. Some farmed or became migrant agricultural workers, but most lived in urban areas and occupied the lower ranks of the unskilled labor force in industries such as meatpacking, steel, and automobiles.

As in the South, unemployed white Anglos demanded jobs held by Hispanics. Thus Mexican unemployment rose quickly to levels far higher than those for Anglos. Some Mexicans were, in effect, forced to leave the country by officials who arbitrarily removed them from relief roles or rounded them up and transported them across the border. There were occasionally signs of organized resistance, most notably in California, where some formed a union of migrant farm workers.

Asian Americans in Hard Times For Asian Americans too, the Depression reinforced long-standing patterns of discrimination. In California, where the largest Japanese-American and Chinese-American populations lived, even educated Asians found it difficult to move into mainstream professions. Like African Americans and Hispanics, they often lost jobs to white Americans desperate for work that a few years ago they would not have considered.

Women and the Workplace The economic crisis served in many ways to strengthen the widespread belief that a woman's place was in the home. Most men and many women believed that with employment so scarce, what work there was should go to men. But the widespread assumption that married women should not work outside the home did not stop them from doing so. Both single and married women worked because they or their families needed the money. By the end of the Depression, 20 percent more women were working than had been doing so at the beginning.

The increase occurred despite considerable obstacles. Professional opportunities declined because unemployed men began moving into professions such as teaching and social work that had previously been considered women's fields. However, the nonprofessional jobs that women traditionally held, such as salesclerks and stenographers, were less likely to disappear than the predominantly male jobs in heavy industry. Fewer men were likely to ask for those jobs.

African American women suffered massive unemployment, particularly in the South due to a great reduction of domestic service jobs. As many as half of all African American working-women lost their jobs in the 1930s.

Escaping the Depression

Americans turned to entertainment to escape the hard times, if only for an hour or two. People who had enough money went to the movies. Others listened to one of the many radio programs that were broadcast.

The Hollywood Fantasy Factory On a movie screen, ordinary Americans could see people who were rich, happy, and success-ful. Comedies provided people with a way to escape their daily worries. Even when films focused on serious subjects, they usually contained a note of optimism. Americans also enjoyed cartoons. Walt Disney produced the first feature-length animat-ed film in 1937.

On the Air Americans listened to the radio every day. Newscasters kept them in touch with events. Comedies and programs dealing with the adventures of heroes such as the Green Hornet and the Lone Ranger were popular. Daytime radio dramas carried their stories over from day to day. The shows' sponsors were often makers of laundry soap, so the shows were nicknamed soap operas. Talking about the lives of radio charac-ters provided Americans with a common ground.

The Depression in Art

Art and literature also flourished in the 1930s. The homeless and unemployed became the subject of pictures and stories as artists and writers tried to portray life around them.

Thomas Hart Benton and Grant Wood were leaders of the regionalist school, which emphasized traditional American values, especially those of the rural Midwest and South. Wood's most famous painting, *American Gothic*, shows a stern farmer and his daughter in front of their humble farmhouse.

Novelists such as John Steinbeck wrote about the lives of people in the Depression. In *The Grapes of Wrath* Steinbeck told the story of an Oklahoma family fleeing the Dust Bowl to find a new life in California. Other writers of this time influenced literary style itself. William Faulkner used a technique known as stream of consciousness, showing what his characters thought and felt before they spoke.

Printed photographs grew in influence. Photojournalists such as Margaret Bourke-White traveled around the country with their cameras, seeking new subjects. In 1936 publisher Henry Luce introduced *Life*, a weekly photojournalism magazine that enjoyed instant success.

Comic Books Beginning in 1938, one of the most popular forms of escape for many young Americans became the comic book. Modern comics began on the "funny pages" of American newspapers in the 1890s. In the first years of the twentieth century, publishers collected previously published strips and began selling them in books. The first successful original material was published in *Action Comics* (1938), which was a book featuring a powerful man in a skin-tight suit lifting a car over his head on the cover. His name was Superman, and he became the most popular cartoon character of all time.

SECTION 3 HOOVER RESPONDS

Promoting Recovery

President Hoover tried to reassure people that industry was "on a sound and prosperous basis." He told the public that the worst effects of the crash would pass in 60 days. He wanted to avoid more bank runs and layoffs.

Voluntary Efforts and Public Works Despite his reassurances to the public, Hoover was seriously worried about the economy. He held conferences with the heads of banks, railroads and other big businesses, as well as with labor and government officials.

Hoover won a pledge from industry to keep factories open and to stop cutting wages. By 1931, however, business leaders had abandoned those pledges. Hoover then tried to increase **public works**—government-financed building projects. He hoped that the construction jobs these projects would create would make up for the jobs lost in private businesses. However, the effort made up for only a small part of the jobs lost in the private sector.

The only way the government could create enough new jobs would be to greatly increase government spending. Hoover refused to do this. He felt that if the government raised taxes to get the money, it would take money away from consumers and hurt businesses that were already struggling. If the government kept taxes low and spent more money than it collected in taxes, it would have to borrow money from banks. This would leave less money for businesses that wanted to expand and for consumers who wanted mortgages or other loans. Hoover was afraid that this deficit spending would delay an economic recovery.

The Midterm Election Americans blamed the party that was in power—the Republican Party—for the worsening unemployment and stumbling economy. In the congressional elections of 1930, the Republicans lost their majority in the House of Representatives and held onto the Senate by a single vote.

Pumping Money into the Economy

Hoover wanted to make sure that banks could make loans to businesses so that they could expand production and rehire workers. He reluctantly recognized the need for federal government actions—too little and too late.

CORE CONCEPTS: PRESIDENTIAL DECISIONS AND ACTIONS

President Hoover issued this statement on Friday, October 25, the day after what came to be called Black Thursday—when the stock market began its plummet following the brokers' first margin calls.

CORE CONCEPTS: PRESIDENTIAL DECISIONS AND ACTIONS

President Hoover's own economic philosophy prevented him from taking drastic action to revive the economy. He believed the "rugged individualism" would be destroyed by direct government aid to the poor. He also was concerned that it might lead to socialism.

CORE CONCEPTS: CONFLICT

In Nebraska, grain growers burned corn to heat their homes in the winter. In Iowa, food growers used force to prevent the delivery of vegetables to distributors. Georgia dairy farmers blocked highways and stopped milk trucks, emptying the milk cans into ditches.

Trying to Rescue the Banks Hoover asked the Federal Reserve Board to put more money into circulation, but the Board refused. By 1932 Hoover decided that the only way to provide money for borrowers was for the government to do the lending to business institutions. Hoover's approach was to lend money at the top that would eventually "trickle down" to workers and the unemployed. He asked Congress to set up the Reconstruction Finance Corporation (RFC) to make loans to banks, railroads, and farming institutions. The RFC made millions of dollars worth of loans. However, it did not increase its loans enough to meet the need. The economy continued to decline.

Direct Help for Citizens Hoover was strongly against federal government participation in **relief**—money that went directly to poor families. He believed that was the job of state and local governments and private charities. These governments, however, were running out of money. In 1932 Congress passed the Emergency Relief and Construction Act, which provided money for public works and loans to states for direct relief. The new program came too late to reverse the continuing collapse.

In an Angry Mood

By 1931 Americans were growing increasingly unhappy about the economy. Open acts of revolt began to take place.

Farmers Revolt Farmers also protested. Prices sank so low after the war that farmers could not even earn back their costs, let alone make a profit. Between 1930 and 1934, creditors **foreclosed** on nearly one million farms. They took possession of the farms and evicted the families. Some farmers began to destroy their crops in an attempt to raise crop prices by lowering the supply.

The Bonus Marchers To thank American soldiers and sailors for their service in World War I, Congress had enacted a $1,000 bonus for each veteran, to be given in 1945. Because of the economic crisis, a bill was introduced in the House of Representatives in 1931 to allow early payment of the money. The bill passed the House and moved to the Senate for debate. In 1932 a group of about 1,000 veterans from Oregon set off on a month-long march to Washington to lobby Congress to pass the bill. The press called the marchers the **Bonus Army**.

Once in Washington, the marchers camped in Hoovervilles. They were joined by veterans from all over the country. The number of veterans grew in a few weeks to almost 15,000. President Hoover refused to meet with them. The Senate voted the bill down. Many veterans returned home. A large number, however, stayed on since they had no jobs to return to. Some moved into unoccupied buildings.

President Hoover ordered the police to clear the buildings. One police officer panicked and fired into a crowd, killing two veterans. The Washington, D.C., government then called in the army. Army chief of staff Douglas MacArthur ignored Hoover's orders to clear the buildings but to leave the camps alone. He sent cavalry, infantry, and tanks to clear the veterans from the city. The army used bayonets and tear gas on the veterans and burned the shacks. The nationwide press coverage and newsreel images of veterans under assault by troops upset the public. The images of the routed Bonus Marchers and the lingering Depression shaped the way the public viewed President Hoover.

CORE CONCEPTS: ECONOMIC SYSTEMS

Most nations in the world operate under a mixed economic system. However, they tend to include more features of one economic system than another. In the United States, for example, the government regulates some aspects of the economy to prevent unfair business practices. The favored form of economic operation, however, is market economy.

Chapter Overview

Unlike Herbert Hoover, Franklin Delano Roosevelt was willing to employ deficit spending and greater federal regulation to revive the depressed economy. In response to his requests, Congress passed a host of new programs. Millions of people received relief to alleviate their suffering, and unemployment dropped from 24 percent to 10 percent, but the New Deal did not really end the Depression. It did, however, permanently expand the federal government's role in providing basic security for citizens.

Certain New Deal legislation still carries great importance in American social policy. The Social Security Act provides retirement benefits, aid to needy groups, and unemployment and disability insurance. The National Labor Relations Act protects the rights of workers to unionize. Safeguards were instituted to help prevent another devastating stock market crash. The Federal Deposit Insurance Corporation protects bank deposits.

As you read through this chapter, ask yourself these questions:
(1) What made Franklin D. Roosevelt appealing to the American public?
(2) Why did the situation of the U.S. banking system worsen in the early 1930s?
(3) What three New Deal programs provided jobs for the unemployed, and how did they do this?
(4) What political challenges did Roosevelt face in the mid-1930s?
(5) How did the New Deal affect Americans' sense of security and their attitude toward the role of government?

Main Ideas and Concepts

- **Identity** Franklin Roosevelt's optimism, determination, and outgoing personality shaped his approach to politics.

- **Individuals, Groups, Institutions** FDR's attempts to end the Depression resulted in many new government agencies.

- **Government** The Second New Deal was a political response to growing criticism from both the left and the right.

- **Individuals, Groups, Institutions** The Democratic Party's victory in 1936 resulted from a new alignment in politics that lasted for several decades.

People, Places, Terms

The following names and terms will help you to prepare for the Regents Exam in United States History and Government. You can find an explanation of each name and term in the Glossary at the back of this book, in your textbook, or in another reference source.

bank holiday
Civilian
   Conservation
   Corps (CCC)
Federal Deposit
   Insurance
   Corporation
   (FDIC)

Glass-Steagall
   Banking Act
John Maynard
   Keynes
National Labor
   Relations
   Board (NLRB)
New Deal

Frances Perkins
Social Security Act
Wagner Act
Works Progress
   Administration

SECTION 1 ROOSEVELT TAKES OFFICE

Roosevelt's Rise to Power

In the 1932 presidential election, many voters were against Republican nominee President Hoover, who had a poor record of success in responding to the economic crisis. The Democrats chose as their candidate New York Governor Franklin Delano Roosevelt. In his speech accepting the nomination, Roosevelt pledged himself to "a new deal for the American people." From that time on, Roosevelt's policies for ending the Depression became known as the **New Deal**. He won the election in a landslide.

Roosevelt's Background Franklin Roosevelt was a distant cousin of President Theodore Roosevelt. While at Harvard he

LINKING PAST AND PRESENT

Few people knew about Roosevelt's physical limitations when he became president. After Roosevelt established a foundation for polio victims at Warm Springs, Georgia, entertainer Eddie Cantor suggested that everyone in the country send a dime to the president for polio research. This campaign became the March of Dimes. In 1945 Congress honored Roosevelt by putting his image on the dime. Because of Dr. Jonas Salk's discovery of the polio vaccine, polio is no longer the threat it once was.

CORE CONCEPTS: GOVERNMENT

Between Roosevelt's election in November 1932 and his inauguration in March 1933, the Twentieth Amendment was added to the Constitution. This amendment changed the inauguration date from March 4 to January 20.

became friendly with Theodore Roosevelt's niece, Eleanor. They were married soon after.

FDR's Early Political Career After leaving Columbia Law School, Roosevelt went into politics. When Woodrow Wilson won the presidency in 1912, he appointed Roosevelt assistant secretary of the navy. In 1920, the Democrats nominated Roosevelt as their candidate for vice president. After losing the election, Roosevelt withdrew from politics. A year later, he was stricken with polio, a disease that paralyzed his legs. While recovering, Roosevelt depended on his wife to keep his name in the forefront of the New York Democratic Party.

Governor of New York By the mid-1920s, Roosevelt was again active in politics. He became governor of New York in 1928. His policies made him a popular governor. He cut taxes for farmers and reduced rates charged by public utilities. In 1931 Roosevelt convinced the New York State legislature to create an agency that would help unemployed New Yorkers.

Roosevelt's popularity in New York led to his nomination for president in the 1932 election. His optimism gave Americans hope despite the hard economic times.

Roosevelt Is Inaugurated

Between Roosevelt's election in November 1932 and his inauguration in March 1933, unemployment continued to rise. Bank runs increased greatly. Some bank runs occurred because people feared Roosevelt would abandon the gold standard and reduce the value of the dollar to fight the Depression. Under the gold standard, one ounce of gold equaled a set number of dollars. To reduce the value of the dollar, the United States would have to stop exchanging dollars for gold. Many investors decided to take their money out of the banks and change it into gold before it lost its value. By March 1933, over 4,000 banks had collapsed. In 38 states, governors declared **bank holidays**. They closed the remaining banks before people could make a run on them and put them out of business.

SECTION 2   THE FIRST NEW DEAL

The Hundred Days Begins

Once Roosevelt took office, he began sending bill after bill to Congress. Between March 9 and June 16, 1933—which came to be called the Hundred Days—Congress passed 15 major acts to meet the economic crisis. Together, these programs made up what would later be called the First New Deal.

Origins of the New Deal Roosevelt was willing to experiment and try a variety of approaches to see whether they worked. To come up with new ideas for programs, Roosevelt asked for advice from a wide range of advisers with experience in different fields. He deliberately chose advisers who disagreed with each other in order to hear different points of view. Roosevelt alone made the final decision about what policies to pursue.

Fixing the Banks and the Stock Market

FDR realized that the first thing he had to do was restore people's confidence in the banking system.

The Emergency Banking Relief Act Roosevelt declared a national bank holiday, closing all banks on a temporary basis. Then he called Congress into a special session. On the day that Congress met, the House of Representatives passed the Emergency Banking Relief Act. The Senate approved it the same evening, and Roosevelt signed it into law. The new law required federal examiners to survey the nation's banks and issue Treasury Department licenses to those that were financially sound.

On March 12, President Roosevelt addressed the nation by radio. This was the first of many "fireside chats"—direct talks that FDR held with the American people to let them know what he was trying to accomplish. In his first chat, Roosevelt said that their money would now be safe if they put it back into the banks. The next day, there were far more bank deposits than withdrawals. The banking crisis was over.

Regulating Banks and Brokers Many of Roosevelt's advisers pushed for new regulations for both banks and the stock market. Roosevelt agreed and supported the Securities Act of 1933 and the **Glass-Steagall Banking Act**.

The Securities Act required companies that sold stocks and bonds to provide complete and truthful information to investors. The next year, Congress set up the Securities and Exchange Commission (SEC) to regulate the stock market and prevent fraud.

The Glass-Steagall Act separated commercial banking from investment banking. Commercial banks handle everyday transactions, such as taking deposits and cashing checks. Under the Glass-Steagall Act, these banks could no longer risk depositors' money by using it to speculate on the stock market. The act also created the **Federal Deposit Insurance Corporation** (FDIC). It provided government insurance on bank deposits up to a certain amount.

Managing Farms and Industry

Many of Roosevelt's advisers believed that both farmers and businesses were suffering because prices were too low and production was too high. Some advisers believed that competition was not efficient and was bad for the economy. They favored the creation of federal agencies to manage the economy.

The Agricultural Adjustment Administration Farmers had been hit hard by the Depression. Roosevelt announced plans for a new farm program to help them. He asked Congress to pass the Agricultural Adjustment Act. The act was based on the idea that prices for farm products were low because farmers grew too much food. Under this act, the government would pay farmers *not* to raise certain livestock and *not* to grow certain crops. This program was run by the Agricultural Adjustment Administration (AAA).

Over the next two years, farmers withdrew millions of acres from production. They received more than $1 billion in support payments. The program reached its goal. The farm surplus fell greatly by 1936, and food prices rose. Total farm income also rose. However, not all farmers benefited. Large commercial farmers who concentrated on one crop benefited more than small farmers who raised several products. In addition, thousands of poor tenant farmers became homeless and jobless when their landlords took fields out of production.

A Blueprint for Industrial Recovery In June 1933, Roosevelt and Congress enacted the National Industrial Recovery Act (NIRA). The NIRA suspended antitrust laws. It allowed business, labor, and government to cooperate in setting up voluntary rules for each industry. These rules were known as codes of fair competition. Some codes set prices, set minimum wages, and limited factories to two shifts a day. Other codes shortened workers' hours with the goal of creating additional jobs. The law also guaranteed workers the right to form unions.

The National Recovery Administration (NRA) ran the whole program. Business owners who signed code agreements

LINKING PAST AND PRESENT

Perhaps no New Deal program produced as many visible benefits as the Tennessee Valley Authority (TVA), established in 1933. The purpose of this dam-building project was to control floods, conserve forests and bring cheap electricity to rural areas. Today the TVA's power facilities include hydroelectric dams, 11 fossil-fuel plants, 3 nuclear power plants, and 17,000 miles of transmission lines. These facilities provide power to nearly 8 million people in seven states. Largely because of the "yardstick" provided by the TVA's cheap production of electricity, private power rates declined.

received signs displaying the NRA's symbol. Consumers were urged to buy goods only from companies that displayed the signs.

The NRA had few successes. Small companies complained that large companies wrote codes that favored themselves. Many companies disliked price fixing, which limited competition. Employers disliked codes that gave workers the right to form unions and bargain over wages and hours. The codes were difficult to enforce, and many companies ignored them. Industrial production actually fell after the NRA was set up. The Supreme Court ruled in 1935 that the NRA was unconstitutional. However, it had already lost much of its political support.

Providing Debt Relief

Some of Roosevelt's advisers believed that debt was the main obstacle to economic recovery. With incomes falling, people had to use most of their money to pay their debts. They had little left over to buy goods or pay for services. Many Americans cut back on their spending in order to pay their mortgages. President Roosevelt responded to the crisis by introducing several programs to help Americans with their debts.

The Home Owners' Loan Corporation To help homeowners pay their mortgages, Roosevelt asked Congress to establish the Home Owners' Loan Corporation (HOLC). The HOLC bought the mortgages of many homeowners who were behind in their payments. It then restructured the payments with lower terms of repayment and lower interest rates. The HOLC helped only those people who still had jobs. When people lost their jobs and could no longer pay their mortgages, the HOLC foreclosed on their property, just as a bank would have done. However, the HOLC did help refinance one out of every five mortgages on private homes in the United States.

The Farm Credit Administration Congress also set up the Farm Credit Administration (FCA) to help farmers refinance their mortgages. FCA loans helped many farmers keep their land.

Spending and Relief Programs

Many of Roosevelt's advisers believed that controlling prices and providing debt relief could cure the Depression. Others, however, felt that the base cause of the Depression was that people were not buying enough products to keep the economy going. These advisers insisted that the fastest way out of the Depression

CORE CONCEPTS: CONSTITUTIONAL PRINCIPLES

The NIRA was declared unconstitutional by the Supreme Court in the case of *Scheckter Poultry Corp.* v. *United States*. The Court ruled that excessive delegation of legislative power to the executive branch was unconstitutional. The Court felt that applying the interstate commerce clause to businesses involved only indirectly in interstate commerce would undermine the authority of the states over their domestic concerns.

was to provide money directly to needy individuals. To do this, Roosevelt urged Congress to set up government agencies that would organize work programs for the unemployed.

The CCC The most highly praised work relief program was the **Civilian Conservation Corps** (CCC). Starting in 1933, the CCC offered employment to young men 18 to 25 years old. They would work under the direction of the national forestry service, planting trees, fighting forest fires, and building reservoirs. Men lived in camps near their work areas and earned $30 a month. By the time it closed down in 1942, the CCC had provided outdoor work for 3 million men.

Public Works and Emergency Relief Congress set up the Federal Emergency Relief Administration (FERA) to provide federal money to state and local relief agencies for their relief projects. The Public Works Administration (PWA) was set up in June 1933 to put construction workers back to work. To do this, the PWA began a series of construction projects to build and improve highways, dams, sewer systems, waterworks, schools, and other government facilities. In most cases, the PWA did not hire workers directly but instead gave contracts to construction companies. The PWA did insist that contractors hire African Americans, which broke down some of the long-standing racial barriers in the construction trades.

The programs passed during the First New Deal did not restore prosperity. However, they did inspire Americans with hope and optimism and restore their faith in the country.

THE FIRST NEW DEAL, 1933–1935		
Agency	**Established**	**Function**
Civilian Conservation Corps (CCC)	March 1933	Employed single men, ages 18–25, for natural resource conservation
Tennessee Valley Authority (TVA)	May 1933	Built hydroelectric plants and dams aimed at improving seven Southern states and attracting industry to the South
Agricultural Adjustment Act (AAA)	May 1933	Reduced agricultural surplus and raised prices for struggling farmers
Federal Emergency Relief Agency (FERA)	May 1933	Granted federal money to state and local governments to be used to help the unemployed
National Recovery Administration (NRA)	June 1933	Controlled industrial production and prices with industry-created codes of fair competition
Federal Deposit Insurance Corporation (FDIC)	June 1933	Guaranteed bank deposits up to $2,5000
Public Works Administration (PWA) Civil Works Administration (CWA)	June 1933 November 1933	Provided employment in construction of airports, parks, schools, and roads
Securities and Exchange Commission (SEC)	June 1934	Regulated the stock market to avoid dishonest practices

SECTION 3   THE SECOND NEW DEAL

Challenges to the New Deal

Although Roosevelt had been highly popular during his first two years in office, opposition to his policies began to grow. After two years of New Deal programs, the economy had improved only slightly.

Criticism from Left and Right People from both the right and left of the political spectrum opposed the president's policies. People on the right believed that the New Deal had placed too many regulations on business. Opposition from the right increased when Roosevelt began deficit spending. He had given up on a balanced budget and had begun borrowing money to pay for his programs. In August 1934, business leaders and anti–New Deal politicians, such as Alfred Smith, former governor of New York and a rival Democratic presidential candidate in 1932, joined together to form the American Liberty League. Its purpose was to organize opposition to the New Deal.

Another serious challenge to the New Deal came from the left. People on the left believed that Roosevelt had not gone far enough. They wanted the government to do even more to shift wealth from the rich to middle-income and poor Americans. Norman Thomas, a six-time presidential candidate for the Socialist Party and founder of the American Civil Liberties Union (ACLU), pushed for socialist policies.

Huey Long What was perhaps the most serious threat from the left came from Democratic Senator Huey Long. As governor of Louisiana, he had fought for the poor. Long's attacks on the rich gave him a national following. Many people believed that if Long ran for president in 1936 as a third-party candidate, he would take 10 percent of Roosevelt's vote. That would be enough to ensure a Republican victory.

Father Coughlin Another New Deal opponent from the left was Father Charles Coughlin, a Catholic priest in Detroit. Coughlin had a popular radio show that reached millions of Americans. Coughlin called for heavy taxes on the wealthy and nationalization of the banking system. He organized the National Union for Social Justice, which some Democrats feared was a step toward creating a new political party.

The Townsend Plan A third left-wing challenge came from Dr. Francis Townsend, a former public health official. He proposed that the federal government pay citizens over age 60 a pension of $200 a month. These citizens would have to retire and spend their entire pension check each month. Townsend believed the plan would increase spending, remove people from the labor force, and free up jobs for the unemployed. Townsend's plan had many supporters, especially among the elderly. If his supporters joined the supporters of Long and Coughlin, there was a possibility that they would draw enough votes away from Roosevelt to keep him from being reelected in 1936.

CORE CONCEPTS: GOVERNMENT

Long had made improvements to schools, colleges, and hospitals. He had also built roads and bridges. These benefits made Long very popular. They also enabled him to build a powerful and corrupt political machine.

Launching the Second New Deal

President Roosevelt knew that he might lose political support because of the attacks from left and right. He was also bothered by the failure of the New Deal to improve the nation's economy. In 1935 he began another series of programs and reforms that he hoped would speed up economic recovery. This came to be called the Second New Deal.

THE SECOND NEW DEAL	
Agency/Legislation	**Function**
Works Progress Administration (WPA)	Combated unemployment; created jobs throughout economy
Rural Electrification Administration (REA)	Brought electricity to isolated agricultural areas
Social Security Act	Created unemployment system disability insurance, old-age pension, and child welfare benefits
Public Utility Holding Company Act	Eliminated unfair practices and abuses of utility companies
Banking Act	Strengthened the Federal Reserve
Resettlement Act	Assisted poor families and sharecroppers in beginning new farms or purchasing land

The WPA In January 1935, Roosevelt asked Congress for funds to provide work relief and increase employment. Much of the money would be given to the **Works Progress Administration** (WPA), a new federal agency. The WPA's 8.5 million workers built miles of highways, roads, and streets, thousands of public buildings, and parks. The WPA also provided work for artists, musicians, theater people, and writers. Under the WPA, artists created murals and sculptures for public buildings. Musicians set up city symphony orchestras and smaller musical groups.

The Supreme Court's Role Because of opposition to Roosevelt's programs, Congress did not pass the bill that created the WPA until April 1935. Then the Supreme Court invalidated the Agricultural Adjustment Act, ruling that it was illegal to tax one group in order to pay another. In 1938, another AAA was passed that was financed by general taxes, which was acceptable to the Supreme Court.

Schechter v. *United States* In May 1935, the Supreme Court unanimously struck down the National Industrial Recovery Act in *Schechter* v. *United States*. The Schechter brothers, who had a poultry business in Brooklyn, New York, had been convicted in 1933 of violating the NIRA's Live Poultry Code. They had sold diseased chickens and violated the code's wage-and-hour provisions. In what became known as the "sick chicken case," the Court ruled that the Constitution did not allow Congress to delegate its power to the executive branch. Thus it considered the NIRA codes unconstitutional.

These rulings suggested to Roosevelt that the Court would soon strike down the rest of the New Deal as well. The president knew that he needed a new set of programs to keep voters' support. He called Congressional leaders to the White House and told them that Congress could not go home until it passed his new bills. That summer, Congress worked quickly to pass Roosevelt's programs.

The Rise of Industrial Unions

Just as Republican policies of the 1920s had favored big business, the New Deal offered assistance to labor, the farmer, and small businesses, as well as providing a program for the regulation and recovery of larger businesses, such as banks and investment systems.

The National Labor Relations Act In July 1935 Congress passed the National Labor Relations Act, also called the **Wagner Act**. This act guaranteed workers the right to form unions and to bargain collectively. The law set up the **National Labor Relations Board** (NLRB), which organized factory elections by secret ballot to determine whether workers wanted a union. The NLRB then certified the successful unions.

The law set up a manner in which dissatisfied union members could take their complaints to binding arbitration. In this process, a neutral party would listen to both sides and decide the

REGENTS WARM-UP

The following question from a past Regents Exam tests your ability to recall important details.

The National Labor Relations Act (Wagner Act) of 1935 strengthened labor unions because it legalized

(1) collective bargaining
(2) blacklisting
(3) the open shop
(4) the sit-down strike

issues. The NLRB was also authorized to investigate employers' actions and to end unfair practices.

The CIO Union activity increased by the mid-1930s. The United Mine Workers union began working with other unions to organize workers in industries where there were no unions. They formed the Committee for Industrial Organization (CIO) in 1935. The CIO set out to organize industrial unions. These unions included all workers in a particular industry, both skilled and unskilled. The CIO began by focusing on the automobile and steel industries, where workers were not yet organized.

Sit-Down Strikes When two union men were demoted at a General Motors (GM) plant in Cleveland, Ohio, 135 workers sat down and started a new kind of strike. They stopped working but refused to leave the factory. A few days later, workers at GM's Flint, Michigan, plant held their own sit-down strike. Workers at other GM plants also went on strike.

Violence broke out in Flint between police and striking workers. In the end, however, the company gave in and recognized the CIO's United Auto Workers (UAW). The UAW became one of the most powerful unions in the nation.

Between 1933 and 1939, total union membership tripled. In 1938 the CIO changed its name to the Congress of Industrial Organizations. It became a federation of industrial unions.

The Social Security Act

In August 1935 Congress passed the **Social Security Act**. Its goal was to provide some security for the elderly and for unemployed workers. Under this act, workers earned the right to receive benefits by paying premiums. The act also provided welfare payments to other needy people, such as people with disabilities. The core of Social Security was the monthly retirement benefit. People could collect this benefit when they stopped working at age 65. Another important benefit was unemployment insurance, which gave unemployed workers a temporary income while they looked for new jobs.

Although Social Security helped many people, it left out farm and domestic workers. About 65 percent of African American workers in the 1930s fell into these two categories. However, Social Security set the principle that the federal government should be responsible for people who, through no fault of their own, were unable to work.

SECTION 4 THE NEW DEAL COALITION

Roosevelt's Second Term

By 1936 most African American voters had switched their support to the Democratic Party because of the New Deal. Both African Americans and women had made some gains during the New Deal. Roosevelt appointed a number of African Americans to positions in his administration. He also tried to see that New Deal relief programs did not leave out African Americans. Roosevelt appointed the first woman to a cabinet post. **Frances Perkins** became the Secretary of Labor. Roosevelt also appointed many women to lower-level jobs in the federal government.

The Indian Reorganization Act Government policies toward Native Americans were largely a continuation of the long-established effort to encourage them to assimilate. However, John Collier, a former social worker who had become committed to the cause of Native Americans after working with them in the 1920s, promoted legislation that he hoped would reverse the pressures on Native Americans to assimilate. He was strongly influenced by the idea of cultural relativism—the idea that every culture should be accepted and respected on its own terms and that no culture was inherently superior to another.

The Indian Reorganization Act of 1934, which Collier promoted, restored to tribes the right to own land collectively, reversing the allotment policy adopted in 1887. Under the old policy, over 90 million acres had been lost to white speculators and others. The act increased tribal land by more than 4 million acres and Native American agricultural income increased dramatically. Much of the land that Native Americans possessed, however, remained that which whites did not want.

The Election of 1936 The New Deal was very popular with the American people. On Election Day, Roosevelt won in one of the largest landslides in American history.

The Court-Packing Plan The Supreme Court was not in support of some of Roosevelt's programs. Roosevelt was angry that the justices were blocking the wishes of a majority of citizens. He decided to change the balance of the Supreme Court. Roosevelt sent Congress a bill to increase the number of justices. If any justice had served for 10 years and did not retire within six months after reaching the age of 70, the president could name an additional justice to the Court. Since four justices were in their 70s and two were in their late 60s, the bill would allow Roosevelt

CORE CONCEPTS: GOVERNMENT

Franklin D. Roosevelt won the 1932 election with an electoral vote of 472 to 59 and a popular vote of 23 million to 16 million for Herbert Hoover. The popular vote for Roosevelt in 1936 was 28 million against 17 million for Alfred Landon. In the electoral college, Roosevelt won every state but Maine and Vermont. This gave him an electoral victory of 523 to 8. Politicians who supported the New Deal also won both houses of Congress and all but six governorships.

REGENTS WARM-UP

The following question from a past Regents Exam tests your ability to determine cause-effect relationships.

The Supreme Court declared some New Deal laws unconstitutional because these laws

(1) overextended the power of the federal government
(2) forced the federal government into heavy debt
(3) ignored the rights of minority groups and women
(4) failed to solve the problems for which they were intended

to appoint as many as six new justices. The court-packing plan, as the press called it, was Roosevelt's first serious political mistake. The plan made it look as if he were trying to interfere with the separation of powers and with the Supreme Court's independence.

The issue split the Democratic Party. Southern Democrats feared that the plan would put justices on the Court who would overturn segregation. African American leaders worried that a future president might pack the Court with justices opposed to civil rights. Many Americans believed the plan would give the president too much power.

Roosevelt's actions appeared to force the Supreme Court to back down. It upheld the Wagner Act and the Social Security Act as constitutional. The Senate quietly killed the court-packing bill. However, the fight over Roosevelt's plan had hurt his reputation with the American people. It also encouraged conservative Democrats in Congress to work with Republicans to oppose further New Deal proposals.

The Roosevelt Recession Roosevelt suffered another setback in 1937 when unemployment suddenly increased dramatically. Roosevelt had decided that although unemployment was still high, it was time to balance the budget. Concerned about the dangers of too much debt, he ordered the WPA and the PWA to be cut considerably. Just as he cut spending, the first Social Security payroll taxes removed $2 billion from the economy. Almost at once the economy dropped severely. By the end of 1937, two million people were out of work.

The recession of 1937 led to a debate among Roosevelt's advisers about what to do. Some wanted to balance the budget and cut spending. Others pushed for more government spending. They pointed to a new theory called "Keynesianism" to support their arguments.

Keynesianism was based on a theory proposed by British economist **John Maynard Keynes**. Keynes argued that the government should spend heavily during a recession, even if it had to go into debt, in order to jump-start the economy by stimulating consumption. According to Keynesian economics, Roosevelt had done the wrong thing when he cut back programs in 1937. Roosevelt did not want to begin deficit spending again. Many critics of his policies had argued that the recession proved the American people were becoming too dependent on government spending. Roosevelt was worried that they might be right.

The Last New Deal Reforms

The recession of 1937 had weakened Roosevelt politically. In 1938 he asked Congress to provide more funds for the PWA, the WPA, and other programs, but his successes were limited.

The National Housing Act One of the president's goals for his second term was to provide better housing for the poor. In 1937 the National Housing Act—which was promoted by Eleanor Roosevelt—set up the United States Housing Authority. The authority received $300 million to subsidize loans for builders willing to buy blocks of slums and build low-cost housing.

The Farm Security Administration The Agricultural Adjustment Administration's price-support program had raised farm income, but it badly hurt tenant farmers. Landlords often evicted tenants from the land in order to take it out of production. Many tenant farmers left farming for this reason. To stop this trend, Congress set up the Farm Security Administration in 1937. Its purpose was to give loans to tenant farmers so they could buy farms.

The Fair Labor Standards Act The Fair Labor Standards Act of 1938 provided more protection for workers. It also abolished child labor and established a 40-hour workweek for many workers and the minimum wage as well.

Congress, however, was beginning to turn against the New Deal. Republicans won many seats in Congress in the congressional election of 1938. Together with conservative Southern Democrats, they began blocking further New Deal legislation. By 1939 the New Deal era had ended.

The Legacy of the New Deal

In terms of its goal of ending the Depression, the New Deal was only a limited success. Unemployment remained high, and the economy did not recover completely until after World War II. The New Deal did, however, give many Americans a stronger sense of security and stability.

Government's New Role The New Deal brought about a new public attitude regarding the government. Roosevelt's programs gave Americans a safety net that provided safeguards and relief programs to protect them from economic disaster. Another legacy of the New Deal is a debate that continues to the present over how much the government should intervene in the economy or support the poor and needy.

The Election of 1940 President Roosevelt decided to run for a third term as president. He believed that at this point, a change of leadership might not be in the country's best interest. During the 1940 campaign, Roosevelt called for a course between neutrality and intervention. He was reelected by a wide margin.

The Twenty-second Amendment Roosevelt ran for an unprecedented fourth term in 1944 and was elected. However, he died suddenly while in office and was succeeded by Vice President Harry Truman. After Roosevelt died, many pushed for a constitutional amendment limiting presidents to two terms in office. The Twenty-second Amendment was proposed by Congress in 1947 and was ratified by the states in 1951.

LINKING PAST AND PRESENT

Most early first ladies limited their activities to that of hostess and social role model. Some, however, took more politically active roles. Eleanor Roosevelt was the first to hold regular press conferences, allowing only women to attend in order to force news agencies to hire more women reporters. Eleanor Roosevelt paved the way for modern activist first ladies such as Lady Bird Johnson, Rosalynn Carter, and Hillary Rodham Clinton.

PRACTICING FOR THE REGENTS

Part I   Multiple-Choice Questions

The following multiple-choice questions come from past Regents Examinations. Test your understanding of United States history and geography by answering each of these items. Circle the number of the word or expression that best completes each statement or question. Test-taking tips can be found in the margins for some questions. For additional help, see Taking the Regents Exam on pages ix–xxxi of this Review Book.

REGENTS WARM-UP

Question 1 tests your knowledge of American history vocabulary. Terms such as *nativism* are defined in your textbook at the point where they are first used, and in the Glossary.

1   Which event represents an expression of nativism during the 1920s?
   (1) trial of John Scopes for teaching evolution
   (2) adoption of a quota system to limit immigration
   (3) Charles Lindbergh's solo transatlantic flight
   (4) rise in popularity of spectator sports

2   What was a major result of Prohibition in the United States during the 1920s?
   (1) restriction of immigration
   (2) growth of communism
   (3) destruction of family values
   (4) increase in organized crime

Base your answer to question 3 on the poem below and on your knowledge of social studies.

One Way Ticket
I am fed up
With Jim Crow laws,
People who are cruel
And afraid,
Who lynch and run,
Who are scared of me
And me of them.
I pick up my life
And take it away
On a one-way ticket
Gone Up North
Gone Out West
Gone!
—Langston Hughes, 1926

REGENTS WARM-UP

The poem tests your ability to interpret the poet's message. Question 3 also requires you to use your knowledge of social conditions in the 1920s.

3   The author states that he has "Gone" because
   (1) jobs were available in northern industries
   (2) there was no racial prejudice in the West
   (3) farmland was more available in the North
   (4) racial discrimination drove him away

4 The works of Duke Ellington and Langston Hughes reflected the
   (1) expanding role of women in the 1920s
   (2) achievements of the Harlem Renaissance
   (3) architectural innovations of the 1930s
   (4) influence of southern European immigrant groups

5 The Harlem Renaissance of the 1920s can best be described as
   (1) an organization created to help promote African American businesses
   (2) a movement that sought to draw people back to the inner cities
   (3) a period of great achievement by African American writers, artists, and performers
   (4) a relief program to provide jobs for minority workers

6 Which long-awaited goal of the women's rights movement was achieved during the Progressive Era?
   (1) right to vote
   (2) right to own property
   (3) equal pay for equal work
   (4) equal access to employment and education

7 The treaties signed at the Washington Conference (1921–1922) and the Kellogg-Briand Pact (1928) were efforts to
   (1) limit the spread of military dictatorships
   (2) maintain peace through international agreements
   (3) form new military alliances after World War I
   (4) bring democratic government to eastern Europe

8 A significant contribution to the industrialization of the United States was Henry Ford's development of
   (1) the assembly line
   (2) electric-powered vehicles
   (3) the first holding company
   (4) a new process for making steel

9 Which statement most accurately describes conditions of American farmers during the economic boom of the mid-1920s?
   (1) Shortages of fertile land and farm equipment lowered farm income.
   (2) Overproduction helped keep farmers from participating in the prosperity of the times.
   (3) Subsidies and other government programs dramatically increased farmers' incomes.
   (4) Higher prices for farm products resulted in a higher standard of living for farmers.

10 Which generalization can best be drawn from the experiment with national Prohibition (1919–1933)?
    (1) Social attitudes can make laws difficult to enforce.
    (2) Americans resent higher taxes.
    (3) Morality can be legislated successfully.
    (4) People will sacrifice willingly for the common good.

11 In the 1920s, which economic factor led to the Great Depression?
    (1) lack of investment in the stock market
    (2) attempt by the United States to promote free trade
    (3) failure to develop new consumer goods industries
    (4) overproduction of farm products and manufactured goods

12 During the Great Depression, expressions such as *Hoovervilles* and *Hoover blankets* showed that President Hoover
    (1) was seen as a role model
    (2) used the military to aid the unemployed
    (3) was blamed for the suffering of the poor
    (4) supported relief and public housing for the needy

13 One difference between the administrations of President Franklin D. Roosevelt and President Herbert Hoover is that Roosevelt was
    (1) unwilling to allow government agencies to establish jobs programs
    (2) unable to win congressional support for his economic program
    (3) able to ignore economic issues for most of his first term in office
    (4) more willing to use government intervention to solve economic problems

Base your answer to question 14 on the cartoon below and on your knowledge of social studies.

Source: Clifford Kennedy Berryman, *The Washington Star,*
March 9, 1937

14 This cartoon illustrates that President Franklin D. Roosevelt caused a controversy based on
    (1) increased military spending in the early 1930s
    (2) a plan to assume some of the powers reserved to the states
    (3) efforts to counter the Dust Bowl with federal conservation measures
    (4) proposals that violated the principle of separation of powers

15 The strongest opposition to President
    Franklin D. Roosevelt's New Deal
    programs came from
    (1) western farmers
    (2) business leaders
    (3) factory workers
    (4) recent immigrants

16 Critics charged that the New Deal
    policies favored socialism because the
    federal government
    (1) took ownership of most major
         industries
    (2) favored farmers over workers and
         business owners
    (3) increased its responsibility for the
         welfare of the economy
    (4) declined to prosecute business
         monopolies

17 The major purpose of President
    Franklin D. Roosevelt's bank holiday
    of 1933 was to
    (1) restore public confidence in the
         nation's banks
    (2) reinforce strict laws to punish banks
         charging high interest rates
    (3) reduce the number of banks to a
         manageable number
    (4) encourage the nation's banks to loan
         more money to failing businesses

18 The National Labor Relations Act
    (Wagner Act) of 1935 strengthened labor
    unions because it legalized
    (1) collective bargaining
    (2) blacklisting
    (3) the open shop
    (4) the sit-down strike

19 In the 1930s, which geographic factor
    most influenced the westward migra-
    tion of thousands of people from the
    southern Great Plains?
    (1) extended drought in farming areas
    (2) excessive flooding of the Mississippi
         River
    (3) serious earthquakes in Pacific
         coastal areas
    (4) destructive hurricanes in the Gulf of
         Mexico

20 President Franklin D. Roosevelt's
    response to Supreme Court decisions
    that declared several New Deal laws
    unconstitutional was to
    (1) ask Congress to limit the Court's
         jurisdiction
    (2) demand the resignation of several
         justices
    (3) propose legislation to increase the
         size of the Court
    (4) ignore the Court's rulings

21 Between 1934 and 1937, Congress
    passed a series of neutrality acts that
    were designed primarily to
    (1) strengthen the nation's military
         defenses
    (2) provide aid to other democratic
         nations
    (3) create jobs for unemployed
         American workers
    (4) avoid mistakes that had led to
         American involvement in World
         War I

Part II Thematic Essay Question

The following thematic essay question comes from past Regents Examinations. Write your answers on a separate sheet of paper. Essay-writing tips appear in the margin. For additional help, see Taking the Regents Exam on pages ix–xxxi of this Review Book.

Directions: Write a well-organized essay that includes an introduction, several paragraphs addressing the task below, and a conclusion.

Theme: Supreme Court Cases Concerning Constitutional Civil Liberties

> The United States Supreme Court has played a major role in either expanding or limiting constitutional civil liberties in the United States.

Task: Identify *two* Supreme Court cases that have had an impact on civil liberties in the United States. For *each* case identified:

> - Discuss the facts of the case
> - Identify a specific constitutional civil liberty issue addressed by the Supreme Court
> - Discuss how the decision of the Supreme Court either expanded or limited a specific constitutional liberty in the United States

REGENTS WARM-UP

Notice the use of italicized type in the task. You are asked to choose two presidential administrations and to carry out three tasks for each administration you select.

You may use any appropriate Supreme Court case from your study of United States history. Some suggestions you might wish to consider include *Plessy* v. *Ferguson* (1896), *Schenck* v. *United States* (1919), *Korematsu* v. *United States* (1944), *Brown* v. *Board of Education of Topeka* (1954), *Mapp* v. *Ohio* (1961), *Gideon* v. *Wainwright* (1963), *Miranda* v. *Arizona* (1966), *Tinker* v. *Des Moines School District* (1969), or *New Jersey* v. *T.L.O.* (1985).

You are *not* limited to these suggestions.

Guidelines: In your essay, be sure to:

- Address all aspects of the *Task*
- Support the theme with relevant facts, examples, and details
- Use a logical and clear plan of organization
- Introduce the theme by establishing a framework that is beyond a simple restatement of the *Task* and conclude with a summation of the theme

Part III   Document-Based Questions

This exercise is designed to test your ability to work with historical documents. It is similar to the document-based questions that you will see on the Regents Examination. While you are asked to analyze four historical documents, the exercise on the actual exam will include more documents. Some of the documents have been edited for the purposes of the question. As you analyze the documents, take into account the source of each document and any point of view that may be presented in the document.

Historical Context: United States immigration policy has changed over time to reflect the needs and attitudes of American society.

Task: Using information from the documents and your knowledge of United States History, answer the questions that follow each document in Part A. Your answers to the questions will help you write the Part B essay, in which you will be asked to:

> • Discuss immigration policies or actions taken by the United States government that affected the immigration of people to the United States
> • Show how these policies or actions reflected the needs and attitudes of American society at that time

Part A   Short-Answer Questions

Directions: Analyze the documents and answer the short-answer questions that follow each document in the space provided.

Document 1

"Welcome to All," 1880

1   What does the cartoon show about United States immigration policy in 1880?

_____

_____

Document 2

> . . . one of those agents from the big bosses in America came to Bugiarno to get men for some iron mines in Missouri. The company paid for the tickets, but the men had to work for about a year to pay them back, and they had to work another year before they could send for their wives and families. So this time, when that agent came, Santino and some of his friends joined the gang and went off to America.
>
> —Rosa Cristoforo, an Italian immigrant, 1884

2a According to this passage, why did the agents encourage Italians to emigrate to America?

_____

_____

b How did the agents encourage Italians to go to America?

_____

_____

Document 3

Immigration Before and After Quota Laws	From Northern and Western Europe	From Southern and Eastern Europe and Asia
Average annual number of immigrants before quotas (1907–1914)	176,983	685,531
Emergency Quota Act of 1921	198,082	158,367
Emergency Quota Act Amended 1924	140,999	21,847
National Origins Act of 1929	132,323	20,251

—*Historical Statistics of the United States*

3 According to this chart, what effect did the quota laws have on immigration to the United States?

_____

_____

Document 4

We were tried during a time that has now passed into history. I mean by that, a time when there was . . . resentment and hate against the people of our principles, against the foreigner, against slackers, and it seems to me—rather, I am positive, that both you and Mr. Katzmann [have] done all . . . [that was] in your power in order to work out, in order to agitate, still more the passion of the juror, the prejudice of the juror, against us. . . . But my conviction is that I have suffered for things that I am guilty of. I am suffering because I am a radical and indeed I am a radical; I have suffered because I was an Italian and indeed I am an Italian; I have suffered more for my family and for my beloved wife than for myself. . . .

—Bartolomeo Vanzetti, to Judge Thayer upon being sentenced to death,
Sacco-Vanzetti case, April 9, 1927

4   State two reasons the speaker in this passage believed he was brought to trial.

(1) _____

_____

(2) _____

_____

Part B   Essay

Directions: Write a well-organized essay that includes an introduction, several paragraphs, and a conclusion.

Use evidence from at least *three* documents in the body of the essay. Support your response with relevant facts, examples, and details. Include additional outside information.

Historical Context: United States immigration policy has changed over time to reflect the needs and attitudes of American society.

Task: Using information from the documents and your knowledge of United States history and geography, write an essay in which you:

> • Discuss immigration policies or actions taken by the United States government that affected the immigration of people to the United States
> • Show how these policies or actions reflected the needs and attitudes of American society at that time

Guidelines: In your essay, be sure to:

- Address all aspects of the *Task* by accurately analyzing and interpreting at least *three* documents
- Incorporate information from the documents in the body of the essay
- Incorporate relevant outside information
- Support the theme with relevant facts, examples, and details
- Use a logical and clear plan of organization
- Introduce the theme by establishing a framework that is beyond a simple restatement of the *Task* or *Historical Context* and conclude with a summation of the theme

UNIT 6 GLOBAL STRUGGLES
1933–1960

Unit 6 Overview

The rise of dictatorships in the 1930s led to World War II, the most destructive war in the history of the world. The postwar decades immensely affected the lives of Americans. Learning about the events of this crucial period in our nation's history will help you understand the events occurring in the nation and around the world today.

Unit 6 Objectives

1.   Identify events leading up to World War II.

2.   Identify the causes and effects of World War II.

3.   Describe life in post-World War II America.

PREPARING FOR THE REGENTS

This entire book is set up to help you grasp the facts, main ideas, and concepts needed to do well on your Regents Exam. Notes in the margin include core concepts, test-taking tips, and more. Use blank spaces in the margins to answer questions raised in the text or to jot down key points. Before each unit of study, skim through the exams at the back of the book to develop a sense of what your state wants you to know about your nation.

Section 1   **America and the World**
Section 2   **World War II Begins**
Section 3   **America Enters the War**

REGENTS WARM-UP

Past Regents Exams have asked students to discuss the factors surrounding major historical events. As you read this chapter, keep an outline like the one shown here to help you organize and understand the relationships among events.

America and the World

I. The Rise of Dictators
  A. Mussolini and Fascism
    in Italy
  B. _____
  C. _____
  D. _____
II. _____

Chapter Overview

After World War I, Europe was unstable. Fascists, led by Benito Mussolini, seized power in Italy, and by 1933 Adolf Hitler and the Nazis had assumed control in Germany. Meanwhile, Japan expanded its territory in Asia. When Germany attacked Poland, World War II began. The United States clung to neutrality until Japan attacked Pearl Harbor.

As you read through this chapter, ask yourself these questions:
(1) Why did many Americans support a policy of isolationism in the 1930s?
(2) What were the early events of World War II and why was Britain able to resist the Nazis?
(3) What groups of people were persecuted by the Nazis?
(4) How did Roosevelt help Britain while maintaining official neutrality?
(5) What events ultimately led to war between the United States and Japan?

Main Ideas and Concepts

- **Decision Making** German and Japanese actions in the 1930s led President Roosevelt to work to prevent aggression.

- **Foreign Policy** The desire of the French and British to avoid another war helped encourage Hitler's aggression in Europe. The U.S. focus on economic issues contributed to its isolationist policies.

- **Human Rights** The Nazis systematically deprived Jews of their rights, while other nations refused to accept many Jewish refugees.

- **Presidential Decisions and Actions** Even while the United States was officially neutral, President Roosevelt found ways to help the British fight Germany.

People, Places, Terms

The following names and terms will help you to prepare for the Regents Exam in United States History and Government. You can find an explanation of each name and term in the Glossary at the back of this book, in your textbook, or in another reference source.

appeasement	internationalism	Manchuria
Atlantic Charter	Lend-Lease Act	Benito Mussolini
blitzkrieg	Vladimir Lenin	Neutrality Act
Winston Churchill	General Douglas	of 1939
Fascism	MacArthur	

SECTION 1 AMERICA AND THE WORLD

The Rise of Dictators

The terms of the peace treaty that ended World War I and the economic depression contributed to the rise of dictatorships in Europe and Asia.

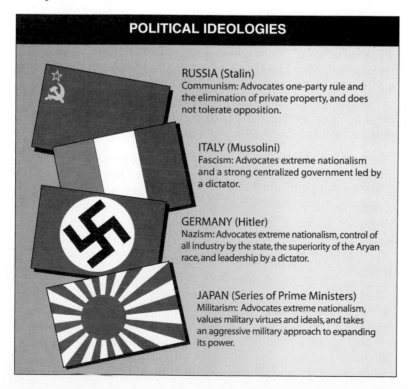

POLITICAL IDEOLOGIES

RUSSIA (Stalin)
Communism: Advocates one-party rule and the elimination of private property, and does not tolerate opposition.

ITALY (Mussolini)
Fascism: Advocates extreme nationalism and a strong centralized government led by a dictator.

GERMANY (Hitler)
Nazism: Advocates extreme nationalism, control of all industry by the state, the superiority of the Aryan race, and leadership by a dictator.

JAPAN (Series of Prime Ministers)
Militarism: Advocates extreme nationalism, values military virtues and ideals, and takes an aggressive military approach to expanding its power.

Mussolini and Fascism in Italy In Italy, **Benito Mussolini** founded Italy's Fascist party. **Fascism** was a kind of aggressive nationalism. Fascists believed that the nation was more important than the individual and that to be strong, a nation needed a strong government led by a dictator to impose order on society. Fascists also believed that a nation became strong by expanding its territory and building up its military.

Mussolini marched on Rome in 1922, claiming that he was coming to defend Italy against a Communist revolution. Conservative leaders of the Italian parliament persuaded the king to appoint Mussolini as the premier and head of the government. Once Mussolini took over, he quickly set up a dictatorship. Business leaders and landowners supported him. In 1929, he made a concordat (an agreement between a leader and the Pope) with the Roman Catholic Church.

Stalin Takes Over the USSR After the Russian Revolution began in 1917, the Bolshevik Party, led by **Vladimir Lenin**, set up Communist governments throughout the Russian empire. They renamed these territories the Union of Soviet Socialist Republics (USSR). To control these territories, the Communists set up a one-party rule, suppressed individual rights, and punished those who opposed them.

Hitler and Nazism in Germany Adolf Hitler opposed communism and admired Mussolini. He hated the Allies for their treatment of Germany after World War I. Germany's condition after the war led to the start of many new political parties. One such party was the National Socialist German Workers' Party, or the Nazi Party. Hitler was one of the first members of the party, which was anti-Communist and nationalistic.

In 1923, Hitler attempted an unsuccessful coup d'état. He was arrested and went to prison, where he wrote *Mein Kampf*, which called for the unification of all Germans under one government and claimed that certain Germans, especially blond, blue-eyed ones, were part of a "master race" called Aryans. Hitler's racism was especially directed toward Jews. He believed that they were responsible for many of the world's problems, including Germany's.

By 1932 the Nazis were the largest party in the German Parliament. Many German leaders supported Hitler and his nationalism. In 1933 they appointed him chancellor, or prime minister, and the Nazi-dominated Parliament gave Hitler the powers of a dictator.

CORE CONCEPTS: POWER

After Hitler became prime minister, he ordered storm troopers to crack down on the Communist Party and to intimidate voters, assuring him a Nazi-dominated Parliament.

Militarists Gain Control of Japan In Japan, the economy was suffering. The country did not make enough money from its exports to pay for the imports it needed. The Depression made the situation worse. Many military leaders believed that Japan should seize territory to get the resources it needed, so a group invaded **Manchuria.** After assassinating the prime minister, the Japanese military was in control.

America Turns to Neutrality

After World War I, many Americans supported isolationism, or the belief that the United States should avoid international commitments that might drag the nation into another war. Many had grown disillusioned with the League of Nations and its inability to stop Japanese aggression in Asia. Support for isolationism became even stronger when many European nations announced that they could not repay money that they had borrowed during World War I. Then several books emerged, arguing that arms manufacturers had tricked the U.S. into entering World War I. The huge profits that arms factories had made during the war gave that impression. In response, Congress passed the Neutrality Act of 1935, which made it illegal for Americans to sell arms to any country at war.

Legislating Neutrality The Spanish Civil War, which started in 1936, was a conflict between the Republican government in Spain and a group of Fascist rebels. Although the Republicans had sought aid from Britain, France, and the United States, only the Soviet Union gave support, which fueled Fascist propaganda against the republic. That same year, Germany, Italy, and Japan agreed to cooperate on several international issues. The three nations became known as the Axis Powers. Germany also assisted the Fascists in the Spanish Civil War, providing new tanks and mechanized armor.

The United States passed the Neutrality Act of 1937, which continued to ban the sale of arms. It also required that countries at war had to send their own ships to pick up nonmilitary supplies in the United States, and that they pay cash. Loans were not allowed. The United States wanted to avoid a situation that had helped bring it into World War I.

Roosevelt and Internationalism Although President Roosevelt knew that ending the Depression was his first priority, he was not an isolationist. Instead, he supported **internationalism.** This was the belief that trade between nations creates prosperity and

CORE CONCEPTS: GOVERNMENT

President Roosevelt explained that the Neutrality Act of 1937 did not apply because neither China nor Japan had actually declared war.

helps to prevent war. Roosevelt knew that isolationism was too strong to resist, however, so he did not veto the Neutrality Acts.

In July 1937, Japan launched a full-scale attack on China. Roosevelt decided to help the Chinese, claiming that the Neutrality Act of 1937 did not apply. Roosevelt ordered the sale of weapons to China, yet Americans still wanted nothing to do with another war.

Roosevelt's Quarantine Speech Roosevelt believed that the United States could not allow the Japanese invasion of China to go unpunished. In a speech in October 1937, he warned forcefully of the dangers that Japanese aggression posed to world peace. Aggressors, he proclaimed, should be "quarantined" by the international community to prevent war from spreading. Public response to the speech was disturbingly hostile, and Roosevelt drew back.

SECTION 2 WORLD WAR II BEGINS

"Peace in Our Time"

European leaders did not try to stop Hitler for several reasons. First, they thought that by giving in to his demands, they would avoid another war. Second, some thought that Hitler's desire to unite all German-speaking regions of Europe with Germany was reasonable. Finally, they believed that if the Nazis received more territory, they would be more interested in peace.

The Munich Crisis and Appeasement Hitler then announced the unification of Austria and Germany and his desire for an area of Czechoslovakia that had many German-speaking people. The Czechs, who were allied with the Soviet Union and France, resisted Germany's demands for a portion of their nation. To help stop another war, in September 1938, Britain, France, Italy, and Germany sent representatives to a meeting in Munich, Germany, to decide what to do about Czechoslovakia. At the meeting, Britain and France agreed to Hitler's demands. This policy became known as **appeasement**, or giving concessions in exchange for peace. Germany violated the agreement in March 1939, when German troops marched into Czechoslovakia.

LINKING GEOGRAPHY TO HISTORY

Hitler was interested in negotiating the nonaggression pact with the USSR before invading Poland because Germany did not want to fight a war on its eastern and western fronts simultaneously.

Danzig and the Polish Corridor In May 1939, Hitler ordered the German army to prepare to invade Poland. He then began negotiations with the USSR. In August 1939, Germany and the USSR signed the nonaggression pact. Britain and France believed that Hitler made the deal with the USSR to free himself to fight a war against them and Poland. They did not know that the nonaggression pact included a deal between Germany and the USSR to divide Poland between themselves.

The War Begins

Germany invaded Poland on September 1, 1939. It invaded from the west, and the Soviets invaded Poland from the east. Hitler assumed that Britain and France would use appeasement toward him as they did before. However, on September 3, Britain and France declared war on Germany. World War II had started.

Blitzkrieg in Poland The Germans used a new type of warfare called **blitzkrieg**, or lightning war. This type of warfare used large numbers of tanks to break through and encircle enemy positions. In addition, waves of aircraft bombed enemy positions. Blitzkrieg depended on radio communication to coordinate tanks and aircraft. The Polish army was not able to defend itself against the German attack. By October 5, 1939, the Polish army had been defeated.

After invading Poland, Germany attacked Norway and Denmark, and controlled both nations within a month. Hitler then turned his attention to France. The Germans sent their troops through the mountains in Luxembourg and eastern Belgium. The French did not think the Germans could get their tanks through the mountains and left few troops to defend that area. The Germans got through easily and moved west across northern France to the English Channel. On June 22, 1940, France surrendered to Hitler. Germany then installed a puppet government to govern France. The Germans believed it would be easy to take Britain.

Britain Remains Defiant

Hitler expected Britain to surrender just as France had. For British Prime Minister **Winston Churchill**, this was not an option. When Hitler realized that Britain would not surrender, he prepared to invade.

Hitler stopped attacks on British military targets and concentrated them on London itself. Hitler wanted to terrorize the British people into surrendering. His plan did not work.

The British Royal Air Force inflicted more damage on the Germans than they endured. On October 12, 1940, Hitler canceled his plans to invade Britain.

SECTION 3   AMERICA ENTERS THE WAR

FDR Supports England

Neutrality Act of 1939 President Roosevelt officially proclaimed the United States neutral two days after Britain and France declared war on Germany. Despite this, he was determined to help the two countries in their struggle against Hitler. Soon after the war began, Roosevelt called Congress into a special session to revise the neutrality laws. He asked Congress to eliminate the ban on arms sales to nations at war. Public opinion strongly supported the president. Congress passed the new law, but isolationists demanded a price for the revision. Under the **Neutrality Act of 1939**, warring nations could buy weapons from the United States only if they paid cash and carried the arms on their own ships (this became known as the "cash and carry" policy).

The Isolationist Debate

LINKING GEOGRAPHY TO HISTORY

Isolationist sentiment in the United States arose in part from the fact that the nation was an ocean away from the conflict in Europe and Asia.

The Range of Opinion By 1940 most Americans supported offering limited aid to the Allies. Yet there was a wide range of opinions. At one end was the Fight for Freedom Committee, which wanted to repeal the neutrality laws and take strong action against Germany. The Committee to defend America by Aiding the Allies pushed for increased American aid to the Allies but not military intervention.

Churchill asked Roosevelt for old American destroyers because Britain's had been lost. Roosevelt agreed to exchange the destroyers for the right to build American bases in some British-controlled territories. Roosevelt's deal led to the establishment of the America First Committee. This was an isolationist group that opposed any American intervention or aid to the Allies.

Edging Toward War

After he was re-elected, Roosevelt began to expand the nation's role in the war. He said that only Britain stood between the United States and a German attack.

The Lend-Lease Act By December 1940, Britain had no funds left to fight Germany. President Roosevelt came up with a way to get around the cash-and-carry policy, which Britain could no longer meet. **The Lend-Lease Act** allowed the United States to lend or lease arms to any country that was considered vital to the defense of the United States. As a result, the United States could send weapons to Britain if Britain promised to return or pay rent for them after the war. Lend-lease aid eventually included aid to the Soviet Union as well. In June 1941, Hitler violated the Nazi-Soviet pact and started a massive invasion of the Soviet Union. Although Churchill detested communism, he promised to aid any nation that helped fight Nazism. Roosevelt agreed with him.

The Atlantic Charter In August 1941 Roosevelt and Churchill met on board American and British warships anchored near Newfoundland. During these meetings, the two leaders agreed on the text of the **Atlantic Charter**. It committed the two countries to a postwar world of democracy, non-aggression, free trade, economic advancement, and freedom of the seas.

Japan Attacks the United States

America Embargos Japan Roosevelt's goal between August 1939 and December 1941 was to help Britain and its allies defeat Germany. Much of the British navy had been moved from Asia to the Atlantic to defend against Germany. As a result, Roosevelt introduced policies to discourage the Japanese from attacking the British Empire. In July 1940, Congress passed the Export Control Act, giving Roosevelt the power to restrict the sale of strategic materials to other nations. Roosevelt blocked the sale of airplane fuel and scrap iron to Japan. This angered the Japanese, who had signed an alliance with Germany and Italy and became a member of the Axis Powers.

By July 1941, Japan had sent troops to southern Indochina. This was a threat to the British Empire. Japan was now in a position to bomb Hong Kong and Singapore. Roosevelt responded by freezing Japanese assets in the United States. He reduced the amount of oil being shipped to Japan, and sent **General Douglas MacArthur** to the Philippines to build up American defenses there. Roosevelt said the ban on oil would be lifted if Japan would leave Indochina and make peace with China.

REGENTS WARM-UP

A graphic organizer like the one below can help you keep track of the events that caused the United States to become involved in World War II.

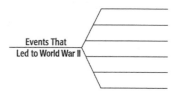

Events That Led to World War II

LINKING GEOGRAPHY TO HISTORY

To gain direct access to natural resources, Japanese military leaders aimed to build an empire in the Pacific. The U.S. Pacific Fleet, headquartered at Oahu island in Hawaii, was seen as an obstacle that had to be destroyed.

Japan Attacks Pearl Harbor The Japanese government appeared to be negotiating with the United States. The United States, however, had decoded Japanese communications that showed Japan was preparing to go to war against the United States. On December 7, 1941, Japan launched a surprise attack on Pearl Harbor. Japan sank or damaged 21 ships of the U.S. Pacific Fleet, destroyed 188 airplanes, killed 2,403 Americans, and injured 1,178. The next day, Congress voted to declare war on Japan. On December 11, Germany and Italy declared war on the United States.

CHAPTER 24 AMERICA AND WORLD WAR II

Chapter Overview

The United States entered World War II unwillingly and largely unprepared. The American people, however, quickly banded together to transform the American economy into the most productive and efficient war-making machine in the world. As the Nazis gained power, they began a campaign of violence against Jews. American forces turned the tide in Europe and the Pacific, playing a crucial role in the defeat of Germany, Italy, and Japan.

Many changes, good and bad, that began during World War II are still shaping our lives today. For example, the United Nations was founded, nuclear weapons were invented, and the United States became the most powerful nation in the world.

As you read through this chapter, ask yourself these questions:
(1) How did the United States mobilize its economy?
(2) How were the Allies able to fight a war on two fronts and turn the war against the Axis in the Pacific, Russia, and the North Atlantic?
(3) How did the wartime economy create opportunities for women and minorities?
(4) What were the goals of the two major offensives the Allies launched in Europe in 1943?
(5) In their planning for peace, what major decisions did the Allied leaders make at their Big Three wartime conference?
(6) Why did the Allies create the United Nations and hold war crimes trials?

Main Ideas and Concepts

- **Citizenship** The success of the United States in mobilizing for war was due largely to the cooperation of individual American citizens.

- **Citizenship** Many American soldiers made heroic sacrifices in order to turn the tide against the Axis Powers.

- **Citizenship** To win the war, American citizens at home made countless changes in work patterns and lifestyles.

- **The Uses of Geography** The United States fought the war by landing troops in Italy and France and island-hopping across the Pacific toward Japan.

- **Individuals, Groups, and Institutions** Allied leaders forged plans for an international organization to prevent future wars.

People, Places, Terms

The following names or terms will help you to prepare for the Regents Exam in United States History and Government. You can find an explanation of each name and term in the Glossary at the back of this book, in your textbook, or in another reference source.

Battle of the Bulge	**kamikaze**	**"Rosie the Riveter"**
charter	*Korematsu* **v.**	**Sunbelt**
concentration camps	*United States*	**Harry S Truman**
convoy system	**Liberty ships**	**United Nations**
D-Day	**Manhattan Project**	**V-E Day**
disenfranchised	**Nuremburg Laws**	**V-J Day**
Holocaust	**rationing**	

SECTION 1 MOBILIZING FOR WAR

Converting the Economy

Even before the attack on Pearl Harbor, the United States had begun to mobilize the economy. When the German blitzkrieg hit France, President Roosevelt declared a national emergency. He announced a plan to build 50,000 warplanes per year. Roosevelt and his advisers believed that the quickest way to mobilize the economy was to give industries motivation to move quickly. Instead of asking companies to bid for contracts, the government signed cost-plus contracts. The government agreed to pay a company whatever it cost to make a product plus a guaranteed percentage of the costs as profit. Under this system, the more a company produced and the faster it did the work, the more money it would make. The system helped get things produced quickly.

To convince companies to switch their factories to make military goods, Congress gave the Reconstruction Finance Corporation (RFC) new authority. The government gave the agency permission to make loans to companies to help them cover the cost of converting to war production.

American Industry Gets the Job Done

Tanks Replace Cars By 1941 the nation's economy was only partially mobilized. Many companies were still producing consumer goods instead of military equipment. By the summer of 1942, however, most major industries had converted to war production. Automobile companies began to make trucks, jeeps, and tanks. They also made rifles, mines, helmets, and other pieces of military equipment. The Ford Motor Company created an assembly line to build the B-24 bomber. By the end of the war, the company had built more than 8,600 aircraft.

Building the Liberty Ships Henry Kaiser's shipyard built ships. They were best known for making **Liberty ships**, basic cargo ships used during the war. They were welded rather than riveted, making them cheap and easy to build and very hard to sink.

The War Production Board To make mobilization more efficient, President Roosevelt set up the War Production Board (WPB). This agency had the authority to set priorities and production goals. It also had the authority to control the distribution of raw materials and supplies.

Building an Army

In addition to changing industries to war production, the country had to build up its military. After France surrendered to Germany, two members of Congress introduced the Selective Service and Training Act. This was a plan for the first peacetime draft in American history. Congress approved the draft in September 1940.

Draftees were sent to a reception center where they were given a physical exam and shots. The draftees were then given uniforms, boots, and equipment. The clothing was labeled "G.I.," which meant "Government Issue." For this reason, American

CORE CONCEPTS: SCIENCE AND TECHNOLOGY

During World War II, U.S. General George C. Marshall believed that the jeep was "America's greatest contribution to modern warfare."

CORE CONCEPTS: GOVERNMENT

From 1948 until 1973, during both peacetime and periods of conflict, men were drafted to fill vacancies in the armed forces that could not be filled through voluntary means. The draft ended in 1973 and the U.S. converted to an all-volunteer military.

CORE CONCEPTS: PRESIDENTIAL DECISIONS AND ACTIONS

Although the military did not end all segregation during the war, it paved the way for President Truman's decision to fully integrate the military in 1948.

LINKING PAST AND PRESENT

From 1942 to 1944, more than 1,000 women pilots trained to fly all kinds of aircraft. Although not allowed to fly combat missions, these women freed male pilots for combat. In 1991 the law excluding women from flying combat aircraft was repealed. By 1998, 21 women were flying fighter jets for the air force and 27 for the navy.

soldiers were called "GIs." Recruits were sent to basic training for eight weeks. There, they learned how to handle weapons, read maps, and dig trenches. They also learned how to work as a team. Recruits came from all over the country. Training made them a unit.

A Segregated Army Although training promoted unity, white recruits did not train alongside African Americans. The army was completely segregated. African Americans had separate barracks, mess halls, and recreational facilities. They were organized into their own military units, commanded by white officers. Many military leaders did not want African American soldiers in combat. They assigned them to construction and supply units.

Pushing for "Double V" Some African Americans did not want to support the war. They noted that African Americans were segregated in the army and that lynchings continued. They also noted that African Americans were **disfranchised**, or denied their right to vote. Many African American leaders combined patriotism with protest. A leading African American newspaper in Pittsburgh started a "Double V" campaign. The paper argued that African Americans should join the war effort to achieve a double victory. This would be a victory over Hitler's racism and a victory over racism in the United States. President Roosevelt responded by ordering the military to begin recruiting African Americans and to put them into combat. He also appointed Colonel Benjamin O. Davis, the highest-ranking African American officer in the U.S. Army, to the rank of brigadier general.

African Americans in Combat The army air force created an African American unit that trained in Tuskegee, Alabama. The fighter pilots became known as the Tuskegee Airmen. They were sent to the Mediterranean in April 1943, where the unit played an important role in a battle in Italy. African Americans also performed well in the army, receiving commendations for distinguished service.

Women Join the Armed Forces The army enlisted women for the first time during World War II, but they were banned from combat. Many women in the army held administrative and clerical jobs, freeing men for combat. The army set up the Women's Army Corps (WAC) in 1943. The Coast Guard, navy, and marines set up their own women's organizations. In addition, thousands of women served as nurses in the army and navy.

SECTION 2 THE EARLY BATTLES

Although the United States fleet at Pearl Harbor was badly damaged by the Japanese, American aircraft carriers were not. The carriers were on a mission in the Pacific. There was little they could do to stop Japanese advances into Southeast Asia. The Japanese attacked American airfields in the Philippines and landed troops in the islands.

The American and Filipino forces defending the Philippines were outnumbered and retreated to the Bataan peninsula. By May the Philippines fell to the Japanese.

A Change in Japanese Strategy The commander of the Japanese fleet wanted to attack Midway Island, the site of the last American base in the North Pacific west of Hawaii. He believed that attacking the base would bring the American fleet into battle. Then the Japanese fleet would destroy it. Japan also planned to attack New Guinea and cut American supply lines to Australia.

The Battle of Midway A team of code breakers learned of the plan to attack Midway. The Pacific commander of the navy decided to ambush the Japanese fleet and ordered carriers to move near Midway. When the Japanese aircraft flew near Midway, they were met with antiaircraft fire. Thirty-eight Japanese planes were shot down. As they were preparing a second wave of attacks on Midway, American aircraft attacked Japanese carriers. The American attacks greatly damaged the Japanese navy, and its commander ordered the ships to retreat.

Turning Back the German Army

President Roosevelt wanted to get American troops into battle in Europe. British Prime Minister Churchill did not believe that the United States and Britain were ready for a full-scale European invasion. He wanted to attack the edges of the German empire. Roosevelt agreed with Churchill and ordered the invasion of Morocco and Algeria.

The Struggle for North Africa Morocco and Algeria were French territories indirectly under German control. The invasion did not involve a large number of troops and placed American troops in North Africa, where they could help the British fight Germans in Egypt. Egypt was important to Britain because of the Suez Canal, used by most of Britain's empire to get supplies to Britain.

CORE CONCEPTS: POWER

When the Allied defenders of Bataan finally surrendered, thousands died on the Bataan Death March to a Japanese prison camp.

LINKING GEOGRAPHY AND HISTORY

The Battle of Midway was a turning point in the war. The Japanese had lost four of its largest carriers. The Americans had stopped the Japanese advance in the Pacific. However, the battle killed 362 Americans and more than 3,000 Japanese.

The American invasion of North Africa began in November 1942. After battles in several North African cities, American and British forces finally pushed the Germans back. In May 1943, the German forces in North Africa surrendered.

The Battle of the Atlantic The war against German submarines in the Atlantic Ocean increased. German submarines entered American coastal waters after Germany declared war on the United States. By August 1942, German submarines had sunk 360 American cargo ships. Because of the loss, the U.S. Navy decided to set up a **convoy system**.

Soon, the United States was building more ships than German submarines managed to sink. American airplanes and warships also began to use new technology, such as radar and sonar, to pinpoint and attack submarines. Eventually the technology took its toll on German submarines. The Battle of the Atlantic turned in favor of the Allies.

REGENTS WARM-UP

The convoy system set up by the U.S. Navy refers to the practice of sending cargo ships out in groups that are escorted by navy warships.

SECTION 3 LIFE ON THE HOME FRONT

Women and Minorities Gain Ground

Women in the Defense Plants World War II changed American society at home. Before the war, most Americans believed married women should not work outside the home. However, the labor shortage during the war forced factories to hire married women to do the jobs that traditionally were done by men.

THE GOOD AND THE BAD IN AMERICAN WARTIME SOCIETY	
Reasons to Celebrate	**Causes for Concern**
End of Great Depression	Racial tension over jobs and equality
Creation of 19 million new jobs	Labor shortage
Average family income doubled	Housing shortages

"Rosie the Riveter" was the great symbol of the campaign to hire women. Images of Rosie appeared on posters and in newspaper ads. Although most women left the factories after the war, their work permanently changed American attitudes about women in the workplace.

African Americans Demand War Work Many factories were willing to hire women but they did not want to hire African Americans. A. Philip Randolph, the head of the Brotherhood of Sleeping Car Porters—a major union for African American railroad workers—decided to do something. He told President Roosevelt that he was going to organize a march on Washington. Roosevelt responded by issuing an order saying that discrimination in hiring workers in defense industries or government would not be tolerated. Roosevelt created the Fair Employment Practices Commission to enforce the order. This was the first civil rights agency set up by the federal government since Reconstruction.

Mexicans Become Farmworkers To help farmers in the Southwest overcome the labor shortage, the government started the Bracero Program in 1942. It arranged for Mexican farmworkers to help in the harvest. Migrant farmworkers became important to farming in the Southwest.

CORE CONCEPTS: ECONOMIC SYSTEMS

World War II had a positive effect on American society. It ended the Depression, led to the creation of almost 19 million new jobs, and doubled the income of most American families.

CORE CONCEPTS: MOVEMENT OF PEOPLE AND GOODS

More than 200,000 Mexicans came to the United States to help with the harvest and to build and maintain railroads.

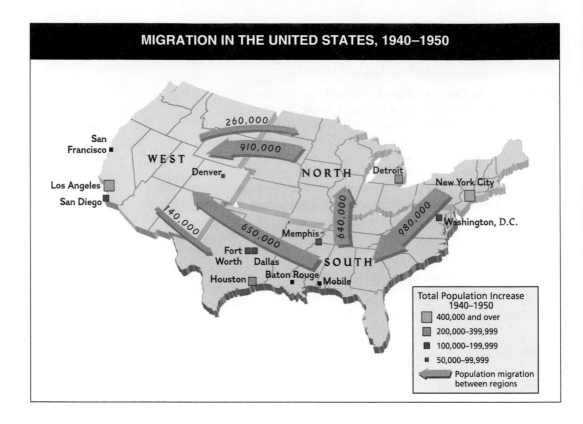

MIGRATION IN THE UNITED STATES, 1940–1950

Total Population Increase 1940–1950

- 400,000 and over
- 200,000–399,999
- 100,000–199,999
- 50,000–99,999

Population migration between regions

A Nation on the Move

Many Americans moved during the war to places that had jobs. Many headed west and south. Southern California and cities in the Deep South made up a new industrial region, the **Sunbelt**. This region led the way in manufacturing and urbanization in the United States.

The Housing Crisis Cities that had war industries had to deal with the problem of providing houses to the thousands of new workers. The federal government gave $1.2 billion to build public housing and schools during the war. About two million people lived in government-built housing during the war.

Racism Explodes Into Violence During World War II, African Americans arrived in cities in the North and West in search of jobs. They were often met with intolerance that sometimes led to violence.

The Zoot Suit Wartime prejudice was evident in other areas of American society. In Los Angeles, racism against Mexican Americans and the fear of juvenile crime became linked because of the zoot suit. This was an overstuffed jacket that had wide lapels and reached to the knees. It also included baggy, pleated pants. Those who wore zoot suits often wore wide-brimmed hats and a long key chain. Many Americans considered the zoot suit unpatriotic. To save fabric for the war, many men wore a suit that had no vest or cuffs and included a short jacket with narrow lapels.

Japanese American Relocation After the attack on Pearl Harbor, many Americans turned their anger against Japanese Americans. Some attacked Japanese American businesses and homes. Some newspapers printed rumors about Japanese spies in the Japanese American community. Many people, including members of Congress, demanded that people of Japanese ancestry be removed from the West Coast. They believed that Japanese Americans would not remain loyal to the United States. Japanese Americans served in the war, and none was ever tried for spying. However, President Roosevelt signed Executive Order 9066, which allowed the War Department to declare any part of the United States a military zone. The department declared most of the West Coast a military zone. People of Japanese ancestry were relocated to 10 internment camps.

Korematsu v. United States Some Japanese Americans protested the relocation. Fred Korematsu claimed that his rights had been violated. He took his case to the Supreme Court. In December 1944, the Court ruled that the relocation was constitutional because it was based on military urgency, not on race. Afterward, the Court ruled that loyal American citizens could not be held against their will. In early 1945, the government began releasing the Japanese Americans from the camps.

CORE CONCEPTS: CHANGE

The worst racial violence occurred in Detroit in June 1943. By the time it ended, 25 African Americans and 9 whites had been killed.

CORE CONCEPTS: DIVERSITY

Hostility toward Mexican Americans did not stop them from joining the war effort. About 500,000 Hispanic Americans served in the American armed forces during the war.

CORE CONCEPTS: HUMAN RIGHTS

When President Roosevelt signed Executive Order 9066, Japanese Americans, many of whom were American citizens, were relocated to internment camps. In some cases, they lost their homes or were forced to sell them quickly at low prices. Many lost their businesses and livelihood.

Daily Life in Wartime America

Wage and Price Controls President Roosevelt worried that mobilizing the economy might result in inflation. Wages and prices began to rise quickly during the war because of the demand for workers and raw materials. To stabilize this, Roosevelt set up the Office of Price Administration (OPA) and the Office of Economic Stabilization (OES). The agencies regulated wages and the price of products. They managed to keep inflation under control.

The War Labor Board tried to prevent labor strikes. Most unions pledged not to strike. The War Labor Board settled over 17,000 disputes by the end of the war.

CORE CONCEPTS: ECONOMIC SYSTEMS

Rationing affected everyone. Women painted seams on their legs to make it appear they were wearing stockings, because silk was needed to make parachutes instead of stockings. Meat, sugar, gasoline, fats, and oils were other goods that were rationed.

Blue Points, Red Points The demand for raw materials and supplies created shortages. The OPA began **rationing**, or limiting the availability of many consumer products to make sure that there were enough supplies for the military. Households were given a book of ration coupons each month. When people bought foods, they also had to give enough coupon points to cover their purchases.

Victory Gardens and Scrap Drives Americans volunteered to plant victory gardens to produce more food for the war effort. Land in backyards, schoolyards, city parks, and empty lots were used for these gardens.

The government organized scrap drives for materials that were important to the war effort. These materials included spare rubber, tin, aluminum, and steel. Also included were oils and fats, which were needed to make explosives.

Paying for the War The war cost more than $300 billion. To raise money, the government raised taxes, but the taxes covered less than half of the cost. The government issued bonds to raise the rest of the money. When Americans bought bonds, they were loaning money to the government. The government promised that the bonds could be redeemed at a future date for the price of the bond plus interest. The most common bonds were E bonds. Private citizens bought nearly $50 billion worth of war bonds, while banks and other financial institutions bought about $100 billion worth of bonds to help finance the war effort.

Wartime Life and Culture The war created considerable anxiety in American life. Families worried about loved ones and struggled to adjust to their absence. However, the abundance of the war years also created a buoyancy in American life that the conflict only partially subdued. Suddenly people had money to spend again and, despite the shortages of wartime, some things to spend it on. The book, theater, and movie industries did record business. Audiences equal to about half the population attended movies each week, often to watch heroic war films.

Swing and Big Band To many young Americans, nothing more strongly evoked the image of life as they remembered it and wished it to be than big bands, the most popular musical groups of the era. The big bands played several different kinds of jazz, but played "swing" above all—a new form of jazz that seemed made for dancing. Like other kinds of jazz (and later, rock and roll), it had its origins in the African American musical world. Musicians such as Benny Goodman, Count Basie, Duke Ellington, and Glenn Miller made swing music wildly popular. Swing music also became one of the first forms of popular music to challenge racial taboos—Goodman hired an African American pianist to play with his band and others soon followed.

SECTION 4 THE HOLOCAUST

Millions of Jews suffered terrible persecution before and during World War II. During the **Holocaust**, the catastrophe that devastated Europe's Jewish population, the Nazis killed nearly 6 million Jews. They also killed millions of other people from groups that they considered inferior. The Hebrew term for the Holocaust is *Shoah*, meaning "catastrophe." It is often used specifically to refer to the Nazi campaign to exterminate the Jews during World War II.

Nazi Ideology In Germany, the Nazis executed the racial policies that Hitler had outlined in his book *Mein Kampf*. The Nazis persecuted anyone who opposed them, such as Protestant and Catholic religious leaders, as well as disabled people, Gypsies, homosexuals, and Slavic peoples. However, they focused most of their hatred on the Jews.

REGENTS WARM-UP

Questions on past Regents Exams have asked students to interpret maps, cartoons, and other graphics. Examine the poster from the World War II era. Then answer the question that follows.

The main message conveyed in the poster is that

(1) all able-bodied Americans should join the army
(2) the purchase of bonds will speed the end of the war
(3) loose lips sink ships
(4) the Nazis are monsters committing horrible atrocities

The Nuremberg Laws In September 1935, the Nazis set up the **Nuremberg Laws**. These took citizenship away from Jewish Germans and banned marriage between Jews and other Germans. Another law defined a Jew as a person with at least one Jewish grandparent and did not allow Jews to hold public office or vote. Jews' passports were marked with a red "J" to clearly identify them as Jewish. Jews lost their right to work as journalists, farmers, teachers, lawyers, or doctors, and from operating businesses. With no income, life became very difficult. Many Jews chose to stay in Germany during the early years of Nazi rule. They did not want to give up the lives they had built there.

Jewish Refugees Try to Flee As the discrimination and violence against Jews increased, many decided to leave Germany and flee to the United States. By 1939 about 350,000 Jews had escaped Germany. However, there was a backlog of visa applications from Jews trying to leave. As a result, millions of Jews remained trapped in Nazi-dominated Europe.

Jewish immigration to the United States was hampered by several factors. Nazis did not allow Jews to take more than about four dollars out of Germany. The United States was reluctant to accept Jewish immigrants because laws prohibited immigration by people who might need financial assistance. High unemployment rates in the United States made immigration unpopular. Also, immigration quotas were in place, limiting the number of immigrants that could be accepted.

CORE CONCEPTS: IMMIGRATION AND MIGRATION

Because they were persecuted in Germany, a number of brilliant Jewish German scientists, such as Albert Einstein, immigrated to the United States in the 1930s.

The Final Solution

In January 1942, Nazi leaders met at the Wannsee Conference to determine the "final solution of the Jewish question." The Nazis made plans to round up Jews throughout Nazi-controlled Europe and take them to detention centers known as **concentration camps.** The elderly, children, and the unhealthy would be sent to extermination camps, attached to the concentration camps, to be executed in massive gas chambers.

Concentration Camps The Nazis built concentration camps throughout Europe. One of the largest was Buchenwald, in Germany. Prisoners worked 12-hour shifts as slave laborers in nearby factories. Hundreds died every month as a result of exhaustion, disease, and malnutrition.

Extermination Camps The Nazis built extermination camps in several concentration camps, mostly in Poland. Sometimes up to 12,000 people were gassed in a single day at Auschwitz. About 1,300,000 of the 1,600,000 people who died at Auschwitz were Jews. The others included Poles, Gypsies, and Soviet prisoners-of-war.

In the midst of intense fighting, the American government was confronted with the Holocaust. As early as 1942, high officials had strong evidence that Hitler's forces were rounding up Jews and others from all over Europe, transporting them to concentration camps, and systematically murdering them. However, the American government resisted pressure from the public to end the killing or attempt to rescue some of the victims.

People continue to debate why and how the Holocaust could have happened. Most historians believe that several factors contributed to it: The German people felt they were harmed by the harsh treaty after World War I; Germany faced severe economic problems; Hitler had a strong hold on Germany; Germany did not have a strong tradition of representative government; Germans feared Hitler's secret police; Europe had a long history of anti-Jewish prejudice and discrimination.

CORE CONCEPTS: HUMAN RIGHTS

After exterminating Jews and other "undesirables" in extermination camps, Nazis took whatever articles of value the victims had, such as gold fillings from teeth and wedding rings.

SECTION 5 PUSHING THE AXIS BACK

Striking Back at the Third Reich

To win the war, the Allies had to land troops in Europe and on islands in the Pacific. To plan this, President Roosevelt met with Prime Minister Winston Churchill at the Casablanca Conference in Morocco. At this meeting, the two leaders decided to increase the bombing of Germany. The Allies also agreed to attack the Axis in Sicily. Churchill believed that the Italians would quit the war if Italy were invaded. Churchill also wanted the invasion of Italy to be extended up into the "soft underbelly" of Europe into Southern France and Eastern Europe to prevent the Soviets from establishing control of all of Eastern Europe in the post-World War II period.

Strategic Bombing The Allies increased the bombing of Germany. The bombing did not destroy German morale, but it created an oil shortage, destroyed the railroad system, and destroyed many German aircraft factories. Germany's air force could not replace the planes they lost, allowing the Allies to have total control of the air.

REGENTS WARM-UP

Essay questions on past Regents Exams required that students make inferences about the reasoning behind historical decisions. List some reasons why it was important that the Allies required unconditional surrender from both Germany in the Atlantic theater and Japan in the Pacific theater.

LINKING PAST AND PRESENT

The date for the invasion of Normandy became know as D-Day because Eisenhower's planning staff referred to the day of *any* invasion with the letter *D*.

LINKING GEOGRAPHY TO HISTORY

The invasion of France along the Normandy coast of northern France was the largest seaborne invasion in history.

Striking at the Soft Underbelly The invasion of Sicily started on July 10, 1943. After the British and American troops came ashore, American tanks pushed through enemy lines and captured the western half of the island. By August, the Germans had left the island. The defeat of the Germans in Sicily caused the king of Italy to arrest Mussolini and to begin negotiating with the Allies for Italy's surrender. Hitler responded by taking control of northern Italy and putting Mussolini back in power.

Roosevelt Meets Stalin at Tehran Roosevelt and Churchill met with Stalin in Tehran, Iran, in late 1943. The leaders reached several agreements. Stalin promised to attack the Germans when the Allies invaded France. They agreed that Germany would be broken up after the war. Stalin promised that after Germany was beaten, the Soviet Union would help the United States defeat Japan. Stalin also agreed to support an international organization to keep peace after the war.

Landing in France

Roosevelt met with Churchill in Egypt to continue to plan the invasion of France. The Germans knew about the plans to invade France, so Hitler had fortified the coast. The Germans guessed that the Allies would land in Pas de Calais, an area of France closest to Britain. To make the Germans think they were right, the Allies placed inflated rubber tanks and dummy landing craft along the coast across from Calais. The Germans were fooled. The Allies actually planned to land in Normandy.

By the spring of 1944, the invasion was ready to begin. The invasion could take place only in certain weather conditions, and the best opportunity appeared to be between June 5 and June 7, 1944. Eisenhower chose June 6. The date became known as **D-Day.**

The Longest Day Thousands of ships sailed for Normandy and fighter-bombers dropped bombs up and down the coast. American troops began to knock out the German defenses. By the end of the day, more than 58,000 American troops had landed. The invasion was successful.

Driving the Japanese Back

At the same time that plans were in progress for the invasion of France, the United States was developing a two-part plan to defeat Japan. The Pacific Fleet would move through the central Pacific, hopping from one island to the next, closer and closer to Japan. Meanwhile, General MacArthur's troops would advance through the Solomon Islands, capture the north coast of New Guinea, and then launch an invasion to retake the Philippines.

MacArthur Returns to the Philippines General MacArthur's troops started their campaign in the southwest Pacific. It began with the invasion of Guadalcanal. MacArthur then captured the Japanese base on the north coast of New Guinea. To take back the Philippines, the United States put together a huge invasion force. For the first time, the Japanese used **kamikaze** attacks. These were attacks in which pilots would deliberately crash their planes into American ships, killing themselves but also inflicting huge damage. Just as the situation for the Americans looked hopeless, the Japanese commander ordered a retreat, because he believed that more American ships were on the way.

SECTION 5 THE WAR ENDS

The Third Reich Collapses

The Allies knew that to defeat the Germans, they would need to liberate France and conquer Germany. On July 25, 1944, American bombers blew a hole in the German lines, opening a gap for American tanks. The Allies then liberated Paris, and three weeks later American troops were within 20 miles of the German border. The Soviets advanced on Germany from the East to meet the western allies in Berlin.

The Battle of the Bulge Hitler decided to cut off Allied supplies that were coming through the port of Antwerp, Belgium. The Germans caught the American defenders by surprise. As Germans moved west, their lines bulged outward, so the attack became known as the **Battle of the Bulge**. Germans decided to capture the town of Bastogne, where several roads met. American troops quickly moved to the town before the Germans. The Germans surrounded the town and demanded that the Americans surrender. When the Americans refused, General Eisenhower ordered General Patton to rescue the surrounded Americans. Patton hit the German lines, and Allied

CORE CONCEPTS: NATIONALISM

During World War II, Japanese fighter pilots called "Kamikaze pilots" offered their lives to their nation in fatal airplane attacks on enemy ships. Since then, the word *kamikaze* has crept into the English language to describe any doomed effort.

aircraft hit German fuel depots. The German troops were forced to stop, and the United States won the Battle of the Bulge. The Germans, who suffered 100,000 casualties, began to withdraw. They had very little left to prevent the Allies from entering Germany.

V-E Day: The War Ends in Europe As the Allies fought to liberate France, Soviet troops had driven the Germans out of Russia and kept pushing them west. By February 1945, Soviet troops were only 35 miles from Berlin. As they crossed Germany's eastern border, American forces attacked the western border. On May 7, 1945, Germany surrendered unconditionally. The next day was proclaimed **V-E Day**, for "Victory in Europe." As the Soviets "liberated" Eastern Europe, they established a Communist foothold in these areas.

Japan Is Defeated

On April 12, 1945, President Roosevelt died after suffering a stroke. Vice President **Harry S Truman** became president. Truman had the responsibility of ending the war with Japan.

The Manhattan Project In 1941 a scientific committee set up by President Roosevelt met with British scientists who were working on an atomic bomb. The research convinced Roosevelt to begin a program to build an atomic bomb. The program was code-named the **Manhattan Project**. In 1942 two physicists— Hungarian Leo Szilard and Italian Enrico Fermi (both of whom had emigrated to the United States)—built the world's first nuclear reactor at the University of Chicago. General Leslie R. Groves, the head of the Manhattan Project, organized a group of engineers and scientists to build an atomic bomb at a secret laboratory in Los Alamos, New Mexico. On July 16, 1945, they detonated the world's first atomic bomb.

The Decision to Drop the Bomb American officials debated how to use the bomb. Some opposed it because it would kill civilians. Some wanted to warn the Japanese about the bomb. Truman's advisers told him that the United States would experience huge casualties if the United States invaded Japan. Truman believed that he should use every weapon available to save American lives.

Truman ordered the military to drop the atomic bomb. On August 6, 1945, a bomber named the *Enola Gay* dropped an atomic bomb on Hiroshima, an important industrial city in Japan. The bomb destroyed about 63 percent of the city. It killed

**CORE CONCEPTS:
INDIVIDUALS, GROUPS,
INSTITUTIONS**

Adolf Hitler, realizing the end was near, killed himself. His successor, Grand Admiral Karl Doentiz, tried to surrender to the Americans and the British while still fighting the Soviets, but he was forced to surrender unconditionally on May 7, 1945.

**CORE CONCEPTS:
SCIENCE AND
TECHNOLOGY**

Use of the atomic bomb by the United States against Japan is still hotly debated. Regardless of people's opinion, development of nuclear weapons changed the nature of war. No nation was completely safe from radioactive fallout—the atomic particles carried by global air currents.

between 80,000 and 120,000 people instantly, and thousands more died later. Then on August 9, the Soviet Union declared war on Japan. On the same day, the United States dropped an atomic bomb on Nagasaki. Between 35,000 and 74,000 people were killed. Japan surrendered on August 15, **V-J Day**. World War II had ended.

Building a New World

Creating the United Nations Even before the war ended, President Roosevelt wanted to ensure that a world war would not happen again. In 1944 he took part in a meeting with delegates from 39 countries in Washington, D.C., to discuss a new international political organization, which was to be called the **United Nations** (UN). On April 25, 1945, representatives from 50 countries met in San Francisco to organize the United Nations. The United Nations would have a General Assembly, where every nation would have one vote. It would have a Security Council with 11 members. Five members would be permanent: Britain, France, China, the Soviet Union, and the United States. The five members would have veto power. The members at the San Francisco meeting also designed the **charter**, or constitution, of the United Nations. The General Assembly was given the power to vote on resolutions and to choose the non-permanent members of the Security Council. The Security Council was responsible for international peace and security.

The United States Senate ratified the United Nations charter in July 1945 by a vote of 80 to 2, a striking contrast to the slow and painful defeat it had administered to the charter of the League of Nations twenty-five years earlier.

Universal Declaration of Human Rights In December 1948, the United Nations adopted the Universal Declaration of Human Rights. This document was the first to introduce on an international level the notion of human rights and that those rights are universal. Included in the rights of individuals are the rights to life, liberty, freedom of thought and opinion, assembly and association. The document also prohibits torture, slavery, and inhumane treatment.

First Lady Eleanor Roosevelt was the chair of the committee that drafted the Declaration and, in a speech before the General Assembly, called it the "international Magna Carta." She was an avid supporter of the United Nations and was an official member of the United States delegation.

REGENTS WARM-UP

Weigh the pros and cons of using the atomic bomb against Japan. Also consider the outcome of Truman's decision both on the United States (which became a global superpower) and world history.

CORE CONCEPTS: INDIVIDUALS, GROUPS, INSTITUTIONS

The United Nations is headquartered in New York City. Since 1945, its membership has more than tripled. New members are mostly African and Asian countries that were formerly European colonies.

Putting the Enemy on Trial In August 1945, the United States, Britain, France, and the Soviet Union created the International Military Tribunal (IMT). At the Nuremberg Trials, the IMT tried German leaders suspected of committing war crimes. Many of these leaders were executed and many others were given prison sentences. Several other Nazi leaders who avoided capture, such as Klaus Barbie and Adolf Eichmann, were tried and executed years later.

Similar trials were held in Tokyo for the leaders of wartime Japan. Twenty-five Japanese leaders were charged with a variety of war crimes, but the Allies did not indict the Japanese emperor. They feared that any attempt to put him on trial would lead to an uprising by the Japanese people. Eighteen people were sentenced to prison; the rest were put to death.

CHAPTER 25   POSTWAR AMERICA

Chapter Overview

After World War II, the country enjoyed a period of economic prosperity. Many more Americans could now aspire to a middle-class lifestyle, with a house in the suburbs and more leisure time. Television became a favorite form of entertainment. This general prosperity, however, did not extend to many Hispanics, African Americans, Native Americans, or people in Appalachia and other economically deprived areas.

The effects of this era can still be seen today. The middle class continues to represent a large segment of the American population, and television—perhaps more than ever—is a popular form of entertainment and a source of news for many Americans.

As you read through this chapter, ask yourself these questions:
(1) What were President Truman's and President Eisenhower's domestic agendas, and what were the effects?
(2) What caused the nation's economic boom in the postwar years?
(3) How did American families change in the 1950s?
(4) What factors contributed to poverty among various groups in a period of economic abundance?

Main Ideas and Concepts

- **Economic Systems** Following World War II, the federal government supported programs that helped the economy make the transition to peacetime production.

- **Change** Americans became avid consumers in the atmosphere of postwar abundance.

- **Culture** The 1950s added such elements as rock 'n' roll music and sitcom television to modern culture.

- **Individuals, Groups, Institutions** For some groups, poverty continued during the apparent abundance of the 1950s.

People, Places, Terms

The following names and terms will help you to prepare for the Regents Exam in United States History and Government. You can find an explanation of each name and term in the Glossary at the back of this book, in your textbook, or in another reference source.

baby boom	John Kenneth	Jonas Salk
blue-collar	Galbraith	Taft-Hartley Act
closed shop	GI Bill	union shop
"Do-Nothing	Levittown	urban renewal
Congress"	poverty line	white-collar
Fair Deal	right-to-work laws	

SECTION 1 TRUMAN AND EISENHOWER

Return to a Peacetime Economy

After the war ended, the United States economy continued to grow. Consumer spending, fueled by pent-up demand from the war years, helped this growth. Americans, who lived with shortages throughout the war, were eager to buy the luxury goods that they had wanted. The economy also got a boost from the Servicemen's Readjustment Act, which was popularly called the **GI Bill**. It provided loans to veterans to help them buy homes, start businesses, or go to college.

Inflation and Strikes The large demand for goods led to higher prices. This led to growing inflation. As the cost of living increased, so did labor unrest. Work stoppages occurred across the country as workers went on strike for better wages. Strikes occurred in the automobile, steel, and mining industries.

Republican Victory The labor unrest and inflation led many people to call for a change in leadership. In the 1946 congressional elections, Republicans took control of both houses of Congress. The new Congress set out to decrease the power of unions. They proposed the **Taft-Hartley Act**. It outlawed the **closed shop**, or the practice of forcing business owners to hire only union members. The law allowed the states to pass **right-to-work laws**, which outlawed both closed shops and **union shops**, or shops in which new workers were required to join the union. The law also prohibited featherbedding, or the practice of limiting work output in order to create more jobs. President

CORE CONCEPTS: CHANGE

The Taft-Hartley Act was the federal government's first attempt to regulate certain practices of large unions. Compare it with the Wagner Act that was passed ten years earlier (found on page 292).

Truman vetoed the bill. Congress overrode the veto and passed the Taft-Hartley Act in 1947. Labor leaders were upset, saying that the law had done away with many of the gains that unions had made since 1933.

Truman's Domestic Program

Although Republicans controlled Congress, President Truman continued to work to push his programs through Congress. He wanted to expand Social Security benefits, increase the minimum wage, set up long-range environmental and public works, and set up a system of national health insurance. However, many of Truman's suggested programs were shut down by a coalition of Republicans and Southern Democrats in Congress.

The Election of 1948 Many people did not think that President Truman would win the 1948 election. The Democratic Party itself was divided over whom to nominate because of Truman's stand on civil rights and perceptions that he was expanding federal power. Southern Democrats formed a new party and nominated Strom Thurmond. The liberal members of the Democratic Party formed a new Progressive Party and nominated Henry A. Wallace. The Republican nominee was the popular New York Governor Thomas Dewey. Dewey was expected to win by a landslide.

Truman believed he could win. He waged an energetic campaign, traveling more than 20,000 miles. He blamed the Republican Congress, referring to it as the **"Do-Nothing Congress,"** for refusing to pass his programs. His claims were not exactly true. Congress did pass many parts of his foreign-policy programs, such as the Marshall Plan. However, these programs did not affect Americans directly. Truman won by a narrow margin in a surprising victory. In addition, the Democrats had regained control of both houses of Congress.

CORE CONCEPTS: PRESIDENTIAL DECISIONS AND ACTIONS

President Truman appointed a Commission on Civil Rights that produced a report entitled "To Secure These Rights." The report would define the civil rights agenda that would emerge in the 1950s and 1960s. In addition, by executive order, Truman, in his constitutional role as Commander in Chief, ordered the immediate integration of the armed services and banned discrimination in federal employment.

TRUMAN'S COMPETITION FOR THE 1948 ELECTION				
Candidate	Harry Truman	Strom Thurmond	Henry Wallace	Thomas Dewey
Party Affiliation	Democrat	Dixiecrat	Progressive	Republican
Important Because	Proposed new civil rights bill	Against civil rights bill	Critical of anti-Soviet foreign policy	Popular

The Fair Deal Truman continued to work for passage of his programs. He said that all Americans had the right to expect a fair deal from the government. The **Fair Deal** became the name of Truman's programs. Congress passed some aspects of the Fair Deal. It increased the minimum wage and approved an expansion of Social Security benefits. Congress also passed the National Housing Act, which provided funding for the building of low-income housing. Congress refused to pass national health insurance or civil rights bills.

THE FAIR DEAL	
Reforms Passed Under the Fair Deal	**Fair Deal Reforms Refused by Congress**
Increase in minimum wage to 75¢ an hour	Passage of national health insurance
Increase in Social Security benefit by 75%	Provision of subsidies to farmers
National Housing Act to facilitate low-income housing	Establishment of federal aid to schools

The Eisenhower Years

Harry Truman did not run for reelection in 1952. The Republicans nominated World War II hero General Dwight Eisenhower for president and Richard Nixon for vice president. The Democrats nominated Illinois governor Adlai Stevenson. Eisenhower won in a landslide. The Republicans had a majority in the House, while the Senate was evenly divided between Democrats and Republicans.

Ike as President President Eisenhower's political beliefs fell between conservative and liberal. He believed in dynamic conservatism, which meant balancing economic conservatism with some activism.

Eisenhower's conservatism showed itself in several ways. He appointed several business leaders to his cabinet. Following their advice, Eisenhower ended government price and rent controls that had been enacted during World War II. Many conservatives had viewed these controls as unnecessary federal control over business. He cut the amount of money allocated for the Tennessee Valley Authority (TVA), another Depression-era agency.

Eisenhower showed his activist side as well. To provide better travel routes for the rapidly increasing number of cars, Eisenhower asked Congress to pass the Federal Highway Act in 1956. This was the largest public works program in American history. The act called for the building of more than 40,000 miles of interstate highway, including Routes 81, 87, 88, and 90 in New York state. He also authorized the building of the Great Lakes–St. Lawrence Seaway, which connected the Great Lakes with the Atlantic Ocean.

Although Eisenhower wanted to limit the federal government's role in the economy, he did agree to broaden the Social Security system. He also extended unemployment compensation and increased the minimum wage.

SECTION 2 THE AFFLUENT SOCIETY

In 1958 economist **John Kenneth Galbraith** published *The Affluent Society* in which he argued that the nation was experiencing an unprecedented economic prosperity. An abundance of goods and services allowed people to have a higher standard of living than they ever thought possible. Galbraith's observation seemed to be true.

The Spread of Wealth Between 1940 and 1955, income tripled for many Americans. They produced more than they could use and more people than ever before owned their own homes. Being able to afford a house was easier in the 1950s due to the low-interest loans offered by the GI Bill. In 1956 more Americans were working in **white-collar** jobs—sales and management, for example—than in **blue-collar** jobs, or those that required physical labor in industry.

Having more available income, Americans bought luxury items such as swimming pools, refrigerators, TVs, and air conditioners. The result of this consumption was that advertising became a major industry. Ads were aimed at people who had money to spend. "Suburbia" became the goal for millions of Americans, and suburban developments, like **Levittown**, New York, grew at an enormous pace.

The 1950s Family In the 1950s, the American family was changing. During the Great Depression and World War II, the birthrate had been relatively static. The birthrate increased greatly after World War II. The time between 1945 and 1961 is known as the **baby boom**. During the 1950s, many women focused on establishing families and staying home to care for them. Even so, the number of women who had jobs outside the home increased during the 1950s.

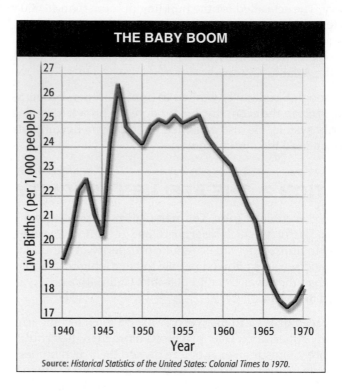

THE BABY BOOM

Source: *Historical Statistics of the United States: Colonial Times to 1970.*

Technological Breakthroughs

Several important scientific advances occurred in the 1950s, including an early computer.

Medical Advances New antibiotics to fight infections and new drugs to fight cancer, diabetes, and heart disease were developed in the 1950s. **Jonas Salk** developed an injectable vaccine to prevent polio, a crippling and often fatal disease that targeted children. Later, an oral vaccine for polio was developed as well. In the following years, the threat of polio almost completely disappeared.

The Space Age After the Soviet Union launched *Sputnik*, the United States hurried to catch up. On January 31, 1958, the U.S. launched its own satellite.

SECTION 3 POPULAR CULTURE OF THE 1950s

By the end of the 1950s, the television was a popular household item. Americans enjoyed watching comedies, cowboy shows, adventures, variety shows, and quiz shows on their black-and-white sets.

Teenagers In the years after World War II, a new social and economic group came into prominence—"teenagers." Before then, a person was perceived as either a child or an adult. Now this new group emerged, with its own lifestyle and values. As advertisers quickly learned, they also had a lot of disposable income.

The 1950s gave rise to a new style of music—rock 'n' roll—that became wildly popular with the nation's teenagers. The decade is also known for a group of white artists who lived unconventional lives and criticized what they saw as the emptiness of American life. These poets, writers, and artists called themselves the beats.

SECTION 4 THE OTHER SIDE OF AMERICAN LIFE

Poverty Amidst Prosperity

Although many Americans benefited from the economic boom in the 1950s, about 30 million Americans still lived below the **poverty line** by 1959. This is a figure set by the government to reflect the minimum income required to support a family. Poverty existed in both urban slums and rural areas.

The Decline of the Inner City Poverty was most obvious in the nation's urban centers. Many white people who could moved to the suburbs. The inner cities became home to poorer minority groups. Sometimes, government efforts to help made things worse. During the 1950s, **urban renewal** programs tried to eliminate poverty by tearing down slums and building new high-rise buildings for poor residents. These high-rises resulted in crowded conditions and violence. The government also ended up encouraging residents to remain in poverty by evicting them from the projects as soon as they earned any money.

Many residents of the inner cities were African Americans, a result of the large migration to Northern cities in search of better jobs and an escape from the racial violence and discrimination they faced in the South. However, fewer and fewer jobs were available as factories and mills left for the suburbs and smaller towns to cut costs. Long-standing patterns of racial discrimination in schools, housing, hiring, and salaries in the North kept inner-city African Americans poor. Several groups, such as the NAACP, pushed for greater equality and economic opportunity for African Americans but had few successes.

Hispanics and Native Americans Hispanics and Native Americans also faced poverty in the 1950s. Nearly 5 million Mexicans who immigrated to the U.S. to work on farms and ranches worked long hours for little pay in horrible conditions. By the mid-1900s, Native Americans made up the poorest group in the nation.

Appalachia Poverty also affected white families of Appalachia, remote rural areas in the eastern part of the United States. During the 1950s, about a million people left Appalachia to start a better life in the cities. They left behind the elderly and other residents. Medical care, nutrition, and schooling in Appalachia were sub-standard.

PRACTICING FOR THE REGENTS

Part I: Multiple-Choice Questions

The following multiple-choice questions come from past Regents Examinations. Test your understanding of United States history and geography by answering each of these items. Circle the number of the word or expression that best completes each statement or question. Test-taking tips can be found in the margins for some questions. For additional help, see Taking the Regents Exam on pages ix–xxxi of this Review Book.

REGENTS WARM-UP

Controversial means debatable, or having strong conflicting points or opinions.

1   The election of Franklin D. Roosevelt to a third term as president in 1940 was controversial primarily because this action
   (1) upset the system of checks and balances
   (2) violated an amendment to the Constitution
   (3) challenged a long-held political tradition
   (4) interfered with the functioning of the electoral college

2   The neutrality laws passed in the 1930s were based on the assumption that the surest way to avoid war was for the United States to
   (1) maintain a superior army and navy
   (2) restrict loans to and limit trade with warring nations
   (3) discourage aggressors by threatening military reprisals
   (4) enter alliances with other democratic nations

3   Which event is most closely associated with the end of the Great Depression?
   (1) passage of the Social Security Act
   (2) the beginning of World War II
   (3) reelection of President Franklin D. Roosevelt
   (4) announcement of the Marshall Plan

4   During the first three decades of the twentieth century, what was the main reason many African Americans left the South?
   (1) The Dawes Act made free land available in the West.
   (2) More factory jobs were available in the North.
   (3) Many white landowners refused to accept them as sharecroppers.
   (4) Racial discrimination did not occur in states outside the South.

5   In 1939, the immediate response
    of the United States to the start of
    World War II in Europe was to
    (1) modify its neutrality policy by
        providing aid to the Allies
    (2) declare war on Germany and Italy
    (3) strengthen its isolationist position
        by ending trade with England
    (4) send troops to the Allied Nations to
        act as advisers

6   In the 1930s, the United States respond-
    ed to the rise of fascism in Europe by
    (1) invading Germany and Italy
    (2) forming military alliances
    (3) passing a series of neutrality laws
    (4) joining the League of Nations

7   President Franklin D. Roosevelt's
    election to an unprecedented third term
    was most strongly influenced by
    (1) his policy on immigration
    (2) his popularity among business
        executives
    (3) the beginning of the Great
        Depression
    (4) the advent of World War II in
        Europe

8   A reason that President Harry Truman
    decided to use atomic weapons against
    Japan was to
    (1) end the war while limiting the loss
        of American lives
    (2) punish the Japanese people by
        destroying their country
    (3) increase Japan's potential as a future
        aggressor
    (4) divert forces to fight Germany

9   • Cash and Carry (1937)
    • Destroyers for Naval Bases Deal (1940)
    • Lend-Lease Act (1941)

    Which change in United States foreign
    policy is demonstrated by the passage of
    these acts prior to World War II?
    (1) a shift from neutrality toward more
        direct involvement
    (2) an effort to become more neutral
    (3) a movement from isolationism to
        containment of communism
    (4) a desire to provide aid to both
        Allied and Axis powers

10 During World War II, many women
    experienced a change in role in that they
    (1) served in military combat positions
    (2) worked in jobs formerly held by
        men
    (3) controlled most corporations
    (4) chaired several congressional
        committees

11 What was a key challenge faced by the
    United States during World War II?
    (1) lack of public support for the war
        effort
    (2) fighting the war on several fronts
    (3) difficulty gaining congressional
        support
    (4) total reliance on naval power

12 Which statement identifies a change in
    American society during World War II?
    (1) Economic opportunities for women
        increased.
    (2) Government regulation of the
        economy decreased.
    (3) The Great Depression worsened.
    (4) Racial tensions were eliminated.

Base your answer to question 13 on the quotation below and on your knowledge of social studies.

"Korematsu was not excluded from the military area because of hostility to him or his race. He was excluded because we are at war with the Japanese Empire, because the . . . authorities feared an invasion of our West Coast, and felt constrained to take proper security measures."

—Justice Hugo Black, *Korematsu* v. *United States*, 1944

13 Which generalization is supported by this quotation?
   (1) Individual rights need to be maintained in national emergencies.
   (2) The Supreme Court lacks the power to block presidential actions taken during wartime.
   (3) Individual rights can be restricted under certain circumstances.
   (4) Only the Supreme Court can alter the constitutional rights of American citizens.

14 During the early years of World War II, the Destroyer Deal and the Lend-Lease Act were efforts by the United States to
   (1) help the Allies without formally declaring war
   (2) maintain strict neutrality toward the war
   (3) negotiate a settlement of the war
   (4) provide help to both sides in the war

15 The war crimes trials of German and Japanese military officials following World War II established that
   (1) it is difficult to convict leaders of crimes against humanity
   (2) civil liberties must be expanded for civilians during wartime
   (3) individuals can be held responsible for wartime atrocities against civilians
   (4) genocidal acts are acceptable during wartime

Base your answers to questions 16 and 17 on the speakers' statements below and on your knowledge of social studies.

Speaker A: "The use of the bomb shortened the war and saved American lives."

Speaker B: "The United States might have been able to force the Japanese to surrender simply by demonstrating the power of the bomb on a deserted island."

Speaker C: "The use of the bomb was justified because of the Japanese attack on Pearl Harbor."

Speaker D: "In Hiroshima, the bomb instantly incinerated more than 60,000 people. Most were civilians."

16 Which speakers hold the view that using the bomb was an appropriate military action?
(1) *A* and *B*
(2) *A* and *C*
(3) *B* and *C*
(4) *B* and *D*

17 These statements most likely were made during the
(1) Versailles Peace Conference (1919)
(2) 1920s
(3) Great Depression
(4) post–World War II period

18 Which factor encouraged an American policy of neutrality during the 1930s?
(1) disillusionment with World War I and its results
(2) decline in the military readiness of other nations
(3) repeal of Prohibition
(4) economic prosperity of the period

19 In the 1944 case *Korematsu* v. *United States*, the Supreme Court ruled that wartime conditions justified the
(1) use of women in military combat
(2) ban against strikes by workers
(3) limitations placed on civil liberties
(4) reduction in the powers of the president

20 During World War II, posters of Rosie the Riveter were used to
(1) recruit women into wartime industries
(2) encourage women to serve in the armed forces
(3) promote women's suffrage
(4) support higher education for women

21 What was one result of World War II?
    (1) The arms race ended.
    (2) The Cold War ended.
    (3) Communism was eliminated.
    (4) Two superpowers emerged.

22 The baby boom primarily resulted from
    (1) economic prosperity of the 1920s
    (2) Great Depression of the 1930s
    (3) delay in marriages during World
         War II
    (4) counterculture movement of the
         1960s

23 How did the post-World War II baby
    boom affect American society between
    1945 and 1960?
    (1) It decreased the demand for
         housing.
    (2) It bankrupted the Social Security
         System.
    (3) It increased the need for educational
         resources.
    (4) It encouraged people to migrate to
         the Sun Belt.

REGENTS WARM-UP

Question 21 focuses on a cause-and-effect
relationship. The use of the word "result" in a
question is a tip that you are looking for an effect
of some condition or event. In this case, you need
to determine an effect of World War II.

Part II: Thematic Essay Question

The following essay question comes from past Regents Examinations. Write your answers on a separate sheet of paper. Essay-writing tips appear in the margin. For additional help, see Taking the Regents Exam on pages ix–xxxi of this Review Book.

Theme: Equal Rights

> Since 1900, various groups in the United States have struggled to achieve full equality.

Task: Identify *one* group of people in American society that has been denied equal rights.

- Discuss a major problem this group has encountered since 1900 in its struggle for full equality
- Discuss *two* specific actions that have been taken by an individual, an organization, or the government in an effort to help this group overcome the problem
- Evaluate the extent to which this group has achieved equality today

REGENTS WARM-UP

To do well on Regents Exam essay questions, you need to read directions carefully. The essay question is a three-part question. Make sure you answer all parts.

Be sure to support your essay with specific names of persons, laws, amendments, and Supreme Court cases whenever possible.

You may use any group from your study of United States history. Some suggestions you might wish to consider include African Americans, Asian Americans, Latinos, Native American Indians, persons with disabilities, and women.

You are *not* limited to these suggestions.

Guidelines: In your essay, be sure to:

- Address all aspects of the *Task*
- Support the theme with relevant facts, examples, and details
- Use a logical and clear plan of organization
- Introduce the theme by establishing a framework that is beyond a simple restatement of the *Task* and conclude with a summation of the theme

Part III   Document-Based Questions

This exercise is designed to test your ability to work with historical documents. It is similar to the document-based questions that you will see on the Regents Examination. While you are asked to analyze three historical documents, the exercise on the actual exam will include more documents. Some of the documents have been edited for the purposes of the question. As you analyze the documents, take into account the source of each document and any point of view that may be presented in the document.

Historical Context: Throughout its history, the United States has followed different foreign policies to promote its interests. These policies have included neutrality, imperialism, containment, and internationalism. Specific actions have been taken and specific programs have been established to carry out these policies.

Task: Using information from the documents and your knowledge of United States History, answer the questions that follow each document in Part A. Your answers to the questions will help you write the Part B essay, in which you will be asked to:

- Describe *two* different United States foreign policies
- Discuss *one* specific action or program the United States has used to carry out *each* foreign policy
- Evaluate the extent to which the action or program used was successful in carrying out *each* foreign policy

Part A   Short-Answer Questions

Directions: Analyze the documents and answer the short-answer questions that follow each document in the space provided.

Document 1

> . . . The great rule of conduct for us in regard to foreign nations is, in extending our commercial relations, to have with them as little political connection as possible. So far as we have already formed engagements let them be fulfilled with perfect good faith Here let us stop. . .
>
> Our detached and distant situation invites and enables us to pursue a different course. . .
>
> Why, be interweaving our destiny with that of any part of Europe, entangle our peace and prosperity in the toils of European ambition, rivalship, interest, humor, or caprice [whim]>
>
> It is our true policy to steer clear of permanent alliances with any portion of the foreign world. . . .
>
> —*George Washington's Farewell Address, 1796*

1   According to this document, what United States foreign policy did President George Washington favor?

_____

_____

Document 2

> . . . the American continents . . . are . . . not to be considered as subjects for future colonization by any European powers . . . .
>
> In the wars of the European powers in matters relating to themselves we have never taken any part, nor does it comport [fit] with our policy so to do. . . . We owe it, therefore, . . . to the amicable [friendly] relations existing between the United States and those powers to declare that we should consider any attempt on their part to extend their system to any portion of this hemisphere as dangerous to our peace and safety. With the existing colonies or dependencies of any European power we . . . shall not interfere . . .
>
> —*James Monroe's message to Congress, 1823*

2*a*   According to the document, what foreign policy did President James Monroe support?

_____

_____

b   What did President Monroe say about wars in Europe?

_____

_____

Document 3

> . . . I believe that it must be the policy of the United States to support free peoples who are resisting attempted [control] by armed minorities or by outside pressures.
>
> I believe that we must assist free peoples to work out their own destinies in their own way.
>
> I believe that our help should be primarily through economic and financial aid which is essential to economic stability and orderly political processes . . .
>
> —*Harry Truman's request for funds to support Greece and Turkey against communism, Message to Congress, 1947*

3a According to this document, what foreign policy did President Harry Truman support?

_____

_____

b What type of assistance did President Truman think the United States should provide to free peoples?

_____

_____

Part B   Essay

Directions: Write a well-organized essay that includes an introduction, several paragraphs, and a conclusion.

Use evidence from at least *two* documents in the body of the essay. Support your response with relevant facts, examples, and details. Include additional outside information.

Historical Context: Throughout its history, the United States has followed different foreign policies to promote its interests. These policies have included neutrality, imperialism, containment, and internationalism. Specific actions have been taken and specific programs have been established to carry out these policies.

Task: Using information from the documents and your knowledge of United States History, answer the questions that follow each document in Part A. Your answers to the questions will help you write the Part B essay, in which you will be asked to:

- Describe *two* different United States foreign policies
- Discuss *one* specific action or program the United States has used to carry out *each* foreign policy
- Evaluate the extent to which the action or program used was successful in carrying out *each* foreign policy

Guidelines: In your essay, be sure to:

- Address all aspects of the *Task* by accurately analyzing and interpreting at least *two* documents
- Incorporate information from the documents in the body of the essay
- Incorporate relevant outside information
- Support the theme with relevant facts, examples, and details
- Use a logical and clear plan of organization
- Introduce the theme by establishing a framework that is beyond a simple restatement of the Task or Historical Context and conclude with a summation of the theme

UNIT 7   A CHANGING SOCIETY, *1950–PRESENT*

Unit 7 Overview

From a presidential assassination to massive governmental programs, from the Vietnam War to the civil rights movement, the events of post–World War II America had a huge impact on the lives of Americans. Abstract ideals battled realities, leading to military actions overseas and social conflict at home. Understanding how these events unfolded provides a window to the world you live in today.

Unit 7 Objectives

1. Explain how the Cold War began.

2. Summarize President Kennedy's economic policies.

3. Discuss the changing role of the federal government in civil rights enforcement.

4. Describe how President Johnson deepened American involvement in Vietnam.

5. Describe the workplace concerns that fueled the growth of the women's movement.

6. Describe President Nixon's foreign policy achievements.

7. Explain President Reagan's economic recovery plans.

8. Describe the ways in which technology has affected American business and communications.

PREPARING FOR THE REGENTS

This entire book is set up to help you grasp the facts, main ideas, and concepts needed to do well on your Regents Exam. Notes in the margin include key concepts, test-taking tips, and more. Use blank spaces in the margins to answer questions raised in the text or to jot down key points. Before each unit of study, skim through the exams at the back of the book to develop a sense of what your state wants you to know about your country.

CHAPTER 26   THE COLD WAR BEGINS

CORE CONCEPTS: FOREIGN POLICY

The only two superpowers left after World War II were the United States and the Soviet Union; they had as much productive capacity between them as the rest of the world combined.

REGENTS WARM-UP

As you read the next section, use a graphic organizer similar to the one below to list events that led to the Cold War.

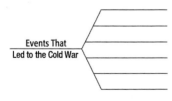

Events That Led to the Cold War

Chapter Overview

After World War II, an intense rivalry developed between the United States and the Soviet Union—two superpowers with very different political and economic systems. This rivalry, known as the Cold War, led to a massive buildup of military weapons on both sides. The determination of American leaders to contain communism also led to the Korean War, in which over 36,500 Americans died.

Two major events resulted from the Cold War that are still currently relevant: the NATO alliance continues today to work to guarantee the security of many democratic countries; the math and science training important to the space race remains an educational priority.

As you read through this chapter, ask yourself these questions:
(1)   What tensions existed between the United States and the Soviet Union at the end of World War II?
(2)   What were the goals of Stalin's foreign policy immediately after the war?
(3)   How did the United States respond to the expansion of communism?
(4)   What were the causes of the Korean War?
(5)   How did American society reflect fears of the nuclear age?
(6)   Was Eisenhower's foreign policy effective? Why or why not?
(7)   How did the United States respond to the communist threat at home?

Main Ideas and Concepts

- **Presidential Decisions and Actions** As World War II was ending, the United States and the Soviet Union began to negotiate to influence the shape of the postwar world.

- **Foreign Policy** Beliefs about Soviet goals and actions had a lasting effect on American policies abroad and on the agencies used to carry them out.

- **Civic Values** In the early part of the Cold War, fear of communism led to a hunt for spies and to intolerance and suspicion of people with radical ideas in the United States.

- **Science and Technology** Nuclear technology enabled Eisenhower to change American military policy, while new missile technology marked the beginning of the space age.

People, Places, Terms

The following names and terms will help you to prepare for the Regents Exam in United States History and Government. You can find an explanation of each name and term in the Glossary at the back of this book, in your textbook, or in another reference source.

brinkmanship	iron curtain	J. Robert
censure	limited war	Oppenheimer
Central Intelligence	loyalty review	perjury
Agency	program	Point Four program
Cold War	Marshall Plan	Potsdam
containment	massive retaliation	satellite nations
covert	McCarthyism	Smith Act
developing nations	military-industrial	sphere of influence
fallout shelters	complex	*Sputnik*
Alger Hiss	NATO	

SECTION 1   ORIGINS OF THE COLD WAR

Converting the Economy

After World War II, the relations between the United States and the Soviet Union became more and more strained. This led to an era of confrontation and competition that lasted from 1946 to 1990. It was known as the **Cold War**.

Soviet Security Concerns The tensions existed because the two countries had different goals. The Soviet Union wanted to control the countries between it and Germany and keep Germany weak to make sure it did not invade the Soviet Union again. The Soviet Union wanted to establish a secure **"sphere of influence"** in Central and Eastern Europe as protection against

CORE CONCEPTS: CULTURE

The term *Cold War* was first used by Walter Lippman, a newspaper columnist. He used it to refer to a state of war that did not involve actual bloodshed, but an icy rivalry between the United States and the Soviet Union.

future aggression. The Soviets also believed that communism was a superior system to capitalism, and they wanted communism to spread to other nations. Believing that capitalism would try to destroy communism, Soviet leaders became suspicious of capitalist nations.

American Economic Concerns The United States focused on economic problems. President Roosevelt and his advisers believed that economic growth was important to keeping peace in the world. They believed that world trade would lead to economic prosperity. The American leaders wanted to promote democracy throughout the world. They believed that democratic nations were more stable and less likely to go to war, and that the free enterprise system was necessary for economic growth.

The Yalta Conference

In February 1945, before the war was finally over, Roosevelt, Churchill, and Stalin met at Yalta, a resort in the Soviet Union, to plan the postwar world.

Poland When the Soviet Union liberated Poland from German control, they wanted Polish communists to set up a new government. As a result, two governments—communist and non-communist—claimed the right to govern Poland. Churchill and Roosevelt compromised with Stalin by recognizing the Polish government that the Soviets set up. Stalin agreed to include members of the old Polish government and to allow free elections in Poland as soon as possible.

Dividing Germany The three leaders agreed to divide Germany into four zones, with Great Britain, the United States, the Soviet Union, and France each controlling one zone, and dividing the city of Berlin amongst them. Stalin wanted Germany to pay heavy reparations. Roosevelt insisted that reparations should be based on Germany's ability to pay and that Germany pay reparations with trade goods and products instead of cash. The Allies would also be allowed to take machinery and other equipment from Germany as reparations. The question of German reparations would contribute to tensions between the United States and the Soviet Union.

Tensions Begin to Rise Two weeks after the meeting at Yalta, the Soviet Union pressured Romania into installing a communist government. The United States accused the Soviet Union of going against the Declaration of Liberated Europe. The Soviet Union also did not allow free elections to be held in Poland, as

CORE CONCEPTS: FOREIGN POLICY

During the meeting at Yalta, Roosevelt, Churchill, and Stalin agreed to issue the Declaration of Liberated Europe. It declared the right of all people to choose the kind of government under which they wanted to live. The meeting then focused on Germany.

promised. President Roosevelt informed the Soviets that their actions were not acceptable. Eleven days later, President Roosevelt died, and Harry S Truman became president.

Truman Takes Control

Truman, strongly anticommunist, was suspicious of Stalin. He demanded that Stalin hold free elections in Poland as he had promised in Yalta.

The Potsdam Conference In 1945, Truman and Stalin met at a conference at **Potsdam**, located near Berlin, to work out a deal on Germany. Truman and his advisers believed that if Germany's economy stayed weak, the rest of Europe would never recover and Germany might turn to communism. Stalin and his advisers believed that Germany had devastated the Soviet Union and should pay reparations.

To solve the problem of reparations, Truman suggested that the Soviet Union take its reparations from its own zone. The Soviets opposed this because their zone was mostly agricultural and could not provide what the Soviets needed. Truman responded by offering Stalin a small amount of German industrial equipment from the other zones. He also accepted the new German-Polish border the Soviets had set up. Stalin did not like Truman's proposal and suspected that the Americans were trying to limit reparations to keep the Soviet Union weak. In the end, the Soviet Union had no choice but to accept the deal. Still, the Potsdam conference was yet another event that increased tensions between the Soviet Union and the United States.

The Iron Curtain Descends The Soviets refused to commit to uphold the Declaration of Liberated Europe. Pro-Soviet communist governments would eventually be established in Poland, Romania, Bulgaria, Hungary, and Czechoslovakia. These countries of Eastern Europe came to be called **satellite nations**. While they had their own governments and were not under the direct control of the Soviet Union, they had to remain communist and friendly to the Soviet Union. Churchill called the communist takeover in Eastern Europe the creation of the **iron curtain**, separating the communist nations of Eastern Europe from the West.

CORE CONCEPTS: PRESIDENTIAL DECISIONS AND ACTIONS

When Stalin was not pleased with Truman's proposal, Truman told Stalin of the successfully tested atomic bomb. This led Stalin to think it was a threat to get him to agree to the deal, increasing tensions between the two nations.

CAUSES AND EFFECTS OF THE COLD WAR	
• Soviet Union controls Eastern Europe after World War II. • Chinese Communists win control of mainland China. • United States and Soviet Union explode atomic bombs.	• Marshall Plan provides aid to Western Europe. • Western nations form NATO; Communist nations respond with Warsaw Pact. • Korean War erupts. • American and Soviet arms race begins. • Red Scare leads to hunt for Communists in the United States.

SECTION 2 THE EARLY COLD WAR YEARS

Containing Communism

REGENTS WARM-UP

Use a graphic organizer like the one below to review the strategies used to contain communism.

Both Britain and the United States urged the Soviet Union to hold free elections in Eastern Europe, but the Soviets refused to do so. The United States asked the American Embassy in Moscow to explain Soviet behavior. Diplomat George Kennan explained his views of Soviet goals. He believed that communists were in an historical struggle against capitalism and that it was impossible to reach any permanent settlement with them. Kennan believed that the Soviet system had several economic and political weaknesses and that if the United States could keep the Soviets from increasing their power, the Soviet system would fall apart. Kennan's suggestions led to the formulation of the policy of **containment**. The policy called for preventing the spread of communism through the use of diplomatic, economic, and military actions.

To stem Soviet aggression in the East, the United States, Great Britain, France, Pakistan, Thailand, the Philippines, Australia, and New Zealand formed the Southeast Asia Treaty Organization (SEATO). The Central Treaty Organization (CENTO), which included Turkey, Iraq, Iran, Pakistan, Great Britain, and the United States, was meant to prevent the Soviet Union from expanding to the south. By the mid-1950s, the United States found itself allied militarily with 42 countries around the world.

The Truman Doctrine Stalin wanted to control the straits of the Dardanelles, which was an important route from Black Sea ports to the Mediterranean. The Soviet Union demanded that Turkey share control of this route. The United States saw this as a way for the Soviets to control the Middle East and in response, sent aircraft carriers into the eastern Mediterranean. In the meantime, Britain tried to help Greece in its fight against communists, but it proved to be too much for Britain's economy. As a result, Truman went before Congress to ask for funds to fight the Soviets in Turkey and in Greece. His speech, which pledged that the United States would fight communism worldwide, became known as the Truman Doctrine.

The Marshall Plan The European economy was in ruins after the war. In June 1947, Secretary of State George C. Marshall proposed the **Marshall Plan**, which would give European nations American aid to rebuild their economies. The Marshall Plan, passed by Congress in 1948, offered the aid to all nations that planned a recovery program. The Soviet Union and its satellite nations rejected the offer, and instead developed their own economic program. The Marshall Plan put billions of dollars worth of supplies and food into Western Europe. It weakened the appeal of communism there and opened new markets for trade.

Point Four Plan In his inaugural address in 1949, Truman announced a new program that became known as the "Point Four plan." The emergency foreign aid of the Marshall Plan was universalized and the plan also aimed to make scientific and technical advances available to what are now known as Third World countries in Latin America, Asia, and Africa.

The Berlin Crisis

West Germany Is Founded By 1948 the United States believed that the Soviets were trying to undermine Germany's economy. As a result, the United States, Great Britain, and France announced that they were combining their zones in Germany and allowing the Germans to have their own government. They also combined their zones in Berlin and made West Berlin a part of the new German nation, which became known as West Germany. The Soviet zone became known as East Germany.

The Berlin Airlift The Soviets were angry. They cut all road and rail traffic to West Berlin and set up a blockade of the city. They wanted to force the Americans to change Germany's status.

CORE CONCEPTS: GOVERNMENT

Senator Robert A. Taft opposed the Marshall Plan, calling it a "global give-away program." He was concerned that the plan would bankrupt the United States.

CORE CONCEPTS: INTERDEPENDENCE

During the Berlin airlift, planes bringing food and other supplies to West Berlin landed every three minutes.

President Truman ordered the Berlin airlift. Cargo planes supplied the people in Berlin with goods and other supplies. The airlift continued for eleven months. Stalin finally lifted the blockade.

NATIONAL GEOGRAPHIC

DIVIDED GERMANY AND THE BERLIN AIR LIFT

EAST GERMANY

FRENCH SECTOR
EAST BERLIN
BRITISH SECTOR
SOVIET SECTOR
WEST BERLIN
AMERICAN SECTOR

EAST GERMANY

0   10 miles
0   10 kilometers
Lambert Azimuthal Equal-Area projection

DENMARK

Hamburg
British Zone
NETHER-LANDS
Hannover
Braunschweig
WEST GERMANY (FEDERAL REPUBLIC OF GERMANY)
BELG.
LUX. French Zone
Frankfurt
American Zone
FRANCE
SWITZ.

Berlin
POLAND
EAST GERMANY (GERMAN DEMOCRATIC REPUBLIC)
CZECHOSLOVAKIA
50°N
AUSTRIA
ITALY
YUGOSLAVIA
45°N

Allied occupation zone
Soviet occupation zone
Routes of the Berlin Airlift, 1948–1949
Iron Curtain
Division of Allied zone

0   100 miles
0   100 kilometers
Chamberlin Trimetric projection

NATO The blockade convinced many Americans that the Soviets were trying to conquer other nations. They began supporting the idea of America becoming part of a military alliance with Western Europe. An agreement had been reached that created **NATO**, the North Atlantic Treaty Organization. It was made up of 12 countries, including the United States. The members agreed to help any member who was attacked. A few years later, NATO allowed West Germany to join the alliance. The Soviets responded by setting up its own alliance in Eastern Europe, which became known as the Warsaw Pact.

Unity in Western Europe After the formation of NATO, many Europeans saw the need for further unity in Europe. National feeling was too strong for nations to give up their political sovereignty, however. The focus shifted to economic unity. In 1957, France, West Germany, Belgium, the Netherlands, Luxembourg, and Italy formed the European Economic Community (EEC), also known as the Common Market. The EEC was a free-trade area; no tariffs, or import charges, were levied on each other's goods, and as a group, they were protected by a tariff imposed on goods from non-EEC nations. In the late 1950s, the EEC joined with other groups to form the European Parliament. By the 1960s, the EEC had become an important trading bloc, and its success paved the way for the formation of the European Union.

The Cold War Spreads to East Asia

Civil War and Revolution in China The Cold War eventually spread to Asia. In China, Mao Zedong had led communist forces against Chiang Kai-shek's Nationalist government since the 1920s. The two sides stopped their conflict during World War II in order to halt Japanese occupation. After World War II ended, the two groups resumed their fighting. To stop the spread of communism in Asia, the United States sent Chiang money. However, the communists captured Beijing, the Chinese capital, and moved southward. The United States discontinued aid to the Chinese Nationalists, who left mainland China for the island of Taiwan. In 1949 the communists set up the People's Republic of China.

After the Fall In the same year, the Soviet Union announced that it had tested its first atomic weapon. In 1950 it signed a treaty of alliance with China. Western nations feared that China and the Soviet Union would support communist revolutions in other parts of the world. The United States set up formal relations with the Nationalists in Taiwan. It helped keep communist China out of the United Nations.

CORE CONCEPTS: ECONOMIC SYSTEMS

The United States encouraged economic recovery in Japan. It saw Japan as a way to defend Asia against communism.

Japan The United States changed its policy toward Japan. After World War II, General Douglas MacArthur took charge of occupied Japan and wanted to introduce democracy there. A new constitution established a parliamentary system and guaranteed basic civil and political rights. In September 1951, the United States and other former World War II allies (but not the Soviet Union) signed a peace treaty restoring Japanese independence. On the same day, Japan and the United States signed a defensive alliance in which the Japanese agreed that the United States could maintain military bases in Japan.

To aid in the economic recovery of Japan, Allied officials planned to dismantle the large business conglomerates that dominated industry. However, with the rise of the Cold War, they scaled back on that policy. The destruction of many industries in World War II required Japan to build new, modern factories. At the end of the Allied occupation of Japan, the gross national product was one-third of that of Great Britain or France. Today, it is larger than both put together. It is the greatest exporting nation in the world.

The Korean War

After the war, the Allies divided Korea at the 38th parallel. The Soviets controlled the north, and set up a communist government. An American-backed government was set up in the south. The Soviets gave military aid to North Korea, which built up a huge army. This army invaded South Korea on June 25, 1950.

CORE CONCEPTS: INDIVIDUALS, GROUPS, INSTITUTIONS

Douglas MacArthur and his father are the only father and son to have both received the Medal of Honor, reserved for people who perform extraordinary acts of heroism.

The UN Intervenes President Truman saw the invasion of South Korea as a test of the containment policy. He asked the United Nations for troops to help the American troops. In September 1950, General MacArthur ordered an invasion that took the North Korean troops by surprise. Within weeks, they retreated back across the 38th parallel.

China Enters the War The communist Chinese ordered the UN troops to retreat. Their warnings were ignored and China started a massive attack across the Yalu River. They were able to drive the UN forces back across the 38th parallel.

Truman Fires MacArthur General MacArthur wanted to expand the war into China. He criticized President Truman for wanting a **limited war**, a war fought to achieve a limited objective such as containing communism. President Truman fired MacArthur and chose General Matthew Ridgway to replace him.

Changes in Policy By mid-1951, the Korean War had settled into small bloody battles. An armistice was not signed until July 1953. More than 35,000 Americans died in the war.

After the Korean War, the United States began a military buildup. Until then, the United States believed that it had to focus on Europe to contain communism. Now it also focused militarily on Asia. Defense agreements were signed with Japan, South Korea, Taiwan, the Philippines, and Australia. The United States also began providing aid to the French forces fighting communists in Vietnam.

SECTION 3 THE COLD WAR AND AMERICAN SOCIETY

A New Red Scare

During the 1950s, people in the United States began to fear that the communists were trying to take over the world. The new Red Scare began in September 1945, when a clerk working in the Soviet Embassy in Canada defected. He had documents that showed that the Soviet Union was trying to infiltrate organizations and government agencies in Canada and the United States to find information about the atomic bomb.

Smith Act In 1940, Congress passed the **Smith Act**, which made it a crime to call for the violent overthrow of the government or to belong to a group that advocated the same thing. This act was often used to prosecute members of Communist or Socialist parties. In 1957 the Supreme Court restricted the powers of the law to include only very specific activities.

The Loyalty Review Program The search for spies soon turned into a general fear of a communist takeover of the government. In 1947 President Truman set up a **loyalty review program** to screen all federal employees. More than 6 million federal employees were screened. People became suspects simply for reading certain books or belonging to various groups. Thousands were subject to intense FBI investigations.

HUAC J. Edgar Hoover, the FBI Director, wanted to go further than screen federal employees. He went before the House Un-American Activities Committee (HUAC) to urge the committee to hold public hearings on communist subversion. FBI agents

LINKING PAST AND PRESENT

The term "Red" is used to describe communism.

CORE CONCEPTS: INDIVIDUALS, GROUPS, INSTITUTIONS

Of the people in the film industry who were investigated by HUAC, ten went to prison. This group was often referred to as "The Hollywood Ten."

were sent to infiltrate groups suspected of subversion. They also wiretapped thousands of telephones.

Watkins **v.** *United States* In 1954, labor organizer John Watkins was called before the House Un-American Activities Committee to answer questions about his connections with the Communist Party. He agreed to answer questions about himself, but refused to identify other members of the party. He was convicted of violating a federal law that made it a crime to refuse to answer questions before a congressional committee. He appealed, arguing that his conviction violated the due process clause of the Fifth Amendment. The Supreme Court agreed and ruled that Watkins' conviction was invalid because congressional committees must uphold the Bill of Rights and grant citizens freedom of speech.

Alger Hiss In 1948 Whittaker Chambers, a *Time* magazine editor, testified before HUAC that several government officials, including **Alger Hiss**, had been communists or spies at that time. Chambers claimed that Hiss, who had served in President Roosevelt's administration, had given him secrets from the State Department. Hiss denied being a member of the Communist Party, but eventually admitted that he had met Chambers in the 1930s. Hiss then sued Chambers, claiming that his accusations were unfounded. To defend himself, Chambers showed copies of secret documents that he had hidden. He believed the documents proved that he was telling the truth. A jury agreed with him. It convicted Hiss of **perjury**, or lying under oath.

The Rosenbergs Another spy case had to do with accusations that American communists had sold secrets of the atomic bomb to the Soviet Union. Many people believed that the Soviet Union could not have developed an atomic bomb in 1949 without this help. In 1950, a British scientist's testimony that he had sent information to the Soviet Union led the FBI to arrest Julius and Ethel Rosenberg, who were members of the Communist Party, and to charge them with passing on atomic secrets. Although the Rosenbergs denied the charges, they were condemned to death and executed in June 1953. Many Americans debated the Rosenbergs' guilt. Future investigation and documents, however, provided strong evidence that they were guilty.

The Oppenheimer Case J. Robert Oppenheimer was the scientific director of the Manhattan Project, the World War II effort to develop nuclear weapons. During the Red Scare, J. Edgar Hoover and the FBI investigated Oppenheimer because of his sympathies (when he was a young man) toward communist

CORE CONCEPTS: GOVERNMENT

In 1946 American cryptographers cracked the Soviet spy code, allowing them to read messages between Moscow and the United States. In 1995 the government revealed existence of **Project Venona**, which provided strong evidence against the Rosenbergs.

groups. Oppenheimer's security clearance was suspended. In the very public hearing that followed to assess his loyalty, Oppenheimer's colleague Edward Teller testified against him and severely damaged his reputation. Although Oppenheimer identified several other left-leaning colleagues, his security clearance was revoked and he never recovered any of his political power.

"A Conspiracy So Immense"

After the Soviet Union tested an atomic bomb in 1949 and China fell to communism, many Americans feared that the United States was losing the Cold War. They believed that communists had infiltrated the government unnoticed. Then in February 1950, Wisconsin Senator Joseph R. McCarthy made a statement that he had a list of 205 communists in the State Department. McCarthy never actually produced the list, but he accused many politicians and military officials of being communists or leaning toward communism.

McCarthy's Tactics In 1952, McCarthy became chairman of the Senate subcommittee on investigations. He used his position to force government officials to testify about so-called communist influences. McCarthy turned the investigation into a witch hunt. His investigations were based on weak evidence and irrational fears. His method of destroying reputations with unfounded charges became known as **McCarthyism**. McCarthy would badger witnesses and then refuse to accept their answers. The methods he used when questioning witnesses left the impression of guilt.

McCarthy's Downfall In 1954, McCarthy began targeting the United States Army. The army's own investigation found no spies. McCarthy then brought his investigation to television. Millions of Americans watched as McCarthy bullied witnesses. His popularity began to decrease. Finally, people began to challenge McCarthy and his methods. In 1954 the Senate passed a vote for **censure**, or formal disapproval, against McCarthy. McCarthy's influence was gone, and he faded from public view.

CORE CONCEPTS: CONSTITUTIONAL PRINCIPLES

Senator Margaret Chase Smith of Maine spoke out against Senator Joseph McCarthy and his "witch hunt" for communists. In her speech called the "Declaration of Conscience," Smith said she was ashamed of the way the Senate had become "a publicity platform for irresponsible sensationalism."

CORE CONCEPTS: GOVERNMENT

Politicians were afraid to challenge McCarthy. Even Dwight D. Eisenhower, running for president in 1952, did not speak out against him, though Eisenhower disliked McCarthy's tactics. Once he was elected president, he worked with congressional leaders to undermine McCarthy's authority.

**CORE CONCEPTS:
SCIENCE AND
TECHNOLOGY**

To protect themselves from
fallout, some people built
fallout shelters in their
yards. They stocked these
shelters with canned food.

Life During the Early Cold War

Facing the Bomb The fear of communism dominated everyday
life in the United States in the 1950s. Americans were upset
when the Soviet Union tested the more powerful hydrogen
bomb. They got ready for a surprise Soviet attack, setting up
special areas as bomb shelters. Students practiced bomb drills.

SECTION 4 EISENHOWER'S POLICIES

Eisenhower's "New Look"

In the 1952 presidential election, the Democrats nominated
Adlai Stevenson, the governor of Illinois. The Republicans
nominated General Dwight D. Eisenhower. Americans wanted a
leader who they believed would lead the nation through the
Cold War. Eisenhower won in a landslide.

"More Bang for the Buck" Eisenhower believed that both a
strong military and a strong economy were essential to win the
Cold War. He also believed that preparing for a large-scale
conventional war would cost too much money. Therefore, he
believed the United States had to be prepared to use atomic
weapons. Nuclear weapons, he said, gave "more bang for the
buck."

**CORE CONCEPTS:
SCIENCE AND
TECHNOLOGY**

New technology led to the
B-52 bomber, which could fly
across continents and drop
nuclear bombs anywhere in
the world. Intercontinental
ballistic missiles and submarines capable of launching
nuclear missiles were also
created.

Massive Retaliation Eisenhower's secretary of state and (except
for the president himself) the dominant figure in the nation's
foreign policy in the 1950s was John Foster Dulles, an aristocratic
corporate lawyer who despised communism. The most prominent of his ideas was the policy of "**massive retaliation**." This
meant the United States would threaten to use nuclear weapons
if a communist state tried to take a territory by force. It allowed
Eisenhower to cut military spending by billions of dollars. He
cut back the army but increased the nation's nuclear weapons.

The H-Bomb In 1952, the United States successfully detonated
the first hydrogen bomb. (The Soviet Union tested its first H-
bomb a year later.) Unlike the bombs developed during World
War II, the H-bomb was capable of producing explosions of
vastly greater power than earlier bombs.

Atoms for Peace Eisenhower was deeply concerned about the
dangers of atomic warfare and the arms race. In his "Atoms for
Peace" speech before the United Nations on December 8, 1953,
Eisenhower suggested that nations contribute materials to a UN

agency that would develop peaceful uses of nuclear energy. In 1957, the International Atomic Energy Agency was established as an independent agency whose goal was to promote the peaceful use of atomic energy and limit its use for military purposes.

The *Sputnik* Crisis On October 4, 1957, the Soviets launched *Sputnik*, the first artificial satellite to orbit the earth. Many Americans saw that as a sign that the United States was falling behind the Soviet Union in missile technology and in scientific research. In response, Congress set up the National Aeronautics and Space Administration (NASA). The agency conducted research in rocket and space technology. Congress also passed the National Defense Education Act (NDEA), which provided money for education and training in science, math, and foreign languages.

Brinkmanship in Action

Eisenhower supported the policy of **brinkmanship**, the willingness to go to the brink of war to force the other side to back down. Some thought the policy was too dangerous. John Foster Dulles strongly defended the policy, however.

The Korean War Ends Eisenhower used the threat of nuclear war to try to end the Korean War. He believed that the war was costing too many lives, so he threatened China with a nuclear attack. The threat seemed to work, because in July 1953, an armistice was signed. The line between the two sides became the border between North Korea and South Korea. A demilitarized zone separated them.

The Suez Crisis In 1955, problems developed in the Middle East. Eisenhower wanted to prevent Arab nations from siding with the Soviet Union. He offered Egypt financial help to build the Aswan Dam on the Nile River. Congress, however, did not agree to provide financial aid. A week later, Egypt took control of the Suez Canal from an Anglo-French company. Egypt wanted to use the profits from the canal to pay for the dam. In response, in October 1956, British and French troops invaded Egypt. The conflict became worse when the Soviet Union threatened to attack France and Britain and to send troops to help Egypt. Again, Eisenhower threatened a nuclear attack. Britain and France called off the invasion. Other Arab nations soon began accepting Soviet aid.

CORE CONCEPTS: SCIENCE AND TECHNOLOGY

In 1666, Isaac Newton came up with the theory that if a cannonball were fired at a high enough speed, the cannonball would not hit the ground at all because of the curvature of the earth. About 300 years later, scientists applied Newton's theory to the launching of satellites.

LINKING GEOGRAPHY AND HISTORY

The Suez Canal, which connects the Mediterranean and Red Seas, opened in 1869. It cut approximately 4,000 miles off voyages between Britain and India. Upon its opening, it greatly reduced travel times and quickly became one of the world's major shipping lanes.

Fighting Communism Covertly

President Eisenhower knew that brinkmanship would not always work to prevent communists from starting revolutions within countries. To prevent revolutions, Eisenhower used **covert**, or hidden, operations that were run by the **Central Intelligence Agency** (CIA). The CIA was formed in 1947 to replace the World War II-era Office of Strategic Services. It was responsible for collecting information through both open and covert methods, but as the Cold War continued, the CIA would engage secretly in political and military operations on behalf of American goals.

Containment in Developing Nations Many of these covert operations took place in **developing nations**, or nations with economies that depend primarily on agriculture. Many of these nations blamed American capitalism for their problems, and they looked to the Soviet Union as a model to industrialize their economies. American leaders feared that these countries would side with the Soviet Union or stage a communist revolution. To prevent this, President Eisenhower offered financial aid to some of these nations. In nations where the communist threat was stronger, the CIA used covert operations to overthrow anti-American leaders. They then replaced them with pro-American leaders.

Uprisings in Hungary and Poland Sometimes covert operations did not work. After Stalin died, Nikita Khrushchev became the Soviet leader. He delivered a secret speech to Soviet leaders in which he attacked Stalin's policies. The CIA obtained a copy of the speech and had it broadcast in Eastern Europe. In June 1956, riots started in Eastern Europe. A full-scale uprising developed in Hungary. Soviet troops moved into Budapest, the capital, and crushed the uprising. Hungarian revolutionaries were disappointed that the United States did not provide support for their revolution.

In 1956, protests also erupted in Poland. In response, the Polish Communist Party adopted a series of reforms and elected a new leader who declared that Poland had the right to follow its own socialist path. Fearful of Soviet armed response, however, the Poles compromised. Poland pledged to remain loyal to the Soviet Union.

The Eisenhower Doctrine In a speech to Congress in January 1957, President Eisenhower announced that the United States would use armed forces upon request in response to aggression

LINKING PAST AND PRESENT

Both the Soviet Union and the United States knew that no winner would emerge from an all-out nuclear war. In 1963 the U.S., the Soviet Union, and Britain signed the Nuclear Test-Ban Treaty, which prohibited nuclear weapons tests in the atmosphere, in space, and underwater—but not underground. In 1968 the three powers signed a Nuclear Non-proliferation Treaty, agreeing not to assist other nations in developing nuclear weapons. Later treaties now limit production and reduce stockpiles of nuclear weapons. The 1996 Comprehensive Test Ban Treaty (CTBT) prohibits all nuclear explosions.

from Communist forces in the Middle East. This policy became known as the Eisenhower Doctrine. The policy was applied in 1958 when Lebanon's leader requested that the United States send troops to his country to stop an insurrection led by Muslims who wanted to pressure the country to join the newly formed United Arab Republic.

Continuing Tensions

The U-2 Crisis In 1958 Khrushchev demanded that the United States, Great Britain, and France remove their troops from West Germany. The United States rejected the demands and threatened to use military force if the Soviets threatened Berlin. The Soviets backed down. Khrushchev suggested a summit with Eisenhower in Paris and invited him to visit the Soviet Union. Eisenhower agreed. Only days before the meeting, however, the Soviet Union announced that it had shot down an American U-2, a high-altitude spy plane, over Russian territory and had captured the American pilot. Khrushchev angrily withdrew his invitation for Eisenhower to visit the Soviet Union. The summit was over before it began.

President Eisenhower left office in January 1961. He delivered a farewell address to the nation in which he pointed out the new relationship that had developed between the military and the defense industry. He warned Americans against the influence of this **military-industrial complex** in a democracy.

Chapter Overview

President John F. Kennedy urged Americans to work for progress and to stand firm against the Soviets. Cold War tensions and the threat of nuclear war peaked during the Cuban missile crisis. Kennedy's assassination changed the nation's mood, but President Lyndon Johnson embraced ambitious goals, including working toward the passage of major civil rights legislation and eradicating poverty.

Initiatives introduced in this era remain a part of American society. Medicaid and Medicare legislation provides major health benefits for elderly and low-income people; and the Head Start program provides early educational opportunities for disadvantaged children.

As you read through this chapter, ask yourself these questions:
(1) What were President Kennedy's economic programs?
(2) How did the Cold War influence foreign aid and the space program?
(3) What programs did the Johnson administration institute?
(4) What inspired Johnson's Great Society programs?

Main Ideas and Concepts

- **Civic Values** The Supreme Court made decisions that protected individual rights, including the Miranda decision.

- **Science and Technology** During the Cold War, the nation devoted much of its scientific and technological resources to competing with the Soviet Union, especially in getting to the moon.

- **Justice** In a time of prosperity, President Johnson won support for extending government aid to the poor and elderly.

People, Places, Terms

The following names and terms will help you to prepare for the Regents Exam in United States History and Government. An explanation of each name and term can be found in the Glossary at the back of this book, in your textbook, or in another reference source.

Bay of Pigs	Peace Corps	Earl Warren
Berlin Wall	reapportionment	Warren
due process	space race	Commission
Great Society	VISTA	
New Frontier	war on poverty	

SECTION 1 THE NEW FRONTIER

The Election of 1960

For the first time, television played an important part in the 1960 presidential election. This was the first election in which a majority of voters used television as a voting tool. The Democrats nominated John F. Kennedy, and the Republicans nominated Richard M. Nixon. Both parties spent money on television ads.

The Main Issues The main issues in the campaign were the economy and the Cold War. The candidates had few differences regarding these issues. Kennedy believed that the Soviets were a serious threat to the United States. He was concerned about a possible "missile gap," in which the United States lagged behind the Soviet Union in weaponry. Nixon argued that the United States was on the right track. He warned that enacting the Democrats' policies would increase inflation. Kennedy faced a religious issue. The United States had never had a Catholic president. Four televised debates between the candidates influenced the outcome of the campaign, and Kennedy won by a narrow margin.

The Kennedy Mystique President Kennedy was very popular with the American people. His youth and attractive family led to constant coverage by the media. Kennedy used the media well. He was the first to have his press conferences televised. He also inspired many of his staff.

CORE CONCEPTS: CONSTITUTIONAL PRINCIPLES

Kennedy faced the issue of his religion by pointing out that in the United States, separation of church and state was absolute as provided by the establishment clause of First Amendment to the Constitution.

Success and Setback on the Domestic Front

President Kennedy was not popular with all Americans. Congress also was less taken with him. After Kennedy became president, he sent a legislative package to Congress. His domestic programs became known as the **New Frontier**. Kennedy wanted to increase aid to education, provide health insurance to the elderly, and create a Department of Urban Affairs. Convincing Congress to pass the legislation was not easy.

Struggles With Congress Kennedy was not able to push through many of his domestic programs. Because he had won by such a narrow margin, he was not helpful in getting many Democrats elected to Congress. As a result, lawmakers found it easy to look out for their own interests instead of considering the interests of the president. Republicans and conservative Southern Democrats believed that the New Frontier was too costly. They also opposed an increase of federal power.

Strengthening the Economy Although Kennedy was unsuccessful in getting Congress to pass many of his programs, he was successful in passing some economic programs. The economic boom of the 1950s had slowed by 1960. To boost the economy, Kennedy pushed Roosevelt's strategy of deficit spending. Kennedy convinced Congress to spend more on defense and space exploration, which created more jobs and stimulated the economy.

CORE CONCEPTS: ECONOMIC SYSTEMS

First implemented during the Great Depression, supply-side (or "trickle-down") economics lowers taxes and can also increase government spending to boost the economy; businesses and individuals spend and invest more money and create higher tax revenue.

BUYING POWER IN 1957						
3¢	19¢	25¢	35¢	50¢	$2,845	$19,500
First-class stamp	Loaf of bread	maga-zine	Movie ticket	Gallon of milk	New car	Median price of a home

Kennedy followed supply-side ideas. He was successful in getting Congress to increase the minimum wage and support his proposal for an Area Redevelopment Act and a Housing Act to create jobs and revitalize urban areas.

CAUSE AND EFFECT	
Economic Problems →	**Kennedy's Solutions**
GNP growth rate was only 2 percent	Proposed tax rate cuts
Unemployment rate was second highest since World War II	Asked labor leaders to hold down pay increases; asked business to hold down prices
Funds needed in poor areas of the country	Area Redevelopment and Housing Acts

Warren Court Reforms

In 1953, President Eisenhower nominated **Earl Warren** to be the Chief Justice of the United States. The Warren Court was an active one, helping shape national policy by taking a stand on several issues.

MAJOR DECISIONS OF THE WARREN COURT, 1954–1967	
Civil Rights	
Brown v. *Board of Education (1954)*	Segregation in public schools unconstitutional
Baker v. *Carr (1962)*	Established that federal courts can hear lawsuits seeking to force state authorities to redraw electoral districts
Reynolds v. *Sims (1964)*	State legislative districts should be equal in population
Heart of Atlanta Motel v. *United States (1964)*	Desegregation of public accommodations established in the Civil Rights Act of 1964 is legal
Due Process	
Mapp v. *Ohio (1961)*	Unlawfully seized evidence is inadmissible at trial
Gideon v. *Wainwright (1963)*	Suspects are entitled to court-appointed attorney if unable to afford one on their own
Miranda v. *Arizona (1966)*	Police must inform suspects of their rights during the arrest process
Freedom of Religion	
Engel v. *Vitale (1962)*	State-mandated prayer in school banned

CORE CONCEPTS: CONSTITUTIONAL PRINCIPLES

In another similar case, *Reynolds* v. *Sims*, the Supreme Court required state legislatures to reapportion electoral districts so that all citizens' votes would have equal weight. The Court's decision shifted political power throughout the country from rural and often conservative areas to urban areas, where more liberal voters resided. It also boosted the political power of African Americans and Hispanics, who typically lived in cities.

REGENTS WARM-UP

Past Regents Exams have included questions about landmark Supreme Court cases. You may wish to create a chart like the one on page 377 to keep track of the issues and rulings in the cases discussed in this chapter and throughout this review book.

"One Man, One Vote" An important decision of the Warren Court had to do with **reapportionment**, or the way in which states draw up political districts based on changes in population. By 1960 more people lived in urban rather than rural areas. Many states had not changed their electoral districts to match this change, however.

In Tennessee, for example, a rural county with only 2,340 voters had 1 representative in the state assembly, while an urban county with 133 times more voters had only 7. The vote of a city dweller counted for less than the vote of a rural resident. Some Tennessee voters took the matter to court.

Baker **v.** *Carr* The *Baker* v. *Carr* case reached the Supreme Court after a federal court ruled that the issue should be solved by legislation. The Fourteenth Amendment specifically gives Congress authority to enforce voting rights. In 1962 the Supreme Court ruled that the federal courts did have jurisdiction and sent the matter back to the lower courts.

Extending Due Process In a series of historic rulings, the Supreme Court began to use the Fourteenth Amendment to apply the Bill of Rights—which originally applied only to the federal government—to the states. The **due process** protection of the Fourteenth Amendment provides that no state could deprive an individual of rights without due process. This means that law may not treat individuals unfairly or unreasonably, and that courts must follow proper procedures and rules when trying cases.

Mapp **v.** *Ohio* In 1957, Cleveland police entered the home of Dolree Mapp after receiving a tip that a bomber was hiding in her home. Mapp tried to block them from entering. As the police were searching the house, they discovered obscene materials and arrested her for possessing them. Mapp argued that her Fourth Amendment rights were violated by the search. The Supreme Court agreed, ruling that both the Fourth and Fourteenth Amendments protected people from unwarranted state and federal intrusion of their property. The Court also ruled that state courts could not use evidence that was obtained illegally.

Gideon **v.** *Wainwright* In 1961 Clarence Gideon was arrested in Florida and charged with breaking and entering. He did not have enough money for a lawyer and requested that one be appointed to defend him. A judge denied his request, saying that under state law, only people who were accused of capital crimes (those where they would face the death penalty) had the right to a court-appointed lawyer. The Supreme Court disagreed. In an unanimous decision, the Court ruled that a defendant in a state court had the right to a lawyer, regardless of his ability to pay.

Miranda **v.** *Arizona* Ernesto Miranda was convicted of rape and kidnapping. His conviction was partly based on incriminating statements he made to police during their interrogation. Police officers never told Miranda that he did not have to talk to them or that he had the right to a lawyer while he was being questioned. The Supreme Court ruled that authorities had to give suspects a four-part warning that included their right to remain silent and their right to have a lawyer. These warnings are now known as the Miranda rights. Police are now required to inform suspects of their Miranda rights before they are questioned.

Engel **v.** *Vitale* The Board of Education of New Hyde Park, New York, told schools in the district to have students begin the day with a prayer. Several parents disputed this policy, saying that the prayer was against their religious beliefs and that the policy violated the First Amendment separation of church and state. The Supreme Court ruled that the school district did violate students' First Amendment rights and that states could not require prayers to be said in state public schools.

SECTION 2 JFK AND THE COLD WAR

Kennedy Confronts Global Challenges

Much of President Kennedy's foreign policy had to do with the Cold War. He tried to reduce the threat of nuclear war and stop the spread of communism.

Flexible Response Believing that Eisenhower depended too much on nuclear weapons, which could be used only in extreme situations, Kennedy wanted to take a more flexible approach that would allow for conventional troops and weapons to be used against communist movements. To do this, Kennedy supported the Special Forces, a small army unit that was created to deal with guerrilla warfare.

Aid to Latin America To improve relations between Latin America and the United States, President Kennedy proposed an Alliance for Progress, a series of cooperative aid projects with Latin American governments. While the people in some countries benefited from the aid, government leaders in other countries used the money to keep themselves in power.

The Peace Corps President Kennedy set up the **Peace Corps** to help fight poverty in less-developed nations. Volunteers were trained to spend two years in a nation that had requested help. Their work included teaching, building roads, training medical technicians, and laying out sewage systems. The Peace Corps is still active today.

The Space Race As the Cold War intensified, the United States and the Soviet Union started a **space race**, vying for dominance of space to increase their competitive positions on Earth. Kennedy was determined that the United States would be first nation to have a human reach the moon. His goal was realized in July 1969.

Crises of the Cold War

President Kennedy faced several crises in the Cold War. The first started in Cuba.

The Bay of Pigs In 1959 Fidel Castro had overthrown the Cuban dictator Fulgencio Batista and immediately established political, economic, and military ties with the Soviet Union. He took over foreign-owned businesses, many of which were American. The United States was concerned that the Soviets would set up a base in Cuba from which to spread communist beliefs throughout the Western Hemisphere. President Eisenhower authorized the Central Intelligence Agency (CIA) to train and arm Cuban exiles and to invade the island, hoping that the invasion would start an uprising in Cuba against Castro.

Shortly after Kennedy became president, Kennedy's advisers approved the invasion plan. On April 17, 1961, armed Cuban exiles landed at the **Bay of Pigs**, on the south coast of Cuba, but the invasion failed. It showed that the United States had tried to overthrow a neighbor's government and it made the United States look weak.

The Berlin Wall Shortly after the failed invasion, Kennedy faced another problem. In June 1961, Kennedy met in Vienna, Austria, with Soviet leader Nikita Khrushchev. Khrushchev wanted to keep the Germans from moving out of communist East Germany into West Berlin. He wanted Western countries to recognize East Germany. He also wanted the United States, Britain, and France to leave Berlin. Kennedy refused. Khrushchev responded by building the **Berlin Wall**. It stopped movement between the Soviet part of the city and rest of the city. Guards along the wall shot at many of those trying to escape

LINKING GEOGRAPHY AND HISTORY

The island of Cuba lies only 90 miles south of Key West, Florida. When Fidel Castro established ties with the Soviets, communism became too close for comfort. This close proximity led to two of the most intense crises of the Cold War.

CORE CONCEPTS: PLACES AND REGIONS

The city of Berlin was actually inside East Germany. In 1947 the Soviet Union had tried to cut West Berlin off by closing off roads leading to it. This led to the Berlin Airlift. In 1961 the Soviet Union built the Berlin Wall, leading to President Kennedy's visit to West Berlin in 1962 and his famous comment, "Ich bin ein Berliner (I am a Berliner)." In 1987, in a speech in West Berlin, President Reagan said, "Mr. Gorbachev [the Soviet leader], tear down this wall." The Berlin Wall was taken down in 1989 and East and West Berlin and Germany were reunited.

from the East. The Berlin Wall stood for nearly 30 years afterward, a visible symbol of the Cold War division between East and West.

The Cuban Missile Crisis The most frightening crisis happened in 1962, and again dealt with Cuba. The United States had learned that Soviet technicians and equipment had arrived in Cuba. They also learned that a military buildup was in progress. On October 22, 1969, President Kennedy told the American people that photos taken from spy planes showed that the Soviet Union had placed long-range missiles in Cuba. These posed a serious threat to the United States. Kennedy ordered a naval blockade to stop the Soviet Union from delivering more missiles. He warned that if the Soviet Union launched missiles on the United States, he would respond against the Soviet Union. However, work on the missile sites continued.

The leaders of the two countries started secret negotiations. They reached an agreement on October 28. Kennedy agreed not to invade Cuba and to remove U.S. missiles from Turkey. The Soviet Union agreed to remove its missiles from Cuba.

The Cuban missile crisis brought the world close to nuclear war and made both countries face the consequences of a nuclear war. As a result, both countries worked to lessen tensions and agreed to the Test Ban Treaty to ban the testing of nuclear weapons in the atmosphere. In 1967, a "hot line" was installed that established a direct communications link between Washington and Moscow. It has often proved useful in tense or emergency situations.

The Death of a President

On November 22, 1963, President Kennedy and his wife traveled to Texas to make some political appearances. As the presidential motorcade rode through Dallas, President Kennedy was shot. He was pronounced dead at a local hospital. Lee Harvey Oswald, the man accused of killing Kennedy, was shot to death two days later while in police custody. In 1964, the **Warren Commission**, a national commission headed by Chief Justice Warren, concluded that Oswald acted alone. However, theories about a more widespread conspiracy to kill the president have continued.

CORE CONCEPTS: CONSTITUTIONAL PRINCIPLES

When President Kennedy was killed in office, Vice President Lyndon Johnson assumed office. The Twenty-fifth Amendment, ratified in 1967, provided for election of a new vice-president.

CORE CONCEPTS: REFORM MOVEMENTS

The issue of civil rights for African Americans came to the forefront following the *Brown* case in 1954.

CORE CONCEPTS: IMMIGRATION AND MIGRATION

Political turmoil in Cuba in the 1950s greatly increased Cuban immigration to the United States. Wealthy families and well-educated people were some of the first to flee Castro's regime, but thousands more followed and were granted asylum by the U.S. government. Several other countries, such as Jamaica, the Dominican Republic, and Puerto Rico, have established large communities in the United States, especially in urban areas such as New York City.

SECTION 3 THE GREAT SOCIETY

After President Kennedy's death, President Johnson knew that he had to reassure the nation that he could hold it together. He went before Congress and urged the nation to move on. President Johnson pushed a number of Kennedy's programs through Congress. He won passage of a major civil rights bill and an anti-poverty bill. Johnson had known poverty firsthand and he made the elimination of poverty a major goal.

A War on Poverty In 1964 Johnson announced that he was declaring a **"war on poverty** in America." Plans for an anti-poverty program were already in place when Johnson took office, and he knew that he would be able to command strong support for any program that could be linked to Kennedy. That same year, Congress passed the Economic Opportunity Act, which established a wide range of programs aimed at creating jobs and fighting poverty.

Johnson also set up programs that were aimed at creating jobs and strengthening education. **VISTA** (Volunteers in Service to America) was a kind of domestic Peace Corps. The program put young people to work in poor school districts.

The Great Society

Johnson won the 1964 election by a landslide and began working on the **Great Society**—Johnson's plan for domestic programs.

During Johnson's administration, the civil rights movement achieved many of its goals through the Civil Rights Act of 1964, which forbade racial discrimination in public accommodations such as hotels and restaurants. The Voting Rights Act of 1965 ensured African Americans the right to vote.

The Immigration Reform Act of 1965 kept a strict limit on the number of immigrants admitted to the United States each year. However, it eliminated the national origins system, which gave preference to immigrants from northern Europe. The new law allowed immigrants from all parts of Europe, as well as from Asia and Africa. The Immigration Reform Act of 1965 was the first major change since the Immigration Act of 1924.

More than 60 of Johnson's programs were passed between 1965 and 1968. Many of them remain today. These include Medicare, a health insurance program for the elderly; Medicaid,

a health-care program for people on welfare; and Project Head
Start, a preschool program for disadvantaged children.

MAJOR GREAT SOCIETY PROGRAMS			
Health and Welfare	**Education**	**The "War on Poverty"**	**Consumer and Environmental Protection**
Medicare (1965) established a comprehensive health insurance program for all elderly people; financed through the Social Security system.	**The Elementary and Secondary Education Act** (1965) targeted aid to students and funded related activities such as adult education and education counseling.	**The Office of Economic Opportunity** (1964) oversaw many programs to improve life in inner cities, including Job Corps, an education and job-training program for at-risk youth.	**The Water Quality Act and Clean Air Acts** (1965) supported development of standards and goals for water and air quality.
Medicaid (1965) funded by federal and state governments, provided health and medical assistance to low-income families.	**Higher Education Act** (1965) supported college tuition scholarships, student loans, and work-study programs for low- and middle-income students.	**Housing and Urban Development Act** (1965) established new housing subsidy programs and made federal loans and public housing grants easier to obtain.	**The Highway Safety Act** (1966) supported highway safety by improving federal, state, and local coordination and by creating training standards for emergency medical technicians.
Child Nutrition Act (1966) established a school breakfast program and expanded the school lunch program and milk program to improve poor children's nutrition.	**Project Head Start** (1965) funded a preschool program for the disadvantaged.	**Demonstration Cities and Metropolitan Development Act** (1966) helped revitalize urban areas through a variety of social and economic programs.	**The Fair Packaging and Labeling Act** (1966) required all consumer products to have true and informative labels.

The Moon Landing The centerpiece of the space program soon
became manned space exploration. After the National
Aeronautics and Space Administration (NASA) was established
in 1958, astronauts quickly became the nation's most revered

heroes. In February 1962, John Glenn (later to become a U.S. Senator) became the first American to orbit the globe.

The goal of the Apollo space program was to land a man on the moon. After some terrible setbacks, on July 20, 1969, Neil Armstrong, Edwin Aldrin, and Michael Collins successfully traveled in a space capsule into orbit around the moon. Armstrong and Aldrin then detached a smaller craft, landed on the surface of the moon, and became the first men to walk on the moon. Six more missions soon followed, but the government began cutting funding for missions and popular enthusiasm faded.

CHAPTER 28   THE CIVIL RIGHTS MOVEMENT

Chapter Overview

In the 1950s and 1960s, African Americans made major strides. They began by challenging segregation in the South. With the Montgomery bus boycott, Martin Luther King, Jr., achieved national and worldwide recognition. His peaceful resistance inspired many, especially students. After King's assassination, the civil rights movement shifted focus. Many people in the movement began to see economic opportunity as the key to equality.

Changes brought about by the civil rights movement are still with us. Civil rights legislation provides protection against discrimination for all citizens, and economic programs for inner-city residents by government and social service agencies continue.

As you read through this chapter, ask yourself these questions:

(1) What was the changing role of the federal government in civil rights enforcement?
(2) What efforts were made to establish voting rights for African Americans?
(3) What issues divided Martin Luther King, Jr., and the black power movement?
(4) How has the civil rights movement progressed since 1968?

Main Ideas and Concepts

- **Justice** In the 1950s, African Americans began a movement to win greater social equality.

- **Science and Technology** The civil rights movement gained momentum in the early 1960s due to national television coverage.

- **Civic Values** In the late 1960s, the civil rights movement tried to address the persistent economic inequality of African Americans.

People, Places, Terms

The following names and terms will help you to prepare for the Regents Exam in United States History and Government. You can find an explanation of each name and term in the Glossary at the back of this book, in your textbook, or in another reference source.

Black Panthers	Freedom Riders	NAACP
black power	Dr. Martin Luther	poll tax
Linda Brown	King, Jr.	separate but equal
Stokely Carmichael	Little Rock,	Twenty-fourth
Civil Rights Act	Arkansas	Amendment
of 1964	Malcolm X	Voting Rights Act
de facto segregation	Thurgood Marshall	of 1965

SECTION 1 THE MOVEMENT BEGINS

The Origins of the Movement

The Supreme Court's 1896 decision in *Plessy* v. *Ferguson* set up a **separate but equal** policy. Laws that segregated African Americans were allowed as long as they provided for "equal" facilities. (In practice, facilities for African Americans were rarely equal.) After this decision, laws segregating African Americans became common. These Jim Crow laws segregated buses, schools, and restaurants. Signs saying "Whites Only" or "Colored" appeared on entrances to many places. Jim Crow laws were common in the South, but segregation also existed in other places. Areas that did not have segregation laws, such as in many places in the North, often had **de facto segregation**, or segregation by custom and tradition.

One important color barrier had been broken as early as 1947, when the Brooklyn Dodgers signed the great Jackie Robinson as the first African American to play Major League Baseball. By the mid-1950s, African Americans had established themselves as a powerful force in almost all professional sports.

Court Challenges Begin Since 1909 the National Association for the Advancement of Colored People **(NAACP)** had supported court cases that had to do with overturning segregation. It was successful in some cases. In addition to these successes, African Americans began experiencing more political power and began using this power to demand more rights. In 1942, James Farmer and George Houser started the Congress of Racial Equality (CORE). The Urban League, which was formed in 1910, also worked to end racial discrimination and increase the political and economic power of African Americans.

In the 1950s and 1960s, members of the organization used sit-ins as a protest strategy. If a restaurant refused to serve African Americans, members of CORE and others would sit down and refuse to leave. Through this strategy, CORE successfully integrated public facilities in several Northern cities.

SUPREME COURT DECISIONS ON CIVIL RIGHTS	
Plessy v. *Ferguson (1896)*	"Separate-but-equal doctrine": Segregation was permitted as long as equal facilities were provided for African Americans
Norris v. *Alabama (1935)*	African Americans should not be excluded from serving on juries.
Morgan v. *Virginia (1946)*	Segregation on interstate buses was unconstitutional.
Sweatt v. *Painter (1950)*	State law schools had to admit qualified African American candidates
Brown v. *Board of Education (1954)*	Segregation in public schools was unconstitutional and violated the equal-protection clause of the Fourteenth Amendment

The Civil Rights Movement Begins

Brown v. *Board of Education* The chief counsel of the NAACP from 1939 to 1961 was African American attorney **Thurgood Marshall**. He focused his attention on desegregating public schools.

In 1954 the Supreme Court heard cases regarding segregation in schools. One case involved **Linda Brown**. She was a young African American girl who was denied admission to her neighborhood school in Topeka, Kansas, because of her race. Together with the NAACP, her parents sued the Topeka school board. In May 1954, the Supreme Court ruled in the case of *Brown* v. *Board of Education of Topeka, Kansas*, that segregation in public schools

REGENTS WARM-UP

Past Regents Exams have included questions that test your knowledge of landmark Supreme Court cases. *Brown* v. *Board of Education of Topeka, Kansas* and *Plessy* v. *Ferguson* are two such landmark cases.

CORE CONCEPTS: CITIZENSHIP

The Fourteenth Amendment, ratified in 1868 and one of the so-called Civil War Amendments, guaranteed "equal protection of the laws." This was the basis of the *Brown* decision. The Supreme Court said that the doctrine of separate but equal was "inherently unequal" and ordered integration to proceed "with all deliberate speed."

CORE CONCEPTS: REFORM MOVEMENTS

Dr. King developed his ideas about nonviolent passive resistance and civil disobedience from the ideas of American Henry David Thoreau, who in the 1840s wrote an essay entitled *Civil Disobedience* in opposition to the war with Mexico that he felt supported slavery; and Indian Mohandas Gandhi, who opposed British colonial rule in India in the first half of the 20th century. Dr. King used the ideas in his fight against racism and segregation.

was unconstitutional. It also ruled that segregation violated the equal protection clause of the Fourteenth Amendment.

This decision reversed the decision in *Plessy* v. *Ferguson* and signaled that it was time to challenge other forms of segregation.

The Montgomery Bus Boycott

During the conflict over the *Brown* v. *Board of Education* case, a woman named Rosa Parks decided to challenge the segregation of the bus system in Montgomery, Alabama. On December 1, 1955, Parks boarded a bus in Montgomery on her way home from work. Buses there at that time reserved the front section for whites and back section for African Americans. Parks took a seat right behind the white section. When she was asked to give up her seat to a white man who was standing, she refused and was arrested. She decided to challenge bus segregation in court.

After her arrest, African Americans in Montgomery started a boycott of the bus system. Several African American leaders formed the Montgomery Improvement Association to negotiate with city leaders to end segregation. The organization's leader was **Martin Luther King, Jr.**, a minister. King believed that the way to end segregation and racism was through nonviolent passive resistance.

African Americans in Montgomery continued their boycott for more than a year. Rosa Parks' lawsuit led to a Supreme Court ruling in 1956 that Alabama's laws requiring segregation on buses were unconstitutional.

The SCLC Many of the leaders of the Montgomery bus boycott were ministers like Martin Luther King, Jr. Led by King, the ministers set up the Southern Christian Leadership Conference (SCLC) in 1957. The organization worked to do away with segregation in American society and to encourage African Americans to register to vote.

Eisenhower's Role President Eisenhower personally opposed segregation, but he disagreed with those who wanted to end it through protests and court rulings. Although he did not support the decision in *Brown* v. *Board of Education*, he believed the federal government had the duty to uphold it.

In September 1957, the **Little Rock, Arkansas**, school board won a court order to admit nine African American students to Central High School, a school whose entire student population was white.

The governor of Arkansas ordered the National Guard to keep the nine African American students from entering the school. When a violent riot ensued, Eisenhower sent U.S. Army troops to Little Rock. The African American students walked into school that day protected by the U.S. Army.

The Civil Rights Act of 1957 That same year, Congress passed the Civil Rights Act of 1957. It was intended to protect the right of African Americans to vote. Although its final form was much weaker than originally intended, the act still brought the power of the federal government into the civil rights debate. The act created a civil rights division within the Department of Justice and gave it the authority to seek court injunctions against anyone interfering with the right to vote. It also created the United States Commission on Civil Rights to investigate allegations of denial of voting rights After the bill passed, the SCLC announced a campaign to register 2 million new African American voters.

SECTION 2 CHALLENGING SEGREGATION

The Sit-in Movement The sit-in strategies to end segregation spread to several cities. During sit-ins, African Americans purposefully sat down in restaurants, at lunch counters, and at other segregated facilities. Despite being punched, kicked, and beaten by bystanders, the mostly student protesters at sit-ins remained peaceful and attracted the nation's attention.

SNCC As students continued to become more active in protesting segregation, they came to see that they needed to create an organization of their own. They established the Student Nonviolent Coordinating Committee (SNCC). The SNCC's membership included both African American and white college students. The group was instrumental in desegregating public facilities in many urban communities and in registering voters in the rural areas of the Deep South.

The Freedom Riders In 1961 James Farmer, the leader of CORE, asked groups of African Americans and white Americans to travel into the South on public buses to draw attention to the South's segregation of bus terminals. These groups became known as **Freedom Riders**. When buses carrying Freedom Riders arrived at various cities in the South, white mobs attacked them. In Birmingham, Alabama, Freedom Riders leaving the bus

CORE CONCEPTS: GOVERNMENT

One way for a senator to defeat a bill he or she opposes is by filibuster. Filibuster means to keep talking until a majority of the Senate either abandons the bill or agrees to modify it. Senator Strom Thurmond of South Carolina set the record for a filibuster when he spoke against the Civil Rights Act of 1957 for 24 hours and 18 minutes.

CORE CONCEPTS: SCIENCE AND TECHNOLOGY

Much momentum for the civil rights movement in the 1950s and 1960s was due to television, a medium that was still in its infancy. The American public saw, for the first time, just how ugly segregation could be, and many joined in the outcry against it.

were viciously beaten by a gang of young men. Later evidence showed that the head of police in Birmingham had contacted the local Ku Klux Klan and had told them he wanted the Freedom riders attacked. The violence shocked many Americans. President Kennedy decided that he had to take action.

John F. Kennedy and Civil Rights

In his campaign, John Kennedy promised to support the civil rights movement if he was elected president. African Americans overwhelmingly voted for him. At first, Kennedy was as cautious as Eisenhower on civil rights. He knew he needed the support of Southern senators to get some other programs he wanted passed. However, Kennedy did name about 40 African Americans to high-level positions in the federal government. He appointed Thurgood Marshall to an Appeals Court in New York, which was only one level below the United States Supreme Court. He also set up the Committee on Equal Employment Opportunity (CEEO) to stop the federal government from discriminating against African Americans.

The Justice Department Takes Action Kennedy was reluctant to challenge Southern Democrats in Congress. He allowed the Justice Department, which was led by his brother Robert Kennedy, to support the civil rights movement. Robert Kennedy helped African Americans register to vote by having the Justice Department file lawsuits throughout the South.

After the Freedom Riders were attacked in Birmingham, the Kennedys urged them to stop the ride, but they refused. They planned their next trip to Mississippi. To prevent any violence, the president made a deal with a senator from Mississippi: if he used his influence to prevent violence, he would not object if the Mississippi police arrested the Freedom Riders. The deal was successful. However, the cost of bailing out the Freedom Riders used up most of CORE's funds. Thurgood Marshall offered money from the NAACP's Legal Defense Fund to keep the rides going.

When President Kennedy realized that the Freedom Riders were still active, he ordered the Interstate Commerce Commission to tighten its regulations against segregated bus terminals. By late 1962, segregation on interstate travel had come to an end.

James Meredith In early 1961, African American James Meredith applied to the University of Mississippi. At the time,

CORE CONCEPTS: GOVERNMENT

The Department of Justice is one of the departments in the president's Cabinet. As its head, Robert Kennedy held the title of Attorney General of the United States.

the university had not yet obeyed the Supreme Court ruling to desegregate. When Meredith tried to register at the university, he was blocked from entering by the governor of Mississippi. President Kennedy sent 500 federal marshals to escort Meredith into the school. When a riot began, Kennedy ordered the Army to send troops to the campus. Meredith attended classes at the university under federal guard for the rest of the year.

Violence in Birmingham Martin Luther King, Jr., and other civil rights leaders were frustrated over the events in Mississippi and disappointed that the president did not push for a new civil rights law. King observed that the president intervened in civil rights issues only when protestors were attacked. To prove his point, King ordered demonstrations in Birmingham, Alabama, that he knew would lead to violence. He believed it was the only way to get Kennedy to actively support civil rights.

King was arrested shortly after the protests began. While in prison, King began writing on scraps of paper that had been smuggled into his cell. The "Letter From Birmingham City Jail" that he produced is one of the most eloquent defenses of nonviolent protest ever written. In his letter, King explained that although the protesters were breaking the law, they were following a higher moral law based on divine justice.

The violence against the protesters escalated and was seen by millions of Americans who watched it on TV. President Kennedy responded as King had hoped, ordering his aides to prepare a new civil rights bill to send to Congress.

The Civil Rights Act of 1964

In June 1963, Alabama governor George Wallace stood in front of the University of Alabama's admissions office to stop two African Americans from enrolling. Federal marshals ordered him to move. The following day a white segregationist murdered Medgar Evers, a civil rights activist in Mississippi. President Kennedy took that opportunity to present his civil rights bill.

The March on Washington To support the passage of the bill through Congress, Martin Luther King, Jr., organized a massive march on Washington. On August 28, 1963, more than 200,000 people gathered peacefully at the nation's capital. Dr. King delivered his powerful "I Have a Dream" speech. The march built support for the bill, but opponents in Congress used filibuster to slow the bill down.

CORE CONCEPTS: CONSTITUTIONAL PRINCIPLES

The president can propose legislation, but only the Congress—the House of Representatives and the Senate—can enact new laws.

CORE CONCEPTS: CHANGE

The filibuster is not as strong a weapon as it used to be. Today a filibuster can be stopped if at least three-fifths of the senators vote for cloture, a motion that cuts off debate and forces a vote.

The Civil Rights Bill Becomes Law After President Kennedy was assassinated in 1963, African Americans worried that the civil rights bill would never pass. But President Johnson committed himself to getting Congress to pass it and on July 2, 1964, signed the **Civil Rights Act of 1963** into law. The law was the most comprehensive civil rights law Congress had ever enacted. Among its provisions:

- Congress had the power to outlaw segregation in most public places.

- All citizens had equal access to public facilities such as restaurants, parks, and theaters.

- The Attorney General had more power to bring lawsuits to force schools to desegregate.

- It set up the Equal Employment Opportunity Commission (EEOC) to oversee the ban on job discrimination by race, religion, gender, and national origin.

Heart of Atlanta Motel, Inc. v. United States A Georgia motel (Heart of Atlanta Motel) drew business from other states, but refused to rent rooms to African Americans. The passage of the Civil Rights Act of 1964 made this illegal. The owner of the motel filed suit, claiming that Congress did not have the power to regulate an individual's business. The Supreme Court disagreed, explaining that Congress had the authority to prohibit such discrimination under both the equal protection clause and the commerce clause. With respect to the commerce clause, the Court explained that Congress had ample evidence to conclude the racial discrimination by hotels and motels impedes interstate commerce.

The Struggle for Voting Rights

The Civil Rights Act of 1964 did little to guarantee the right to vote. The **Twenty-fourth Amendment**, ratified in 1964, helped somewhat, by abolishing **poll taxes**—fees that had to be paid by voters in order to vote in national elections. The SNCC and SCLC increased their voter registration drives in the South. Those that tried to register African American voters were often attacked and sometimes murdered.

Martin Luther King, Jr., and others believed that a new law was necessary to protect African American voting rights. Dr. King decided to stage another protest in Selma, Alabama.

CORE CONCEPTS: CONSTITUTIONAL PRINCIPLES

The Civil Rights Act of 1964 was based on the authority given to Congress by the Constitution to regulate commerce. The Supreme Act reasoned that people who could not access hotels and restaurants could not travel, which, therefore, interrupts the flow of interstate commerce. Congress has the power the regulate commerce. Therefore, Congress may pass laws against racial discrimination.

The Selma March A protest march from Selma to Montgomery began on March 7, 1965. As protesters approached the bridge that led out of Selma, the sheriff ordered them to break up. While the marchers knelt in prayer, state troopers and deputized citizens attacked them. The nation again witnessed the violence on television and was shocked. An outraged President Johnson came before Congress to present a new voting rights act.

The Voting Rights Act of 1965 Congress approved the **Voting Rights Act of 1965** in August of that year. It ordered federal examiners to register qualified voters and it got rid of discriminatory practices such as the literacy test. By the end of 1965, almost 250,000 new African American voters had registered to vote. The number of African American elected officials in the South also increased.

SECTION 3 NEW ISSUES

Problems Facing Urban African Americans

By 1965 the civil rights movement had achieved the passage of several civil rights laws, but African Americans across the nation still faced prejudice, discrimination, and economic inequalities. Hope gave way to frustration and anger when civil rights laws failed to change the everyday hardships of African Americans.

Urban Riots Race riots broke out in dozens of American cities between 1965 and 1968 as some became impatient in the struggle for civil rights. One took place in Watts, an African American neighborhood in Los Angeles. The riots lasted six days, during which entire neighborhoods were looted and burned. Thirty-four people were killed and hundreds were injured.

Kerner Commission In 1967 President Johnson appointed the National Advisory Commission on Civil Disorders, headed by Governor Otto Kerner of Illinois, to study the causes of the urban riots and to make recommendations to prevent them from happening again in the future. The Kerner Commission conducted a detailed study of the problem. The commission blamed white society and white racism for the majority of the problems in the inner city. The commission recommended the creation of 2 million new units of public housing, and a renewed federal commitment to fight de facto segregation. However, saddled with massive spending for the Vietnam War, President Johnson never endorsed the recommendations of the commission.

Black Power Frustration with nonviolent protests led some African American leaders to turn to more aggressive forms of protest. African Americans began to advocate **black power**. Most African Americans, including SNCC leader **Stokely Carmichael**, believed that black power stressed black pride and black nationalism.

A man named **Malcolm X** became the symbol of black power. After a difficult childhood and time in prison, he educated himself and became a member of the Nation of Islam, or Black Muslims. The Nation of Islam preached black nationalism. Like Marcus Garvey in the 1920s, Black Muslims believed that African Americans should separate themselves from whites and form their own self-governing communities.

However, by 1964, Malcolm X had broken with the Nation of Islam after a trip to the Muslim holy city of Mecca in Saudi Arabia. After seeing Muslims from many different races worshipping together, he concluded that an integrated society was possible. He began speaking out against the Nation of Islam. Because of this, three organization members shot and killed him in 1965. Malcolm X's ideas have continued to influence African Americans to take pride in their culture and to believe in their ability to make their way in the world.

Other African Americans called for violent action to end racial oppression. One group, the **Black Panthers**, believed a revolution against white society was necessary.

The Assassination of Martin Luther King, Jr.

By the late 1960s, the civil rights movement was divided into competing organizations that were at odds with one another. In 1968 an assassin's bullet took the life of Dr. Martin Luther King, Jr., as he stood on his hotel balcony. The assassination touched off riots in more than 100 cities and ended an era of unified and visionary civil rights achievements that had transformed American society.

In the wake of Dr. King's death, Congress passed the Civil Rights Act of 1968. The act contained the Fair Housing Act provision outlawing discrimination in housing sales and rentals and gave the Justice Department authority to bring suits against such discrimination.

CHAPTER 29 THE VIETNAM WAR

Chapter Overview

The Vietnam War created very bitter divisions within the United States. Supporters argued that the communist belief in world domination meant that communism must be halted. Opponents argued that intervening in Vietnam was immoral. Many young people protested or resisted the draft. Victory was not achieved, although more than 58,000 American soldiers died. After the war, the nation had many wounds to heal.

As you read through this chapter, ask yourself these questions:
(1) What were the origins of America's involvement in Vietnam during the 1950s?
(2) How did the Vietcong and the North Vietnamese frustrate the American military?
(3) Why did support for the war begin to weaken?
(4) What lessons did the United States learn from the Vietnam War experience?

Main Ideas and Concepts

- **Government** American involvement in Vietnam was a reflection of Cold War strategy.

- **Civic Values** Many Americans protested their country's involvement in the Vietnam War.

- **Government** The Vietnam War led to changes in the way the U.S. military is deployed.

People, Places, Terms

The following names and terms will help you to prepare for the Regents Exam in United States History and Government. You can find an explanation of each name and term in the Glossary at the back of this book, in your textbook, or in another reference source.

Ho Chi Minh	Gulf of Tonkin	Tet offensive
credibility gap	Resolution	Vietcong
domino theory	hawks	Vietnamization
doves	Henry Kissinger	War Powers Act
guerillas	Ngo Dinh Diem	

SECTION 1 THE UNITED STATES FOCUSES ON VIETNAM

Early American Involvement in Vietnam

Vietnam had often been ruled by foreign powers. China controlled it off and on for hundreds of years. From the late 1800s until World War II, France ruled Vietnam and neighboring Laos and Cambodia. This region became known as French Indochina. Japan took power in Vietnam during World War II.

By the early 1900s, nationalism had spread through Vietnam. Several political parties pushed for independence from France. One of the leaders of the movement was **Ho Chi Minh**. In 1930 he helped start the Indochinese Communist Party and worked to overthrow French rule. In 1941, after Japan had taken control of Vietnam, Ho organized a nationalist group called the Vietminh. The group's goal was to get rid of the Japanese forces. The United States sent military aid to the Vietminh.

The United States Supports the French When Japan was defeated in World War II in August 1945, it gave up control of Indochina. Ho announced that Vietnam was an independent nation. France wanted to regain its colonial empire in Southeast Asia. France sent troops to Vietnam in 1946 and drove the Vietminh's forces into hiding in the countryside. By 1949 France had set up a new government in Vietnam. The Vietminh fought against the French and slowly increased their control over large areas of the countryside. As fighting increased, France asked the United States for help.

The request put the United States in a difficult position. The United States did not think France should control Vietnam, but it did want not the country to be Communist.

President Truman decided to help France for two reasons: the fall of China to Communism and the Korean War. President Eisenhower continued to support the French. He stressed the **domino theory**—the belief that if Vietnam fell to Communism, other Southeast Asian nations would, too.

The Vietminh Drive Out the French

The Vietminh used the tactics of **guerillas**. These are irregular troops who usually blend into the civilian population and are often difficult for regular armies to fight.

Defeat at Dien Bien Phu In 1954, French troops occupied the Vietnamese town of Dien Bien Phu. They hoped to interfere with the Vietminh's supply lines. Soon after, a large Vietminh force surrounded the town and began bombarding it. The French forces fell to the Vietminh and the French withdrew from Indochina.

Geneva Accords Negotiations to end the conflict took place in Geneva, Switzerland. The Geneva Accords temporarily divided Vietnam in North Vietnam and South Vietnam. Ho Chi Minh and the Vietminh controlled North Vietnam. A pro-Western regime controlled South Vietnam. Elections were to be held in 1956 to reunite the country under a single government.

The United States stepped in to support the new government in South Vietnam. Its leader was **Ngo Dinh Diem**, who was anti-Communist. When the time came to hold elections in 1956, Diem refused. Eisenhower supported Diem, and the United States increased military and economic aid to South Vietnam. Tensions between the North and South increased.

SECTION 2   GOING TO WAR IN VIETNAM

American Involvement Deepens

After Diem refused to hold national elections, Ho Chi Minh began an armed struggle to reunify the nation. He and his followers organized a new guerrilla army, which became known as the **Vietcong**. Fighting between the Vietcong and South

CORE CONCEPTS: FOREIGN POLICY

A central idea of American foreign policy after World War II was containment, or stopping the further spread of communism.

REGENTS WARM-UP

Past Regents Exams have included questions that test your knowledge of the causes and effects of the Vietnam War. Create a cause-and-effect diagram like the one below to help you take notes as you read through this chapter.

THE VIETNAM WAR	
Causes	Effects

Vietnam's forces began. President Eisenhower increased military aid and sent military advisors to the South Vietnamese, but the Vietcong's power increased.

Kennedy Takes Over President Kennedy increased military aid and sent more advisers. In addition, the United States urged Diem to introduce more democratic reforms. Diem's government was corrupt and unpopular, and it discriminated against Buddhism, one of the most-practiced religions in Vietnam.

By 1963, several Vietnamese generals were plotting to over-throw Diem. Supported by the United States, the generals not only overthrew Diem, but executed him as well. His death made the government even more unstable and the United States became even more involved.

Johnson and Vietnam

After President Kennedy was assassinated, the problem in Vietnam became President Johnson's problem. Johnson was determined to stop South Vietnam from becoming Communist.

The Gulf of Tonkin On August 2, 1964, President Johnson announced that North Vietnamese torpedo boats had fired unprovoked on two American destroyers in the Gulf of Tonkin. He ordered American aircraft to attack North Vietnamese ships. What Johnson did not reveal was that American warships had been helping South Vietnam in spying and raids on North Vietnam. President Johnson had to ask Congress for the authority to use force to defend American troops. A few days later Congress passed the **Gulf of Tonkin Resolution**, authorizing the president to use whatever force necessary to protect American lives. A confident United States began sending combat troops to fight against the Vietcong, while aircraft carried out sustained bombing raids on North Vietnam.

A Bloody Stalemate Emerges By 1966 more than 300,000 American soldiers were fighting in Vietnam alongside the South Vietnamese troops. With such a large fighting force, Americans believed that the United States couldn't lose. The Vietcong's strength and stamina surprised the United States, and their use of surprise tactics and guerilla warfare frustrated American troops. American forces countered with chemical weapons and napalm, bombing jungle areas in Vietnam, Laos, and Cambodia to cut off the "Ho Chi Minh Trail," the infiltration routes by which the North Vietnamese sent troops and supplies into the south. However, President Johnson refused to order an invasion of North Vietnam because he feared an attack would bring China into the war.

By the mid-1960s American casualties mounted, and the Vietcong and North Vietnamese showed no sign of surrendering.

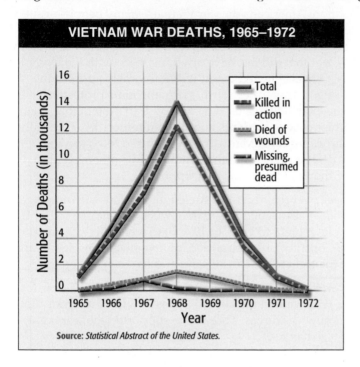

VIETNAM WAR DEATHS, 1965–1972

Legend:
- Total
- Killed in action
- Died of wounds
- Missing, presumed dead

Y-axis: Number of Deaths (in thousands)
X-axis: Year (1965, 1966, 1967, 1968, 1969, 1970, 1971, 1972)

Source: *Statistical Abstract of the United States.*

SECTION 3 VIETNAM DIVIDES THE NATION

A Growing Credibility Gap

Opposition to the Vietnam War grew in the United States in the late 1960s. One of the main reasons for the increased opposition was that many Americans were suspicious of the government's truthfulness about the war. Although many Americans supported the military effort when the first American troops landed in Vietnam in the spring of 1965, those numbers decreased as the war dragged on. In 1967, the American commander in South Vietnam reported that the United States was near victory. However, grim television coverage of the war began to conflict with optimistic government reports. Many

CORE CONCEPTS: SCIENCE AND TECHNOLOGY

Television brought the Vietnam War directly into American living rooms every evening during the nightly news, considerably affecting public opinion about the war.

Americans believed a **credibility gap** had developed, and Congress grew uncertain about the war as well.

An Antiwar Movement Emerges

As more Americans died in Vietnam, many people—especially college students—began to protest against the war. People opposed the war for different reasons. Some believed that it was a civil war that did not have anything to do with the United States. Others believed that it was immoral to support the corrupt government of South Vietnam. Some protesters believed that the United States used a corrupt draft system that exempted wealthier college students and drafted minorities, especially African Americans. Many draftees refused to go to Vietnam. Some draft-dodgers fled the country while others went to prison rather than fight in a war they opposed.

Anger over the draft also fueled discussions of voting age. Many draftees argued that if they were old enough to fight, they were old enough to vote. In 1971 the Twenty-sixth Amendment to the Constitution was ratified, giving all citizens age 18 and older the right to vote in all state and federal elections.

By 1968, Americans seemed to be divided into two camps. Those who wanted the United States to withdraw from Vietnam were known as **doves**. Those who supported the war were known as **hawks**.

1968: The Pivotal Year

The most turbulent year of the 1960s was 1968. Troubling events in 1968 sent the nation reeling.

The Tet Offensive On January 30, 1968, the Vietcong and North Vietnamese launched a huge surprise attack during Tet, the Vietnamese New Year. In the **Tet offensive**, guerrilla fighters attacked all American airbases in South Vietnam, and most of the nation's major cities. North Vietnam scored a major political victory after about a month of fighting. Americans were shocked that the North Vietnamese, who were supposedly near defeat, could launch such a huge attack. The media criticized the military effort and indicated that the United States could not win the war.

President Johnson's approval rating fell drastically after the Tet offensive. As a result, Johnson announced that he would not run for reelection.

CORE CONCEPTS: PRESIDENTIAL DECISIONS AND ACTIONS

Some Americans were against the war on the grounds that it was "illegal," meaning that Congress had never declared war against North Vietnam. The president, as Commander in Chief, had the power to involve the nation in undeclared wars.

A Season of Violence In April 1968, Dr. Martin Luther King, Jr., was shot and killed, leading to riots in several cities. Two months later, Senator Robert Kennedy was shot and killed just after winning California's Democratic primary. Violence continued with a clash between police and protesters at the Democratic National Convention in Chicago as protesters demanded that the Democrats adopt an anti-war platform.

Republican Richard Nixon won the 1968 presidential election. He promised to unify the nation, restore law and order, and end the Vietnam War.

SECTION 4 THE WAR WINDS DOWN

Nixon Moves to End the War

President Nixon appointed **Henry Kissinger** as special assistant for national security affairs. Kissinger would use diplomacy to end the United States' involvement in Vietnam. Hoping to bring a diplomatic end to the war, President Nixon authorized secret negotiations between the United States and the North Vietnamese. A plan called **Vietnamization** called for a gradual withdrawal of American troops as the South Vietnamese army took over more of the fighting. Nixon wanted to keep America's strength in Vietnam visible during negotiations. To do this, Nixon increased air strikes against North Vietnam and ordered the bombing of the Vietcong in Cambodia.

Turmoil at Home Continues Protests and violence continued at home when the American media reported that an American platoon massacred more than 200 unarmed South Vietnamese civilians. The My Lai massacre increased the belief among many Americans that the war was brutal and senseless.

Many Americans viewed the bombing of the Vietcong in Cambodia as an action that enlarged the war, and more protests occurred. At one—at Kent State University in Ohio—four students were killed by Ohio National Guard soldiers. Two more students were killed at a demonstration ten days later at Jackson State College in Mississippi.

The Pentagon Papers Support for the war weakened further in 1971 when a disillusioned former Defense Department worker leaked documents that would become known as the Pentagon Papers. The documents showed that the government had not been honest about the Vietnam War with the American people.

CORE CONCEPTS: CONSTITUTIONAL PRINCIPLES

At issue in the publication of the Pentagon Papers was the extent to which newspapers were protected under the First Amendment dealing with freedom of the press.

New York Times **v.** *United States*   The Pentagon Papers were leaked to reporters at the *Washington Post* and the *New York Times.* The United States wanted to prevent the newspapers from publishing the report, which was critical of many of the decisions the government had made during the Vietnam War. A lower court had sided with the government, but the papers appealed to the Supreme Court. The Court ruled in favor of the newspapers' right to publish the Pentagon Papers, saying that "prior restraint" (prohibiting information from being published) must be strongly justified. Since national security was not threatened by the release of the report, the Court ruled, the government's attempt to restrain publication violated the First Amendment.

The United States Pulls Out of Vietnam

By 1971 a majority of Americans wanted to end the Vietnam War. Soon after Nixon was elected to a second term in 1972, peace talks broke down. Under mounting pressure to end the war, Nixon agreed to drop some of his conditions for peace, and in 1973 leaders signed the Paris Peace Accords. In March 1975, shortly after the United States pulled out the last of its troops, North Vietnam started a full-scale invasion of South Vietnam. Although South Vietnam asked for help from the United States, Congress refused. On April 30, 1975, North Vietnam captured Saigon, the capital of South Vietnam, and renamed it Ho Chi Minh City. The country of Vietnam was now united under Communist rule.

CORE CONCEPTS: CONSTITUTIONAL PRINCIPLES

The War Powers Act was an attempt to set limits on the power of the president. Congress held that the Constitution never intended for the president to have the power to involve the nation in undeclared wars. Every president since Nixon has argued that the War Powers Act is unconstitutional, but neither the Congress nor the president has tested it in court.

The Legacy of Vietnam

The Vietnam War left lasting effects on the United States. More than 58,000 Americans and about one million North and South Vietnamese had died. Many Americans considered the war a defeat.

In 1973 Congress passed the **War Powers Act**. The law required the president to inform Congress of any commitment of troops within 48 hours. It also required the president to withdraw troops in 60 to 90 days unless Congress approved the troop commitment.

After the war, many Americans became more reluctant to involve the United States in the affairs of other nations, and became more cynical about their own government.

CHAPTER 30   THE POLITICS OF PROTEST

Chapter Overview

Protest characterized the 1960s. Young people often led the civil rights and antiwar movements. Some wanted to change the entire society and urged more communal, less materialistic values. Young people were not the only protesters, however. Using the civil rights movement as a model, women, Hispanic Americans, and Native Americans also organized to gain greater recognition and equality. Increased awareness and new attitudes changed the lives of disabled Americans.

As you read through this chapter, ask yourself these questions:
(1) What were the goals of the counterculture?
(2) What were the major achievements of the women's movement?
(3) What were the goals of affirmative action?
(4) What steps were taken to combat environmental problems?

REGENTS WARM-UP

Several questions on the Regents Exam focus on your understanding of core concepts and themes in United States history. Change is an example of a core concept. As you read this chapter, note how various groups protested and called for changes in society, and how those protests often created conflict.

Main Ideas and Concepts

- **Constitutional Principles** Although protest movements often challenged the opinions and values of many Americans, the courts protected the protesters' rights of self-expression under the Constitution.

- **Civic Values** Women organized to claim their rights and responsibilities as citizens and employees.

- **Human Rights** African Americans, Hispanics, and Native Americans organized to fight discrimination and to gain access to better education and jobs.

- **Environment and Society** Increased awareness of environmental issues inspired a grassroots campaign to protect nature.

People, Places, Terms

The following names and terms will help you to prepare for the Regents Exam in United States History and Government. You can find an explanation of each name and term in the Glossary at the back of this book, in your textbook, or in another reference source.

affirmative action	fossil fuels	Equal Rights
American Indian	Ralph Nader	Amendment
Movement	National	
César Chávez	Organization	
counterculture	for Women	
feminism	Title IX	

SECTION 1 THE STUDENT MOVEMENT AND THE COUNTERCULTURE

The Growth of the Youth Movement

FACTORS BEHIND THE YOUTH MOVEMENT OF THE 1960s

- Economic boom of the 1950s
- Population factors: by 1970 over 58% of U.S. population was under 34 years old
- Rapid increase in college enrollments; increase of 2 million between 1960 and 1966

During the 1960s, a youth movement developed that challenged the United States' politics, its social system, and the values of the time. There were several reasons for the development of this new movement.

During the 1950s, the nation had a boom in its economy that not all Americans enjoyed. Some Americans, especially writers and artists of the "beat" movement, openly criticized American society. Also, there were huge numbers of people in the postwar generation, also called the "baby boom" generation. By 1970, 58.4 percent of the American population was 34 years old or younger. Finally, the economic boom of the 1950s led to a dramatic increase in college enrollment. College gave young people the opportunity to share their feelings and fears about the future, including fear over the growing nuclear arms race between the United States and the Soviet Union.

Students for a Democratic Society Students concerned about injustices in political and social issues formed the Students for a Democratic Society (SDS). Their views were written in the 1962 declaration known as the Port Huron Statement. Written by Tom Hayden, editor of the University of Michigan's student newspaper, the statement called for an end to apathy and urged citizens to stop accepting a country run by corporations and big government.

The Free Speech Movement A group of activists at the University of California at Berkeley, led by Mario Savo, began the Free Speech Movement. The group, disgruntled by several practices at the university, staged a sit-in at the administration building. After some 700 protesters were arrested, a campus-wide strike stopped classes for two days. The administration gave in to the students' demands, and the Supreme Court validated the students' rights to freedom of speech and assembly on campus. The Berkeley revolt became the model for college demonstrations around the country.

Tinker **v.** *Des Moines School District* In December 1965, Marybeth and John Tinker planned to wear black armbands to school to protest the Vietnam War. School officials found out beforehand and passed a rule banning the armbands. If students broke the rule, they would be suspended and not allowed to return to school until they removed the armbands. The Tinkers argued that their First Amendment rights to free speech and free expression were violated by the rule. The Supreme Court agreed with the Tinkers, ruling that wearing the armband was a demonstration of symbolic speech protected under the First Amendment. In the decision, Justice Abe Fortas wrote, "It can hardly be argued that either students or teachers shed their constitutional rights to freedom of speech or expression at the schoolhouse gate."

The Counterculture

Some young Americans did not challenge the system. Instead, they sought to create their own society. The **counterculture,** or hippies, was mostly made up of white youths from middle- and upper class backgrounds. They lived a life that promoted flamboyant dress, rock music, drug use, and free and independent living.

At the core of the counterculture was a utopian ideal of a society that was free, closer to nature, and full of love, empathy, tolerance, and cooperation. Communes, or group living arrangements in which members shared everything and worked together, were formed as hippies dropped out of society. As the movement grew, newcomers did not always understand the ideals of the movement and focused on the outward signs, including long hair, Native American headbands, shabby jeans, and drugs.

The counterculture declined as some hippie communities became places where criminal activity was common. Drug use declined as the excitement faded and as more young people became addicted or died from overdoses.

CORE CONCEPTS: IDENTITY

Shirley Chisholm became the first African American woman to serve in Congress. In Congress, she was an early opponent of selling arms to South Africa's racist regime, and crusaded to help women and minorities. She once remarked, "Of my two 'handicaps,' being female put more obstacles in my path than being black."

SECTION 2 THE FEMINIST MOVEMENT

Even before the adoption of the Nineteenth Amendment in 1920, **feminism**—the belief that men and women should be equal politically, economically, and socially—had been an issue. When many men went off to fight in World War II, women joined the nation's workforce. When the men returned, many women lost their jobs. But women gradually returned to the labor market, and by 1960 they made up almost one-third of the nation's workforce.

The Women's Movement Reawakens

A new feminist movement began in the 1960s. Women had become increasingly resentful of old stereotypes. As more women entered the workforce, the protest for equality increased.

IMPORTANT WOMEN'S RIGHTS MILESTONES OF THE 1970s		
Title IX of the Educational Amendment	1972	Prohibited federally funded schools from discriminating against women in admissions, athletics, and other areas
Roe v. *Wade*	1973	Repealed the law against abortion; guaranteed abortion rights for women in first trimester, a time interpreted as within a woman's constitutional right to privacy
Equal Rights Amendment (ERA)	1972	Passed by Congress and ratified by 35 states

Fighting for Workplace Rights Two forces helped bring the women's movement back to life. One was the mass protest of ordinary women. The second was a government initiative called the President's Commission on the Status of Women. The group, headed by Eleanor Roosevelt, urged President Kennedy to study the status of women.

The commission's report helped create networks of feminists, who lobbied Congress for legislation. In 1963, the Equal Pay Act was passed. It outlawed paying a man more than a woman for doing the same job. Title VII of the 1964 Civil Rights Act outlawed job discrimination. It became the legal basis for advances by the women's movement.

Attitudes about what was "proper women's work" took time to change. The Equal Employment Opportunity Commission still held that jobs could be distinguished by gender. Throughout the years, women still felt, despite the progress that was made, that they bumped up against a "glass ceiling," an unofficial barrier to upper levels of management or prominent positions.

The Time is NOW In 1966, feminist leaders began considering the need for women to form a national organization. This led to the start of the **National Organization for Women** (NOW). The organization demanded greater educational opportunities for women and denounced the exclusion of women from certain professions and political positions.

Successes and Failures

The women's movement experienced many successes and failures as it fought for women's rights.

Striving for Equality in Education An important success was greater equality for women in the educational system. Lawmakers enacted federal legislation banning sex discrimination in education. In 1972 Congress passed the Educational Amendments. One of the sections, **Title IX**, prohibited federally funded schools from discriminating against girls in nearly all aspects of their operations, from admissions to athletics, and led to a tremendous increase in the number of girls and women involved in sports programs.

REGENTS WARM-UP

As you read this chapter, make note of the major court cases and legislation connected with rights movements. Past Regents Exams have focused on such cases and legislation.

CORE CONCEPTS: CONSTITUTIONAL PRINCIPLES

In the *Roe* v. *Wade* case, the Supreme Court referred to the right to privacy as a constitutional right protected by the Ninth Amendment dealing with "other . . . rights retained by the people."

Roe **v.** *Wade* By the late 1960s, some states began adopting liberal abortion laws regarding a woman's mental health or in the case of rape or incest. The biggest change came with the 1973 Supreme Court decision *Roe* v. *Wade.* The Supreme Court ruled that state governments could no longer regulate abortion during the first three months of pregnancy, a time that was interpreted as being within a woman's constitutional right to privacy. This gave rise to the right-to-life movement, whose members considered abortion morally wrong.

The Equal Rights Amendment In 1972 Congress approved the **Equal Rights Amendment** (ERA), which protected against discrimination based on gender. In order for it to become part of the Constitution, 38 states had to ratify it.

Many people saw the ERA as a threat to traditional American values, and opposition to the act began to grow. Phyllis Schlafly, one of the most vocal critics of the amendment, organized a national Stop-ERA campaign. The amendment failed to be ratified by 38 states and finally died in 1982.

The Impact of the Women's Movement Although the women's movement helped to change societal attitudes about women, a large income gap between men and women remains. Most working women still have lower-paying jobs, but professional women have advanced the most since the 1970s. By 2000, over 40 percent of the Americans graduating with law or medical degrees were women. The women's movement also succeeded in shining light on the problem of domestic abuse.

SECTION 3 NEW APPROACHES TO CIVIL RIGHTS

CIVIL RIGHTS FOR MINORITY GROUPS		
Native Americans	**Hispanic Americans**	**African Americans**
Declaration of Indian Purpose Called for policies to create greater economic opportunities on reservations	**United Farm Workers** Fought for: • Increased wages • Better benefits	**People United to Save Humanity** Worked to: • Register African American voters • Develop African American businesses • Broaden educational opportunities
American Indian Movement Demanded: • Changes in the administration of reservations • Government to honor treaty obligations • Native American self-determination • Land and water rights	**La Raza Unida** • Mobilized Hispanic American voters • Called for job-training programs • Promoted greater access to financial institutions	**Congressional Black Caucus** Promoted: • Health care • Economic development • Crime reduction

Fighting for Greater Opportunity

During the 1960s and 1970s, Native Americans, Hispanic Americans, and African Americans organized to improve their position within society.

Affirmative Action African American leaders looked to **affirmative action** to gain good jobs and adequate housing. This initiative, enforced through executive orders and federal policies, called for companies and institutions doing business with the federal government to recruit African American employees to help improve their social and economic status. It was later expanded to include other minority groups and women.

Equal Access to Education Even after the Supreme Court ruling in *Brown* v. *Board of Education of Topeka, Kansas*, many

CORE CONCEPTS: DIVERSITY

In one example of affirmative action's impact, Atlanta witnessed a significant increase in minority job opportunities shortly after Maynard Jackson became its first African American mayor in 1973. When Jackson took office, less than one percent of all city contracts went to African Americans, although they made up about half of Atlanta's population. Jackson used the expansion of the city's airport to fix this imbalance.

CORE CONCEPTS: CONSTITUTIONAL PRINCIPLES

The Supreme Court upheld the constitutionality of busing in the 1971 case of *Swann* v. *Charlotte-Mecklenburg Board of Education*. The case also ordered that reorganizing of school boundaries and racial ratios be used as methods to achieve desegregated school systems.

schools in the 1960s remained racially segregated. In the early 1970s, there was a push for educational improvements for African American students. Inequality was apparent as schools in white neighborhoods had better supplies, facilities, and teachers. To desegregate schools, local governments implemented a policy known as busing, where children were transported to schools outside their neighborhoods to gain racial balance. In Boston, about 20,000 white students left the public school system for parochial and private schools. This "white flight" occurred in other cities as well.

New Political Leaders African Americans gained influence in Congress. In 1971 African American members of Congress formed the Congressional Black Caucus. It was organized to better represent the legislative concerns of African Americans. It promoted African American interests in areas such as health care and economics.

Hispanic Americans Organize

Hispanics in the 1960s also worked to gain greater rights. Hispanics came to the United States from different places and for different reasons. Hispanics, like other immigrant groups, experienced prejudice and a lack of access to housing and employment. Encouraged by the civil rights movement, they began to organize a "brown power" protest movement.

César Chávez and the UFW Hispanics began working to win rights for farm workers. Most Mexican American farm workers earned little money and had few benefits. In the early 1960s, **César Chávez** and Dolores Huerta organized two groups that fought for the rights of farm workers. They staged successful protests and a nationwide boycott against California grape growers. In 1966 Chávez and Huerta merged their organizations into the United Farm Workers (UFW). They continued their boycott until 1970, when the grape growers agreed to a contract to raise wages and improve working conditions.

Growing Political Activism Hispanic Americans also became more politically active. In 1969, a new political party called La Raza Unida was organized. The group mobilized Mexican American voters to support programs that called for job training and greater access to financial institutions.

Another issue that both Hispanic students and political leaders worked for was bilingualism. This is the practice of teaching immigrant students in their own language while they learn English. Congress responded by passing the Bilingual Education Act in 1968. Some American voters opposed bilingual education because they believed it made it more difficult for a child to adjust to American culture. The U.S. Supreme Court ruled in favor of bilingualism in 1974.

Cuban and Haitian Immigration Following the revolution in Cuba, thousands of Cubans fled the country to come to the United States. Here they were granted political asylum (protection from persecution because of a person's religious or political beliefs). A good number of Haitian immigrants have also fled their home country for the United States due to political upheaval. Both groups have established communities in Florida and New York.

REGENTS WARM-UP

Past Regents Exams have focused on the reform movements that characterized this period in U.S. history. As you read this chapter, use a graphic organizer such as the one shown on this page to identify the causes and effects of the major movements discussed in this chapter.

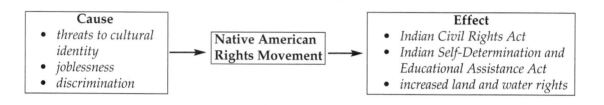

Cause	Native American Rights Movement	Effect
• *threats to cultural identity* • *joblessness* • *discrimination*	→	• *Indian Civil Rights Act* • *Indian Self-Determination and Educational Assistance Act* • *increased land and water rights*

Native Americans Raise Their Voices

Native Americans suffered many injustices. Their unemployment rate was 10 times the national rate. Unemployment was especially high on reservation lands. More than half of Native Americans lived on these lands. Life expectancy for Native Americans was about seven years below the national average.

A Protest Movement Emerges In the late 1960s and early 1970s, many Native Americans began to organize to improve conditions for Native Americans. Many wanted greater independence from the mainstream society of the United States. In 1968, Congress passed the Indian Civil Rights Act. The law guaranteed Native Americans on reservations the protection of the Bill of Rights. It also recognized local reservation law.

Some Native Americans believed the government wasn't doing enough. They formed more militant groups, such as the **American Indian Movement** (AIM). In 1969, members of several tribes made a symbolic protest by occupying the

CORE CONCEPTS: NEEDS AND WANTS

In 1961, more than 400 members of 67 Native American groups gathered in Chicago to discuss ways to address their many problems. They issued a manifesto, known as the Declaration of Indian Purpose, calling for policies to create better economic opportunities on reservations.

abandoned federal prison on Alcatraz Island in San Francisco Bay and proclaimed it Indian land.

In February 1973, AIM members occupied the town of Wounded Knee, South Dakota. The AIM members demanded changes in the way the reservations were run. They also wanted the government to honor its treaty obligations to Native Americans. A clash occurred between the Native Americans and the FBI. Two Native Americans were killed and several people were wounded.

Native Americans Make Notable Gains In 1975, Congress passed the Indian Self-Determination and Educational Assistance Act. The law increased funds for Native American education. It increased the role of Native Americans in administering federal programs. By working through the courts, Native Americans won a number of land and water rights that they had worked for. They also developed businesses on reservations, operated under the reservation laws. The Indian Civil Rights Act gave Native American tribes greater control over their own affairs on reservations.

SECTION 4 PROGRESS FOR AMERICANS WITH DISABILITIES

The movement for the rights of disabled citizens did not gain widespread support until the mid-twentieth century. Historically, people with disabilities were regarded with suspicion and disapproval, and they were often persecuted or discriminated against for their conditions. During the eighteenth and nineteenth centuries, disabled people were largely segregated from the rest of society in institutions such as asylums, hospitals, and prisons. The eugenics movement and the theory of Social Darwinism—both of which emphasized the survival of the "fittest" members of society—contributed to the improper treatment of disabled citizens.

In the mid-1800s and early 1900s, the rights of people with disabilities began to gain more attention. In 1848 a Boston school became the first to experiment with formal education of people with mental retardation. Schools for blind and deaf students and associations advocating their rights were founded. It was not until the 1960s and 1970s, however, that Americans became aware of the concept of "normalization," which supported the integration of people with disabilities as much as possible in mainstream society. Parents began to demand an equal education for their children with disabilities.

Disabled war veterans brought much attention to the issues that disabled people faced. Legislative initiatives that were meant to support these veterans, including rehabilitation and job training programs, also included benefits for those with mental retardation. Several advocacy groups were formed by veterans to lobby legislators for access to medical care and more support programs.

In 1961, President John F. Kennedy organized the President's Panel on Mental Retardation to investigate the status of people with mental disabilities and develop programs and reforms to improve their situation. President Johnson issued an Executive Order in 1966 that formally established the panel, which was renamed the President's Committee for People with Intellectual Disabilities by George W. Bush in 2003.

IMPORTANT LEGISLATIVE LANDMARKS FOR PEOPLE WITH DISABILITIES

Education of the Handicapped Act, 1966	established a federal grant program for children with disabilities to be educated at local schools as opposed to state-operated schools or institutions
Education for All Handicapped Children Act, 1971	now known as Individuals with Disabilities Education Act, the act established the right of equal education for those with disabilities and required states to develop and implement policies that provided a "free, appropriate public education" to receive federal funds
Rehabilitation Act of 1973, Section 504	bars any recipients of federal assistance from discriminating on the basis of physical disability in their programs and employment practices and requires anyone received federal funding to have disabled-accessible buildings
Americans with Disabilities Act, 1990	prohibits private employers, state and local governments, employment agencies and labor unions from discriminating against individuals with disabilities and requires public buildings and mass transit be accessible

Another effort to recognize the contributions and abilities of citizens with disabilities was the creation of the Special Olympics. The First International Special Olympics were held in July 1968 in Chicago, Illinois, although the concept for these games had emerged in 1962 under the influence of Eunice Kennedy Shriver, the sister of President John F. Kennedy. In 1962, she started Camp Shriver, a summer day camp at her home for children and adults with intellectual disabilities to take part in various physical activities and competitions. The movement has grown considerably since then; at the 2003 Special Olympics World Summer Games, 7,000 athletes from 150 countries competed.

Advocates continue to push for more mainstreaming of disabled people. Long-term care is now often in a community-based setting, with nursing care and therapy, rather than the institutions of the past where patients were treated harshly and often lived in terrible conditions. Nine states have completely closed their state-run institutions and have helped patients move back into their communities. Job placement programs, rehabilitative care, and supported-living facilities have all proved successful in helping disabled people make this transition.

SECTION 5 SAVING THE EARTH

The Beginnings of Environmentalism

By the late 1960s, environmental troubles existed in every region of the nation. Acres of forestland were being cut down. An increasing use of pesticides had damaged a wide range of wildlife. A rise in pollution had fouled both the air and the water. Potentially deadly nuclear energy was being used more and more. Many people believed it was time to take action to protect the environment.

The Government Steps In In 1970, the federal government established the Environmental Protection Agency. Its job was to set and enforce pollution standards. The agency also coordinated anti-pollution activities with state and local governments.

- In 1970, the Clean Air Act became law. It established emission standards for factories and automobiles.

- The Clean Water Act of 1972 restricted the discharge of pollutants into the nation's lakes and rivers.

- The Endangered Species Act of 1973 established measures for saving threatened animal species.

Love Canal During the 1970s, residents at a local housing development near Niagara Falls, New York, called Love Canal, began noticing a high incidence of health problems. It was discovered that the community was built on a toxic waste dump. Through dramatic community activism, the state permanently relocated 200 families. President Jimmy Carter later relocated the remaining 600 families.

Concerns Over Nuclear Energy The use of nuclear energy became an issue in the 1970s. Supporters claimed it was cleaner and less expensive than **fossil fuels**, such as coal, oil, and natural gas, which have a limited supply. Opponents warned of risks, including consequences of an accidental radiation release.

On March 28, 1979, one of the reactors at Pennsylvania's Three Mile Island nuclear facility overheated. Low levels of radiation escaped. Although the plant was eventually declared safe, the incident left the public in doubt about the safety of nuclear energy.

Environmental Problems Environmentalists also brought public attention to some longer-term dangers of unchecked industrial development: the rapid depletion of oil and other irreplaceable

CORE CONCEPTS: SCIENCE AND TECHNOLOGY

Concerns about the environment and safe energy led to a strong interest in solar energy. The use of photovoltaic cells allows energy from the sun to be used for a wide range of energy needs, from powering generators to running agricultural water pumps to powering simple calculators.

fossil fuels; the destruction of lakes and forests as a result of "acid rain" (rainfall polluted by chemical contaminants); the rapid destruction of vast rain forests, in Brazil and elsewhere, which limited the earth's capacity to replenish its oxygen supply; the depletion of the ozone layer as a result of the release of chemicals into the atmosphere, which threatened to limit the earth's protection from dangerous ultraviolet rays from the sun; and global warming, which—if unchecked—would create dramatic changes in the earth's climate and would threaten existing cities and settlements in coastal areas all over the world by causing a rise in ocean levels.

The Consumer Movement

During the 1960s and 1970s, many Americans demanded product safety, accurate information, and a voice in the government formulation of consumer policy.

The leader in the consumer protection movement, **Ralph Nader**, researched the alarming number of deaths from car accidents. He presented his findings in a book titled *Unsafe at Any Speed*. Nader's work helped to get Congress to pass the national Traffic and Motor Vehicle Safety Act in 1966. The law set mandatory standards and established a system for notifying car owners about defects. Carmakers had to incorporate safety standards into their car designs.

Nader's success led to calls for a closer examination of numerous other consumer goods during the 1960s and 1970s. Organizations lobbied Congress and state legislatures to pass laws that regulated products such as dangerous toys, flammable fabrics, and unsafe meat and poultry.

CORE CONCEPTS: CIVIC VALUES

Shortly after his book came out, a car company hired private detectives to follow Ralph Nader. They were hoping to uncover information that would discredit him. They found nothing. But when the corporate spying came to light, the publicity pushed Nader's book onto the bestseller list. As a result, the public became more aware of auto safety issues. Nader sued the car company and used the settlement money to fund several consumer protection organizations.

CHAPTER 31   POLITICS AND ECONOMICS

Chapter Overview

The protests of the 1960s were passionate and sometimes violent. The nation elected President Nixon on a promise to uphold the values of what Nixon called "Middle America." In foreign policy, Nixon charted a new path with a historic visit to China. At home, he introduced "New Federalism." In 1974, the Watergate scandal forced Nixon to resign. Presidents Ford and Carter faced an economic downturn and a major energy crisis.

As you read through this chapter, ask yourself these questions:
(1) What were Nixon's foreign policy achievements?
(2) What was the Watergate scandal and what were its effects?
(3) What were the causes of the 1970s' economic problems?
(4) What changes in culture and belief systems occurred in the 1970s?

REGENTS WARM-UP

Several questions on the Regents Exam focus on your understanding of core concepts and themes in United States history. Presidential decisions and actions is an example of a core concept. As you read this chapter, note the national and global impact of the decisions and actions of Presidents Nixon, Ford, and Carter.

Main Ideas and Concepts

- **Foreign Policy** One of President Nixon's most dramatic accomplishments was changing the relationship between the United States, China, and the Soviet Union.

- **Government** The Watergate scandal intensified the lingering distrust of government that had grown in the United States during the Vietnam War.

- **Economic Systems** A weakening economy and growing energy crisis marred the terms of Presidents Ford and Carter.

- **Culture** Even after the turbulent 1960s, American culture continued changing to reflect new trends and ideas.

People, Places, Terms

The following names and terms will help you to prepare for the Regents Exam in United States History and Government. You can find an explanation of each name and term in the

Glossary at the back of this book, in your textbook, or in another reference source.

Camp David	**Helsinki Accords**	**Strategic Arms**
Accords	**impeach**	**Limitation Treaty**
détente	**inflation**	*United States* **v.**
embargo	**Henry Kissinger**	*Nixon*
executive privilege	**Nixon Doctrine**	

SECTION 1 THE NIXON ADMINISTRATION

Appealing to Middle America

Many Americans supported the government and longed for an end to the violence of the 1960s. The 1968 Republican presidential candidate, Richard Nixon, appealed to the people whom he called "Middle America." He promised them peace in Vietnam, law and order, a streamlined government, and a return to conservative values.

The Southern Strategy Nixon received a great amount of support in the election from the South. He promised to appoint conservatives to the Supreme Court, to oppose court-ordered busing of students, and to choose a vice president acceptable to the South. As a result, a large number of white Southerners left the Democratic Party and voted for Nixon. The South had been a Democratic stronghold since the Civil War. Nixon won the election.

A Law-and-Order President To keep his promise of law and order, Nixon set out to battle crime. He criticized the Supreme Court regarding expanded rights for accused criminals and appointed several conservative judges to the Supreme Court.

The New Federalism Nixon's Republican leaders dismantled several federal programs and gave more control to state and local governments. Under Nixon's New Federalism program, Congress passed a series of revenue-sharing bills that provided federal funds to state and local agencies. Intended to give state and local agencies increased power, it actually led to a greater dependency on federal funds.

Legislation that was passed during the Nixon administration also created new government agencies. The Occupational Safety and Health Administration (OSHA) works to prevent work-related illnesses and injury. The Drug Enforcement Agency (DEA) is charged with eliminating the trafficking of illegal recreational drugs. The Federal Energy Office was responsible for allocating reduced petroleum supplies and controlling the price of oil and gasoline.

The Family Assistance Plan In 1969 Nixon proposed replacing the existing Aid to Families with Dependent Children (AFDC) welfare program with the Family Assistance Plan. The plan would give needy families a guaranteed yearly grant of $1,600. The program won House approval but was later defeated in the Senate.

Nixon's Foreign Policy

President Nixon was more interested in foreign affairs than in domestic ones. He chose **Henry Kissinger** as his national security adviser. Kissinger took the lead in helping Nixon shape his foreign policy.

The Establishment of Détente Nixon thought the nation's policy against Communism was too rigid. He believed friendly negotiation was a better way to contain Communism and ensure world peace. Nixon and Kissinger developed an approach called **détente**, or relaxation of tensions between the United States and its two major Communist rivals, the Soviet Union and China. In a speech in 1969, Nixon told the American people that the United States had to build a better relationship with its main rivals in the interest of world peace.

Nixon Doctrine Nixon also set forth a policy that became known as the **Nixon Doctrine**, in which Asian allies were responsible for their own defense. Nixon said that the United States would honor all its treaties and commitments to military and economic assistance, but would "look to the nation directly threatened to assume the primary responsibility of providing the manpower for its defense."

Nixon Visits China To ease tensions with China, Nixon lifted trade and travel restrictions and withdrew the Seventh Fleet from defending Taiwan. In February 1972, Nixon took a historic trip to China, where both leaders agreed to better relations between the nations.

U.S.–Soviet Tensions Ease Shortly after negotiations with China took place, the Soviet Union proposed an American–Soviet summit, or high-level diplomatic meeting. In

CORE CONCEPTS: FOREIGN POLICY

President Nixon affirmed the idea from the Constitution that the president directs foreign policy. His actions in regard to China and the Soviet Union provided a new direction for the United States relative to the Cold War.

CORE CONCEPTS: PRESIDENTIAL DECISIONS AND ACTIONS

President Nixon often tried to work around Congress and use greater executive authority. For instance, when Congress appropriated money for programs he opposed, Nixon impounded, or refused to release, the funds. The Supreme Court eventually declared impound-ment unconstitutional.

May 1972, Nixon flew to Moscow for the summit, becoming the first U.S. president to visit the Soviet Union. During the summit, the countries signed the first **Strategic Arms Limitation Treaty** (SALT I) to limit nuclear arms. The countries also agreed to increase trade and the exchange of scientific information.

SECTION 2 THE WATERGATE SCANDAL

The Roots of Watergate

President Nixon's administration became involved in a scandal known as Watergate. It was an attempt by members of the administration to cover up its involvement in the break-in at Democratic National Committee headquarters in the Watergate office-apartment complex. The scandal also revealed other illegal actions committed during Nixon's re-election campaign.

Nixon and His "Enemies" Nixon had become defensive, secretive, and resentful of his critics. He went as far as creating an "enemies list," naming people from politicians to members of the media.

In an effort to win re-election, Nixon and his team looked for ways to gain an edge. On June 17, 1972, five Nixon supporters broke into the Democratic Party's headquarters to locate campaign information and install wiretaps on telephones. Discovered by a security guard, the burglars were arrested.

The Cover-Up Begins One of the burglars, James McCord, was an ex-CIA official and a member of the Committee for the Re-election of the President. As the questions about the break-in began, the cover-up started. Although it is thought that Nixon did not order the break-in, it is believed that he did order the cover-up.

Most Americans believed the president when he claimed he had no involvement in the break-in, and Nixon won re-election in 1972.

The Cover-Up Unravels

In 1973, the Watergate burglars went on trial. James McCord agreed to cooperate with the grand jury investigation and the Senate's Select Committee on Presidential Campaign Activities, established under Senator Sam J. Ervin. McCord's testimony

CORE CONCEPTS: POWER

The Watergate burglars were paid from a secret fund controlled by the White House. When the FBI investigated the source of the money, Nixon administration officials asked the CIA to stop the FBI. Their justification was that such an investigation would threaten national security.

opened a floodgate of confessions, and officials and White House staff exposed illegalities.

The counsel to the president, John Dean, leveled allegations against Nixon. Dean testified that Attorney General John Mitchell ordered the Watergate break-in and Nixon was active in its cover-up.

The fall of 1973 proved to be a disastrous time for Nixon for other reasons as well. His vice president, Spiro Agnew, was forced to resign in disgrace. Investigators had discovered that Agnew had taken bribes from state contractors while he was governor of Maryland and that he had continued to accept bribes while serving in Washington. Gerald Ford, the Republican leader of the House of Representatives, became the new vice president.

The Case of the Tapes White House aide Alexander Butterfield testified that Nixon had ordered a taping system installed in the White House to record all conversations, in order to help him write his memoirs once he left office. These tapes were sought by all groups investigating the scandal. Nixon refused to hand over the tapes, pleading **executive privilege** —the principle that White House conversations be kept confidential to protect national security.

A special investigator, Archibald Cox, took Nixon to court to force him to give up the recordings. In 1974, the case of *United States* v. *Nixon* went before the Supreme Court. It ruled that presidential power is not above the law and that it cannot be used to protect evidence that may be used in a criminal trial. Nixon had to turn over the unedited tapes.

Nixon Resigns The House Judiciary Committee voted to **impeach**, or officially charge Nixon with presidential miscon- duct. The next step was for the entire House of Representatives to vote whether or not to impeach the president. Investigators finally found indisputable evidence against the president. One of the unedited tapes revealed that Nixon had ordered the CIA to stop the FBI's investigation of the break-in. Impeachment and conviction seemed inevitable. On August 9, 1974, Nixon resigned, and Vice President Gerald Ford became the 38th president of the United States.

CORE CONCEPTS: GOVERNMENT

The Constitution creates separation of powers and checks and balances that prevent any branch of the government from becoming too powerful. One provision is impeachment and trial of officers (including the president) in the executive branch by the legislative branch of Congress.

CORE CONCEPTS: GOVERNMENT

In 1967, the Twenty-fifth Amendment was added to the Constitution. It allowed for the election of a new vice president in the event that office fell vacant. After Vice President Agnew was forced to resign, Nixon nominated Gerald Ford to replace Agnew and he was confirmed by both houses of Congress. When Ford became president upon Nixon's resignation, he nominated Nelson Rockefeller to be vice president and his nomination was confirmed by Congress.

The Impact of Watergate

Watergate prompted the implementation of several new laws limiting the power of the executive branch and reestablishing a greater balance of power in the government:

- The Federal Campaign Act Amendments limited campaign contributions and set up an independent agency to administer stricter election laws.

- The Ethics in Government Act required financial disclosure by high government officials in all three branches of government.

- The FBI Domestic Security Investigation Guidelines restricted the bureau's political intelligence-gathering activities.

Watergate left many Americans distrustful of public officials. Other Americans felt that Nixon's impeachment and resignation proved that in the United States, no one is above the law.

SECTION 3 FORD AND CARTER

The Economic Crisis of the 1970s

The United States had enjoyed a strong economy during the 1950s and 1960s. This was partly because the United States had easy access to raw materials around the world and had a strong manufacturing industry at home. By the 1970s, these conditions had changed.

A Mighty Economic Machine Slows The economic troubles began in the mid-1960s. President Johnson increased federal deficit spending to fund the Vietnam War and the Great Society program without raising taxes. Pumping large amounts of money into the economy created **inflation**, or a rise in the cost of goods.

In 1973, the Organization of Petroleum Exporting Countries (OPEC) announced an **embargo**, or a halt in shipping, of petroleum to countries that supported Israel. OPEC also raised the price of crude oil by 70 percent, and then by another 130 percent a few months later. As a result, the United States suffered its first fuel shortage since World War II.

Although the embargo ended a few months after it began, oil prices continued to rise. OPEC raised prices three more times in the 1970s and again in 1980. By that time, the price of a barrel of crude oil had risen from $3 in 1973 to $30 in 1980. The high prices for oil-based products meant that Americans had less money to spend on other goods, tipping the economy into a recession.

A Stagnant Economy By the 1970s, the United States manufacturing industry faced increased international competition. In 1971, for the first time since 1889, the United States imported more goods than it exported. U.S. factories closed, and workers lost their jobs. The U.S. economy faced stagflation, which is a combination of rising prices and economic stagnation.

President Nixon focused on controlling inflation by cutting spending, raising taxes, and freezing prices and wages. His methods did not work. By the time Nixon resigned, the inflation rate remained high and the unemployment rate was increasing.

Ford Takes Over

President Ford attempted to restore Americans' faith in their government. He granted a full pardon to Richard Nixon, hoping to bring that chapter of the nation's history to an end. However, the pardon caused Ford's popularity to plunge. Ford also granted amnesty to Vietnam War draft dodgers and deserters.

Ford Tries to "Whip" Inflation By 1975, the American economy was in its worst recession since the Great Depression. Ford attempted to revive the economy by pushing for voluntary controls of wages and prices. But his plan, known as Whip Inflation Now (WIN), failed. He also tried to limit federal authority, balance the budget, and keep taxes low.

Ford's Foreign Policy Ford continued the foreign policy of Nixon. In August 1975, Ford met with leaders of NATO and the Warsaw Pact to sign the **Helsinki Accords**. Under the accords, the parties recognized the borders of eastern Europe established at the end of World War II. The Soviets promised to uphold certain basic human rights but later went back on this promise, which turned many Americans against détente.

The Election of 1976 In 1976, many Americans were unsure of the future. Rising inflation and unemployment forced many Americans to change their lifestyle. The United States also faced instability in foreign affairs. As the 1976 presidential election approached, Americans hoped for a leader who could meet these challenges. Gerald Ford ran against Democratic candidate Jimmy

CORE CONCEPTS: ECONOMIC SYSTEMS

Resolving the combined recession and inflation of the 1970s was a dilemma for economists. Increased spending might help end the recession, but it would increase inflation. Raising taxes might slow inflation, but it would keep the economy in a recession.

Carter. Carter's image as a moral and upstanding person attracted many voters, and he won the election.

REGENTS WARM-UP

The Regents Exam might ask you to interpret information from a table or chart. To practice this skill, look at the Campaign Propaganda Techniques table and answer the following question.

Which technique is most likely to be used by one candidate to harm the opposing candidate's campaign?

CAMPAIGN PROPAGANDA TECHNIQUES	
Technique	**How to Recognize It**
Labeling	Name calling; identifying a candidate with a term such as "un-American"
Glittering Generality	Vague or broad statements containing little substance
Card Stacking	Giving only one side of the facts to support a candidate's position
Transfer	Associating a patriotic symbol with a candidate
Plain Folks	Identifying the candidate as "just one of the common people"
Testimonial	Endorsement of a candidate by a celebrity
The Bandwagon	Urging voters to support a candidate because everyone else is

Carter Battles the Economic Crisis

Carter first tried to deal with the economic crisis by increasing government spending and cutting taxes. When inflation rose in 1978, he reduced the money supply and raised interest rates. His attempts were unsuccessful.

A "War" Against Energy Consumption Carter believed that the nation's most serious problem was its dependence on foreign oil. He proposed a national energy program to conserve oil and to promote the use of coal and renewable energy sources. He had Congress create the Department of Energy. He asked Americans to reduce energy consumption, a request that most Americans ignored.

Carter's Foreign Policy

President Carter's foreign policy was more clearly defined than his domestic policy, and it focused on human rights.

Carter singled out the Soviet Union as a violator of human rights because it imprisoned people who protested against the

CORE CONCEPTS: ECONOMIC SYSTEMS

Many business leaders and economists urged President Carter to deregulate the oil industry. The regulations limited the ability of oil companies to pass on oil price increases to American consumers. As a result, oil companies found it difficult to make a profit and to invest in new oil wells.

government. Tensions deepened as the Soviet Union invaded the Central Asian nation of Afghanistan in December 1979. Carter responded with an embargo on grain to the Soviet Union and a boycott of the 1980 Summer Olympics Games in Moscow.

Triumph and Failure in the Middle East In 1978, Carter helped set up a historic peace treaty between Israel and Egypt known as the **Camp David Accords**. Most Arab nations opposed the treaty, but it marked the first step toward peace in the Middle East.

In 1979 Iran's monarch, the Shah, was forced to flee, and an Islamic republic was declared. The new government distrusted the United States because it supported the Shah. Religious leader Ayatollah Khomeini ordered revolutionaries to enter the American embassy in Tehran and take 52 Americans hostage.

President Carter tried unsuccessfully to negotiate for the hostages' release. In April 1980, he approved a daring military rescue mission. The mission failed and resulted in the death of eight American servicemen. Carter's failure to gain the release of the hostages contributed to his loss to Ronald Reagan in the 1980 presidential election. After 444 days in captivity, the hostages were released on January 20, 1981—the day Carter left office.

CORE CONCEPTS: PLACES AND REGIONS

Increasingly, the economic and political fortunes are tied to the events in the Middle East. That part of the world has much of the world's oil resources, and the United States is increasingly dependent on them. In addition, the Arab-Israeli conflict has been on-going for more than half a century and the United States is a major player in it.

SECTION 4 THE "ME" DECADE: LIFE IN THE 1970s

The Search for Fulfillment

Most Americans in the 1970s believed that the United States would eventually move beyond the Watergate scandal and the effects of the Vietnam War. Americans found ways to cope with the tense times. Writer Tom Wolfe named the 1970s the "me decade." He was referring to the self-absorbed attitude of many Americans as they looked for greater personal satisfaction.

Changing Families By 1970, about 60 percent of women between the ages of 16 and 24 had joined the workforce. American family life changed with the increase in women working outside of the home. Americans were having smaller families. Parents and children were spending less time together. The divorce rate doubled over a period of 10 years.

Cultural Trends in the 1970s

Popular culture reflected the changes taking place in the 1970s. Television began to portray women in independent roles, or took on formerly taboo topics, such as racism, abortion, and poverty. Americans listened and danced to new forms of music and sought escape in a variety of new fads.

TELEVISION SHOWS OF THE 1970s	
The Mary Tyler Moore Show	depicted an unmarried career woman
All in the Family	addressed controversial social issues through racially bigoted protagonist Archie Bunker
The Jeffersons	portrayed African Americans as successful and respectable
Maude	featured a strong-willed liberal woman married four times
Good Times	showed the typical life of a low-income urban African American family

CORE CONCEPTS: EMPATHY, IDENTITY

By carefully mixing humor and sensitive issues and by not preaching to its audience, the popular television show *All in the Family* made viewers examine their own feelings about social issues. Producer Norman Lear claimed that the show "holds a mirror to our prejudices. . . . We laugh now, swallowing just the littlest bit of truth about ourselves."

Music of the 1970s The music of this period marked the end of the 1960s' youth and protest movements. It had a softer, more reflective, less political sound. As a member of the rock group Chicago said, "These days, nobody wants to hear songs that have a message."

CHAPTER 32   RESURGENCE OF CONSERVATISM

Chapter Overview

The 1980s saw the rise of a new conservatism. President Reagan, standing for traditional values and smaller government, symbolized this movement. While tax cuts and new technologies fueled an economic boom, Reagan embarked on a massive military buildup and expanded efforts to contain Communism. During President George Bush's term, the United States fought the Persian Gulf War, and the Cold War came to a dramatic end with massive changes in and ultimately the demise of the Soviet Union.

As you read through this chapter, ask yourself these questions:
(1) How did discontent with the government lead to a conservative shift in Americans' political convictions?
(2) How did the nation's population shifts affect voting patterns?
(3) What was President Reagan's plan for improving the economy?
(4) How was money important to the culture of the 1980s?
(5) What events led to the end of the Cold War?

REGENTS WARM-UP

Several questions on the Regents Exam focus on your understanding of core concepts and themes in United States history. Change is an example of a core concept. As you read this chapter, note the economic and societal changes that occurred during this period.

Main Ideas and Concepts

- **Change** High taxes as well as economic and moral concerns led the country toward a new conservatism.

- **Foreign Policy** President Reagan believed the country should take strong action to resist Communist influence overseas.

- **Economic Systems** The deficit and an economic slowdown hurt George Bush's attempt to win re-election in 1992.

People, Places, Terms

The following names and terms will help you to prepare for the Regents Exam in United States History and Government. You can find an explanation of each name and term in the

Glossary at the back of this book, in your textbook, or in another reference source.

capital gains tax	Mikhail Gorbachev	Moral Majority
conservative	Iran-Contra scandal	Reaganomics
glasnost	liberal	

SECTION 1 THE NEW CONSERVATISM

Conservatism and Liberalism

CORE CONCEPTS: CONSTITUTIONAL PRINCIPLES, GOVERNMENT

Liberals are strong supporters of free speech and privacy, and they are opposed to the government supporting or endorsing religious beliefs, no matter how indirectly.

CORE CONCEPTS: ECONOMIC SYSTEMS

Conservatives believe the government should play a very limited role in controlling the economy. They fear that the government might end up restricting people's economic freedom so much that they could not improve their standard of living and get ahead in life.

Liberals had dominated the United States for much of the 1900s. In 1980, a **conservative** candidate, Ronald Reagan, became president. Conservative ideas gained strength in the 1980s.

Liberals believe that:

- government should regulate the economy to protect people from the power of large corporations and wealthy elites

- government should help the disadvantaged through social programs and taxing the wealthy

- most social problems have their roots in economic inequality and societal behavior

- individual rights need to be protected

Conservatives believe that:

- if government regulates the economy, the economy is less efficient

- the free enterprise system is the way to organize society

- taxes should be kept low, and wealth should not be transferred from the wealthy to the less wealthy through government programs

- most social problems result from issues of morality and character

- rights of society need to be protected

Conservatism Revives

Conservative ideas were revived shortly after World War II. Some Americans thought that liberal ideas were leading the United States toward communism. Because communism rejected religion and materialism and stressed economic welfare, many Americans with religious convictions opposed it. As a result, these same Americans rejected liberalism, which focused on economic welfare, and turned to conservatism.

Conservatism Gains Support

Sunbelt Conservatism During World War II, many Americans moved south and west to get jobs in the war factories. The movement to the South and West, which was known as the Sunbelt, continued after the war. Southerners and Westerners tended to look at government more conservatively than people living in the more liberal Northeast. By 1980 the Sunbelt population surpassed that of the Northeast, giving conservative regions of the country more electoral votes and more influence. Southerners, who in the past had tended to vote for Democrats, shifted their votes to Republicans.

Suburban Conservatism During the 1960s and 1970s, many Americans moved to the suburbs to escape the drug problems and increasing crime in the cities. They found their middle-class existence was in danger, because rapid inflation in the 1970s caused their buying power to decrease.

LINKING GEOGRAPHY TO HISTORY

In the 1950s and 1960s, Americans living in the West were proud of their frontier heritage and spirit of "rugged individualism." They resented federal environmental regulations that limited ranching, controlled water use, and restricted development of the region's natural resources. Anger over such policies led to the "Sagebrush Rebellion" of the early 1970s—a widespread protest against federal laws hindering the region's development. At the same time, those states were heavily dependent on various forms of government subsidies, such as dams, highways, and agricultural price support.

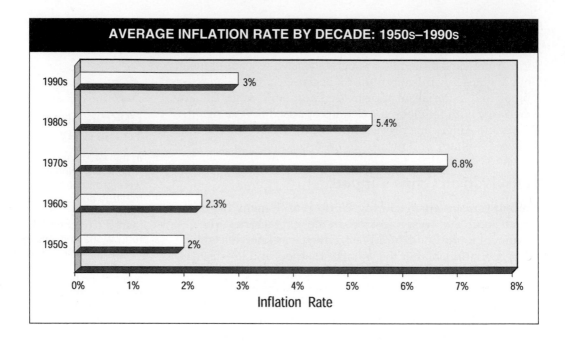

AVERAGE INFLATION RATE BY DECADE: 1950s–1990s

- 1990s — 3%
- 1980s — 5.4%
- 1970s — 6.8%
- 1960s — 2.3%
- 1950s — 2%

Inflation Rate

The Religious Right Many Americans looked to conservative ideas out of fear that society had lost touch with traditional values during the 1960s and 1970s. Very religious Americans were shocked by the Supreme Court decision in *Roe* v. *Wade*, which made abortion a constitutional right, and the Court's decision to limit prayer in public schools.

SECTION 2   THE REAGAN YEARS

The Road to the White House

Ronald Reagan had worked as a broadcaster, an actor, and a motivational speaker, all of which helped him with public speaking and his image. He had been a Democrat and a supporter of the New Deal. But his experiences dealing with Communists as head of an actors' union made him more conservative. Later, as he traveled the country talking to workers, he heard many stories about high taxes and how government regulations made it hard for people to get ahead. This experience made Reagan even more conservative.

The Election of 1980 Reagan caught the attention of several wealthy entrepreneurs, who convinced him to run for governor of California in 1966. In 1980, he ran for president as the Republican candidate. He promised to cut taxes and increase defense spending. He called for a constitutional amendment banning abortion. Reagan's campaign appealed to Americans who were frustrated with the economy and a weakened nation. He won the election.

Reagan's Domestic Policies

Ronald Reagan's first priority was the economy and its combination of high unemployment and high inflation. Conservative economists disagreed on how to address the problem. On the one side, monetarists believed that too much money in circulation caused inflation, and raising interest rates was the solution. The other group of economists supported supply-side economics, arguing that the economy was weak because taxes were too high.

Reagan's conservative beliefs led him to support policies that many considered to work against civil rights. He said the Voting Rights Act of 1965 had been "humiliating to the South." His support (in a tax dispute with the IRS) of Bob Jones University, a Southern college that forbade interracial dating and marriage, outraged many people. He also supported a constitutional amendment to allow prayer in schools.

During Reagan's administration, the Environmental Protection Agency relaxed or entirely eliminated enforcement of major environmental laws and regulations. The Civil Rights Division of the Justice Department eased enforcement of civil rights laws.

Immigration Reform and Control Act In November 1986 Congress passed the Immigration Reform and Control Act. The act granted amnesty to illegal aliens who came to the country before 1982, but it also made it illegal to hire an illegal alien. It requires employers to verify a potential employee's information to determine that they are eligible to work in the United States.

Reaganomics Reagan combined two types of economics by encouraging the Federal Reserve to raise interest rates and by asking Congress to pass a massive tax cut. Critics called his approach **Reaganomics**, or "trickle-down economics." They believed it would help wealthy Americans but little would "trickle down" to average Americans.

**CORE CONCEPTS:
ECONOMIC SYSTEMS**

Supply-side economists believed that high taxes took too much money away from investors. If taxes were cut, businesses and investors could use their extra capital to make new investments, and businesses could expand and create new jobs. The result would be a larger supply of goods for consumers, who would now have more money to spend because of the tax cuts.

By 1982, the nation had sunk into the most severe recession since the 1930s. The economic crisis hit farmers especially hard. Advances in technology and low interest rates in the 1970s allowed agriculture to boom, but a failing economy, lower demand for exports, and lower prices reversed that trend. Rising interest rates took their toll as well, as many farmers could not repay debts that they had taken on in boom years to purchase new advanced equipment and expand their farms.

Cutting Programs Cutting taxes meant less money for the government and an increase in the budget deficit, the amount by which expenditures exceed income. To control the deficit, Reagan cut social programs. Welfare benefits, including the food stamp program and the school lunch program, were cut back. Medicare payments, student loans, housing subsidies, and unemployment compensation were also reduced. These cuts were still not enough to balance the budget.

Deregulation Reagan saw government regulations as another cause of economic problems. He signed an executive order eliminating price controls on oil and gasoline, which resulted in lower gas prices. Other deregulation occurred in the automobile industry, airline industry, and the easing of regulations on pollution.

The Economy Booms In 1983, the economy began to recover. By 1989, the median income of American families had risen by 15 percent. Millions of new businesses and new jobs were created. By 1988, the unemployment rate had fallen to about 5.5 percent, but the federal deficit soared.

Shifting the Judicial Balance Reagan took his conservative ideas to the federal judiciary. He wanted justices to follow a conservative interpretation of the Constitution. He filled a vacant spot on the Court with a very conservative justice, William Rehnquist. He also changed the face of the Court by nominating the first female Supreme Court justice, Sandra Day O'Connor.

New Jersey v. T.L.O. In 1980, a teacher in a New Jersey high school found two girls smoking in the bathroom and took them to the principal's office. The principal searched a student's (known as T.L.O.) purse and found rolling papers, marijuana, and other items that led him to believe she was involved in dealing drugs. T.L.O. argued that the search of her purse was

CORE CONCEPTS: JUSTICE

Sandra Day O'Connor's nomination to the Supreme Court was opposed by the **Moral Majority** because she had supported the Equal Rights Amendment and refused to back an antiabortion amendment. Others, however, praised her legal judgment and conservative approach to the law. As a moderate conservative, she quickly became an important swing-vote on the Court, between more liberal and more conservative justices.

unconstitutional, violating her Fourth Amendment right of protection from unreasonable search, her Fifth Amendment right of protection against self-incrimination, and her Fourteenth Amendment right to due process. The Supreme Court disagreed, ruling that if school officials have a "reasonable suspicion" that a student has done something wrong, the officials have the right to search that student. School officials are not held to the same, higher standard to which the police are held.

Reagan Wins Re-election In the 1984 election, the Democratic candidate was Walter Mondale, who chose as his running mate Geraldine Ferraro, the first woman to run for vice president for a major party. However, the growing economy made Reagan the favorite candidate. He won in a landslide.

Reagan Builds Up the Military

Reagan did not follow containment or détente in his foreign policy. He viewed the Soviet Union as evil and believed that the United States should not negotiate with it. Reagan's approach to relations with the Soviet Union was "peace through strength." He launched the largest peacetime military buildup in American history. Reagan's defense spending pushed the nation's budget deficit from $80 billion to more than $200 billion.

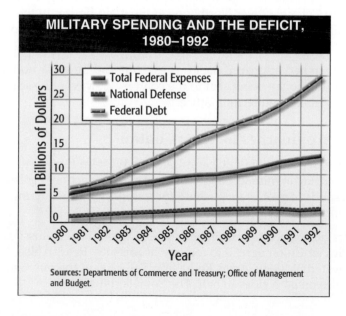

MILITARY SPENDING AND THE DEFICIT, 1980–1992

Legend:
- Total Federal Expenses
- National Defense
- Federal Debt

In Billions of Dollars (y-axis: 0, 5, 10, 15, 20, 25, 30)

Year (x-axis: 1980, 1981, 1982, 1983, 1984, 1985, 1986, 1987, 1988, 1989, 1990, 1991, 1992)

Sources: Departments of Commerce and Treasury; Office of Management and Budget.

The Reagan Doctrine

Reagan believed that the United States should support guerilla groups trying to overthrow Communist or pro-Soviet governments. This became known as the Reagan Doctrine. Reagan sent $570 million to aid Afghan guerillas in Afghanistan, who would later turn against the United States and provide refuge to al-Qaeda. The Soviet invasion of Afghanistan was unsuccessful due to a huge Afghan resistance. The Soviets withdrew from the region in 1988.

The Sandinistas and the Contras Rebels known as Sandinistas had overthrown a pro-American dictator in Nicaragua and set up a socialist government. They also accepted aid from Cuba and the Soviet Union, and began supporting anti-government rebels in nearby El Salvador.

Concerned about Soviet influence in Nicaragua, Reagan began secretly arming an anti-Sandinista guerilla force known as the contras. After Congress learned of that policy, it banned further aid to the contras.

The Iran-Contra Scandal The **Iran-Contra scandal** became news in November 1986. It was discovered that individuals in the Reagan administration were illegally supporting Nicaraguan contras. They had sold weapons to Iran in violation of federal law. The profits from the arms sales were sent to the contras. Marine Colonel Oliver North, one of the main figures in the scandal, testified that he and other officials had attempted to cover up their actions.

Reagan had approved the arms sale but said he knew nothing about the money being sent to the contras. However, the scandal tainted his second term in office.

New Approaches to Arms Control

Reagan positioned nuclear missiles in Western Europe to counter Soviet missiles in Eastern Europe. This action resulted in thousands of protesters pushing for a stop to the positioning of new nuclear missiles.

Reagan agreed to cancel the positioning of the new missiles if the Soviet Union agreed to remove its missiles. Reagan also suggested Strategic Arms Reduction Talks to cut the number of missiles on both sides in half. The Soviets refused.

CORE CONCEPTS: FOREIGN POLICY

Aiding the contras was not Reagan's only action in Latin America. In 1983, radical Marxists overthrew the left-wing government on the tiny Caribbean island of Grenada. Reagan sent in troops to defeat the rebels. A new anti-Communist government was then put into place.

Star Wars Despite his decision to position missiles in Europe, Reagan disagreed with the military strategy known as nuclear deterrence, or mutual assured destruction. This strategy assumed that as long as the United States and the Soviet Union could destroy each other with nuclear weapons, they would be afraid to use them.

Reagan also felt that if nuclear war did begin, there would be no way to defend the United States. In 1983, he proposed the Strategic Defense Initiative. This plan, nicknamed Star Wars, called for the development of weapons that could intercept and destroy incoming missiles.

A New Soviet Leader In 1985, **Mikhail Gorbachev** became the leader of the Soviet Union and agreed to resume arms control talks. He believed that the Soviet economy was on the edge of collapse and could not afford an arms race with the United States. Reagan eventually became convinced that Gorbachev truly wanted to reform the Soviet Union and end the arms race.

The two leaders signed the Intermediate-Range Nuclear Forces Treaty. It called for the destruction of some nuclear weapons and marked the beginning of the end of the Cold War. Gorbachev introduced economic and political reforms in the Soviet Union that led to the end of Communism.

Japan For decades, the United States and Japan have imported each other's goods, especially cars and computer equipment (from Japan) and computers and medicine (from the United States). However, trade barriers set up by the Japanese government place significant restrictions on many goods. In the 1980s, this resulted in a large trade imbalance—the United States was buying much more from Japan than Japan was buying from the United States.

South Africa South Africa's economy had boomed in the decades from the 1950s to the 1980s. Many people and companies in the United States invested money in the country. However, a slowdown that hit in the 1980s, combined with worldwide protests against apartheid (a system of racial segregation), led many foreign investors to withdraw their money. When apartheid was repealed in 1991, foreign investment returned.

CORE CONCEPTS: FOREIGN POLICY

The negotiations that occurred between Soviet leader Gorbachev and President Reagan marked the end of the Cold War, which had been the dominant feature of American foreign policy since the years immediately following World War II. Regents questions sometimes deal with such elements of that policy as the Truman Doctrine, the McCarthy Red Scare, the Korean War, the Vietnam War, and the Strategic Arms Limitation (SALT) treaties.

SECTION 3 LIFE IN THE 1980s

A Decade of Indulgence

The rapid economic growth of the 1980s was partly caused by the baby boom. By the 1980s, baby boomers had finished college and were entering the workforce. They often placed an emphasis on acquiring material items and advancing professionally.

Technology and the Media

In the 1980s, technology changed broadcast news and entertainment. Cassette tapes and the Sony Walkman made music portable. Many houses had VCRs, making it possible to view movies anytime. The creation of cable and satellite television brought many more choices to viewers.

A Society Under Stress

The United States continued to deal with many social problems in the 1980s. Drug abuse made many city neighborhoods dangerous. Drug abuse spread from cities to small towns and rural areas. In 1981 researchers identified a disease called AIDS, or acquired immune deficiency syndrome. AIDS weakens the immune system, lowering resistance to illnesses such as pneumonia and some cancers. HIV, the virus that causes AIDS, is spread through bodily fluids. In the United States, AIDS was first seen among homosexual men, then it began to spread among heterosexual men and women.

American Economy Moves Into a Post-Industrial World

One of the economic trends that became increasingly apparent in the 1980s was that the United States was moving increasingly into a service-oriented economy. Manufacturing, which had been an economic mainstay since the nineteenth century, decreased in importance and the number of factory jobs declined precipitously. More and more Americans were employed in service jobs that involved no manufacturing.

Social Activism

Although Ronald Reagan's election began a conservative movement in the United States, many Americans continued to

CORE CONCEPTS: ECONOMIC SYSTEMS

The strong economic growth of the 1980s mostly benefited middle- and upper-class Americans. As a result, the emphasis on acquiring wealth had another effect on society. From 1967 to 1986, the amount of money earned by the top 5 percent of Americans fluctuated between 15.6 and 17.5 percent of the nation's total income. In the late 1980s, their share of the nation's income began to rise. By the mid-1990s, the top 5 percent of Americans earned well over 21 percent of the nation's income.

CORE CONCEPTS: ENVIRONMENT AND SOCIETY

Environmentalists had become frustrated during the Reagan years. Secretary of the Interior James Watt had encouraged the development of public lands, saying, "We will mine more, drill more, cut more timber." Under pressure from environmental groups, Congress blocked many of Watt's plans.

organize and promote social causes. The environmental movement born in the 1970s continued to grow in the 1980s. Many people joined environmental groups such as the Sierra Club, protested nuclear power plants, worked to protect wetlands and rain forests, and started recycling programs.

As people began living longer and birthrates declined, the senior citizen population became a stronger presence. Senior Americans became more active in politics, and opposed cuts in Social Security and Medicare. Because they voted in large numbers, they were an influential group.

SECTION 4 THE END OF THE COLD WAR

In 1988, Democrats had high hopes going into the election, but Vice President George H. W. Bush won a decisive victory over Michael Dukakis, the Democratic candidate. Political Action Committees, organizations that are formed by corporations, unions, and other organizations to raise money for political campaigns or candidates, played a larger role in the election than ever before. An advertisement attacking Dukakis that was run by a conservative PAC was particularly damaging. However, Democrats kept control of Congress. Bush faced many changes that took place with the sudden end to the Cold War.

By the late 1980s, the Soviet economy was collapsing. Soviet leader Gorbachev instituted *perestroika*, or restructuring, to help save the economy by allowing some private enterprise and profit-making. Gorbachev also introduced *glasnost*, or openness, which allowed for more freedom of speech and religion. *Glasnost* spread to Eastern Europe in 1989. Communist governments were peacefully replaced with democratically elected governments in several countries. The revolution spread to East Germany and the Berlin Wall was finally torn down. In 1991, a group of Communist officials and army officers staged a coup in the Soviet Union. Gorbachev was arrested, but Russian president Boris Yeltsin defied the coup and it collapsed. In December 1991, the Soviet Union ended, replaced by fifteen separate, independent nations.

CORE CONCEPTS: PRESIDENTIAL DECISIONS AND ACTIONS

In reaction to the massacre in Tiananmen Square, many congressional leaders urged much stronger sanctions against China's government. President Bush resisted the harsher measures. He believed that trade and diplomacy would eventually moderate China's behavior.

LINKING GEOGRAPHY TO HISTORY

The oil reserves of the Middle East were an important factor in the Persian Gulf war. American officials feared that the invasion of Kuwait was only a first step, and that Iraq's ultimate goal was to capture Saudi Arabia and its vast oil reserves.

The New World Order

After the Cold War, the world became increasingly unpredictable. President Bush said a "new world order" was developing as he tried to redefine American foreign policy.

Tragedy in Tiananmen Square China's communist leaders were determined to stay in power. China continued to repress political speech and dissent. In June 1989, government tanks and soldiers attacked people who were demonstrating for democracy in Beijing's Tiananmen Square. Many people were killed in the attack and many were arrested and later sentenced to death. As a result, the United States and several countries halted arms sales and reduced their contacts with China.

The Bosnian Crisis In 1991, after the fall of communism, Yugoslavia split apart. In Bosnia, one of the former Yugoslav republics, a vicious three-way civil war erupted between Orthodox Christian Serbs, Catholic Croatians, and Bosnian Muslims. Despite international pressure, the fighting continued until 1995. The Serbs began what they called ethnic cleansing—the brutal expulsion of an ethnic group from a geographic area. In some cases, Serbian troops slaughtered the Muslims instead of moving them.

The United States convinced its NATO allies that military action was necessary. NATO warplanes attacked the Serbs in Bosnia, forcing them to negotiate. Peace talks were held in Dayton, Ohio, and in 1996, some 60,000 NATO troops, including 20,000 Americans, entered Bosnia to enforce the plan.

The Persian Gulf War In August 1990, Iraq's leader, Saddam Hussein, sent his army to invade the oil-rich country of Kuwait. Bush convinced other nations to join a coalition to stop Iraq. Economic sanctions were imposed and a deadline was set for Hussein to withdraw his troops. Hussein refused, so in January of 1991 the coalition began Operation Desert Storm. An air attack followed by a massive ground attack left thousands of Iraqi soldiers dead. Just 100 hours after the ground attack began, Bush declared that Kuwait had been liberated. Saddam Hussein, however, remained in power in Iraq.

Domestic Challenges

The defense industry was hard hit by the end of the Cold War, when the need for military equipment decreased. This recession hit other companies as well, and they began downsizing, or

laying off workers to become more efficient. The nation's high
level of debt made the situation worse.

Savings and Loan Scandal The economic slowdown caused
hundreds of savings and loans institutions to collapse. After
these institutions had been deregulated by President Reagan,
many had made risky or even dishonest investments. When
these investments failed, depositors collected on federal programs to insure deposits. The cost to the public may have
reached $500 billion.

To improve the economy, Bush called for a cut in the **capital
gains tax**, the tax paid by businesses and investors when they
sell stocks or real estate for a profit. The Democrats in Congress
defeated it. Bush agreed to a tax increase, which broke his
campaign promise of "no new taxes."

Bush and Congress did cooperate on other laws. One was the
Americans with Disabilities Act, signed in 1990. The law forbade
discrimination in workplaces and public places against people
who were physically and/or mentally challenged. The law
resulted in a broad range of actions that allowed disabled
Americans to more easily participate in everyday life. The Clean
Air Act of 1990 amended the 1970 Clean Air Act, placing limits
on chemicals and other pollutants that cause acid rain and
establishing committees to monitor interstate pollution. The act
also called for reductions in several other types of pollutants.
Finally, the Immigration Act of 1990 set permanent worldwide
levels of immigration with specific formulas for family-related
and employment-based immigrants, with exceptions made for
refugees.

Cruzan v. *Director, Missouri Dept. of Health* In 1983, a car
accident left Nancy Beth Cruzan in a vegetative state from which
she could not recover. After several weeks of being on a life
support system, Cruzan's parents tried to have Cruzan discon-
nected from the life support system, arguing that Cruzan had
said she would not want to be kept alive on machines. Hospital
officials refused to disconnect her. Her parents appealed, saying
that Cruzan's Fourteenth Amendment due process and liberty
interest rights allowed her to refuse unwanted medical treatment. The Supreme Court agreed that a person did have the right
to refuse medical treatment, but that there must be "clear and
convincing" evidence (such as a living will) that the person did
not want to be kept alive by artificial means. In this particular
case, Cruzan's parents did not have such evidence.

Planned Parenthood of Southeastern Pennsylvania v. *Casey* In 1982, Pennsylvania amended its abortion law to require several new regulations, including a 24-hour waiting period and parental consent for minors seeking abortions. Married women would be required to inform their husbands if they decided to have an abortion. Planned Parenthood and other clinics and physicians challenged the regulations. The Supreme Court reaffirmed a woman's basic freedom to have an abortion, but upheld most of the Pennsylvania regulations because the Court said they were not a "substantial obstacle" to a woman seeking an abortion. The only regulation struck down was the requirement of a wife to notify her husband.

The 1992 Election President Bush won the Republican nomination for the 1992 presidential election. Democratic nominee Bill Clinton promised to cut taxes and blamed Bush for the recession. Political maverick H. Ross Perot, running as an independent candidate, ran a quixotic campaign that caught the attention of millions of voters. A grassroots movement, or groups of people organizing at the local level, put Perot on the ballot in all 50 states. However, Bill Clinton won the election, and the Democrats kept control of Congress.

CHAPTER 33   INTO A NEW CENTURY

Chapter Overview

During the 1990s, a technological revolution transformed society. President Clinton pushed for budget cuts, health care and welfare reforms, and global trade. He also worked for peace in the Middle East and the Balkans. In 2000, George W. Bush won the presidency. He supported tax cuts, a new energy program, increased trade, and a missile defense system. After terrorists killed thousands of people in the United States, the new president launched a war on terrorism.

As you read through this chapter, ask yourself these questions:
(1) How has the computer revolutionized science, medicine, and communications?
(2) What environmental issues have become important internationally?
(3) What led to the development of economic blocs around the world?
(4) What programs did George W. Bush initiate?
(5) What factors contributed to the rise of Middle East terrorism?

REGENTS WARM-UP

Several questions on the Regents Exam focus on your understanding of core concepts and themes in United States history. Science and technology is an example of a core concept. As you read this chapter, note the impact that computers and telecommunication have had on the nation and the world.

Main Ideas and Concepts

- **Science and Technology** The computer has helped reshape the nation's economy.

- **Economic Systems** The United States, along with much of the industrialized world, experienced economic prosperity in the 1990s.

- **Nationalism** Economic, health, and environmental developments in recent years have led to the world's nations becoming more independent.

- **Conflict** International terrorists targeted the United States and other Western nations.

People, Places, Terms

The following names and terms will help you to prepare for the Regents Exam in United States History and Government. You can find an explanation of each name and term in the Glossary at the back of this book, in your textbook, or in another reference source.

biotechnology	ethnic cleansing	North American Free
Department of	euro	Trade Agreement
Homeland	Al Gore	Osama bin Laden
Security	Kyoto Protocol	trade deficit

SECTION 1 THE TECHNOLOGICAL REVOLUTION

The Rise of the Compact Computer

In 1959, Robert Noyce designed the first integrated circuit, a complete electronics circuit on a single chip of the element silicon. This innovation made circuits much smaller and easier to make.

In 1968, Noyce and a colleague formed Intel, a company that revolutionized computers with the creation of microprocessors. These chips further reduced the size of computers and increased their speed.

Computers for Everyone Stephen Wozniak and Steven Jobs set out to build a small computer using the microprocessor technology. By 1976, the pair had founded Apple Computer. Apple's success created intense competition in the computer industry.

In 1981, IBM introduced the "Personal Computer" (PC). Apple responded with the Macintosh, featuring a much simpler operating system that used on-screen graphic symbols called icons, which users could control with a hand-operated device called a mouse.

At the same time Apple was being created, a 19-year-old named Bill Gates co-founded Microsoft to design PC software, the instructions used to program computers to perform certain tasks. In 1985 Microsoft introduced Windows, which brought mouse-activated on-screen graphics to PCs.

LINKING GEOGRAPHY TO HISTORY

Robert Noyce's company that made integrated circuits was located in an area south of San Francisco. Many new companies sprang up nearby to make products using the integrated circuits. This led to a nickname for the area: Silicon Valley.

Computers soon transformed the workplace, linking employees within an office or among office branches. By the late 1990s, many workers used a home computer and electronic mail to telecommute, or do their jobs at home via computer.

The Telecommunications Revolution

From the 1970s through the 1990s, the deregulation of telecommunications created an explosion of creativity and competition in the telephone and television industries.

In 1996 Congress passed the Telecommunications Act. The act allowed telephone companies to compete with each other and to send television signals. It also permitted cable television companies to offer telephone service.

The Rise of the Internet

Digital electronics made worldwide communications possible with the creation of the Internet, a global information system. The roots of this networking system began with the U.S. Defense Department's Advanced Research Project Agency in 1969. Known as ARPNET, this system linked government agencies, defense contractors, and scientists at various universities.

When the National Science Foundation funded several supercomputer centers across the country, it paved the way for the system to operate commercially rather than through the government. With the development of the hypertext transport protocol (http) and new software known as Web browsers, the Internet rapidly expanded. Use of the Internet grew almost 300 percent between 1997 and 2000.

The Internet also created a "dot-com" economy. Many companies made millions of dollars for stock investors. Internet-related stocks helped fuel the economy of the 1990s. However, the stocks of these companies dropped drastically in 2000.

Breakthroughs in Biotechnology

Computers aided scientists involved in **biotechnology**, the managing of biological systems to improve human life. Researchers have used biotechnology to develop new medicines, animal growth hormones, genetically engineered plants, and industrial chemicals.

CORE CONCEPTS: INTERDEPENDENCE

All the data from the Human Genome Project was placed on the Internet, free of charge, making it available to scientists all over the world. This was done to prevent any single nation or private laboratory from controlling the outcome or limiting the use of genome findings.

The development of supercomputers helped scientists to map out the human genome by recording the human DNA sequence. The Human Genome Project began at the National Institutes of Health in 1990. This project completed its first map of the human genome in February 2001. The information helps medical researchers determine which genes make people more susceptible to disease.

SECTION 2 THE CLINTON YEARS

Clinton's Agenda

When President Bill Clinton took office, he focused on domestic issues, including the economy, the family, education, crime, and health care.

Raising Taxes, Cutting Spending Clinton felt the problem with the economy was due to the federal deficit. The high deficit caused the government to borrow large sums of money, which drove up interest rates. Clinton felt that the key to economic growth was to lower interest rates.

Clinton had difficulty cutting government spending that went to entitlement programs, such as Social Security and Medicare. Although he had promised to cut taxes, instead he had to increase taxes. The tax increases were unpopular, and congressional Republicans refused to pass them. Finally, Congress passed a revised version of Clinton's plan.

Stumbling on Health Care Clinton appointed his wife, Hillary Rodham Clinton, to head a task force to prepare a health care plan. The plan guaranteed health care for all Americans, but it was widely opposed by employers, small business owners, the insurance industry, doctors' organizations, and Republicans. In the end, the plan died without ever coming to a vote.

Families and Education Clinton pushed through several pieces of legislation to help the American family. His first success was the Family Medical Leave Act. It gave workers up to 12 weeks per year of unpaid family leave for the birth or adoption of a child, or to help care for an ill family member.

Clinton also had Congress create AmeriCorps, a program that put students to work improving low-income housing, teaching children to read, and cleaning up the environment. AmeriCorps workers earned salaries and were awarded scholarships.

CORE CONCEPTS: NEEDS AND WANTS

During his campaign, Clinton promised to reform the health care system. At the time, an estimated 40 million Americans, or about 15 percent of the nation, did not have private health insurance. Because Clinton's program failed to pass, there are still millions of Americans who do not have basic health care.

Crime and Gun Control Democrats in Congress passed a gun-control law known as the Brady Bill. The law imposed a waiting period before people could buy handguns as well as police background checks on people trying to buy handguns.

Clinton introduced a bill that provided extra funds to states to build new prisons and put 100,000 more police officers on the streets.

IMPORTANT LEGISLATIVE INITIATIVES IN CLINTON ERA	
Family Medical Leave Act	gave workers unpaid family leave for up to 12 weeks following new child's birth or adoption or for illness in the family
Brady Bill	imposed a waiting period before people could buy handguns and required background checks
Crime Bill	provided states with extra funds to build new prisons and put 100,000 more police officers on the streets
Health Insurance Portability Act	improved healthcare coverage for people who changed jobs and reduced discrimination against people with pre-existing illnesses
Welfare Reform Act	limited people to two consecutive years on welfare and required them to work to receive welfare benefits; helped with childcare costs
Contract With America	proposed lower taxes, welfare reform, anti-crime laws and balanced budget amendment

Vernonia **v.** *Acton* The Vernonia school district in Oregon wanted to reduce the drug problem in its schools and created a student-athlete drug policy that allowed schools to test athletes for drugs using urinalysis. A student named James Acton refused to take the test, arguing that the test was unreasonable search and seizure, and was not allowed to play football because of his refusal. The Supreme Court held that drug testing of student athletes was constitutional, accepting the school's reasoning that to maintain safety in schools, students' rights can be reduced and that the search was a "promotion of legitimate governmental interests."

The Republicans Gain Control of Congress

By late 1994, Clinton had become unpopular. He had raised taxes and failed to fix the health care system. Although the economy was improving, many companies continued to downsize. Several scandals weakened public confidence in him.

The Contract with America As the 1994 elections neared, congressional Republican leaders, led by Newt Gingrich, created an election program that they called Contract with America. The program proposed 10 major changes, including lower taxes, term limits for members of Congress, and a balanced budget amendment.

These proposals, along with decreased public confidence in Clinton, gave the Republicans a stunning victory in the elections. For the first time in 40 years, Republicans had won a majority in both houses of Congress.

The Budget Battle In 1995, instead of backing down to the Republicans in Congress, Clinton allowed the federal government to close when a budget agreement could not be reached. The Republicans in Congress and the president eventually worked together to balance the budget.

In their first 100 days in office, House Republicans passed almost the entire Contract with America, but they soon ran into trouble. The Senate defeated several proposals, including the balanced budget amendment, while the president vetoed others.

Prior to the 1996 election, Clinton and the Republicans worked to pass the Health Insurance Portability Act. This act improved coverage for people who changed jobs, and reduced discrimination against people with pre-existing illnesses.

They also passed a welfare reform bill that marked the most important change in aid to the poor since the Social Security Act of 1935. It ended the fifty-year federal guarantee of assistance to families with dependent children and limited people to no more than two consecutive years on welfare. Most of all, it shifted the bulk of welfare benefits away from those without jobs and toward support for low-wage workers.

The 1996 Election

During the 1996 presidential election, Clinton took credit for the booming economy. The economic boom of the 1990s was the longest sustained period of growth in United States history. Unemployment and inflation were at their lowest levels in 40 years, the stock market soared, wages increased, and crime declined.

Clinton won re-election against Republican candidate Bob Dole, but Republicans retained control of Congress.

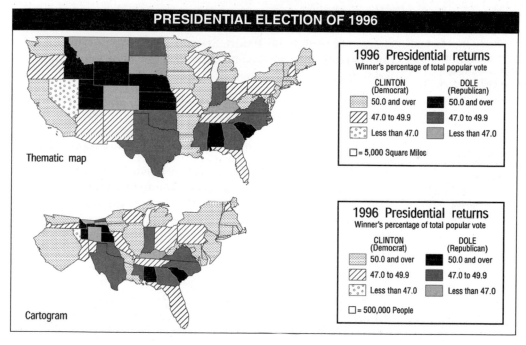

PRESIDENTIAL ELECTION OF 1996

Thematic map

1996 Presidential returns
Winner's percentage of total popular vote

CLINTON (Democrat)	DOLE (Republican)
50.0 and over	50.0 and over
47.0 to 49.9	47.0 to 49.9
Less than 47.0	Less than 47.0

☐ = 5,000 Square Miles

Cartogram

1996 Presidential returns
Winner's percentage of total popular vote

CLINTON (Democrat)	DOLE (Republican)
50.0 and over	50.0 and over
47.0 to 49.9	47.0 to 49.9
Less than 47.0	Less than 47.0

☐ = 500,000 People

Clinton's Second Term

During Clinton's second term in office, the economy continued to expand. In 1997, for the first time in 24 years, the president submitted a balanced budget to Congress. In 1998, the government ran a surplus, meaning it collected more money than it spent. Clinton suggested putting some of the surplus money into the Social Security system to extend its life (the system is due to run out of money some decades in the future).

Putting Children First In his second term, Clinton aimed his proposals toward children's needs. He signed an Adoption and Safe Families Act, and the Children's Health Insurance Program, providing insurance for children whose parents could not afford it.

CORE CONCEPTS: PRESIDENTIAL DECISIONS AND ACTIONS

In his second term, Clinton continued his efforts to help students. He asked for a tax credit for students, a large increase in student grants, and an expansion of the Head Start program for preschoolers.

CORE CONCEPTS: CONSTITUTIONAL PRINCIPLES

The impeachment of President Clinton is a good opportunity to review what the constitutional provisions are for removing a person from office. Two presidents have been impeached—that is, had formal charges brought against them—Andrew Johnson and Bill Clinton. The House of Representatives has power of impeachment. Neither man was convicted of the charges. Trial on impeachment charges occurs in the Senate, with the Chief Justice of the Supreme Court presiding. Refer to the last paragraphs of Article I, Sections 1 and 2 of the Constitution.

Clinton is Impeached In 1998 a scandal involving President Clinton threatened his presidency. Beginning in his first term, Clinton was accused of arranging for illegal loans to Whitewater Development—an Arkansas real estate company— while he was governor of that state. Attorney General Janet Reno appointed an independent counsel, Kenneth Starr, to investigate the president. Ultimately, no evidence of any wrongdoing was uncovered in this matter.

In early 1998, a scandal involving a personal relationship with a White House intern suggested that the president had committed perjury, or lied under oath. Starr began investigating these charges as well. In his report, Starr argued that Clinton had obstructed justice, abused his power as president, and committed perjury.

In 1998, the House passed two articles of impeachment. In February 1999, the senators cast their votes, with the result well short of the two-thirds needed to remove Clinton from office. Although Clinton kept his job, his reputation was damaged.

Campaign Finance Reform The issue of campaign finance reform had been debated for years without any major changes being made. However, in 2002, Congress passed the Bipartisan Campaign Reform Act of 2002, whose chief supporters, John McCain and Russ Feingold, were long-time advocates of reform. The act eliminated soft money donations (money donated to political parties that avoided certain restrictions) and eliminated "issue" advertisements that were often thinly veiled attacks on a candidate by a special interest group. Several groups challenged the law as unconstitutional, but in December 2003, the Supreme Court upheld most of the key provisions of the law.

Clinton's Foreign Policy

The Haitian Intervention In 1991, military leaders in Haiti overthrew Jean-Bertrand Aristide, the country's first democratically elected president in many decades. The new rulers used violence to suppress the opposition.

President Clinton convinced the United Nations to impose a trade embargo on Haiti, creating a severe economic crisis. Thousands of Haitian refugees fled to the United States. Clinton ordered an invasion of Haiti, but before troops arrived, former president Jimmy Carter convinced Haiti's rulers to step aside.

Problems in Bosnia and Kosovo In the southeastern European country of Bosnia, a vicious civil war erupted in the early 1990s. Fighting among Orthodox Christian Serbs, Catholic Croatians, and Bosnian Muslims continued until 1995. The Serbs attacked non-Serbs and began calling for **ethnic cleansing**—the brutal expulsion of an ethnic group from a geographic area.

The United States convinced NATO allies that intervention was necessary, resulting in NATO warplanes attacking Serbs. The Clinton administration arranged for peace talks in Dayton, Ohio, and a peace plan called the Dayton Accords was signed.

In 1998 another war began in the Serbian province of Kosovo between Serbs and Albanians. The Serbs' treatment of Albanians angered people around the world, and leaders tried unsuccessfully to bring the two sides together. In 1999, NATO began bombing Serbia. Serbian troops pulled out of Kosovo.

Problems in the Middle East Although Iraq was defeated in the Persian Gulf War, Iraqi president Saddam Hussein remained in power, threatening Iraq's neighbors. United Nations sanctions that had been put in place after the Gulf War created significant shortages of common products in Iraq.

Relations between Israel and the Palestinians were very volatile. In 1993 Israeli Prime Minister Yitzhak Rabin and Palestine Liberation Organization leader Yasir Arafat reached an agreement. Clinton invited them to the White House to sign the Declaration of Principles. There was opposition to the plan from both sides, and in 1995, Rabin was assassinated by an Israeli radical.

Somalia In 1991, after the collapse of the Somali government, tribal clans in a portion of northern Somalia declared independence from the rest of the country. The United Nations sent peacekeeping troops, led by the United States, into Somalia to make sure that food was distributed (there was an ongoing famine) and that peace would be established. However, many Somalis opposed the intervention and in October 2003, 19 U.N. troops and 24 American Special Forces soldiers were killed in gun battles with rebels. After further casualties, troops were withdrawn from the country in 1995.

CORE CONCEPTS: PLACES AND REGIONS

In 1998 Israeli and Palestinian leaders met with President Clinton to work out details of the withdrawal of Israeli troops from the West Bank and the Gaza Strip. This agreement, however, failed to settle the status of Jerusalem, which both sides claimed.

SECTION 3 AN INTERDEPENDENT WORLD

The New Global Economy

In the latter part of the 1900s, computer technology and the Internet helped to create a global economy. The sale of American goods abroad had long been essential to American prosperity. By the 1970s, however, serious **trade deficits** had mounted. The United States purchased more from foreign nations than it sold abroad.

Regional Economic Blocs In 1994, the **North American Free Trade Agreement** (NAFTA) was created to increase international trade. Canada, the United States, and Mexico joined in a free-trade zone. In 1995, the General Agreement on Trade and Tariffs (GATT) established the World Trade Organization, an international body that oversees trade agreements between member nations. Members are required to grant each other "most favored nation" trade status, which means that tariffs on exports will be no higher than those on goods from another "most favored" nation. There are currently 148 member nations.

CORE CONCEPTS: MOVEMENT OF PEOPLE AND GOODS

Many Americans thought that NAFTA would increase unemployment in the United States. They feared that industrial jobs would go to Mexico, where labor costs were lower. Although some jobs were lost to Mexico, unemployment rates fell and wages rose. Many American businesses upgraded their technology and workers shifted to more skilled jobs or to the service industry.

NORTH AMERICA FREE TRADE AGREEMENT (NAFTA)

ADVANTAGES	DISADVANTAGES
★ U.S. exports to Canada rose.	★ Mexico purchased fewer goods from the United States.
★ Rising employment in Mexico reduced the flow of illegal immigrants into the United States.	
	★ Mexico exported more to the United States than it imported.
★ Unemployment in the United States decreased as workers shifted to more skilled jobs.	
★ Small businesses increased their trade with Canada and Mexico.	★ American industrial jobs moved to Mexico where labor costs were lower.

In 1993 the European Union (EU) was created to promote economic and political cooperation among European nations. The EU created a common bank as well as a common currency called the **euro**.

The World Trade Organization administered international trade agreements and helped settle trade disputes. American supporters of the WTO felt it would benefit consumers. On the other hand, the United States had no veto power in the WTO and poorer nations could outvote it.

Trade with China China became important in the global economy. Many Americans were uneasy about China's record of human rights violations and its threats to invade Taiwan. Despite these concerns, President Clinton negotiated a new trade agreement with China.

Economic Aid to Russia During the Cold War, only a few nations had possessed nuclear weapons, and they tried to restrict the spread of nuclear technology to other countries. After the Cold War ended, the United States provided funds to Russia and former satellite states to assist in the reduction of its nuclear stockpile and to secure weapons and radioactive material.

Trade with Latin American After the end of the Cold War, the United States became increasingly concerned with supporting fledgling democracies in Latin America and provided significant financial support to these governments. However, many countries took on massive amounts of debt in efforts to expand their industrial economies and in tough financial times could not make loan payments. Repaying foreign debt halted needed domestic programs in some countries. Many are watching Mexico's economy to see the effect that NAFTA has to determine if similar agreements would work for them. Thus far, Mexico has boosted exports and created thousands of new jobs through NAFTA.

Issues of Global Concern

Nuclear Concerns When Russia agreed to reduce its nuclear arsenal, concerns arose that some of its weapons or radioactive material could be lost, stolen, or sold on the black market. The United States provided funds to Russia to assist in the reduction of its nuclear stockpile. Congress also passed legislation that cut aid to and imposed sanctions on nations looking to acquire nuclear weapons.

Environmental Concerns Many environmentalists began to push for a ban on chlorofluorocarbons (CFCs) because these chemicals had the potential to deplete Earth's ozone layer. The ozone layer protects life on Earth from the cancer-causing ultraviolet rays of the sun. CFCs are used as a refrigerant in air conditioners. In the early 1990s nearly 100 nations, including the United States, agreed to phase out the use of CFCs, and the United States stopped producing them in 1996.

In the early 1990s, some scientists found evidence of global warming, an increase in average world temperatures over time. Concern about global warming led to an international meeting in Kyoto, Japan, in 1997. Thirty-eight nations and the EU signed the **Kyoto Protocol**, promising to reduce carbon dioxide emissions that might cause global warming. Very few of the nations put it into effect. In 2001, President George W. Bush withdrew the United States from the Protocol, citing what his administration said were flaws in the treaty.

CORE CONCEPTS: CITIZENSHIP

Third parties have sometimes had a significant impact on American political life. In 1892 the Populist party was able to elect a number of state legislators and Congressmen in the Midwest and South. In 1912 Theodore Roosevelt ran as a Progressive, which split the Republican party to such a degree that Democrat Woodrow Wilson won the presidency. In 1948 Strom Thurmond ran as a Dixiecrat and Henry A. Wallace ran as a Progressive, splitting the Democrats into three parts. In 1968 George Wallace was on the American Independent party ticket and won 49 electoral votes. In the 2000 election many feel that Ralph Nader, the Green Party candidate, had a profound impact on the election.

SECTION 4   AMERICA ENTERS A NEW CENTURY

A New President for a New Century

The presidential election of 2000 was historically close. Vice President **Al Gore** was the Democratic candidate. The Republican candidate was George W. Bush, son of former president George Bush. Each candidate battled for the undecided independent voters. Both candidates promised to cut taxes and made education and health care central issues in their campaigns. Ralph Nader of the Green Party was the only major challenger to Gore and Bush.

A Close Vote On Election Day, voters were split almost evenly. The election came down to the state of Florida. The results there were so close that state law required a recount of the ballots using vote-counting machines. There were, however, thousands of ballots that had been thrown out because the machines could not discern a vote for president.

Gore asked for a hand recount of ballots in several strongly Democratic counties. Vote counters tried to determine from the ballots what voters intended, but different counties used different standards. When it became clear that not all of the recounts would be finished on time, Gore went to court to overturn the deadline. The Florida Supreme Court set a new deadline, but the U.S. Supreme Court intervened to decide whether the Florida court had acted unconstitutionally. Florida officials certified Bush the winner by 537 votes.

Bush Becomes President

During the 2000 election campaign, the U.S. economy began to slow. The stock market dropped and many Internet-based technology companies went out of business. President Bush's first priority in office was to cut taxes to boost the economy. Congress passed a large tax cut.

Soon after, Bush proposed two major reforms in education. He wanted public schools to hold annual standardized tests, and he wanted to allow parents be able to use federal funds to pay for private schools if their public schools were doing poorly. Congress refused to give federal funds for private schools. But it voted in favor of annual reading and math tests in public schools for grades three through eight.

Bush wanted to reform Medicare. In November 2003, Congress finally passed a bill that added prescription drug benefits to Medicare.

Congress also reacted to a rash of corporate scandals by tightening accounting regulations and increasing the penalties for dishonest corporate executives.

Bush called for a new military program designed to meet the needs of the post-Cold War world. He strongly favored strategic defense, the effort to develop missiles and other devices that can shoot down nuclear missiles before they hit the United States. As the debate about military programs continued, a horrific event changed everything. On September 11, 2001, terrorists crashed passenger jets into the World Trade Center and the Pentagon. Another hijacked plane crashed in a Pennsylvania field when the passengers resisted the hijacking. A new war had begun.

SECTION 5 THE WAR ON TERRORISM

The attacks of September 11, 2001, killed more than 3,300 people. These attacks were acts of terrorism—the use of violence by nongovernmental groups against civilians to achieve a political goal.

CORE CONCEPTS: CITIZENSHIP

Under the Constitution, most Americans age 18 and over have the right to vote. In the 2000 presidential election, the winner in several states, including Florida, was decided by no more than a few thousand votes. Slightly more than 50 percent of the voting age population actually voted, and 76 percent of registered voters actually voted.

CORE CONCEPTS: JUSTICE

In *Bush* v. *Gore*, the United States Supreme Court ruled that the hand recounts in Florida violated the equal protection clause of the Constitution. The Court argued that because different vote counters used different standards, the recount did not treat all votes equally.

CORE CONCEPTS: BELIEF SYSTEMS, IDENTITY

Although many Middle Eastern terrorist groups are Muslim, most Muslim people do not support terrorism. They believe it is against their faith, Islam.

Middle East Terrorism

Oil has been important to the American economy since the 1920s, and the United States has invested heavily in the Middle East oil industry. Some Middle Easterners have grown increasingly resentful of the United States for helping certain ruling families in the Middle East become richer while most of the people remained poor. Many people in the Middle East have also become increasingly angered by U.S. support of Israel.

Some devout Muslims in the Middle East have grown resentful of contact with Western societies, fearing that their traditional values and beliefs are being weakened. Throughout the Middle East, new movements have arisen calling for a return to traditional Muslim religious laws. The movements have also sought to overthrow pro-Western governments in the Middle East. Muslims who support these movements are called fundamentalist militants.

The al-Qaeda Threat In 1988 **Osama bin Laden**, a wealthy Saudi Arabian, founded al-Qaeda. The organization recruited Muslims to fight in Afghanistan against the Soviets and channeled money and arms to the resistance.

Bin Laden believed Western ideas had contaminated Muslim society. He changed al-Qaeda into a terrorist organization and eventually began operating out of Afghanistan, a country that was then under the control of Muslim fundamentalists known as the Taliban. In 1998, bin Laden called on Muslims to kill Americans anywhere in the world. After al-Qaeda simultaneously bombed American embassies in Kenya and Tanzania, the United States began air strikes against training bases connected with bin Laden.

In 1999, al-Qaeda terrorists were arrested while trying to smuggle explosives in an attempt to bomb Seattle. In October 2000, al-Qaeda terrorists attacked the USS *Cole*, an American warship docked in the Middle Eastern country of Yemen.

A New War Begins

When terrorists attacked the United States on September 11, 2001, the government put the armed forces on high alert. The FBI began a massive investigation, which soon identified the attacks as the work of Osama bin Laden and al-Qaeda. On September 14, President Bush declared a national emergency, and Congress voted to use force to fight the terrorists.

Secretary of State Colin Powell built an international coalition to support the United States' fight against terrorism. Secretary of Defense Donald Rumsfeld began deploying troops, aircraft, and warships to the Middle East. President Bush announced that the war on terrorism would start against al-Qaeda, and warned the Taliban regime of Afghanistan to turn over bin Laden and his supporters. Bush also announced that the war on terrorism would be waged against every terrorist group around the world, as well as the countries that aided or harbored terrorists.

In early October, U.S. warplanes began bombing targets in Afghanistan, including al-Qaeda camps and the military forces of the Taliban. At the same time, the United States began sending aid to the Northern Alliance, a coalition of Afghan groups that had been fighting the Taliban.

The Taliban regime collapsed by early December, but difficult fighting against al-Qaeda troops went on. Al-Qaeda forces in Afghanistan were eventually defeated and forced to scatter, but Osama bin Laden was not found. By mid-2004, the worldwide hunt for bin Laden and other al-Qaeda members continued.

Fighting Terrorism at Home Congress drafted a new antiterrorist law, called the USA Patriot Act, in late October 2001. It permitted secret searches and allowed authorities to obtain a single nationwide search warrant. It also made it easier to wiretap suspects, and allowed authorities to track Internet communications and seize voice mail.

There were several federal agencies working to prevent terrorism. President Bush asked Congress to combine them all under the umbrella of the **Department of Homeland Security**. To alert Americans to the level of terrorist threat and any changes in that level, a color-coded system was developed. When officials received credible information about a possible terrorist attack, they would alert the public and sometimes raise the threat level.

Weapons of Mass Destruction The September 11, 2001, attacks led to fears that al-Qaeda and other terrorist groups could acquire weapons of mass destruction (nuclear, chemical, or biological weapons), which could kill tens of thousands of people at once.

In January of 2002, Bush warned of the grave threat to the world posed by Iraq, Iran, and North Korea. Iran and Libya had sponsored terrorists and were also suspected of developing weapons of mass destruction. Later that year, North Korea

CORE CONCEPTS: GOVERNMENT

Sometimes governments secretly support terrorist groups with money, weapons, and training. Such support is known as state-sponsored terrorism. The governments of Libya, Syria, and Iran have all sponsored terrorism.

announced that it had resumed its nuclear weapons program. The Bush administration was not able to persuade North Korea to stop the program.

Confronting Iraq

President Bush considered Iraq a more immediate threat than North Korea in developing and distributing weapons of mass destruction. Iraq's dictator, Saddam Hussein, had used chemical weapons twice in the 1980s, and after the Gulf War, United Nations inspectors had found evidence that Iraq had biological weapons and was working on a nuclear bomb.

In October of 2002, Congress authorized the use of force against Iraq. A UN resolution threatened "serious consequences" if Iraq did not declare all of its weapons of mass destruction, stop supporting terrorism, and stop oppressing its people.

Weapons inspectors returned to Iraq. The Bush administration pushed for a war resolution in the UN Security Council. France and Russia refused to back it, but the United States and about 30 other countries prepared for war as many antiwar protests took place around the world.

War and Its Aftermath On March 20, 2003, the U.S.-led coalition forces attacked Iraq and quickly seized control. On May 1, Bush declared that major combat was over. Hussein, however, was not captured until December 2003.

The fighting and controversy continued. Bombings, sniper attacks, and battles plagued American troops, and deaths and expenses mounted. Meanwhile, no evidence of weapons of mass destruction was found during the occupation of Iraq. Many Americans wondered whether the invasion had been necessary. Though President Bush's popularity began to suffer, he narrowly won reelection in 2004.

A New Iraqi Government On June 28, 2004, the United States handed over power to an interim, or temporary, Iraqi government made of members of different political, ethnic, and religious groups. The interim government was set up to rule only until new leaders could be elected democratically by Iraqis. Despite the election of an Iraqi government in early 2005, the path toward a free and stable Iraq remained long and difficult. Terrorist attacks and violence continued, and by the fall of 2005, more than 1,800 American soldiers had died in Iraq.

CORE CONCEPTS: ECONOMIC SYSTEMS

One important way to fight terrorists is to cut off their funding. President Bush froze the financial assets of several individuals and groups suspected of terrorism. Eighty other nations did the same.

CORE CONCEPTS: JUSTICE

On July 1, 2004, Saddam Hussein was read his rights in an Iraqi court. An Iraqi judge told him that he would be charged with war crimes and crimes against humanity and put on trial. The former Iraqi president's trial was expected to begin in 2005.

PRACTICING FOR THE REGENTS

Part I   Multiple-Choice Questions

The following multiple-choice questions come from past Regents Examinations. Test your understanding of United States history and geography by answering each of these items. Circle the number of the word or expression that best completes each statement or question. Test-taking tips can be found in the margins for some questions. For additional help, see Taking the Regents Exam on pages ix–xxxi of this Review Book.

Base your answer to question 1 on the cartoon below and on your knowledge of social studies.

1   The main idea of this cartoon from the late 1940s is that
(1)   Europe is slipping into chaos and revolution
(2)   American economic aid is assisting European recovery
(3)   containment is failing as a policy for stopping Soviet expansion into Western Europe
(4)   Europeans are not making serious attempts to solve their economic problems

REGENTS WARM-UP

Many past Regents Examinations have included questions that test your ability to interpret a cartoonist's message, or point of view. Thinking about the position of the "Marshall Plan" and "Europe" will help you interpret the main idea of the cartoon.

2   The main reason that the North Atlantic Treaty Organization (NATO) was formed after World War II was to
    (1) provide collective security against international Communist aggression
    (2) increase trade between European nations
    (3) encourage "people-to-people" peaceful diplomacy
    (4) rebuild Western European economies

Base your answer to question 3 on the excerpt below and on your knowledge of social studies.

> "There shall be a loyalty investigation of every person entering the civilian employment of any department or agency of the Executive Branch of the Federal Government."
> — *The Truman Loyalty Order,*
> *March 22, 1947*

3   President Harry Truman issued his executive order in response to the
    (1) fear of Communist Party influence in government
    (2) election of Socialist Party representatives to Congress
    (3) discovery of spies in defense industries
    (4) arrest and trial of high-ranking government employees for terrorism

4   Immediately after World War II, the relationship between the United States and the Soviet Union became strained because
    (1) both nations were competing for supremacy in space exploration
    (2) the United States prevented the Soviet Union from joining the United Nations
    (3) each nation believed that the other was a threat to its national security
    (4) the United States used military forces in Cuba and South Vietnam

5   During the Cold War era, the United States and the Soviet Union were hesitant to become involved in direct military conflict mainly because of
    (1) the threat of China to both nations
    (2) pressure from nonaligned nations
    (3) the potential for global nuclear destruction
    (4) mutual dependence on Middle East petroleum

6   One result of the Cold War between the United States and the Soviet Union was that the two nations
    (1) broke all diplomatic ties
    (2) refused to trade with each other
    (3) formed competing military alliances
    (4) clashed over control of the Mediterranean Sea

7   Which foreign policy term would be the most appropriate title for the partial outline below?

    I. _____
        A. Truman Doctrine
        B. Marshall Plan
        C. Berlin Blockade
        D. Korean War

    (1) Imperialism
    (2) Appeasement
    (3) Noninvolvement
    (4) Containment

8   Who led a "witch hunt" for Communist spies in the United States government during the early 1950s?
    (1) Supreme Court Justice Earl Warren
    (2) President Dwight Eisenhower
    (3) Senator Joseph McCarthy
    (4) Secretary of State Dean Acheson

9   In the post–World War II era, Senator Joseph McCarthy and the House Un-American Activities Committee attempted to
    (1)   develop an effective system for spying on other countries
    (2)   make Cold War programs a priority in United States foreign policy
    (3)   identify Communists in the government and elsewhere in American society
    (4)   establish a policy of détente with the Soviet Union

10   In the period following World War II, the United States established a long-term military presence in West Germany in an effort to
    (1)   support the unification of Europe, by force if necessary
    (2)   stop communist expansion in Europe
    (3)   prevent the renewal of German aggression in Europe
    (4)   allow the United Nations to resolve international disputes

Base your answer to question 11 on the cartoon below and on your knowledge of social studies.

11   Which event of 1948–1949 is illustrated by this cartoon?
    (1)   Berlin airlift
    (2)   collapse of the Berlin Wall
    (3)   reunification of Germany
    (4)   allied invasion of Normandy

12 Martin Luther King, Jr., first emerged as a leader of the civil rights movement when he
   (1) led the bus boycott in Montgomery, Alabama
   (2) refused to give up his seat on a bus to a white man
   (3) challenged the authority of the Supreme Court
   (4) was elected as the first black congressman from the South

13 Which initiative was part of President Lyndon Johnson's Great Society program?
   (1) providing medical care to the poor and elderly
   (2) reducing federal aid to education
   (3) increasing foreign aid to the Soviet Union
   (4) opposing civil rights legislation

   "I would agree with Saint Augustine that 'An unjust law is no law at all.' "
   — Dr. Martin Luther King, Jr.
   "Letter From Birmingham City Jail"

REGENTS WARM-UP

Question 14 is a data-based question that evaluates your ability to draw inferences from a quote. You must also draw upon your knowledge of the person to whom the quote is attributed to interpret it correctly.

14 This statement was used by Dr. King to show support for
   (1) Social Darwinism
   (2) Jim Crow laws
   (3) separation of church and state
   (4) civil disobedience

15 The federal voting rights laws passed in the 1950s and 1960s were designed to
   (1) return control of voting regulations to the states
   (2) remove racial barriers to voting
   (3) extend suffrage to American women
   (4) prevent recent immigrants from voting

16   President Lyndon B. Johnson's Great Society is similar to President Franklin D. Roosevelt's New Deal in that both programs
    (1)   sought ratification of the Equal Rights Amendment to guarantee equality for women
    (2)   advocated passage of civil rights laws to help African Americans
    (3)   supported federal funding of programs for the poor
    (4)   approved efforts by states to reduce taxes for the middle class

   "Sputnik Launch Propels Soviets Ahead in Space Race"

17   In 1957, the United States government responded to the event described in this headline by
    (1)   reducing military spending
    (2)   building a joint space station with the Soviet Union
    (3)   constructing President Ronald Reagan's "Star Wars" defense system
    (4)   providing funds to improve the educational system in the United States

REGENTS WARM-UP

Question 16 evaluates your ability to compare and contrast. This question asks you to identify one way in which the programs of presidents Lyndon B. Johnson and Franklin Roosevelt were the same.

Base your answer to question 18 on the chart below and on your knowledge of social studies.

African-American Voter Registration

State	Years	
	1960	**1966**
Alabama	66,000	250,000
Mississippi	22,000	175,000
N. Carolina	210,000	282,000
S. Carolina	58,000	191,000
Tennessee	185,000	225,000

18   The changes shown in the chart were most directly the result of the
   (1)   enactment of voting-reform laws by these southern states
   (2)   Supreme Court decision in *Brown* v. *Board of Education*
   (3)   passage of the Voting Rights Act of 1965
   (4)   executive branch's resistance to protecting the civil rights of minorities

19   What was the main reason for President Kennedy's action toward Cuba?
   (1)   Cuba is located close to the United States.
   (2)   The United States needed to protect business investments in Cuba.
   (3)   The cost of building missile defense bases in Florida was high.
   (4)   Cuba threatened to seize United States merchant ships in the Caribbean.

20   Which conclusion can best be drawn from the United States involvement in the Korean War and the Vietnam War?
   (1)   The Cold War extended beyond direct conflict with the Soviet Union.
   (2)   Popular wars have assured the re-election of incumbent presidents.
   (3)   War is the best way to support developing nations.
   (4)   The threat of nuclear war is necessary to settle a military conflict.

21   In foreign affairs, the domino theory was mainly applied to
   (1)   United States involvement in Latin America
   (2)   Japanese expansion in East Asia
   (3)   the Communist threat in Southeast Asia
   (4)   the movement for national independence in Africa

22 Which conclusion can be drawn from a study of the Vietnam War?
    (1) The policy of containment was successful.
    (2) Foreign policy can be altered by public opinion.
    (3) The power of the president is reduced during wartime.
    (4) Military superiority ensures military victory.

23 One reason the United States became involved in the Vietnam War was to
    (1) prevent the spread of Communism in Indochina
    (2) reduce French influence in Vietnam
    (3) stop China from seizing Vietnam
    (4) support the government of North Vietnam

24 An effect of the War Powers Act of 1973 was that
    (1) the authority of the president as commander in chief was limited
    (2) the North Atlantic Treaty Organization (NATO) became more involved in world conflicts
    (3) congressional approval was not needed when appropriating funds for the military
    (4) women were prevented from serving in combat roles during wartime

25 What was a lasting effect of the Watergate scandal under President Richard Nixon?
    (1) The system of checks and balances was weakened.
    (2) The scope of executive privilege was broadened.
    (3) Trust in elected officials was undermined.
    (4) Presidential responsiveness to public opinion was lessened.

26 During the 1980s, President Ronald Reagan used the ideas of supply-side economics to justify
    (1) increases in social welfare spending
    (2) expansion of the Social Security program
    (3) tax cuts for businesses
    (4) reductions in military spending

27 The Civil Rights Act of 1964, the Fair Housing Act, and the Americans with Disabilities Act were government efforts to
    (1) eliminate restrictions on immigration
    (2) end discrimination against various groups
    (3) provide federal aid for children
    (4) require equal treatment of men and women

28 President Bill Clinton's decision to send troops to Bosnia in 1995 and to participate in the bombing of Kosovo in 1999 were both in response to international concern over
    (1) trade agreement violations
    (2) access to world oil reserves
    (3) human rights violations
    (4) monetary policies

29 Which change in the demographic pattern of the United States is currently contributing most to the problems facing the Social Security system?
    (1) aging of the baby boomers
    (2) shorter life span of the elderly
    (3) migration to the Sunbelt
    (4) decline in the rate of immigration

30 President Richard Nixon supported the policy of détente as a way to
   (1) undermine Soviet influence among nonaligned countries in Africa and Asia
   (2) introduce democratic elections to Communist nations
   (3) encourage satellite nations to break their ties with the Soviet Union
   (4) reduce tensions between the United States and the Soviet Union

31 Support for the North American Free Trade Agreement (NAFTA) reflected the United States commitment to
   (1) globalization
   (2) Manifest Destiny
   (3) collective security
   (4) isolationism

32 The loss of jobs in manufacturing industries has been caused by the introduction of
   (1) radio and television
   (2) automobiles and airplanes
   (3) automation and computers
   (4) improved medicine and space travel

Base your answer to question 33 on the cartoon below and on your knowledge of social studies.

Source: Chip Bok, Creators Syndicate (adapted)

33 Which situation faced by President Bill Clinton is expressed in the cartoon?
   (1) Impeachment hampered his ability to carry out programs.
   (2) International problems interfered with domestic policy goals.
   (3) Health care costs took away funds needed for peacekeeping commitments.
   (4) Budget deficits prevented military action in world trouble spots.

34 The main goal of affirmative action
programs is to
   (1) enforce racial segregation laws
   (2) secure equal voting rights for
       African Americans
   (3) provide affordable childcare
   (4) promote economic gains for minori-
       ties and women

"I think it will be a safer world and a
better world if we have a strong,
healthy United States, Europe, Soviet
Union, China, Japan, each balancing
the other, not playing one against the
other, an even balance."
—Richard Nixon, 1972

35 President Nixon put this idea into
practice by
   (1) expanding economic relations with
       Communist nations
   (2) abandoning his policy of détente
   (3) declaring an end to the Korean War
   (4) ending collective security agreements

Part II   Thematic Essay Question

The following thematic essay question comes from past Regents Examinations. Write your answers on a separate sheet of paper. Essay-writing tips appear in the margin. For additional help, see Taking the Regents Exam on pages ix–xxxi of this Review Book.

Theme: Social Change

> Events have influenced social change in American society.

Task: Identify *one* event in United States history that has influenced *social* change and for the event identified:

> • Discuss the historical circumstances surrounding the event
> • Show how the event was intended to bring about specific social change
> • Evaluate the extent to which the event was successful in bringing about that change

REGENTS WARM-UP

Discuss means "to make observations about something using facts, reasoning, and arguments to present in some detail." *Show* means "to point out a position or idea by stating it and giving information that supports it." *Evaluate* means "to make a judgment about something's value or worth."

You may use any example from your study of United States history. Some suggestions you might wish to consider include passage of the Civil War amendments; development of the automobile; passage of the 18th Amendment [national Prohibition]; passage of the 19th Amendment [women's suffrage]; passage of the Social Security Act (1935); President Dwight D. Eisenhower's decision to send troops to Little Rock, Arkansas; and the Supreme Court's decision in *Roe* v. *Wade*.

You are *not* limited to these suggestions

Guidelines: In your essay, be sure to:

- Address all aspects of the *Task*
- Support the theme with relevant facts, examples and details
- Use a logical and clear plan of organization
- Introduce the theme by establishing a framework that is beyond a simple restatement of the *Task* and conclude with a summation of the theme

Part III Document-Based Questions

This exercise is designed to test your ability to work with historical documents. It is similar to the document-based questions that you will see on the Regents Examination. While you are asked to analyze five historical documents, the exercise on the actual exam will include more documents. Some of the documents have been edited for the purposes of the question. As you analyze the documents, take into account the source of each document and any point of view that may be presented in the document.

Historical Context: The women's rights movement had all but disappeared after the adoption of the 19th Amendment in 1920. However, in the post–World War II period, women increasingly realized that they continued to face obstacles in achieving equality in American society.

Task: Using information from the documents and your knowledge of United States history, answer the questions that follow each document in Part A. Your answers to the questions will help you write the Part B essay, in which you will be asked to:

- Discuss why women were dissatisfied with their roles after World War II
- Discuss specific attempts by women to achieve equality after World War II

Part A   Short-Answer Questions

Directions: Analyze the documents and answer the short-answer questions that follow each document in the space provided.

Document 1

> Within two months after the war, some 800,000 women had been fired from jobs in the aircraft industry; the same thing was happening in the auto industry and elsewhere. In the two years after the war, some two million women had lost their jobs. In the post-war years, the sheer affluence [wealth] of the country meant that many families could now live in a middle-class existence on only one income. In addition, the migration to the suburbs physically separated women from the workplace. The new culture of consumerism told women they should be homemakers and saw them merely as potential buyers for all the new washers and dryers, freezers, floor waxers, pressure cookers, and blenders.
>
> —David Halberstam, *The Fifties*

1*a*   According to David Halberstam, when World War II ended, what happened to many of the women who had been employed during the war?

_____

_____

b   What does this passage indicate about the role women were expected to play in the 1950s?

_____

_____

Document 2

> Each suburban wife struggled with it [a sense of dissatisfaction] alone. As she made the beds, shopped for groceries, matched slipcover material, ate peanut butter sandwiches with her children, chauffeured Cub Scouts and Brownies, lay beside her husband at night—she was afraid to ask even of herself the silent question—"Is this all [there is]?"
>
> —Betty Friedan, *The Feminine Mystique*, 1963

2   According to this document, why were some American women dissatisfied with their lives during the 1950s and 1960s?

_____

_____

Document 3

> Women comprise less than 1% of federal judges; less than 4% of all lawyers; 7% of doctors. Yet women represent 51% of the U.S. population. . . . Discrimination in employment on the basis of sex is now prohibited by . . . the Civil Rights Act of 1964. But although nearly one-third of the cases brought before the Equal Employment Opportunity Commission during the first year dealt with sex discrimination, . . . the Commission has not made clear its intention to enforce the law with the same seriousness on behalf of women as of other victims of discrimination. Join us in taking action to work toward these goals:
>
> - Ratification of the Equal Rights Amendment
> - Equal employment opportunities
> - Developmental child care
> - Paid maternity leave
> - Right to control our own reproductive lives
> - Improvement of the image of women in the mass media
>
> —National Organization for Women, 1966

3*a*   Why did the National Organization for Women (NOW) believe it had to continue to support equal opportunities for women after the passage of the Civil Rights Act of 1964?

_____

_____

b   State *one* significant goal of the National Organization for Women.

_____

_____

Document 4

Why is it acceptable for women to be secretaries, librarians and teachers, but totally unacceptable for them to be managers, administrators, doctors, lawyers, and members of Congress? The unspoken assumption is that women are different. They do not have executive ability, orderly minds, stability, leadership skills, and they are too emotional. Prejudice against women is still acceptable. There is very little understanding yet of the immorality involved in double pay scales and the classification of most of the better jobs as "for men only." . . . It is for this reason that I wish to introduce today a proposal that has been before every Congress for the last forty years and that sooner or later must become part of the basic law of the land—the equal rights amendment.

—Congresswoman Shirley Chisholm, 1969

4   Why did Congresswoman Chisholm support the passage of an equal rights amendment?

_____

_____

Document 5

Earnings by Occupation, 1981 Weekly Medians	Women's Pay	Men's Pay
Clerical workers	$220	$328
Computer specialists	355	488
Editors, reporters	324	382
Engineers	371	547
Lawyers	407	574
Nurses	326	344
Physicians	401	495
Sales workers	190	366
Teachers (elementary)	311	379
Waiters	144	200

Source: Time, July 12, 1982

5   Based on this chart, what conclusion can be drawn from comparing the earnings of women with the earnings of men in 1981?

_____

_____

Part B Essay

Directions: Write a well-organized essay that includes an introduction, several paragraphs, and a conclusion.

Use evidence from at least *three* documents to support your response. Support your response with relevant facts, examples, and details. Include additional outside information.

Historical Context: The women's rights movement had all but disappeared after the adoption of the 19th Amendment in 1920. However, in the post–World War II period, women increasingly realized that they continued to face obstacles in achieving equality in American society.

Task: Using information from the documents and your knowledge of United States history and geography, write an essay in which you:

> • Discuss why women were dissatisfied with their roles after World War II
> • Discuss specific attempts by women to achieve equality after World War II

Guidelines: In your essay, be sure to:

- Address all aspects of the *Task* by accurately analyzing and interpreting at least *three* documents
- Incorporate information from the documents in the body of the essay
- Incorporate relevant outside information
- Support the theme with relevant facts, examples, and details
- Use a logical and clear plan of organization
- Introduce the theme by establishing a framework that is beyond a simple restatement of the *Task* or *Historical Context* and conclude with a summation of the theme

STUDENT REVIEW OUTLINE
OF THE CONSTITUTION

You can use the following outline to help you find information in the Constitution or to help you prepare for the Regents Examination in United States History and Government.

Preamble

States the purpose of the Constitution

ARTICLE 1–THE LEGISLATIVE BRANCH

Section 1: Congress Established

Section 2: House of Representatives
Clause 1: Election and Term of Office
Clause 2: Qualifications for the House
Clause 3: Number of Representatives per State (Parts changed by Amendments 13, 14, 16)
Clause 4: Vacancies in the House
Clause 5: Officers for the House; Impeachment

Section 3: Senate
Clause 1: Election of Senators (Parts changed by Amendment 17)
Clause 2: Term of Office; Vacancies (Parts changed by Amendment 17)
Clause 3: Qualifications for the Senate
Clause 4: President of the Senate
Clause 5: Office for the Senate
Clause 6: Impeachment Trials
Clause 7: Impeachment Penalties

Section 4: Congressional Elections and Meetings
Clause 1: State Powers over Elections
Clause 2: Annual Meetings (Changed by Amendment 20)

Section 5: Rules for Conducting Business in Congress
Clause 1: Organization
Clause 2: Rules of Governance
Clause 3: Keeping the *Congressional Record*
Clause 4: Adjournment

Section 6: Privileges and Restrictions of Congress
Clause 1: Pay; Privileges
Clause 2: Restrictions on Employment of Congress

Section 7: Passing Laws
Clause 1: Raising Money
Clause 2: How a Bill Becomes Law
Clause 3: Presidential Veto

Section 8: Enumerated Powers of Congress
Clause 1: Tax; Pay Debts
Clause 2: Borrow Money
Clause 3: Regulate Trade
Clause 4: Regulate Citizenship; Bankruptcies
Clause 5: Regulate Money, Weights and Measures
Clause 6: Punish Counterfeiting
Clause 7: Establish a Postal Service
Clause 8: Issue Copyrights and Patents
Clause 9: Establish Minor Courts
Clause 10: Define and Punish Crimes on the Oceans
Clause 11: Declare War
Clause 12: Create and Support an Army
Clause 13: Create and Support a Navy
Clause 14: Make Rules for the Military
Clause 15: Utilize State Militia
Clause 16: Regulate State Militia
Clause 17: Establish the Federal Capital; Regulate Federal Lands
Clause 18: "Elastic Clause"

Section 9: Powers Denied to the Federal Government
Clause 1: Regulating Slave Trade (Amendment 13 made this invalid)
Clause 2: Issue of a Writ of Habeas Corpus
Clause 3: Bills of Attainder; Ex Post Facto
Clause 4: Creation of Direct Taxes
Clause 5: Taxes on Exports
Clause 6: State Commerce
Clause 7: Spending Money
Clause 8: Titles of Nobility

Section 10: Powers Denied to the States
Clause 1: Treaties; Coining Money; Making Laws that Violate the Federal Constitution
Clause 2: Taxes on Imports and Exports
Clause 3: Declations of War

ARTICLE II–THE EXECUTIVE BRANCH

Section 1: The President and Vice-President
        Clause 1: Term of Office
        Clause 2: Electors
        Clause 3: Election Process (Amendment 12 changed this clause)
        Clause 4: Time of Elections
        Clause 5: Qualifications for President
        Clause 6: Vacancy in Office (Amendment 25 gives further directions)
        Clause 7: Salary for the Executive
        Clause 8: Oath of Office

Section 2: Powers of the President
        Clause 1: Commander in Chief; Appoint Cabinet; Issue Pardons
        Clause 2: Make Treaties; Appoint Certain Officials
        Clause 3: Filling Temporary Vacancies in Government

Section 3: Duties of the President

Section 4: Impeachment of Federal Officers

ARTICLE III–THE JUDICIAL BRANCH

Section 1: Federal Courts
        Clause 1: Supreme Court

Section 2: Jurisdiction of the Federal Courts
        Clause 1: Powers of the Courts
        Clause 2: The Supreme Court
        Clause 3: Trial by Jury

Section 3: Treason
        Clause 1: Definition of Treason
        Clause 2: Punishment for Treason

ARTICLE IV–RELATIONS AMONG THE STATES

Section 1: Official Actions of States

Section 2: Rights of Citizens
Clause 1: Privileges
Clause 2: Extradition
Clause 3: Return of Escaped Slaves (Changed by Amendment 13)

Section 3: Admission of New States and Territories
Clause 1: Admission of New States
Clause 2: Congressional Power over Federal Lands

Section 4: Guarantees and Protection for the States

ARTICLE V–AMENDING THE CONSTITUTION
Proposing Amendments
Ratification of Amendments
Prohibited Amendments (This is no longer valid)

ARTICLE VI–NATIONAL SUPREMACY
Clause 1: Debts Owed Before the Constitution
Clause 2: Constitution is Supreme Law of the Land
Clause 3: Officals Take Oaths of Office

ARTICLE VII–RATIFICATION PROCESS FOR THE CONSTITUTION
Amendment 1–Religious and Political Freedom
Amendment 2–Right to Bear Arms
Amendment 3–Quartering Troops
Amendment 4–Searches and Seizures
Amendment 5–Rights of the Accused
Amendment 6–Right to Speedy and Fair Trial
Amendment 7–Right to Trial by Jury
Amendment 8–Bail and Punishment
Amendment 9–Rights Not Specified
Amendment 10–Powers Reserved to the States
Amendment 11–Suits Against States
Amendment 12–Election of the President and Vice-President

Amendment 13–Abolition of Slavery
Amendment 14–Rights of Citizens
Amendment 15–Right to Vote
Amendment 16–Income Tax
Amendment 17–Direct Election of Senators
Amendment 18–Prohibition
Amendment 19–Women's Right to Vote
Amendment 20–"Lame-Duck" Amendment
Amendment 21–Repeal of Prohibition
Amendment 22–Limit on Presidential Term
Amendment 23–Voting in the District of Columbia
Amendment 24–Abolition of the Poll Tax
Amendment 25–Presidential Disability and Succession
Amendment 26–Eighteen-Year-Old Vote
Amendment 27–Restraint on Congressional Salaries

SUPREME COURT CASE SUMMARIES

Marbury **v.** *Madison* **(1803)** established one of the most important principles of American constitutional law. The Supreme Court held that the Court itself has the final say on what the Constitution means. It is also the Supreme Court that has the final say whether or not an act of government—legislative or executive at the federal, state, or local level—violates the Constitution

McCullough **v.** *Maryland* **(1819)** established the basis for the expansive authority of Congress. The Supreme Court held that the necessary and proper clause (U.S. Const. art. I, sec. 8, cl. 18) allows Congress to do more than the Constitution specifically authorizes it to do. This case holds that Congress can enact almost any law that will help it achieve the ends established by Article I, Section 8 of the Constitution. For example, Congress has the power to regulate interstate commerce; the necessary and proper clause permits Congress to do so in ways not specified in the Constitution.

Gibbons **v.** *Ogden* **(1824)** made it clear that the authority of Congress to regulate interstate commerce (U.S. Const. art. I, sec. 8, cl. 3) includes the authority to regulate intrastate commercial activity that relates to interstate commerce. Before this case, it was thought that the Constitution would allow a state to close its borders to interstate commercial activity. This ruling says that a state can only regulate internal commercial activity, but Congress can regulate commercial activity that has both intrastate and interstate dimensions.

Worcester **v.** *Georgia* **(1832)** overturned the conviction of Samuel A. Worcester, a missionary among the Cherokee. Worcester was imprisoned under a Georgia law forbidding whites to reside in Cherokee country without taking an oath of allegiance to the state and obtaining a permit. The Supreme Court voided the state law, ruling that the Cherokee were an independent nation based on a federal treaty and free from the jurisdiction of the state. Georgia ignored the decision, and President Jackson refused to enforce it, instead supporting the removal of the Cherokee to the Indian Territory.

Dred Scott **v.** *Sanford* **(1857)** was decided before the Fourteenth Amendment. The Fourteenth Amendment provides that anyone born or naturalized in the United Sates is a citizen of the nation and of his or her state. In this case, the Supreme Court held that a slave was property, not a citizen, and thus had no rights under the Constitution. The decision was a prime factor leading to the Civil War.

Civil Rights Cases **(1883)** held that private discrimination does not violate the Thirteenth Amendment's prohibition against slavery and involuntary servitude. Even though the Civil Rights Act of 1875 declared it a crime to deny equal access and enjoyment of public accommodations to "citizens of every race or color," it was determined that the Fourteenth Amendment could not prevent discriminatory actions taken by individuals in the private sector.

Wabash, St. Louis & Pacific R.R. **v.** *Illinois* **(1886)** held that states have no authority to regulate railroad rates for interstate commerce. The Supreme Court held that the commerce clause (U.S. Const. art. I, sec. 8, cl. 3) allowed states to enforce "indirect" but not "direct" burdens on interstate commerce. State railroad rates were ruled "direct" burdens and therefore could not be enforced by states. The decision created a precedent by establishing rate regulation of interstate commerce as an exclusive federal power.

United States v. *E.C. Knight Co.* **(1895)** determined that the states, under the Tenth Amendment, should have the right reserved to them to regulate "local activities" such as manufacturing. The American Sugar Refining Co. purchased stock in smaller companies and eventually controlled 90 percent of the sugar processed in the United States. The ruling determined that the federal government could not regulate the refiners since they were "manufacturing operations" that were not directly related to interstate commerce.

In Re Debs (U.S. v. *Debs)* **(1895)** upheld the authority of the federal government to halt the strike of the Pullman Railroad Car workers after they refused to honor a federal court "injunction" ordering a halt to the strike. The Court reasoned that the federal government "has enumerated powers" found in Article 1, Section 8, "to regulate commerce . . . among the several states," and to establish post offices and post roads. When the strike occurred, it interfered with the railroad's ability to carry commerce and mail, which benefited the needs and "general welfare" of all Americans.

Plessy v. *Ferguson* **(1896)** upheld the "separate but equal" doctrine used by Southern states to perpetuate segregation after the Civil War officially ended law-mandated segregation. The decision upheld a Louisiana law requiring passenger trains to have "equal but separated accommodations for the white and colored races." The Court held that the Fourteenth Amendment's equal protection clause required only equal public facilities for the two races, not equal access. This case was overruled by *Brown* v. *Board of Education* (1954).

Northern Securities Co. v. *United States* **(1904)** dealt with the application of congressional antitrust legislation. The party involved held three-fourths of the stock in two parallel railroad lines. By a narrow 5–4 decision, the Court upheld the application of the Sherman Antitrust Act. The Court ruled that the holding company clearly intended to eliminate competition between the two railroads, violating the constitutional right of Congress to regulate interstate commerce.

Lochner v. *New York* **(1905)** ruled that states did not have the right to infringe upon employer/employee contracts. This case dealt with a New York law that set a limit on how many hours bakery employees could work. The employer in this case was convicted and fined for permitting an employee to work more than the lawful number of hours in one week. The ruling declared that even though states have the power to regulate the areas of health, safety, morals, and public welfare, this New York law was not within the limits of powers of the state.

Muller v. *Oregon* **(1908)** dealt with whether the state of Oregon, through its regulation of women's work hours, violated the "privileges and immunities" clause of the Fourteenth Amendment by forbidding the employment of women for more than ten hours a day in laundries and factories. The Court ruled in favor of the Oregon law and distinguished it from the case of *Lochner* v. *New York*, where an employer's "liberty to contract" outweighed the state's interest to regulate bakery employees' hours, by taking into account in *Muller* the physical differences between men and women.

Schenck v. *United States* **(1919)** upheld convictions under the Federal Espionage Act. The defendants were charged under the act with distributing leaflets aimed at inciting draft resistance during World War I; their defense was that antidraft speech was protected under the First Amendment.

The Supreme Court unanimously rejected the defense, explaining that whether or not speech is protected depends on the context in which it occurs. Because the defendants' antidraft rhetoric created a "clear and present danger" to the success of the war effort, it was not protected.

Schechter Poultry Corporation v. *United States* **(1935)** overturned the conviction of the employers, who were charged with violating the wage and hour limitations of a law adopted under the authority of the National Industrial Recovery Act. The Court held that because the defendants did not sell poultry in interstate commerce, they were not subject to federal regulations on wages and hours.

Korematsu v. *United States* **(1944)** allowed the federal government's authority to exclude Japanese Americans, many of whom were citizens, from designated military areas that included almost the entire West Coast. The government defended the orders as a necessary response to Japan's attack on Pearl Harbor. Yet, in upholding the orders, the Court established that government actions that discriminate on the basis of race would be subject to strict scrutiny.

Brown v. *Board of Education of Topeka* **(1954)** overruled *Plessy* v. *Ferguson* (1896) and abandoned the "separate but equal" doctrine in the context of public schools. In deciding this case, the Supreme Court rejected the idea that equivalent but separate schools for African Americans and white students would be constitutional. The Court stated that the Fourteenth Amendment's command that all persons be accorded the equal protection of the law (U.S. Const. amend XIV, sec. 1) is not satisfied by ensuring that African American and white schools

"have been equalized, or are being equalized, with respect to buildings, curricula, qualifications, and salaries, and other tangible factors."

The Court then held that racial segregation in public schools violates the equal protection clause because it is inherently unequal. In other words, the separation of schools by race marks the separate race as inferior. The ruling in this case has been extended beyond public education to virtually all public accommodations and activities.

Watkins v. *United States* **(1957)** held that, in order to guarantee that people summoned to testify before a congressional committee are treated fairly and are given all their rights, Congress has to specifically spell out its purposes. Watkins was summoned to testify before the House Committee on Un-American Activities, and while he willingly talked about his own socialist activities, he refused to answer questions about other people because he believed they were outside the scope of the committee's activities and not relevant to its work. Such committees are restricted to the areas of investigation delegated to the committees, and no witness can be made to testify on matters outside those areas.

Mapp v. *Ohio* **(1961)** established that evidence seized in violation of the Fourth Amendment could not be used by the prosecution as evidence of a defendant's guilt at the federal, state, or local level.

Baker v. *Carr* **(1962)** established that federal courts can hear suits seeking to force state authorities to redraw electoral districts. In this case, the plaintiff wanted the population of each district to be roughly equal to the population in all other districts. The plaintiff claimed that the votes of voters in the least populous districts counted as much as the votes of voters in the most populous districts.

Engel **v.** *Vitale* **(1962)** held that the establishment clause (U.S. Const. amend. I, cl. 1) was violated by a public school district's practice of starting each school day with a prayer which began, "Almighty God, we acknowledge our dependence upon Thee." The Supreme Court ruled that religion is a personal matter and that government should not align itself with a particular religion in order to prevent religious persecution.

Gideon **v.** *Wainwright* **(1963)** ruled that poor defendants in criminal cases have the right to a state-paid attorney under the Sixth Amendment. The ruling in this case has been refined to apply only when the defendant, if convicted, can be sentenced to more than six months in jail.

Heart of Atlanta Motel **v.** *United States* **(1964)** upheld the Civil Rights Act of 1964, which prohibits racial discrimination by those who provide goods, services, and facilities to the public. The Georgia motel in the case drew its business from other states but refused to rent rooms to African Americans. The Supreme Court explained that Congress had the authority to prohibit such discrimination under both the equal protection clause (U.S. Const. amend. XIV, sec. 1) and the commerce clause (art. I, sec. 8, cl. 3). With respect to the commerce clause, the Court explained that Congress had ample evidence to conclude that racial discrimination by hotels and motels impedes interstate commerce.

Miranda **v.** *Arizona* **(1966)** held that a person in police custody may not be held unless reminded of his or her rights. These rights include: 1) the right to remain silent, 2) the right to an attorney (at government expense if the person is unable to pay), and 3) that anything the person says after acknowledging that he or she understands

these rights can be used as evidence of guilt at a trial.

The Supreme Court explained that a person alone in police custody may not understand, even if told, that he or she can remain silent and thus might be misled into answering questions. The presence of an attorney is essential.

Tinker **v.** *Des Moines* **(1969)** ruled that the suspension of students for wearing black armbands to school as a protest of the Vietnam War was unconstitutional. The wearing of black armbands is an exercise of the right to free, silent, symbolic speech, which is protected under the First Amendment.

New York Times **v.** *United States* **(1971)** held that prior restraints (prohibiting information from being broadcast or published in any form) was almost always forbidden. In this particular case, the Court ruled that publication of the "Pentagon Papers" was not a threat to national security, so the attempted censorship by the government was unconstitutional. However, the Court did leave open the possibility that, under certain strict circumstances, the government could prohibit the publication of information.

Roe **v.** *Wade* **(1973)** held that women have the right under various provisions of the Constitution—most notably, the due process clause of the Fourteenth Amendment—to decide whether or not to terminate a pregnancy. The Court's ruling in this case was the most significant in a long line of decisions over a period of 50 years that recognized a constitutional right of privacy, even though the word *privacy* is not found in the Constitution.

United States **v.** *Nixon* **(1974)** ruled that presidential power is not above the law and that executive power cannot protect evidence that may be used in a criminal trial. Certain tapes and documents of specific meetings held in the White House were subpoenaed after it was found that staff members of President Nixon were connected to a break-in at the Democratic National Headquarters. Nixon's lawyer sought to deny the subpoena, saying that it violated Nixon's constitutional right of executive power.

New Jersey **v.** *TLO* **(1985)** ruled that school officials who have "reasonable suspicion" that a student has done something wrong can conduct a reasonable search of the suspicious student. A school's main objective is to educate students in a legal, safe learning environment, whereas police need a "probable cause" to search people, places and things. Therefore, a student's property under reasonable suspicion that is searched by a school official does not violate the student's right of protection from "unreasonable search, the right of protection from self-incrimination, and the right to due process."

Cruzan **v.** *Director, Missouri Department of Health* **(1990)** ruled that a person has the right to refuse medical treatment under the due process clause of the Fourteenth Amendment, provided the person was

competent and that there was "clear and convincing" evidence that the person did not want artificial support to keep them alive. Without this evidence, a state's obligation to preserve human life overrules the wishes of the patient or parents.

Planned Parenthood of Southeastern Pennsylvania, et. al. **v.** *Casey* **(1992)** reaffirmed a woman's "liberty" to have an abortion as it had in the *Roe* v. *Wade* decision. However, the Court upheld Pennsylvania's abortion control law provisions requiring a 24-hour waiting period prior to the abortion, and that minors seeking an abortion would need consent of at least one parent. The Court ruled that these provisions do not create an "undue burden" or "substantial obstacle" for women seeking an abortion. The only provision to fail was the requirement of married women seeking an abortion to notify their husbands of their intentions to abort the fetus.

Vernonia School District **v.** *Acton* **(1995)** ruled that drug testing of student athletes was constitutional. The Court accepted the argument that student rights were lessened at school if it was necessary to maintain student safety and to fulfill the educational mission of the school.

GLOSSARY/GLOSARIO

A

abolition   the immediate ending of slavery

abolitionist   a person who strongly favors doing away with slavery

affirmative action   an active effort to improve employment or educational opportunities for minorities

Albany Plan of Union   a proposal for the colonies to unite to form a federal government

Alien and Sedition Acts   four laws that included giving the president the right to deport aliens and made criticism of the government a criminal act

alien   person living in a country who is not a citizen of that country

amendment   a change to the Constitution

American Federation of Labor   an organization of trade unions that fought for better wages and working conditions for laborers

American Indian Movement   a militant Native American group, formed in response to the 1968 Indian Civil Rights Act

amnesty   the act of granting a pardon to a large group of people

annexation   incorporating a territory within the domain of a country

appeasement   accepting demands in order to avoid conflict

arbitration   settling a dispute by agreeing to accept the decision of an impartial outsider

armistice   a temporary agreement to end fighting

Articles of Confederation and Perpetual Union   a plan for a loose union of the states under the authority of Congress

abolición   la terminación inmediata de la esclavitud

abolicionista   una persona que está firmemente a favor de la abolición de la esclavitud

acción afirmativa   un esfuerzo activo para mejorar las oportunidades educacionales o de empleo para las minorías

Plan de Unión de Albany   una propuesta para unir a las colonias en un gobierno federal

Actos de Extranjeros y Sedición   cuatro leyes que incluyeron la otorgación al presidente del derecho a deportar extranjeros y definieron la crítica al gobierno como una acción criminal

extranjero   una persona que vive en un país del cual no es ciudadano

enmienda   un cambio a la Constitución

Federación Americana de Sindicatos   una organización de sindicatos que luchó por mejores sueldos y condiciones de trabajo para los obreros

Movimiento de Indios Americanos   un grupo militante de indios americanos, formado en respuesta a la Ley de Derechos Civiles de los Indios de 1968

amnistía   el acto de otorgar perdón a un número grande de personas

anexión   incorporar un territorio dentro del dominio de un país

apaciguamiento   demandas aceptadas a fin de evitar conflictos

arbitraje   arreglar una disputa acordando aceptar la decisión de una persona imparcial

armisticio   acuerdo temporal de paz para terminar con una lucha

Artículos de Confederación y Unión Perpetua   un plan para una unión informal de los estados bajo la autoridad del Congreso

assembly line   a production system with machines and workers arranged so that each person performs an assigned task again and again as the item passes before him or her

assimilation   the act of a group absorbing into the culture of a larger population

Atlantic Charter   an agreement between President Franklin Roosevelt and English Prime Minister Winston Churchill that committed both nations to a postwar world of democracy, free trade, economic advancement, and freedom of the seas

línea de montaje (ensamble)   sistema de producción con máquinas y trabajadores arreglados para que cada persona haga su trabajo designado una y otra vez mientras el artículo pasa frente a ellos

asimilación   la incorporación de un grupo a la cultura de una población más grande

La Carta del Atlántico   un acuerdo entre el Presidente Franklin Roosevelt y el primer ministro inglés Winston Churchill que comprometió a las dos naciones a un mundo de posguerra con democrácia, comercio libre, avances económicos, y libertad marítima

B

baby boom   a marked rise in birthrate, such as occurred in the United States following World War II

bank holiday   during the Depression, the closing of banks before bank runs (massive numbers of people pulling their money out of the banks) could put them out of business

barbed wire   twisted wire with points or sharp projections

Battle of the Bulge   a defining battle of World War II between Germany and the United States

Bay of Pigs   site in Cuba where in 1961 the United States launched a failed plot to overthrow Cuba's Communist government

Berlin Wall   a wall built by the Soviet Union through Berlin to keep Germans from leaving East Germany into West Berlin

auge de nacimientos   aumento marcado en la taza de natalidad, tal como ocurrió en los Estados Unidos después de la Segunda Guerra Mundial

fiesta bancaria   durante la Depresión, el cierre de bancos antes de las corridas de bancos (grandes cantidades de personas tratando de retirar su dinero de los bancos) podían arruinar su negocio

alambre de espina   alambre retorcido con puntas o proyecciones afiladas

Batalla del Bulge   una batalla definitiva de la Segunda Guerra Mundial entre Alemania y los Estados Unidos

Bahía de Cochinos   sitio en Cuba donde los Estados Unidos emprendieron un intento fallido en 1961 para derrocar al gobierno comunista de Cuba

Muro de Berlín   una pared construida por la Unión Soviética a través de Berlin para evitar la salida de los alemanes del este de Alemania al oeste Berlin

big stick diplomacy   President Theodore Roosevelt's strategy that said that the United States would intervene in the affairs of Latin American countries when necessary to maintain economic and political stability in the Western Hemisphere

biotechnology   the managing of biological systems to improve human life

Black Panthers   a militant African American group that preached black power, black nationalism, and economic self-sufficiency

black power   the mobilization of the political and economic power of African Americans, especially to compel respect for their rights and to improve their condition

blitzkrieg   name given to sudden violent offensive attacks the Germans used during World War II; literally "lightning war"

blue-collar   jobs in the manual labor field, particularly those requiring protective clothing

bonds   notes issued by the government which promise to pay off a loan with interest

boycott   to refuse to buy items from a particular country; to refuse to use in order to show disapproval or force acceptance of one's terms

brinkmanship   the willingness to go to the brink of war to force an opponent to back down

__diplomacia de palo grande__   la estrategia del Presidente Theodore Roosevelt que establecía que los Estados Unidos iban a intervenir en los asuntos de los países de Latinoamérica cuando fuera necesario para mantener la estabilidad económica y política en el hemisferio del oeste

__biotecnología__   el manejo de sistemas biológicos para mejorar la vida humana

__panteras Negras__   un grupo militante de afroamericanos que predicaba el poder negro, el nacionalismo negro, y una economía de autosuficiencia

__poder negro__   movilización del poder económico y político de los afroamericanos especialmente para imponer respeto por sus derechos y para mejorar sus condiciones

__guerra relámpago__   término alemán utilizado para ataques ofensivos violentos, "guerra relámpago," una táctica utilizada por los alemanes durante la Segunda Guerra Mundial

__cuello azul__   trabajos de mano de obra, particularmente aquellos que requieren ropa de protección

__bonos__   obligaciones emitidas por el gobierno que prometen pagar un préstamo con interés

__boicot__   rechazo a la compra de artículos a un país específico; rechazo al uso como muestra de esaprobación o la aceptación forzada de términos

__política arriesgada__   la buena voluntad para ir al borde de la guerra para forzar a un oponente a que se retracte

C

cabinet   a group of advisers to the president

Camp David Accords   a historic peace treaty between Israel and Egypt brokered by President Carter in 1978

__gabinete__   grupo de consejeros para el presidente

__Acuerdo del Campo David__   un tratado de paz histórico entre Israel y Egipto llevado a cabo por el Presidente Carter en 1978

capital gains tax a federal tax paid by businesses and investors when they sell stocks or real estate

carpetbaggers name given to many Northerners who moved to the South after the Civil War and supported the Republicans

cash crops crops grown primarily for profit

caucus system a system in which members of a political party meet to choose their party's candidate for president or to decide policy

censure to express formal disapproval of some action

Central Intelligence Agency the government agency that aids American foreign policy by collecting, evaluating, and passing on information about other countries to the president

charter a constitution

checks and balances the system in which each branch of government has the ability to limit the power of the other branches to prevent any from becoming too powerful

Civil Rights Act of 1964 law that made segregation illegal in most public places

closed shop an agreement in which a company agrees to hire only union members

Cold War the ideological and often confrontational conflict between the United States and the Soviet Union between 1946 and 1990

concentration camps camps where persons are detained or confined

Confederacy nation declared to have been formed by the southern states that seceded from the Union in 1860–1861

impuesto sobre las plusvalías un impuesto federal pagado por negocios e inversionistas cuando venden valores o bienes inmuebles

carpetbagger nombre dado a muchos norteños que se mudaron al sur después de la Guerra Civil y apoyaron a los republicanos

cultivo comercial cosecha cultivada para ganancia

sistema de junta electoral sistema en el cual los miembros de un partido político se reúnen para escoger al candidato para la presidencia de su partido o para decidir políticas

censura expresar la desaprobación formal sobre una acción

Agencia Central de Inteligencia la agencia del gobierno en apoyo a la política americana por medio de la obtención, evaluación y transmisión de información de otros países al presidente

carta de privilegio una constitución

restricciones y equilibrios el sistema en el cual cada rama del gobierno tiene el poder para limitar el poder de las otras ramas con el objetivo de prevenir que ninguna de ellas se vuelva demasiado poderosa

Acto de Derechos Civiles de 1964 ley que establece la segregación como ilegal en la mayoría de lugares públicos

taller cerrado acuerdo en el que una compañía contrata solamente a miembros sindicales

Guerra Fría conflicto ideológico caracterizado por frecuentes confrontaciones entre los Estados Unidos y la Unión Soviética entre 1946 y 1990

campos de concentración campamentos donde personas están detenidas o encerradas

Confederación nación formada por los estados sureños que se separaron de la Unión en 1860–1861

conservative   a person who believes government power, particularly in the economy, should be limited in order to maximize individual freedom

containment   the policy or process of preventing the expansion of a hostile power

convoy system   a system in which merchant ships travel with naval vessels for protection

corporation   an organization that is authorized by law to carry on an activity but treated as though it were a single person

cotton gin   a machine that removed seeds from cotton fiber

counterculture   a culture with values and beliefs different than the mainstream

covert   not openly shown or engaged in

credibility gap   lack of trust or believability

conservador   una persona que cree que el poder del gobierno, particularmente en la economía, debe estar limitado para maximizar la libertad individual

contención   la política o proceso para prevenir la expansión de una potencia hostil

sistema de convoy   un sistema en el cual barcos mercantes viajan con buques navales para su protección

sociedad anónima   organización autorizada por la ley a dirigir una actividad, tratada como si fuera una persona moral

despepitadora de algodón   máquina que sacaba las semillas de las fibras de algodón

contracultura   una cultura con valores y creencias diferentes a los de la cultura principal

encubierto   no expuesto o involucrado abiertamente

barrera de credibilidad   falta de confianza

D

D-Day   June 6, 1944, the day that 150,000 American soldiers invaded and gained control of a 60-mile stretch of coast in Normandy, France, marking a major turning point in World War II

de facto segregation   segregation by custom and tradition

Declaration of Independence   document that stated the American colonies were free of British rule and were now the United States of America

Democratic-Republicans   political party formed by supporters of Andrew Jackson

Department of Homeland Security   a counter-terrorism agency formed in response to the terrorist attacks on the United States on September 11, 2001

D-Day   el 6 de junio de 1944, el día que 150,000 soldados americanos invadieron y ganaron el control de 60 millas en la costa de Normandy, Francia, representando un hecho de trascendencia en la Segunda Guerra Mundial

segregación de facto   segregación por costumbre y tradición

Declaración de Independencia   documento que declaró a las colonias americanas libres del mandato británico y las declaraba los Estados Unidos de America

Republicanos-Democráticos   un partido político formado por los partidarios de Andrew Jackson

Departamento de Seguridad al País   una agencia de contraterrorismo formada en respuesta a los ataques terroristas en los Estados Unidos el 11 de septiembre del 2001

department store   a store selling a wide variety of goods organized into departments

détente   a policy which attempts to relax or ease tensions between nations

developing nations   nations whose economies are primarily agricultural

direct primary   a vote held by all members of a political party to decide their candidate for public office

disenfranchised   deprived of the right to vote

"Do-Nothing Congress"   the name President Truman gave to the Republican Congress

dollar diplomacy   a policy of joining the business interests of a country with its diplomatic interests abroad

domino theory   the belief that if one nation in Asia fell to the Communists, neighboring countries would follow

doves   people in favor of the United States withdrawing from the Vietnam War

Dred Scott decision   stated that slaves are property and, even if they reside in a free territory or state, they must be returned to their owners

dry farming   a way of farming dry land in which seeds are planted deep in the ground where there is some moisture

due process   the idea that the law may not treat individuals unfairly or unreasonable and that courts must follow proper procedures when trying cases

Dust Bowl   name given to the area of the southern Great Plains severely damaged by droughts and dust storms during the 1930s

duty   a tax on imports

grandes almacenes   una tienda que vende una gran variedad de mercancías organizada por departamentos

relajación   una política que intenta relajar o borrar la tensión entre naciones

naciones en desarrollo   naciones en donde la economía es principalmente agrícola

elección primaria   voto hecho por todos los miembros de un partido político para elegir a su candidato para un puesto público

privación civil   privar el derecho al voto

"Congreso de No Hacer Nada"   el nombre que el Presidente Truman le dio al Congreso Republicano

diplomacia del dólar   política para unir los intereses comerciales de un país con sus intereses diplomáticos en el extranjero

teoría domino   la creencia de que si una nación en Asia se doblegaba a los comunistas, sus países vecinos lo harían en seguida

paloma   persona a favor de que los Estados Unidos se retiraran de la guerra en Vietnam

La decisión de Dred Scott   declaró que los esclavos son posesiones y, aunque residan en un territorio o estado libre, deben ser devueltos a sus dueños

cultivo seco   manera de cultivar tierra seca plantando las semillas en la profundidad de la tierra donde hay algo de humedad

proceso justo   requerimiento judicial de que las leyes no deben tratar a los individuos injustamente, arbitrariamente, o irracionalmente y que las cortes deben seguir los procesos y reglamentos justos al someter casos a juicio

Cuenca Polvorosa   nombre dado al área sureña de las Grandes Planicies severamente dañada por sequías y tormentas de arena durante los años de 1930

impuesto   un impuesto sobre importaciones

E

economies of scale the reduction in the cost of a good brought about especially by increased production at a given facility

emancipation the act or process of freeing enslaved persons

Emancipation Proclamation a decree freeing all enslaved persons in states still in rebellion after January 1, 1863

embargo a government ban on trade with other countries

Enlightenment a movement during the 1700s that promoted science, knowledge, and reason

entrepreneur one who organizes, manages, and assumes the risks of a business or enterprise

enumerated powers powers listed in the Constitution as belonging to the federal government

Era of Good Feelings phrase used to describe James Monroe's presidency because of the harmony in national politics

ethnic cleansing the expulsion, imprisonment, or killing of ethnic minorities by a dominant majority group

euro the basic currency shared by the countries of the European Union since 1999

evolution the scientific theory that humans and other forms of life have evolved over time

executive branch the branch of government that implements and enforces laws

executive privilege principle stating that communications of the executive branch should remain confidential to protect national security

economía a gran escala reducción del costo de un producto a causa de la producción por mayoreo en una fábrica de producción

emancipación el proceso de liberar a personas esclavizadas

Proclamación de Emancipación un decreto que liberaba a todos los esclavos en los estados que aun estaban en rebelión después del primero de enero de 1863

embargo prohibición gubernamental contra el comercio con otros países

Renacimiento movimiento durante el siglo XVII que promovió la ciencia, el conocimiento y el razonamiento

empresario persona que organiza, dirige y asume el riesgo de un negocio o empresa

poderes enumerados poderes enlistados en la Constitución que pertenecen solamente al gobierno federal

Era de Buenos Sentimientos frase utilizada para describir la presidencia de James Monroe en la cual hubo una armonía en la política nacional

purificación étnica expulsión, encarcelamiento o asesinato de minorías étnicas por un grupo mayoritario dominante

Euro moneda básica compartida por los países de la Unión Europea desde 1999

evolución teoría científica de que los humanos y otras formas de vida han evolucionado a través del tiempo

rama ejecutiva rama del gobierno que implementa y hace cumplir las leyes

privilegio ejecutivo el principio de que las comunicaciones de la rama ejecutiva deben permanecer confidenciales para proteger la seguridad nacional

F

"Fifty-four Forty or Fight"   slogan used to support the acquisition of Oregon to the line of 54° 40' north latitude

54th Massachusetts   the first African American regiment officially organized in the North

Fair Deal   the name given to President Truman's programs

fallout   radioactive particles dispersed by a nuclear explosion

fascism   a political philosophy, movement, or regime that exalts nation and race above the individual and stands for a centralized autocratic government headed by a dictatorial leader, severe economic and social regimentation and forcible suppression of opposition

federalism   political system in which power is divided between the national and state governments

feminism   the belief that men and women should be equal politically, economically, and socially

Fifteenth Amendment   prohibits government from denying a person's right to vote on the basis of race

foreclose   to take possession of a property from a mortgagor because of defaults on payments

fossil fuels   fuels formed in the earth from decayed plant or animal remains

Fourteen Points   the peace plan to end World War I and restructure the countries of Europe, proposed by Woodrow Wilson

"Cincuenta y Cuatro o Lucha"   eslogan usado para apoyar la adquisición de Oregon hasta la línea 54° 40' de latitud norte

El Cincuentavo cuarto de Massachussets   el primer regimiento afroamericano oficialmente organizado en el Norte

Convenio Justo   el nombre dado a los programas del Presidente Truman

caída radioactiva   partículas radioactivas dispersadas por una explosión nuclear

fascismo   una filosofía política, un movimiento o régimen que exalta a la nación y a la raza por encima del individuo y es representado por un gobierno autocrático centralizado con un líder dictatorial, organización económica y social muy rígida y represión de la oposición

federalismo   sistema político en el cual el poder está dividido entre los estados y el gobierno federal

feminismo   la creencia de que los hombres y las mujeres deben ser iguales política, económica y socialmente

Enmienda Decimoquinta   prohíbe que el gobierno niegue el derecho al voto a una persona por causa racial

ejecutar una hipoteca   tomar posesión de una propiedad por falta de pagos hipotecarios

combustible fósil   combustibles formados en la tierra de plantas en descomposición o restos de animales

Los Catorce Puntos   el plan de paz para terminar la Primera Guerra Mundial y reconstruir los países de Europa, propuesto por Woodrow Wilson

Fourteenth Amendment   originally intended to protect the legal rights of freed slaves, its interpretation has been extended to protect the rights of citizenship in general by prohibiting a state from depriving any person of life, liberty, or property without "due process of law"

Enmienda Decimocuarta   originalmente destinada a proteger los derechos legales de los esclavos libres, su interpretación se ha extendido para proteger los derechos de la ciudadanía en general con la prohibición al estado de privar a cualquier persona de la vida, la libertad o la propiedad sin "el debido procedimiento de la ley"

Freedom Riders   name given to a group of people who traveled to the South in 1961 to protest the South's refusal to integrate bus terminals

Jinetes de la Libertad   nombre dado a un grupo de personas que viajaron al sur en 1961 para protestar la negativa del sur para integrar las estaciones de autobuses

Free Soil Party   a political party that opposed the spread of slavery in the western territories

El Partido de la Tierra Libre   un partido político que se opuso a la propagación de la esclavitud en los territorios occidentales

Fugitive Slave Act   law that required citizens to help catch runaway slaves

Acto de Esclavos Fugitivos   ley que requería que los ciudadanos ayudaran a capturar esclavos que habían escapado

fundamentalism   a movement emphasizing the literal interpretation of the Bible

fundamentalismo   un movimiento que hacia hincapié en la interpretación literal de la Biblia

G

GI Bill   a bill that provided loans to veterans to help them start businesses, buy homes, and attend college

Proyecto de Ley GI   un acto que proporcionó prestamos a los veteranos para ayudarlos a comenzar negocios, comprar casas y asistir a la universidad

glasnost   Russian term for a new "openness," part of Mikhail Gorbachev's reform plans

glasnost   término ruso para una nueva "apertura"; parte de los planes de reforma de Mikhail Gorbachev

graft   the acquisition of money in dishonest ways, as in bribing a politician

soborno   adquisición de dinero de manera deshonesta tal como el sobornar a un político

grandfather clause   a clause that allowed individuals who did not pass the literacy test to vote if their fathers or grandfathers had voted before Reconstruction began; an exception to a law based on preexisting circumstances

cláusula del abuelo   cláusula que permitió votar a los que no aprobaron el examen de lectura-escritura si sus padres o sus abuelos habían votado antes de que empezara la Reconstrucción; excepción a una ley basada en circunstancias preexistentes

Great Compromise   a compromise that solved the problem of representation in Congress

Gran Compromiso   un compromiso que resolvióel problema de representación en el Congreso

Great Migration   the emigration of thousands of people from England

Gran Migración   la emigración de miles de personas de Inglaterra

Great Society   the domestic programs and goals of President Lyndon Johnson's administration

Gran Sociedad   los programas domésticos y los objetivos de la administración del Presidente Lyndon Johnson

greenback   a piece of U.S. paper money first issued by the North during the Civil War

billete dorso verde   billete de papel moneda de EEUU expedido por primera vez en el norte durante la Guerra Civil

guerillas   members of an armed band that carries out surprise attacks and sabotage rather than open warfare

guerrillas   banda armada que lleva a cabo ataques sorpresa y sabotaje en vez de guerra organizada

Gulf of Tonkin Resolution   a Congressional resolution that allowed President Johnson to use force to defend American troops in Vietnam

Resolución del Golfo de Tonkin   una resolución del Congreso que permitió al Presidente Johnson usar la fuerza para defender las tropas americanas en Vietnam

H

habeas corpus   a legal order for an inquiry to determine whether a person has been lawfully imprisoned

habeas corpus   orden legal para una investigación para determinar si una persona ha sido encarcelada legalmente

hawk   a person who believed the United States should continue its military efforts in Vietnam

halcón   persona que creía que los Estados Unidos debían continuar sus esfuerzos militares en Vietnam

Helsinki Accords   agreement signed in 1975 between the United States and leaders of NATO and the Warsaw Pact

Acuerdos de Helsinki   acuerdo firmado en 1975 entre los Estados Unidos y los líderes de la OTAN y el Pacto de Varsovia

Holocaust   the mass killings of 6 million Jews by Germany's Nazi leaders during World War II

Holocausto   el asesinato masivo de 6 millones de judíos por los líderes Nazi de Alemania durante la Segunda Guerra Mundial

I

immigration   movement of people from one country into another country

inmigración   el movimiento de gente de un país a otro

impeach   to formally charge a public official with misconduct in office

acusar   acusar formalmente a un oficial público por mala conducta en el cargo

imperialism   the actions used by one nation to exercise political or economic control over a smaller or weaker nation

imperialismo   acciones usadas por una nación para ejercer el control político o económico sobre naciones más pequeñas o más débiles

implied powers powers not specifically listed in the Constitution but claimed by the federal government

indentured servants individuals who contract to work for a colonist for a specified number of years in exchange for transportation to the colonies, food, clothing, and shelter

Indian Removal Act law that provided money to relocate Native Americans

individualism a belief that the interests of the individual are or should be of primary importance

industrialization the change from an agrarian (agricultural) society to one based on industry

Industrial Revolution the change from an agrarian society to one based on industry which began in Great Britain and spread to the United States around 1800

inflation the loss of the value of money

initiative a measure or issue put on the ballot by citizens for the approval of the voters or the legislature

interchangeable parts uniform pieces that can be made in large quantities to replace other identical pieces

internationalism a national policy of actively trading with foreign countries to foster peace and prosperity

Interstate Commerce Commission a commission created to regulate interstate trade

Iran-Contra scandal during the Reagan administration, deals made to exchange arms for hostages

iron curtain the political and military barrier that isolated Soviet-controlled countries of Eastern Europe after World War II

isolationism a national policy of avoiding involvement in world affairs

poderes implícitos poderes no enlistados específicamente en la Constitución pero reclamados por el gobierno federal

sirviente contratado individuo contratado para trabajar para un colono durante un cierto número de años a cambio de transportación a las colonias, alimento, ropa y refugio

Decreto de Traslado de Indios ley que proporcionó fondos para reubicar a los indios americanos

individualismo la creencia de que los intereses del individuo son o beben de ser de importancia primaria

industrialización el cambio de una sociedad agraria a una industrial

Revolución Industrial el cambio de una sociedad agraria a una industrial que comenzó en Gran Bretaña y se extendió a los Estados Unidos alrededor de 1800

inflación pérdida del valor del dinero

iniciativa una propuesta o asunto que los ciudadanos ponen a votación ante los votantes o el cuerpo legislativo para su aprobación

partes intercambiables piezas uniformes que pueden ser hechas en grandes cantidades para reemplazar otras piezas idénticas

internacionalismo política nacional de intercambio comercial activo con países extranjeros para promover la paz y la prosperidad

Comisión de Comercio Entre Estados una comisión creada para regular el comercio entre los estados

Escándalo de Irán-Contra durante la administración de Reagan, acuerdos hechos para intercambiar armas por rehenes

cortina de hierro barrera política y militar que aisló a los países de Europa Oriental controlados por los soviéticos después de la Segunda Guerra Mundial

aislacionismo política nacional para evitar el involucramiento en asuntos mundiales

J

jingoism extreme nationalism marked by an aggressive foreign policy

judicial branch the branch of government that interprets laws and renders judgment in cases involving those laws

judicial review power of the Supreme Court to determine whether laws of Congress are constitutional and to strike down those that are not

patriotismo nacionalismo extremo marcado por una política agresiva extranjera

rama judicial rama del gobierno que interpreta las leyes y administra juicios en casos que involucren esas leyes

revisión judicial derecho de la Corte Suprema para determinar si las leyes del Congreso son constitucionales y para anular aquellas que no lo son

K

kamikaze during World War II, a Japanese suicide pilot whose mission was to crash into his target

Kansas-Nebraska Act bill proposed by Stephen Douglas to allow popular sovereignty in the territories of Kansas and Nebraska, thereby repealing the Missouri Compromise

Know-Nothings an anti-Catholic and nativist political party

Ku Klux Klan an organization founded in the South during Reconstruction to threaten former slaves and keep them from voting; the group reemerged in the early 1900s to promote white supremacy

Kyoto Protocol an anti-pollution pact signed by 38 nations and the European Union in 1997 in response to global warming

kamikaze durante la Segunda Guerra Mundial un piloto suicida japonés cuya misión era estrellarse contra su objetivo

Decreto de Kansas-Nebraska una ley propuesta por Stephen Douglas para permitir la soberanía en los territorios de Kansas y Nebraska, revocando por lo tanto el Compromiso de Missouri

Saben Nada un partido político anticatólico y nativista

Ku Klux Klan una organización fundada en el sur durante la Reconstrucción para amenazar a los que anteriormente eran esclavos e impedirles que votaran; el grupo resurgió en los primeros años del siglo XIX para promover la supremacía blanca

Protocolo de Kioto un pacto anticontaminación firmado por 38 naciones y la Unión Europea en 1997 en respuesta al calentamiento global

L

laissez-faire literally, "let [people] do [what they want]," the concept that the state should not impose government regulations but should leave the economy alone

laissez-faire literalmente, "dejar [a las personas] hacer [lo que quieran]," el concepto de que el estado no debe imponer regulaciones gubernamentales si no que debe dejar a la economía libre

League of Nations   an association of nations to preserve peace and resolve international disputes proposed in Wilson's Fourteen Points

legislative branch   the branch of government that makes the nation's laws

Lend-Lease Act   legislation enacted in 1940 allowing the United States to lend or lease arms to any country vital to the defense of the U.S.

liberal   a person who generally believes the government should take an active role in the economy and in social programs but should not dictate social behavior

Liberty ships   basic cargo ships used by the United States during World War II

limited war   a war fought with a limited commitment of resources to achieve a limited objective, such as containing communism

literacy test   a method used to prevent African Americans from voting by requiring prospective voters to read and write at a specified level

long drive   driving cattle long distances to a railroad depot for fast transport and great profit

Louisiana Purchase   the land purchased from France in 1803 that more than doubled the size of the United States and gained U.S. control of the entire Mississippi River

loyalty review program   1947 program to screen federal employees in order to find communists who may have infiltrated the government

Liga de Naciones   una asociación de naciones para conservar la paz y resolver disputas internacionales propuesta en los Catorce Puntos de Wilson

rama legislativa   rama del gobierno que hace las leyes de una nación

Ley de Préstamo y Arrendamiento   legislación promulgada en 1940 permitiendo a los Estados Unidos prestar o arrendar armas a cualquier país vital para la defensa de los Estados Unidos

liberal   persona que generalmente cree que el gobierno debe desempeñar un papel activo en la economía y programas sociales pero que no debe dictar el comportamiento social

barco de Libertad   barco de carga básica utilizado por los Estados Unidos durante la Segunda Guerra Mundial

guerra limitada   guerra peleada con un compromiso limitado de recursos para alcanzar un objetivo limitado, tal como la contención del comunismo

prueba de alfabetización   un método utilizado para impedir a los afroamericanos que votaran con el requisito de que los votantes potenciales leyeran y escribieran a un nivel especifico

viaje largo   conducción de ganado por grandes distancias a estaciones de ferrocarril para una transportación rápida y grandes ganancias

Compra de Louisiana   la tierra que se compró a Francia en 1803 que duplico y más el tamaño de los Estados Unidos y ganó el control de todo el río Mississippi

programa para revisar la fidelidad   el programa de 1947 para investigar a empleados federales con el propósito de encontrar comunistas que se hubieran infiltrado en el gobierno

M

Manhattan Project   the American project to build an atomic bomb

Proyecto Manhattan   el proyecto americano para construir una bomba atómica

Manifest Destiny   the idea popular in the United States during the 1800s that the country must expand its boundaries to the Pacific Ocean

Destino Manifiesto   idea popular en los Estados Unidos durante el siglo XVIII que el país debe expandir sus fronteras hasta el Océano Pacífico

margin   buying a stock by paying only a fraction of the stock price and borrowing the rest

margen   comprar acciones pagando solamente una fracción del precio y pidiendo prestado el resto

Marshall Plan   post-World War II plan to give European nations American aid to help rebuild their economies

El Plan Marshall   un plan después de la Segunda Guerra Mundial para otorgar ayuda americana a las naciones europeas para reconstruir sus economías

mass production   the production of large quantities of goods using machinery and often an assembly line

fabricación en serie   producción de grandes cantidades de productos usando máquinas y a menudo una línea de montaje

massive retaliation   a policy of threatening a massive response, including the use of nuclear weapons, against a Communist state trying to seize a peaceful state by force

represalia masiva   una política que amenaza una respuesta masiva, incluyendo el uso de armas nucleares, contra un estado comunista que trate de tomar un país pacífico por la fuerza

McCarthyism   anti-Communist tactics of Senator Joseph McCarthy of damaging reputations with vague and unfounded charges in the 1950s

McCarthyism   tácticas anticomunistas del senador Joseph McCarthy para dañar reputaciones con cargos vagos e infundados durante los años de 1950

military-industrial complex   an informal relationship that some people believe exists between the military and the defense industry to promote greater military spending and influence government policy

complejo militar-industrial   relación informal que algunas personas creen que existe entre el ejercito y la industria de la defensa para promover mayores gastos militares y para influenciar la política gubernamental

Missouri Compromise   the agreement for admitting Maine to the Union as a free state and Missouri as a slave state

Compromiso de Missouri   el acuerdo que admite a Maine a la Unión como un estado libre y a Missouri como un estado de esclavitud

monopoly   total control of a type of industry by one person or one company

monopolio   control total de una industria por una persona o una compañía

Moral Majority   a political label applied to people with conservative values in the late 1970s

Mayoría Moral   una etiqueta política aplicada a las personas con valores conservadores en los últimos años de 1970

N

NAACP   the National Association for the Advancement of Colored People

National Organization for Women   the national women's organization started in the mid-1960s

nativism   the belief that those born in a given country are superior to immigrants

natural rights   rights with which all humans are supposedly born, including the rights to life, liberty, and property

New Deal   the name given to the new laws aimed at relieving the Depression, which were passed by Congress during the Hundred Days and the months that followed

New Frontier   President Kennedy's domestic programs

New Jersey Plan   the plan of government developed by the New Jersey delegates to the Constitutional Convention

Nineteenth Amendment   guaranteed women the right to vote

normalcy   the state or fact of being normal

North American Free Trade Agreement the agreement that joined Canada, the United States, and Mexico in a free-trade zone

NATO (North Atlantic Treaty Organization)   an international organization created in 1949 by the North Atlantic Treaty for purposes of collective security

Northwest Ordinance   the law that provided the basis for governing much of the western territory

nullification   the theory that states have the right to declare a federal law invalid

Nuremberg Laws   1935 laws that deprived German Jews of many rights of citizenship

ANAGC   la Asociación Nacional para el Avance de la Gente de Color

Organización Nacional de Mujeres   la organización nacional que empezó a mediados de 1960

nativismo   creencia de que aquellos que nacen en cierto país son superiores a los inmigrantes

derechos naturales   derechos con los que todos los humanos supuestamente nacen, incluyendo el derecho a la vida, la libertad y la propiedad

Nuevo Acuerdo   el nombre dado a las nuevas leyes dirigidas al alivio de la Depresión, que se aprobaron por el Congreso durante los Cien Días y los meses que siguieron

Frontera Nueva   los programas domésticos del Presidente Kennedy

Plan de Nueva Jersey   el plan del gobierno desarrollado por los delegados de Nueva Jersey para la Convención Constitucional

Enmienda Decimonovena   garantizó el derecho al voto a las mujeres

normalidad   estado o hecho de ser normal

Tratado de Libre Comercio   el acuerdo que unió a Canadá, los Estados Unidos y México en una zona de comercio libre

OTAN   una organización internacional creada en 1949 por el Tratado del Atlántico Norte para seguridad colectiva

Ordenanza Noroeste   la ley que estableció la base para el gobierno de mucho del territorio del oeste

anulación   teoría que los estados tienen el derecho de declarar como nula una ley federal

Leyes de Nuremberg   leyes de 1935 que privaron a los judíos de Alemania de muchos de sus derechos como ciudadanos

O

Open Door policy   a policy that allowed each foreign nation in China to trade freely in the other nations' spheres of influence

política de Puertas Abiertas   política que permitió a cada nación extranjera en China intercambiar libremente en las esferas de influencia de otras naciones

open range   vast areas of grassland owned by the federal government

terreno abierto   gran extensión de pastos propiedad del gobierno federal

P

patronage   another name for the spoils system, in which government jobs or favors are given out to political allies and friends

patronazgo   otro nombre para el sistema político en el cual puestos y favores gubernamentales son dados a aliados políticos y amigos

Peace Corps   an organization that sent young Americans to perform humanitarian services in less developed nations

organización gubernamental estadounidense una organización que envía jóvenes americanos a realizar servicios humanitarios en países subdesarrollados

Pendleton Act   a law which set up a system for filling government jobs based on passing an examination

Acto de Pendleton   una ley que establece un sistema para cubrir puestos gubernamentales por medio de un examen

perjury   lying when one has sworn under oath to tell the truth

perjurio   mentir bajo juramento

philanthropy   providing money to support humanitarian or social goals

filantropía   proporcionar dinero para apoyar objetivos humanitarios o sociales

plantations   large, commercial, agricultural estates

plantaciones   haciendas comerciales y agrícolas muy grandes

police powers   a government's power to control people and property in the interest of public safety, health, welfare, and morals

fuerza policía   poder gubernamental para controlar a personas y propiedades para la seguridad, salud, bienestar, y moralidad públicas

political machine   an organization linked to a political party that often controlled local government

maquinaria política   organización aliada a un partido político que a menudo controlaba al gobierno local

poll tax   a tax of a fixed amount per person that had to be paid before the person could vote

impuesto de capitación   impuesto de cantidad fija por persona, el cual tenía que ser pagado antes de que una persona pudiera votar

pool groups sharing in some activity; for example, among railroad owners who made secret agreements and set rates among themselves

popular sovereignty government subject to the will of the people; before the Civil War, the idea that people living in a territory had the right to decide by voting if slavery would be allowed there

populism political movement founded in the 1890s representing mainly farmers, favoring free coinage of silver and government control of railroads and other large industries

poverty line a level of personal or family income below which one is classified as poor by the federal government

prairie an inland grassland area

presidio a fort built by the Spanish in the Americas

prohibition laws banning the manufacture, transportation, and sale of alcoholic beverages

propaganda the spreading of ideas about an institution or individual for the purpose of influencing opinion

protective tariff tax on imports designed to protect American manufacturers

protectorate a country that is technically independent but is actually under the control of another country

public works projects such as highways, parks, and libraries built with public funds for public use

Puritans people who wanted to purify the Anglican Church during the 1500s and 1600s

consorcio grupo que comparte una actividad; por ejemplo, dueños de ferrocarril que hacían acuerdos secretos y fijaban tarifas fijas entre ellos

soberanía popular teoría política de que el gobierno está sujeto a la voluntad del pueblo; antes de la Guerra Civil, la idea de que la gente que vivía en un territorio tenía el derecho de decidir por medio del voto si ahí sería permitida la esclavitud

populismo movimiento político fundado en los años de 1890 representando principalmente a los granjeros que favorecía la libre acuñación de plata y el control gubernamental de ferrocarriles y otras grandes industrias

línea de pobreza nivel de ingreso individual o familiar bajo del cual uno es clasificado por el gobierno federal como pobre

pradera pastizal tierra adentro

presidio fuerte construido por los españoles en las Américas

prohibición leyes que prohibían la manufactura, transportación y venta de bebidas alcohólicas

propaganda diseminación de ideas sobre una institución o individuo con el propósito de influenciar la opinión

arancel protector impuesto a importaciones creado para proteger a los manufactureros americanos

protectorado país que es técnicamente independiente pero que en realidad está bajo el control de otro país

obras públicas proyectos como carreteras, parques y bibliotecas construidos con fondos públicos para el uso público

puritano persona que quería purificar la Iglesia Anglicana en los siglos XV y XVI

R

rationing the giving out of scarce items on a limited basis

Reaganomics name given to President Reagan's economic policies by critics

realism an approach to literature, art, and theater that attempts to accurately portray things as they really are and holds that society will function best if left to itself

reapportionment the method states use to draw up political districts based on changes in population

recall the right that enables voters to remove unsatisfactory elected officials from office

referendum the practice of letting voters accept or reject measures proposed by the legislature

relief aid for the needy; welfare

reparations payment by the losing country in a war to the winner for the damages caused by the war

republic form of government in which power resides in a body of citizens entitled to vote

Republican Party a political party formed in 1854 as an antislavery party

revenue tariffs taxes on imports for the purpose of raising money

right-to-work laws laws making it illegal to require employees to join a union

racionamiento proporcionar escasos artículos de manera limitada

Reagonomics nombre dado a las políticas económicas del Presidente Reagan por sus críticos

realismo perspectiva de literatura, arte, y teatro que intenta representar las cosas tal como son y que mantiene que la sociedad funcionará mejor si la dejan como tal

nueva repartición método usado por los estados para formar distritos políticos considerando los cambios de población

elección de revocación derecho que permite a los votantes quitar del cargo a los oficiales elegidos por ser inadecuados

referéndum práctica de permitir a los votantes aceptar o rechazar medidas propuestas por el cuerpo legislativo

asistencia pública ayuda para los necesitados; beneficencia

indemnización pago hecho por el país perdedor de una guerra al país ganador por los daños causados en la guerra

república forma de gobierno en el cual el poder reside en un cuerpo de ciudadanos con derecho al voto

Partido Republicano un partido político formado en 1854 como un partido contra la esclavitud

arancel de ingresos impuesto a las importaciones con el propósito de recaudar dinero

derecho a trabajar ley que hace ilegal la exigencia a los trabajadores de afiliarse a un sindicato

S

satellite nations   the Communist countries of Eastern Europe

scalawags   name given to Southerners who supported Republican Reconstruction of the South

secede   to leave or withdraw

secession   withdrawal from the Union

Second Great Awakening   a movement in the early 1800s to revive Americans' commitment to religion

sedition   incitement to rebellion

self-determination   belief that people in a territory should have the ability to choose their own government

separate but equal   doctrine established by the 1896 Supreme Court case *Plessy* v. *Ferguson* that permitted laws segregating African Americans as long as equal facilities were provided

separation of powers   government principle in which power is divided among different branches

shantytown   an economically depressed section of town consisting of crudely built dwellings usually made of wood

sharecropping   farmer who works land for an owner who provides equipment and seed and receives a share of the crop

skyscraper   a very tall building

slave codes   a set of laws that formally regulated slavery and defined the relationship between enslaved Africans and free people

naciones satélite   los países comunistas de Europa del este

scalawags   nombre dado a los sureños que apoyaron la Reconstrucción republicana del sur

separarse   abandonar o retirar

secesión   separación de la Unión

El Segundo Gran Despertar   un movimiento a los principios del siglo XVIII para restablecer el compromiso de los americanos a la religión

sedición   incitación a la rebelión

autodeterminación   creencia de que las personas en un territorio deberían tener la habilidad para escoger su propio gobierno

separados pero iguales   doctrina establecida por la Corte Suprema en el caso *Plessy contra Ferguson* en 1896 cuyas leyes permitían la segregación de los afroamericanos siempre y cuando se les proveyeran las mismas facilidades

separación de poderes   principio de gobierno en el cual el poder está dividido en diferentes ramas

villa miseria   barrio pobre de un pueblo que consiste de viviendas mal construidas, normalmente hechas de madera

aparcero   agricultor que labra la tierra para un dueño que proporciona el equipo y las semillas y recibe una porción de la cosecha

rascacielos   edificio de gran altura

código de esclavos   leyes aprobadas que regularon formalmente la esclavitud y definieron la relación entre los africanos esclavizados y la gente libre

Social Darwinism the theory that social progress came from "the struggle for survival" as the "fit"—the strong—advanced while the weak declined; often used by extremists to justify imperialism and racism

darvinismo social la teoría que explicaba que el progreso social venia de la "lucha por la sobrevivencia" ya que los sanos—los más fuertes—avanzaban mientras los más débiles descendían; muchas veces se usó por los extremistas para justificar el imperialismo y el racismo

Social Security Act a law requiring workers and employers to pay a tax; the money provides a monthly stipend for retired people

Ley del Seguro Social ley que requiere que los trabajadores y empleados paguen un impuesto; el dinero proporciona un ingreso mensual para la gente jubilada

space race refers to the Cold War competition over dominance of space exploration capability

carrera espacial se refiere a la competencia durante la Guerra Fría por el dominio de la exploración espacial

speculation act of buying stocks at great risk with the anticipation that the price will rise

especulación compra de acciones de alto riesgo con la esperanza de que los precios suban

speculators people who risk money in hopes of a financial profit

especulador persona que arriesga dinero con la esperanza de obtener un ganancia financiera

sphere of influence section of a country where one foreign nation enjoys special rights and powers

esfera de influencia sección de un país donde una nación extranjera tiene derechos y poderes especiales

spoils system practice of handing out government jobs to supporters; replacing government employees with the winning candidate's supporters

sistema de despojos práctica de dar puestos gubernamentales a los partidarios; reemplazando a los empleados del gobierno con los partidarios del candidato victorioso

Sputnik name of the first artificial satellite to orbit the earth, launched by the Soviet Union in 1957

Spútnik nombre del primer satélite artificial que orbitó la tierra, lanzado por la Unión Soviética en 1957

Square Deal Theodore Roosevelt's promise of fair and equal treatment for all

Trato Justo promesa de Theodore Roosevelt para un trato justo e igualitario para todos

steppe wide, grassy plains of Eurasia; also, similar semi-arid climate regions elsewhere

estepa vastas llanuras de pastizales de Eurasia; también regiones en otros lugares con climas semiáridos similares

stock market a system for buying and selling stocks in corporations

bolsa de valores sistema para comprar y vender acciones de corporaciones

Strategic Arms Limitation Treaty treaty signed by the United States and the Soviet Union in 1972 to limit nuclear arms

Tratado de Limitación de Armas Estratégicas tratado firmado por los Estados Unidos y la Unión Soviética en 1972 para limitar armas nuclear

subsistence farming   farming only enough food to feed one's family

suffrage   the right to vote

Sunbelt   mild climate region, southern United States

agricultura de subsistencia   labranza que solo produce la cosecha que se necesita para alimentar a la familia de uno

sufragio   derecho al voto

Franja del Sol   parte sur de los Estados Unidos, denominada así debido a su clima

T

Taft-Hartley Act   the 1947 bill that limited the actions workers could take against their employers

tariff   a tax on imports or exports

Tariff of Abominations   tariff of 1828 that made imports extremely expensive

temperance   moderation in or abstinence from alcohol

tenement   multi-family apartments, usually dark, crowded, and barely meeting minimum living standards

Tet offensive   a surprise attack in January 1968, by the Vietcong and the North Vietnamese of all American airbases in south Vietnam and most of the nation's major cities

Thirteenth Amendment   outlaws slavery

Three-Fifths Compromise   a compromise that solved the problem of how enslaved people were to be counted in determining representation in Congress

time zones   geographical regions in which the same standard time is kept

Acto de Taft-Hartley   el acto de 1947 que limitó las acciones que los trabajadores podían tomar contra sus patrones

arancel   un impuesto a importaciones y exportaciones

Arancel de Abominaciones   arancel de 1828 que provoco que las importaciones fueran muy caras

templanza   moderación o abstinencia del uso del alcohol

casa de vecindad   apartamentos para varias familias, normalmente oscuros, apretados que apenas cumplen con los estándares mínimos de la vivienda

Ofensiva de Tet   un ataque sorpresa en enero de 1968 por los Vietcong y los vietnamitas del norte a todos los campos de aviación en el sur de Vietnam y a la mayor parte de las ciudades de la nación

Enmienda Decimotercera   prohíbe la esclavitud

Compromiso de Tres Quintos   un compromiso que resolvió el problema de cómo la gente esclavizada tenia que ser calculada para determinar la representación en el Congreso

huso horario   región geográfica en la cual la misma norma del tiempo es mantenida

Title IX section of the 1972 Educational Amendments prohibiting federally funded schools from discriminating against girls and young women in nearly all aspects of their operations

trade deficit the difference between the value of a country's imports versus its exports

transcontinental railroad a railway system extending across the continent

Treaty of Ghent treaty that ended the War of 1812

Treaty of Guadalupe Hidalgo agreement signed by Mexico and the United States after the war with Mexico that ceded the United States more than 500,000 square miles of territory, including what are now the states of California, Utah, and Nevada; most of New Mexico and Arizona; and parts of Colorado and Wyoming

Treaty of Versailles treaty that ended World War I

trickle-down economics economic theory that lower taxes will boost the economy as businesses and individuals invest their money, thereby creating higher tax revenue

trusts a combination of firms or corporations formed by a legal agreement, especially to reduce competition

Twenty-fourth Amendment prohibits poll taxes in federal elections; these taxes were previously used to keep low-income African Americans from voting

Título IX sección de las Enmiendas Educacionales de 1972 que prohibían que las escuelas que recibían fondos federales discriminaran a niñas y mujeres jóvenes en casi todas las áreas de su operación

déficit de intercambio diferencia entre el valor de las importaciones de un país y sus exportaciones

ferrocarril transcontinental sistema de ferrocarriles que se extiende a través del continente

Tratado de Ghent tratado que terminó la guerra de 1812

Tratado de Guadalupe Hidalgo acuerdo firmado por México y los Estados Unidos después de la guerra con México que cedió más de 500,000 millas cuadradas de territorio a los Estados Unidos, incluyendo lo que hoy en día son los estados de California, Utah, y Nevada; la mayoría de Nuevo México y Arizona; y partes de Colorado y Wyoming

Tratado de Versailles tratado que terminó la Primera Guerra Mundial

economía de goteo una teoría económica que dice que impuestos más bajos dan un impulso a la economía porque negocios e individuos invierten su dinero, generando por lo tanto mayores ingresos de impuestos sobre las ganancias

cartel combinación de empresas o sociedades anónimas formada por acuerdo legal, especialmente para reducir la competencia

Enmienda Vigésimo Cuarta prohíbe impuestos en las elecciones federales; estos impuestos anteriormente se usaban para impedir a los afroamericanos pobres que votaran

U

Uncle Tom's Cabin   a novel written by Harriet Beecher Stowe that depicted the horrors of slavery

La cabaña del Tío Tom   una novela escrita por Harriet Beecher Stowe que describió los horrores de la esclavitud

Underground Railroad   a system that helped enslaved African Americans follow a network of escape routes out of the South to freedom in the North

Ferrocarril Clandestino   sistema que ayudó a los afroamericanos esclavizados a seguir una red de rutas de escape fuera del sur hacia la libertad en el norte

union shop   a business that requires employees to join a union

taller sindicalizado   comercio que requiere que los trabajadores se afilien a un sindicato

United Nations   organization formed in 1945 to promote international cooperation

Naciones Unidas   organización formada en 1945 para promover la cooperación internacional

urban renewal   government programs that attempt to eliminate poverty and revitalize urban areas

renovación urbana   programas gubernamentales que intentan eliminar la pobreza y revitalizar las áreas urbanas

V

V-E Day   Victory in Europe Day, May 7, 1945

V-E Day   Día de Triunfo en Europa, 7 de mayo de 1945

veto   to reject a bill and prevent it from becoming a law

veto   poder del jefe ejecutivo para rechazar leyes aprobadas por el cuerpo legislativo

Vietcong   the guerilla soldiers of the communist faction in Vietnam, also known as the National Liberation Front

Vietcong   soldados guerrilleros de la facción comunista en Vietnam, también conocidos como Frente Nacional de Liberación

Vietnamization   the process of making South Vietnam assume more of the war effort by slowly withdrawing American troops from Vietnam

vietnamización   el proceso por el cual el sur de Vietnam asumia más el esfuerzo en la guerra, desalojando paulatinamente a las tropas americanas de Vietnam

VISTA   a Great Society program in which young people were put to work in poor school districts

VISTA   un programa de la Gran Sociedad en el cual se pusieron jóvenes a trabajar en distritos escolares pobres

V-J Day   Victory in Japan Day, August 15, 1945

V-J Day   Día de Triunfo en Japón, 15 de agosto de 1945

W

war on poverty antipoverty program under President Lyndon Johnson

guerra contra la pobreza programa contra la pobreza bajo la presidencia de Lyndon Jonson

War Powers Act a law that required the president to inform Congress of any troop commitment with 48 hours and to withdraw the troops in 60 days unless Congress approved the troop commitment

Decreto de Poderes de Guerra una ley que requiere que el presidente informe al Congreso de cualquier compromiso de tropas dentro de 48 horas y que retire las tropas en 60 días a no ser que el Congreso apruebe dicho compromiso

Warren Commission a commission headed by Chief Justice Warren that concluded that Oswald was the lone assassin of President Kennedy

Comisión de Warren una comisión encabezada por el Jefe de Justicia Warren que concluyo que Oswald fue el único asesino del Presidente Kennedy

welfare capitalism a system in which companies enable employees to buy stock, participate in profit sharing, and receive benefits such as medical care; common in the 1920s

capitalismo de beneficencia sistema en el cual las compañías permiten a los trabajadores comprar acciones, compartir las ganancias, y recibir beneficios tal como atención médica; común en los años de 1920

Whiskey Rebellion a protest by farmers against the government's tax on whiskey

Rebelión de Whiskey una protesta de agricultores en contra del impuesto gubernamental al whiskey

white-collar jobs in fields not requiring work clothes or protective clothing, such as sales

Cuello blanco trabajos que no requieren ropa de trabajo o de protección, tales como los vendedores

Y

yellow journalism a type of sensational, biased, and often false reporting for the sake of attracting readers

periodismo amarillista tipo de reportaje sensacionalista, tendencioso, y a menudo falso con el propósito de atraer a los lectores

REGENTS IN U.S. HISTORY AND GOVERNMENT

The University of the State of New York

REGENTS HIGH SCHOOL EXAMINATION

UNITED STATES HISTORY
AND
GOVERNMENT

Thursday, January 27, 2005 — 1:15 to 4:15 p.m., only

Student Name _____

School Name _____

Print your name and the name of your school on the lines above. Then turn to the last page of this booklet, which is the answer sheet for Part I. Fold the last page along the perforations and, slowly and carefully, tear off the answer sheet. Then fill in the heading of your answer sheet. Now print your name and the name of your school in the heading of each page of your essay booklet.

This examination has three parts. You are to answer **all** questions in all parts. Use black or dark-blue ink to write your answers.

Part I contains 50 multiple-choice questions. Record your answers to these questions on the separate answer sheet.

Part II contains one thematic essay question. Write your answer to this question in the essay booklet, beginning on page 1.

Part III is based on several documents:

Part III A contains the documents. Each document is followed by one or more questions. In the test booklet, write your answer to each question on the lines following that question. Be sure to enter your name and the name of your school on the first page of this section.

Part III B contains one essay question based on the documents. Write your answer to this question in the essay booklet, beginning on page 7.

When you have completed the examination, you must sign the statement printed on the Part I answer sheet, indicating that you had no unlawful knowledge of the questions or answers prior to the examination and that you have neither given nor received assistance in answering any of the questions during the examination. Your answer sheet cannot be accepted if you fail to sign this declaration.

DO NOT OPEN THIS EXAMINATION BOOKLET UNTIL THE SIGNAL IS GIVEN.

Part I

Answer all questions in this part.

Directions (1–50): For each statement or question, write on the separate answer sheet the *number* of the word or expression that, of those given, best completes the statement or answers the question.

1 Because of fertile land and a long growing season, plantations in the thirteen colonies developed in

(1) New England
(2) the Middle Atlantic region
(3) the South
(4) the upper Mississippi River valley

Base your answer to question 2 on the map below and on your knowledge of social studies.

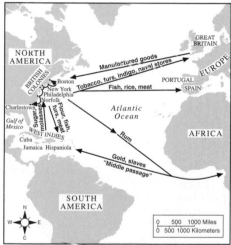

Source: *U.S. History: Preparing for the Advanced Placement Examination*, AMSCO (adapted)

2 What would be the best title for this map?

(1) British Domination of the Americas
(2) Colonial Trade Routes
(3) Spanish Colonies in the New World
(4) The United States in 1750

Base your answer to question 3 on the quotation below and on your knowledge of social studies.

> . . . I challenge the warmest advocate [supporter] for reconciliation, to shew [show], a single advantage that this continent can reap [gain], by being connected with Great Britain. I repeat the challenge, not a single advantage is derived [acquired]. Our corn will fetch its price in any market in Europe, and our imported goods must be paid for, buy them where we will. . . .
>
> — Thomas Paine, *Common Sense*, 1776

3 This speaker is most likely opposed to

(1) mercantilism
(2) capitalism
(3) direct democracy
(4) representative government

4 A major argument for American independence found in the Declaration of Independence was that the British

(1) stopped participating in the slave trade
(2) refused to sell products to Americans
(3) deprived Americans of their natural rights
(4) censored American representatives in Parliament

5 The Preamble of the United States Constitution states the purposes of government and is based on the belief that

(1) the states have ultimate authority
(2) members of Congress should be appointed
(3) Supreme Court Justices should be elected
(4) the people are sovereign

Base your answers to questions 6 and 7 on the statements below and on your knowledge of social studies.

Speaker A: We want a strong national government to provide order and protect the rights of the people.

Speaker B: We want a weak national government so that it will not threaten the rights of the people or the powers of the states.

Speaker C: We want to add a bill of rights to the Constitution to protect the people against abuses of power.

Speaker D: A bill of rights is unnecessary because the new government's powers are limited by the Constitution.

6 A common theme in the statements is a concern about
   (1) excessive state power
   (2) the Land Ordinance of 1785
   (3) the rights of the individual
   (4) creation of the Articles of Confederation

7 These statements represent points of view that differ between
   (1) pro-independence Patriots and pro-British Tories
   (2) leaders of the North and the West
   (3) supporters of Congress and the president
   (4) Federalists and Antifederalists

_____

8 How did President George Washington react to the conflict between France and England in 1793?
   (1) He used the opportunity to begin the war for American independence.
   (2) He declared the neutrality of the United States.
   (3) He aided the French because they had supported the American Revolution.
   (4) He negotiated a peace settlement between the warring nations.

9 The framers of the United States Constitution included the concepts of federalism, checks and balances, and separation of powers in the document because they
   (1) feared a government with unlimited power
   (2) favored the poor over the rich
   (3) wanted to increase the powers of the states
   (4) hoped to expand the democratic process

10 The power of judicial review allows the Supreme Court to
   (1) repeal amendments to the Constitution
   (2) determine the constitutionality of a law
   (3) break tie votes in the electoral college
   (4) impeach the president and other high-level officials

11 The development of political parties and of the committee system used in Congress illustrates the application of
   (1) constitutional amendments
   (2) federal legislation
   (3) the unwritten constitution
   (4) Supreme Court decisions

12 A loose interpretation of the Constitution was applied when
   (1) George Washington appointed John Jay to the Supreme Court
   (2) John Adams signed the Alien and Sedition Acts
   (3) Thomas Jefferson purchased the Louisiana Territory
   (4) James Monroe delivered his State of the Union message

13 One reason James Madison and Thomas Jefferson objected to Alexander Hamilton's financial policies was that they believed
   (1) the establishment of a national bank was unconstitutional
   (2) a laissez-faire policy would not help the country's economy
   (3) the government should encourage industrial development
   (4) high tariffs were needed to protect America's economic interests

14 As a result of President Andrew Jackson's policies, Native American Indians were

(1) relocated to reservations in Mexico
(2) forcibly removed to areas west of the Mississippi River
(3) gradually allowed to return to their ancestral lands
(4) given United States citizenship

15 The Missouri Compromise (1820), the Compromise of 1850, and the Kansas-Nebraska Act (1854) were all efforts to

(1) end fighting between midwestern farmers and Native American Indians
(2) encourage manufacturing in the West
(3) increase the number of people who voted in presidential elections
(4) settle disputes over the spread of slavery to the western territories

16 The institution of slavery was formally abolished in the United States by the

(1) Compromise of 1850
(2) Emancipation Proclamation of 1863
(3) creation of the Freedmen's Bureau in 1865
(4) ratification of the 13th amendment in 1865

17 In an outline, which main topic would include the other three?

(1) Erie Canal
(2) 19th-Century Internal Improvements
(3) Transcontinental Railroad
(4) National Road

18 Which leader founded a vocational training institution in the late 1800s to improve economic opportunities for African Americans?

(1) George Washington Carver
(2) Frederick Douglass
(3) W. E. B. Du Bois
(4) Booker T. Washington

19 In the last half of the 1800s, which development led to the other three?

(1) expansion of the middle class
(2) growth of industrialization
(3) formation of trusts
(4) creation of labor unions

20 The "new immigrants" to the United States between 1890 and 1915 came primarily from

(1) southern and eastern Europe
(2) northern and western Europe
(3) East Asia
(4) Latin America

21 Both the Interstate Commerce Act and the Sherman Antitrust Act were

(1) inspired by the effectiveness of earlier state laws
(2) designed to protect business from foreign competition
(3) declared unconstitutional by the Supreme Court in the late 1800s
(4) passed by the federal government to regulate big business

22 Why was there increased interest in building a canal across Central America in the late 1800s?

(1) The United States had acquired colonies in the Pacific region.
(2) Tariffs on Chinese and Japanese products had ended.
(3) The main source of immigration had shifted from northern Europe to southern Europe.
(4) Transcontinental railroads had not yet been completed.

23 Much of the economic growth of the 1920s was based on

(1) increased trade with other nations
(2) the production of new consumer goods
(3) rising prices of agricultural products
(4) the rapid development of the West

24 Langston Hughes and Duke Ellington are noted for their contributions to the cultural movement of the 1920s known as the

(1) Gospel of Wealth
(2) Lost Generation
(3) Harlem Renaissance
(4) Gilded Age

Base your answer to question 25 on the graph below and on your knowledge of social studies.

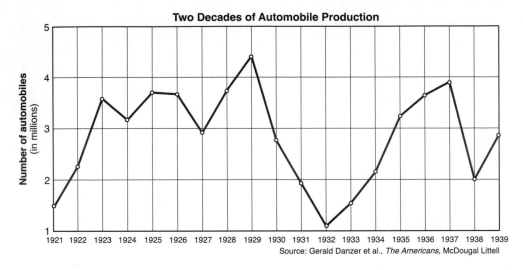

Two Decades of Automobile Production

Source: Gerald Danzer et al., *The Americans*, McDougal Littell

25 Which conclusion is best supported by the information on the graph?

(1) The level of automobile production remained constant.
(2) The average American family found the automobile too expensive to purchase.
(3) By 1929, most of the automobiles in the world were produced in the United States.
(4) Changes in economic conditions led to changes in automobile production.

26 The failure of national Prohibition led to a public awareness that

(1) crime rates decline when the sale of alcoholic beverages is banned
(2) economic prosperity encourages social conformity
(3) unpopular laws are difficult to enforce
(4) geographic conditions affect law enforcement

27 A lasting effect of the New Deal has been a belief that government should

(1) own the principal means of producing goods and services
(2) allow natural market forces to determine economic conditions
(3) maintain a balanced federal budget during hard economic times
(4) assume responsibility for the well-being of its citizens

28 ". . . The American people are sick and tired of being afraid to speak their minds lest they be politically smeared as 'Communists' or 'Fascists' by their opponents. Freedom of speech is not what it used to be in America. It has been so abused by some that it is not exercised by others. The American people are sick and tired of seeing innocent people smeared and guilty people whitewashed. But there have been enough proved cases to cause nationwide distrust and strong suspicion that there may be something to the unproved, sensational accusations. . . ."

— Senator Margaret Chase Smith,
United States Senate, June 1, 1950

When Senator Smith spoke these words, she was reacting to

(1) the Yellow Peril
(2) McCarthyism
(3) the Eisenhower Doctrine
(4) Progressivism

Base your answers to questions 29 and 30 on the cartoon below and on your knowledge of social studies.

Source: *PM*, May 15, 1941 (adapted)

Ho Hum! No Chance of Contagion.

29 In the cartoon, most of the "diseases" refer to the
 (1) military dictatorships of the 1930s
 (2) Allied powers of World War II
 (3) nations banned from the United Nations after World War II
 (4) Communist bloc countries in the Cold War

30 Which action is most closely associated with the situation shown in the cartoon?
 (1) signing of the Atlantic Charter
 (2) passage of the Neutrality Acts of 1935–1937
 (3) first fireside chat of Franklin D. Roosevelt
 (4) declaration of war on Japan

31 Which foreign policy decision by President Harry Truman is an example of the policy of containment?
 (1) relieving General MacArthur of his Korean command
 (2) recognizing the new nation of Israel
 (3) supporting the trials of war criminals in Germany and Japan
 (4) providing military aid to Greece and Turkey

32 Before ratification of the 22nd amendment in 1951, most presidents served no more than two terms because of
 (1) a federal law
 (2) a Supreme Court decision
 (3) the elastic clause
 (4) custom and tradition

33 Which constitutional principle was tested in the cases of *Plessy* v. *Ferguson* and *Brown* v. *Board of Education of Topeka*?
 (1) separation of powers
 (2) popular sovereignty
 (3) equal protection of the law
 (4) separation of church and state

34 ". . . My fellow citizens of the world: ask not what America will do for you, but what together we can do for the freedom of man. . . ."
— John F. Kennedy, Inaugural Address, 1961

To implement the idea expressed in this statement, President Kennedy supported the
 (1) creation of the Marshall Plan
 (2) formation of the Peace Corps
 (3) removal of United States troops from Korea
 (4) establishment of the South East Asia Treaty Organization

Base your answer to question 35 on the cartoon below and on your knowledge of social studies.

Declined with Thanks
The Antis—"Here take a dose of this anti-fat and get thin again!"
Uncle Sam—"No, Sonny! I never did take any of that stuff, and I'm too old to begin."

Source: J. S. Pugh, *Puck*, September 5, 1900 (adapted)

35 Which foreign policy is the main issue of this cartoon?

(1) containment   (3) internationalism
(2) imperialism   (4) neutrality

---

36 The police enter an individual's home without invitation or a warrant and seize evidence to be used against the individual.

Which Supreme Court decision may be used to rule this evidence inadmissible in court?

(1) *Baker* v. *Carr*
(2) *Gideon* v. *Wainwright*
(3) *Mapp* v. *Ohio*
(4) *Roe* v. *Wade*

37 The war in Vietnam led Congress to pass the War Powers Act of 1973 in order to

(1) affirm United States support for the United Nations
(2) strengthen the policy of détente
(3) increase United States participation in international peacekeeping operations
(4) assert the role of Congress in the commitment of troops overseas

38 The ratification of the 26th amendment, which lowered the voting age to 18, was a result of the

(1) participation of the United States in the Vietnam War
(2) fear of McCarthyism
(3) reaction to the launching of Sputnik by the Soviet Union
(4) reporting of the Watergate scandal

39 The decisions of the United States Supreme Court in *Tinker* v. *Des Moines* and *New York Times Co.* v. *United States* were based on interpretations of the

(1) meaning of a republican form of government
(2) powers delegated specifically to Congress
(3) president's right to executive privilege
(4) rights guaranteed by the 1st amendment

Base your answer to question 40 on the cartoon below and on your knowledge of social studies.

Source: Joe Heller, *Utica Observer-Dispatch*, March 27, 2001 (adapted)

40 According to the cartoonist, the United States has

(1) an ethnically diverse population
(2) an overly restrictive immigration policy
(3) a national requirement that high school students learn foreign languages
(4) a census report printed in languages that are spoken in the United States

41 One responsibility of the Federal Reserve System is to

(1) balance the federal budget
(2) raise or lower income taxes
(3) control the supply of money
(4) regulate the stock market

Base your answers to questions 42 and 43 on the table below and on your knowledge of social studies.

Participation in High School Sports

School Year	Boys	Girls
1971–72	3,666,917	294,015
2003–04	4,038,253	2,865,299

Source: National Federation of State High School Associations (adapted)

42 The data included in the table suggest that since 1971

(1) boys are losing interest in participating in sports
(2) participation in sports by boys and girls is nearly equal
(3) girls' participation in sports equals that of boys
(4) girls' participation in sports is increasing at a faster rate than that of boys

43 Which development contributed most to the changes shown in the table?

(1) passage of the Civil Rights Act of 1964
(2) inclusion of Title IX in the Education Amendments of 1972
(3) the beginning of Head Start programs in the 1960s
(4) increase in the number of nonpublic schools since the 1970s

Base your answer to question 44 on the cartoon below and on your knowledge of social studies.

"But we're not just talking about buying a car—we're talking about confronting this country's trade deficit with Japan."

Source: Mort Gerberg in *Macroeconomics, Principles and Policy*, Dryden Press (adapted)

44 The cartoonist is trying to encourage American consumers to consider that

(1) the United States buys more from Japan than Japan buys from the United States
(2) cars produced in the United States are often inferior to foreign-made automobiles
(3) single purchases of automobiles do not have an impact on calculating foreign trade balances
(4) automobile dealerships in the United States should offer more incentives for purchasing American-made cars

45 Since 1980, most new jobs in the United States have been in

(1) education   (3) service industries
(2) heavy industry   (4) civil service

46 President George Washington in his Farewell Address, President James Monroe in the Monroe Doctrine, and the opponents of the League of Nations all wanted the United States to

(1) avoid European conflicts
(2) avoid trade with foreign nations
(3) refuse diplomatic recognition of non-democratic nations
(4) reduce foreign influence by establishing immigration quotas

Base your answer to question 47 on the cartoon below and on your knowledge of social studies.

SHOPPING ONLINE REALLY TAKES THE HASSLE OUT OF BUYING A SENATOR...

CLICK CLICK

Source: Mike Luckovich, *The Atlanta Constitution*

47 In this cartoon, what is the main concern of the cartoonist?

(1) The technology needed to run the federal government is too expensive.
(2) Consumers should be protected from false advertising in the media.
(3) Technology makes it easier to influence legislators.
(4) The government is unable to safeguard the privacy of Internet users.

48 How were the presidential elections of 1876 and 2000 similar?

(1) The winner of the popular vote lost the electoral vote.
(2) Third-party candidates did not affect the outcome.
(3) The outcome of the election was decided by Congress.
(4) The winner was decided by the Supreme Court.

Base your answers to questions 49 and 50 on the graph below and on your knowledge of social studies.

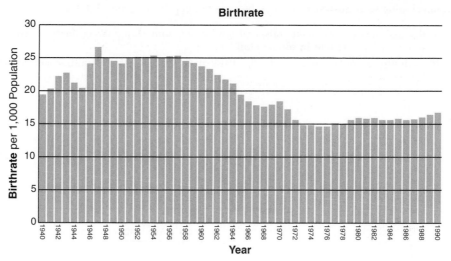

Birthrate

Source: U.S. Census Bureau, *Statistical Abstract of the United States* (adapted)

49 Which situation can be inferred from the population trend shown on the graph?

(1) In the 1980s, more new schools were needed than in the early 1960s.
(2) In the 1970s, there was increased migration to the northeast.
(3) In the 1980s, the number of baby boomers was recognized as a threat to the future of Social Security benefits.
(4) In the 1990s, death rates increased.

50 Information on the graph shows that the birthrate peaked in

(1) 1940
(2) 1947
(3) 1957
(4) 1970

Answers to the essay questions are to be written in the separate essay booklet.

In developing your answer to Part II, be sure to keep these general definitions in mind:

(a) __discuss__ means "to make observations about something using facts, reasoning, and argument; to present in some detail"

(b) __evaluate__ means "examine and judge the significance, worth, or condition of; to determine the value of"

Part II

THEMATIC ESSAY QUESTION

Directions: Write a well-organized essay that includes an introduction, several paragraphs addressing the task below, and a conclusion.

Theme: Foreign Policy

> Since 1900, United States foreign policy actions have often been based on national self-interest. These actions have had immediate and long-term results.

Task:

> Identify *two* important United States foreign policy actions **since 1900** and for *each*
> - Discuss the historical circumstances surrounding the action
> - Discuss *one* immediate **or** *one* long-term result of the action
> - Evaluate the extent to which the action promoted the nation's self-interest

You may use any important foreign policy action since 1900 from your study of United States history. Some suggestions you might wish to consider include Theodore Roosevelt's Corollary to the Monroe Doctrine (1904), Woodrow Wilson's Fourteen Points (1918), the Lend-Lease Act (1941), the Marshall Plan (1947), the blockade of Cuba (1962), the Strategic Arms Limitation Talks (SALT) agreements (1972), and the Persian Gulf War (1991).

You are *not* limited to these suggestions.

Guidelines:

In your essay, be sure to:
- Develop all aspects of the task
- Support the theme with relevant facts, examples, and details
- Use a logical and clear plan of organization, including an introduction and a conclusion that are beyond a restatement of the theme

In developing your answer to Part III, be sure to keep this general definition in mind:

> <u>discuss</u> means "to make observations about something using facts, reasoning, and arguments; to present in some detail"

Part III

DOCUMENT-BASED QUESTION

This question is based on the accompanying documents. This question is designed to test your ability to work with historical documents. Some of the documents have been edited for the purposes of the question. As you analyze the documents, take into account the source of each document and any point of view that may be presented in the document.

Historical Context:

> During the late 1800s and early 1900s, Progressive reformers worked to improve American society. Their goals included **protecting consumers**, **regulating child labor**, **improving working conditions**, and **expanding democracy**.

Task: Using information from the documents and your knowledge of United States history, answer the questions that follow each document in Part A. Your answers to the questions will help you write the Part B essay in which you will be asked to

> Choose *three* goals mentioned in the historical context and for *each*
> - Discuss the conditions that led Progressive reformers to address the goal
> - Discuss the extent to which the goal was achieved

Part A

Short-Answer Questions

Directions: Analyze the documents and answer the short-answer questions that follow each document in the space provided.

Document 1

> . . . There were the men in the pickle rooms, for instance, where old Antanas had gotten his death; scarce a one of these that had not some spot of horror on his person. Let a man so much as scrape his finger pushing a truck in the pickle rooms, and he might have a sore that would put him out of the world [lead to his death]; all the joints in his fingers might be eaten by the acid, one by one. Of the butchers and floorsmen, the beef boners and trimmers, and all those who used knives, you could scarcely find a person who had the use of his thumb; time and time again the base of it had been slashed, till it was a mere lump of flesh against which the man pressed the knife to hold it. The hands of these men would be criss-crossed with cuts, until you could no longer pretend to count them or to trace them. They would have no nails,—they had worn them off pulling hides; their knuckles were swollen so that their fingers spread out like a fan. There were men who worked in the cooking rooms, in the midst of steam and sickening odors, by artificial light; in these rooms the germs of tuberculosis might live for two years, but the supply was renewed every hour. There were the beef luggers, who carried two-hundred-pound quarters into the refrigerator cars, a fearful kind of work, that began at four o'clock in the morning, and that wore out the most powerful men in a few years. . . .

Source: Upton Sinclair, *The Jungle,* 1906

1 Based on this document, state *two* effects of poor working conditions in this factory. [2]

(1) _____

_____

Score ☐

(2) _____

_____

Score ☐

Document 2

... In just one week a scandalized public had snapped up some 25,000 copies of *The Jungle*. Almost all of those readers missed the socialist message. Sinclair had hoped to draw their attention to "the conditions under which toilers [workers] get their bread." The public had responded instead to the disclosures about corrupt federal meat inspectors, unsanitary slaughter houses, tubercular cattle, and the packers' unscrupulous [unethical] business practices.

One of the most outraged readers was President Theodore Roosevelt. Few politicians have ever been as well-informed as TR, who devoured books at over 1,500 words per minute, published works of history, and corresponded regularly with leading business, academic, and public figures. Roosevelt recognized immediately that the public would expect government at some level—local, state, or federal—to clean up the meat industry. He invited Sinclair for a talk at the White House, and though he dismissed the writer's "pathetic belief" in socialism, he promised that "the specific evils you point out shall, if their existence be proved, and if I have the power, be eradicated [eliminated]."

Roosevelt kept his promise. With the help of allies in Congress, he quickly brought out a new bill, along with the proverbial [well-known] big stick. Only four months later, on June 30, he signed into law a Meat Inspection Act that banned the packers from using any unhealthy dyes, chemical preservatives, or adulterants. The bill provided $3 million toward a new, tougher inspection system, where government inspectors could be on hand day or night to condemn animals unfit for human consumption. Senator Albert Beveridge of Indiana, Roosevelt's progressive ally in Congress, gave the president credit for the new bill. "It is chiefly to him that we owe the fact that we will get as excellent a bill as we will have," he told reporters. Once again, Americans could put canned meats and sausages on the dinner table and eat happily ever after. Or so it would seem. ...

Source: James Davidson and Mark Lytle, *After the Fact: The Art of Historical Detection*, Alfred A. Knopf

2 According to this document, what action did President Theodore Roosevelt take to keep his promise to Upton Sinclair? [1]

_____

_____

Score ☐

Document 3a

... During the same winter three boys from a Hull-House club were injured at one machine in a neighboring factory for lack of a guard which would have cost but a few dollars. When the injury of one of these boys resulted in his death, we felt quite sure that the owners of the factory would share our horror and remorse, and that they would do everything possible to prevent the recurrence of such a tragedy. To our surprise they did nothing whatever, and I made my first acquaintance then with those pathetic documents signed by the parents of working children, that they will make no claim for damages resulting from "carelessness."

The visits we made in the neighborhood constantly discovered women sewing upon sweatshop work, and often they were assisted by incredibly small children. I remember a little girl of four who pulled out basting threads hour after hour, sitting on a stool at the feet of her Bohemian mother, a little bunch of human misery. But even for that there was no legal redress [remedy], for the only child-labor law in Illinois, with any provision for enforcement, had been secured [achieved] by the coal miners' unions, and was confined to children employed in mines. ...

There was at that time no statistical information on Chicago industrial conditions, and Mrs. Florence Kelley, an early resident of Hull-House, suggested to the Illinois State Bureau of Labor that they investigate the sweating system [sweatshops] in Chicago with its attendant [use of] child labor. The head of the Bureau adopted this suggestion and engaged Mrs. Kelley to make the investigation. When the report was presented to the Illinois Legislature, a special committee was appointed to look into the Chicago conditions. I well recall that on the Sunday the members of this commission came to dine at Hull-House, our hopes ran high, and we believed that at last some of the worst ills under which our neighbors were suffering would be brought to an end. ...

Source: Jane Addams, *Twenty Years at Hull-House with Autobiographical Notes*, MacMillan, 1912

3a Based on this document, identify *one* social problem Jane Addams wanted to reform. [1]

_____

_____

Score ▢

Document 3b

First Factory Law of Illinois

FACTORIES AND WORKSHOPS

... 4. Children under 14 years of age prohibited from being employed in any manufacturing establishment, factory or work shop in the state. Register of children under 16 years shall be kept. The employment of children between ages of 14 and 16 years prohibited unless an affidavit by the parent or guardian shall first be filed in which shall be stated the age date and place of birth. Certificates of physical health may be demanded by the inspectors. ...

Source: "Factories and Workshops," *Laws of the State of Illinois*, Thirty-Eighth General Assembly, 1893

b Based on this document, state *one* provision of the Illinois factory law. [1]

_____

_____

Score ▢

Document 4

<table>
<tr><td colspan="2" align="center">State Actions Affecting Working Conditions</td></tr>
<tr><td>1911</td><td>Recommendations of Illinois Commission on Occupational Disease (1909) result in Illinois Occupational Disease Act (ventilation, sanitation, fumes, temperature)</td></tr>
<tr><td>1911</td><td>Wisconsin becomes first state to pass workman's compensation legislation</td></tr>
<tr><td>1911</td><td>Wisconsin legislature limits hours of labor for women and children</td></tr>
<tr><td>1911–1915</td><td>Recommendations of New York State Factory Investigating Commission result in dozens of new laws creating healthier and safer factory working conditions during New York's "golden era in remedial factory legislation"</td></tr>
<tr><td>1912</td><td>New York State Factory Investigating Commission requires automatic sprinklers for all floors above seventh floor of buildings; broadens regulation and inspection of workplace safety (fire escapes, safe gas jets, fireproof receptacles, escape routes, fire drills)</td></tr>
<tr><td>1912</td><td>Massachusetts passes first state minimum wage law</td></tr>
<tr><td>1913</td><td>Oregon law requires payment of overtime for workers in mills or factories (over ten hours a day)</td></tr>
</table>

4 Based on this document, identify *two* examples of how a state action resulted in the improvement of working conditions. [2]

(1) _____

_____

Score ☐

(2) _____

_____

Score ☐

Document 5

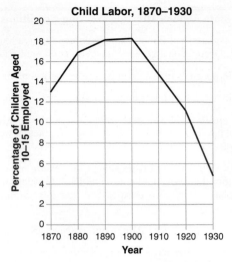

Child Labor, 1870–1930

Percentage of Children Aged 10–15 Employed

Year

Source: United States Bureau of the Census
(adapted)

5 Based on this graph, how did the use of child labor change between 1900 and 1920?   [1]

_____

_____

Score ☐

Document 6a

Bosses of the Senate

Source: Joseph J. Keppler, *Puck*, 1889 (adapted)

Document 6b

... The Senate of the United States shall be composed of two Senators from each State, elected by the people thereof, for six years; and each Senator shall have one vote. The electors in each State shall have the qualifications requisite for electors of the most numerous branch of the State legislatures. ...

— 17th Amendment, Section 1, 1913

6　State **one** way the 17th amendment addressed the concern expressed in the cartoon.　[1]

_____

_____

Score ☐

Document 7

. . . Indeed, the growth of fundamental democracy in this country is astonishing. Thirty years ago the secret ballot was regarded as a passing craze by professional politicians. Twenty years ago it was a vital issue in nearly every American state. To-day the secret ballot is universal in American politics. Ten years ago the direct primary was the subject of an academic discussion in the University of Michigan by a young man named La Follette of Wisconsin. Now it is in active operation in over two-thirds of our American states, and over half of the American people use the direct primary as a weapon of self-government. Five years ago the recall was a piece of freak legislation in Oregon. To-day more American citizens are living under laws giving them the power of recall than were living under the secret ballot when [President] Garfield came to the White House, and many times more people have the power to recall certain public officers to-day than had the advantages of the direct primary form of party nominations when [President] Theodore Roosevelt came to Washington. The referendum is only five years behind the primary. Prophecy with these facts before one becomes something more than a rash guess. [With these facts in mind, predicting the future becomes something more than rash guessing.] . . .

Source: William Allen White, *The Old Order Changeth*, Macmillan, 1910

7 According to William Allen White, what were **two** reforms the Progressives supported to expand democracy? [2]

(1) _____

_____

Score ☐

(2) _____

_____

Score ☐

Document 8

... Women compose one-half of the human race. In the last forty years, women in gradually increasing numbers have been compelled to leave the home and enter the factory and work-shop. Over seven million women are so employed and the remainder of the sex are employed largely in domestic services. A full half of the work of the world is done by women. A careful study of the matter has demonstrated the vital fact that these working women receive a smaller wage for equal work than men do and that the smaller wage and harder conditions imposed on the woman worker are due to the lack of the ballot. ...

The great doctrine of the American Republic that *"all governments derive their just powers from the consent of the governed,"* justifies the plea of one-half of the people, the women, to exercise the suffrage. The doctrine of the American Revolutionary War that taxation without representation is unendurable [intolerable], justifies women in exercising the suffrage. One great advantage, however, of the suffrage is in raising women to a position of greater honor and dignity so that the children of the land shall show and feel greater reverence and honor for their mothers, and that the mothers may teach the elementary principles of good government while they are teaching them good manners, morality and religion. ...

Source: Senator Robert Owen, Speech, 1910

8 Based on this document, state *two* reasons for giving women the right to vote. [2]

(1) _____

_____

Score ☐

(2) _____

_____

Score ☐

Part B

Essay

Directions: Write a well-organized essay that includes an introduction, several paragraphs, and a conclusion. Use evidence from at least *five* documents in the body of the essay. Support your response with relevant facts, examples, and details. Include additional outside information.

Historical Context:

During the late 1800s and early 1900s, Progressive reformers worked to improve American society. Their goals included **protecting consumers**, **regulating child labor**, **improving working conditions**, and **expanding democracy**.

Task: Using information from the documents and your knowledge of United States history, write an essay in which you

> Choose *three* goals mentioned in the historical context and for *each*
> - Discuss the conditions that led Progressive reformers to address the goal
> - Discuss the extent to which the goal was achieved

Guidelines:

In your essay, be sure to:
- Develop all aspects of the task
- Incorporate information from *at least five* documents
- Incorporate relevant outside information
- Support the theme with relevant facts, examples, and details
- Use a logical and clear plan of organization, including an introduction and conclusion that are beyond a restatement of the theme

The University of the State of New York

REGENTS HIGH SCHOOL EXAMINATION

UNITED STATES HISTORY AND GOVERNMENT

Tuesday, June 21, 2005 — 1:15 to 4:15 p.m., only

Student Name _____

School Name _____

Print your name and the name of your school on the lines above. Then turn to the last page of this booklet, which is the answer sheet for Part I. Fold the last page along the perforations and, slowly and carefully, tear off the answer sheet. Then fill in the heading of your answer sheet. Now print your name and the name of your school in the heading of each page of your essay booklet.

This examination has three parts. You are to answer **all** questions in all parts. Use black or dark-blue ink to write your answers.

Part I contains 50 multiple-choice questions. Record your answers to these questions on the separate answer sheet.

Part II contains one thematic essay question. Write your answer to this question in the essay booklet, beginning on page 1.

Part III is based on several documents:

Part III A contains the documents. Each document is followed by one or more questions. In the test booklet, write your answer to each question on the lines following that question. Be sure to enter your name and the name of your school on the first page of this section.

Part III B contains one essay question based on the documents. Write your answer to this question in the essay booklet, beginning on page 7.

When you have completed the examination, you must sign the statement printed on the Part I answer sheet, indicating that you had no unlawful knowledge of the questions or answers prior to the examination and that you have neither given nor received assistance in answering any of the questions during the examination. Your answer sheet cannot be accepted if you fail to sign this declaration.

The use of any communications device is strictly prohibited when taking this examination. If you use any communications device, no matter how briefly, your examination will be invalidated and no score will be calculated for you.

DO NOT OPEN THIS EXAMINATION BOOKLET UNTIL THE SIGNAL IS GIVEN.

Part I

Answer all questions in this part.

Directions (1–50): For each statement or question, write on the separate answer sheet the *number* of the word or expression that, of those given, best completes the statement or answers the question.

Base your answer to question 1 on the series of maps below and on your knowledge of social studies.

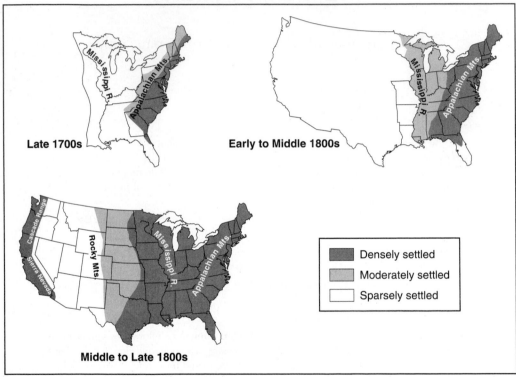

Source: *Atlas of Our Country*, NYSTROM (adapted)

1 What is the best title for this series of maps?

(1) Industrialization of the United States
(2) Sectional Conflicts in the United States
(3) Transportation Revolution in the United States
(4) Shifting Frontier of the United States

2 Which statement is most accurate about the movement for independence in the thirteen colonies?

(1) The independence movement began soon after the founding of the Plymouth Colony.
(2) Protests against British colonial policies gradually led to demands for independence.
(3) The King of England required the colonists to become economically self-sufficient.
(4) The movement for independence was equally strong in all of the colonies.

3 According to the Declaration of Independence, the fundamental purpose of government is to

(1) protect people's natural rights
(2) equalize opportunities for all citizens
(3) provide for the defense of the nation
(4) establish a system of free public education

4 To address the weaknesses of the Articles of Confederation, delegates at the Constitutional Convention agreed to

(1) eliminate the slave trade
(2) increase the powers of the central government
(3) decrease the number of states
(4) allow states to set tariff rates

5 During the Constitutional Convention of 1787, the major disagreement between the large and small states occurred over the issue of

(1) continuation of slavery
(2) guaranteeing States rights
(3) representation in Congress
(4) control of interstate commerce

6 ". . . it is the opinion of this committee that a national government ought to be established consisting of a Supreme Legislature, Judiciary, and Executive. . . ."

— Resolution submitted by Edmund Randolph, delegate to the Constitutional Convention, 1787

In adopting this resolution, the framers of the Constitution showed their belief in the idea of

(1) judicial review
(2) an elastic clause
(3) States rights
(4) separation of powers

7 The requirement to conduct a census was included in the United States Constitution to

(1) control the numbers of immigrants
(2) determine income tax rates
(3) determine the number of members from each state in the House of Representatives
(4) record the birth and death rates of the population

8 Which role of the president is considered part of the unwritten constitution?

(1) nominating federal judges
(2) signing or vetoing legislation
(3) acting as the leader of his political party
(4) serving as commander in chief of the armed forces

9 ". . . Now, one of the most essential branches of English liberty is the freedom of one's house. A man's house is his castle; and whilst he is quiet, he is as well guarded as a prince in his castle. . . ."

James Otis, *Against the Writs of Assistance*, 1761

Which provision in the Bill of Rights includes this same belief?

(1) right to a fair trial
(2) protection against unreasonable search and seizure
(3) guarantee against double jeopardy
(4) prohibition of cruel and unusual punishment

10 Which proposal was included in Secretary of the Treasury Alexander Hamilton's financial plans in the 1790s?

(1) incentives to encourage agricultural expansion
(2) creation of a national bank
(3) direct taxes on the states to support government operations
(4) free trade with other nations

11 President George Washington's principal reason for issuing the Proclamation of Neutrality (1793) was to

(1) repay France for help in the Revolutionary War
(2) protect United States interests in the Caribbean area
(3) safeguard the newly won independence
(4) punish the British for failing to withdraw from American territory

12 The Supreme Court decision in *Marbury* v. *Madison* (1803) was important because it

(1) established the principle of judicial review
(2) led to the reelection of President Thomas Jefferson
(3) showed that the states were stronger than the federal government
(4) proved that the legislative branch was the most powerful branch of government

13 During the first half of the 19th century, the construction of canals and roads led to the

(1) expansion of trade between midwestern farmers and eastern merchants
(2) growth of plantation agriculture in Texas and New Mexico
(3) severe economic decline of the South
(4) bankruptcy of several railroad companies in the Mississippi Valley

14 Which term did Americans use in the 1840s to describe the idea that the United States should possess the entire continent?

(1) containment
(2) globalization
(3) Manifest Destiny
(4) popular sovereignty

15 During the 1840s, abolitionists opposed annexation of new western territory because they

(1) feared the admission of new slave states
(2) wanted to limit the power of the national government
(3) were concerned with the legal rights of Native American Indians
(4) supported an isolationist foreign policy

16 In the ten years following the Civil War, a large numbers of former slaves earned a living by becoming

(1) conductors on the Underground Railroad
(2) workers in Northern factories
(3) sharecroppers on Southern farms
(4) gold miners in California

17 During the late 1800s, the defenders of Social Darwinism would most likely have supported

(1) labor unions
(2) progressive income taxes
(3) laissez-faire capitalism
(4) environmental conservation

Base your answers to questions 18 and 19 on the passage below and on your knowledge of social studies.

". . . This, then, is held to be the duty of the man of Wealth: First, to set an example of modest, unostentatious living, shunning display or extravagance; to provide moderately for the legitimate wants of those dependent upon him; and after doing so to consider all surplus revenues which come to him simply as trust funds, which he is called upon to administer, and strictly bound as a matter of duty to administer in the manner which, in his judgment, is best calculated to produce the most beneficial results for the community— . . ."

— Andrew Carnegie, "Wealth," *North American Review*, June 1889

18 According to this passage, the responsibility of the wealthy is to

(1) invest in future industry to increase wealth
(2) share their excess wealth with the community
(3) maintain a lifestyle consistent with their wealth
(4) influence government to assist all people

19 Andrew Carnegie carried out the ideas expressed in this statement by

(1) funding numerous libraries and educational institutions
(2) serving many years in the federal government
(3) investing his fortune in several new industries
(4) promoting programs to benefit the wealthy

20 The Interstate Commerce Act and the Sherman Antitrust Act were attempts by Congress to

(1) regulate the activities of big business
(2) protect consumers against unsafe products
(3) impose government regulations on agricultural production
(4) bring transportation activities under government ownership

Base your answers to questions 21 and 22 on the cartoon below and on your knowledge of social studies.

ONE SEES HIS FINISH UNLESS GOOD GOVERNMENT RETAKES THE SHIP.

Source: George B. Luks, *The Verdict*, June 5, 1899 (adapted)

21 What is the main idea of the cartoon?

(1) Government policies have created a recession.
(2) Americans support the activities of trusts.
(3) Good government has saved the country from trusts.
(4) Trusts are a threat to the nation.

22 Which group would most likely have favored government action to address the issue shown in the cartoon?

(1) bankers   (3) industrialists
(2) unions   (4) railroad owners

23 A goal of President Theodore Roosevelt's Big Stick policy and President William Howard Taft's Dollar Diplomacy policy toward Latin America was to

(1) join Western Hemisphere nations in a military alliance
(2) protect American economic and political interests
(3) encourage foreign nations to establish colonies
(4) raise Latin America's standard of living

24 A major reason the United States entered World War I was to

(1) gain additional colonial possessions
(2) react to the bombing of Pearl Harbor
(3) safeguard freedom of the seas for United States ships
(4) honor prewar commitments to its military allies

25 Which factor contributed most to the growth of nativist attitudes in the United States in the years immediately following World War I?

(1) the establishment of national Prohibition
(2) a decline of organized religions
(3) the increase in the number of settlement houses
(4) the large numbers of immigrants from southern and eastern Europe

26 What was a principle reason for rapid economic growth in the United States during the 1920s?

(1) prosperity of American agriculture
(2) increase of American imports
(3) development of many new consumer goods
(4) increased spending on defense

27 What was one factor that led to the Great Depression?

(1) government limitations on the amount of money in circulation
(2) high wages paid by employers
(3) increases in the tax rate for corporations
(4) excessive speculation in the stock market

28 Much of the domestic legislation of the New Deal period was based on the idea that the federal government should

(1) favor big business over labor and farming
(2) assume some responsibility for the welfare of people
(3) own and operate the major industries of the country
(4) require local communities to be responsible for social welfare programs

29 Which wartime policy toward Japanese Americans was upheld by the Supreme Court in its 1944 ruling in *Korematsu* v. *United States*?

(1) deportation to Japan
(2) mandatory military service
(3) denial of voting rights
(4) confinement in internment camps

Base your answers to questions 30 and 31 on the cartoon below and on your knowledge of social studies.

Source: Fred O. Seibel, *Richmond Times-Dispatch,*
January 8, 1937

30 What is the main idea of this cartoon?

(1) The legislative branch disagreed with the executive branch during the presidency of Franklin D. Roosevelt.
(2) President Franklin D. Roosevelt wanted the Supreme Court to support his programs.
(3) Justices of the Supreme Court were not asked for their opinion about New Deal programs.
(4) The three branches of government agreed on the correct response to the Great Depression.

31 President Roosevelt responded to the situation illustrated in the cartoon by

(1) calling for repeal of many New Deal programs
(2) demanding popular election of members of the judicial branch
(3) asking voters to elect more Democrats to Congress
(4) proposing to increase the number of justices on the Supreme Court

32 The goal of President Harry Truman's Fair Deal was to

(1) continue reforms begun during Franklin D. Roosevelt's presidency
(2) decrease government spending on social welfare programs
(3) reduce taxes on large corporations and wealthy individuals
(4) restore domestic policies that existed in the 1920s

33 A controversial issue that resulted from World War II was the

(1) future role of the League of Nations
(2) morality of nuclear warfare
(3) commitment of troops without congressional approval
(4) civilian control of the military

34 McCarthyism in the early 1950s resulted from

(1) new commitments to civil rights for African Americans
(2) opposition to the Marshall Plan
(3) charges that Communists had infiltrated the United States government
(4) increased public support for labor unions

35 What was a major outcome of the Korean War (1950–1953)?

(1) Korea continued to be a divided nation.
(2) North Korea became an ally of the United States.
(3) South Korea became a communist nation.
(4) Control of Korea was turned over to the United Nations.

36 "... Let every nation know, whether it wishes us well or ill, that we shall pay any price, bear any burden, meet any hardship, support any friend, oppose any foe to assure the survival and the success of liberty. ..."

— President John F. Kennedy, Inaugural Address, 1961

This statement by President Kennedy suggests a continued commitment to the foreign policy of

(1) isolationism   (3) containment
(2) appeasement   (4) imperialism

37 The Supreme Court decisions in *Gideon* v. *Wainwright* (1963) and *Miranda* v. *Arizona* (1966) have been criticized because these rulings

(1) expanded the rights of the accused
(2) granted more powers to federal judges
(3) lengthened prison sentences for the guilty
(4) reinstated the use of capital punishment

Base your answer to question 38 on the table below and on your knowledge of social studies.

Federal Debt, 1970–1998
(billions of dollars)

Year	Debt
1970	$ 380.9
1975	$ 541.9
1980	$ 909.0
1982	$1,137.3
1984	$1,564.6
1986	$2,120.5
1988	$2,601.1
1990	$3,206.3
1992	$4,001.8
1994	$4,643.3
1996	$5,181.5
1998	$5,478.2

Source: *Historical Tables, Budget of the United States Government*, Fiscal Year 2005 (adapted)

38 Which practice of the federal government has contributed most to the situation shown in the table?

(1) taking steps to reduce growth of the gross domestic product
(2) raising taxes to try to reduce inflation
(3) spending more money than is received in revenues
(4) lowering taxes during election years

39 The Supreme Court decision in *Roe* v. *Wade* (1973) was based on the constitutional principle of

(1) protection of property rights
(2) freedom of speech
(3) right to privacy
(4) freedom of religion

Base your answer to question 40 on the cartoon below and on your knowledge of social studies.

Source: Walt Handelsman, *The Times-Picayune* (adapted)

40 The point of view expressed in this cartoon is that
   (1) President and Mrs. Clinton have made Chicago their new home
   (2) President Clinton supports adoption over abortion
   (3) Republican issues should not be part of the Democratic National Convention
   (4) Democrats sometimes support traditionally Republican issues

41 President Richard Nixon's policy of détente is best characterized by his
   (1) decision to dismantle the nuclear weapons arsenal of the United States
   (2) attempt to reduce tensions with the Soviet Union
   (3) order to bomb Cambodia
   (4) support for membership in the United Nations for communist countries

42 The War Powers Act of 1973 was passed by Congress as a response to the
   (1) spread of nuclear weapons during the Cold War
   (2) invasion of Kuwait by Iraq
   (3) threat of communism in the Middle East
   (4) United States involvement in the Vietnam War

43 "I believe that our young people [18–20 years old] possess a great social conscience, are perplexed by the injustices which exist in the world and are anxious to rectify [correct] these ills."
   — Senator Jennings Randolph, 1971,
   The New York Times

Those who favor this point of view would likely have supported
   (1) a constitutional amendment extending voting rights
   (2) a presidential decision to raise speed limits
   (3) a Supreme Court ruling to reverse desegregation
   (4) a law passed by Congress to increase Social Security benefits

Base your answer to question 44 on the tables below and on your knowledge of social studies.

United States Trends in Farming, 1910 – 1960

Table A Number of Farms	
1910	6,406,000
1920	6,518,000
1930	6,546,000*
1940	6,350,000*
1950	5,648,000*
1960	3,963,000*
*Includes Alaska and Hawaii	

Table B Number of People in Agriculture	
1910	11,770,000
1920	10,790,000
1930	10,560,000
1940	9,575,000
1950	7,870,000
1960	5,970,000

Source: United States Census Bureau (adapted)

44 Which situation is associated with the trends in agriculture shown in these tables?

(1) Farm foreclosures decreased.
(2) Farm size was substantially reduced.
(3) Farm output declined.
(4) Farmers became a smaller percentage of the labor force.

45 The Supreme Court decisions in *New York Times Co.* v. *United States* (1971) and *United States* v. *Nixon* (1974) reinforced the principle that the president of the United States

(1) has unlimited use of the veto power
(2) is protected from unfair media criticism
(3) may not be convicted of a crime
(4) is not above the law

46 The beginning of the collapse of communism in Eastern Europe is most closely associated with the

(1) fall of the Berlin Wall
(2) admission of Warsaw Pact nations to the North Atlantic Treaty Organization (NATO)
(3) intervention of the North Atlantic Treaty Organization (NATO) in Yugoslavia
(4) formation of the European Union

47 Which development led to the other three?

(1) growth of tenements and slums
(2) shift from a rural to an urban lifestyle
(3) rapid industrial growth
(4) widespread use of child labor

48 The dispute over counting Florida voter ballots in the presidential election of 2000 was settled by

(1) an order of the governor of Florida
(2) an agreement between the candidates
(3) a vote of the United States Senate
(4) a United States Supreme Court decision

49 As the average age of the nation's population increases, there will be a need to

(1) create more child care facilities
(2) address the financing of Medicare
(3) increase the number of public schools
(4) reform immigration laws

50 Reducing interest rates to stimulate economic growth is a function of the

(1) Department of Commerce
(2) Federal Reserve System
(3) Federal Deposit Insurance Corporation
(4) Securities and Exchange Commission

Answers to the essay questions are to be written in the separate essay booklet.

In developing your answer to Part II, be sure to keep these general definitions in mind:

(a) <u>discuss</u> means "to make observations about something using facts, reasoning, and argument; to present in some detail"

(b) <u>describe</u> means "to illustrate something in words or tell about it"

(c) <u>evaluate</u> means to "examine and judge the significance, worth, or condition of; to determine the value of"

Part II

THEMATIC ESSAY QUESTION

Directions: Write a well-organized essay that includes an introduction, several paragraphs addressing the task below, and a conclusion.

Theme: Reform Movements in the United States

Reform movements are intended to improve different aspects of American life. Through the actions of individuals, organizations, or the government, the goals of these reform movements have been achieved, but with varying degrees of success.

Task:

Identify *two* reform movements that have had an impact on American life and for *each*
- Discuss *one* major goal of the movement
- Describe *one* action taken by an individual, an organization, or the government in an attempt to achieve this goal
- Evaluate the extent to which this goal was achieved

You may use any reform movement from your study of United States history. Some suggestions you might wish to consider include the abolitionist movement, woman's suffrage movement, temperance movement, Progressive movement, civil rights movement, women's rights movement, and environmental movement.

You are *not* limited to these suggestions.

Guidelines:

In your essay, be sure to:
- Develop all aspects of the task
- Support the theme with relevant facts, examples, and details
- Use a logical and clear plan of organization, including an introduction and a conclusion that are beyond a restatement of the theme

In developing your answer to Part III, be sure to keep this general definition in mind:

> <u>discuss</u> means "to make observations about something using facts, reasoning, and argument; to present in some detail"

Part III

DOCUMENT-BASED QUESTION

This question is based on the accompanying documents. It is designed to test your ability to work with historical documents. Some of the documents have been edited for the purposes of the question. As you analyze the documents, take into account the source of each document and any point of view that may be presented in the document.

Historical Context:

> After World War I, events in Europe caused the United States to review its foreign policy. This review led to controversies between those who supported a return to isolationism and those who wanted to see the United States take a more active role in world affairs.

Task: Using information from the documents and your knowledge of United States history, answer the questions that follow each document in Part A. Your answers to the questions will help you write the Part B essay in which you will be asked to

> • Discuss United States foreign policy toward Europe prior to World War II. In your discussion, include the arguments used by those who *supported* isolationism *and* those who were *opposed* to it.

Part A
Short-Answer Questions

Directions: Analyze the documents and answer the short-answer questions that follow each document in the space provided.

Document 1

> . . . No people came to believe more emphatically than the Americans that the Great War [World War I] was an unalloyed [absolute] tragedy, an unpardonably costly mistake never to be repeated. More than fifty thousand American doughboys [soldiers] had perished fighting on the western front, and to what avail? So far from being redeemed by American intervention, Europe swiftly slid back into its historic vices of authoritarianism and armed rivalry, while America slid back into its historic attitude of isolationism. Isolationism may have been most pronounced in the landlocked Midwest, but Americans of both sexes, of all ages, religions, and political persuasions, from all ethnic groups and all regions, shared in the postwar years a feeling of apathy toward Europe, not to mention the rest of the wretchedly quarrelsome world, that bordered on disgust. "Let us turn our eyes inward," declared Pennsylvania's liberal Democratic governor George Earle in 1935. "If the world is to become a wilderness of waste, hatred, and bitterness, let us all the more earnestly protect and preserve our own oasis of liberty." . . .

Source: David M. Kennedy, *Freedom from Fear*, Oxford University Press, 1999

1 Based on this document, state *one* reason many Americans wanted to return to a policy of isolationism after World War I. [1]

_____

_____

Score ☐

Document 2

... It seems to be unfortunately true that the epidemic of world lawlessness is spreading.

When an epidemic of physical disease starts to spread, the community approves and joins in a quarantine of the patients in order to protect the health of the community against the spread of the disease.

It is my determination to pursue a policy of peace. It is my determination to adopt every practicable measure to avoid involvement in war. It ought to be inconceivable that in this modern era, and in the face of experience, any nation could be so foolish and ruthless as to run the risk of plunging the whole world into war by invading and violating, in contravention [violation] of solemn treaties, the territory of other nations that have done them no real harm and are too weak to protect themselves adequately. Yet the peace of the world and the welfare and security of every nation, including our own, is today being threatened by that very thing. ...

War is a contagion [virus], whether it be declared or undeclared. It can engulf states and peoples remote from the original scene of hostilities. We are determined to keep out of war, yet we cannot insure ourselves against the disastrous effects of war and the dangers of involvement. We are adopting such measures as will minimize our risk of involvement, but we cannot have complete protection in a world of disorder in which confidence and security have broken down. ...

Source: President Franklin D. Roosevelt, Quarantine Speech, October 5, 1937

2 According to this document, what was President Franklin D. Roosevelt's viewpoint about United States involvement in war? [1]

_____

_____

Score ▢

Document 3

In this speech, Senator Robert A. Taft agrees with President Franklin D. Roosevelt's policy concerning the war in Europe.

> . . . Secondly, it has been widely argued that we should enter the war to defend democracy against dictatorship. The President himself, less than a year ago, suggested that it was our duty to defend religion, democracy, and good faith throughout the world, although he proposed methods short of war. I question the whole theory that our entrance into war will preserve democracy. The purpose of the World War [I] was to save democracy, but the actual result destroyed more democracies and set up more dictatorships than the world had seen for many days. We might go in to save England and France and find that, when the war ended, their governments were Communist and Fascist. Nothing is so destructive of forms of government as war. . . .
>
> The arguments for war are unsound and will almost certainly remain so. The horrors of modern war are so great, its futility is so evident, its effect on democracy and prosperity and happiness so destructive, that almost any alternative is to be desired. . . .

Source: Senator Robert A. Taft, speech in Minneapolis, September 6, 1939

3 Based on this document, state **one** reason Senator Taft was opposed to the United States entering the war in Europe. [1]

_____

_____

Score ▢

Document 4

This cartoon is a view of United States foreign policy from the perspective of a British cartoonist in 1940.

"So this is isolation."

Source: David Low, *Evening Standard*, July 4, 1940

4 According to this cartoon, what is threatening the United States policy of isolationism? [1]

_____

_____

Score [ ]

Document 5

In the spring of 1940 opinion polls indicated, as they had for some time, that two thirds of the American public believed it was more important to keep out of war than to aid Britain; by September less than half of the American public held this view; and by January 1941 70 per cent were prepared to aid Britain at the risk of war. The German victory in the West, climaxed by the fall of France in June 1940, brought about a change in American public opinion and in public policy which the nation's most influential political leader of the twentieth century [President Franklin D. Roosevelt] had tried but failed to bring about since at least 1937. By every index [opinion poll], a substantial majority of Americans came at last to the view that the avoidance of British defeat was sufficiently in the American interest to justify the risk of war. On the basis of that shift in public opinion the presidential campaign of 1940 was fought and the groundwork laid for Lend-Lease and accelerated rearmament. . . .

Source: W. W. Rostow, *The United States in the World Arena*, Harper & Brothers, 1960

5a According to this document, how did public opinion change between the spring of 1940 and January 1941? [1]

_____

_____

Score ☐

b Based on this document, identify **one** event that caused public opinion to change during this time period. [1]

_____

_____

Score ☐

Document 6

... The lend-lease-give program is the New Deal's triple A foreign policy; it will plow under every fourth American boy.

Never before have the American people been asked or compelled to give so bounteously [much] and so completely of their tax dollars to any foreign nation. Never before has the Congress of the United States been asked by any President to violate international law. Never before has this Nation resorted to duplicity [deception] in the conduct of its foreign affairs. Never before has the United States given to one man the power to strip this Nation of its defenses. Never before has a Congress coldly and flatly been asked to abdicate.

If the American people want a dictatorship—if they want a totalitarian form of government and if they want war—this bill should be steam-rollered through Congress, as is the wont [desire] of President Roosevelt.

Approval of this legislation [Lend-Lease bill] means war, open and complete warfare. I, therefore, ask the American people before they supinely [passively] accept it, Was the last World War worth while? ...

Source: Senator Burton K. Wheeler, speech in Congress, January 21, 1941

6 Based on this document, state **one** reason Senator Wheeler was opposed to the Lend-Lease bill. [1]

_____

_____

Score ☐

Document 7

... War is not inevitable for this country. Such a claim is defeatism in the true sense. No one can make us fight abroad unless we ourselves are willing to do so. No one will attempt to fight us here if we arm ourselves as a great nation should be armed. Over a hundred million people in this nation are opposed to entering the war. If the principles of democracy mean anything at all, that is reason enough for us to stay out. If we are forced into a war against the wishes of an overwhelming majority of our people, we will have proved democracy such a failure at home that there will be little use fighting for it abroad. ...

Source: Charles Lindbergh, speech at a rally of the America First Committee, April 23, 1941

7 Based on this document, state **one** reason Charles Lindbergh believed that the United States should stay out of the war. [1]

_____

_____

Score [ ]

Document 8

... It has been said, times without number, that if Hitler cannot cross the English Channel he cannot cross three thousand miles of sea. But there is only one reason why he has not crossed the English Channel. That is because forty-five million determined Britons in a heroic resistance have converted their island into an armed base from which proceeds a steady stream of sea and air power. As Secretary Hull has said: "It is not the water that bars the way. It is the resolute determination of British arms. Were the control of the seas by Britain lost, the Atlantic would no longer be an obstacle — rather, it would become a broad highway for a conqueror moving westward."

That conqueror does not need to attempt at once an invasion of continental United States in order to place this country in deadly danger. We shall be in deadly danger the moment British sea power fails; the moment the eastern gates of the Atlantic are open to the aggressor; the moment we are compelled to divide our one-ocean Navy between two oceans simultaneously. ...

Source: *The New York Times*, "Let Us Face the Truth," editorial, April 30, 1941

8 According to this editorial excerpt, what is **one** reason Americans should oppose the United States policy of isolationism? [1]

_____

_____

Score ☐

Part B

Essay

Directions: Write a well-organized essay that includes an introduction, several paragraphs, and a conclusion. Use evidence from *at least five* documents in your essay. Support your response with relevant facts, examples, and details. Include additional outside information.

Historical Context:

After World War I, events in Europe caused the United States to review its foreign policy. This review led to controversies between those who supported a return to isolationism and those who wanted to see the United States take a more active role in world affairs.

Task: Using information from the documents and your knowledge of United States history, write an essay in which you

> • Discuss United States foreign policy toward Europe prior to World War II. In your discussion, include the arguments used by those who *supported* isolationism **and** those who were *opposed* to it.

Guidelines:

In your essay, be sure to:
- Develop all aspects of the task
- Incorporate information from *at least five* documents
- Incorporate relevant outside information
- Support the theme with relevant facts, examples, and details
- Use a logical and clear plan of organization, including an introduction and a conclusion that are beyond a restatement of the theme

The University of the State of New York

REGENTS HIGH SCHOOL EXAMINATION

UNITED STATES HISTORY AND GOVERNMENT

Tuesday, August 16, 2005 — 12:30 to 3:30 p.m., only

Student Name _____

School Name _____

Print your name and the name of your school on the lines above. Then turn to the last page of this booklet, which is the answer sheet for Part I. Fold the last page along the perforations and, slowly and carefully, tear off the answer sheet. Then fill in the heading of your answer sheet. Now print your name and the name of your school in the heading of each page of your essay booklet.

This examination has three parts. You are to answer **all** questions in all parts. Use black or dark-blue ink to write your answers.

Part I contains 50 multiple-choice questions. Record your answers to these questions on the separate answer sheet.

Part II contains one thematic essay question. Write your answer to this question in the essay booklet, beginning on page 1.

Part III is based on several documents:

Part III A contains the documents. Each document is followed by one or more questions. In the test booklet, write your answer to each question on the lines following that question. Be sure to enter your name and the name of your school on the first page of this section.

Part III B contains one essay question based on the documents. Write your answer to this question in the essay booklet, beginning on page 7.

When you have completed the examination, you must sign the statement printed on the Part I answer sheet, indicating that you had no unlawful knowledge of the questions or answers prior to the examination and that you have neither given nor received assistance in answering any of the questions during the examination. Your answer sheet cannot be accepted if you fail to sign this declaration.

The use of any communications device is strictly prohibited when taking this examination. If you use any communications device, no matter how briefly, your examination will be invalidated and no score will be calculated for you.

DO NOT OPEN THIS EXAMINATION BOOKLET UNTIL THE SIGNAL IS GIVEN.

Part I

Answer all questions in this part.

Directions (1–50): For each statement or question, write on the separate answer sheet the *number* of the word or expression that, of those given, best completes the statement or answers the question.

1 One of the principles stated in the Declaration of Independence is that government should

(1) guarantee economic equality among citizens
(2) have unlimited power to rule the people
(3) be based upon the consent of the governed
(4) be led by educated citizens

2 The Great Compromise at the Constitutional Convention of 1787 was important because it

(1) established suffrage for all males over the age of twenty-one
(2) ended the controversy over slavery
(3) created a single-house national legislature
(4) balanced the interests of states with large and small populations

3 To provide for change, the authors of the United States Constitution included the amendment process and the

(1) commerce clause
(2) elastic clause
(3) supremacy clause
(4) naturalization clause

4 Filibusters were used by United States Senators from the South in the 1950s and 1960s to

(1) block passage of civil rights bills
(2) protest United States involvement in Vietnam
(3) override presidential vetoes of environmental bills
(4) gain approval of presidential appointments to the Supreme Court

5 Judicial review gives the United States Supreme Court the power to

(1) declare state laws unconstitutional
(2) override a congressional veto
(3) impeach and remove the president from office
(4) approve treaties with foreign nations

6 Thomas Jefferson opposed Alexander Hamilton's plan to create a national bank primarily because the plan would

(1) weaken the nation's currency
(2) increase the national debt
(3) promote the interests of farmers
(4) depend on a loose interpretation of the Constitution

7 " 'Tis [It is] our true policy to steer clear of permanent alliances with any portion of the foreign world. . . ."

— President George Washington, Farewell Address, 1796

The United States was able to follow this advice from President Washington for several decades primarily because of

(1) industrial and agricultural self-sufficiency
(2) strong support from other Western Hemisphere nations
(3) geographic isolation from Europe
(4) peaceful relations between the European powers

8 The completion of the Erie Canal in the early 19th century aided the economic development of the United States by

(1) supplying water for the irrigation of western farms
(2) lowering the cost of shipping goods from the Midwest to the Atlantic coast
(3) providing a shipping route for cotton from the South to Europe
(4) supplying waterpower for running factories and mills

9 The annexation of Texas and the Mexican Cession are best described as efforts by the United States to

(1) remove European threats
(2) limit the spread of slavery
(3) end wars of aggression
(4) fulfill Manifest Destiny

Base your answer to question 10 on the table below and on your knowledge of social studies.

CASUALTIES OF THE CIVIL WAR

	Union Troops	Confederate Troops
Total Troops	1,566,678	1,082,119
Wounded	275,175	194,000*
Died of Wounds	110,070	94,000
Died of Disease	249,458	164,000

— Garraty and McCaughey, *The American Nation,* Harper and Row, 1987;
*Shelby Foote, *The Civil War: A Narrative,* Vintage Books, 1986

10 Which statement is best supported by the data in the table?

(1) The Confederate troops lost the Civil War as a result of their higher numbers of injuries and fatalities.
(2) The Union army had better generals during the Civil War.
(3) The Civil War had more casualties than any other war.
(4) More soldiers died from disease than from wounds.

---

11 The Seneca Falls Convention of 1848 is often viewed as the beginning of the

(1) temperance movement
(2) women's rights movement
(3) antislavery movement
(4) Native American Indian movement

12 ". . . Liberty *and* Union, now and forever, one and inseparable!"

— Daniel Webster, 1830

The principle expressed in this statement was also reflected in

(1) Thomas Jefferson's call for nullification of the Alien and Sedition Acts
(2) Federalist Party threats during the War of 1812
(3) John Calhoun's defense of States rights
(4) Abraham Lincoln's attitude toward Southern secession

13 From 1820 to 1865, the debates over nullification, protective tariffs, and the spread of slavery into the new territories concerned the constitutional issue of the

(1) balance of power between the federal and state governments
(2) balance between the rights of individuals and the need to maintain order
(3) protection of the rights of ethnic and racial groups
(4) separation of power between the executive and legislative branches

14 Which group's numbers increased the most as a result of the Industrial Revolution?

(1) skilled craftsmen
(2) landed aristocracy
(3) urban middle class
(4) owners of small farms

Base your answers to questions 15 and 16 on the graphs below and on your knowledge of social studies.

Corn Production and Prices, 1870–1900

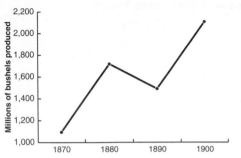 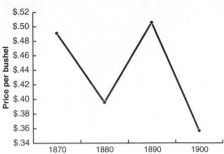

Source: *Statistical Abstract of the United States*, 1900 (adapted)

15 Which trend is shown in these graphs?

(1) When production increases, prices decrease.
(2) When production increases, prices increase.
(3) When production remains unchanged, prices decrease.
(4) Prices and production are usually unrelated.

16 As a result of the trends shown in the graphs, the Populist Party wanted the federal government to increase the money supply to

(1) raise the prices of crops
(2) limit the exportation of corn
(3) discourage the consumption of corn
(4) increase agricultural imports

17 Business leaders John D. Rockefeller, J. P. Morgan, and Cornelius Vanderbilt were referred to as robber barons primarily because they

(1) bought titles of nobility from foreign governments
(2) were ruthless in dealing with competitors
(3) stole money from state and local governments
(4) gained all of their wealth by illegal means

18 During the late 1800s, what was the main reason labor unions had difficulty achieving gains for workers?

(1) Communists had taken control of the major unions.
(2) The government supported business efforts to limit the powers of unions.
(3) Most unions had been organized by big business.
(4) Most workers were satisfied with working conditions.

19 During the late 1800s, Southern voters solidly supported the Democratic Party primarily because Democrats

(1) favored a stronger national government
(2) led efforts to advance civil rights
(3) opposed the Jim Crow legal system
(4) disliked the Reconstruction programs of the Republicans

20 A goal of the Progressive movement was to

(1) reduce the government's involvement in social issues
(2) correct the problems caused by industrialization
(3) promote laissez-faire policies
(4) promote settlement of land west of the Mississippi River

Base your answer to question 21 on the map below and on your knowledge of social studies.

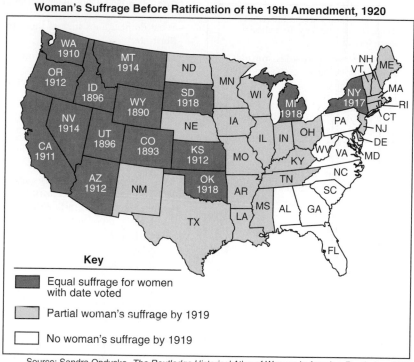

Woman's Suffrage Before Ratification of the 19th Amendment, 1920

Key

- Equal suffrage for women with date voted
- Partial woman's suffrage by 1919
- No woman's suffrage by 1919

Source: Sandra Opdycke, *The Routledge Historical Atlas of Women in America*, Routledge, 2000
(adapted)

21 According to the map, in which region of the United States did women receive the most support for equal suffrage before passage of the 19th amendment?

(1) East
(2) North
(3) South
(4) West

22 Which idea led to the creation of the Interstate Commerce Commission, the Federal Trade Commission, and the Food and Drug Administration?

(1) Business activity must sometimes be regulated in the public interest.
(2) Workers should be allowed to bargain with owners for working conditions.
(3) Domestic industry should be protected from foreign competition.
(4) The economy works best without government regulation.

23 When the Federal Reserve Board lowers interest rates, it is most likely attempting to

(1) stimulate consumer spending
(2) lower prices
(3) encourage saving
(4) reduce investment

24 Which heading best completes the partial outline below?

> I. _____
> A. Sea power is the key to national greatness.
> B. United States missionaries spread Christian principles.
> C. The Anglo-Saxon civilization is the best in the world.
> D. Sugar plantations in Hawaii were developed by Americans.

(1) Reasons to Declare War on Spain
(2) Justification for American Imperialism
(3) Theodore Roosevelt's Political Platform
(4) Yellow Journalism in Newspapers

25 At the beginning of World War I, President Woodrow Wilson followed a traditional United States foreign policy by

(1) refusing to permit trade with either side in the conflict
(2) sending troops to aid Great Britain
(3) declaring American neutrality
(4) requesting an immediate declaration of war against the aggressors

26 The initiative, the referendum, and the recall were adopted by several states during the Progressive Era as ways to

(1) limit immigration
(2) promote the formation of trusts
(3) restrict the use of presidential vetoes
(4) make government more democratic

27 The influence of nativism during the 1920s is best illustrated by the

(1) increase in the popularity of the automobile
(2) emergence of the flappers
(3) expansion of trusts and monopolies
(4) growth of the Ku Klux Klan

28 **"Public Ignores Prohibition Restrictions"**
"Evolution and Creation Debated in Scopes Trial"
"Women Bring Change to the Industrial Workforce"

What do headlines such as these from the 1920s illustrate?

(1) conflict between traditional and modern values
(2) trend toward mass consumption of consumer goods
(3) hostility of certain groups toward ethnic minorities
(4) debate over the role of government in the economy

29 The Federal Deposit Insurance Corporation (FDIC) and the Securities and Exchange Commission (SEC), established during the New Deal, were important because they

(1) increased the supply of money in the economy
(2) guaranteed loans to failing businesses and banks
(3) attempted to restore public confidence in financial institutions
(4) provided grants to unemployed workers

30 At the beginning of World War II, national debate focused on whether the United States should continue the policy of

(1) coexistence   (3) imperialism
(2) containment   (4) isolationism

31 Before entering World War II, the United States acted as the "arsenal of democracy" by

(1) creating a weapons stockpile for use after the war
(2) financing overseas radio broadcasts in support of democracy
(3) providing workers for overseas factories
(4) supplying war materials to the Allies

Base your answer to question 32 on the map below and on your knowledge of social studies.

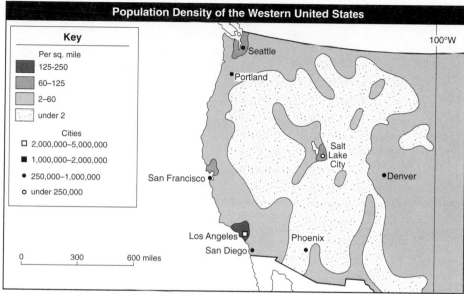

Population Density of the Western United States

Key

Per sq. mile
- 125–250
- 60–125
- 2–60
- under 2

Cities
- ☐ 2,000,000–5,000,000
- ■ 1,000,000–2,000,000
- ● 250,000–1,000,000
- ○ under 250,000

Seattle
Portland
San Francisco
Salt Lake City
Denver
Los Angeles
San Diego
Phoenix

100°W

0   300   600 miles

Source: Andrew Cayton et al., *America: Pathways to the Present*, Prentice Hall (adapted)

32 Which geographic feature is primarily responsible for the lowest population density in the area shown on the map?

(1) Columbia River
(2) Pacific Ocean
(3) Rocky Mountains
(4) Mississippi River Valley

33 "The Parties to this Treaty reaffirm their faith in the purposes and principles of the Charter of the United Nations and their desire to live in peace with all peoples and all governments.

"They are determined to safeguard the freedom, common heritage and civilisation of their peoples, founded on the principles of democracy, individual liberty and the rule of law. . . ."

— Preamble to the North Atlantic Treaty, 1949

This statement shows the commitment of the United States to the principle of

(1) colonialism
(2) neutrality
(3) militarism
(4) collective security

34 One reason the Nuremberg trials following World War II were held was to

(1) bring Hitler, Mussolini, and Tojo to justice
(2) force Japan to pay for the attack on Pearl Harbor
(3) make German leaders accountable for the Holocaust
(4) punish the German government for bombing England

Base your answer to question 35 on excerpts from the song lyrics below and on your knowledge of social studies.

Lyric A:
    . . . Father, father
We don't need to escalate
You see, war is not the answer
For only love can conquer hate
You know we've got to find a way
To bring some lovin' here today. . .

— "What's Going On," Al Cleveland, Marvin Gaye, Renaldo Benson, 1971

Lyric B:
    . . . Yeah, my blood's so mad
Feels like coagulatin'
I'm sittin' here, just contemplatin'
I can't twist the truth
It knows no regulation
Hand full of senators don't pass legislation
And marches alone can't bring integration
When human respect is disintegratin'
This whole crazy world
Is just too frustratin'. . .

— "Eve of Destruction," P.F. Sloan, 1965

35 Which conclusion is most clearly supported by an examination of these song lyrics?

(1) In the 1960s and early 1970s, Americans shared common views on foreign policy.
(2) Social conflict existed over war and civil rights in the 1960s and early 1970s.
(3) The music of the 1960s and early 1970s supported government policies.
(4) Most songwriters of the 1960s and early 1970s used their music to advocate violent revolution.

---

36 During the civil rights movement of the 1960s, activities of the Congress of Racial Equality, the National Urban League, and the National Association for the Advancement of Colored People (NAACP) illustrated that

(1) all civil rights groups use the same tactics
(2) different approaches can be used to achieve a common goal
(3) organizational differences usually lead to failure
(4) violence is the best tool for achieving social change

37 In 1954, the Supreme Court decision in *Brown* v. *Board of Education of Topeka* advanced the civil rights movement by

(1) guaranteeing equal voting rights to African Americans
(2) banning racial segregation in hotels and restaurants
(3) declaring that racial segregation in public schools violated the 14th amendment
(4) upholding the principle of separate but equal public facilities

Base your answers to questions 38 and 39 on the cartoon below and on your knowledge of social studies.

A Show of Hands

YES! TO TRADE WITH CHINA! GODLESS COMMUNISTS! VICIOUS DICTATORS! ENEMIES OF FREEDOM!

NO! TO TRADE WITH CUBA! GODLESS COMMUNISTS! VICIOUS DICTATORS! ENEMIES OF FREEDOM!

Source: Jeff Danziger, *L. A. Times Syndicate*, 2000 (adapted)

38 The cartoonist is expressing the opinion that
(1) the United States should place tariffs on goods from communist nations
(2) most Americans favor trading with both China and Cuba
(3) American foreign trade policies are sometimes inconsistent
(4) democratic nations should receive preferential trade agreements

39 What is the explanation for the situation shown in the cartoon?
(1) Strong anti-Castro sentiment existed in Congress.
(2) China had met all United States human rights demands.
(3) Castro refused to allow Cuba to trade with the United States.
(4) The United States was dependent on food imports from China.

40 President Richard Nixon's visit to the People's Republic of China in 1972 was significant because it
(1) convinced the Chinese to abandon communism
(2) brought about the unification of Taiwan and Communist China
(3) reduced tensions between the United States and Communist China
(4) decreased United States dependence on Chinese exports

41 One similarity in the Supreme Court decisions in *Gideon* v. *Wainwright* and *Miranda* v. *Arizona* is that both decisions
(1) expanded the rights of the accused
(2) improved the ability of the police to gather evidence
(3) lengthened sentences for violent felony offenses
(4) set limits on the use of the death penalty

42 **"Lincoln Suspends Writ of Habeas Corpus"**

"Supreme Court Rules for Government in Draft Resister Case"

"Relocation of Japanese Americans Upheld by Supreme Court"

These headlines illustrate that during wartime

(1) the liberties of individuals can be restricted
(2) the role of the government in regulating the economy increases
(3) most Americans support participation in wars
(4) new job opportunities are created by increased demand

Base your answer to question 43 on the quotations below and on your knowledge of social studies.

. . . Unjust laws exist; shall we be content to obey them, or shall we endeavor to amend them, and obey them until we have succeeded, or shall we transgress them at once? . . .

— Henry David Thoreau, 1849

. . . But the great glory of American democracy is the right to protest for right. My friends, don't let anybody make us feel that we [are] to be compared in our actions with the Ku Klux Klan or with the White Citizens Council. There will be no crosses burned at any bus stops in Montgomery. There will be no white persons pulled out of their homes and taken out on some distant road and lynched for not cooperating. There will be nobody amid, among us who will stand up and defy the Constitution of this nation. We only assemble here because of our desire to see right exist. . . .

— Martin Luther King, Jr., December 1955

43 Which statement most accurately summarizes the main idea of these quotations?

(1) Revolution is inevitable in a democratic society.
(2) Government consistently protects the freedom and dignity of all its citizens.
(3) Violence is the most effective form of protest.
(4) Civil disobedience is sometimes necessary to bring about change.

Base your answer to question 44 on the poster below and on your knowledge of social studies.

Source: Andrew Cayton, et al., *America: Pathways to the Present*, Prentice Hall, 1995 (adapted)

44 This poster was used during the

(1) abolitionist movement
(2) woman's suffrage movement
(3) civil rights movement
(4) environmental movement

45 What is the most likely result of the United States raising tariff rates on imported steel?

(1) The price of consumer goods made with American steel is lowered.
(2) American steel companies are protected from foreign competition.
(3) The quality of consumer goods made with steel is improved.
(4) Foreign steel companies are encouraged to buy American steel companies.

Base your answers to questions 46 and 47 on the table below and on your knowledge of social studies.

FINAL ELECTION RETURNS

| ELECTION OF 1876 | Popular Vote | | Electoral College Vote |
	Total	Percentage	
Hayes*	4,033,497	47.95	185
Tilden	4,288,191	50.98	184
Cooper	78,501	0.90	—

| ELECTION OF 1888 | Popular Vote | | Electoral College Vote |
	Total	Percentage	
Harrison*	5,449,825	47.82	233
Cleveland	5,539,118	48.61	168
Fisk	249,492	2.19	—
Streeter	146,602	1.29	—

| ELECTION OF 2000 | Popular Vote | | Electoral College Vote |
	Total	Percentage	
George W. Bush*	50,456,062	47.89	271
Albert Gore	50,996,582	48.40	266
Ralph Nader	2,858,843	2.71	—

*elected by electoral college

Source: 1876 and 1888, Presidential Elections, 1789–2000, CQ Press, 2002; 2000, "Historical Election Results," U.S. Electoral College, National Archives (adapted)

46 Which criticism of the electoral college system is illustrated by the information in the table?

(1) Presidential electors frequently do not vote for the person they were pledged to support.
(2) A person can win the presidency without winning the most popular votes.
(3) The vote of the people in each state has little relationship to the election outcome.
(4) Minor-party candidates often receive too many electoral votes.

47 Which change is most often proposed to correct the problem shown by the table?

(1) adopt a constitutional amendment to elect the president by popular vote
(2) pass a law requiring state electors to vote for the candidate with the most popular votes
(3) place limits on the number of political parties allowed in presidential elections
(4) allow the elected members of Congress to select the president

48 What was a direct result of the census of 2000?

(1) Personal income tax rates were changed.
(2) New United States District Courts were created.
(3) Seats in the House of Representatives were reapportioned.
(4) The number of United States Senators was increased.

49 During the 20th century, federal prosecutions of corporations such as Standard Oil, AT&T, and Microsoft were based on alleged violations of

(1) stock market practices
(2) environmental regulations
(3) labor union protections
(4) antitrust laws

Base your answer to question 50 on the cartoon below and on your knowledge of social studies.

"...And Best of All, We Merged the Cost of Two Tickets into One!"

Source: Matson, *Car and Travel*, 2001 (adapted)

50 What is the main idea of the cartoon?

(1) Airline technology has resulted in more efficient service.

(2) Reduced competition in the airline industry has hurt the consumer.

(3) A growing economy has led to the start-up of new airlines.

(4) An increase in the number of airlines has led to computer malfunctions.

In developing your answer to Part II, be sure to keep these general definitions in mind:

(a) <u>explain</u> means "to make plain or understandable; to give reasons for or causes of; to show the logical development or relationships of"

(b) <u>describe</u> means "to illustrate something in words or tell about it"

(c) <u>evaluate</u> means "to examine and judge the significance, worth, or condition of; to determine the value of"

Part II

THEMATIC ESSAY QUESTION

Directions: Write a well-organized essay that includes an introduction, several paragraphs addressing the task below, and a conclusion.

Theme: Cold War

> Following World War II, the United States and the Soviet Union were engaged in a conflict that became known as the Cold War. The Cold War created problems that the United States addressed with specific actions. These actions had varying degrees of success.

Task:

> Identify *two* problems faced by the United States during the Cold War and for *each*
> - Explain how the problem led to conflict between the United States and the Soviet Union
> - Describe *one* action taken by the United States in response to the problem
> - Evaluate the extent to which the action taken was successful in solving the problem

You may use any Cold War problems from your study of United States history. Some suggestions you might wish to consider include the postwar economic upheaval in Western Europe (1945–1947), Soviet takeover of Eastern Europe (1945–1948), threat of Communist takeover in Greece (1947), Soviet blockade of Berlin (1948), nuclear arms race (1950s–1970s), and placement of Soviet missiles in Cuba (1962).

You are *not* limited to these suggestions.

Guidelines:

In your essay, be sure to:
- Develop all aspects of the task
- Support the theme with relevant facts, examples, and details
- Use a logical and clear plan of organization, including an introduction and a conclusion that are beyond a restatement of the theme

In developing your answer to Part III, be sure to keep these general definitions in mind:

    (a) <u>discuss</u> means "to make observations about something using facts, reasoning, and argument; to present in some detail"

    (b) <u>explain</u> means "to make plain or understandable; to give reasons for or causes of; to show the logical development or relationships of"

PART III

DOCUMENT-BASED QUESTION

This question is based on the accompanying documents. It is designed to test your ability to work with historical documents. Some of the documents have been edited for the purposes of the question. As you analyze the documents, take into account both the source of each document and any point of view that may be presented in the document.

Historical Context:

    After the crash of the stock market in 1929, the Great Depression began. The Depression brought devastation to the economy of the United States and resulted in severe problems for the American people. Throughout the 1930s, the American people and the government dealt with the Depression in various ways.

Task: Using information from the documents and your knowledge of United States history, answer the questions that follow each document in Part A. Your answers to the questions will help you write the Part B essay, in which you will be asked to

> • Discuss problems faced by the American people during the Great Depression of the 1930s
> • Explain how the American people **and** the government dealt with the problems of the Depression

Part A
Short-Answer Questions

Directions: Analyze the documents and answer the short-answer questions that follow each document in the space provided.

Document 1

> . . . This is not an issue as to whether the people are going hungry or cold in the United States. It is solely a question of the best method by which hunger and cold can be prevented. It is a question as to whether the American people on the one hand will maintain the spirit of charity and of mutual self-help through voluntary giving and the responsibility of local government as distinguished on the other hand from appropriations out of the Federal Treasury for such purposes. My own conviction is strongly that if we break down this sense of responsibility, of individual generosity to individual, and mutual self-help in the country in times of national difficulty and if we start appropriations of this character we have not only impaired something infinitely valuable in the life of the American people but have struck at the roots of self-government. Once this has happened it is not the cost of a few score millions, but we are faced with the abyss of reliance [trap of relying] in [the] future upon Government charity in some form or other. The money involved is indeed the least of the costs to American ideals and American institutions. . . .

Source: President Herbert Hoover, Press Statement, February 3, 1931

1 According to this document, how did President Hoover hope the American people would respond to the problems of the Depression? [1]

_____

_____

Score ☐

Document 2

... Kentucky coal miners suffered perhaps the most. In Harlan County there were whole towns whose people had not a cent of income. They lived on dandelions and blackberries. The women washed clothes in soapweed suds. Dysentery bloated the stomachs of starving babies. Children were reported so famished they were chewing up their own hands. Miners tried to plant vegetables, but they were often so hungry that they ate them before they were ripe. On her first trip to the mountains, Eleanor Roosevelt saw a little boy trying to hide his pet rabbit. "He thinks we are not going to eat it," his sister told her, "but we are." In West Virginia, miners mobbed company stores demanding food. Mountain people, with no means to leave their homes, sometimes had to burn their last chairs and tables to keep warm. Local charity could not help in a place where everyone was destitute. . . .

"No one has starved," Hoover boasted. To prove it, he announced a decline in the death rate. It was heartening, but puzzling, too. Even the social workers could not see how the unemployed kept body and soul together, and the more they studied, the more the wonder grew. Savings, if any, went first. Then insurance was cashed. Then people borrowed from family and friends. They stopped paying rent. When evicted, they moved in with relatives. They ran up bills. It was surprising how much credit could be wangled. In 1932, about 400 families on relief in Philadelphia had managed to contract an average debt of $160, a tribute to the hearts if not the business heads of landlords and merchants. But in the end they had to eat "tight." . . .

A teacher in a mountain school told a little girl who looked sick but said she was hungry to go home and eat something. "I can't," the youngster said. "It's my sister's turn to eat." In Chicago, teachers were ordered to ask what a child had had to eat before punishing him. Many of them were getting nothing but potatoes, a diet that kept their weight up, but left them listless, crotchety [cranky], and sleepy. . . .

Source: Caroline Bird, *The Invisible Scar*, David McKay Company

2 State *two* ways the families described in this passage dealt with the problems of the Depression. [2]

(1) _____

_____

Score ☐

(2) _____

_____

Score ☐

Document 3

Source: H. W. Felchner, New York City, February, 1932

3 Based on the photograph, state **one** effect the Great Depression had on many Americans. [1]

_____

_____

Score ☐

Document 4

... Brigades of Bonus Marchers converged on Washington [in 1932]. Congress had voted the bonus money, but for later. Some of these men might have been hustlers and perhaps there were a few Communists among them, but most were ex-soldiers who had served the nation [in World War I], frightened men with hungry families. The ragged hordes blocked traffic, clung like swarming bees to the steps of the Capitol. They needed their money now. They built a shacktown on the edge of Washington. Many had brought their wives and children. Contemporary reports mention the orderliness and discipline of these soldiers of misfortune. ...

Source: John Steinbeck, "Living With Hard Times," *Esquire*

4 Based on this document, state the reason the Bonus Marchers went to Washington. [1]

_____

_____

Score ⬜

Document 5

... Working women at first lost their jobs at a faster rate than men — then reentered the workforce more rapidly. In the early years of the Depression, many employers, including the federal government, tried to spread what employment they had to heads of households. That meant firing any married woman identified as a family's "secondary" wage-earner. But the gender segregation in employment patterns that was already well established before the Depression also worked to women's advantage. Heavy industry suffered the worst unemployment, but relatively few women stoked blast furnaces in the steel mills or drilled rivets on assembly lines or swung hammers in the building trades. The teaching profession, however, in which women were highly concentrated and indeed constituted a hefty majority of employees, suffered pay cuts but only minimal job losses. And the underlying trends of the economy meant that what new jobs did become available in the 1930s, such as telephone switchboard operation and clerical work, were peculiarly suited to women. ...

Source: David M. Kennedy, *Freedom From Fear*, Oxford University Press

5 Based on this document, state *two* ways women in the labor force were affected by the Great Depression. [2]

(1) _____

_____

Score ⬜

(2) _____

_____

Score ⬜

Document 6

... For black people, the New Deal was psychologically encouraging (Mrs. Roosevelt was sympathetic; some blacks got posts in the administration), but most blacks were ignored by the New Deal programs. As tenant farmers, as farm laborers, as migrants, as domestic workers, they didn't qualify for unemployment insurance, minimum wages, social security, or farm subsidies. Roosevelt, careful not to offend southern white politicians whose political support he needed, did not push a bill against lynching. Blacks and whites were segregated in the armed forces. And black workers were discriminated against in getting jobs. They were the last hired, the first fired. Only when A. Philip Randolph, head of the Sleeping-Car Porters Union, threatened a massive march on Washington in 1941 would Roosevelt agree to sign an executive order establishing a Fair Employment Practices Committee. But the FEPC had no enforcement powers and changed little. ...

Source: Howard Zinn, *A People's History of the United States,* HarperCollins Publishers

6a Based on this document, state **one** reason many African Americans did not benefit from New Deal programs. [1]

_____

_____

Score ☐

b According to this document, how did the government respond to the threat from the Sleeping-Car Porters Union? [1]

_____

_____

Score ☐

Document 7

... Suddenly the papers were filled with accounts of highway picketing by farmers around Sioux City. A Farmers' Holiday Association had been organized by one Milo Reno, and the farmers were to refuse to bring food to market for thirty days or "until the cost of production had been obtained." ...

The strike around Sioux City soon ceased to be a local matter. It jumped the Missouri River and crossed the Big Sioux. Roads were picketed in South Dakota and Nebraska as well as in Iowa. Soon Minnesota followed suit, and her farmers picketed her roads. North Dakota organized. Down in Georgia farmers dumped milk on the highway. For a few days the milk supply of New York City was menaced. Farmers in Bucks County, Pennsylvania, organized, and potato farmers in Long Island raised the price of potatoes by a "holiday." This banding together of farmers for mutual protection is going on everywhere, but the center of this disturbance is still Iowa and the neighboring States.

The Milk Producers' Association joined forces with the Farmers' Holiday. All the roads leading to Sioux City were picketed. Trucks by hundreds were turned back. Farmers by hundreds lined the roads. They blockaded the roads with spiked telegraph poles and logs. They took away a sheriff's badge and his gun and threw them in a cornfield. Gallons of milk ran down roadway ditches. Gallons of confiscated milk were distributed free on the streets of Sioux City. ...

Source: Mary Heaton Vorse, "Rebellion in the Cornbelt," *Harper's Magazine*, December 1932

7 Based on this document, state *two* actions taken by farmers to deal with their economic situation during the Great Depression. [2]

(1) _____

_____

Score ☐

(2) _____

_____

Score ☐

Document 8

Lorena Hickok, a former Associated Press reporter, was hired by Harry Hopkins (head of the Federal Emergency Relief Administration) to travel throughout the United States and send Hopkins private reports on the state of the nation and effects of the New Deal programs. This is an excerpt from one of those reports, dated January 1, 1935.

> . . . Only among the young is there evidence of revolt, apparently. These young people are growing restive [restless]. Out of some 15 weekly reports from industrial centers all over the country, hardly one omitted a paragraph pointing out that these young people may not tolerate much longer a condition that prevents them from starting normal, active, self-respecting lives, that will not let them marry and raise families, that condemns them to idleness and want. At present there is no leadership among them. College men are shoveling sand, checking freight cars, working in filling stations. High school graduates are offering themselves to industry "for nothing, just experience"—and are being accepted. Boys who normally would be apprentices in the trades are tramping [wandering] the pavements, riding the freights back and forth across the country, hanging about on street corners. One day in November a 21-year-old boy in Baltimore walked 20 miles, looking for work. "I just stopped at every place," he said, "but mostly they wouldn't even talk to me." . . .

Source: Lowitt and Beasley, eds., *One Third of a Nation*, University of Illinois Press, 1981

8 Based on this document, state **one** way the Great Depression affected young people. [1]

_____

_____

Score ▢

Part B

Essay

Directions: Write a well-organized essay that includes an introduction, several paragraphs, and a conclusion. Use evidence from *at least **five*** documents in the body of the essay. Support your response with relevant facts, examples, and details. Include additional outside information.

Historical Context:

After the crash of the stock market in 1929, the Great Depression began. The Depression brought devastation to the economy of the United States and resulted in severe problems for the American people. Throughout the 1930s, the American people and the government dealt with the Depression in various ways.

Task: Using information from the documents and your knowledge of United States history, write an essay in which you

- Discuss problems faced by the American people during the Great Depression of the 1930s
- Explain how the American people ***and*** the government dealt with the problems of the Depression

Guidelines:

In your essay, be sure to:

- Develop all aspects of the task
- Incorporate information from *at least **five*** documents
- Incorporate relevant outside information
- Support the theme with relevant facts, examples, and details
- Use a logical and clear plan of organization, including an introduction and a conclusion that are beyond a restatement of the theme

INDEX